HISTORIOGRAPHY AND
SELF-DEFINITION

Supplements to
Novum Testamentum

EDITORIAL BOARD
C. K. Barrett, Durham
P. Borgen, Trondheim
J. K. Elliott, Leeds
H. J. de Jonge, Leiden
M. J. J. Menken, Heerlen
J. Smit Sibinga, Amsterdam

EXECUTIVE EDITORS
D. P. Moessner, Atlanta
A. J. Malherbe, New Haven

VOLUME LXIV

HISTORIOGRAPHY AND
SELF-DEFINITION

Josephos, Luke-Acts, and
Apologetic Historiography

HISTORIOGRAPHY AND SELF-DEFINITION

Josephos, Luke-Acts, and Apologetic Historiography

BY

Gregory E. Sterliing

Society of Biblical Literature
Atlanta

HISTORIOGRAPHY AND
SELF-DEFINITION

Library of Congress Cataloging-in-Publication Data

Sterling, Gregory E.
    Historiography and self-definition : Josephos, Luke-Acts, and apologetic historiography / by Gregory E. Sterling.
        p. cm.
    Originally published: Leiden ; New York : E. J. Brill, 1992, in series: Supplements to Novum Testamentum.
    Includes bibliographical references and indexes.
    ISBN-13: 978-1-58983-193-3 (paper binding : alk. paper)
    ISBN-10: 1-58983-193-4 (paper binding : alk. paper)
    1. Bible. N.T. Luke–Criticism, interpretation, etc. 2. Bible. N.T. Acts–Criticism, interpretation, etc. 3. History–Biblical teaching. 4. Apologetics–History–Early church, ca. 30–600. 5. Josephus, Flavius. Antiquitates Judaicae. 6. Judaism–Apologetic works–History and criticism. 7. Historiography–Greece. 8. Historiography–Middle East. I. Title.
BS2589.6.H55S74 2005
226.4'067–dc22   2005029537

Printed in the United States of America
on acid-free paper

For Dee Dee

TABLE OF CONTENTS

ACKNOWLEDGEMENTS

This volume is a lightly revised version of my dissertation which the Graduate Theological Union accepted in the fall of 1989. I have attempted to incorporate the most significant works since then. There are, however, a couple of studies which came to my attention too late, e.g., William Adler's *Time Immemorial*.

The transition from the dissertation to this monograph has involved a number of people. In particular, I owe a special word of thanks to Julian Deahl and Hans van der Meij, editors at E. J. Brill, for their encouragement and assistance during both the writing of the manuscript and the process of publication. I likewise want to express my appreciation to the editors of *Novum Testamentum* for accepting the work into the *Supplements* series. The interest and assistance of Robert Burke and Jennifer Warlick of the Institute for Scholarship in the Liberal Arts at the University of Notre Dame was indispensable for making it possible to publish the manuscript in its present form. Kim Pattenroth, a graduate student at the University of Notre Dame, assisted in the proof-reading of galleys and compiled the index of modern authors.

The task of writing a dissertation is never undertaken alone. Perhaps only those who have also written prefaces of acknowledgement understand the extent to which each author is indebted to other individuals or can sense the feeling of gratitude that these few lines are intended to convey.

For several years, John R. Donahue, S.J., served as a discerning mentor and helpful coordinator. This work owes a great deal to his careful scholarship, perceptive judgments, and expert tutelage. My debt, however, extends beyond the academic realm: he has been a friend and priest as well. It is for both his expertise and his friendship that I am grateful and proud that he served as chairperson for the dissertation. He stands in a unique place in my life as my *Doktorvater*.

I would also like to recognize the debt I owe to the other members of my committee for their assistance first in courses and then with the dissertation. David Winston introduced me to and helped guide me in the fascinating world of Hellenistic Judaism. Wilhelm Wuellner taught me a great deal about methodology and continually challenged my thinking. To the extent that the thesis in this work is clear and carefully argued, Erich Gruen should be largely credited. He unstintingly lent his masterful knowledge of antiquity to the formation of my argument. The ambiguities and errors which have survived should be attributed to the recalcitrant nature of the author and not to the members of the committee.

Finally, I want to thank my family. For Audra and Amber who patiently endured an absent or preoccupied Daddy, I am thankful. For my wife who typed my papers before the age of computers and freely sacrificed to allow me to pursue my intellectual passion, I am thankful and dedicate this monograph to her for her love.

31 March 1991
Easter Sunday

ABBREVIATIONS[1]

ANRW	*Aufstieg und Niedergang der römischen Welt*
ALGHJ	Arbeiten zur Literatur und Geschichte des Hellenistischen Judentums
GLAJJ	M. Stern, *Greek and Latin Authors on Jews and Judaism*
JSP	*Journal for the Study of the Pseudepigrapha*
KP	K. Ziegler and W. Sontheimer, eds. *Der kleine Pauly*
KRS	G.S. Kirk, J.E. Raven, and M. Schofield, *The Presocratic Philosophers*
LingBib	*Linguistica Biblica*
OCT	Oxford Classical Texts
OTP	J.P. Charlesworth, *The Old Testament Pseudepigrapha*
RE	G. Wissowa *et al.*, eds., *Paulys Real-Encyclopädie der classischen Altertumswissenschaft*

---

[1] Only abbreviations which either do not appear in the *Catholic Biblical Quarterly* or which vary from the practice of that journal are listed.

CHAPTER ONE

GENRE AND HISTORIOGRAPHY

For diff'rent *Styles* with diff'rent *Subjects* sort,
As several Garbs with Country, Town, and Court.

Alexander Pope, *Essay on Criticism* 322-323

For several centuries now, students of Luke-Acts have recognized
the apologetic nature of sections of the work, especially the latter half
of Acts.[1] In recent years this has assumed the form of a full-blown
debate. Most studies have used some form of redaction criticism to
examine the texts which have a social or political bearing and have
argued from an interpretation of those texts to an understanding of
the document(s) as a whole. There is, however, a prior task that
needs to be addressed which reverses the current methodology: this
is to ask if Luke-Acts is an apologetic work as a whole and then to
determine what light such an understanding might cast on specific
texts.

The first step this procedure implies is to determine the nature of
Luke-Acts. What type of work is it? In the nineteenth century the
merits (or demerits) of Luke and Acts as historical works were widely debated. The fulcrum on which the debate rested was the interpretation of the development of Christianity by Ferdinand Christian Baur and the Tübingen school. Baur's students argued that
Acts was a *Tendenzschrift* and historically reliable for the time of its
composition—the second century—rather than for the events it
reports.[2] The most significant attempts to establish the credibility
of Acts as a historical work were the monographs of Sir William
Ramsay and Adolf von Harnack at the turn and beginning of the

---

[1] The earliest attempt to deal with the apologetic nature of Luke-Acts was the
article of C.A. Heumann, "Dissertatio de Theophilo, cui Lucas Historiam Sacram
Inscripsit," *Bibliotheca Historico-Philogico-Theologica*, Class. 4 (1721): 483-505. The
most important early monograph analyzing Acts from this perspective is Matthias
Schneckenburger, *Über den Zweck der Apostelgeschichte* (Bern: Christian Fischer,
1841). A summary of more recent work is presented in chapter seven.

[2] A history of the Tübingen school and the controversy it spawned may be
found in W. Ward Gasque, *A History of the Criticism of the Acts of the Apostles* (Grand
Rapids: Wm. B. Eerdmans Publishing Co., 1975; rev. ed., 1989), pp. 21-95.

present century.[3] The legacy of this debate on subsequent studies has been the tendency to assess the nature of Luke and Acts on the basis of their historical veracity, i.e., if they are judged accurate the works are history; if not, attacks on their historicity have become an argument for labeling them as something other than history.

This has become particularly problematic since the development of *Stilkritik* by Martin Dibelius and composition or redaction criticism by Hans Conzelmann and Ernst Haenchen.[4] The emphasis on the shaping of the texts through theological agendas naturally shifted the focus to theological inquiries. At the same time it delivered the *coup de grâce* to the older view of Acts as objective reporting and led to the question of whether Luke and Acts should be considered historical works.[5] The concentration on the creative role of the author has naturally led to the exploration of literary and rhetorical analyses which are so popular in contemporary scholarship.

Recently, however, there have been several efforts to balance the scales. In Germany, Martin Hengel and Gerd Lüdemann have reacted against overplaying the theological component by defending the historical integrity of Acts as a principal source for reconstructing the history of the early community.[6] The latter, in particular, has made a cogent case for distinguishing between the reliability of authorial redaction and the traditions incorporated in the text. In England, Colin J. Hemer's posthumous analysis of Acts again defends the integrity of the work as a historical source.[7]

In this dissertation, I will argue that Luke-Acts is a historical

---

[3] *Ibid.*, pp. 136-163.

[4] Martin Dibelius, *Studies in the Acts of the Apostles*, edited by H. Greeven and trans. by Mary Ling (London: SCM, 1956 [originally published in 1951; the essays in the collection date from 1923-1949]); Hans Conzelmann, *The Theology of St. Luke*, trans. by Geoffrey Buswell (New York: Harper and Row, 1960 [originally published in 1953]); and Ernst Haenchen, *The Acts of the Apostles: A Commentary*, rev. trans. by R. McL. Wilson (Philadelphia: The Westminster Press, 1971 [originally published in 1956]).

[5] Haenchen, *The Acts of the Apostles*, pp. 103-112, thought of the author as an edifier more than a historian in the sense of Xenophon. See chapter seven for subsequent assessments.

[6] Martin Hengel, *Acts and the History of Earliest Christianity*, trans. by John Bowden (Philadelphia: Fortress Press, 1979) and Gerd Lüdemann, *Das frühe Christentum nach den Traditionen der Apostelgeschichte: Ein Kommentar* (Göttingen: Vandenhoeck & Ruprecht, 1987; ET 1989), pp. 9-24; *Early Christianity according to the Traditions in Acts: A Commentary*, trans. John Bowden (Minneapolis: Fortress Press, 1989), pp. 1-18.

[7] *The Book of Acts in the Setting of Hellenistic History*, edited by Conrad H. Gempf. WUNT 49 (Tübingen: J.C.B. Mohr [Paul Siebeck], 1989).

work. This study does not, however, enter the tradition of scholarship within the framework of the debate over reliability, but on the
basis of contemporary literary criticism. To place Luke-Acts into the
framework of ancient historiography does not presuppose a settlement of the issue of veracity. The relevance of this study to that
question is to ask what we mean by the category of history into which
we place Luke-Acts. The issue of reliability can only be fully addressed once we understand the historiographical tradition of Luke-
Acts and comprehend what the tasks and expectations of that tradition were.

This leads us to the second task: to situate Luke-Acts within a
specific historiographical tradition. An obvious author for comparison is Josephos. The *Antiquitates Judaicae* invites comparison because
like its contemporary counterpart, Luke-Acts, it relates the story of
an identifiable group of people within the Greco-Roman world and
is apologetic. But in what sense is *AJ* apologetic? Does it stand in an
identifiable apologetic tradition? Surprisingly little attention has
been paid to this question in spite of the enormous bulk of literature
devoted to Josephos. This hiatus necessitated an examination of the
possible predecessors of Josephos.

What appeared to emerge was the presence of a distinct historiographical tradition which I have called apologetic historiography.
It therefore became necessary to establish the existence of this tradition as a whole. This necessitated a metamorphosis in the monograph. Instead of being a monograph about Luke-Acts with an introduction presenting earlier authors, it became an attempt to
determine whether or not there was a distinct tradition of apologetic
historiography and to indicate how *AJ* and Luke-Acts fit within it.
Before setting out this tradition it is essential to summarize ancient
and modern views on historiographical traditions.

Ancient Classifications

Prose did not enjoy the position of honor in antiquity that it does in
modernity. For that reason the ancients did not feel compelled to
analyze prose with the same care and attention they did writing
rhythmically in sophisticated patterns cast in meter—nor have we
for that matter.[8] This does not mean that they totally neglected it.

---

[8] Northrop Frye, *Anatomy of Criticism: Four Essays* (Princeton: Princeton Univer-

Aristotle defined poetry by comparing it to history.[9] He rejected the
facile distinction between verse and prose as the essential variation
and said τούτῳ διαφέρει, τῷ τὸν μὲν τὰ γενόμενα λέγειν, τὸν δὲ οἷα
ἂν γένοιτο. The distinction is thus between the particular and the
universal. For this reason he argued poetry was more philosophical
and serious than history.[10]

Fortunately, not all ancients shared Aristotle's dim view of history. Did they draw any differentiae within the broader category of
history?[11] Writing at the end of the first century B.C.E., Dionysios
of Halikarnassos looked back at the period prior to Thukydides. He
grouped all of his predecessors into one category with the exception
of Herodotos.[12] He distinguished them primarily on the basis of
their subject matter: the former dealt with separate countries/peo-
ples; the latter πολλὰς δὲ καὶ διαφόρους πράξεις ἔκ τε τῆς Εὐρώπης
ἔκ τε τῆς 'Ασίας εἰς μιᾶς περιγραφὴν πραγματείας συναγαγεῖν.
Thukydides again altered the pattern by writing on a single war.
Dionysios' perception accurately reflects Thukydides' own criticism
of his predecessors. He called them λογογράφοι and charged them
with unreliability in contrast to his own work.[13] There is thus some
credibility to the division which Dionysios made, although we
should point out that his distinction is temporal and based on subject
matter rather than a formal generic classification.[14]

---

sity Press, 1957), pp. 13-14, pointed out that we use the term "novel" to cover virtually all prose fiction and maintain a library distinction between fiction and non-
fiction.

[9] *Poet.* 9.1-3.

[10] Aristotle said very little about history—not the term ἱστορία which he used
frequently but the concept of historical writing. He apparently knew of the work
of Herodotos (*Poet.* 9.2; 23.2-3 [Herodotos 7.166]; *Rh.* 3.9.2) and Thukydides (*Ath.
Pol.* 33.2 [Thukydides 8.97.2]). He did think that history was useful for political
debates. *Rh.* 1.4.13.

[11] I have based my discussion on major statements of the ancients concerning
distinctions. This is by no means exhaustive. The limitations with this approach
are that history never established itself as an independent science in antiquity and
we do not have everything written about history let alone know unwritten assumptions. For semantic studies which follow the evolution of the term ἱστορία see
TDNT, s.v. ἱστορέω, by Friedrich Büchsel, 3: 391-396 and Gerald A. Press, *The
Development of the Idea of History in Antiquity*. McGill-Queen's Studies in the History
of Ideas 2 (Kingston/Montreal: McGill-Queen's University Press, 1982), pp.
23-119, who examines the entire word group in both Greek and Latin.

[12] *Thuk.* 5-6.

[13] *Thuk.* 1.21.1.

[14] On Dionysios' statements, especially on the controversy about whether or
not the earliest writers wrote local history see W. Kendrick Pritchett, *Dionysius of*

The most self-conscious historian of antiquity is Polybios. Unfortunately, his statements are sometimes at odds with each other or placed in a polemical setting which makes certainty in interpretation difficult if not impossible.[15] In his opening comments Polybios stated the reasons for his history. In the first place, the unification of the world πρὸς ἕνα καὶ τὸν αὐτὸν σκοπόν should compel the historian to bring before his/her readers under a single synoptic view the means by which Tyche had accomplished this.[16] Second, none of his predecessors had written a universal history (τὰ καθόλου πράγματα), but had only composed monographs (κατὰ μέρος).[17] This universal perspective is a distinction which Polybios repeatedly insists on and indicates his own conception of genre: universal history vs. monographs.[18] He thus draws a line on the basis of scope.

He returns to the uniqueness of his own work in a very significant statement at the beginning of the ninth book. He opens by confessing that his πραγματεία will have only limited appeal. He explains this by comparing his subject matter and its appeal with that of others. There are three types in his analysis: ὁ γενεαλογικὸς τρόπος which suits those who like a good story, ὁ περὶ τὰς ἀποικίας καὶ κτίσεις καὶ συγγενείας (such as Ephoros) which appeals to the curious and recondite, and ὁ περὶ τὰς πράξεις τῶν ἐθνῶν καὶ πόλεων καὶ

Halicarnassus: On Thucydides (Berkeley/Los Angeles: University of California Press, 1975), pp. 50-58.
[15] The most important treatments of Polybios are: Paul Pédech, La Méthode historique de Polybe (Paris: Les Belles Lettres, 1964); F.W. Walbank, Polybius. The Sather Classical Lectures (Berkeley/Los Angeles/London: University of California Press, 1972); and Kenneth Sacks, Polybius on the Writing of History. University of California Publications in Classical Studies 24 (Berkeley/Los Angeles/London: University of California Press, 1981).
[16] Polybios 1.4.1-2. The movement from content to form may indicate that Polybios was first interested in the subject and then discovered the form. See also Sacks, Polybius on the Writing of History, p. 104, who argues that Polybios' emphasis on his own historigraphical accomplishments over against the theoretical advice of others also suggests this.
[17] Polybios 1.4.2-3. In 5.33.2, he acknowledges Ephoros as a predecessor, but roundly rejects all others (5.33.3-8). Diodoros Sikelos 5.1.4, also classifies Ephoros as a universal historian.
[18] Cf. also 2.37.4. On Polybios' work as a universal history see Pédech, La Méthode historique de Polybe, pp. 496-514 and Sacks, Polybius on the Writing of History, pp. 96-121. Sacks gives the various terms Polybios used to denote his universal history on pp. 100-101: τὰ καθόλου, κοινὴ ἱστορία, οἰκουμένη, τὰ παρὰ πᾶσι γεγονότα, οἰκονομία. On world history as a theme with attention given to Polybios see A.B. Breebaart, "Weltgeschichte als Thema der antiken Geschichtsschreibung," Acta Historiae Neerlandica 1 (1966): 1-21.

δυναστῶν which attracts those interested in politics.[19] He places himself in the final division.[20] He continues his contrast by lumping the first two categories into one and comparing it to ὁ πραγματικὸς τρόπος.[21] In his opinion, contemporary history is far superior to ancient history since it alone permits a fresh exposition. His aim is therefore not to entertain, but to profit his readers.[22]

How does ἡ πραγματικὴ ἱστορία relate to τὰ καθόλου?[23] The former refers to the subject matter and the latter to the scope. Does Polybios also make a generic distinction between *pragmatikē historia* and other forms? I think that he does. This is his *terminus technicus* for his work and should be seen in that light.[24] How could he make both claims? It is essential to remember that Polybios defines his own work by comparing it to others. Perhaps the most helpful way for us to view Polybios is to compare him to Thukydides. In subject matter, Polybios stands in a direct line with Thukydides; where he differs is in scope: Thukydides clearly wrote κατὰ μέρος.[25] Polybios thus, on the one hand, defined his own work over against monographs; and, on the other, over against all ancient histories even as Thukydides had done.

The final type of history Polybios deals with is tragic historical writing.[26] Although many have taken a cue from Polybios' criticisms to posit a formal school of historical writing, his strictures are general in nature and probably are directed at the sensational aspect

---

[19] Polybios 9.1.4.

[20] 9.1.5-6.

[21] 9.2.1-3 vs. 4-7.

[22] 9.2.6: διόπερ ἡμεῖς οὐχ οὕτως τῆς τέρψεως στοχαζόμενοι τῶν ἀναγνωσομένων ὡς τῆς ὠφελείας τῶν προσεχόντων . . .

[23] On ἡ πραγματικὴ ἱστορία see also 1.2.8, 35.9; 3.47.8; 12.25e.1; 36.17.1; 39.1.4.

[24] A key text which helps to define the term is 12.25e.1-7. Pédech, *La Méthode historique de Polybe*, p. 32, defines it: "Πραγματική précise et limite la portée d'ἱστορία: c'est l'étude qui s'attache exclusivement aux événements publics et aux actes politiques et qui fait la matière de la διήγησις τῶν πραγμάτων." Walbank, *Polybius*, pp. 66-96, considers this to be the type of history Polybios wrote. (It is the title of his chapter.) Sacks, *Polybius on the Writing of History*, pp. 178-180, denies that it has generic significance. He points out that it is also used of the monographic works of Aulus Postumius (39.1.4) and others (3.47.8). This, however, is not a decisive objection in my opinion since genre is not necessarily coterminous with scope.

[25] On Polybios and Thukydides see Walbank, *Polybius*, pp. 40-43. (32-65, for his historiographical position in general)

[26] 2.56.1-63.6 (especially 56.6-16). Other texts discussed under this heading are 2.16.13-15; 3.47.6-48.12, 58.9; 7.7.1-8; 10.27.8; 12.24.5; 15.34.1-36.11.

of writing which characterized so much of Hellenistic historiography rather than a single school of writing.[27]

The distinction between αἱ παλαιαὶ μυθολογίαι and αἱ νεώτεραι πράξεις reappears in Diodoros Sikelos.[28] Plutarch makes the same observation and adds that historians of the past are principally hindered by the distance between themselves and their subjects while those who write contemporary history are liable to distort their works through bias.[29]

Since history was supposed to be a record of τὰ γενόμενα and was measured in terms of truthfulness, it is not surprising to find a classification made on this basis.[30] This system of classification appears in Sextos Empirikos who has preserved the grouping of Asklepiades of Myrleia (1st century B.C.E.).[31] Asklepiades thought there were three classes: true history represented by πραγματική, false illustrated by history περὶ πλάσματα καὶ μύθους, and what is as if true such as ἡ κωμῳδία καὶ οἱ μῖμοι. He further subdivided the true into three parts: περὶ τὰ πρόσωπα θεῶν καὶ ἡρώων καὶ ἀνδρῶν ἐπιφανῶν, περὶ τοὺς τόπους καὶ χρόνους, and περὶ τὰς πράξεις. Of false history he said there was only one form: τὸ γενεαλογικόν. Sextos went on to offer his own schematization based upon subjects: one form of history is τοπική, another χρονική, a third is περὶ τὰ πρόσωπα, and a fourth περὶ τὰς πράξεις.[32]

Some authors defined their own works in contradistinction to the basic pattern. So Strabon thought of his work as ἡ γεωγραφικὴ

---

[27] This is a debatable point. I have followed Walbank, *Polybius*, pp. 34-40 and Sacks, *Polybius on the Writing of History*, pp. 144-170. B.L. Ullman, "History and Tragedy," *TAPA* 73 (1942): 25-53, traced the tragic school back to Isokrates rather than Aristotle as is commonly argued.

[28] 4.1.1-4. Diodoros draws the difference and places Ephoros, Kallisthenes, and Theopompos in the second group and himself in the first. He also contrasts writing on a single war (monograph) with his task of encompassing all of history (universal) in 1.3.1-8.

[29] *Per.* 13.12. The issue of bias was only addressed by writers of contemporary history. On bias see T.J. Luce, "Ancient Views on the Causes of Bias in Historical Writing," *Classical Philology* 84 (1989): 16-31.

[30] We have done the same thing. Note the recent work of Emilio Gabba, "True History and False History," *JRS* 71 (1981): 50-62. One contribution of Gabba is to note that we have tended to measure ancient historians by Thukydides and Polybios "precisely because their historical method is close to our own." He thinks this is wrongheaded: "they are untypical and exceptional; and one has moreover to ask to what extent they were even properly understood in antiquity." (p. 50)

[31] *Math.* 1.252-253.

[32] *Math.* 1.257.

ἰστορία.[33] More surprising to us is the declaration of Plutarch who in the preface to his *Alexander* wrote: οὔτε γὰρ ἰστορίας γράφομεν, ἀλλὰ βίους.[34]

Some of the most important statements for our purposes are those which compare the Greek tradition to those of other nations. The first and most famous is Cicero's contrast between Greek and Roman historiography.[35] In the course of a dialogue, Antonius asked Catulus what type of orator the writing of history required. Catulus responded: Si, ut Graeci scripserunt, summi . . . si, ut nostri, nihil opus est oratore: satis est, non esse mendacem.[36] Antonius went on to explain that the contrast between the highly rhetorical form of Greek historiography and the annalistic style of Roman works had not always been true. The Greeks originally wrote simply.[37] The reason that the Greeks had excelled in historical writing is that eloquent Greeks chose to write history rather than stand before the bar.[38] The present problem for Roman rhetoricians is that there are no rules to follow in writing history even though its basic laws are known to all. Nam quis nescit, primam esse historiae legem, ne quid falsi dicere audeat? Deinde ne quid veri non audeat?[39] This commitment to truth must be evident in the absence of bias.[40] Antonius then offered some directives for res[41] and verba[42] in the writing of history. What is important about this text is that it not only speaks of the rhetorical nature of history, but actually classifies history as a category of rhetoric.[43] We should probably think of Isokrates as a

---

[33] Strabon 1.1.12.

[34] *Alex.* 1.2. Cf. also Polybios 10.21.5-8. On the relationship between biography and history see Arnaldo Momigliano, *The Development of Greek Biography* (Cambridge: Harvard University Press, 1971), pp. 1-7, especially p. 6, and Bruno Gentili and Giovanni Cerri, *History and Biography in Ancient Thought*. London Studies in Classical Philology 20 (Amsterdam: J.C. Gieben, 1988), pp. 61-85.

[35] *De Or.* 2.51-64.

[36] 2.51. On early Roman historiography see J.P.V.D. Baldson, "Some Questions about Historical Writing in the Second Century B.C.," *CQ* n.s. 3 (1953): 158-164.

[37] 2.52-54a.

[38] 2.55-58.

[39] 2.62.

[40] *Ibid.*: Ne qua suspicio gratiae sit in scribendo? Ne qua simultatis?

[41] 2.63.

[42] 2.64.

[43] I can not agree with P.G. Walsh, *Livy: His Historical Aims and Methods* (Cambridge: The University Press, 1961), p. 32, that Cicero is distinguishing history from rhetoric in this text. The analysis of A.J. Woodman, *Rhetoric in Classical*

forerunner—whether direct or indirect—who openly affirmed the elaborate nature of his writing.[44] Perhaps this is why Quintillian can properly censure Greek historians for practising poetic license.[45]

Of even greater significance are the observations of Josephos who contrasts Near Eastern historiography with that of the Greeks in his polemic against Greek historiography in the opening section of *Contra Apionem*. In a statement which reminds us of Cicero's assessment, the Jewish historian affirms: λόγων μὲν οὖν ἕνεκα καὶ τῆς ἐν τούτοις δεινότητος δεῖ παραχωρεῖν ἡμᾶς τοῖς συγγραφεῦσι τοῖς Ἑλληνικοῖς, οὐ μὴν καὶ τῆς περὶ τῶν ἀρχαίων ἀληθοῦς ἱστορίας καὶ μάλιστά γε τῆς περὶ τῶν ἐκάστοις ἐπιχωρίων.[46] This polarization of East and West is largely due to the conflicting accounts of Near Eastern countries and those of the Greeks concerning the earliest periods of time[47] and the defensive posture of the former towards the victorious latter. Josephos' comments indicate that he—at least formally—made a distinction between the two traditions.

This brief survey of ancient attempts to classify history has demonstrated that there were not hard and fast categories of historical writing among the Greeks in antiquity. The primary distinction was between writing about antiquities versus current events. Beyond this, the Greeks did not bother to trouble themselves with defining specific categories.[48] Other nations were forced to compare their own traditions with that of the Greeks. The issue is whether such comparisons establish separate historiographical traditions or merely indicate that different ethnic groups wrote within Greek conventions.

Historiography: Four Studies (Portland, Oregon: Areopagitica Press, 1988), pp. 70-116, especially 78-82, is much more satisfactory. Woodman argues that Cicero here subsumes history to rhetoric as a type of *narratio* in judicial oratory. Cf. also *Inv. Rhet.* 1.19.27 where the three forms of *narratio* are *fabula, historia,* and *argumentum*. So also Quintillian 2.4.2. For an analysis of the major Roman historians as rhetoricians see George A. Kennedy, *The Art of Rhetoric in the Roman World (300 B.C.-A.D. 300)* (Princeton: Princeton University Press, 1972), pp. 292-297 (Sallust), 420-427 (Livy), 515-526 (Tacitus).

[44] *Panathenaic* 1-2.

[45] 2.4.19: Nam Graecis historiis plerumque poeticae similis licentia est.

[46] *CA* 1.27. Cf. also 6 and 58.

[47] We should remember that Diodoros Sikelos gave the mythological material of barbarian nations in books 1-3 and the Greek in 4-6 rather than combining them into a single narrative.

[48] It is interesting that in Lucian's *Quomodo Historia conscribenda sit* no categories are given.

GENRE AND HISTORIOGRAPHY

Modern classifications[49]

At the beginning of this century Felix Jacoby attempted to introduce some order into the confusing state of works which we have
come to label rather loosely "history" by grouping them into the
categories of *Genealogie, Ethnographie, Griechische Zeitgeschichte,* and
Horographie.[50] Jacoby's analysis has become orthodoxy among scholars with one major exception: he refused to bestow the term
Historie (he substituted *Zeitgeschichte*) on ancient works. So in his
influential survey of Greco-Roman historiography, Charles Fornara
offered five genres which developed in this sequence: genealogy or
mythography, ethnography, history, horography, and chronology.[51] David Aune accepted Fornara's system and then attempted to
further analyze "history" into three subgenres: historical monographs, general history, and antiquarian history.[52] While Polybios
certainly sets monographs over against his own work, Aune's insistence that this is "general" history rather than "universal" is unac-
ceptable.[53] As we have seen, Polybios argued that the scope of his
work was unique with the exception of Ephoros. Further, a specific
division of historiography which lumps together works dealing with
the entire habitable world and works on individual countries under
one rubric runs the danger of becoming amorphous.[54]

---

[49] Besides the works summarized below, mention should also be made of Ulrich
von Wilamowitz-Moellendorff, *Greek Historical Writing and Apollo: Two Lectures Delivered Before the University of Oxford June 3 and 4, 1908,* trans. by Gilbert Murray
(Oxford: The Clarendon Press, 1908), pp. 3-26 and Arnaldo Momigliano, "Greek
Historiography," *History and Theory* 17 (1978): 1-28 (pp. 23-28 have an excellent
bibliography).

[50] "Über die Entwicklung der griechischen Historiographie," *Klio* 9 (1909):
80-123. This article served to introduce Jacoby's plan for his monumental *Die Fragmente der griechischen Historiker,* 3 vols. in 16 parts (Leiden: E.J. Brill, 1923-1969).
When his *magnum opus* became a partial reality, Jacoby offered three major
categories: I. Genealogie und Mythographie; II. Zeitgeschichte; III. Geschichte
von Städten und Völkern (Hororaphie und Ethnographie). This does not represent
his final assessment since the work remains incomplete.

[51] *The Nature of History in Ancient Greece and Rome.* Eidos: Studies in Classical
Kinds (Berkeley/Los Angeles/London: University of California Press, 1983), pp.
1-46.

[52] *The New Testament in Its Literary Environment.* Library of Early Christianity
(Philadelphia: The Westminster Press, 1987), pp. 84-89.

[53] *Ibid.,* pp. 88-89.

[54] I can not see how Aune can place Polybios and Berossos in the same subdivision! The gulf which separates them is far greater than what they might share in
common.

The distinction between Western and Near Eastern traditions has been noted by two studies. R.A. Oden, Jr. made a significant contribution to Hellenistic historiography when he pointed out that Philo of Byblos shared five characteristics with authors writing in the Near East in the Hellenistic and Roman worlds: euhemerism, a universal scale (i.e., while they concentrate on their own lands and peoples, the historians begin with the origins of the universe), a tendency to patriotic cultural history, a defensive posture towards Greek culture, and a claim to more reliable source material than their competitors or adversaries.[55] Oden's analysis clearly pointed out a group of common concerns for historians of subject nations and suggested that their works comprised a distinct tradition, but did not attempt to trace or establish it other than to note Philo's ties. More recently D. Mendels has argued that there was a fundamental distinction between historiography in the West and the East.[56] He has chosen to call the latter "creative historiography," i.e., a rewriting of canonical histories within the new realities of the Hellenistic world. He has correctly argued that the Hellenistic Jewish historians belong to this effort. He does not, however, offer an analysis of the tradition as a whole and provides only programmatic statements.

These articles have suggested but not established the tradition to which Josephos alluded in *CA*. Was there a Near Eastern tradition of Hellenistic historiography and how can we establish it?[57]

---

[55] "Philo of Byblos and Hellenistic Historiography," *PEQ* 110 (1978): 115-126. I have not presented an analysis of Philo in this monograph although I would place him within the category of apologetic historiography. The rationale for inclusion is the relationship to Josephos and Luke-Acts. Philo's work is too late to influence them although it does attest to the same tradition.

[56] "'Creative History' in the Hellenistic Near East in the Third and Second Centuries BCE: The Jewish Case," *JSP* 2 (1988): 13-20. I can not concur with his analysis that Thukydides and Polybios are representative of the West and Herodotos and Ktesias the East. (pp. 13-14) Thukydides and Polybios are the exceptions in antiquity—in both the West and the East. I do, however, think that the distinction between West and East is valid.

[57] Since the completion of the dissertation, two works have appeared which sketch the material treated here as the background to the Christian apologetic tradition of the second and following centuries. See Arthur J. Droge, *Homer or Moses? Early Christian Interpretations of the History of Culture*, HUT 26 (Tübingen: J.C.B. Mohr (Paul Siebeck), 1989) and Peter Pilhofer, *Presbyteron Kreitton: Der Alterbeweis der jüdischen und christlichen Apologeten und seine Vorgeschichte*. WUNT II/39 (Tübingen: J.C.B. Mohr (Paul Siebeck), 1990).

Toward a Theory of Genre

The difficulty lies in deciding what criteria to use to separate one group of historical writing from another.[58] Ever since Aristotle opened his Περὶ ποιητικῆς with the statement, "Let us discuss poetry both as poetry and its different forms with the individual quality of each," the concept of genre has been a part of literary criticism.[59] It became well enough entrenched in antiquity that Horace could advise would-be poets: "Let each separate literary type keep its proper place."[60] While there have been denials of its validity in the twentieth century,[61] it has established itself as an essential component of literary criticism.[62] Since our task is essentially a question of genre (εἶδος or γένος for Aristotle), we should be able to employ genre criticism as a means of locating specific traditions. Unfortunately, there is little agreement among critics about exactly what genre is, how to recognize it, or how it functions. Since it is beyond the purpose of this monograph to enter into this con-

---

[58] Volker Ladenthin, "Betrachtungen zur antiken Geschichtsschreibung," *Geschichte in Wissenschaft* 36 (1985): 737-760, has recently addressed this problem and offered a list of questions which he believes will help this process. (p. 756)

[59] *Poet.* 1.1: Περὶ ποιητικῆς αὐτῆς τε καὶ τῶν εἰδῶν αὐτῆς ἥν τινα δύναμιν ἕκαστον ἔχει . . . . As we would expect, Aristotle was anticipated by his teacher who divided poetry into three categories: narration (διήγησις), narration through mimesis (διὰ μιμήσεως), and a combination of the two (δι' ἀμφοτέρων). *Resp.* 392D. See 392C-401A. These are identified as tragedy and comedy, dithyramb, and epic, respectively. (394C-D) This classification occurs in the midst of Plato's critique of poetry on moral grounds. Cf. also 376C-403C, 595A-608B; *Prt.* 347C-348A. On Plato's classification see D.A. Russell, *Criticism in Antiquity* (Berkeley/Los Angeles: University of California Press, 1981), pp. 102-104. On ancient categories of literature in general see pp. 148-158.

[60] *Ars P.* 92: singula quaeque locum teneant sortita decenter. The context is his warning against mixing tragic and comic elements.

[61] One of the most celebrated criticisms was leveled by Benedetto Croce, *Aesthetic: As science of expressions and general linguistic*, rev. ed., trans. by Douglas Ainsile (Farrar, Strauss and Giroux, 1922), pp. 32-38. Croce's attack was based on the distinction between intuitive and logical knowledge. He argued that systems of classifications such as genres belonged to logical processes not to aesthetic or intuitive thought. "The logical or scientific form, as such, excludes the aesthetic form. He who begins to think scientifically has already ceased to contemplate aesthetically. . ." (p. 36). I do not believe that written works are either written or read from an entirely intuitive or aesthetic perspective.

[62] One of the most important treatments of genre in this century is that of Frye, *Anatomy of Criticism*. Frye appears to view his work as a continuation of Aristotle's *Poetics*: "We discover that the critical theory of genres is stuck precisely where Aristotle left it" (p. 13). There are now several journals devoted to genre and genre studies. In this country see *Genre* published by the University of Oklahoma.

troversy, I will simply state my own understanding and proceed.[63]

Every literary text is a form of communication involving three major components: the author, the text, and the readers.[64] Genre theories in the past have frequently been built primarily on one of these elements.[65] There are hazards with each position. If we place the emphasis principally on the author,[66] we must explain not only how we can know the author's intention—it is not always stated— but the relationship between the author and the text. Texts can and do function in societies in ways that authors never imagined. The Bible is a classic example.[67] If, on the other hand, we focus exclusively on structural similarities among texts we run the risk of seeing similarities among texts which share common elements but function in entirely different ways.[68] To use a modern example, a historical novel shares many formalistic similarities with a novel; at the same time it is a distinct category with its own set of presuppositions. Finally, if we concentrate on the readers, we place ourselves in a very precarious position.[69] How can we determine the expectations

---

[63] For overviews of genre theory see W.G. Doty, "The Concept of Genre in Literary Analysis," in *Society of Biblical Literature 1972 Proceedings*, ed. by L.C. McGaughy (Missoula, Montana: Society of Biblical Literature, 1972), pp. 413-448; Paul Hernadi, *Beyond Genre: New Directions in Literary Classsification* (Ithaca/London: Cornell University Press, 1972), pp. 10-151; and H. Dubrow, *Genre* (New York/London: Methuen, 1982), pp. 45-104.

[64] Here my analysis is similar to the New Rhetoric. See Chaim Perelman, *The Realm of Rhetoric*, trans. by William Kluback (Notre Dame: University of Notre Dame Press, 1982), pp. 9-20, who speaks of argumentation, speaker, and audience.

[65] Hernadi, *Beyond Genre*, pp. 6-7, gives four possible bases: the mental attitude of the author ("expressive"), the effect on the reader ("pragmatic"), the similarity between literary works as verbal constructs ("structural"), and the similarity between the imaginative worlds that different verbal constructs evoke ("mimetic"). Adena Rosmarin, *The Power of Genre* (Minneapolis: University of Minnesota Press, 1985), pp. 25, 48-49, has added yet another possibility: genre is the critic's heuristic tool which enables her/him to persuade the audience to see the work in a new way. While the practical function of genre is its potentiality as a hermeneutical tool, I still believe that there is enough similarity in some texts (rather than critics) which leads critics or readers to group them.

[66] The most famous representative of this position is E.D. Hirsch, Jr. *Validity in Interpretation* (New Haven/London: Yale University Press, 1967), pp. 99-102.

[67] Note also Plato's comments in *Phdr.* 275D-E.

[68] Doty, "The Concept of Genre in Literary Analysis," pp. 413-448, thought that genre primarily concentrates on formal, structural aspects.

[69] Aristotle classified rhetoric into the three categories of deliberative, forensic, and epideictic on the basis of audience in *Rh.* 1.3.1: Ἔστι δὲ τῆς ῥητορικῆς εἴδη τρία τὸν ἀριθμόν· τοσοῦτοι γὰρ καὶ οἱ ἀκροαταὶ τῶν λόγων ὑπάρχουσιν ὄντες. He does

of ancient audiences? Further, what of the instances where an author creates a new form?[70]

All of these factors are compounded by a further observation: these are ancient texts. For this reason I have tried to adopt a method which would cover all of the primary bases. I have chosen to follow the basic format developed by the Apocalypse Group of the SBL Genres Project which was published in *Semeia* 36. Their model consists of analyzing the content, form, and function of a text.[71] By content I mean the basic material of the text. More specifically it involves establishing the text—most of the authors exist in fragments—determining the scope of the work, and reconstructing the basic contours. By form I mean how the texts assume the specific shape which they do. In this particular tradition this means examining rewritten texts. This raises several particular questions such as determining what other sources have been influential in the writing of the text. What historiographical techniques has the author consistently employed? By function I mean how was the text designed to function in its original *Sitz im Leben*. This involves reconstructing as much as we can about the life of both the author and the audience. It forces us to ask about the social location of both and whether the tradition has a specific social location. Additionally it demands that we look for discernible tendencies within the text and why emphases measured in the quantity of content have been given.

By formalistically separating these elements, I do not mean that the texts recognize this division. The line between content and form can become opaque—some would claim invisible—at times. I have maintained the distinction as a heuristic device for organizing the analysis of the texts. More importantly, I do not believe that any one item should be severed from the others. Genre deals with the text as a whole; analyses of genre should do likewise. The arguments I have made, therefore, do not stand on any specific facet of the work. I have tried to provide an integrated analysis which makes sense of the

---

go on to add other differences, especially purpose: Τέλος δὲ ἑκάστοις τούτων ἕτερόν ἐστι, καὶ τρισὶν οὖσι τρία (5).

[70] E.g., Dionysios of Halikarnassos 1.8.3, who tells his readers that his history has a different form from what they would expect.

[71] Adela Yarbro Collins, ed., *Early Christian Apocalypticism: Genre and Social Setting. Semeia* 36 (Decatur, GA: Scholars Press, 1986). In particular see the "Introduction" by Collins, pp. 1-11. The work in this issue is an extension of the earlier work of John J. Collins, ed., *Apocalypse: The Morphology of a Genre. Semeia* 14 (Missoula, Montana: Scholars Press, 1979). Again see in particular the "Introduction: Morphology of a Genre," pp. 1-20.

entire work and measures each author against the others on that basis.

I have, however, modified this basic model in two significant ways. First, I have introduced the issue of literary dependence. By determining whether or not an author is aware of the tradition—in this instance other specific authors—I have not intended to argue for a genetic relationship among texts as much as for a greater likelihood of a position within the tradition. It goes without saying that an author can know a tradition and not write in it; however, if it can be established that the author was aware of the tradition it strengthens the possibility that he/she wrote in it. Second, I have pre-empted the schema of content, form, function in the chapters on Josephos and Luke-Acts by placing their own historiographical comments at the beginning of the discussion. This enables the reader to get a sense of the whole of each work.

The methodology which I have adopted is not without some problems. First, the incorporation of a schema can lead a researcher to bend pliant texts—fragments can be very yielding—into a preconceived mold. I have tried to avoid this by letting the texts themselves establish the agenda as much as possible. I refrained from reading secondary literature until I had completed my initial investigation of the texts themselves.

Second, one of the greatest difficulties confronting any study of genre is the presence of mixed forms. This study is no exception. As early as the first part of this century Felix Jacoby pointed out the tendency among Hellenistic authors to mix *Gattungen*.[72] This is even more acute in our tradition since the tradition itself demands that an author take a native text and transform it into a Hellenistic form. Each historian had to determine how Hellenized he would allow his narrative to become—depending upon both his own skill and fidelity to the native sources. It should go without saying that authors did not all arrive at the same position: some are more faithful to their native material than others. Nor are the specific ways in which they recast it identical. The crucial issue is to determine when a given work has moved from one genre into another because of the presence of material from another genre. The most helpful suggestion for solving this problem is that of Heather Dubrow who wrote of and defined host genres: "those forms one of whose roles is to provide

---

[72] "Über die Entwicklung der griechischen Historiographie," p. 122.

a hospitable environment for the other form or forms that are regularly incorporated within them."[73] In this study, I have argued that apologetic historiography is a host genre for natives who wrote the story of their own people in the form of Hellenistic historiography.

The purpose of this study is to do more than simply classify these texts. Traditionally, genre criticism has been paradagmatic in its orientation and taxonomic in its *telos*. Northrop Frye attempted to move beyond this in his major study when he wrote: "The purpose of criticism by genres is not so much to classify as to clarify such traditions and affinities, thereby bringing out a large number of literary relationships that would not be noticed as long as there were no context established for them."[74] This study has attempted to accomplish this for a specific tradition.

More recently, critics have pointed out another function of genre. E.D. Hirsch in his *Validity in Interpretation* suggested that "an interpreter's preliminary generic conception of a text is constitutive of everything that he(/she—GES) subsequently understands."[75] Hirsch has been seconded by a number of other scholars working on genre.[76] The significance of this claim is that it makes genre an indispensable aspect of interpretation. The following study is therefore not simply an attempt to delineate a specific historiographical tradition, but to understand it. I think this is what Robert Frost meant when he said: "Poetry is what gets lost in translation."

Apologetic Historiography

The application of this genre model uncovered the presence of apologetic historiography. Initially I found it necessary to work my way back through the material beginning with the end of the first century C.E. and culminating in the sixth century B.C.E. I have

---

[73] *Genre*, p. 116. I found her analogy to human personalities to be particularly helpful: "A genre closely resembles a human personality in the way it may incorporate elements from many other personality types while still conforming to one basic type itself: someone whose fundamental configuration is obsessive may include elements of the depressive, much as a genre that is primarily epic may also participate in romance and pastoral. . . " (p. 117).

[74] *Anatomy of Criticism*, pp. 247-248.

[75] *Validity in Interpretation*, p. 74. Note also p. 76: "All understanding of verbal meaning is necessarily genre-bound." He makes this point repeadtedly (pp. 78, 80-81, 98). For Hirsch the key is the "intrinsic genre" which he defines as "that sense of the whole by means of which an interpreter can correctly understand any part in its determinacy" (p. 86).

reversed that procedure here and attempted to set the texts out in chronological order. I have presented my analysis of the works of twelve authors through three major phases of ancient Mediterranean and Near Eastern history: the Persian empire (chapter two), the Hellenistic world (chapters three-five), and the Roman empire (chapters six-seven).

Using the model it became evident that there was a group of texts which all told the story of a particular group of people (content) by recasting native texts into a mold more palatable in the Greco-Roman world (form). All of the authors were natives or "insiders" who related the story of their own group in an effort to offer a self-definition of that group (function). The texts were addressed to outsiders in some cases and to members of the same group in others. The common element in all cases was the need that each author felt to relate her/his group to the larger world. The works are therefore apologetic, but may be either directly or indirectly apologetic depending upon the primary audience.

We may now hazard a definition of apologetic historiography. *Apologetic historiography is the story of a subgroup of people in an extended prose narrative written by a member of the group who follows the group's own traditions but Hellenizes them in an effort to establish the identity of the group within the setting of the larger world.* This definition presupposes an understanding of what I mean by self-definition.[77] In this study I use the term with a restricted range. The phrase denotes the attempt of an author to provide identity for the group to which the author belongs in contrast to outside perceptions. It is not intended to convey the impression that the author's proposal was normative for the group, but that the author offered it as a normative understanding. In each instance, this definition represents a shift from previously held views since the group in question is now seen as a subgroup within a larger body rather than as an insulated unit. The phrase thus connotes an effort to shape as well as to describe.

Apologetic historiography was not like the biblical Melchizedek,

---

[76] Dubrow, *Genre*, pp. 8-44, especially 29-30 and the important work of Mary Gerhart, "Generic Studies: Their Renewed Importance in Religious and Literary Interpretations," *JAAR* 45 (1977): 309-325 and "Generic Competence in Biblical Hermeneutics," in *Genre, Narrativity, and Theology. Semeia* 43 (Atlanta, GA: Scholars Press, 1988), pp. 29-44.

[77] A very important discussion of self-definition is Ben F. Meyer, *et al.*, *Self-Definition in Early Christianity.* Protocol of the Colloquy of the Center for Hermeneu-

without father and mother, but was to an extent the offspring of Greek ethnography. Greek ethnography served as a direct *model* for the works which served as transitional links from ethnography to apologetic historiography (Hekataios of Abdera and Megasthenes) and for the first author within apologetic historiography proper (Berossos). Nor was the influence only immediate; the legacy of ethnography lived on in the determination of the content of apologetic historiography (the story of a particular people) and in its function (the attempt to define the people). It would, however, be incorrect to think of apologetic historiography only as an offspring—or at least as an obedient child: it also arose as a *reaction* to Greek ethnography. Indigenous authors were dissatisfied with the way they had been represented by Greeks in the ethnographic tradition and responded by setting out their own definition of who they were. The polemics against Greek accounts in works primarily addressed to the Hellenistic world make this evident.

For these reasons we must begin with a recapitulation of Greek ethnography as it began with Hekataios of Miletos and his successors, most notably Herodotos whose ethnographic *logoi* are the most complete examples of Ionian ethnography we have. While Herodotos was important for the early apologetic historians, his *Histories* did not serve as the immediate parent.

That distinction belongs to Hekataios of Abdera whose *Aigyptiaka* exploited Greek ethnography on behalf of the aggrandizement of Egypt. This shift in function compelled Hekataios to criticize Greek ethnography—especially Herodotos' account of Egypt—by setting native sources over against his predecessors method of investigation. While he was inconsistent in his application, his polemic reached fruition in the works of Berossos and Manethon who may be regarded as the founders of apologetic historiography. These priests collected their sacred traditions and wove them into a single narrative in which they presented Babylon and Egypt to the Hellenistic world. Their amalgamations of native sources in Greek dress—however crude—offered an alternative to previous ethnographic perceptions.

---

tical Studies in Hellenistic and Modern Culture 37 (Berkeley: The Center for Hermeneutical Studies in Hellenistic and Modern Culture, 1980), pp. 1-13 and the following discussion. Meyer posited three moments for self-definition when it functions as a process rather than a terminus: horizons, self-understanding, and self-shaping. His work was related to the project which he helped edit: E.P. Sanders, *et al.*, eds., *Jewish and Christian Self-Definition*, 3 vols. (Philadelphia: Fortress Press, 1980-1982).

They provided a self- rather than a alien-definition. At the same time the conflict became more complex: each ethnic group made competing claims, most frequently by contending for their more remote antiquity.

The genre flourished in antiquity as indigenous authors attempted to carve out a niche for their people within the Hellenistic world. The most significant—although by no means the only—group to do this was the Jews. The earliest representatives are the Hellenistic Jewish historians who experimented with different Hellenistic forms in their efforts to recast their sacred narratives. In each case the Jewish story was retold in an effort to redefine Judaism within the context of the Hellenistic world. Very importantly, they appear to have addressed their histories first to Jewish audiences and only secondarily to outside groups.

The greatest representative of this tradition is the *Antiquitates Judaicae* of Josephos. Writing the full story of his own people, Josephos sought to win a place of respectability for them by Hellenizing their native traditions. Like a Janus head, *AJ* also addressed the Jews hoping that its Hellenized definition of Judaism would help to reconcile them with their place in the world. Josephos followed Berossos and Manethon by insisting on native sources and the Hellenistic Jewish historians by Hellenizing Israel's sacred texts. Yet he dwarfed them all quantitatively and qualitatively and stands at the apex of apologetic historiography.

At the point of this summit a third generation Christian author made use of the same tradition. Luke-Acts tells the story not simply of the founder of Christianity, but of Christians as a people. This is accomplished through a conscious Hellenization of Christian texts and traditions. Like other authors within this tradition of historiography, the penman had come to recognize Christians as a subgroup within the larger world and set out their story in an effort to provide them with a definition of who they were—a definition which must have struck them as new and different if they heard what was being said.

CHAPTER TWO

GREEK ETHNOGRAPHY

"In this way, our book will recount
to you [all the greatest marvels and
diversities of Greater Armenia] clearly and in orderly fashion, just as Sire
Marco Polo, the wise and noble
Venetian from Venice, describes
them, for he has seen them with his
own eyes."

Marco Polo, *The Description of the
World*

For millenia travelers have regaled audiences with stories about
strange and exotic lands and peoples they have seen. Ionian Greeks
cultivated and developed this tradition into a definable literary
genre which we know as ethnography.[1] Arising at the dawn of
Greek historiography, ethnography burned brightly for centuries.
In its initial stages it represented the first efforts by the Greeks to systematically describe the peoples of the Mediterranean world. The
presentation was naturally filtered through a distinctly Hellenic
lens. It should, therefore, hardly occasion a surprise to realize that
following the Macedonian juggernaut, indigenous authors began to
react to this Greek tradition. It is accordingly imperative that we understand Greek ethnography in its earliest form.

Literary Precursors

The initial traces of ethnography in a literary form extend back to
the Homeric references to foreign peoples such as the Phoenicians[2]

---

[1] On ethnography cf. K. Trüdinger, "Studien zur Geschichte der griechisch-
römischen Ethnographie." (Dissertation, Basel, 1918); Klaus Erich Müller,
Geschichte der antiken Ethnographie und ethnologischen Theoriebildung. Vol. 1: *Von den
Anfängen bis auf die byzantinischen Historiographen.* Studien zur Kulturkunde 29
(Wiesbaden: Steiner, 1972).
[2] E.g., Homer, *Od.* 15.403-484. That γεωγραφία began with Homer was recognized in antiquity. Cf. Strabon 1.1.11.

and Egyptians.[3] Such cursory glances were expanded by two new literary forms.[4] The first of these were known as περίπλοι which could be either simple reports of navigators who braved uncharted coastlines or manuals, *Lotsenbücher*, for use by navigators as they made their way around coastlines unknown to them.[5] These accounts primarily focused on the coast itself, although some did contain descriptions of the adjoining lands and peoples. The best-known of these is that of Skylax who was sent by Dareios I c. 515 B.C.E. down the Indus to its mouth and then along the coast until the party reached Egypt some thirty months later.[6] Although the περίπλους which bears his name is a fourth century compilation, we do have references to the authentic work.[7]

The second new form, a map of the known world, arose in connection with the emergence of Ionian philosophy. Thales has been justly regarded as the first philosopher since he broke with mythological explanations of the earth.[8] It is a younger contemporary, however, who applied the new *Weltanschauung* in a creative literary form. The traditions which we have about Anaximander have ultimately come to us—in all likelihood—from Eratosthenes (c. 295-194 B.C.E.), the successor of Apollonios Rhodios as head of the Alexandrian library.[9] Although Agathemeros claims Anaximander was a disciple of Thales,[10] it may well be that he was simply a con-

---

[3] E.g., Homer, *Iliad* 9.382-384. For fuller evidence see R. Drews, *The Greek Accounts of Eastern History* (Washington: Center for Hellenic Studies, 1973), p. 5. In addition to these literary references, the cultural borrowings of the Phoenician alphabet, Egyptian sculpture, and Lydian coinage suggest that archaic Greeks had a favorable image of their Eastern neighbors.

[4] Fuller treatment of these same two literary forebears may be found in Kurt von Fritz, *Die griechische Geschichtsschreibung*. Bd. 1: *Von den Anfängen bis Thukydides* (Berlin: Walter de Gruyter & Co., 1967), 1: 23-47.

[5] Brief but helpful discussions of this form of writing are in *KP*, s.v. "Periplus," by F. Lasserre, 4: 640-641 and *The Oxford Classical Dictionary*, 2nd ed., s.v. "Periploi," by Eric Herbert Warmington. A more comprehensive discussion is in *RE*, s.v., "Periplus," by F. Gisinger, 19: 841-850. It is worth pointing out that there are Homeric foreshadowings of this genre. Cf. *Od.* 1.80-81; 12.447-448.

[6] Herodotos 4.44.

[7] *FGrH* 709.

[8] Cf. G.S. Kirk, J.E. Raven, and M. Schofield, *The Presocratic Philosophers*, 2nd ed. (Cambridge: Cambridge University Press, 1983), pp. 76-99 for texts and commentary. Hereafter abbreviated *KRS*.

[9] Cf. Strabon 1.1.11 (= *KRS* 99). On Anaximander see *KRS*, pp. 100-142.

[10] Agathemeros 1.1 (= *KRS*, 98): Ἀναξίμανδρος ὁ Μιλήσιος ἀκουστὴς Θαλέω. Cf. also Theophrastos (= *KRS* 101A and B); Strabon 14.1.7; and Eustath. *Comm. Dion. Perieg.*, p. 208.

temporary.[11] He was the πρῶτος who ἐτόλμησε τὴν οἰκουμένην ἐν πίνακι γράψαι.[12] The form of his πίναξ is probably that ridiculed by Herodotos as he scorned his Ionian forerunners: οἳ Ὠκεανόν τε ῥέοντα γράφουσι πέριξ τὴν γῆν, ἐοῦσαν κυκλοτερέα ὡς ἀπὸ τόρνου, καὶ τὴν Ἀσίην τῇ Εὐρώπῃ ποιεύντων ἴσην.[13] Crude though his map was, it represented the first effort to comprehensively describe the world. It was from this πίναξ that the first glimmerings of ethnography—and consequently history—were to arise.

HEKATAIOS OF MILETOS

Life

Hekataios,[14] the son of Hegesander (TT 4, 45), was a Milesian[15] of high standing. His social standing is indicated by the length of his family's history (T 2) as well as the role he played in the Ionian revolt of 499. He advised Miletos not to revolt against Persia καταλέγων τά τε ἔθνεα πάντα τῶν ἦρχε Δαρεῖος καὶ τὴν δύναμιν αὐτοῦ.[16] The

---

[11] Strabon 1.1.11 (= *KRS* 99) only says that he is a γνώριμος καὶ πολίτης. Cf. also the version of Theophrastos in Ps.-Plutarch, *Strom.* 2 (= *KRS* 101C).

[12] Agathemeros 1.1 (= *KRS* 98). Cf. also Strabon 1.1.11 (= *KRS* 99) and Diogenes Laertios 2.2 (= *KRS* 94). The last also claims he made a sphere as well: ἀλλὰ καὶ σφαῖραν κατεσκεύασε. This is, however, unsubstantiated by other traditions.

[13] Herodotos 4.36.2. I do not mean that Herodotos specifically attacked Anaximander, but that the later was representative of those who followed him. Cf. below the discussion of Hekataios and Anaximander.

[14] For the text cf. *FGrH* 1 and Giuseppe Nenci, *Hecataei Milesii Fragmenta* (Florence, 1954). I have used Nenci for my analysis of Hekataios. Major studies on Hekataios are: *RE*, s.v., "Hekataios von Miletus," by Felix Jacoby, 7: 2667-2750; reprinted in his *Griechische Historiker* (Stuttgart: Alfred Druckenmüller, 1956), pp. 186-227; Lionel Pearson, *The Early Ionian Historians* (Oxford: The Clarendon Press, 1939), pp. 25-108; and the articles by Pierluigi Tozzi, "Studi su Ecateo di Mileto: Ecateo ed Euripide," *Anthenaeum* n.s. 41 (1963): 39-50; "Studi su Ecateo di Mileto: Ecateo e la Cultura Ionica," *Anthenaeum* n.s. 41 (1963): 318-326; "Studi su Ecateo di Mileto: Lingua e Stile di Ecateo," *Anthenaeum* n.s. 42 (1964): 101-117; "Studi su Ecateo di Mileto: La ΙΣΤΟΡΙΗ di Ecateo," *Anthenaeum* n.s. 43 (1965): 41-76; "Studi su Ecateo di Mileto: La Fortuna," *Anthenaeum* n.s. 45 (1967): 313-334. Other significant works are listed in *KP*, s.v., "Hekataios," by W. Spoerri, 2: 980-982. Add: Pilhofer, *Presbyteron Kreitton*, pp. 26–33.

[15] He was known as ὁ Μιλήσιος. Cf. TT 7, 9, 12, 15, 16, 27, 28, 30, 33, 34, 35, 38, 41, 45, and 46 which is likely a reference to Hekataios and not Hellanikos. The following description suits Hekataios much better than Hellanikos. TT 11, 14, 39 also state he was from Miletos.

[16] Herodotos 5.36.2. von Fritz, *Die griechische Geschichtsschreibung*, 1: 49, pointed out that this implies Hekataios had "eine intime Kenntnis des inneren Funktionierens des persischen Reiches."

sagacity of his counsel appears not to have impressed the insurrectionists, however, since when we meet him a second time, he is vainly urging Aristagoras to vacate to Leros and lie low until affairs calmed down enough to allow him to return to Miletos.[17] While Hekataios may not have enjoyed the approbation of his peers, the Herodotean narrative makes it clear that he was both knowledgeable and respected.

There are several corroborating traditions which help to confirm this impression. Some ancient authorities attempt to link him directly with Ionian philosophers. While the specific points of these statements are dubious[18] or clearly wrong,[19] we may at least say that Hekataios drank enough from the cup of the Ionian philosophy that he could write: Ἑκαταῖος Μιλήσιος ὧδε μυθεῖται· τάδε γράφω, ὥς μοι δοκεῖ ἀληθέα εἶναι· οἱ γὰρ Ἑλλήνων λόγοι πολλοί τε καὶ γελοῖοι, ὡς ἐμοὶ φαίνονται, εἰσίν (F 1).[20] How we interpret the offense he took and sought to rectify depends upon how much weight we place on πολλοί and how much on γελοῖοι. The former suggests he found the numerous and contradictory genealogies objectionable,[21] whereas the latter forces us to think about rationalizations of the myths.[22] I propose that such perspectives are not mutually exclusive and that both have a place – not because the evidence is too opaque, but because both are stated and are part of Hekataios' work.

---

[17] Herodotos 5.125. Hekataios may have had a special connection with Leros. Cf. T 5. The account of Ephoros preserved in Diodoros 10.25.4, that Hekataios represented the Milesians before Artaphernes after their defeat, is probably an invention based on Herodotos 6.42-43. Cf. Jacoby in *FGrH*, 1a: 317.

[18] T 42. Whether Hekataios shared Herakleitos' views on celestial bodies is uncertain. T 1 makes it clear that Herakleitos did not have a high regard for Hekataios. For Herakleitos' views see *KRS*, pp. 200-202.

[19] The statement in the Suda (T 45), καὶ ἦν ἀκουστὴς Πρωταγόρου ὁ Ἑκαταῖος, is impossible since Protagoros was born c.485 B.C.E.

[20] Jacoby goes beyond the evidence when he considers Hekataios to belong to the school of Thales. Cf. *RE*, s.v. "Hekataios," 7: 2669.

[21] So Fornara, *The Nature of History in Ancient Greece and Rome*, pp. 5-7. This is the preface to the Γενεαλογίαι. Fornara regarded the distinction between the heroic age and the *spatium historicum* in Hekataios as his major accomplishment whether it was "latent or explicit." One issue which must be addressed by this interpretation is what criterion did Hekataios apply to decide among conflicting accounts. It appears *ratio* was his yardstick. Cf. von Fritz, *Die griechische Geschichtsschreibung*, pp. 71-76.

[22] A good example is F 31. The problem with this interpretation is that Hekataios is inconsistent. He employs myths also. Cf. TT 9, 12, 32.

Of more immediate importance is the epithet Agathemeros assigns to him: πολυπλανής (T 34). We know that Hekataios visited Egypt,[23] but beyond this it is hard to be specific. It is certainly possible to argue that he had visited parts of the Persian empire based on Herodotos' report of his speech in 5.36.2, but this is not decisive. *A priori* it is likely that he visited other areas in the eastern half of the Mediterranean, but we cannot say more.[24]

These *facta* allow us to place Hekataios at the time ancient tradents situate him: the second half of the sixth century and the beginning of the fifth (TT 45, 47).[25] This means that he lived during the nascence of the Persian empire, an event which created not only a sense of curiosity, but also a need to know about other groups within the orb of the new sovereign power.[26]

Hekataios undertook to fill this gap in a new literary effort.[27] As we have seen, Anaximander was the first τὴν οἰκουμένην ἐν πίνακι γράψαι. Agathemeros then added: μεθ' ὃν Ἑκαταῖος ὁ Μιλήσιος ἀνὴρ πολυπλανὴς διηκρίβωσεν, ὥστε θαυμασθῆναι τὸ πρᾶγμα (1.1 = T 34). The obvious question to raise is what is meant by διηκρίβωσεν? While it may mean that he merely made some adjustments or additions to Anaximander's map, it is likely that he drew up his own, although he appears to have followed along his predecessor's general lines.[28] The new ground which Hekataios broke was

---

[23] Herodotos 2.143.

[24] Jacoby, *RE*, s.v. "Hekataios," 7: 2689-90, and Drews, *The Greek Accounts of Eastern History*, p. 15, think he traveled extensively. Nenci, *Hecataei Milesii Fragmenta*, p. xi, disagrees arguing that he only went to Egypt.

[25] Nenci, *Hecataei Milesii Fragmenta*, p. ix-x, assigns him the dates 560-480.

[26] So Pearson, *The Early Ionian Historians*, p. 18.

[27] Lionel Pearson, review of *Hecataei Milesii Fragmenta*, by G. Nenci, in *Classical Review*, n.s. 5 (1955): 263, offers a reconstruction of Hekataios' map. Cf. also his "Herodotus on the Source of the Danube," *Classical Philology* 29 (1934): 328-37. von Fritz, *Die griechische Geschichtsschreibung*, 1: 50, draws a distinction between "einer verbesserten Erdkarte" which should be denoted by περίοδος γῆς and "einer diese begleitenden oder sie ergänzenden Erdschreibung" which is correctly designated περιήγησις γῆς. While his interpretation is possible it is far from secure since ancient sources do not consistently make such a distinction—a problem he realizes.

[28] Cf. also TT 35, 48. Jacoby contrasted the two in *RE*, s.v. "Hekataios," 7: 2690-91, in these words: "Denn während es Anaximander wohl mehr auf die allgemeine Gestalt der Erde, auf die Lage der Οἰκουμένη, ihre Form und ihr Verhältnis zur Erdoberfläche überhaupt, vielleicht auch auf die sonstigen geographischen Probleme ankam, verband H.—um die griechischen Termini beizubehalten—mit dem geographischen das chorographische Interesse . . . Anaximander ist der Erfinder der Geographie; H. der Erfinder der beschreibenden Länderkunde."

not so much in his map but in an accompanying work designed to serve as a running commentary on the map. Strabon—following Eratosthenes—suggests this in his comments on the origins of γεωγραφία. He wrote: . . . τοὺς πρώτους μεθ' Ὅμηρον δύο φησιν Ἐρατοσθένης, Ἀναξίμανδρον . . . καὶ Ἑκαταῖον τὸν Μιλήσιον. He then explains: τὸν μὲν οὖν ἐκδοῦναι πρῶτον γεωγραφικὸν πίνακα, τὸν δὲ Ἑκαταῖον καταλιπεῖν γράμμα. . . (1.1.11 = T 15) This γράμμα has come down to us in fragmentary form as the Περιήγησις Γῆς. Hekataios also composed a Γενεαλογίαι which has also only reached us in bits and pieces.

These works earned Hekataios titles such as λογοποιός (TT 2, 3, 4, 25, 32), ἱστορικός (TT 31, 46(?), 49), and ἱστοριογράφος (T 45). He is said to have written γεωγραφικήν (TT 14, 15 [Strabon]), ἱστορίαν (T 11 [Strabon]), and an ἀρχαιολογίαν (T 24 [Josephos]). The multiplicity of these ascriptions make it clear that Hekataios does not fall into a prefabricated mold.

The Περιήγησις Γῆς

1. *Textual Problem.* The first step in exploring Hekataios' work is grappling with the fragments. While Nenci in his *Hecataei Milesii Fragmenta* was able to collect 388 fragments, they are limited both quantitatively and qualitatively. The former is due to the fact that over 300 of these are from the Ἐθνικά of Stephan of Byzantium whose alphabetical listing of place-names with the adjectives which are derived from them offers a very limited view into Hekataios' work.[29] Although we can be certain that later authors preserved sections of Hekataios in their works, it is extremely difficult to extract Hekataion passages with confidence.[30] We are also restricted qualitatively because we do not have the original word order in the fragments.[31] What this means is that we have relatively few of the

---

[29] Cf. Stephan von Byzanz, *Ethnika: Stephani Byzantii Ethnicorum quae supersunt ex Recensione Augusti Meinekii* (Berlin: G. Reimar, 1849; reprint ed., Graz, Austria: Akademische Druck-u. Verlagsanstalt, 1958). The situation is compounded one step more since Stephan's work was lost and we are now dependent upon an epitome which was made in the second half of the first millennium C.E.

[30] Cf. below on Herodotos' relationship to Hekataios.

[31] Cf. von Fritz, *Die griechische Geschichtsschreibung*, 1: 50-52. It is sometimes difficult to decide where the material from Hekataios ends in the fragments. For example, the derivation in F 70, the *mirabilia* in F 137, and the νόμοι in F 196 may stem from others. Cf. Pearson, *The Early Ionian Historians*, pp. 39-41, 47, 62 respec-

ipsissima verba of Hekataios. We also lack any coherent recapitulation of the work as a whole.[32] Although these limitations do not prevent us from obtaining a general concept of Hekataios' work, they caution us against dogmatic views based upon limited data.

A second problem is that in antiquity there was some debate over the authenticity of the material circulating under Hekataios' name (TT 28, 29; FF 240, 304, 314). The basis for the question is preserved in a statement by Athenaios who after mentioning the Περιήγησις of Asia says: εἰ γνήσιον τοῦ συγγραφέως τὸ βιβλίον. Καλλίμαχος γὰρ (Νησιώτου) ἀντ᾽ ἀναγράφει (2.70A = T 28). Apparently Kallimachos (c. 305-240 B.C.E.) questioned the authenticity of the second volume of the Περιήγησις in the Alexandrian library.[33] His doubts, however, were not shared by his student Eratosthenes (c. 275-194 B.C.E.) whose views are preserved by Strabon. After mentioning Hekataios' γράμμα, he says πιστούμενον ἐκείνου εἶναι ἐκ τῆς ἄλλης αὐτοῦ γραφῆς (1.1.11 = T 15). The defense was offered ἐκ τῆς ἄλλης αὐτοῦ γραφῆς. This suggests that it was only the particular volume at Alexandria which was at stake and not the entire corpus. Although modern scholars have at times tried to resurrect Kallimachos' uncertainties in an effort to stress the independence of Herodotos, the allignment of the twofold division with Ionian geographical thought (see below) and weight of the tradition as a whole argue for authenticity.[34]

2. *Content*. At some point before Hekataios' work came to Alexandria, it was divided into two volumes. The controversy over the second scroll helps to substantiate this.[35] The first scroll has come down to us under the headings Εὐρώπη,[36] Περιήγησις Εὐρώπης,[37]

---

tively. The best criterion is to eliminate what is characteristic of the author preserving Hekataios and anything unsuited to his time-frame.

[32] Cf. the warning of Jacoby, *RE*, s.v. "Hekataios," 7: 2702.

[33] On the division of the work see under Content.

[34] Cf. Pearson, *The Early Ionian Historians*, pp. 31-34, for an overview with bibliographic references.

[35] Jacoby, *RE*, s.v. "Hekataios," 7: 2672.

[36] FF 44, 45, 46, 47, 48, 49, 51, 52, 53, 54, 55, 56, 57, 58, 59, 60, 61, 63, 64, 65, 66, 67, 68, 69, 70, 71, 72, 73, 75, 76, 77, 78, 79, 80, 81, 82, 83, 84, 85, 86, 87, 88, 89, 90, 91, 92, 94, 96, 97, 98, 100, 101, 102, 103, 104, 105, 108, 113, 115, 116, 117, 118, 119, 120, 122, 123, 124, 125, 127, 128, 131, 132, 134, 137, 138, 142, 144, 145, 146, 147, 148, 149, 151, 152, 153, 154, 157, 158, 159, 161, 163, 164, 167, 168, 170, 171, 172, 173, 174, 175, 176, 179, 181, 182, 183, 184, 186, 187, 188, 189, 190, 191, 192, 193, 194, 195, 196, 197, 198, 199, 200, 201, 202, 203.

[37] FF 121, 139, 143, 177.

Περίοδος Εὐρώπης,[38] and Περίοδος τῆς Γῆς.[39] The second has a more prolific number of denominations: Ἀσία,[40] Ἀσίας Περιήγησις,[41] Περιήγησις,[42] Περίοδος Ἀσίας,[43] δεύτερος Περιήγησις,[44] Περιήγησις Αἰγύπτου,[45] Περιήγησις Λιβύης,[46] Αἰολικοί,[47] and the simple ἐν γῆς περιόδῳ.[48] The division of the work into these two halves doubtless reflects the Ionian concept that there were two continents: Europe and Asia.[49] It is, therefore, possible that Hekataios himself made the division, although this is not a necessary deduction.[50] The proliferation of headings for the second volume may reflect sectional headings since F 328 indicates that Egypt was discussed in Ἀσία.[51]

The fragments of the first book, Εὐρώπη, deal primarily with cities[52] and peoples.[53] Geographical features also constitute a significant amount of the preserved fragments: islands,[54] plains and bays,[55] mountains,[56] rivers,[57] regions,[58] and even ἄκραι.[59] The

[38] FF 156, 165.
[39] F 135.
[40] FF 204, 208, 210, 211, 212, 214, 215, 217, 218, 222, 223, 225, 226, 227, 228, 229, 231, 234, 236, 242, 243, 244, 245, 246, 247, 249, 250, 251, 252, 254, 255, 257, 258, 259, 260, 262, 264, 265, 266, 267, 268, 269, 270, 271, 272, 273, 275, 276, 277, 278, 279, 280, 282, 283, 284, 287, 288, 291, 293, 295, 298, 299, 301, 302, 303, 307, 309, 311, 312, 340, 347, 354, 360, 362, 372, 373.
[41] FF 233, 240, 263, 292, 296, 304, 306, 328, 351, 352, 353, 361, 368, 371.
[42] FF 285, 294, 330, 339, 349, 350, 358, 363, 364, 370.
[43] F 297.
[44] FF 317, 336.
[45] FF 318, 324, 325, 329, 332, 334, 341, 342.
[46] FF 291, 322, 327, 333, 345, 348, 356, 357, 359, 366, 367, 369.
[47] FF 239, 241.
[48] F 230.
[49] Herodotos 4.36.2. Europe was the upper half and Asia the lower half.
[50] It could have been someone who was influenced by Ionian conceptions.
[51] Could a librarian have inserted the titles for the sake of reference?
[52] FF 44, 45, 46, 49, 50, 51, 52, 53, 54, 56, 63, 64, 65, 66, 69, 70, 72, 73, 74, 75, 76, 77, 78, 79, 80, 81, 83, 87, 88, 92, 94, 95, 97, 99, 106, 107, 114, 118, 119, 121, 122, 123, 132, 133, 136, 139, 140, 141, 142, 143, 144, 145, 148, 159, 160, 161, 162, 166, 167, 169, 170, 171, 172, 173, 174, 175, 176, 177, 180, 183, 199.
[53] FF 47, 48, 55, 57, 58, 61, 62, 96, 98, 100, 102, 103, 104, 105, 108, 109, 113, 117, 146, 158, 168, 181, 182, 185, 186, 187, 188, 189, 190, 191, 192, 193, 194, 196, 197, 198, 200, 201, 202, 203.
[54] FF 59, 60, 67, 68, 71, 134, 135, 153, 154.
[55] FF 115, 126.
[56] FF 155, 178.
[57] F 156.
[58] F 184.
[59] FF 84, 91.

work extended beyond simple identifications, however; it also dealt with the early history of a country,[60] wonders,[61] and the etymology of various names.[62]

'Ασία proceeded along similar lines. Cities once again dominate the remnants[63] with ἔθνη again claiming the second position.[64] Geographical considerations are likewise prominent including νῆσοι,[65] rivers,[66] bays,[67] lakes,[68] χῶραι,[69] τόποι,[70] and one fragment each for oceans,[71] mountains,[72] and ἄκραι.[73] On three occasions, Hekataios offers measurements—in terms of sailing days.[74] We encounter a brief historical note,[75] wonders,[76] and very importantly, νόμοι.[77] Etymological discussions are once again dispersed within these fragments.[78]

What then comprised Hekataios' work? The primary focus is to describe the physical and human world as the ancient Ionian knew it. It is the human element which significantly distances him from

---

[60] F 130.

[61] FF 99, 112, 147, 165.

[62] Names of countries FF 43, 81(?), 124; cities, FF 82, 85, 86, 89, 90, 93, 111, 116, 120, 125, 126, 127, 128, 131, 137, 138, 149, 151, 157, 163, 179; ἔθνη, FF 101, 102, 196; spring, F 90; ἄκρα, F 110; plains, F 115; and islands, FF 147, 150, 152. Cf. also F 126 where he corrects an etymology.

[63] FF 208, 210, 211, 212, 214, 219, 220, 225, 226, 227, 231, 234, 235, 236, 237, 238, 239, 242, 243, 244, 246, 247, 248, 249, 250, 251, 252, 254, 256, 257, 258, 259, 260, 261, 262, 263, 264, 265, 266, 267, 268, 269, 270, 271, 272, 273, 274, 275, 276, 277, 278, 280, 281, 282, 283, 286, 287, 288, 289, 290, 291, 292, 293, 295, 296, 298, 300, 306, 309, 310, 317, 319, 324, 325, 326, 327, 328, 329, 330, 331, 332, 333, 334, 347, 349, 351, 353, 354, 355, 357, 360, 361, 362, 364, 365, 366, 367, 368, 370, 372, 373. Cf. also 316 where he deals with a κώμη.

[64] FF 204, 213, 215, 217, 218, 222, 223, 228, 229, 232, 284, 301, 302, 303, 307, 308, 312, 340, 342, 352. Cf. also F 311 for γένος and 350 for νομάδες.

[65] FF 255, 280, 285, 291, 316, 318, 320, 323, 341, 346, 356, 358, 363, 369.

[66] FF 221, 230, 274, 314, 315.

[67] FF 224, 256, 348.

[68] FF 216, 279, 371.

[69] FF 216, 299, 373.

[70] FF 322, 345.

[71] F 205.

[72] F 245.

[73] F 233.

[74] FF 206, 207, 348.

[75] F 313.

[76] FF 209, 240, 305, 305, 339.

[77] Clothing, FF 297, 300; Food, FF 335, 336, 337, 338; Other customs, FF 343, 344, 361.

[78] Cities, FF 242, 269, 270, 276, 280; bays, FF 241, 353; ocean, F 205; place, F 321.

Anaximander. It is this element which also raises the important issue of whether or not Hekataios related the history of the peoples he described. While the fragments are frustratingly limited, they do afford some evidence of historical reporting.[79] These hints are buttressed by the account of Egypt in Herodotos which is indebted to Hekataios. (See below) It, therefore, appears safe to conclude that Hekataios related the royal traditions of nations where he could obtain information.[80]

The scope of his work covers the entire Mediterranean world. The fragments reach from Spain (FF 44-60) to India (FF 310-312) on an east-west axis and from Pontus (F 206) to Ethiopia (FF 340-344) on a north-south axis. If we can believe Agatharchides, the work provided more material on the East than the West (T 44).

3. *Form.* How did he organize such a comprehensive effort? Our first clue is a possible dependence upon Skylax and therefore an awareness of περίπλοι. The evidence for this is as follows: both writers list groups of people in succession with their locale simply given as having come after the next, both works are divided into the same two halves,[81] and FF 305, 309 appear to reflect Hekataion dependence upon Skylax.[82] What this means is that Hekataios oriented his work along the coastline and moved sequentially around the Mediterranean as if he were circumnavigating it.

This impression is strengthened by the fragments themselves. Hekataios used adverbs and prepositional phrases to locate cities and ethnic groups. Three of the most important are μετά,[83] προσεχές,[84] and πρός.[85] This indicates his sequential pattern as he moved from ethnic group and their locale to ethnic group. The frag-

---

[79] So F 338. There are several difficulties here. First, is the Hekataios of this fragment Hekataios of Miletos or Abdera? Nenci opts for the former and Jacoby the latter (*FGrH* 264, F 5). Second, even if this is our author, did he relate the history of the custom or Eudoxos? If Hekataios gave this sketch he may have also given some royal history since the custom is tied to it.

[80] So also J. B. Bury, *The Ancient Greek Historians* (reprint ed., New York: Dover Publications, 1958), p. 12. *Contra* Drews, *The Greek Accounts of Eastern History*, pp. 11-14, who denies a historical element in Hekataios.

[81] On these two points see von Fritz, *Die griechische Geschichtsschreibung*, 1: 52-53.

[82] Cf. Jacoby, *FGrH*, 1a: 365. (Nenci 305 and 309 = Jacoby 296 and 295 respectively.

[83] FF 50, 56, 82, 97, 116, 122, 159, 177, 279, 288.

[84] FF 98, 102, 104, 113, 146, 153, 215, 229, 300, 301.

[85] E.g., FF 127, 134, 291, 303, 322, 358.

ments also indicate a pattern oriented to the coast.[86] It is likely that
he moved from W to E in the north and E to W in the south since
the tome was divided in this fashion and this constitutes the basic
pattern utilized by subsequent authors.[87] As he made his way, he
would first describe the coast and then interior features with rivers
serving as the key geographical markers.[88] Each area was named
and in some cases, he offered measurements. He then appears to
have located and identified the cities and major points of interest.
His last section appears to have dealt with the *nomoi* of the people.[89]

We should not presume, however, that Hekataios had a fixed
order from which he never varied. The diversity in the arrangements of his successors argues against such a naive assumption. Nor
should we think of his ethnographic commentary as a tight-knit
piece of writing. In fact, ancient *testimonia* suggest the opposite: the
work was loosely stitched with the seams clearly visible (TT 6, 9).

What did impress his ancient readers was the new medium in
which he chose to write. Hekataios elected not to write in meter but
in prose (TT 18,45). His style was σαφῆ καὶ κοινὴν καὶ καθαρὰν καὶ
σύντομον καὶ τοῖς πράγμασι προσφυῆ καὶ μηδεμίαν σκευωρίαν ἐπι-
φαίνουσαν τεχνικήν.[90] The fact that his selection of prose coincides
with Ionian familiarity with works from the East may be more than
simple coincidence.[91] It clearly lent itself more readily to the task of
simply describing what was known.

4. *Function.* The content and form of Hekataios' work make it evident that the Περιήγησις Γῆς attempted to describe the known world
via the insights of Ionian philosophy and the new knowledge which

---

[86] Cf. FF 46, 48, 59, 60, 72, 73, 74, 75, 76, 77, 78, 79, 80.

[87] Examples are Ephoros, Skylax, Pseudo-Skymnos, and the Latin Avienus.
Cf. Pearson, *The Early Ionian Historians*, p. 30. Jacoby thinks that Hekataios began
this pattern. *RE*, s.v. "Hekataios," 7: 2691.

[88] E.g., FF 230, 302, 312.

[89] For attempts to reconstruct a pattern see *RE*, s.v. "Hekataios," by Jacoby,
7: 2691-2692; Trüdinger, "Studien zur Geschichte der griechisch-römischen Ethnographie," pp. 9-10; Pearson, *The Early Ionian Historians*, p. 30; and Fornara, *The
Nature of History in Ancient Greece and Rome*, p. 14.

[90] Dionysios *De Thuc.*, 5 (= T 9). While the statement of Dionysios is a general
description of the style of the early logographers, it certainly fits Hekataios. Cf. also
TT 10 and 30.

[91] This connection is made by J. B. Bury, "Greek Literature from the Eighth
Century to the Persian Wars," in *The Persian Empire and the West*, ed. J.B. Bury,
S.A. Cook, and F.E. Adcock. CAH (Cambridge: The University Press, 1969),
4: 521.

came through reports and Hekataios' own ἱστορία.⁹² It is a marked improvement over his predecessor's efforts in detail and in ethnographic information, e.g., customs. The spirit was not as critical as it was learned.⁹³ Dionysios of Halikarnassos accurately summarized the general thrust of Hekataios and his successors, even if some of the language is anachronistic when applied to the former. He wrote . . . ἕνα καὶ τὸν αὐτὸν φυλάττοντες σκοπόν, ὅσαι διεσῴζοντο παρὰ τοῖς ἐπιχωρίοις μνῆμαι κατὰ ἔθνη τε καὶ κατὰ πόλεις, expanding, εἰ τ' ἐν ἱεροῖς εἴ τ' ἐν βεβήλοις ἀποκείμεναι γραφαί, ταύτας εἰς τὴν κοινὴν ἁπάντων γνῶσιν ἐξενεγκεῖν, and then elaborating with Herodotean language, οἵας παρέλαβον, μήτε προστιθέντες αὐταῖς τι μήτε ἀφαιροῦντες.⁹⁴ It was this encyclopedic effort to bring the traditions of others to the common knowledge of all that makes Hekataios significant for us. The impetus for his work came from the rise of Persia which he apparently felt he needed to know and understand.⁹⁵ While his work is more comprehensive in scope, it can hardly be only τύχη which saw his literary efforts take place after the rise of Persia.⁹⁶

Significance

Was Hekataios the first historian?⁹⁷ This depends in part on how far we are willing to stretch the term "history." I prefer to see him as the author of a περιήγησις from which both ethnography and history sprang.⁹⁸ He is, then, a seminal figure who helped set in

⁹² I use ἱστορία here in its original sense of investigation. I have in mind Hekataios' trip to Egypt.
⁹³ Herakleitos' criticism is thus partly validated when he accused Hekataios of having only πολυμαθίη νόον (T 1).
⁹⁴ Dionysios, *De Thuc.* 5 (= T 9) The inclusion of the distinction in sources will emerge in chapter three.
⁹⁵ Herodotos 5.36.2.
⁹⁶ F. W. Walbank, *Polybius.* The Sather Classical Lectures (Berkeley/Los Angeles/London: The University of California Press, 1972), p. 2, emphasized the importance of the Persian empire and the rise of history. Earlier control of Ionia by Lydia would not be parallel since the extent of the territories were so different and the proximity of Lydia would not have the same impact.
⁹⁷ T 45 (Suda). It is more accurate to speak of him as one of the historiae conditores. (T 36)
⁹⁸ Cf. Jacoby, "Über die Entwicklung der griechischen Historiographie," p. 82, who correctly saw Hekataios as the first in a process and Fornara, *The Nature of History in Ancient Greece and Rome*, p. 14, who calls Hekataios' work a "geography containing subordinate ethnographies."

motion a movement which extended for centuries. Authors soon began to concentrate on specific peoples—both Hellenic and barbarian—using the same basic format as Hekataios. These works did not have a specific genre name in antiquity, but are easily identifiable since they were entitled by the adjectival form of the people.

Three of these early prose authors are of particular importance for our study. One of the earliest was Charon of Lampsakos who wrote a Περσικὰ ἐν βιβλίοις β′ and ῏Ωροι Λαμψακηνῶν ἐν βιβλίοις δ′.[99]

The second was actually a native who appropriated Greek ethnography to write about his own *patria*. Xanthos is epitomized by Suda in these words: Ξάνθος, Κανδαύλου, Λυδὸς ἐκ Σάρδεων, ἱστορικός, γεγονὼς ἐπὶ τῆς ἁλώσεως Σάρδεων. Λυδιακὰ βιβλία δ′.[100] While he may have also authored a Μαγικά and a life of Empedokles, it is his Λυδιακά which arrests our attention. The fragments are too scanty to allow a reconstruction, but do offer insights into the content. He dealt with the land,[101] early history,[102] myths,[103] rivers,[104] the location of cities,[105] a temple,[106] νόμοι,[107] and has an etymological discussion.[108] What immediately strikes us is the role which history played in his work. Dionysios of Halikarnassos gave him a rather unusual bouquet when he wrote: Ξάνθος δ' ὁ Λυδός, ἱστορίας παλαιᾶς εἰ καί τις ἄλλος ἔμπειρος ὤν; adding, τῆς δὲ πατρίου καὶ βεβαιωτὴς ἂν οὐδενὸς ὑποδεέστερος νομισθείς. . .[109]

---

[99] *FGrH* 262. There were other works ascribed to him, but probably incorrectly. Cf. Pearson, *The Early Ionian Historians*, pp. 139-151. We only have one fragment of the Περσικά which mentions the first appearance of white doves in Greece in connection with Mardonios, the nephew and son-in-law of Dareios I. I have not entered the debate on which of these early authors preceded Herodotos.

[100] *FGrH*, 765. The quote is T 1. The date can not be trusted. Cf. Pearson, *The Early Ionian Historians*, pp. 115-117. He discusses Xanthos on pp. 109-138.

[101] FF 1, 12, 13.

[102] FF 14, 15, 16, 18, 19, 26(?), 30.

[103] FF 3, 8, 17, 20, 21, 29.

[104] F 24.

[105] FF 2, 5, 6, 7, 8, 9, 10, 11, 23, 25, 26, 27. The large number devoted to cities is due to the fact that Stephan of Byzantium preserved these.

[106] F 28.

[107] FF 4, 22.

[108] F 15.

[109] Dionysios 1.28.2 (= T 8). This is a quite different view than the more critical appraisal in *De Thuc.* 5. Dionysios must have read either Xanthos or the epitome of Menippos. Cf. Pearson, *The Early Ionian Historians*, pp. 120-121. On the increased role of history in ethnographies over the *periodos* see Jacoby, "Über die Entwicklung der griechischen Historiographie," p. 90.

His contemporary, Hellanikos of Lesbos, was even more prolific.[110] Among his numerous works are an Αἰγυπτιακά and a Περσικά in two books.[111] We have seven fragments from the Αἰγυπτιακά which relate myth,[112] history,[113] wonders,[114] νόμοι,[115] and discoveries or firsts.[116] The Περσικά offer the same basic material: lands,[117] myths of eponymous ancestors,[118] history,[119] and a etymological discussion.[120]

Scanty and broken as these works are, they appear to establish the presence of a genre which arose in the first half of the fifth century B.C.E. which we may label ethnography.[121] The content of these works—while not inflexible – covered four basic areas: the land, the history, θαυμάσια, and νόμοι of a people.[122] Ethnographies were intended to inform Greeks about peoples with whom they had now been brought into meaningful contact. The validity of these conclusions, however, depends upon an analysis of the only complete ethnographic *logoi* extant, those of Herodotos.

---

[110] *FGrH*, 4. Cf. also Pearson, *The Early Ionian Historians*, pp. 152-235.

[111] The number of his works is disputed. The Suda did not bother to list all of the titles which were attached to his name but simply wrote: συνεγράψατο δὲ πλεῖστα πεζῶς τε καὶ ποιητικῶς (T 1).

[112] FF 173, 176.

[113] F 55.

[114] FF 54, 174.

[115] F 53.

[116] F 175.

[117] FF 60, 179.

[118] FF 59 and 132 deal with eponymous ancestors. F 60 deals with mythical beginnings.

[119] FF 177 (Assyrian); 178, 180, 181, 182, 183, 184 (Persian).

[120] F 59.

[121] Cf. Jacoby, "Über die Entwicklung der griechischen Historiographie," p. 88: "Nicht minder zahlreich als die, Nachkommenschaft der Γενεαλογίαι ist die der Περίοδος Γῆς. Ich meine jetzt nicht die eigentlichen Periegesen; die haben wir schon ausgesondert und dem Geographenbande zugewiesen. Vielmehr die Werke, die nicht mehr die ganze bekannte Welt, sondern ein einzelnes Land geographisch-ethnographisch darstellen, die das Bindeglied sind auch zwischen der Περίοδος und Herodot. Ich will sie Ethnogrpahien nennen, obwohl der Terminus in dieser Form nicht antik ist."

[122] *Ibid.*, p. 89.

HERODOTOS[123]

Life[124]

The greatest successor to Hekataios is none other than the pater historiae.[125] Herodotos of Halikarnassos was born—according to the traditional date—in 484 B.C.E.[126] He was the son of Lyxes and, like his forerunner Hekataios, was from a family of some standing. In the course of a civil dispute, a relative, the epic poet Panyassis, was slain by the tyrant Lydamis: an event which precipitated Herodotos' removal to Samos.[127] Lydamis was removed from his position by 454, but Herodotos chose not to make his native city his permanent residence.[128]

Instead he spent his time traveling and lecturing. His journeys can only be gleaned or inferred from his *Histories*. We can be certain that he spent time in Scythia,[129] Egypt,[130] and Greece.[131] The importance these journeys had for Herodotos is hard to overstate. Based upon them, he developed a hierarchy of reliability for his sources: placing autopsy and personal investigation at the top and

---

[123] There is a very helpful recent essay introducing both Herodotean studies and providing bibliographical information: Carolyn Dewald and John Marincola, "A Selective Introduction to Herodotean Studies," *Arethusa* 20 (1987): 9-40. The entire issue is devoted to Herodotos and contains a number of important papers. Cf. esp. Christian Meier, "Historical Answers to Historical Questions: The Origins of History in Ancient Greece," pp. 41-57. See also Pilhofer, *Presbyteron Kreitton*, pp. 34-49.

[124] The main source for Herodotos' life is the Suda. All references to the text of Herodotos are to Carol Hude, ed., *Herodoti Historiae*, 3rd ed., 2 vols. OCT (Oxford: The Clarendon Press, 1927).

[125] The title was conferred on him by Cicero, *De leg.* 1.5.

[126] Aulus Gellius *Noct. Att.* 15.23. Dionysios, *De Thuc.* 5, wrote: ὁ δ' Ἁλικαρνασεὺς Ἡρόδοτος, γενόμενος ὀλίγῳ πρότερον τῶν Περσικῶν, παρεκτείνας δὲ μέχρι τῶν Πελοποννησιακῶν . . .

[127] 3.60 demonstrates his familiarity with Samos.

[128] Halikarnassos appears in an Athenian tribute list of this year without a ruler. Cf. R. Meiggs and D. Lewis, eds., *A Selection of Greek Historical Inscriptions* (Oxford: The Clarendon Press, 1969), n.32.

[129] Cf. 4.76.4.

[130] The journeys of Herodotos in Egypt have been carefully analyzed by Alan B. Lloyd, *Herodotus: Book II*, 3 vols. (Leiden: E. J. Brill, 1975-1988), 1: 61-76. He summarized his findings thus: "Herodotus came to Egypt by sea but we cannot tell whether he ascended the Nile via the Canopic or Pelusiac Branch. Much of his travelling in the Delta was determined by these two branches. In Upper Egypt he travelled as far as Elephantine and either going or returning visited the Fayyum where he saw the Labyrinth and Memphis. In the latter city he spent a great deal of time."

[131] The evidence for Greece is the tradition of his lectures.

native reports below them. This is clearly borne out by his statement in 2.99.1: μέχρι μὲν τούτου ὄψις τε ἐμὴ καὶ γνώμη καὶ ἱστορίη ταῦτα λέγουσά ἐστι, τὸ δέ ἀπὸ τοῦδε Αἰγυπτίους ἔρχομαι λόγους ἐρέων κατὰ τὰ ἤκουον.[132]

There is an ancient tradition that Herodotos lectured in Athens. Plutarch, who disputes the integrity of the tradition, has preserved it for us in these words: ὅτι μέντοι δέκα τάλαντα δωρεὰν ἔλαβεν ἐξ Ἀθηνῶν Ἀνύτου τὸ ψήφισμα γράψαντος, ἀνὴρ Ἀθηναῖος, οὐ τῶν παρημελημένων ἐν ἱστορίᾳ, Δίυλλος εἴρηκεν.[133] While the reliability of the details is far from secure,[134] the tradition is buttressed by Aristophanes' parody of the cherchez-la-femme view of the cause of animosities which Herodotos mentions but rejects in his introduction.[135] His work must have been known for the comic's lampoon to have been effective.[136] It may even be possible that the original divisions of the work were guided by considerations of public recitations.[137]

At either the founding of Thurioi in southern Italy or shortly thereafter, Herodotos joined the venture as a citizen.[138] While it is likely that he continued to travel some, he apparently made the new colony his home. One tradition places his death here,[139] although it

---

[132] K. H. Waters, *Herodotus, the Historian: His Problems, Methods, and Originality* (Norman: University of Oklahoma Press, 1985), pp. 90-91, suggests a more nuanced gradation of three steps: autopsy, hearing, and reports.

[133] Plutarch, *De malign H.* 862B. Diyllos was a fourth century Athenian historian. The tradition of his lectures grew wildly out of hand as is evidenced by the report of his address at the Olympian games in which παρεῖχεν ἑαυτὸν ᾄδων τὰς ἱστορίας καὶ κηλῶν τοὺς παρόντας, ἄχρι τοῦ καὶ Μούσας, κληθῆναι τὰς βίβλους αὐτοῦ, ἐννέα καὶ αὐτὰς οὔσας. Lucian, *Herod.* 1. Cf. 1-2.

[134] The sum is extraordinarily high and the identification of Anytos is problematic if he is the wealthy Athenian at the turn of the fifth to fourth centuries.

[135] Aristophanes, *Ach.* 515-529.

[136] It is possible to argue for another source behind Aristophanes' lines. The proximity of dates and tradition, however, argue against such a view.

[137] This has been proposed recently. Silvana Cagnazzi, "Tavola dei 28 Logoi di Erodoto," *Hermes* 103 (1975): 385-423, argued that Herodotos originally wrote 28 *logoi*. Waters, *Herodotus, the Historian*, p. 70, has followed this lead and concluded: ". . . it seems probable enough that the general plan of Herodotos' work was modified, if not totally controlled, by the appropriate length of a lecture." Cf. further discussion under the heading Form.

[138] Aristotle has the following title for Herodotos' work: Ἡροδότου Θουρίου ἥδ' ἱστορίης ἀπόδειξις. *Rhe.* 3.9.2. Cf. also Plutarch, *De epil.* 604F.

[139] Stephan of Byzantium, s.v. "Θούριοι."

has not gone unrivaled.[140] Since his work mentions events down to
c. 430 B.C.E., he presumably died in the following decade.

The Histories

1. *Relationship to Hekataios*. Past generations have sometimes thought
it fashionable to conceive of creative geniuses working *a novo*. In-
novative and epoch-making as Herodotos was, he did not begin with
a *tabula rasa*. The most important of his predecessors or contemporaries was Hekataios. That Herodotos knew about Hekataios is
beyond dispute since he mentions him by name on four occasions.[141] The final reference is the most important since Herodotos
says: Ἑκαταῖος μὲν ὁ Ἡγησάνδρου ἔφησε ἐν τοῖς λόγοισι . . .
(6.137.1)[142] The statement not only lets us know that Herodotos
knew of the Milesian's work, but calls express attention to it by naming it as a source: a rarity in the Herodotean narrative.[143]

A number of ancient scholars believed that Herodotos' familiarity
with Hekataios was more than passing. Eusebios, following Porphery, could even place Herodotean dependence upon Hekataios in
the form of a rhetorical question: ἢ ὡς Ἡρόδοτος ἐν τῇ δευτέρᾳ πολλὰ Ἑκαταίου τοῦ Μιλησίου κατὰ λέξιν μετήνεγκεν ἐκ τῆς Περιη-
γήσεως, βραχέα παραποιήσας, and then spelling it out, τὰ τοῦ
φοίνικος ὀρνέου καὶ περὶ τοῦ ποταμίου ἵππου καὶ τῆς θήρας
κροκοδείλων.[144] Is this a valid observation or does it merely assume that similarity of content entails dependence? The only way to
answer this question is to examine possible points of contact between
Hekataios and Herodotos and determine whether or not the similarities are close enough to posit dependence.

Since we know that both visited Egypt, both wrote about Egypt,
and Porphery points us here, I will examine the fragments of Hekataios which are similar to the account of Herodotos in book 2. Arrian
observed that Αἴγυπτόν τε Ἡρόδοτός τε καὶ Ἑκαταῖος οἱ λογοποῖοι
. . . δῶρόν τε τοῦ ποταμοῦ ἀμφότεροι ὡσαύτως ὀνομάζουσιν, which

---

[140] Pella of Macedonia is the alternate recorded by the Suda.
[141] 2.143; 5.36, 125; 6.137.
[142] 2.143 also indicates—in all probability that Herodotos had read Hekataios.
[143] Jacoby calls attention to this in *RE*, s.v. "Hekataios," 7: 2675.
[144] Eusebios *PE* 10.3 (466B) (= T 38 in *FGrH* 1 [Hekataios]). See T 30 for the
testimony of Hermogenes: Ἑκαταῖος δὲ ὁ Μιλήσιος, παρ' οὗ δὴ μάλιστα ὠφέληται
ὁ Ἡρόδοτος. Suda (T 45) similarly wrote: Ἡρόδοτος δὲ ὁ Ἁλικαρνασεὺς ὠφέληται
τούτου (i.e., Ἑκαταίου—GES).

he then qualifies: καὶ οὐκ ἀμαυροῖς τεκμηρίοις ὅτι ταύτῃ ἔχει Ἡροδότῳ ἐπιδέδεκται.[145] Although the last clause may imply Herodotos offered a more complete account, the common use of such a striking phrase raises our eyebrows.[146] We have a similar type of comparison in Diodoros Sikelos who tells us that both commented on the sources of the Nile, although not identically.[147]

There are two descriptions where we can actually make comparisons. The first concerns the temple of Leto and the island of Chembis. I have set the texts out in synoptic form:

HEKATAIOS	HERODOTOS
318	155.2-156.2
	2 οὔνομα δὲ τῇ πόλι ταύτῃ
ἐν βούτοις	ὅκου τὸ χρηστήριόν ἐστι βούτω,
	ὡς καὶ πρότερον ὠνόμασταί μοι.
περὶ τὸ ἱερὸν	ἱρὸν δὲ ἔστι ἐν τῇ βουτοῖ ταύτῃ
	Ἀπόλλωνος καὶ Ἀρτέμιδος.
τῆς Λητοῦς	καὶ ὅ γε νηὸς τῆς Λητοῦς
	. . . (Description of temple)
	1 οὕτω μέν νυν ὁ νηὸς
	τῶν φανερῶν μοι τῶν
	περὶ τοῦτο τὸ ἱρόν ἐστι
	θωμαστότατον,
	τῶν δὲ δευτέρων
ἔστι νῆσος Χέμβις ὄνομα,	νῆσος ἡ Χέμμις καλευμένη.
ἵρη τοῦ Ἀπόλλωνος,	(Cf. 4)
	2 ἔστι μὲν ἐν λίμνῃ
	βαθέῃ καὶ πλατέῃ κειμένη
	παρὰ τὸ ἐν βουτοῖ ἱρόν,
	λέγεται δὲ ὑπ᾿ Αἰγυπτίων
ἔστι δὲ ἡ νῆσος μεταρσίη	εἶναι αὕτη ἡ νῆσος πλωτή.
καὶ περιπλεῖ	αὐτὸς μὲν ἔγωγε οὔτε πλέουσαν
καὶ κινέεται ἐπὶ τοῦ ὕδατος.	οὔτε κινηθεῖσαν εἶδον,
	τέθηπα δὲ ἀκούων
	εἰ νῆσος ἀληθέως ἐστὶ πλωτή.

---

[145] Arrian *Anab.* 5.6.5 (= F 314 in Nenci, *Hecataei Milesii Fragmenta*) Cf. Herodotos 2.5.1: . . . Αἴγυπτος ἐς τὴν Ἕλληνες ναυτίλλονται ἐστὶ Αἰγυπτίοισι ἐπίκτητός τε γῆ καὶ δῶρον τοῦ ποταμοῦ. . .

[146] Too much should not be made of this phrase since it was such a memorable expression that it may have immediately passed into common usage after Hekataios (or a predecessor of his) used it.

[147] Diodoros 1.37.1-4. Hekataios approached the matter mythologically and Herodotos rationally—although incorrectly. Cf. esp. 3-4.

The first impression these texts create is the similarity of the order
and basic congruence. This is broken only once when the Hekataion
fragment simply asserts the νῆσος is ἴρη τοῦ ᾿Απόλλωνος; whereas
Herodotos delays this point until he can give a description of the
temple on the island (156.4). Such general parallels could proceed
from independent eye-witness reports. The description of the island,
however, carries us beyond this. Note the synonyms:

Hekataios	Herodotos
μεταρσίη	πλωτή
περιπλεῖ	πλέουσαν
κινέεται	κινηθεῖσαν

The fact that these three pairs are all in the same order makes it appear that the text of Hekataios served as the ἀφορμή for Herodotos.
    The identical pattern appears again in the description of Egyptian
νόμοι.

HEKATAIOS	HERODOTOS
Athenaios 10.418E (F 337)	77.4

Αἰγυπτίους δὲ ῾Εκαταῖος	
ἀρτοφάγους φησὶν εἶναι	ἀρτοφαγέουσι δὲ
	ἐκ τῶν ὀλυρέων ποιεῦντες ἄρτους,
κυλλήστιας ἐσθίοντας,	τοὺς ἐκεῖνοι κυλλήστις ὀνομάζουσι.
τὰς δὲ κριθὰς	οἴνῳ δὲ ἐκ κριθέων
εἰς ποτὸν καταλέοντας.	πεποιημένῳ διαχρέωνται.

Cf. also 3.114C (335 = *FGrH* 322)
        10.447C (336 = *FGrH* 323)
    Again note the parallels:

Hekataios	Herodotos
ἀρτοφάγους	ἀρτοφαγέουσι
κυλλήστους	κυλλήστις
κριθάς	κριθέων

This kind of agreement is too close for happenstance.
    We may now look at more distant parallels with a different per-
spective. Compare F 1 of Hekataios with Herodotos 2.45.1

HEKATAIOS

οἱ γὰρ Ἑλλήνων λόγοι
πολλοί τε καὶ γελοῖοι,

ὡς ἐμοὶ φαίνονται, εἰσίν.

HERODOTOS

λέγουσι δὲ
πολλὰ καὶ ἄλλα ἀνεπισκέπτως
οἱ Ἕλληνες

Both of these asseverations are earmarks of incipient rationalism. While they could derive from a common intellectual milieu, they add some weight to our preceding comparisons. There is also a curious statement about sources in 2.147.1: ταῦτα μέν νυν αὐτοὶ Αἰγύπτιοι λέγουσι, ὅσα δὲ οἵ τε ἄλλοι ἄνθρωποι καὶ Αἰγύπτιοι λέγουσι ὁμολογέοντες τοῖσι ἄλλοισι κατὰ ταύτην τὴν χώρην γενέσθαι, ταῦτ' ἤδη φράσω. Who are οἱ ἄλλοι ἄνθρωποι? Two factors lead me to include Hekataios: he had just mentioned him (2.143) and the discussion of the temple of Leto and island of Chembis follows (2.155-156).

Do these data—admittedly scanty—allow us to proclaim dependence. I believe they do.[148] The more difficult issue is: What was the extent of the borrowing? Is *Quellenforschung* an accurate enough tool to allow us to dissect the Herodotean narrative and remove the Hekataion segments? While I am confident they are there, I am reluctant to claim as Hekataion a text for which there is no corresponding fragment.[149] In any case, this effort goes beyond my purpose.

It is more relevant to realize what alterations Herodotos made to the framework he inherited. We have already seen that ethnogra-

---

[148] This has long been an accepted conclusion. Cf. Bury, *The Ancient Greek Historians*, pp. 49-50. For a recent discussion see Lloyd, *Herodotus: Book II*, 1: 127-139. Jacoby went a step further. He wrote in *RE*, s.v. "Hekataios," 7: 2685: "Es steht jetzt fest (wofür II 143 stets hätte genügen sollen), daß Herodot auf seinen Reisen das Buch des H. mit sich geführt hat; daß seine eigene Forschung von diesem Buche ausgegangen und in ihrer Richtung teilweise durch dies Buch bestimmt ist; daß er es schließlich bei der Ausarbeitung seiner λόγοι stark benützt hat." He may well be right.

[149] Jacoby pointed out that the bulk of usage comes in Books 1-4. He thought that Book 1 contains "nur einige geographischen Einlagen." Concerning Book 2 he wrote: "Dagegen ist in Buch II die Benützung durchgehend, soweit es sich um die Natur des Landes, die νόμοι seiner Bewohner, die Beziehungen der Hellenen zu Agypten handelt: H. hat das Alter des Volkes, die φύσις τῆς χώρης, den Nil, die νόμοι Αἰγυπτίων besprochen, und diese Behandlung bildet die Grundlage für Herodot." He also saw 3.89-116, the Λιβυκά and Σκυθικά of Book 4, and 5.57-61 as deriving from Hekataios. Cf. *RE*, s.v. "Hekataios," 7: 2686. I think these are very probable deductions. They can not be proven, however, without fragments.

phies developed from Hekataios' Περιήγησις. While it does not appear possible to firmly establish Herodotean dependence upon a specific author or ethnography,[150] he was unquestionably familiar with the form and function of ethnographies.[151] What Herodotos did with this old wine was to put it into a new wineskin.[152] His new creation is what we may legitimately call history.[153]

2. *Content.* The marriage of ethnographic material and historical narrative has occasioned a major debate in Herodotean scholarship in this century. Since this polemic bears on our understanding of the evolution of the genre I am attempting to trace, I will sketch the basic contours of the exchange.

The gauntlet was appropriately thrown down by Felix Jacoby, whose views are recorded in his book-length article on Herodotos for the supplement of the *Real-Encyclopädie der classischen Altertumswissenschaft.*[154] Jacoby argued that Herodotos began as a traveler whose primary concerns were ethnographic. As an ethnographer, he first wrote independent *logoi* on different ethnic groups, probably as a basis for lectures. A showcase example of the independence of the

---

[150] Attempts stem from antiquity. So Athenaios reports the view of Ephoros (12.11 = T 5 *FGrH*, 765): ὡς ἱστορεῖ Ξάνθος ὁ Λυδὸς ἢ ὁ τὰς εἰς αὐτὸν ἀναφερομένας ἱστορίας συγγεγραφώς—Διονύσιος δ' ὁ Σκυτοβραχίων, ὡς 'Αρτέμων φησὶν ὁ Κασανδρεύς, ἐν τῷ περὶ συναγωγῆς βιβλίων, ἀγνοῶν ὅτι "Εφορος ὁ συγγραφεὺς μνημονεύει αὐτοῦ ὡς παλαιοτέρου ὄντος καὶ 'Ηροδότῳ τὰς ἀφορμὰς δεδωκότος. It is likewise possible to claim Charon and Hellanikos as precursors. The difficulty lies in establishing specific contributions. The evidence is just too fragmentary.

[151] A comparison of Herodotos' ethnographic λόγοι and those of Charon, Xanthos, and Hellanikos strongly suggests this. (Their fragmentary nature stops us short of demonstration.)

[152] Cf. Jacoby, *RE*, s.v. "Hekataios," 7: 2700: "Die Περίοδος hatte, wenn man schon vergleichen will, weit mehr Ähnlichkeit mit Skylax' Περίπλους als mit Herodots 'Ιστορίαι. Die Entwicklungslinie, an deren Anfang sie steht, läuft über eine Reihe ähnlicher Werke sec. V, über Eudoxus, Dikaiarchos und die ganz selbständigen geographischen Bücher des Ephoros zu Eratosthenes Γεωγραφουμενα und von da weiter zu Strabon . . . Herodot steht nicht in dieser Reihe. Sein Zweck ist ein anderer; und damit ist eine völlig verschiedene Form gegeben."

[153] Cf. R. G. Collingwood, *The Idea of History* (Oxford: Oxford University Press, 1946), pp. 17-20. Collingwood believes history consists of four elements: it is scientific, i.e., asks questions; it is humanistic, i.e., it asks about humans in specific contexts; it is rational; and it is self-revelatory, i.e., it tells humans who they are by what they have done. There is an important study on Herodotos' representation of other peoples. See Francois Hartog, *The Mirror of Herodotus: The Representation of the Other in the Writing of History,* trans. by Janet Lloyd. The New Historicism: Studies in Cultural Poetics 5 (Berkeley/Los Angeles/London: University of California Press, 1988).

[154] *RE. Suppl.,* s.v. "Herodotos," by Felix Jacoby, 2: 205-520.

logoi is Book 2.[155] Jacoby thought that Herodotos originally intended to unite them in the mold of Hekataios, i.e., he would write his
own Περιήγησις, only he would improve the work of his forerunner
with more attention given to history.[156] A major change took place,
however, when Herodotos visited Greece. Here while giving his ethnographic lectures, Herodotos conceived of his *Histories* as we now
have them.[157] This shift came about as a result of Herodotos' desire
to incorporate Greek material into his work. He wanted to inform
a now ignorant generation of the great service Athens had rendered.[158] Herodotos thus moved through two major stages in his
development: he began as an ethnographer in the Ionic tradition,
and then through his ties with Greece became the historian we
know.

While Jacoby's *Entwicklungstheorie* has been very influential,[159] it
has by no means gone uncontested. The first major challenge came
from Max Pohlenz who could not see the *Histories* as a conglomerate
of *disjecta membra*, but argued that Herodotos was a historian *ab ini-
tio*.[160] The *Leitmotiv*—according to Pohlenz—was the Hellenic quest
for freedom against Asiatic imperialism.[161] This is not to deny
Herodotos' debt to Hekataios; it is to recognize that Herodotos went
far beyond his predecessors in his historical interests.[162] Pohlenz
countered Jacoby's deduction from the unity of individual *logoi* with
the observation that literary units within a larger corpus do not
necessitate original independence.[163] Rather, Herodotos incorporated diverse materials in the interests of clarity: everything which
helped to explicate was included.[164] There is no evidence that

---

[155] *Ibid.*, 2: 330-332. Jacoby thought Herodotos wrote major independent *logoi*
on Egypt, Lydia, Persia, Babylon, the Massagetae, Ethiopia, (Samos), Skythia,
Cyrene and Lydia, and Thrace.

[156] *Ibid.*, 2: 342-343.

[157] *Ibid.*, 2: 353-355.

[158] *Ibid.*, 2: 358-359.

[159] This is exemplified in the work of Trüdinger, "Studien zur Geschichte der
griechisch-römischen Ethnographie," who accepts Jacoby's two stage analysis (pp.
14-16) and then moves beyond him by recognizing that a distinction should be
made between *logoi* which were independent and those which were not (pp. 16-21).

[160] Max Pohlenz, *Herodot, der erste Geschichtsschreiber des Abendlandes*, Neue Wege
zur Antike 2 Series, 7-8 (Leipzig/Berlin: B.G. Teubner, 1937; reprint ed., Stuttgart: B.G. Teubner, 1961).

[161] *Ibid.*, p. 10.

[162] *Ibid.*, pp. 50-52.

[163] *Ibid.*, p. 66.

[164] *Ibid.*, p. 70. Cf. also pp. 83-85.

Herodotos wrote a Περιήγησις. In fact, Herodotos differs from Hekataios by focusing more on the human element than the geographical.[165] He already had these interests on his journeys when he began accumulating information for his *Histories*.[166] His work is, therefore, "die Schöpfung eines Meisters, der wie der Plato nach einem durch sein Thema gegebenen Plane ein Kunstwerk aufgebaut hat."[167]

Critics of Jacoby were not limited to the continent. In his *Form and Thought in Herodotus*, Henry Immerwahr likewise rejected Jacoby's genetic method.[168] He reminded us that ethnographic *logoi* join the narrative at the point where the respective nation is attacked by the East and terminate when the nation ceases to be autonomous.[169] This does not preclude the recognition that the basic unit of the *Histories* is the *logos*.[170] In fact, Immerwahr contended that the entire work is a series of *logoi*. "These are arranged in a single row from which are suspended, as it were, separate ethnographic and Greek historical *logoi* at irregular intervals."[171] This paratactic method of linking *logoi* is a heritage from Hekataios.[172] The theme which couples these links is the encomiastic portrayal of the Greek way of life.[173] The reason the ethnographic material is included is Herodotos' anthropocentric view of geography, i.e., human beings can only be understood as part of the world in which they live.[174] It

---

[165] *Ibid.*, pp. 78-79.

[166] *Ibid.*, pp. 79-81, 83.

[167] *Ibid.*, pp. 90-91.

[168] Henry R. Immerwahr, *Form and Thought in Herodotus*. Philological Monographs 23 (Cleveland: The American Philological Association, 1966). Cf. p. 8: "Genetic theories operate upon the assumption that traces of such earlier conceptions survive in the final version, and that we can recognize them unequivocally for what they are. This is true, however, only when the final stage is very incompletely finished, and a number of remnants of earlier conceptions are evident which conflict with the final stage and have neither been eliminated nor adjusted."

[169] *Ibid.*, p. 34. Cf. also p. 317.

[170] *Ibid.*, p. 42: "The structure of the *Histories* is very simple. The work is a chain of *logoi* with special emphasis at the beginning and a similar, if greater, emphasis at the end."

[171] *Ibid.*, p. 79. It should be noted that Immerwahr argued that Herodotos simply extended the principle of ethnographic *logoi* to the Greek material (pp. 34-38). *Contra* Jacoby, *RE Suppl.*. 2: 351.

[172] Immerwahr, *Form and Thought in Herodotus*, p. 47.

[173] *Ibid.*, pp. 44-45.

[174] *Ibid.*, p. 315. In Herodotos' *Weltanschauung*—according to Immerwahr—animals, geography, and humans are all governed by the same laws (p. 315).

is therefore a mistake to sever the close-knit bond between ethnography and history.[175]

The evolutionary view has not, on the other hand, lacked defenders. The most important of these is Kurt von Fritz who has advanced Jacoby's case by analyzing the journeys of Herodotos to determine his purposes. He concluded that the ancient historian's travels could not be tied to the Persian war since he failed to investigate crucial areas.[176] Von Fritz thinks, rather, that Herodotos went to Egypt in order to refute the prevailing continent theory of the Ionians.[177] This eliminates postulating historical interests in the Persian wars for the early Herodotos. What did happen was that in his account of Egypt Herodotos wedded history to ethnography.[178] Eventually he extended this on a much grander scale.

The most ambitious attempt to argue for the unity of the *Histories* is the work of J. Cobet.[179] His work is two-pronged basically. He contends that Herodotos is concerned with the entire human situation, not just historical events. The ethnographic *logoi*, are, therefore, an attempt to grasp the totality of human experience.[180] They relate to the Persian wars because the Persian empire is what brought this world into meaningful relationships.[181] The second point is that we should not measure Herodotos by ourselves. Excurses are an integral part of the *Histories*. We are bothered by them because they interrupt the flow of the narrative: they are static and not dynamic.[182] Yet it is this very point which should help us to see that Herodotos is interested in more than events. He presents the entire human situation.[183]

Charles Fornara has attempted to cast light on this continuing controversy by pointing out that the genetic approach seeks to explain how the material came into its present form, while the uni-

[175] *Ibid.*, p. 323.
[176] "Herodotus and the Growth of Greek Historiography," *TAPA* 67 (1936): 322-326 and *Die griechische Geschichtsschreibung*, 1: 131.
[177] *Ibid.*, 1: 141.
[178] *Ibid.*, 1: 153.
[179] J. Cobet, *Herodots Exkurse und die Frage der Einheit seines Werkes*. Historica Einzelschriften 17 (1971).
[180] *Ibid.*, p. 120.
[181] *Ibid.*, pp. 120-121.
[182] *Ibid.*, pp. 156-157.
[183] *Ibid*, p. 180.

tarian perspective describes the finished product.[184] He thus concurs with Jacoby that Herodotos began writing ethnographic
logoi[185] which he considered organizing into a περίοδος γῆς, but
kept finding Persia obtruding. Persian expansion thus became the
organizing principle. The theme was inspired by epic poetry which
also offered some of the techniques for carrying it out.[186] We may,
accordingly, appreciate the unity of the work and the placement of
the ethnographic *logoi* in synchronization with Persian expansion,
but this does not explain the genesis of the *Histories*.[187]

Some of the difficulties in subsuming all of the ethnographic
material neatly under the banner of Persian expansion have recently
been pointed out by K. H. Waters. The greatest obstacle is the fact
that there are ethnographic treatments of groups who never came
under Persian sway.[188] Waters thinks Herodotos included these
materials to illustrate the power of νόμος.[189] In any case, the independence of units such as Book 2 led Waters to follow the general
lines of the genetic school.[190]

It would be an act of the highest *hybris* to presume to resolve this
debate in the present framework. What we can realize is that the
Histories are not a monolithic work of homogeneous parts, but a unified collection of rather disparate members. This is really no surprise
since Herodotos tells us in his opening sentence that ἱστορίης
ἀπόδειξις ἥδε is for two reasons: first, ὡς μήτε τὰ γενόμενα ἐξ ἀνθρώπων τῷ χρόνῳ ἐξίτηλα γένηται, μήτε ἔργα μεγάλα τε καὶ θωμασία, τὰ μὲν Ἕλλησι, τὰ δὲ βαρβάροισι ἀποδεχθέντα, ἀκλεᾶ γένηται;
and second, τά τε ἄλλα καὶ δι' ἣν αἰτίην ἐπολέμησαν ἀλλήλοισι.
True to his word, the *Histories* do present θωμασία as well as the
conflict.

There are two points which need more attention in the debate and
which have a bearing on our subject. The first has been raised by

---

[184] Charles W. Fornara, *Herodotus: An Interpretative Essay* (Oxford: The Clarendon Press, 1971), p. 13.
[185] *Ibid.*, p. 3, where he points out that Book Two was composed with ethnographic interests.
[186] *Ibid.*, pp. 32-36.
[187] *Ibid.*, p. 31. Cf. also pp. 6-13 and esp. pp. 9 and 28.
[188] Waters, *Herodotos, the Historian*, pp. 38-39. He mentions "the various inhabitants of South Russia and those of North Africa westwards from Kyrene."
[189] He suggested that the work was like a sermon on the text 'Custom rules.'
Ibid., p. 39.
[190] *Ibid.*, p. 53.

von Fritz, i.e., why did Herodotos travel? In connection with Kambyses' campaign, Herodotos says: ἄλλοι τε συχνοὶ ἐς τὴν Αἴγυπτον ἀπίκοντο Ἑλλήνων; he then explains, οἱ μὲν, ὡς οἰκός, κατ' ἐμπορίην, οἱ δέ στρατευόμενοι, οἱ δὲ τινες καὶ αὐτῆς τῆς χώρης θεηταί . . . (3.139.1). Why did Herodotos go at a later date? The express statements indicate that he went as a θεητής. So he tells us that he sought out the sources of the Nile (2.29.1), visited Tyre to enquire about Herakles (2.44.1), Arabia to investigate the flying snakes (2.75.1), and asked the Egyptian priests about the reliability of the Iliad (2.118). In fact, he claims that his account of Egypt up to 2.99.1 is due to his own investigation.[191] These statements clearly match the first half of his opening statement better than the second.

The second point which has not received its due is the recognition that the ethnographic *logoi* of Herodotos stand in a literary tradition which has both predecessors and successors.[192] Placing Herodotos within this tradition enables us both to understand his debt to that tradition and the extent of his genius as he transcended it.

This is not to deny the unity of the final product which we now have. It is to suggest that the *Histories* as we now know them are partly a result of *Redaktionsgeschichte*. The ethnographic *logoi* which—in my judgment—do reflect an earlier phase of Herodotos' work, have now become the digressions. Herodotos freely acknowledges the presence of προσθῆκαι in 4.30.1: προσθήκας γὰρ δή μοι ὁ λόγος ἐξ ἀρχῆς ἐδίζητο.[193] It is to Herodotos' credit that he has so successfully incorporated two literary genres within a single literary work.[194]

3. *Form.* We are now in a position to examine the form(s) of the ethnographic *logoi* to determine whether or not a consistent pattern emerges.[195] for the sake of clarity and simplification, I have at-

---

[191] Cf. also 4.81.1, where he indicates that he investigated the population of Scythia.

[192] For his successors see under "Significance" below.

[193] Digressions were also part of Polybios' work. He has three major units: Book 6, Roman institutions; Book 12, Timaios; and Book 34, Geography.

[194] E.g., 1.185 (from 1.178-187, 192-200: Babylon), describes the lake of Nitokris which is essential to the account of Babylon's fall in 1.191. Even Book 2 is neatly tucked into the narrative: 3.10 presupposes it and offers a continuation of sorts. Again 4.108.1 (the neighbors of Skythia) is picked up by 4.123.1. I should also point out that not all ethnographic digressions should be considered independent. 1.142-148 is a good example since it is clearly linked to the Persian advance (143.1).

[195] Earlier studies of the forms themselves include Jacoby, "Über die Entwicklung der griechischen Historiographie," p. 89; Trüdinger, "Studien zur

tempted to place Herodotos' major treatments of non-Hellenic peoples[196] into a chart.

Major Ethnographic *Logoi* in Herodotos

	Persia	Babylon	Massagetae	Egypt	Skythia	Libya
Text	1.131-140	1.178-187; 1.192-200	1.201-204.1; 1.215-216	2.1-182	4.5-82; 99-101	4.168-199
Land		178-183 (City)	201-204.1	4.3-34	(36-45) 46-58	181.1-2a
Peoples			(201-203)		16-35	168-180 181.2b-185 191-196 197-199
Customs	131-140	195-200	215-216	35-98	(16-35) 59-81	186-190
History		184-187		99-182	5-15	
Wonders		192-194				

At first glance, we realize that there is not an unwavering pattern which is rigidly followed; rather, the form is somewhat fluid. I say somewhat because closer inspection does reveal a basic group of elements and order. The first element is the description of the land or a listing of the peoples within their respective locales. The only exception to this is the Skythian *logos* which places mythological history before locating the people and describing the land.[197] The second

---

Geschichte der griechisch-römischen Ethnographie," esp. p. 21 (where he offers the ideal form based on the Skythian *logos* in 4.5-82: I. Das Land. 1. Begrenzung, Vermessung, Gestalt 2. Natur des Landes 3. Flüsse 4. Klima 5. Tierwelt II. Das Volk 1. Zahl 2. Alter; Archaeologie 3. Lebensweise 4. Sitten III. Die Merkwürdigkeiten des Landes); Pohlenz, *Herodot*, pp. 71ff.; Immerwahr, *Form and Thought in Herodotos*, pp. 67-68 (who bases his analysis on the Egyptian *logos* of Book 2 and concludes: "it consists of Origins, Description of Country, Customs, and History, and the Customs section is divided into Religious Customs and Secular Customs, in that order."); and John L. Myers, *Herodotus: Father of History* (Oxford: Clarendon Press, 1953; reprint ed., Chicago: Henry Regnery Company, 1971), pp. 72-73.

[196] I have omitted 1.56-58 on the Pelasgians and Dorians; 1.142-148 on the Ionians; 1.149 on the Aeolians; and 4.145-167 on Cyrene.

[197] The placement of 4.181.1-2a in the Skythian *logos* is due to the fact that it introduces the desert whose people are described in 181.2b-185.

element is the νόμοι which appear to be the most dominant motif within the ethnographic *logoi* proper.[198] This suggests that Herodotos' primary focus was anthropocentric rather than geocentric. In fact, even his attention to the land may be fairly labeled anthropogeographical. Νόμοι denote the practices which have become habitual for a group of people: these range from religion to table etiquette.[199] They are of critical importance because they establish the identity of each group. It is for this reason that comparisons are made with the customs of others.[200] The third element is history. The accounts are biographical in nature[201] and concentrate on the θαυμάσια associated with the figures.[202] The final element is "wonders" which are not mentioned within a larger context, but are listed separately. Our analysis thus suggests that there is a degree of congruity between Herodotos and the fragmentary remains of other early ethnographers.

We can find additional support for these observations as we scan the minor ethnographic *logoi* (see Table, p. 48).

---

[198] Herodotos said: καὶ ὀρθῶς μοί δοκέει Πίνδαρος ποιῆσαι νόμον πάντων βασιλέα φήσας εἶναι (3.38.4). Cf. also Plato, *Gorgias*, 484B. On the use of customs in Herodotos see esp. Immerwahr, *Form and Thought in Herodotus*, pp. 319-320.

[199] Religion appears to come first (1.131-132, Persia; 2.35-76, Egypt; 4.59-63, Skythia) and then matters of daily living.

[200] The most significant statements Herodotos makes along these lines are the openness of the Persians to foreign νόμοι (1.135) and the resolute resistance of the Egyptians (2.35.2; 2.91.1) and Skythians (4.76-80). When listing various groups, Herodotos sometimes gives customs held in common, 3.101 (Indians S. of Persia), 4.186-190 (desert peoples of Libya), and 5.6 (Thracians).

[201] On the importance of individuals in Herodotos see Waters, *Herodotos*, pp. 136-151. Cobet, *Herodots Exkurse*, pp. 158-176, has shown how the structure of the finished product moves through Kroisos, Kyros, Kambyses, Dareios, and Xerxes.

[202] The basic criterion appears to be the ἀξιαπηγητότατα of the individuals or groups. Lloyd, *Herodotus: Book II*, 1: 141-147, offers four criteria for τὸ θωμάσιον: a reversal from Greek customs, size, extraordinary people and accomplishments, and τὸ παράδοξον. Cf. Barth Hannelore, "Zur Bewertung und Auswahl des Stoffes durch Herodot (Die Begriffe θῶμα, θωμάζω, θωμάσιος und θωμαστός)," *Klio* 50 (1968): 93-110. Interestingly, Barth makes a distinction between Herodotos' use of the concept in the ethnographic and historical sections. Cf. p. 109: ". . . In den geographisch-ethnographischen Partien gilt Herodot offenbar jedes Abweichen vom Durchschnitt überhaupt als mitteilenswert, während ihm im historischen Bereich in der Hauptsache das Überdurchschnittliche, Außergewöhnliche im positiven 'Sinne,' Kriterium bei der Auswahl des Stoffes zu sein scheint."

Minor Ethnographic *Logoi* in Herodotos

	Lydian	Carian	Caunian	Lucian	Arabian	Indian	Ethiopian	Extremities of Europe	Asian Plain	Getne	Skythian Neighbors	Thrace
Text	1.93-94	1.171	1.172	1.173	3.8 3.107-113	3.98-106	3.114	3.115-116	3.117	4.94-95	4.103-117	5.3-10
List and location of Peoples	93.5					98-106			117		103-117	3-10
Customs			2	4-5	8.1-3	(98-105)				94-95	(103-104,) (106-117)	(3-10)
History		2-3, 5-6		1-3							(105)	
Wonders	93.1-4				107-113	(98-106)	114	115-116				
Discoveries	94.1-7	4										

Each of these peoples is geographically located by Herodotos—the chart only concentrates on the central thurst of his discussion. The first group, 1.171-173, deals primarily with origins. The second and larger group, 3.98-117, the far reaches of the known world, deals with *exotica* (θαύματα) on the principle enunciated in 3.116.3: αἱ δὲ ὧν ἐσχατιαὶ οἴκασι, περικληίουσαι τὴν ἄλλην χώρην καὶ ἐντὸς ἀπέργουσαι, τὰ κάλλιστα δοκέοντα ἡμῖν εἶναι καὶ σπανιώτατα ἔχειν αὐτά. The presentation thus identifies groups with the precious metals or spices which come from them: the groups are important as they connect with the Greek world. The last three brief accounts are a very clear example of how νόμοι define groups, especially the latter two. As Herodotos lists various peoples he includes νόμοι which help give them identity.

There is one element in this chart which I omitted in the first: discoveries. On two occasions Herodotos deals with "firsts."[203] This was also an element of note in the account of Egypt.[204] While this is not a mainstay of the Herodotean narrative, it is firmly established in the ethnographic treatments.

One of the greatest advances Herodotos made over his predecessors was his style. What Homer did for epic meter, Herodotos did for prose.[205] His skill extended to structure as well: each ethnographic account was carefully placed at the appropriate place in the irrepressible expansion of Persia. As we have seen, it is likely that Herodotos originally composed independent *logoi* which he then joined into his finished masterpiece.[206] The final division into nine books is due to Alexandrian scholars who matched his work with the Muses.[207]

4. *Function.* Any assessment of the *Histories* must take into account

---

[203] The vocabulary in 1.94.1-7 is very significant, 2: ἐξεύρημα, ἐξευρεθῆναι; 3: ἐξευρεθῆναι, ἐξεύρεσιν; 4: ἐξευρόντας.

[204] Compare this vocabulary, 2.4.1 ἐξευρεῖν (*bis*); 2: πρώτους (*bis*); 2.82.1: ἐξευρημένα; 2: ἀνεύρηται; 2.92.1: ἐξεύρηται.

[205] He is dubbed Ὁμηρικώτατος in Longinos 13.3. On the superiority of his style over his predecessors see Dionysios, *De Thuc.* 5, 23. This is even conceded by (Pseudo-) Plutarch, *De Herodoti malignitate*, 874B: γραφικὸς ἀνήρ, καὶ ἡδὺς ὁ λόγος, καὶ χάρις ἔπεστι καὶ δεινότης καὶ ὥρα τοῖς διηγήμασι . . . His ability to tell a good story is superb. The clever thief in 2.121a-z, is a literary gem.

[206] Cagnazzi, "Tavola die 28 Logoi di Erodoto," p. 388, argues that there were 28 *logoi*: three in each book except the fifth which had four. This scheme fits our analysis nicely since Book 2 then becomes three lectures: 1-34, 35-98, 99-182. Cf. pp. 421-423 for an overview of the divisions.

[207] Cf. Lucian, *Hist. Conscr.* 42 and *Herod.* 1.

both the ethnographic element and the overarching theme of conflict. With regard to the former, Herodotos appears to stand in line with his Ionian predecessors. He is writing to Greeks[208] and telling them who these other people are. His task is simply to report what he can learn about them. So he writes: ταῦτα εἰ μὲν ἔστι ἀληθέως οὐκ οἶδα, τὰ δὲ λέγεται γράφω (4.195.2).[209] Such an uncritical methodology incurred the censorious rebuke of his successor, Thukydides. The Athenian wrote: ἐκ δὲ τῶν εἰρημένων τεκμηρίων ὅμως τοιαῦτα ἄν τις νομίζων μάλιστα ἃ διῆλθον οὐχ ἁμαρτάνοι. He contrasts this with the poets and then says: οὔτε ὡς λογογράφοι ξυνέθεσαν ἐπὶ τὸ προσαγωγότερον τῇ ἀκροάσει ἢ ἀληθέστερον, ὄντα ἀνεξέλεγκτα καὶ τὰ πολλὰ ὑπὸ χρόνου αὐτῶν ἀπίστως ἐπὶ τὸ μυθῶδες ἐκνενικηκότα . . .[210] We can learn three things from this stricture: first, that Herodotos wrote ἐπὶ τὸ προσαγωγότερον; second, that he probably recited his work, τῇ ἀκροάσει;[211] and third, that the content tended ἐπὶ τὸ μυθῶδες.[212] Thukydides assessed his own work in the famous line: κτῆμά τε ἐς αἰεὶ μᾶλλον ἢ ἀγώνισμα ἐς τὸ παραχρῆμα ἀκούειν ξύγκειται (1.22.4).[213] Is this a fair critique? Only if we measure Herodotos by Thukydides. Herodotos' task was not to sift through the materials critically, but to weigh them in terms of human interest and repeat what was reported.[214]

---

[208] This is explicit in 3.103. It is also supported by the repeated comparisons of the customs of other nations to those of the Greeks.

[209] Cf. also 2.123; 3.3.1; 4.5.1; 4.25.1; 4.42.4; 4.105.2 et al.

[210] Thukydides 1.21.1. The text is that of Henry Stuart Jones and J. E. Powell, eds. Thucydidis Historiae, OCT (Oxford: The Clarendon Press, 1942).

[211] Since all works were read aloud whether publicly or privately, this can not be construed as an express reference to lectures. However the ἀγώνισμα of 22.4 lends weight to recitations. Cf. A. W. Gomme, A. Andrews, and K. J. Dover, A Historical Commentary on Thucydides, 5 vols. (Oxford: The Clarendon Press, 1945-1981), sub loc.

[212] Aristotle called him ὁ μυθολόγος in De gen. anim. 756b. It is also a charge leveled by (Pseudo-) Plutarch, De Herodoti malignitate, 874B. Cf. also Josephus CA 1.16.

[213] That Thukydides has Herodotos in mind—although not solely—is due to the stature of the Histories. Cf. Gomme, Andrews, and Dover, A Historical Commentary on Thucydides, 1: 148-149.

[214] Cf. Lucian, Hist. Consc., 60, who allows for the simple repetition of a myth without a pronouncement on it. Καὶ μὴν καὶ μῦθος εἴ τις παρεμπέσοι, λεκτέος μέν, οὐ μὴν πιστωτέος πάντως, ἀλλ᾿ ἐν μέσῳ θετέος τοῖς ὅπως ἂν ἐθέλωσιν εἰκάσουσι περὶ αὐτοῦ· σὺ δ᾿ ἀκίνδυνος καὶ πρὸς οὐδέτερον ἐπιρρεπέστερος. This is not fully consistent with the principle he stated in 39: τοῦ δὴ συγγραφέως ἔργον ἕν—ὡς ἐπράχθη εἰπεῖν. Cf. also 9. This is very close to the celebrated dictum of L. von Ranke:

In terms of the larger conflict, Herodotos is pro-Greek; after all, the *Histories* celebrate the Greek victory.[215] How then can the author of the *De Herodoti malignitate* slander him as φιλοβάρβαρος?[216] There is no doubt that Herodotos paints a very positive picture of some non-Hellenic peoples, especially Egypt.[217] It is possible that Herodotos wanted to present each of the major opponents of Persia as worthy opponents. This would heighten the status of the Greeks since they were the only people whom Persia could not subdue and must, therefore, be very special. On the other hand, Herodotos was one of the few people in antiquity whose experiences among foreigners genuinely and sanguinely affected him.

The fact that the theme of the work is the conflict between the East and the West helps to underscore another point. The nexus of Greek historiography proper is the Persian Wars.[218] Later authors in antiquity were conscious of the interrelationship between conquest and geographical knowledge.[219] It was, appropriately, the expansion of Persia which gave rise to both ethnographical inquiry and history proper.

Significance

The importance of Herodotos for our study is immense. He is primarily responsible for joining history to ethnography.[220]

"Wie es eigentlich gewesen." *Geschichten der römanischen und germanischen Völker* (Leipzig, 1874), p. vii.

[215] This was recognized in antiquity. Cf. Pseudo-Plutarch, *De Herodoti malignitate*, 867C: Ἡρόδοτος δὲ ὑφ' οὗ κεκοσμῆσθαί τινες ἀξίουσι τὴν Ἑλλάδα. The author did not share this sentiment. The point is also made by claiming pre-eminence for Greece, e.g., 3.106.1.

[216] Cf. esp. 857A-858F.

[217] E.g., 2.4 openly acknowledges Egyptian calendrical superiority. 2.43.2 and 2.49 indicate Grecian borrowing.

[218] Cf. R. W. Macan, "Herodotus and Thucydides," in *Athens*, ed. J. B. Bury, S. A. Cook, and F. E. Adcock, CAH (Cambridge: University Press, 1969),5: 399-400 and Drews, *Greek Accounts*, pp. 36,91.

[219] E.g., Polybius, 3.59.3-5: ἐν δὲ τοῖς καθ' ἡμᾶς τῶν μὲν κατὰ τὴν Ἀσίαν διὰ τὴν Ἀλεξάνδρου δυναστείαν, τῶν δὲ λοιπῶν τόπων, διὰ τὴν Ῥωμαίων ὑπεροχὴν σχεδὸν ἁπάντων πλωτῶν καὶ πορευτῶν γεγονότων, ἀπολελυμένων δὲ καὶ τῶν πρακτικῶν ἀνδρῶν τῆς περὶ τὰς πολεμικὰς καὶ πολιτικὰς πράξεις, φιλοτιμίας, ἐκ δὲ τούτων πολλὰς καὶ μεγάλας ἀφορμὰς εἰληφότων εἰς τὸ πολυπραγμονεῖν καὶ φιλομαθεῖν περὶ τῶν προειρημένων, δέον ἂν εἴη καὶ βέλτιον γινώσκειν κἀληθινώτερον ὑπὲρ τῶν πρότερον ἀγνοουμένων.

[220] Cf. Drews, *Greek Accounts*, p. 69. See also the comments of Jacoby, "Über die Entwicklung der griechischen Historiographie," p. 118.

Ethnography was subsequently either subsumed under the banner
of history or became more historically oriented. The former is evidenced by the most illustrious successors of Herodotos: Thukydides
gives a brief and necessary sketch of Sicily at the beginning of his
books on the Sicilian War[221]; Hieronymos of Kardia likewise
thought it necessary to insert ethnographical sections in his histories
of the διάδοχοι[222]; Polybios devoted one book to the subject[223]; and
his successor Poseidonios again thought it important to include
major ethnographical sections.[224] If we turn to the West we find so
much ethnographic material in the *Histories* of Timaios of
Tauromenium that Jacoby actually considered him an ethnographer rather than a historian.[225]

---

[221] 6.2-5. K. J. Dover, *A Historical Commentary on Thucydides*, 4: 198-210, thinks
Antiochos of Syracuse (*FGrH* 555) is the source from which Thukydides drew. This
would provide a Herodotean-type background.
[222] *FGrH* 154; *RE*, s.v. "Hieronymous," by Felix Jacoby, 8: 1540-1560; and
Jane Hornblower, *Hieronymus of Cardia*. Oxford Classical and Philosophical Monographs (Oxford: Oxford University Press, 1981). Hieronymous has been largely
preserved in Diodoros Sikelos 18-20. Cf. Jacoby, *op. cit.*, 8: 1549-1556 and
Hornblower, *op. cit.*, pp. 18-75. Hieronymous probably opened his narrative with
a geographical introduction (Diodoros 18.5.2-6.4). The purpose is stated in 5.1:
οὕτως γὰρ μάλιστα εὐπαρακολούθητος τοῖς ἀναγινώσκουσιν ἡ διήγησις ἔσται, πρὸ
ὀφθαλμῶν τεθείσης τῆς ὅλης τοποθεσίας καὶ τῶν διαστημάτων. Hieronymous also
included treatments of the Dead Sea (F 5; cf. also F 6), Corinth (F 16), Thessaly
(F 17), and Crete (F 18). The excursus on Thessaly is similar to Thukydides *Sikelika*; on the other hand, his treatment of the Dead Sea is much closer to Herodotos.
Hornblower suggested that Hieronymous began in the tradition of Thukydides,
but found it necessary to move in the direction of Herodotos as a result of the new
territory opened up by Alexander. *Ibid.*, pp. 152-153.
[223] Polybios 34. Cf. also Bk. 3. Walbank, *Polybius*, p. 32, wrote: ". . . Polybius
was reverting to an earlier tradition which had associated the study of lands with
the study of peoples."
[224] *FGrH* 87. There is now an important treatment of his histories. Jurgen
Malitz, *Die Historien des Poseidonios* (München: Beck, 1983).
[225] "Über die Entwicklung der griechischen Historiographie," p. 93. *Contra*
Fornara, *The Nature of History in Ancient Greece and Rome*, pp. 36-38, who compares
Sikelika with *Hellenika*. On Timaios see *FGrH* 566. Full discussions of Timaios may
be found in *RE*, s.v. "Timaios," by Richard Laquer, II 6: 1076-1203; Truesdell
Sparhawk Brown, *Timaeus of Tauromenium* (Berkeley: University of California
Press, 1958); Arnaldo Momigliano, "Athens in the Third Century B.C. and the
Discovery of Rome in the Histories of Timaeus of Tauromenium," in *Essays in An-
cient and Modern Historiography* (Middletown, Conneticut: Wesleyan University
Press, 1977), pp. 37-66; and Lionel Pearson, *The Greek Historians of the West: Timaeus
and His Predecessors*. Philological Monographs of the American Philological Associa-
tion 35 (Atlanta: the American Philological Association, 1987). Cf. also *KP*, s.v.
"Timaios," by Emilie Boer, 5: 835-837, for a brief but very useful treatment.
Timaios is particularly interesting because he appears to have made an apologetic

The latter phenomenon appears in the specialized treatments of various countries. A prime example is the Περσικά of Ktesias of Knidos, a Greek physician who served at the court of Artaxerxes II. His twenty-three books cover the affairs of kings from Minos to Artaxerxes II.[226] In either case, the fledgling genre was profoundly affected.[227] What this discussion points out is the fact that Herodotos exerted a profound influence on Hellenistic historians.[228]

SUMMARY

The inclusion of Ionian Greeks in the Persian empire and the birth of Ionian philosophy helped to create an awareness of other people and a new way of looking at the world that had not previously existed. This combination of circumstances gave birth to Hekataios' Περιήγησις Γῆς. The generalized presentation of Hekataios served to spur on more specific treatments of individual countries or ethnic groups. Although the remains of these works are too fragmentary to warrant dogmatic conclusions, their fundamental agreement with the ethnographic *logoi* of Herodotos indicates the establishment of a distinct genre.

There were four major areas of concern for ancient ethnographers: the land, the history, the marvels, and the customs of a people. The specific form of the treatise varied from ethnic group to

case for his native Sicily as he wrote his *Histories* in Athens, i.e., the Greek West is as impressive as the homeland. Both Cicero and Polybios attest to his enthusiasm for his *patria* (FF 40 and 94 respectively). More specifically he links figures to the West when he can, e.g., Laida, the famous courtesan, is from Hykaross (F 24) and Lysias is a Syracusan not an Athenian (F 137). Similarly, he includes "discoveries" in the West as a way of claiming glory for it. See Brown, *Timaeus of Tauromenium*, p. 14. Finally, he exploits myths as a means of enhancing the prestige of the West. See Lionel Pearson, "Myth and *Archaeologia* in Italy and Sicily—Timaeus and his predecessors," *Yale Classical Studies* 24 (1975): 171-195, esp. p. 193.

[226] *FGrH*, 688. Ktesias also wrote the first independent Ἰνδικά and a Περίοδος which surveyed Egypt, the Western Mediterranean, and Asia in three books. He thus stands squarely in the Ionic tradition. He differs from Herodotos in freely inventing what he could not glean through ἱστορία.

[227] Fornara, *The Nature of History in Ancient Greece and Rome*, pp. 14-15, makes Xanthos the watershed. I think Herodotos' influence on later developments was more profound.

[228] This point has been made by O. Murray, "Herodotus and Hellenistic Culture," *CQ* n.s. 22 (1972): 204: "I wish to show the influence of Herodotus on the conception which the Hellenistic age had of the world around it. And especially I wish to argue that it is this influence which lies at the basis of the whole tradition of Hellenistic historical ethnography."

ethnic group even within the same author. This may have been due to the fact that the information available varied. The most desirable means of acquiring information was to travel to the locale and offer a hearer the report of the author's own autopsy. Delivering reports of what one heard was also acceptable, even when the author was uncertain about the report's credibility. The function of these works appears to have been to define the peoples living in exotic places. Perhaps this is why there was such an interest in ''marvels'': it titillated the curiosity of the hearer.

The entire process—with the exception of the subject matter— was Hellenic. There is no evidence that the investigators bothered or even attempted to learn any language other than Greek. Hellenic standards were the standards. This was fine as long as Greeks and non-Greeks remained distant. It could not continue indefinitely, however, when that situation changed.

CHAPTER THREE

ETHNOGRAPHY IN TRANSITION

> He (Alexander) brought into one
> matters from everywhere, just as if he
> mingled their life-styles, customs,
> marriages, and way of living in a
> mixing bowl of friendship . . .
>
> Plutarch, *De Alexandri magni fortuna
> aut virtute*, 329C

The rise of Persia and the ensuing Persian Wars not only served as
a key stimulus for the beginnings of historical writing, but also gave
the Greeks a unified sense of the Hellenic way of life over against
that of barbarians.[1] Nor was this view neutral. Aristotle defended
Greek superiority on what he must have considered scientific
grounds in these words: τὰ μὲν γὰρ ἐν τοῖς ψυχροῖς τόποις ἔθνη καὶ
τὰ περὶ τὴν Εὐρώπην θυμοῦ μέν ἐστι πλήρη, διανοίας δὲ ἐνδεέστερα
καὶ τέχνης, διόπερ ἐλεύθερα μὲν διατελεῖ μᾶλλον, ἀπολίτευτα δὲ καὶ
τῶν πλησίον ἄρχειν οὐ δυνάμενα. He then contrasts these with the
nations of Asia: τὰ δὲ περὶ τὴν ᾿Ασίαν διανοητικὰ μὲν καὶ τεχνικὰ τὴν
ψυχήν, ἄθυμα δέ, διόπερ ἀρχόμενα καὶ δουλεύοντα διατελεῖ. He is
now in a position to present the ideal: τὸ δὲ τῶν ῾Ελλήνων γένος
ὥσπερ μεσεύει κατὰ τοὺς τόπους, οὕτως ἀμφοῖν μετέχει, καὶ γὰρ
ἔνθυμον καὶ διανοητικόν ἐστιν, διόπερ ἐλεύθερόν τε διατελεῖ καὶ βέλ-
τιστα πολιτευόμενον καὶ δυνάμενον ἄρχειν πάντων, μιᾶς τυγχάνον
πολιτείας.[2]

---

[1] Hans Diller, "Die Hellenen-Barbaren-Antithese im Zeitalter der Perserkriege," in *Grecs et Barbares*. Entretiens sur l'Antiquité Classique 7 (Genève:
Fondation Hardt, 1962), pp. 37-82, who argues that βάρβαρος came to have a
sense of inferiority which it did not previously carry. Moses Hadas, *Hellenistic Culture: Fusion and Diffusion* (New York/London: W.W. Norton & Co., 1959), p. 12,
also credits the Persian Wars with giving the Greeks their sense of superiority.

[2] *Pol.* 7.6.1 (= 1327b). Aristotle's assessment of barbarians could not have
been helped by the fact that his close friend, Hermeias the tyrant of Assos, was tortured to death by the Persians in Susa in 341 B.C.E., for suspected collusion with
Philip. Cf. also Plato, *Rep.* 470C: ῞Ελληνας μὲν ἄρα βαρβάροις καὶ βαρβάρους
῞Ελλησι πολεμεῖν μαχομένους τε φήσομεν καὶ πολεμίους φύσει εἶναι, καὶ πόλεμον τὴν
ἔχθραν ταύτην κλητέον. The Greeks did not have a monopoly on such attitudes. An

The views of Aristotle are particularly important because in 343 he became the tutor of Alexander the Great. For the next three years, Aristotle taught his illustrious student in Mieza near Pella.[3] The relationship was warm during this period but appears to have cooled later.[4] Subsequent tradition suggests that Aristotle unsuccessfully attempted to persuade Alexander to put into practice his views on barbarians. Plutarch wrote: οὐ γὰρ, ὡς 'Αριστοτέλης συνεβούλευεν αὐτῷ, τοῖς μὲν "Ελλησιν ἡγεμονικῶς τοῖς δὲ βαρβάροις δεσποτικῶς χρώμενος, then expanding with καὶ τῶν μὲν ὡς φίλων καὶ οἰκείων ἐπιμελούμενος τοῖς δ᾽ ὡς ζῴοις ἢ φυτοῖς προσφερόμενος . . .[5] Alexander instead—according to Plutarch—brought them together: . . . εἰς τὸ αὐτὸ συνενεγκὼν τὰ πανταχόθεν, ὥσπερ ἐν κρατῆρι φιλοτησίῳ μείξας τοὺς βίους καὶ τὰ ἤθη καὶ τοὺς γάμους καὶ τὰς διαίτας . . .[6] These and other statements led W.W. Tarn to the conclusion that Alexander envisioned the unity of the human race.[7] While this appears to me to go beyond the evidence,[8] there can be

---

excellent example of the concept of being the supreme civilization is that of the Shang and Zou dynasties in China in the second and first millenia B.C.E.

[3] On Alexander's education and relationship to Aristotle see J.R. Hamilton, *Plutarch Alexander: A Commentary* (Oxford: The Clarendon Press, 1969), pp. 16-20, and the relatively recent biographies on Alexander by R.D. Milns, *Alexander the Great* (London: Robert Hale, 1968), pp. 20-25; Robert Lane Fox, *Alexander the Great* (London: Allen Lane, 1973), pp. 52-60; and J.R. Hamilton, *Alexander the Great* (London: Hutchinson University Library, 1973), pp. 32-34.

[4] Plutarch, Alex. 8.4 wrote: 'Αριστοτέλην δὲ θαυμάζων ἐν ἀρχῇ καὶ ἀγαπῶν οὐχ ἧττον, ὡς αὐτὸς ἔλεγε, τοῦ πατρός, ὡς δι᾽ ἐκεῖνον μὲν ζῶν, διὰ τοῦτον δὲ καλῶς ζῶν, ὕστερον ὑποπτότερον ἔσχεν, οὐχ ὥστε ποιῆσαί τι κακόν, ἀλλ᾽ αἱ φιλοφροσύναι τὸ σφοδρὸν ἐκεῖνο καὶ στερκτικὸν οὐκ ἔχουσαι πρὸς αὐτὸν ἀλλοτριότητος ἐγένοντο τεκμήριον.

[5] Plutarch, *De Alex. fort.* 6 (= 329B-D).

[6] *Ibid.*, 6 (= 329C). Cf. also Strabon 1.4.9 and Arrian, Anab. 7.11.8-9.

[7] He has stated his interpretation in numerous publications. The most important is his *Alexander the Great*, 2 vols. (Cambridge: Cambridge University Press, 1948).

[8] The principle opponents of Tarn are Victor Ehrenberg, *Alexander and the Greeks*, trans. by Ruth Fraenkel von Velsen (Oxford: B. Blackwell, 1938), pp. 62-102; E. Badian, "Alexander the Great and the Unity of Mankind," *Historia* 7 (1958): 425-444; and H.C. Baldry, "The Idea of the Unity of Mankind," in *Grecs et Barbares*. Entretiens sur l'Antiquité Classique 7 (Genève: Fondation Hardt, 1962), pp. 167-204, who argues that the rise of Rome in the 3rd-2nd centuries B.C.E., is the key which made possible the concept of a unified humanity. The problem with the statement of Plutarch is that it is in the first of two encomiastic speeches in which he celebrates the accomplishments of Alexander. As J.R. Hamilton has noted: "It seems most probable that . . .the two speeches are 'epideictic display-pieces,' devoid of any serious purpose." *Plutarch Alexander*, p. xxxi. Cf. also M.M. Austin, *The Hellenistic World from Alexander to the Roman Conquest: A Selection*

no doubt that the conquests of Alexander and the imposition of Hellenism did serve to bring about a cultural unity unknown prior to Alexander.

Yet this unity was not a synthesis nor even an amalgamation of the various cultures of the known world, but Pan-Hellenism. The greatest exponent of this view was Isokrates who claimed pre-eminence for Athens in these words: τοσοῦτον δ᾽ ἀπολέλοιπεν ἡ πόλις ἡμῶν περὶ τὸ φρονεῖν καὶ λέγειν τοὺς ἄλλους ἀνθρώπους, ὥσθ᾽ οἱ ταύτης μαθηταὶ τῶν ἄλλων διδάσκαλοι γεγόνασι, and then offered a new definition of what it means to be a Greek, καὶ τὸ τῶν Ἑλλήνων ὄνομα πεποίηκε μηκέτι τοῦ γένους ἀλλὰ τῆς διανοίας δοκεῖν εἶναι, καὶ μᾶλλον Ἕλληνας καλεῖσθαι τοὺς τῆς παιδεύσεως τῆς ἡμετέρας ἢ τοὺς τῆς κοινῆς φύσεως μετέχοντας.[9] What this meant for the nations Alexander subdued was that they must not only come to grips with Greek hegemony, but with Greek culture as well. This began with Alexander himself who required his Iranian troops to train in Macedonian arms, that sons born in mixed marriages (Macedonian fathers and Iranian mothers) be raised as Macedonians, and that Dareios' family learn Greek.[10] The last skill became a *sine qua non* for any who wished to excel in the Hellenistic world.[11] Social and economic success were directly linked to the acceptance and assimi-

---

of *Ancient Sources in Translation* (Cambridge: Cambridge University Press, 1981), p. 19. On Alexander's plans see Diodoros 18.4.1-6. The authenticity of these plans is questionable since we have the version of Perdikkas who wanted the army to reject them.

[9] Isokrates, *Paneg.* 50. Cf. also *Evagoras* 47. On the relationship between the views of Aristotle and that of Isokrates, see Edmund Buchner, "Zwei Gutachten für die Behandlung der Barbaren durch Alexander den Grossen?," *Hermes* 82 (1954): 378-384. Plutarch, *De Alex. fort.* 329C, offers an ethical definition: ἀλλὰ τὸ μὲν Ἑλληνικὸν ἀρετῇ τὸ δὲ βαρβαρικὸν κακίᾳ τεκμαίρεσθαι . . . Dionysios *AR* 14.5.5-6 and Strabon 1.4.9 (following Eratosthenes) make the same point.

[10] Arrian, *Anab.* 7.6.1; 7.12.2; Diodoros 17.67.1, respectively.

[11] Cf. Diodoros 1.2.5-6 (esp. 6): τούτῳ (i.e., the power of speech—GES) γὰρ οἱ μὲν Ἕλληνες τῶν βαρβάρων, οἱ δὲ πεπαιδευμένοι τῶν ἀπαιδεύτων προέχουσι, πρὸς δὲ τούτοις διὰ μόνου τούτου δυνατόν ἐστιν ἕνα τῶν πολλῶν περιγενέσθαι. Martin Hengel, *Judaism and Hellenism: Studies in their Encounter in Palestine during the Early Hellenistic Period*, 2 vols. trans. by John Bowden (Philadelphia: Fortress Press, 1974), p. 58, wrote: "The bond which held the Hellenistic world together despite the fragmentation which began with the death of Alexander and continued thereafter, was Attic *koine* . . . anyone who sought social respect or even the reputation of being an educated man had to have an impeccable command of it." Cf. also his *Jews, Greeks and Barbarians: Aspects of the Hellenization of Judaism in the pre-Christian Period*, trans. by John Bowden (Philadelphia: Fortress Press, 1980), pp. 76-77.

lation of Hellenism.[12] It is no wonder that such a social matrix gave birth to philhellenism, especially among the upper classes. At the same time a sense of resentment developed among native peoples who resisted the imposition of foreign elements.[13]

Such radical transitions necessarily affected the literature of the period: ethnography was no exception.[14] Two historical factors had a profound effect on the genre. First, the campaigns of Alexander made formerly remote areas of the world part of the accessible world. The new knowledge of these areas meant that the casual perspective of Herodotos would have to yield. Second, the continued development of philosophy and the influence of its insights would shape the selection and presentation of material.[15]

---

[12] For an overview of the unity of the Hellenistic world with the social and economic implications see M. Rostovtzeff, *The Social and Economic History of the Hellenistic World*, 3 vols. (Oxford: The Clarendon Press, 1941), 2:1032-1107. Rostovtzeff's summary statement of how the new world was viewed by Hellenistic authors is particularly apposite: "All these judgments, flattering, censorious, or impartial, take one cardinal point for granted. The new world which they describe or mention was in their eyes an extension, a continuation of the Greek world. The new kings are Greek kings and pursue a Greek policy; they rule over Greeks and are surrounded by Greeks, and they are prepared to offer excellent opportunities to other Greeks who may be willing and ready to emigrate to the new world." 2:1035. Rostovtzeff points out that this unity was superficial, i.e., it was restricted to the upper strata of Hellenistic society. The native populations continued in their old ways primarily in rural areas. See especially 2:1098-1107. Cf. also Arnaldo Momigliano, *Alien Wisdom: The Limits of Hellenization* (Cambridge: Cambridge University Press, 1975).
[13] An excellent example of this paradox is provided by Erich Gruen in his *The Hellenistic World and the Coming of Rome*, 2 vols. (Berkeley/Los Angeles/London: The University of California Press, 1984), 2:250-272.
[14] For a survey of Hellenistic historiography see Albin Lesky, *A History of Greek Literature*, trans. by James Willis and Cornelis de Heer (New York: Thomas Y. Crowell Co., 1966), pp. 764-783 and W.R. Conner, "Historical writing in the fourth century B.C. and in the Hellenistic period," in *The Cambridge History of Classical Literature. Greek Literature*, ed. P.E. Easterling and B.M.W. Knox (Cambridge: Cambridge University Press, 1985), pp. 458-471.
[15] Trüdinger, "Studien zur Geschichte der griechisch-römischen Ethnographie," pp. 43-59, lists three major changes: "1. die Begründung einer geschichtlich orientierten Völkerbetrachtung; 2. die Weiterbildung der Theorien vom Zusammenhang zwischen Volk und Natur; 3. die Fortschritte in der Erfassung fremder Volksindividualität." Albrecht Dihle, "Zur hellenistischen Ethnographie," in *Grecs et Barbares*. Entretiens sur l'Antiquité Classique 7 (Genève: Fondation Hardt, 1962), p. 213, summarized the shift in these words: "Wohl aber zeigt sich bei den hellenistischen Autoren allenthalben der grosse Vorzug einer Gewöhnung an rational-kausales Denken, die es ihnen ermöglicht, mit Hilfe bereitstehender Theorien die neuen Informationen sogleich in einen sinnvollen Zusammenhang mit dem bisher verfügbaren Wissen zu bringen und von vornherein Beobachtungen unter festen physikalischen, anthropologischen oder

HEKATAIOS OF ABDERA

Life

As might be expected, the transition from ethnography to apologetic historiography did not take place in one stroke of a reed. The figure who constructed the bridge from the old to the new genre was not an Easterner, but a Greek who lived in the East.[16] Unfortunately, we know little if anything about the life of Hekataios (*fl.* c. 320-290).[17] He is said to have come from either Abdera or Teos.[18] There are only a few data about his life which are related with any credibility. He is said to have been a student of Pyrrhon (365/360-275/270) (T 3a)[19]; an observation which appears justified

---

moralisch-soziologischen Gesichtspunkten anzustellen." Cf. also pp. 207-208, 226. The most important school early in the Hellenistic period for our literature was the Peripatetic. On the importance of Aristotle see Kurt von Fritz, "Die Bedeutung des Aristoteles für die Geschichtsschreibung," in *Histoire et Historiens dans l'Antiquité*. Entretiens sur l'Antiquité Classique 4 (Genève: Vandoeuvres, 1956), pp. 83-145.

[16] The primary treatments of Hekataios are *RE*, s.v. "Hekataios aus Abdera," by Felix Jacoby, 7:2750-2769 which is reprinted in his *Griechische Historiker*, pp. 227-245; *KP*, s.v. "Hekataios von Abdera," by W. Spoerri, 2:980-982; *EncJud*, s.v. "Hecataeus of Abdera," by Ben Zion Wacholder, 8:236-237; P.M. Fraser, *Ptolemaic Alexandria*, 3 vols. (Oxford: The Clarendon Press, 1972), 1:496-505; Frances Henderson Diamond, "Hecataeus of Abdera: A New Historical Approach," (Ph.D. dissertation, U.C.L.A., 1974); and *RAC*, s.v. "Hekataios von Abdera," by W. Spoerri, 14:275-310.

[17] Spoerri bluntly stated: "Vom Bios des als 'Αβδηρίτης gekennzeichneten Autors ist so gut wie nichts bekannt." *RAC*, s.v. "Hekataios von Abdera," 14:278.

[18] He is called 'Αβδηρίτης (TT 1,3; FF 4, 11, 12, 17, 21, 23) and also linked to Teos (T 2; F 13). The confusion may be partly explained by the fact that Abdera was the colony of Teos (Strabon 14.1.30). Eduard Schwartz, "Hekataeos von Teos," *Rheinisches Museum für Philologie* 40 (1885):233-234, traces him to Teos. Jacoby, FGrH, 3a:31, suggested that "sich H in dem Hyperboreerbuch aus Gründen, die mit der Rahmenerzahlung zusammenhängen (s. zu F 13/14), selbst Teier nannte, während die Aigyptiaka, wie die von ihnen ausgehende Falschung zeigt (T 7a; F 21; 23), als 'Εκαταίου 'Αβδερίτου umliefen."

[19] Pyrrhon was the founder of skepticism. The classic definition of skepticism is that of Sextos Empirikos, *P.H.* 1.8: "Εστι δὲ ἡ σκεπτικὴ δύναμις ἀντιθετικὴ φαινομένων τε καὶ νοουμένων καθ' οἱονδήποτε τρόπον, ἀφ' ἧς ἐρχόμεθα διὰ τὴν ἐν τοῖς ἀντικειμένοις πράγμασι καὶ λόγοις ἰσοσθένειαν τὸ μὲν πρῶτον εἰς ἐποχήν, τὸ δὲ μετὰ τοῦτο εἰς ἀταραξίαν. The difficulty in determining his views is that they have come to us through the influence of the later academy. On Pyrrhon see A.A. Long, *Hellenistic Philosophy: Stoics, Epicureans, Sceptics* (New York: Charles Scribner's Sons, 1974), pp. 75-88 and Fernanda Decleva Caizzi, "Pirroniani ed Accademici nel III Secolo A.C.," in *Aspects de la Philosophie Hellénistique*. Entretiens sur l'Antiquité Classique 32 (Genève: Vandoeuvres, 1986), pp. 147-183. For the primary texts on early Pyrhonnism see A.A. Long and D.N. Sedley, *The Hellenistic Philosophers*, 2 vols.

as the epithet φιλόσοφος (TT 1,7; cf. also 3[20] and 5) and his writings attest. He γέγονε δὲ ἐπὶ τῶν διαδόχων (T 1; cf. also T 7) and came to Thebes under Ptolemy Lagos (TT 4 and 7). Plutarch says that he was once in Sparta (T 5)[21] which may reflect Hekataios' role as an ambassador for Ptolemy I.[22]

A number of works have come down to us bearing Hekataios' name. It is certain, however, that not all were written by the fourth-third century savant. We are confident that he wrote at least three works: Περὶ τῆς ποιήσεως Ὁμήρου καὶ Ἡσιόδου (T 1)[23], Περὶ Ὑπερβορέων (T 6; FF 4-14), and τὰ Αἰγυπτιακά (T 4).[24] The issue of whether or not he wrote a separate Περὶ Ἰουδαίων will be dealt with separately. What is important for our purposes at present is to note that there appear to be some correspondences between the Περὶ Ὑπερβορέων and τὰ Αἰγυπτιακά. The Hyperboreans were a group of legendary people who were associated with Apollo in antiquity.[25] Hekataios wrote an idealized account of these figures in the form of an ethnography.[26] Unfortunately our fragments are very limited.

(Cambridge: Cambridge University Press, 1987-present), 1:13-24; Diogenes Laertios 9.61-108.

[20] That Hekataios taught τέλος ὑπάρχειν . . . αὐτάρκειαν . . .(Clem. Al., *Strom.* 2.130.4 = T 3b) is questionable. Cf. Spoerri in *KP*, s.v. "Hekataios von Abdera," 2:978.

[21] The reference in Jacoby is wrong. It should be *Lycurgus* 20.2 not 20.3.

[22] Jacoby, *FGrH*, 3a:33-34, suggests that Archidamidas who came to Hekataios' defence at Sparta was Achidamos IV who fought against Ptolemy's enemy, Demetrios Poliorketes, in 294 B.C.E. This is a very plausible deduction, especially if Hekataios had an official position with Ptolemy. (See below under Function.) It has been followed by Murray, "Hecataeus of Abdera and Pharaonic Kingship," p. 144, but challenged by Diamond, "Hecataeus of Abdera," pp. 143-144. She argues that his taciturnity in the Spartans' company would not be fitting for a diplomat.

[23] Perhaps we should associate the κριτικὸς γραμματικός of the Suda (T 1) with this work.

[24] He is also said to have written περὶ τῆς τῶν Αἰγυπτίων φιλοσοφίας (F 1). This may, however, only refer to sections of his Αἰγυπτιακά.

[25] On this connection see W.K.C. Guthrie, *The Greeks and their Gods* (Boston: Beacon Press, 1950), pp. 74-82.

[26] The abstract in Diodoros 2.47.1-6 (= F 7), follows the basic pattern of an ethnography: 1, the island (its location, name, and fertility); 2-3, religion (their relation to Apollo); 4-5a, their language and relationship to Greece; 5b-6a, marvels (the proximity of the moon and an aetiological myth explaining the Metonic cycle); 6b, the rulers. The other fragments support this observation: FF 9, 11, 13, 14, would all fit nicely into a discussion of the land—complete with etymological discussions; F 8 probably provides the name of the sacred city mentioned in Diodoros 2.47.3 (so Jacoby, *FGrH*, 3a:56-57); F 12 again covers the descendants of Boreos

The significance of the work is that Hekataios combined philosophical concerns with ethnographic to produce his utopia.[27] What he did with a legendary group, he was also to do for a real group, the Egyptians.[28]

Αἰγυπτιακά

1. *Textual Problem*. The first problem which confronts the reader of Hekataios is to determine what is authentic and what is not. Jacoby collected six fragments which are certain to belong to the Αἰγυπτιακά of Hekataios. The bulk of what we believe to be Hekataion is preserved in the first book of Diodoros Sikelos 1.10-98. The obvious questions are: what is Hekataion within this section of the βιβλιοθήκη and by what criterion(a) do we think it Hekataion.

A little over a hundred years ago, Eduard Schwartz published an article in which he argued that Diodoros preserved Hekataios with but a few exceptions in this section.[29] He developed his views more fully for his article on Diodoros in the *Real-Encyclopädie der classischen Altertumswissenschaft*.[30] In it he contended that with only five major exceptions, we are reading Hekataios in Diodoros.[31] He began with the presupposition that Diodoros is mainly an excerptor who dutifully followed his principal sources.[32] His primary arguments were:

(Diod. 2.47.6b); and F 10 affirms their continued history which could well be tied to F 12 in some form of historical section, however legendary.

[27] Jacoby, *RE*, s.v. "Hekataios aus Abdera," 7:2755, calls it an "ethnographische Utopien." Spoerri, *RAC*, s.v. "Hekataios von Abdera," 14:279, thought that the combination of ethnography and philosophy produced a work in which "Idealvorstellungen von Staat u. Gesellschafft oder andere philosophische Theorien als bei einem realen oder der Vergangenheit verwirklicht erscheinen." The same view is held by W. Edward Brown, "Some Hellenistic Utopias," *The Classical Weekly* 48 (1955): 57-62, who offers a survey of utopian accounts in the period and Gabba, "True History and False History in Classical Antiquity," pp. 55-60, esp. 58-59.

[28] We should not miss seeing the dependence of the Greeks on the Hyperboreans (Diodoros 2.47.4-6) which becomes such an important issue in the *Aigyptiaka*. It is not possible to establish priority of date for one of the two works. Jacoby, *RE*, s.v. "Hekataios aus Abdera," 7:2758, argued that the Hyperborean work preceded the Egyptian as a theoretical model a concrete example.

[29] Schwartz, "Hekataeos von Teos," pp. 224-230. His fundamental argument was the internal cross references which he thought suggested a single source.

[30] *RE*, s.v. "Diodoros," by Eduard Schwartz, 5:663-704, esp. 669-72.

[31] The exceptions are 15.6-8; 17.1-20.5, the theologumena; 24.4 which is attributed to Matris; 32.1-41.9 which should be considered to be from Agatharchides; 56.5 from Ktesias; and 94-95 which are from an unknown source.

[32] The principal sources are Hekataios, Ktesias, Poseidonios, Agatharchides, Megasthenes, Ephoros, Kleitarchos, Duris, and Hieronymous.

the direct reference to Hekataios in 46.8 which denotes him as the source for 47-49; the similarity between 48.6 and 75-76 which suggests he stands behind "die ganze ägyptische Culturgeschichte," i.e., 79-82 and 91-93; the time reference Ptolemy I in 31.7; the juxtaposition of the ἱεραὶ ἀναγραφαί with Ptolemy I in 31.7 as well as the priests with the same time period in 26.1 points to the use of the sacred sources as a criterion for Hekataios (this embraces 43-68); and the concomitant calendrical speculations.

Schwartz was followed by Karl Reinhardt who contended that 1.7-8 were also from Hekataios since they are echoed by later Hekataion passages.[33] The factor which made Schwartz's view all but orthodoxy was its acceptance by Felix Jacoby.[34] He was impressed by the structure of the section, the connections between the individual sections of the ethnography, the pervasive sense of unity,[35] the ability to fit the fragments into the text,[36] and the basic congruence of the section with the ethnographic pattern. Oswyn Murray later pointed out that this pattern also fits what we know about Hekataios' writings on the Hyperboreans and the Jews.[37]

The case appeared air-tight until Walter Spoerri pointed out that some of the philosophical concepts in 1.11-13 are too late for Hekataios.[38] He was seconded by Anne Burton in her commentary on

---

[33] Karl Reinhardt, "Hekataios von Abdera und Demokrit," *Hermes* 47 (1912): 492-513.

[34] Jacoby first argued for this in his article for *RE*, s.v. "Hekataios aus Abdera," esp. 7:2758-2760, and then summarized his position with some expansions in his *FGrH*, 3a:75-76.

[35] His comment in *RE*, s.v. "Hekataios aus Abdera," 7:2760, is worth noting carefully: "Daß Diodor überhaupt der Disposition des H. folgt, wird sich noch zeigen. Alle vier Abschnitte charakterisiert außer einem ausgesprochen rationalistischen Standpunkt in gleicher Weise das Streben, die ägyptischen Meinungen und Institutionen als allein wahr, vortrefflich und nachahmenswert hinzustellen."

[36] Cf. Oswyn Murray, "Hecataeus of Abdera and Pharaonic Kingship," *Journal of Egyptian Archaeology* 56 (1970): 145, who provides a excellent chart summarizing the evidence on p. 146.

[37] *Ibid.*, p. 145.

[38] Walter Spoerri, *Späthellenistische Berichte über Welt, Kultur und Götter*. Schweizerische Beiträge zur Altertumswissenschaft 9 (Basel: Friedrich Reinhardt, 1959), pp.203-204, where he concludes with this deduction: "Damit wird aber die Zurückführung der diodorischen Theologumena auf Hekataios nur noch unbegründeter, weil man ja dann annehmen muß, Hekataios habe aus dem vorstoischen Gedankengut die von ihm vorgetragenen Vorstellungen entnehmen können. Eine derartige Hypothese ist allein für das eigentlich Stoische bei Diodor schon sehr bedenklich; für das spezifisch Späthellenistische ist sie vollends unhaltbar."

Diodoros I.[39] Burton countered the prevailing view with three arguments: her major objection is that Diodoros is known to be an uncritical excerptor in his later books who even allows his narrative to lapse into contradictions, a phenomenon also present in book one[40]; the Hekataion passages are too scant to warrant the hypothesis of a major source stemming from him[41]; and there are too many other passages from other authors imbedded within the text.[42] Finally, M. Sartori has questioned the basic presupposition of the earlier view. She avers that Diodoros has been short-changed, that he is not a mere abstractor but an author writing with a specific agenda in mind.[43]

The importance of our conclusion on this matter determines whether or not we have any basis for a discussion of Hekataios' work. We must begin with the consensus which has been reached concerning the methodology of Diodoros. It is now known that Diodoros did employ principal sources which he supplemented with other material in order to advance his own purposes.[44] The question which we must now raise is not whether Diodoros preserves Hekataios *au pied de la lettre*, but whether the general lines and concerns of the *Aigyptiaka* are discernible. Four factors suggest that they are. First, we do know that Diodoros was familiar with

---

[39] Anne Burton, *Diodorus Siculus: Book I, A Commentary*. Études Préliminaires aux Religions Orientales dans l'Empire Romain 29 (Leiden: E.J. Brill, 1972), pp. 1-34.

[40] Compare 15.1 with 45.4; 23 with 97.4; 61.1 with 66.3 and 89.3; and 45.1 with 61.1 and 97.5.

[41] She reinforces this by observing that Hekataios regularly mentions Ktesias in book two. Why be reticent about naming Hekataios in book one? See pp. 8-9.

[42] She attributes 37-41 and possibly 30-36 to either Agatharchides or Artemidoros; to Hellanikos 13.3 (= F 71b), 94.2-3 (= F 73), 15.8 (= Athen. 1.334); to Aristotle 82.3 (= *Politics* 3.10); to Timaios 28; to Agroitas 19.1; to Manetho—through an intermediate source—12-13.2 (= F 83), and 26 (= F 1).

[43] M. Sartori, "Storia, utopia è mito nei primi libri della Bibliotheca historicà di Diodoro Siculo," *Athenaeum* 62 (1984): 492-536, esp. 533 and Diamond, "Hecataeus of Abdera," pp. 13-132, who also credits Diodoros with editorial creativity in her analysis of 40.3.1-8.

[44] So Robert Drews, "Diodorus and His Sources," *American Journal of Philology* 83 (1962): 383-392, who suggested that the supplements were primarily moral examples; Burton, *Diodorus Siculus*, p. 1; and Hornblower, *Hieronymus of Cardia*, pp. 18-75, esp. pp. 39-62. Her conclusion on p. 32 is worth repeating: "He did not copy them word for word: an analysis of Diodorus' style shows that it is consistent throughout the *Bibliotheke*. He seems, however, to be a reliable vehicle for the subject-matter of the histories he used, taking over both facts and the inbuilt attitudes and assumptions, and his language frequently echoes even when it does not actually repeat, the language of the original."

Hekataios (1.46.8). It is worth pointing out that Diodoros begins relating the Hekataion section (47-49) with the singular φησίν (47.1), but concludes with his ubiquitous plural φασίν (49.6). The unusual singular followed by the long *oratio obliqua* clearly points to Hekataios. Does the plural in the summary merely reflect Diodoron style or does it subtly betray a link with the preceding? The following suggest the latter. Second, on three occasions—all in different sections of the text—events are dated to Ptolemy Lagos.[45] This makes sense for an author contemporary with Ptolemy, but not with one subsequent to him. Third, all of the sections have a common theme: the antiquity and superiority of Egypt.[46] What makes this impressive is that it is at direct odds with Diodoros' own statement that the Greeks are older than the barbarians in 1.9.5![47] He either changed his mind very quickly or allowed the sentiments of his source(s) to radiate through his retelling. The fourth and final point is that the text is clearly in the form of an ethnography: 10-29 present the religion; 30-41, the land; 42-68, the history; 69-95, the *nomoi*; and 96-98 serve as an appendix.

We may, then, confidently reconstruct the overall schema of the *Aigyptiaka* as well as the prominent themes. We must, however, avoid the mistake of assuming that everything in Diodoros 1.10-98 reflects our work.[48]

2. *Content.* We have suggested that Hekataios wrote his *Aigyptiaka* in the form of an ethnography. This implies that he was familiar with previous Greek accounts: a deduction which can be substan-

---

[45] 1.31.7; 46.7 and 8; 84.8. 33.11 and 37.5 date events to Ptolemy Philadelphos.

[46] For the sections see the fourth point below. The spread of Egyptian culture is highlighted by the campaign of Osiris, 17.3-20.6; the colonization movement, 28.1-29.6; the campaign of Sesoosis, 55.1-12; and the visits of distinguished Greeks, 96.1-98.9.

[47] 1.9.5: περὶ πρώτων δὲ τῶν βαρβάρων διέξιμεν, οὐκ ἀρχαιοτέρους αὐτοὺς ἡγούμενοι τῶν Ἑλλήνων, καθάπερ Ἔφορος εἴρηκεν, ἀλλὰ προδιελθεῖν βουλόμενοι τὰ πλεῖστα τῶν περὶ αὐτούς, ὅπως ἀρξάμενοι τῶν παρὰ τοῖς Ἕλλησιν ἱστορουμένων μηδεμίαν ἐν ταῖς ἀρχαιολογίαις ἑτερογενῆ πρᾶξιν παρεμβάλωμεν.

[48] Diodoros claims to have traveled extensively in preparation for his work. (1.4.1) In the first book he alludes to a visit to Egypt in 44.1; 46.7; 83.9. It is, therefore, possible that his own ἱστορία appears in the work. This can not, however, be pushed since his preface is likely more rhetorical than factual and it is only possible to place him at Bubastis in Egypt. See Burton, *Diodorus Siculus*, pp. 38-39, who concludes that he mainly stayed at Rome. Murray, "Hecataeus of Abdera and Pharaonic Kingship," p. 146, offers a chart indicating the insertions of Diodoros.

tiated by references within the text.[49] In particular, Hekataios appears to have known and used Herodotos.[50] Yet, as we have just seen, we must not simply assume the point. What is undeniable is the similarity of the texts in the historical section (42-68, especially 51-68). There are three points which make this clear. First, as the chart will demonstrate, both narratives follow the same basic order of rulers.

Egyptian Kings in Herodotos and Hekataios

Herodotos	Hekataios
	Μηνᾶς (45.1-3)
	Βούσιρις (45.4-50.2)
	Οὐχορεύς (50.3-51.4)
Μοίριος (101.1-2)	Μοῖρις (51.6-52.6)
Σέσωστρις (102.1-110.3)	Σεσόωσις (53.1-58.5)
Φερῶν (111.1-4)	Σεσόωσις (υἱός) (59.1-4)
	Ἄμασις (60.1-2)
	Ἀκτισάνης (60.3-10)
	Μένδης (61.1-4)
Πρωτεύς (112.1-120.5)	Πρωτεύς (62.1-4)
Ῥαμψίνιτος (121.1-123.3)	Ῥέμφις (62.5-6)
	Νεῖλος (63.1)
Χέοψ (124.1-126.2)	Χέμμις (63.2-9)
Χεφρήν (127.1-128)	Κεφρήν or Χαμβρύης (64.1-6a)
Μυκερῖνος (129.1-135.6)	Μυκερῖνος (64.6b-14)
Ἄσυχις (136.1-4)	
	Βόκχορις (65.1)
Σαβακῶς and Ἄνυσις (137.1-140.2)	Σαβάκων (65.2-8)
Σεθών (141.1-6)	
δυώδεκα (147.1-150.4)	δώδεκα (66.1-6)
Ψαμμήτιχος (151.1-157)	Ψαμμήτιχος (66.7-67.11)
Νεκῶς (158.1-159.3)	
Ψάμμις (160.1-4)	
Ἀπρίης (161.1-171.3)	Ἀπρίης (68.1-5a)
Ἄμασις (172.1-182.2)	Ἄμασις (68.5b-6)

Even a cursory glance reveals the basic uniformity. This is not surprising in and of itself. What does compel attention is the fact that

---

[49] See 15.2; 46.8; 53.1; 64.13; 66.10; 69.7. On Greek accounts of Egypt see Truesdell S. Brown, "The Greek Sense of Time in History as Suggested by Their Accounts of Egypt," *Historia* 11 (1962): 257-270. Brown thinks that Hekataios may have used Herodotos and Hellanikos, p. 267.

[50] So Schwartz, "Hekataeos von Teos," p. 235; Jacoby, *FGrH*, 3a:76-77; and Murray, "Herodotus and Hellenistic Culture," p. 207.

they both end with the same ruler. If the text in Diodoros had been
independent, we would have expected it to continue the historical
section down to a point in time closer to that of the author. The
differences between the two are not substantial. The most obvious
are the variations in spelling and the additional rulers which
Diodoros supplies. The only real aberrations are the omissions of
Diodoros which are more apparent than real. Φερῶν in Herodotos
is clearly Σεσόωσις in Diodoros.[51] Ἄσυχις of Herodotos is likely
Σάσυχις of Diodoros 1.94.3.[52] Νεκῶς is mentioned in Diodoros
1.33.9.[53] Finally, the events related about Ψάμμις by Herodotos
are transferred to Ἄμασις (1.95.2) by the text in Diodoros.

Nor is the similarity simply structural. The content of the two narratives is too close to be accidental. An excellent example of this is
the account of Sesostris. The following chart will illustrate how the
two relate the same events.

Event	Herodotos	Diodoros
Preparations		53.1-6
Campaign	102.2-3	53.7-55.4a,6
Monuments	102.4-5	55.7-8
Colchian Nation	103.1-105	55.4b-5
Pillars in Palestine	106	55.9
Revolt of Brother	107	56.6-8
Captives as Laborers	108-109	55.10-57.5
Ruled Ethiopia	110	(55.1)
Foreign Rulers		58.1-3
Fame		58.4-5

The minor transpositions are not enough to offset the dominant impression of agreement.

The final test of dependence is whether or not there are enough
similarities in the actual wording of episodes. The synopsis on pp.
67-68 will answer this.

---

[51] Φερῶν is simply a title, not a personal name as both the biblical use of פרעה
and Diodoros 1.59.1 indicate.

[52] This may be Shepseskaf of the fourth dynasty, c. 2613-2498. It would be very
easy for a Σ to disappear.

[53] This is, however, a section which may not be Hekataion.

Herodotos 2.111.1-4	Hekataios (D.S. 1.59.1-4)
1 Σεσώστριος δὲ τελευτήσαντος ἐκδέξασθαι ἔλεγον τὴν βασιληίην	1 ὁ δ᾽ υἱὸς αὐτοῦ διαδεξάμενος τὴν βασιλείαν
τὸν παῖδα αὐτοῦ Φερῶν,	καὶ τὴν τοῦ πατρὸς προσηγορίαν ἑαυτῷ περιθέμενος
τὸν ἀποδέξασθαι μὲν οὐδεμίαν στρατηίην,	πρᾶξιν μὲν πολεμικὴν ἢ μνήμης ἀξίαν οὐδ᾽ ἡντινοῦν συνετελέσατο, συμπτώματι δὲ περιέπεσεν ἰδιάζοντι.
συνενειχθῆναι δὲ οἱ τυφλὸν γενέσθαι	2 ἐστερήθη μὲν γὰρ τῆς ὁράσεως εἴτε διὰ τὴν πρὸς τὸν πατέρα τῆς φύσεως κοινωνίαν εἴθ᾽, ὥς τινες μυθολογοῦσι,
διὰ τοιόνδε πρῆγμα· τοῦ ποταμοῦ κατελθόντος μέγιστα δὴ τότε ἐπ᾽ ὀκτωκαίδεκα πήχεας, ὡς ὑπερέβαλε τὰς ἀρούρας πνεύματος ἐμπεσόντος κυματίης ὁ ποταμὸς ἐγένετο.	διὰ τὴν εἰς τὸν πόταμον ἀσέβειαν
	ἐν ᾧ χειμαζόμενός
2 τὸν δὲ βασιλέα λέγουσι τοῦτον ἀτασθαλίῃ χρησάμενον λαβόντα αἰχμὴν βαλεῖν ἐς μέσας τὰς δίνας τοῦ ποταμοῦ, μετὰ δὲ αὐτίκα καμόντα αὐτὸν τοὺς ὀφθαλμοὺς τυφλωθῆναι.	ποτε τὸ φερόμενον ῥεῦμα κατηκόντισε·
	διὰ δὲ τὴν ἀτυχίαν ἀναγκασθεὶς καταφυγεῖν ἐπὶ τὴν τῶν θεῶν βοήθειαν,
δέκα μὲν δὴ ἔτεα εἶναί μιν τυφλόν,	ἐπὶ χρόνους ἱκανοὺς πλείσταις θυσίαις καὶ τιμαῖς τὸ θεῖον ἐξιλασκόμενος οὐδεμιᾶς ἐτύγχανε πολυωρίας·
ἑνδεκάτῳ δὲ ἔτεϊ ἀπικέσθαι οἱ μαντήιον ἐκ βουτοῦς πόλιος	3 τῷ δεκάτῳ δ᾽ ἔτει μαντείας αὐτῷ γενομένης
	τιμῆσαί τε τὸν θεὸν τὸν ἐν Ἡλιουπόλει
ὡς ἐξήκει τέ οἱ ὁ χρόνος τῆς ζημίης καὶ ἀναβλέψει γυναικὸς οὔρῳ νιψάμενος τοὺς ὀφθαλμούς,	καὶ γυναικὸς οὔρῳ νίζεσθαι τὸ πρόσωπον
ἥτις παρὰ τὸν ἑωυτῆς ἄνδρα μοῦνον πεφοίτηκε, ἄλλων ἀνδρῶν ἐοῦσα ἄπειρος.	ἥτις
3 καὶ τὸν πρώτης τῆς ἑωυτοῦ γυναικὸς πειρᾶσθαι,	ἑτέρου πεῖραν ἀνδρὸς οὐκ εἴληφε, τῶν μὲν γυναικῶν ἀπὸ τῆς ἰδίας ἀρξάμενος
μετὰ δέ, ὡς οὐκ ἀνέβλεπε, ἐπεξῆς πασέων πειρᾶσθαι·	καὶ πολλὰς ἐξετάσας οὐδεμίαν εὗρεν ἀδιάφθορον πλὴν κηπουροῦ τινος,
ἀναβλέψαντα δὲ συναγαγεῖν τὰς γυναῖκας τῶν ἐπειρήθη,	ἣν ὑγιὴς γενόμενος ἔγημε· τὰς δ᾽ ἄλλας ζώσας

Herodotos 2.111.1-4	Hekataios (D.S. 1.59.1-4)
πλὴν ἢ τῆς τῷ οὔρῳ νιψάμενος ἀνέβλεψε, ἐς μίαν πόλιν, ἣ νῦν καλέεται Ἐρυθρὴ βῶλος, ἐς ταύτην συναλίσαντα ὑποπρῆσαι πάσας σὺν αὐτῇ τῇ πόλι. 4 τῆς δὲ νιψάμενος τῷ οὔρῳ ἀνέβλεψε, ταύτην δὲ ἔσχε αὐτὸς γυναῖκα.	ἐν κώμῃ τινὶ κατέκαυσεν, ἣν Αἰγύπτιοι διὰ τὸ σύμπτωμα τοῦτο προσηγόρευσαν ἱερὰν βῶλον.
ἀναθήματα δὲ ἀποφυγὼν τὴν πάθην τῶν ὀφθαλμῶν ἄλλα τε ἀνὰ τὰ ἱρὰ πάντα τὰ λόγιμα ἀνέθηκε καὶ τοῦ γε λόγου μάλιστα ἄξιόν ἐστι ἔχειν, ἐς τοῦ Ἡλίου τὸ ἱρὸν	4 τῷ δ᾿ ἐν Ἡλιουπόλει θεῷ τὰς χάριτας ἀπονέμων τῆς εὐεργεσίας κατὰ τὸν χρησμὸν
ἀξιοθέητα ἀνέθηκε ἔργα, ὀβελοὺς δύο λιθίνους, ἐξ ἑνὸς ἐόντας ἑκάτερον λίθου, μῆκος μὲν ἑκάτερον πήχεων ἑκατόν, εὖρος δὲ ὀκτὼ πήχεων.	ὀβελίσκους ἀνέθηκε δύο μονολίθους, τὸ μὲν πλάτος ὀκτώ, τὸ δὲ μῆκος πηχῶν ἑκατόν.

The correspondence between the two accounts is self-evident and impressive. It is clear that the text in Diodoros abbreviates except where supplementary information is being supplied. The only variations are minor. The difference in the year of the oracle (Herodotos, in the eleventh year; Diodoros, in the 10th) may be due to the previous statement in Herodotos that Φερῶν was blind for ten years. The only other difference is the name of the village which likely reflects some confusion in translation.[54]

The literary dependence of the text in Diodoros on Herodotos is beyond question. The real issue is: Did Diodoros lift the text from Herodotos[55] or from a source which had drawn from Herodotos?

---

[54] Burton, *Diodorus Siculus*, p. 180, explains: "The difference in the names recorded by the two classical authors might well be the result of confused translations of an Egyptian name: the Egyptian for 'holy' is ḏsr, for 'red' dsr, and by late times the difference in pronunciation between these two words would be minimal." The site has not been located.

[55] So Diamond, "Hecataeus of Abdera," pp. 29-30.

The former seems unlikely to me since there is a polemic in the Diodoran text against Herodotos.[56] There is no reason to attribute this to Diodoros. It is much more reasonable to credit it to a source whose perspective Diodoros has not dimmed and who had reasons for attacking Herodotos. But what is this source? Jacoby thought it was Hekataios who was attempting to displace Herodotos.[57] Burton can not see why Hekataios would have employed Herodotos so extensively if he had wanted to discredit him. Instead, she sees the anti-Herodotean crusade arising with Manethon and the source of Diodoros an unknown figure from the Manethonian school.[58] There are, however, solid grounds for attributing the polemic to Hekataios. As I will show below, Hekataios was attempting to write an official history.[59] Earlier treatments which do not share the same perspective or purpose are no longer acceptable. At the same time, their place in the ethnographic tradition can not be denied. The most effective course is to displace them, not ignore them. This is what Hekataios sought to do. It is, therefore, more reasonable to ascribe the text to a known source rather to one which must be postulated.

Granted, then, that Hekataios did make use of the Ionic tradition and Herodotos in particular, we must ask what transformations took place. The experience of reading Herodotos' Egyptian *logos* and Hekataios' *Aigyptiaka* is by no means identical. The key statement in understanding Hekataios' polemic against Herodotos is 1.69.7: ὅσα μὲν οὖν Ἡρόδοτος καί τινες τῶν τὰς Αἰγυπτίων πράξεις συνταξαμένων ἐσχεδιάκασιν, ἑκουσίως προκρίναντες τῆς ἀληθείας τὸ παραδοξολογεῖν καὶ μύθους πλάττειν ψυχαγωγίας ἕνεκα, παρήσομεν, stating instead, αὐτὰ δὲ τὰ παρὰ τοῖς ἱερεῦσι τοῖς κατ' Αἴγυπτον ἐν ταῖς ἀναγραφαῖς γεγραμμένα φιλοτίμως ἐξητακότες ἐκθησόμεθα. Herodotos carefully distinguished between his own investigations and native reports, placing his ὄψις before the stories of

---

[56] 1.59.2 (*contra* Herodotos 2.111); 66.10 (*contra* 2.151); and 69.7.

[57] So Jacoby, *FGrH*, 3a:77.

[58] Burton, *Diodorus Siculus*, pp. 28-29. She thinks that the text succeeds in "combining an author of the Herodotean school with one of the Manethonian school. The latter would account for the hostile attitude towards Herodotus, which seems to have been established by Manetho. Or these two hypothetical authors may in fact be one . . ." Cf. also pp. 25-29.

[59] See the section on Function.

the inhabitants.[60] Hekataios reverses his procedure and castigates Herodotos for his inaccuracy. The only acceptable base of information is now the native sources. This explains the pervasive use of the impersonal φασί and λέγουσι as surrogates for the priests who are Hekataios' sources.[61] The priests are the interpreters of the sacred writings which are the ultimate source.[62] *In nuce,* outsiders can not define who the Egyptians are or what their history has been, only the Egyptians themselves.

The effect this had on the content of the Αἰγυπτιακά is subtle yet powerful.[63] All of the standard ethnographic elements are present. What changes is the emphasis given to a particular element. Geography is clearly diminished.[64] While it undoubtedly formed a part of Hekataios' work, his account was unsatisfactory to Diodoros who replaced it with a more adequate description.[65] This may be due in part to the fact that his audience lived in Egypt, not in Greece, and would not need a detailed description of the land.

On the other hand, the role of "discoveries" or "firsts" greatly

---

[60] 2.99.1.

[61] I count 101 uses of φασί(ν) or a form of it and 41 occurrences of λέγουσι or a related form of λέγω. (Not counting the passages where the verbs describe Greek versions.) Other verbs such as ἱστορέω (5t.), μυθολογέω (5t.), and φέρω (3t.) are also present, but not in such frequency. The emphasis on native reports is unmistakable.

[62] The ἱεραὶ ἀναγραφαί are mentioned in 31.7; 43.6; 44.4; 46.7, 8; 63.1; 69.7; 73.4; 95.2; 96.2. The priests or Egyptians are mentioned in 10.1; 12.6,10; 13.3; 15.2; 26.1,6; 28.1; 29.5; 46.7; 52.6; 62.2; 63.8; 68.5; 86.2,3; 88.6; 94.3; 96.2. On two of these occasions the priests and the records are mentioned together: in each instance the priests inform on the basis of the sacred records, 46.7; 96.2. (The priests are also mentioned in the non-Hekataion 37.7.) It may be that these are the Theban priests. See 50.1 and Jacoby, *FGrH*, 3a:83-85. There is no evidence to substantiate Schwartz's claim that Hekataios could have read hieroglyphs. "Hekataeos von Teos," p. 236. Rightly Jacoby, *RE*, s.v. "Hekataios aus Abdera," 7:2762.

[63] Jacoby, *FGrH*, 3a:86-87, wrote: "Er will überall nur dieser (i.e., der geschriebenen aegyptischen Priestertradition—GES) folgen (oder behauptet es wenigstens) und damit—denn das ist der entscheidende Gesichtspunkt, unter dem sich all Abweichungen von Herodot und der Ethnographie überhaupt vereinigen lassen—die höchstmögliche Authentizität und Autorität für den gesamten Inhalt seines Buches erreichen."

[64] 30 and most of 31 is likely Hekataion. Murray, "Hecataeus of Abdera and Pharaonic Kingship," pp. 147-148, also recognized the diminution of geography.

[65] Probably from Agatharchides. *FGrH* 86. This may have come to Diodoros through Artemidoros. See Burton, *Diodorus Siculus,* pp. 18-25 for details. She attributes 37-41 to Agatharchides and 30-36—possibly—to Artemidoros.

increases. It plays a part in every section of the work.[66] The *locus classicus* for this is in 1.69.5: λέγουσι τοίνυν Αἰγύπτιοι παρ' αὐτοῖς τήν τε τῶν γραμμάτων εὕρεσιν γενέσθαι καὶ τὴν τῶν ἄστρων παρατήρησιν, continuing with, πρὸς δὲ τούτοις τά τε κατὰ τὴν γεωμετρίαν θεωρήματα καὶ τῶν τεχνῶν τὰς πλείστας εὑρεθῆναι, νόμους τε τοὺς ἀρίστους τεθῆναι. While Herodotos was content to note a νόμος or a claim wherever he encountered it, Hekataios stakes the origin of all civilization to Egypt. Thus, what was an admiring observation has become an important claim.[67] Nor was Hekataios making this claim for the first time. It was a long-standing attitude within Egyptian tradition.[68]

This is further buttressed by the insistence of Greek dependence on Egypt.[69] Yet it is not only Greece, but all of the world which has derived its culture from Egypt. This is made plain by a new element which Hekataios injected into his document. In 28.1-29.6, there is a summary of Egypt's colonization of the rest of the world: Babylon from Belos (28.1), Argos from Danaos (28.2a), the Kolchians and Jews as the custom of circumcision proves (28.2b-3), and Athens from Sais (28.4-29.5a). The editorial introduction and conclusion to

---

[66] The language in the Theologoumena is explicit: εὑρετής, 13.3; 15.8; 16.1; 25.2-6 (where the feminine εὑρετίς is used of Isis in 2 and the verb εὑρίσκω in 6); 27.5; πρῶτον, 14.1,4; 16.1; ἀνευρίσκω, 15.4; εὕρεσις, 16.1. The historical section also has a treatment (43.5-6), although the claims are noticeably weaker here. This is intriguing since this is the section where Hekataios is most clearly dependent upon Herodotos. Finally, the *nomoi* have four texts dealing with the subject: 69.5; 94.3; 97.6; 97.7 (the last two technically belong to the appendix). Cf. also F 1.

[67] On Herodotos' attitude see Waters, *Herodotos the Historian*, pp. 119-121. The recognition of Egypt's contributions was acknowledged by the Greeks. Cf. Plato, *Phdr.* 274C-275B; Isokrates, Busiris, 21-23; and Aristotle, *Metaph.* 1.1.14-16 (= 981b).

[68] An excellent example of this is in *The Journey of Wen-Amon to Phoenicia* which dates to the eleventh century B.C.E. Zakar-Baal says: "Now when Amon founded all lands, in founding them he founded first the land of Egypt, from which you come; for craftsmanship came out of it, to reach the place where I am, and learning came out of it, to reach the place where I am. What are these silly trips which they have had you make?" Cited from *ANET*, 1:27. On Egyptian attitudes towards foreigners see Serge Sauneron, "L'Avis des Egyptiens sur la cuisine Soudanaise," *Kush* 7 (1959): 63-70; W. Helck, "Die Ägypter und die Fremden," *Saeculum* 15 (1964): 103-114; and B.G. Trigger, B.J. Kemp, D. O'Conner, and A.B. Lloyd, *Ancient Egypt: A Social History* (Cambridge: Cambridge University Press, 1983), pp. 194-195, 316-317.

[69] 22.7; 23.8 (especially); 61.3-4; and the beginning and ending of the section on νόμοι deal with Greek visitors who borrow from what they learn in Egypt, 69.2-7; 96.1-9.

the extract make it very clear that we only have a sample of what once must have constituted a much larger section of Hekataios' text.[70] Diodoros—who does not share the same view—can not let these claims pass without expressing his lack of agreement.[71]

3. *Form*. The process of collapsing and expanding elements within the tradition has some obvious implications for the form of Hekataios' tome. As we have already seen, the description of the land, traditionally the first element in ethnography, is altered by Hekataios. Yet not only does he compress it, he moves it from the first position to the second thereby reducing its significance even more. On the other hand, he splits the *nomoi* of Herodotos into two separate sections. Whereas in Herodotos religion is simply the first half of the *nomoi* (2.37-76 followed by 77-98), in Hekataios it is moved to the first position. This is not all. Herodotos offers a simple description of the cult and practices of the Egyptians; Hekataios does not. He instead chooses to develop only the theologoumena in 11-27 and then offers a description of the Egyptian state as well as the standard fare of diet, sexual mores, and peculiar practices or qualities of the people. We must ask what led to such alterations.

The opening section on theogony is the most heavily laden with interpolations and we must be careful about how wide we cast our net. The two points which appear to be the foci of the discussion are that the gods are personifications of matter (12.1-10)[72] or deified humans (13.1-17.2).[73] These rationalizations suggest that Heka-

---

[70] 28.1: Οἱ δ' οὖν Αἰγύπτιοί φασι καὶ μετὰ ταῦτα ἀποικίας πλείστας ἐξ Αἰγύπτου κατὰ πᾶσαν διασπαρῆναι τὴν οἰκουμένην. 29.5b: Καθόλου δὲ πλείστας ἀποικίας Αἰγύπτιοί φασιν ἐκπέμψαι τοὺς ἑαυτῶν προγόνους ἐπὶ πολλὰ μέρη τῆς οἰκουμένης διά τε τὴν ὑπεροχὴν τῶν βασιλευσάντων παρ' αὐτοῖς καὶ διὰ τὴν ὑπερβολὴν τῆς πολυανθρωπίας. Murray, "Hecataeus of Abdera and Pharaonic Kingship," p. 145, also thinks that this was a significant part of Hekataios' work.

[71] 29.5,6.

[72] Zeus is πνεῦμα, 2; Hephaistos is πῦρ, 3; Demeter is γῆ, 4; Okeanos is ὑγρόν (= Nile), 5-6; and Athena is ἀήρ, 7-8.

[73] 13.1: Ἄλλους δ' ἐκ τούτων ἐπιγείους γενέσθαι φασίν, ὑπάρξαντας μὲν θνητούς, διὰ δὲ σύνεσιν καὶ κοινὴν ἀνθρώπων εὐεργεσίαν τετευχότας τῆς ἀθανασίας, ὧν ἐνίους καὶ βασιλεῖς γεγονέναι κατὰ τὴν Αἴγυπτον. A word of caution should be registered here. Diodoros was enamored by Euhemeros as book six attests. It would, therefore, be possible to ascribe this to Diodoros rather than Hekataios. On the other hand, there is no reason why Hekataios could not have made the same point as Euhemeros in the same period. This is particularly true since the ἱεραὶ ἀναγραφαί of Euhemeros is a utopia like the Hyperboreans (and the *Aigyptiaka*) of Hekataios. Euhermeros' claim that Uranos, Kronos, and Zeus were former kings who had subsequently been apotheosized has obvious implications for Hellenistic

taios presented the theologoumena through the lens of Greek philosophy, an impression reinforced by three of the fragments.[74] The second half of his discussion betrays the same perspective. As Oswyn Murray has shown, the fact that he presents a constitutional monarchy and treats the king in his relation to law attests to Greek concerns.[75] This is not to say that he did not receive his information from the priests. It is to affirm that the native Egyptian data passed through a Greek sieve as Hekataios wrote.[76]

We must now ask what sort of work takes information from native sources and then filters it through Greek philosophical issues. At this point it is important to remember the Περὶ Ὑπερβορέων.[77] The latter employed a legendary people in order to present a utopia via Greek philosophy. The Αἰγυπτιακά takes a real people and tells their story through the medium of Greek ethnography shaped by philosophical concerns and claims that they are the fount of all civilization. It is hard not to see the idealistic tendency of a utopia being foisted onto a concrete group of people.[78]

4. *Function*. But why? The Περὶ Ὑπερβορέων could well be an exercise designed to portray a utopian state within the context of contemporary discussions on the state. But does the Αἰγυπτιακά fall into the same category? In other words, is it a theoretical treatise or does it have a specific historical function?

We have already seen that Hekataios came to Egypt during the reign of Ptolemy I Soter (367/6-283/2).[79] Ptolemy became satrap of

---

rulers. Would the same claim in Hekataios have the same implications?

[74] F 1 (= Diogenes Laertios 1.10) presents a cosmogony in terms of Greek philosophical discussion. Diogenes mentions Hekataios' views ἔν τε πρώτῃ Περὶ τῆς Αἰγυπτίων φιλοσοφίας. It would be possible to see a separate work here; however, the subject matter of the fragment matches that in Diodoros and it is preferable to consider it a brief recapitulation of the Αἰγυπτιακά. F 3 (= Diogenes Laertios 1.9) claims the gods are γενετούς and F 4 (= Plutarch, *De Is.* 9) offers a rationalistic explanation for the name Ἀμοῦν (= Zeus).

[75] Murray, "Hecataeus of Abdera and Pharaonic Kingship," pp. 152-166, esp. pp. 164-166.

[76] The author who has emphasized this most is Werner Jaeger, "Greeks and Jews: The First Greek Records of Jewish Religion and Civilization," *The Journal of Religion* 18 (1938): 136-137.

[77] Jacoby, *RE*, s.v., "Hekataios aus Abdera," 7:2758, drew attention to the parallel between the two works.

[78] As Jacoby, *RE*, s.v. "Hekataios aus Abdera," 7:2755.

[79] On Ptolemaic Egypt see *RE*, s.v. "Ptolemais I. Soter," by Hans Volkmann, 23:1603-1643; M. Rostovtzeff, "Ptolemaic Egypt," in *The Hellenistic Monarchies and the Rise of Rome*, ed. by S.A. Cook, F.E. Adcock, and M.P. Charlesworth. CAH

Egypt in 323 and assumed the title of βασιλεύς in 304. The difficulty lies in determining the relationship of the work to Ptolemy. Was the work directed *for* or *against* him or neither? If we conceive of the work as written on Ptolemy's behalf, then we must explain how a work which is unabashedly nationalistic could support Ptolemy's aspirations to recover Alexander's empire. On the other hand, if we perceive a negative stance toward Ptolemy, then we must account for Hekataios' alignment with native resistance.

While the following must be considered tentative, it suggests a reasonable rationale for the work. Ptolemy's power base was Egypt. His right to rule was ultimately based on power. This meant that he had to reward his army financially and socially in order to maintain his source of power. At the same time, he could not successfully accomplish this without the support of the native population. Sheer force was obviously inadequate. The Ptolemies needed to buttress their sovereignty along several non-military lines including a philosophical undergirding.[80]

It appears to be more than coincidental that at the same time Ptolemy needed philosophical support for his state, a known philosopher should write a philosophically oriented ethnography of Egypt. A possible deduction from this is that Hekataios was a court writer.[81]

We must now try to make sense of the *Aigyptiaka* from this perspective. A court author in this period would have three major concerns. First, the writer would need to address the Greeks in Egypt and demonstrate to them that the Ptolemaic kingdom was the ideal state. Second, the same work would need to win the approbation of the indigenous power base (i.e., the priests) by celebrating the

(Cambridge: Cambridge University Press, 1954), 7:109-154, as well as his *The Social and Economic History of the Hellenistic World*, 1:255-422, esp. pp. 261-267.

[80] On this see Rostovtzeff, "Ptolemaic Egypt," pp. 113-114 and Hengel, *Hellenism and Judaism*, 1:18-20. On the concept of kingship, see Erwin R. Goodenough, "The Political Philosophy of Hellenistic Kingship," *Yale Classical Studies* 1 (1928): 53-102 and *RAC* s.v., "Euergetes," by B. Koetting, 6:848-860, esp. 850-856. Koetting's summary of the numerous περὶ βασιλείας is apposite: "Die wenigen Bruchstücke haben immer den gleichen Inhalt, daß die Könige sich der Gerechtigkeit befleißigen u. durch Wohltun sich bewahren müssen." Col. 852.

[81] Diamond, "Hecataeus of Abdera," pp. 117, 139, 140-141, disputes this since—in her view—there is no evidence for it and she can not imagine a philosopher serving as a press agent. While the evidence is admittedly circumstantial, it is nonetheless strong. As I will point out below Hekataios was not a simple mouthpiece.

accomplishments of the native civilization and affirming continuity with it. Third, the first two causes could both be bolstered and a point made against rival hellenistic kingdoms if Egypt were presented as the civilization *par excellence*.

This is what we have in the Αἰγυπτιακά. The common theme is the greatness of Egypt as the mother of all civilization, a claim which was echoed by the other hellenistic kingdoms as we will soon see.[82] The priests served as the informants and it was their information which became the official account. Their nationalism was neither monitored nor censored but exploited.[83] Perhaps the insistence that the king was subject to law was a bow to them; on the other hand, it would also appeal to the Greeks and remove any charge of obsequiousness from Hekataios.[84] Finally, the work was cast in a thoroughly Greek mold in an effort to persuade the upper echelon to live amicably with those beneath them.[85]

What we have, then, in the *Aigyptiaka* is the shell of an ethnography. It would, however, be a mistake to call it an ethnography since it has undergone extensive alterations in content, form, and especially function. It is rather the first decisive step towards apologetic historiography. When should we date it?

5. *The Jewish Excursus*. The question of date leads us into Hekataios' comments on the Jews. We have already seen that Hekataios had a colonization account which included the Jews (28.2-3). In 40.3, Diodoros offers a second account of the Jews which he has

---

[82] Murray, "Hecataeus of Abdera and Pharaonic Kingship," p. 166, claimed "it began a war of books between the Hellenistic monarchies . . ." While there were competing claims, it goes beyond the evidence to posit direct responses. See below.

[83] It should be pointed out that in the campaign of Sesoosis we are told: οὐ μόνον γὰρ τὴν ὕστερον ὑπ' Ἀλεξάνδρου τοῦ Μακεδόνος κατακτηθεῖσαν χώραν ἐπῆλθεν, ἀλλὰ καί τινα τῶν ἐθνῶν ὧν ἐκεῖνος οὐ παρέβαλεν εἰς τὴν χώραν (1.55.3).

[84] Although Ptolemy had not yet assumed the title of king it is worth pointing out that this was a topic of importance in Greek discussions on kingship. Cf. Goodenough, "The Political Philosophy of Hellenistic Kingship," pp. 59-75. Murray, "Hecataeus of Abdera and Pharaonic Kingship," p. 166, suggests that this may have been both the view of the priests and Hekataios. He also points out that if the work is dated prior to Ptolemy's accession, there is no real tension between his advice and place in the court since Ptolemy was anxious to be conciliatory.

[85] Jacoby, *RE*, s.v. "Hekataios aus Abdera," 7:2764-2765, recognized the need Hekataios had to address both Ptolemy and the Greeks. He urged Ptolemy to use his power according to the guidance of philosophy and the Greeks to treat the natives with respect and not arrogance.

taken from Hekataios.[86] The obvious question which arises is: Did Diodoros take the account preserved in 40.3 from the Αἰγυπτιακά? It appears that he did. There are two reasons for this statement. First, we know that Diodoros was familiar with the Αἰγυπτιακά. Second, it would be entirely in keeping with Diodoros' methodology to withhold an excursus on the Jews from book one in order to be able to use it for an introduction to his account of Pompey's campaign in book forty.[87]

Is it possible to be more specific? I believe that it is. It is natural to think that 40.3 must be tied in some way to 1.28.2-3, since both texts mention Danaos and the Jews. We have already noted that the colonization account of 1.28-29 has been significantly reduced by Diodoros. It would certainly be possible to place 40.3 within the framework of this section. That it belongs there is confirmed by the language of the two texts. 1.28.1 opens with the statement: Οἱ δ' οὖν Αἰγύπτιοί φασιν καὶ μετὰ ταῦτα ἀποικίας πλείστας ἐξ Αἰγύπτου κατὰ πᾶσαν διασπαρῆναι τὴν οἰκουμένην. 40.3.3 echoes with: ἡγεῖτο δὲ τῆς ἀποικίας ὁ προσαγορευόμενος Μωσῆς . . . There is, however, a problem: 1.28.2-3, suggests the Jews were colonists who set out from Egypt; 40.3.1-2, indicates that they were expelled by the Egyptians. Jacoby solved the tension by noting that 40.3 is a variant account: the colonization section is designed to glorify Egypt as the cradle of all civilization; 40.3 serves a different purpose. It displays Egyptian contempt for foreigners.[88] The two fit nicely

---

[86] The fragment preserved as 40.3 is attributed by Photios to Hekataios of Miletos. Modern scholars have been loathe to accept this, although see F. Dornseiff, "Antikes zum Alten Testament," *ZAW* n.s. 15 (1938): 76 n. 1, who defended it on stylistic grounds. Jacoby, *FGrH*, 3a:46, has shown that it must be Hekataios of Abdera. The authenticity of the account should not be doubted since—as we will see—the perspective of the account fits Hekataios of Abdera.

[87] Cf. Jacoby, *FGrH*, 3a:47: "Diodor hatte sich—offenbar im Gedanken an jüngste Ereignisse—H.'s Judenexkurs bei Seite gelegt, als er die Aigyptiaka für sein erstes Buch exzerpierte, um ihn als Einleitung für den Judenkrieg des Pompeius zu verwenden; und er hat ihn nicht kassiert, als er bei Poseidonios, den er erst vom 5. Buche an und dann wieder für die Geschichte des 2. Jhdts. aufschlug, ebenfalls einen Judenexkurs fand." Others who link 40.3 to the *Aigyptiaka* include: Francis R. Walton, "The Messenger of God in Hecataeus of Abdera," *HTR* 48 (1955): 256 and Albert-Marie Denis, *Introduction aux Pseudépigraphes Grecs d'Ancien Testament*. SVTP 1 (Leiden: E.J. Brill, 1970), p. 263.

[88] Jacoby, *FGrH*, 3a:50-51. Cf. also John G. Gager, *Moses in Greco-Roman Paganism* (Nashville/New York: Abingdon Press, 1972), pp. 28-29.

together since a feeling of superiority often breeds disdain for those who are considered inferior.

But how does this relate to the dating of the *Aigyptiaka?* Fifty years ago, Werner Jaeger argued that Hekataios was the first Greek author to write on the Jews.[89] He based this position on the relative dating of Hekataios and Theophrastos (c. 370-288). Jaeger contended that the references in Theophrastos' *De lapidibus* 24 and 55 to those who wrote on the Egyptian kings necessitated a Greek literary source. This must be Hekataios since the annals were not available until after Manethon. This led him to conclude that Theophrastos' presentation of the Jewish religion in Περὶ Εὐσεβείας was also based upon Hekataios. He dated Hekataios' work to the accession of Ptolemy to the kingship, i.e., 305/304 B.C.E. Jaeger's views won wide acceptance,[90] but have recently been subjected to some penetrating criticism.[91] M. Stern has attempted to reverse the relative priority back to its traditional order by pointing out that both the Περὶ λίθων and the Περὶ Εὐσεβείας of Theophrastos must be dated to around 320-315 B.C.E.[92] Since Ptolemy did not take control of Egypt until 323 and was not solidly entrenched until 321, dependence of Theophrastos on Hekataios is ruled out. Oswyn Murray has agreed that Jaeger's dating of Hekataios is flawed: only the problem is that he did not date him early enough.[93] Murray thinks that Theophrastos must have used Hekataios in *De lapidibus,* but not

---

[89] He first published his views in *Diokles von Karystos: Die griechische Medizin und die Schule des Aristoteles* (Berlin: Walter de Gruyter & Co., 1938), pp. 116-150 and then again in "Greeks and Jews," pp. 134-136.

[90] Jacoby, *FGrH,* 3a:48; Arthur Darby Nock, "The Cult of Heroes," *HTR* 37 (1944): 174; and Hengel, *Judaism and Hellenism,* 1:256.

[91] M. Stern and Oswyn Murray, "Hecataeus of Abdera and Theophrastus on Jews and Egyptians," *Journal of Egyptian Archaeology* 59 (1973): 159-168. Cf. also Diamond, "Hecataeus of Abdera," pp. 197-198, who denies Theophrastos used Hekataios.

[92] *De lapidibus* should be placed c. 315/314 since 59 dates the discovery of cinnabar to 90 years prior to the insignificant archonship of Praxibylos. If Praxibylos had been out of office for long, the dating would have had no meaning. Περὶ Εὐσεβείας appears to be a response to the charge of impiety leveled against Theophrastos in 319. He thus dates it between 320 and 310. See *ibid.,* pp. 161-162.

[93] Murray offers five arguments: 1. Diodoros 1.84.8 (funeral of the Apis bull) should be placed c. 320 since the bulls lived approximately twenty years and a new era began in 300. 2. Ptolemy is not called βασιλεύς. 3. The Jews always place him early. 4. Hekataios does not mention Alexandria which implies that Memphis is still the capital—it was until 311/310. 5. Ptolemy paid more attention to native traditions in his early days than in his latter ones. *Ibid.,* pp. 164-166.

in Περὶ Εὐσεβείας.[94] This means that we should place Hekataios c. 320-315. Thus the comments of both authors on the Jews should be considered contemporary.

While we may not be able to solve the issue of dependence satisfactorily, the discussion does point us to the period of composition. We should now be able to establish the boundaries. The *terminus a quo* is 321 when Ptolemy received the satrapy of Egypt from Antipater. I would place the *terminus ad quem* at 304 when Ptolemy assumed the royal title.[95] Within these perimeters, I prefer to place Hekataios as early as possible. This allows for both the dependence of Theophrastos in *De lapidibus* and matches the early period of Ptolemy's rule when he was well-disposed to the Egyptians in an effort to consolidate his power base.

Περὶ 'Ιουδαίων

The injection of the Jewish element in the *Aigyptiaka* leads us to the traditions which affirm Hekataios wrote a separate work on the Jews. Before we examine those, however, we need to summarize what we know Hekataios wrote about the Jews in the Αἰγυπτιακά. The account in 40.3 falls into two halves: 1-3 present the origins of the Jews and 4-8 their *politeia*.[96] The initial reaction to reading the text is to note how different it is from the biblical record.[97] Scholars have offered three major interpretations to account for these aberrations: first, the text accurately reflects conditions in Judea at the time

---

[94] *Ibid.*, p. 167.

[95] He is never called βασιλεύς by Hekataios.

[96] The text has been abbreviated by the tradents, especially Diodoros. Cf. Jacoby, *FGrH*, 3a:48. On Photios see Walton, "The Messenger of God in Hecataeus of Abdera," p. 256 and Diamond, "Hecataeus of Abdera," pp. 5-12. Her treatment of Diodoros follows on pp. 13-132. She is excessive in her attempts to attribute material to Diodoros in my opinion.

[97] Some of the differences may be more apparent than real—there is quite obviously more than one way to interpret the biblical data—but those which strike me as being different in spirit if not in fact from the biblical text are: the nature of the exodus, 1-2 (where in the biblical narrative are the Egyptians concerned about the purity of their worship?); the condition of Judea, 2 (the land flowing with milk and honey has become a barren waste); the activities of Moses, 3 and 7 (who now not only takes the land in person, but founds Jerusalem and the temple, then divides the land, and makes forays into foreign territories); the qualifications of the priests, 4 and 5 (who are not chosen by birth but by virtue); the denial that the Jews ever had a king, 5; and the amount of land received by the priests, 7.

of the writing[98]; second, the *interpretatio Graeca* of Hekataios has altered the data[99]; and third, the concepts of the text emanate from some priestly circles at the time of the composition and have been cast in the mold of a Greek *politeia*.[100]

The first view may be discarded since there is no evidence to substantiate it. The presence of the *interpretatio Graeca* is undeniable in my opinion: the language and the forms are clearly Greek.[101] The presentation of the Jewish *politeia* according to the Greek philosophical tradition should not warrant any surprise after we have read the Περὶ Ὑπερβορέων and the Αἰγυπτιακά. The remaining issue is whether the content is due to Hekataios or to Jewish source(s). Doron Mendels has recently shown that there are numerous parallels between 40.3 and the concerns in Ezra-Nehemiah.[102] This opens the door to the third possibility. That Hekataios obtained his information from native sources is paralleled by his handling of Egypt. We must be careful, however, not to overplay the possibility of a Jewish source which provided information to Hekataios that has been shaped by internal Jewish debates.[103] As we have already seen, the expulsion of the Jews most likely stems from Egyptian not Jewish circles. It, therefore, appears most reasonable to conclude that Hekataios obtained his expulsion account from Egyptian priests and then turned to Jewish priests living in Egypt for information about their traditions. He presented this in language and concepts intelligible to Greeks.

To insist that Hekataios has painted his picture of the Jewish *politeia* via Greek concerns raises the question of whether his portrait is positive. *A priori* we would expect it to be. This is in fact what we

---

[98] E.g., Tcherikover, *Hellenistic Civilization and the Jews*, pp. 58-59, who argues from our text that the high priest was the central power in Palestine at this time. There are no satraps.

[99] The best example of this interpretation is that of Jaeger, "Greeks and Jews," pp. 139-143. Cf. also Hengel, *Judaism and Hellenism*, 1:255-256.

[100] Doron Mendels, "Hecataeus of Abdera and a Jewish 'Patrios Politeia' of the Perian Period (Diodorus Siculus XL, 3)," *ZAW* 95 (1983): 96-110.

[101] The most obvious example is the description of Moses who is said to excel in the virtues of φρόνεσις and ἀνδρεία, 3. The latter is one of the four cardinal virtues of Plato (*Rep.* 433) and the former an important concept in the philosophical tradition beginning with Plato and Aristotle. Cf. *TDNT*, s.v., "φρήν," by Georg Bertram, 9:221-224, for its use in the tradition.

[102] Mendels, "Hecataeus of Abdera and a Jewish 'Patrios Politeia' of the Persian Period," pp. 98-110.

[103] Diamond, "Hecataeus of Abdera," pp. 144-159, is guilty of this.

generally find in the text. Moses is described as φρονήσει τε καὶ ἀνδρείᾳ πολὺ διαφέρων (40.3.3). Jewish religion meets the canon of Xenophanes: God is not ἀνθρωπόμορφος.[104] The Jewish state is ruled by priests who were selected on the basis of their virtue not their birth: a good Platonic *politeia*.[105] It is within this positive assessment that Hekataios also noted a characteristic which would later be turned against the Jews, i.e., separatism.[106] The overall impression is good, but not perfect.[107]

1. *Authenticity.* These comments about the Jews are not the only ones which are attributed to Hekataios by ancient sources. Pseudo-Aristeas 31 (= F 23) tells us that the failure of Greek authors to mention the Scriptures is διὸ τὸ ἁγνήν τινα καὶ σεμνὴν εἶναι τὴν ἐν αὐτοῖς θεωρίαν, ὡς φησίν Ἑκαταῖος ὁ Ἀβδηρίτης. Josephos quotes extensively from Hekataios whom he avers described the Jews οὐ παρέργως, ἀλλὰ περὶ αὐτῶν Ἰουδαίων συγγέγραφε βιβλίον in *Contra Apionem* 1.183-205; 2.43 (= FF 21 and 22). Finally, Josephos also informs us that Hekataios wrote a book on Abraham (*AJ* 1.159 = T 8a) which Clement likewise mentions as κατ' Ἄβραμον καὶ τοὺς Αἰγυπτίους (*Strom.* 5.14.113.1-2 = T 8b). These references have served as the occasion for a great deal of learned ink in this century. Nearly every conceivable position has found an adherent as the following chart will show.

While the multiplicity of views is bewildering,[108] it is important

---

[104] On Xenophanes' concept of God see *KRS*, pp. 168-171. Clement, *Strom.* 5.14.109.1 (= *KRS* 170) summarized his views as: εἷς θεός, ἕν τε θεοῖσι καὶ ἀνθρώποισι μέγιστος,/ οὔτι δέμας θνητοῖσιν ὁμοίιος οὐδὲ νόημα.

[105] Cf. *Rep.* 414C-415D.

[106] This is brought out in 4 (*bis*) and 8a.

[107] Jacoby, *FGrH*, 3a:48-49, makes too much of the negative.

[108] The bibliographic material for the authors is Jacoby, *RE*, s.v. "Hekataios aus Abdera," 7:2766-2768 and *FGrH*, 3a:61-66; Hans Lewy, "Hekataios von Abdera περὶ Ἰουδαίων," *ZNW* 31 (1932): 117-132; Berndt Schaller, "Hekataios von Abdera über die Juden. Zur Frage der Echtheit und der Datierung," *ZNW* 54 (1963): 15-31; John G. Gager, "Pseudo-Hecataeus Again," *ZNW* 60 (1969): 130-139; Albert-Marie Denis, *Introduction aux Pseudépigraphes Grecs d'Ancien Testament*, pp. 262-267; Oswyn Murray, "Hecataeus of Abdera and Pharaonic Kingship," p. 144; Martin Hengel, "Anonymität, Pseudepigraphie und 'Literarische Fälschung' in der jüdisch-hellenistischen Literatur," in *Pseudepigrapha I: Pseudopythagorica-Lettres de Platon-Littérature pseudépigraphique juive.* Entretiens sur l'Antiquité Classique 18 (Genève: Vandoeuvres, 1972), pp. 301-303, 324-325; Ben Zion Wacholder, *Eupolemus: A Study of Judaeo-Greek Literature.* Monographs of the Hebrew Union College 3 (New York: Hebrew Union College-Jewish Institute of Religion, 1974), pp. 266-273 and also his earlier article in *EncJud*, s.v. "Hecataeus of Abdera," 8:236-237, where he only distinguishes between two instead of three

Scholar	Text	Title	Author	Date	Purpose
Felix Jacoby	CA 1.183-204	Περὶ Ἰουδαίων	Pseudo-Hekataios I	Betw. Polyhistor and Josephos	Panegyric on Jews
	Strom. 5.14.113	Περὶ Ἀβράμου	Pseudo-Hekataios II		Apologetic: Jews Source of Civilization
Hans Lewy (1932)	CA 1.183-204	Memoirs (Περὶ Ἰουδαίων 1 bk.)	Hekataios		
Berndt Schaller (1963)	CA 1.183-204 Strom. 5.14.113	Περὶ Ἰουδαίων Περὶ Ἀβράμου	Pseudo-Hekataios Pseudo-Hekataios	165-100	
John Gager (1969)	CA 1.183-204 2.43		Hekataios		
Albert-Marie Denis (1970)	CA 1.183-204 2.43	Περὶ Ἰουδαίων	Priest with Onias	170-168?	Apology
Oswyn Murray (1970)	CA 1.183-204 2.43	Περὶ Ἰουδαίων	Pseudo-Hekataios		
Martin Hengel (1972)	CA 1.183-204	Περὶ Ἰουδαίων	Pseudo-Hekataios		
	Strom. 5.14.113	Abraham und die Ägypter	Pseudo-Hekataios		
Ben Zion Wacholder (1984)	CA 1.183-205 Ps.-Aristeas 83-120 CA 1.213ff.		Pseudo-Hekataios I (Jerusalem Priest)	c. 300	Win favor of Ptolemy I

Scholar	Text	Title	Author	Date	Purpose
Menahem Stern (1974)	CA 2.43-47 AJ 12.3-8 Ps.-Aristeas 12-27, 31		Pseudo-Hekataios II	Between Aristeas and Josephos	
	AJ 1.159 Strom. 5.14.113 Origen Contra Cel. 1.15b		Pseudo-Hekataios III	Before Aristobulus	
	CA 1.183-204		Hekataios w/ Jewish revisions		
Nikolaus Walter (1976)	CA 1.183-214 (204?) 2.43 Origen Contra Cel. 1.15		Pseudo-Hekataios I	c. 100 in Alexandria	To demonstrate good relations betw. Jews and Ptolemies
	Strom 5.14.113 AJ 1.159 Ps.-Aristeas 31		Pseudo-Hekataios II	100-50 in Alexandria	
			Pseudo-Hekataios III?		
Hans Conzelmann (1981)	CA 1.183-204 2.43		Pseudo-Hekataios		Ethnographic Apology
Jörg-Dieter Gauger (1982)	CA 1.183-204	Memoirs or Historical Work	Hekataios		
	CA 2.43		Pseudo-Hekataios		Political Propaganda
Carl Holladay (1983)	CA 1.183-204 2.42-43	Περὶ Ἰουδαίων	Pseudo-Hekataios	200-150	Apologetic ethnography
	AJ 1.159 Strom. 5.14.13	Περὶ Ἀβράμου	Pseudo-Hekataios	200-150	Apologetic

Scholar	Text	Title	Author	Date	Purpose
R. Doran	CA 1.183-204 2.42-43		Hekataios	c. 300	
	AJ 1.159 Strom. 5.14.113	Περὶ Ἀβράμου	Pseudo-Hekataios	Ante Josephos	
Revised Schürer	CA 1.183-204 2.42-43	Περὶ Ἰουδαίων	Hekataios (w/slight interpolations)		
	AJ 1.159 Strom. 5.14.113	Περὶ Ἀβράμου	Pseudo-Hekataios		
W. Spoerri	CA 1.183-205, 213ff. 2.43		Pseudo-Hekataios I		
	AJ 1.159 Strom. 5.14.113		Pseudo-Hekataios II		

that we determine whether or not the work is authentic. The significance of determining whether or not Hekataios penned any of the works lies in tracing the development of the genre. The first issue which we must address is how many works are ascribed to Hekataios. In my opinion we must distinguish two separate works. Ancient tradents assign them separate names and both the content and the spirit of the two are different. The fragment handed down by Clement preserves verses under the name of Sophokles which attack idolatry.[109] There is not a suitable place to locate this fragment in *CA* 1.183-204. It could, however, be nicely fitted into a book on Abraham which dealt with his monotheism.[110] Again, the spirit is very different: the verses are unmistakably apologetic, while *CA* 1.183-204 remains within the orb of ethnographic influence.

The unabashed apologetic tone of *Strom.* 5.14.113.1-2, has since the days of J.J. Scaliger and R. Bentley raised serious questions about their authenticity. The *communis opinio* is that they are spurious, a judgment which appears unassailable. The question naturally

---

Pseudo-Hekataion works; Menahem Stern, *Greek and Latin Authors on Jews and Judaism*, 2 vols. (Jerusalem: The Israel Academy of Sciences and Humanities, 1974), 1:20-24; Nikolaus Walter, "Fragmente jüdisch-hellenistischer Historiker," in *Historische und legendarische Erzählungen*, Bd. 1, Lfg. 2. JSHRZ, ed. W.G. Kümmel (Gütersloh: Gerd Mohn, 1976), pp. 144-151; Hans Conzelmann, *Heiden-Juden-Christen: Auseinandersetzungen in der Literatur der hellenistisch-römischen Zeit*. BHT 62 (Tübingen: J.C.B. Mohr, 1981), pp. 164-168; Emilio Gabba *et al.*, *Greek Knowledge of Jews up to Hecataeus of Abdera*. Protocol of the Colloquy of the Center for Hermeneutical Studies in Hellenistic and Modern Culture 40 (Berkeley: The Center for Hermeneutical Studies in Hellenistic and Modern Culture, 1981); Jörg-Dieter Gauger, "Zitate in der jüdischen Apologetik und die Authentizität der Hekataios-Passagen bei Flavius Josephus und im Ps. Aristeas-Brief," *JSJ* 13 (1982): 6-46; Carl R. Holladay, *Fragments from Hellenistic Jewish Authors. Volume 1: Historians*. Texts and Translations/Pseudepigrapha Series 20 (Chico: Scholars Press, 1983), pp. 277-297; Robert Doran, "Pseudo-Hecataeus," in *The Old Testament Pseudepigrapha*, 2 vols. ed. by James H. Charlesworth (Garden City, New York: Doubleday & Company, Inc., 1983-1985), 2:905-919 (Hereafter abbreviated *OTP*); Emil Schürer, *The History of the Jewish People in the Age of Jesus Christ*, 3 vols. Revised and edited by Geza Vermes, Fergus Millar, and Martin Goodman (Edinburgh: T.& T. Clark, 1973-1986), 3a:671-675 (Note that this reverses the original view of Schürer who in the first edition argued that Περὶ Ἀβράμου and Περὶ Ἰουδαίων were identical and were the work of a Jewish forger who based his work on that of the authentic Hekataios, 3:304-305 [Orig. ed.]); and *RAC*, s.v. "Hekataios von Abdera," by Walter Spoerri, 14:275-310.

[109] Clement also cites the verses in *Protrepticus* 7.74.2, but without mentioning Hekataios.

[110] Cf. Walter, *JSHRZ*, 1:149-150, who thinks the work on Abraham constituted a major source for Josephus' retelling of Abraham and offers a reconstruction.

arises, if we are certain that ancient Jewish forgers utilized the name of Hekataios to give authority to their accounts, could the Περὶ 'Ιουδαίων of Josephos be another example?

Three major considerations have led a significant number of researchers to answer affirmatively. Origen tells us that the work of Hekataios on the Jews praised them ἐπὶ τοσοῦτον, ὡς καὶ 'Ερέννιον Φίλωνα ἐν τῷ περὶ 'Ιουδαίων συγγράμματι πρῶτον μὲν ἀμφιβάλλειν εἰ τοῦ ἱστορικοῦ ἐστι τὸ σύγγραμμα, adding the alternative, δεύτερον δὲ λέγειν ὅτι εἴπερ ἔστιν αὐτοῦ, εἰκὸς αὐτὸν συνηρπάσθαι ἀπὸ τῆς παρὰ 'Ιουδαίοις πιθανότητος καὶ συγκατατεθεῖσθαι αὐτῷ τῷ λόγῳ.[111] The basis of Herrenios Philo's (= Philo of Byblos, 64-141 C.E.) doubts is that he can not believe a Greek could write with great favor about the Jews, a sentiment which has been shared by a good number of moderns. This, however, is clearly not in tune with the earliest Greek reports of the Jews. The accounts prior to Poseidonios all picture the Jews as a group of philosophers.[112] The objection, therefore, tells us more about the age of Herrenios Philo than it does about Hekataios.[113]

The second difficulty is the seeming difference in perspective between *CA* 1.183-204; 2.43 and Diodoros 40.3.[114] It is true that the account in Josephos is more panegyric than that in Diodoros—although the latter can not be construed as negative in any significant way. We should, however, remember the tendencies of the extractors themselves along these lines. It would be incredibly naive to think that Josephus did not make the most of his source.[115] Fur-

---

[111] Origen, *Contra Celsum* 1.15.

[112] This is true of Theophrastos in his Περὶ Εὐσεβείας (= *GLAJJ* n. 4); Megasthenes in his 'Ινδικά (= *GLAJJ* n. 14); Klearchos of Soli, *De somno* (= *GLAJJ* n. 15); and Hermippos of Smyrna, *De Pythagora* (= *GLAJJ* n. 25). Hengel, *Judaism and Hellenism*, 1:255-261, has an excellent summary. See also Pilhofer, *Presbyteron Kreitton*, pp. 73-75.

[113] Lewy, "Hekataios von Abdera Περὶ 'Ιουδαίων," p. 118 and Gabba, *Greek Knowledge of Jews up to Hecataeus of Abdera*, p. 10.

[114] Schaller, "Hekataios von Abdera über die Juden," pp. 17-18, lists the following specifics. 1. Form: Diodoros uses the past narrative while Josephos uses "I" and "we." 2. Content: Diodoros' account describes the Jewish past history, Josephos' Jewish life. 3. Tone: Diodoros' record is objective with some criticism, whereas Josephos' has open praise. This has been the decisive factor for Jacoby, RE, s.v., "Hekataios aus Abdera," 7:2766; Denis, *Introduction aux Pseudépigraphes Grecs d'Ancien Testament*, p. 263; and Spoerri, *RAC*, s.v. "Hekataios von Abdera," 14:292.

[115] On Josephos' tendency in this regard see Gauger, "Zitate in der jüdischen Apologetik und die Authentizität der Hekataios-Passagen bei Flavius Josephus und im Ps. Aristeas-Brief," pp. 9-17. He remarks on p. 17: "Dieses Vorgehen, Zitate

ther, as we will suggest below, it is entirely possible that Hekataios
had different reasons for writing the two works and that his emphasis
changed with the needs of the moment.

The third and most substantial objection relates to the possible
anachronisms within the text.[116] The strongest of these are: the
naming of Ezekias as high priest (1.183), priests not Levites receive
the tithe (1.188), Jewish martyrs under Persian—rather than
Syrian—rule (1.191), and the statement that Alexander τὴν
Σαμαρεῖτιν χώραν προσέθηκεν ἔχειν αὐτοῖς ἀφορολόγητον (2.43). At
first glance these appear insurmountable. On closer scrutiny,
however, we find that each has a possible historical explanation. So
we now know that there was a priest named Ezekias thanks to a coin
found at Beth-Zur.[117] Exactly when the priests began receiving the
tithe and not the Levites is a matter of controversy.[118] Besides, it
may be asking too much to expect Hekataios to appreciate the distinction between the two. On the matter of martyrdom under Persian rule, both sides must argue *e silentio*. There are some indications
that this is historically possible,[119] but it should not be used by
either side in the question. Finally, it is possible—although not
provable—that Alexander did reward the Jews for assisting in the
suppression of the Samaritan insurrection.[120]

---

selbst zu kommentieren und ihnen eine andere Richtung zu geben, wird auch bei
der Vermittlung der Hekataios-Berichte zu beobachten sein.''

[116] Schaller, "Hekataios von Abdera über die Juden," p. 18, in presenting the
case against authenticity includes the number of fortresses (1.197) and the description of Jerusalem (1.198) in addition to those mentioned in our text. The former
is too indefinite to be conclusive: ἔστι γὰρ τῶν Ἰουδαίων τὰ μὲν πολλὰ ὀχυρώματα
κατὰ τὴν χώραν καὶ κῶμαι . . . The latter can be reversed on Schaller: Would a
Jewish forger have placed the temple in the center of Jerusalem? Lewy, "Hekataios
von Abdera περὶ Ἰουδαίων," pp. 126-127, argued that this is where a Greek would
have placed it. Cf. also pp. 128-129.

[117] Cf. Gager, "Pseudo-Hecataeus Again," pp. 138-139.

[118] *Ibid.*, pp. 137-138. The key primary texts are Jud. 11:13 and Jub. 32:15.

[119] Esth. 3:8. The text is not parallel to our text, but does point out the possibility of death for loyal Jews.

[120] The relevant texts are these. Quintus Curtius Rufus 4.8.9, tells us that the
Samaritans revolted against Alexander. According to Eusebios (*Chron.* 123d),
Samaria was given to the Macedonians. It could well be that the Jews assisted and
were also given a part of Samaria. So Gager, "Pseudo-Hecataeus Again," p. 136.
This may find some support in I Macc. 10:30,38; 11:34. The first two texts are
statements within a letter Demetrios is sending to the Jews in an effort to win them
over from Alexander Balas. Demetrios renounces taxes in v. 30 and then in v. 38
adds three territories to Judea, καὶ τοὺς τρεῖς νομοὺς τοὺς προστεθέντας τῇ Ἰουδαίᾳ
. . . The aorist participle is intriguing. Unfortunately we are several steps away

There are a couple of other statements which also deserve attention. On the one hand, 1.193 says that Hekataios praised the Jews
for razing foreign temples built within their country. Would a Greek
do this? On the other hand, would a Jewish author say that the Persians carried the Jews off into Babylonian exile (1.194)?[121]

What we can learn from this summary is that the evidence is not
conclusive. The missing element in the debate is an analysis of the
text as a whole. It seems to me that the form and function of the text
could tell us something about its origin.

2. *Content and Form*. The text presents the migration of a large
number of Jews under Ezekias to Egypt (186-189); a description of
the Jewish people on the basis of their leading characteristic, loyalty
to their law, and their population (190-194); a description of the land
(195-199); and Jewish participation in the campaigns of Alexander
and his successors as illustrated by Mosollamos, the Jewish archer
who shot the unforeseeing bird of omen (200-204).

Several items strike us initially. First of all, where could Hekataios
have obtained his information? The most likely explanation is from
Ezekias. Just as priests served as the source for the Αἰγυπτιακά, a
priest or priests probably provided the information for the Περὶ
'Ιουδαίων. Second, the text is clearly modeled on ethnography.[122]
We have a description of the land (195-199), the history of the people
(186-189; 200-204), and their customs (190-194). It is also interesting to note that the land is not the first element. This could, of
course, be due to a number of factors: Josephos' retelling of the text,
imitation of Hekataios by a forger, or Hekataios' own pattern as we
have seen in the Αἰγυπτιακά. We should now ask ourselves what
function this ethnography could serve.

---

from the original wording of the letter. The letter was composed in Greek and then
translated into the Hebrew text which has again been translated into Greek. Since
Hebrew participles lack tense, we can not lean upon the aorist. There are three
ways of interpreting the text as it stands: the territories are being recognized as *de
facto* Jewish (cf. 2:28); the letter recognizes the claim that Alexander bestowed this;
or Demetrios is attempting to remove the three nomes from the control of Jonathan
and assigning them to a Judea which will be ruled by a different high priest of his
appointing. In any case, it appears that the Jews did have some claim to Samaria.
Cf. Jonathan Goldstein, *I Maccabees*. AB 41 (Garden City, New York: Doubleday
& Company, Inc., 1976), pp. 410-411.
  [121] Lewy, "Hekataios von Abdera περὶ 'Ιουδαίων," p. 126, points out that
there could be some basis to this.
  [122] This was observed by Conzelmann, *Heiden-Juden-Christen*, p. 168 and
Spoerri, *RAC*, s.v. "Hekataios von Abdera," 14:291.

3. *Function*. I would like to suggest that this text best fits the authentic Hekataios writing on behalf of Ptolemy between 312 and 302 B.C.E. There are two corroborating lines which lead to this conclusion. We must begin by recalling the political situation Ptolemy and Hekataios faced. Ptolemy was given Egypt by Perdikkas in 323 (Diodoros 18.3.1),[123] but correctly feared that Perdikkas had designs on "the gift of the Nile" himself (18.14.1-2). When Perdikkas' invasion of 321 failed and he was executed by his own men (18.25.6; 29.1; 33.1-36.7), Antipater reassigned the satrapies with Ptolemy again receiving Egypt (18.39.5). Ptolemy now began to solidify his territory. One of his first steps was to invade and take Coele-Syria in 320 (18.43.1-2). The editorial comment in the text of Diodoros summarizes one of his motives with perspicacity: ὁρῶν δὲ τήν τε φοινίκην καὶ τὴν Κοίλην ὀνομαζομένην Συρίαν εὐφυῶς κειμένας κατὰ τῆς Αἰγύπτου πολλὴν εἰσεφέρετο σπουδὴν κυριεῦσαι τούτων τῶν τόπων.[124] For the next five years, Ptolemy essentially controlled the area.[125] In 315, however, circumstances changed. After Antigonos refused to accede to the demands of Ptolemy, Lysimachos, and Kasander—including Ptolemy's right to rule Syria (19.57.1)—he easily took Syria (19.58.1-59.3a). His sovereignty over the area was not long-lived. In 312 Ptolemy and Seleukos defeated Demetrios at the battle of Gaza (19.80.3-84.8). Ptolemy followed up his victory by again taking Coele-Syria (19.85.1-86.5), only to lose it (19.93.1-7). He finally retook it in 302 (20.113.1-4) and although he withdrew on the basis of a ruse, he must have quickly recovered since after the battle of Ipsos he maintained control of it despite the fact that it was granted to Seleukos in the terms decided upon by the victors (21.1.5).[126] The fact that he made three different campaigns

---

[123] The following account is based on the narrative in Diodoros 18-20. The primary source behind Diodoros in this section is Hieronymous of Kardia. On the use of additional sources here see Hornblower, *Hieronymus of Cardia*, pp. 49-75.

[124] The strategic location of this territory for economic reasons should also be mentioned. The coastal cities were particularly important.

[125] In 318 Eumenes wanted to take the coastal area, but was forced to march through the land (18.73.2).

[126] Since Ptolemy did not participate in the battle, he did not have a voice in the terms agreed upon. Ptolemy, however, was not about to hand over Coele-Syria. The text in Diodoros explains Seleukos' decision to yield to Ptolemy in these words: περὶ δὲ τῆς Κοίλης Συρίας διὰ τὴν φιλίαν ἐπὶ τοῦ παρόντος μηδὲν πολυπραγμονήσειν, ὕστερον δὲ βουλεύεσθαι πῶς χρηστέον ἐστὶν τῶν φίλων τοῖς βουλομένοις πλεονεκτεῖν (21.1.5). Although this does not exhaust the reasons why Seleukos gave ground to Ptolemy—military concerns must have also played a factor—it does find support

to take Coele-Syria suggests that it was of great importance to him. How did he treat the inhabitants of this strategic locale? There are two different traditions preserved by Josephos.[127] The first is the opening comment Josephos ascribes to Hekataios when he explains why so many Jews migrated to Egypt: πολλοὶ τῶν ἀνθρώπων πυνθανόμενοι τὴν ἠπιότητα καὶ φιλανθρωπίαν τοῦ Πτολεμαίου (1.186). This would suggest that Ptolemy openly courted the Jews and extended courtesy to them. The second tradition reverses this image. According to Agatharchides, Ptolemy entered Jerusalem under false pretenses on a Sabbath, took control of it, καὶ πικρῶς ἦρχεν αὐτῆς (AJ 12.4). Are these irreconcilable or may both preserve his actions? Victor Tcherikover has shown that the latter is the case.[128] He assigns the taking of Jerusalem to 302 and places his kindness prior to this. We should also remember that there were undoubtedly numerous political views among the residents of Jerusalem: some favorable to Ptolemy and some not. He was probably helped by his supporters and vented his wrath on his opponents.

How does this relate to our text? One of the things Ptolemy needed to accomplish in order to establish himself firmly in Coele-Syria was to win the support of at least some of its inhabitants. Is it merely coincidental that our text opens with an encomiastic statement on Ptolemy by not only Hekataios, but by the highly esteemed Ezekias as well (1.189)? The remainder of the text reinforces this view. Early in his reign Ptolemy was open to native traditions as the Αἰγυπτιακά shows. The section on νόμοι which emphasizes Jewish loyalty to their ancestral law matches the insistence in the Αἰγυπτιακά on the priestly traditions.[129] The Jews have nothing to fear from Ptolemy:

---

in the report of Polybios 5.67.1-13, where the representatives of Antiochos III and Ptolemy IV argue over the right to Syria: the position of Antiochos is that he possesses it *de jure* on the basis of the agreement of the kings, while Ptolemy claims that it is his *de facto* by right of occupation and a private agreement between Seleukos and Ptolemy I. Cf. Victor Tcherikover, *Hellenistic Civilization and the Jews*, trans. by S. Applebaum (Jewish Publication Society of America, 1959; reprint ed., New York: Athenaeum, 1970), pp. 53-55.

[127] AJ 12.4-8 (Agatharchides) and 12.9 (Hekataios). He again sets them together in CA 1.186-189 (Hekataios) and 1.210 (Agatharchides).

[128] Tcherikover, *Hellenistic Civilization and the Jews*, pp. 55-58 and his "The Political Background," in *The Hellenistic Age: Political History of Jewish Palestine from 332 B.C.E. to 67 B.C.E.*, ed. Abraham Schalit. The World History of the Jewish People 6 (New Brunswick: Rutgers University Press, 1972), pp. 63-67.

[129] It is possible to place the reference in Pseudo-Aristeas 31 within the framework of this section. The issue is how much of the statement in Pseudo-Aristeas 31

he will let them maintain their own traditions.[130] What he wants
and needs from them is military support. We know that Jews served
as soldiers and mercenaries in Egypt.[131] The clips which we have in
our text also underscore this point. There must have been a much
larger section which dealt with the service of Jews in the armies of
Alexander and Ptolemy.[132] Why? Could this have been an appeal
of some sort?

We may now offer a tentative reconstruction of the *Sitz Im Leben*
of the Περὶ Ἰουδαίων. Following the battle of Gaza (1.184) but before he took Jerusalem in 302, Ptolemy commissioned Hekataios to
write an ethnography on the Jews in an effort to win support among
them. The tone was, therefore, positive, but stops well short of
celebrating the Jews as the mother of all civilization as we would
expect a Jewish forger to do and as later Jews did.[133] It reassured

---

should be attributed to Hekataios. Lewy, "Hekataios von Abdera περὶ Ἰουδαίων,"
pp. 119-120, argued that Hekataios had only stated that the Jews had holy writings
and that Pseudo-Aristeas made the connection between their holiness and the silence of Greek authors. If he is right, then we should consider Pseudo-Aristeas 31
to refer to the authentic Hekataios. So also Walter, *JSHRZ*, 1:146 and Gauger,
"Zitate in der jüdischen Apologetik und die Authentizität der Hekataios-Passagen
bei Flavius Josephus und im Ps. Aristeas-Brief," pp. 36-38.

[130] The treatment of the laws in this connection is particularly important. Gauger, "Zitate in der jüdischen Apologetik und die Authentizität der Hekataios-
Passagen bei Flavius Josephus und im Ps. Aristeas-Brief," p. 31, has pointed out
that the perspective is not what we would expect from a Jewish author. "Und diese
Beobachtung ist m.E. eine der wichtigsten, die *gegen* einen Fälscher Ps. Hekataios
sprechen. Denn ein jüdischer Propagandist hätte die Gelegenheit nicht vorüber ge-
hen lassen, auf den Gehalt dieser νόμοι einzugehen, um das Verhalten als lohnend
hinzustellen, sie als gottgegeben, rein, tiefsinnig hinzustellen, die θεωρία, gar
σοφία seines Volkes zu preisen, um so in einer Schrift, die (anders als III. Makk.)
nach außen wirken sollte . . . das Festhalten an diesen Gesetzen gegenüber einer
unwissenden Umwelt als notwendig, richtig, einzig möglich darzubieten. Nichts
davon bei unserem Autor."

[131] The best known example is, of course, Elephantine. See Bezalel Porten, *Archives from Elephantine: The Life of an Ancient Jewish Military Colony* (Berkeley/Los Angeles: University of California Press, 1968), pp. 28-42. The Greek papyri also support this observation. Cf. Victor Tcherikover, ed. *Corpus Papyrorum Judaicarum*, 3
vols. (Cambridge: Harvard University Press, 1957-1964), 1:11-15. Other authors
who testify to the presence of Jewish soldiers in Egypt are: Pseudo-Aristeas 13, 37;
III Macc. 6:25; Josephos, *AJ* 12.8, 47; 13.285-286, 349.

[132] Josephos implies this in his opening editorial comment: ἔτι γε μὴν ὅτι καὶ
Ἀλεξάνδρῳ τῷ βασιλεῖ συνεστρατεύσαντο καὶ μετὰ ταῦτα τοῖς διαδόχοις αὐτοῦ
μεμαρτύρηκεν (*CA* 1.200).

[133] Wacholder, *Eupolemus*, p. 273, thinks that Pseudo-Hekataios is an analogue
to Berossos and Manethon. I see a major contrast between what Hekataios claims
for the Jews and what Berossos claims for the Babylonians and Manethon for the
Egyptians.

the Jews that they could maintain their life-style, but made it clear that historically this meant service in the army. The work would have been aimed at the leading Jews in Egypt, e.g., people like the priest Ezekias who were in positions of power and influence. The positive portrayal would also have aided in helping the Jews to establish themselves in Egypt. Respect and acceptance should belong to a nation with such an illustrious tradition.

If this analysis is correct, then we have a second witness from Hekataios on how ethnography can be exploited for political purposes. It would also provide an adequate basis for thinking of the work as a separate volume.[134] Statements such as the razing of the temples should probably be attributed to a later Jewish tradent.[135] If my conclusion about authorship is not sound, then we should consider Pseudo-Hekataios to be a later Jewish author who serves as an example of an apologetic historian heavily influenced by Greek ethnography. In either case, the fragments demonstrate the close connection between Greek ethnography and apologetic historiography.

Significance

The importance of Hekataios for subsequent writers is immense.[136] The Αἰγυπτιακά not only set out a new form of ethnography, but stands as the first of a group of works which champion an individual nation or people over against all others. His attention to the Jews would not be forgotten by them. It helped to set in motion the tradition which we will trace in chapters five and six.[137]

---

[134] The greatest problem with considering the work a separate volume is the way that Josephus introduces it. If Josephus has kept the order, then the work opened with a reference to the battle of Gaza. Gauger, "Zitate in der jüdischen Apologetik und die Authentizität der Hekataios-Passagen bei Flavius Josephus und im Ps. Aristeas-Brief," pp. 26-27 does not believe an independent work could have such an opening. It is possible, however, if the work began by relating the strong and positive Jewish ties to Ptolemy in the migration after the battle.

[135] So also Stern, *GLAJJ*, 1:24 and the revised Schürer, *The History of the Jewish People in the Age of Jesus Christ*, 3a:673.

[136] Murray, "Hecataeus of Abdera and Pharaonic Kingship," p. 167, wrote: "His book, so complete and so well documented, immediately became and remained the standard work on Egypt, and a model for the new Hellenistic historiography of native cultures; its fusion of the traditions of philosophy and historical ethnography with local tradition was more complete than that in any previous work and set a standard for the next two centuries." Cf. also *RAC*, s.v. "Hekataios von Abdera," by W. Spoerri, 14:286-288.

[137] Cf. *Ibid.*, 14:289-290: "Der in jüdisch-hellenistischen Kreisen gängigen

MEGASTHENES[138]

Life

The gauntlet which Hekataios threw down did not lie long on the
ground. One of the first to seize it was a philosopher-ambassador of
Seleukos. As with most ancient figures, we know very little about
Megasthenes. What we do know, however, is important for our understanding of his work. Clement tells us that he was a contemporary of Seleukos Nikator (c. 351-281 B.C.E.) (T 1). He served
two ambassadorial missions according to ancient testimony. He apparently first went to Sibyrtios, the satrap of Arachosia (TT 2a,
5a).[139] He must have proved to be a successful diplomat since we
learn that he was also sent to Sandrakottos (= Chandragupta), the
king of India and founder of the Mauryan empire (T 2a, 2b, 2c. Cf.
also F 5).[140] Although the text of Arrian 5.6.2 (= T 2a) can be
interpreted to mean that he went numerous times to Chandragutpa
in Palimbothra[141] or that he conversed frequently with him while in
Palimbothra, it is his presence in India which is important for his
work.[142]

We can establish the *termini* for his visit with some certainty. The
terminus a quo is the treaty which Seleukos made with Chandragupta
(c. 305) in which he ceded the Kabul valley and the areas west of the

---

These von der direkten bzw. indirekten Abhängigkeit der Griechen von den Juden
in Weisheit u. Kultur entspricht griechischerseits bei Diod. Sic. 1 bzw. H. die Her-
leitung griechischer Weisheit, Kultur u. Religion aus Ägypten.''

[138] The most important works on Megasthenes are E.A. Schwanbeck, *Megasthenis Indica* (Bonn, 1846); Trüdinger, "Studien zur Geschichte der griechisch-
römischen Ethnographie,'' pp. 74-77; *RE*, s.v. "Megasthenes,'' by O. Stein,
15:230-326; B.C.J. Timmer, "Megasthenes en de Indische Maatschappij'' (Dissertation, Amsterdam, 1930); *FGrH*, 715 [I have used Jacoby's text for my discussion.]; R.C. Majumdar, *The Classical Accounts of India* (Calcutta: K.L. Mukhopadhyay, 1960); Allan Dahlquist, *Megasthenes and Indian Religion: A Study in Motives and
Types* (Stockholm: Almquist & Wiksell, 1962); and KP, s.v. "Megasthenes," by
J.D.M. Derrett, 3:1150-1154.

[139] On Sibyrtios and Arachosia see Edwyn Robert Bevan, *The House of Seleucus*,
2 vols. (London: Edward Arnold, 1902; reprint ed., New York: Barnes & Noble,
Inc., 1966), 1:271.

[140] On Seleukos' relationship to India see Bevan, *The House of Seleucus*,
1:292-299.

[141] Palimbothra is also mentioned by Strabon 2.1.9 (= T 2c). It is Pataliputra
or the modern Patna.

[142] The text reads: πολλάκις δὲ λέγει ἀφικέσθαι παρὰ Σανδράκοττον τὸν Ἰνδῶν
βασιλέα. For arguments pro and con see Stein, *RE*, s.v. "Megasthenes,''
15:233-234.

Indus in return for peace and the guarantee of the free flow of trade.[143] The *terminus ad quem* is obviously the death of Chandragupta in the first twelve years of the third century.[144] Megasthenes was sent to the Indian capital to maintain ties and ensure the economic well-being of Seleucid concerns.[145]

Megasthenes used his time in Palimbothra for other reasons as well. He traveled some, although as Arrian says: οὐδὲ Μεγασθένης πολλὴν δοκέει μοι ἐπελθεῖν τῆς Ἰνδῶν χώρης (*Ind.* 5.3 = T 2b).[146] Strabon tells us that both Megasthenes and Deimachos who were sent on missions ὑπομνήματα δὲ τῆς ἀποδημίας κατέλιπον τοιαῦτα (2.1.9 = T 2c). This suggests that Megasthenes' Ἰνδικά should be dated in the first score of the third century. His record provided the Greeks with a full description of India and also enables us to see what happened to one strand of ethnography after the conquests of Alexander.

Ἰνδικά

1. *Textual Problem.* As we should expect, Megasthenes' work has not survived intact down to the present. Besides scattered fragments, we have three authors who preserve a condensed version of Megasthenes' Ἰνδικά: Diodoros Sikelos 2.35-42, Strabon 15.35-60,

---

[143] The terms of the agreement are mentioned by Strabon 15.2.9 and include an intermarriage and Chandragupta giving Seleukos 500 elephants. There must have also been commercial considerations involved since the overland trade routes of the Seleukid empire were at stake. On the trade routes and their importance for this relationship see Rostovtzeff, *The Social and Economic History of the Hellenistic World*, 2:459-461, as well as his "Syria and the East," in *The Hellenistic Monarchies and the Rise of Rome*, CAH, 7:173-176; and W.W. Tarn, *Hellenistic Civilization*, 3rd ed. revised with G.T. Griffith (1952; reprint ed., New York: Meridian, 1974), pp. 241-244.

[144] Stein, *RE*, s.v. "Megasthenes," 15:232, places it between 303 and 292 while Dahlquist, *Megasthenes and Indian Religion*, p. 9, puts it at 302-288.

[145] On India at the time of Megasthenes see J. Allan, T. Wolseley Haig, and H.H. Dowell, *The Cambridge Shorter History of India* (Reprint ed., Delhi: S. Chand & Co., 1969), pp. 31-41.

[146] Stein, *RE*, s.v. "Megasthenes," 15:233, attempted to locate his travels more specifically. He wrote: "Daraus folgt, daß der griechische Gesandte sich dauernd in Pataliputra aufgehalten, seine freie Zeit zu Beobachtungen, Erkundigungen und kleineren Reisen verwendet haben wird, wie seine Nachrichten erkennen lassen. Wenn ihn diese Reisen auch nicht weit über die heutige Provinz Bengalen hinausgeführt haben werden, östlich vom Ganges schon gar nicht, während er die westlich gelegenen Gebiete bei der Durchreise wenigstens oberflachlich kennengelernt hatte, so muß er doch an diesem großen Strom und über ihn genauere Erkundigungen eingezogen haben . . ."

and Arrian Ἰνδική 1-17. That these three preserve Megasthenes
may be easily proven: Strabon and Arrian frequently cite him by
name as their source. The account in Diodoros is so similar that he
is clearly using the same source. It would, however, be incredibly
naive to expect the three sources to concur in their presentations.
They clearly do not extract from Megasthenes *verbatim et litteratim*.
Our first task is to decide what we may consider authentic.

As we have seen, Diodoros does not simply cite his sources, but
freely supplements them with additional material.[147] It is also certain that Arrian has injected material from Eratosthenes and Nearchos into the first half of his Ἰνδική.[148] Strabon likewise makes it
clear that he is combining sources as he offers his version of India.[149] The question thus becomes how to disentangle Megasthenes
from the accounts. O. Stein argued that Megasthenes should be
reconstructed on the basis of the account in Strabon.[150] This,
however, is too simplistic for the evidence. It is so because while the
three differ, they also have a significant amount in common. Since
we do not need to establish the *ipsissima verba* of Megasthenes but
only the basic content of his work, I have set out the three texts in
a chart (p. 95). If a common pattern emerges—as it does—I will use
it to reconstruct the basic lines and material of Megasthenes'
work.[151] A few words are in order to explain the chart. I have set

---

[147] For Diodoros' use of Megasthenes in this matter cf. Stein, *RE*, s.v.
"Megasthenes," 15:267-269 and Majumdar, *The Classical Accounts of India*, pp.
463-464.

[148] Arrian summarized his use of sources for the first half of his Ἰνδική in these
words: ταῦτά μοι ἀπόχρη δεδηλῶσθαι ὑπὲρ Ἰνδῶν, ὅσα γνωριμώτατα Νέαρχός τε καὶ
Μεγασθένης, δοκίμω ἄνδρε, ἀνεγραψάτην . . . He explicitly cites Eratosthenes, 3.1;
Ktesias, 3.6; Onesikritos, 3.6; 6.8; and Nearchos, 3.6; 11.7; 15.1, 4, 8, 10, 11;
16.1, 4. For Arrian's use of Megasthenes see Philip A. Stadter, *Arrian of Nicomedia*
(Chapel Hill: The University of North Carolina Press, 1980), pp. 115-132, but especially pp. 115-124. He attributes 2.1-3.8 to Eratosthenes (p. 120) and 6.4-9 and
15.1-17.7 to Nearchos (pp. 121 and 123 respectively). 5.1-6.3 is Arrian's own
digression on his sources. He ascribes 4.3-12; 7.1-9.12; 11.1-14.9 to Megasthenes.
He argues that Arrian did follow the basic order of Megasthenes (p. 119). Cf. also
the comments of P.A. Brunt in his edition of Arrian, *Anabasis Alexandri et Indica.* 2
vols. LCL (Cambridge: Harvard University Press, 1983), 2:447-449.

[149] This is especially evident in 15.1.35, 37, 43, 68. He explicitly mentions
Krateros, 15.1.35; Onesikritos, 15.1.43, 45; Nearchos, 15.1.43, 44, 45; Aristobulos, 15.1.45; Simonides and Pindar, 15.1.57; and Timagenes, 15.1.57.

[150] Stein, *RE*, s.v. "Megasthenes," 15:267-273.

[151] The conclusion of Timmer, "Megasthenes en de Indische Maatschappij,"
p. 312 *apud* Dahlquist, *Megasthenes and Indian Religion*, p. 35, is worth quoting:
"Megasthenes terminology is best preserved in Strabo and Diodorus, the construc-

the texts out in the order in which they appear without attempting
to favor the sequence of one version over the others. In order to help
determine what Strabon and Arrian directly attribute to
Megasthenes, I have placed an asterisk beside the references where
there is either an explicit citation or where continued *oratio obliqua*
make it certain that they are quoting from him. For the sake of com-
pleteness, I have included some elements which are doubtful—
although possible. My working hypothesis is that we may consider
those passages which are either directly attributed to Megasthenes
(and their parallels) or are attested by more than one author as
authentic.[152]

	Megasthenes		
Content	D.S. 2	Strabon 15	Arrian *Ind.*
1. Shape of India	35.1		
2. Size of India	35.2	1.11-12*	3.6-7*
3. Fertility	35.3-36.7	1.20*	9.8*
4. Rivers	37.1-7	1.35*	4.2-6*
5. Animals	(35.3b-4)	1.37*	
6. Silas River		1.38*	6.2-3*
7. Autochthonous & Isolated	38.1	1.6*	5.4-7;9.12*
8. Earliest Inhabitants	38.2		7.1-3*
9. Dionysos Myth	38.3-6	1.7*	7.4-8.3*
10. Herakles Myth	39.1-4	1.7*	8.4-9.8*
11. Historical Summary			9.9-12
12. Burial Customs			10.1
13. Palimbothra	(39.3)	1.36	10.5-7*
14. No Slavery	39.5	1.54*	10.8-9
15. Seven Castes	40.1-41.5	1.39-41,46-49*	11.1-12.9
16. Elephants	42.1-2 (Cf. 35.4)	1.42-43	13.1-14.9
17. Ants		1.44*	15.5-6
18. Officials	42.3-4	1.50-52	
19. Νόμοι		1.53-55*	
20. θαυμάσια		1.56-57*	
21. Philosophers		1.58-60,68*	

2. *Content and Form.* The agreement demonstrated in the chart suggests that Megasthenes commented on the land of India, its history,
and customs. This impression is reinforced by our ability to fit the

tion of his work by Arrianus and Diodorus, and the construction of the fragments
by Strabo.''
    [152] I recognize that it is possible that both authors drew from a different com-
mon source, but do not believe such took place in this case.

other fragments Jacoby collected into this framework.[153] We are clearly looking at a work which has been shaped by ethnographic concerns.

This immediately raises the issue of sources.[154] Megasthenes was by no means the first Greek to write on India. He was preceded by Ktesias, the Greek physician at the Persian court,[155] as well as Herodotos. He also had several contemporaries who wrote either before or at the same time he did: Nearchos, the close friend of Alexander, sailed from the Indus to the Tigris and left an account[156]; his lieutenant, the Cynic philosopher Onesikritos, also wrote a record which makes Alexander a Cynic philosopher and *Kulturbringer*[157]; and possibly Patrokles, the Greek commander at Babylon under Seleukos and Antiochos I.[158]

Was Megasthenes influenced by the tradition and to what extent? While it is very probable that Megasthenes knew Ktesias and the Alexander historians, we need only establish his tie with the tradition for our purposes. A comparison of Herodotos 3.98-106 with the 'Ινδικά reveals the following common topics:

Subject	Herodotos	Megasthenes
1. Eat the infirm.	3.99	S. 15.1.56
2. Copulate in open.	3.101.1	S. 15.1.56
3. Gold-digging ants.	3.102-105	S. 15.1.44
4. Size of the animals.	3.106.2	DS 2.35.3
5. Wool bearing trees.	3.106.3	A. 7.3

I have intentionally called these topics because there are numerous differences in the details. Megasthenes says that the first two νόμοι are true of people who inhabit the Caucasus. The records of the celebrated μύρμηκες are close. Megasthenes' account could be a condensation of that of Herodotos with one exception: Herodotos

---

[153] I only refer to the fragments which do not have a direct parallel to the three major texts. Fragments which may be connected with the land are FF 22, 24, and 26. F 1 is historical and F 3 summarizes Megasthenes' claim that philosophy began with the barbarians. F 2 relates to customs and FF 7, 25, 28, 29, 30 all treat θαυμάσια. On the order of the work see below on form.

[154] For a general treatment see Stein, *RE*, s.v. "Megasthenes," 15:236-267.

[155] *FGrH* 688.

[156] *FGrH* 133.

[157] *FGrH* 134.

[158] *FGrH* 712.

says that the Indians steal the gold the ants have dug up in the middle of the day when it is hot and the ants are underground; Megasthenes claims that the Indians set out pieces of meat in order to lure the ants away from their holes. The final two references are close, but are much too brief to be definitive. It is not possible to say that Megasthenes lifted his text directly from Herodotos, although the agenda set by his predecessor was influential enough that he followed it.[159]

Perhaps of even greater importance is the fact that Megasthenes basically follows the methodology of Herodotos. That is to say, he practiced autopsy—particularly in his description of the land and customs—and reported what the Brahmans told him about Indian life.[160] This closely matches Herodotos' practice and differs from that of Hekataios who downplayed anything but priestly tradition.[161] At the same time, this incurred the criticism of successors who found his uncritical reporting to be inadequate. Eratosthenes and Strabon both accuse him of recording myths.[162] Arrian, who does hold him in some esteem, nevertheless has doubts as he indicates in his recounting of the ants: ἀλλὰ Μεγασθένης τε ἀκοὴν ἀπηγέεται.[163] Nor has the debate been limited to antiquity. It is still an issue among scholars.[164]

---

[159] Stein, RE, s.v. "Megasthenes," 15:237-239, explains their similarities on the basis of "eine einheimische Überlieferung."

[160] It may not be possible to determine what came from previous Greek accounts and what stems from indigenous sources. The only point I wish to make here is that Megasthenes, like Herodotos, made use of both.

[161] Megasthenes did not, however, practice ἱστορία with the care of Herodotos.

[162] Strabon 2.1.9; 15.1.7 and then 15.1.57 and 58 respectively.

[163] Ind. 15.7.

[164] There is a good survey by J.D.M. Derrett, KP, s.v. "Megasthenes," 3:1150-1151. Megasthenes found his first substantial modern supporter in Schwanbeck, Megasthenis Indica, p. 76, whose statement has been very influential: Nam etsi geographica Graecorum scientia postea demum perfecta est, tamen Indiae cognitio iam Megasthenis libris ad summam perfectionem ita pervenit, ut qui postea de India scripserunt, ad veritatem tanto proprius accedant, quanto accuratius Megasthenis Indica sequantur. Truesdell S. Brown, "The Reliability of Megasthenes," American Journal of Philology 76 (1955): 18-33, has an excellent summary of Megasthenes' relationship to earlier Greek sources on pp. 32-33: 1. Megasthenes does correct Greek sources by his own experience. 2. He is not critical about his sources. Once Megasthenes leaves the India he knows personally, we can not be sure that he is following the best possible source. Specific studies include Timmer, "Megasthenes en de Indische Maatschappij," on Indian society and Dahlquist, Megasthenes and Indian Religion, on the Dionysos and Herakles myths who concludes on p. 289: "In matters of religion, as in all else, Megasthenes has given us the Indians' point of view, whether or not it agreed with that of the Greeks."

Whether we decide for or against Megasthenes' reliability, he is clearly indebted to the Greek ethnographic tradition. We must now ask what he has done with the tradition. Megasthenes began in standard Ionic fashion by describing the land with its boundaries, fertility, rivers, and animals. He offered an historical summary, but unlike the Ionic tradition did not—if our reports are representative—merely summarize the royal traditions, but concentrated on the emergence of culture through the two myths. His presentation of the myths differs from both the tradition and what we have seen in Hekataios. Greek gods or demi-gods are the founders of civilization in India.[165] This does not, however, mean that Indian culture is strictly derived from Greek since philosophy existed among the Indians prior to the Greeks.[166] The *nomoi* witness both continuity and change in the tradition: he reports on the customary topics with a keen eye on θαυμάσια, but like Hekataios heavily emphasizes the structure of the society. As Hekataios had done with the Jews, he found a key hermeneutical virtue by which he presented the Indians, ἁπλότης.[167] Indian society falls into seven groups with an inordinate amount of attention given to philosophers. We are clearly looking at a work which has been shaped by ethnographic concerns, but one which has undergone a metamorphosis.

---

[165] The identification of these gods has been the occasion of a great deal of literature. The major issue is: Should we identify one of these with Krishna? Dahlquist, *Megasthenes and Indian Religion*, identifies Dionysos with Munda Dema and Herakles with Indra. He argues that this reflects conditions in India at the time of Megasthenes on p. 283: "But Megasthenes witnessed a different situation; on the one hand he saw the dwellers on the plains, worshippers of Indra, who were Aryans, and on the other the hill-men, non-Aryans, belonging to a variety of races and speaking a variety of languages. No mention is made of Hinduism. In short, the situation was not unlike that which we imagine to have existed soon after the time of the Aryan invasions, with a sharp distinction drawn between Aryans and non-Aryans."

[166] Clement, *Strom.* 1.15.72.5 (F 3), quotes Megasthenes in a now famous passage: ἅπαντα μέντοι τὰ περὶ φύσεως εἰρημένα παρὰ τοῖς ἀρχαίοις λέγεται καὶ παρὰ τοῖς ἔξω τῆς Ἑλλάδος φιλοσοφοῦσι, τὰ μὲν παρ' Ἰνδοῖς ὑπὸ τῶν Βραχμάνων, τὰ δὲ ἐν τῇ Συρίᾳ ὑπὸ τῶν καλουμένων Ἰουδαίων. Jaeger, *Diokles von Karystos*, p. 141, thought that the comparison between Jews and Brahmans went back to Megasthenes and then entered the stream of popular presentation. An interesting twist of history is that Megasthenes' Ἰνδικά may have served as a source of influence for Porphery and Neo-Platonic thought. Cf. John J. O'Meara, "Indian Wisdom and Porphyry's Search for a Universal Way," in *Neoplatonism and Indian Thought*, edited by R. Baine Harris. Studies in Neoplatonism: Ancient and Modern 2 (Norfolk, Virginia: International Society for Neoplatonic Studies, 1982), pp. 10-12.

[167] Strabon 15.1.53-54. Strabon's version has several terms to suggest this way of life, but the basic concept is the same.

We are now in a position to attempt a reconstruction of the work. If we follow the lead of the three major witnesses, we could easily deduce the general pattern of the second book of Herodotos: land, history, and νόμοι—with the latter two changing positions. However, there is a problem. We possess three fragments which claim to come from a specific book of Megasthenes' work. F 2 deals with eating habits and comes from book two. F 3 is the well-known claim that philosophy did not originate with the Greeks and belongs to book three. F 1 is historical in nature and should be assigned to the fourth book.[168] We now know that we have a four-volume work (at minimum) with a νόμος in the second book, philosophy in the third, and history in the fourth. The first book must have dealt with the land as the major fragments suggest.

The problem which confronts us is that the two schema do not match. F 2 seems to be related to Strabon 15.1.53, where the eating of ὄρυζαν is again mentioned; a position which could not reflect the second book if Strabon is following the order of the original. This can be easily resolved by realizing that Strabon does not strictly follow Megasthenes' order.[169] The more difficult problem is that Diodoros and Arrian both place the *archaeologiai* before the *nomoi*. We could claim that both violate the order of the *Vorlage* or that they have an intermediate *Vorlage* which has condensed the account of Megasthenes' original, but there is no real evidence to support such a claim. It seems more reasonable to me, to split the *archaeologiai* off from the historical section and place it earlier in the Ἰνδικά than the fourth book. Thus I would reconstruct it as follows:[170]

---

[168] There is a problem with the text here. The manuscripts read fourth, but Jacoby thought it should read first. It would be easy to see how an Alpha could become a Delta in uncial script. However, I can not see that Jacoby really gains anything from the transposition and prefer to follow the manuscripts.

[169] This is supported by our chart where there is more agreement between Diodoros and Arrian in structure.

[170] My reconstruction is thus different from that of Stein, *RE*, s.v. "Megasthenes," 15:272, who offers the following: 1. Buch: Geographie, Fauna und Flora, Ethnographie. 2. Buch: Sitten, Städte, Prasiermonographie, Beamtungen. 3. Buch: Gesellschaft, Philosophie. 4. Buch: Archäologie, Mythen und Geschichte. He has been followed by Godfrey Louis Barber, The Oxford Classical Dictionary, 2nd ed., s.v. "Megasthenes," and Derrett, KP, s.v. "Megasthenes," 3:1151.

Book One: Land
Book Two: *Archaeologiai* and Customs
Book Three: Society and Philosophy
Book Four: History

This is not as radical as it may first appear since the origins are cultural origins and the *nomoi* could be seen as a continuation of what Dionysos and Herakles originated, e.g., Dionysos did after all give the Indians seed and the knowledge of cultivation, a gift which could be carried on by customs of eating.

More importantly, Megasthenes presented India via the *interpretatio Graeca*. He thus calls Indian officials by Greek names[171] and uses Greek philosophy—as Hekataios had done—as a prism through which Indian society was refracted.[172] This is proven beyond doubt by the statement of Strabon (15.1.59) that Megasthenes says about the Brahmans περὶ πολλῶν δὲ τοῖς Ἕλλησιν ὁμοδοξεῖν. He then proceeds to enumerate some of the touchstones of Greek philosophy. The issue is not whether he utilizes Greek concepts, but to what extent they color his picture.

3. *Function.* Another way of phrasing the last question is to ask why Megasthenes wrote as he did. As an ambassador, he was in a position to inform his Greek audience about the land which held so much fascination for them and which was of strategic, political and economic importance for the Seleukid kingdom. Cultural exchange is an admittedly anachronistic term, but is part of what his work is about. The work served for several centuries as a—if not the—major repository of Greek knowledge about India.

Yet this does not fully explain the text as it stands. Why does he tie Indian religion to Greek gods? Is this simply a convenient device to enable Greek readers to relate to Indian religion or is something more afoot? O. Stein pointed out Alexander's close connections to the two gods and suggested that this was a way of presenting Alexander as a *Kulturbringer*.[173] While this is possible, it must overcome the fact that the text clearly dates the rise of civilization in India prior to that in Greece. Elias Bickerman, on the other hand, has con-

---

[171] Cf. Stein, *RE*, s.v. "Megasthenes," 15:280-284.

[172] *Ibid.*, 15:275-280, who compares it with Plato's ideal state and concludes that while an imposition of Plato "ist zwar nicht erweisbar, jedoch auch nicht ganz von der Hand zu weisen." (280)

[173] Stein, *RE*, s.v. "Megasthenes," 15:276.

tended that only the Greeks attempted to construct a pre-history. The task of a historian was to graft barbarian origins onto the most suitable branch of Greek pre-history. This preserved the Hellenocentric view of the world which comprised the unifying glue of the Hellenistic world.[174] Since this was such a common practice I am inclined to accept Bickerman's suggestion.

We still need to account for the fact that Indian culture was older and that India was a society ruled by philosophers. While Megasthenes is not as overt as Hekataios in claiming Egypt to be the mother of all civilization, he makes it very plain that India has claims of her own. Is he directly responding to Hekataios? There is no direct evidence that he was. There are some indirect factors which may suggest that he was.[175] We have already seen that Hekataios' Αἰγυπτιακά antedates Megasthenes' Ἰνδικά by at least twenty years. An official work written by a fellow philosopher in a competing kingdom would have attracted some attention in rival centers. While there are no direct repartees in the fragments which we have, there are some similarities: both employ philosophy as a means of heightening the image of their respective societies and both claim precedence for their countries of residence. Whether Megasthenes is responding directly to Hekataios or whether both serve as witnesses to a common milieu, Egypt was no longer the only competitor in the bid for cultural superiority: India has now made her case.

Significance

Megasthenes thus takes his place along side that of Hekataios as a Greek who not only admired foreign culture, but was willing to present this culture with its claims of superiority to the ancient world.

SUMMARY

While the Persian empire had opened the eyes of Greeks to other peoples, the conquests of Alexander opened the doors to their lands. Just as Ionian philosophy had enabled early ethnographers to look at the world in an empirical way, the expansion of philosophy gave

---

[174] Elias J. Bickerman, "Origenes Gentium," *Classical Philology* 47 (1952): 65-81.

[175] So also Murray, "Herodotus and Hellenistic Culture," p. 208.

Hellenistic ethnographers specific categories and standards by which to judge their material. These shifts can be clearly seen by comparing the authors of the last two chapters. Hekataios of Miletos and Herodotos were both aristocratic travelers; Hekataios of Abdera and Megasthenes were court philosophers who lived in the lands they described. The result was an expansion and renewal of ethnography.

The expansion is attested in the new ethnographies. While the basic categories remained in place, the prism of philosophy and openness to native sources (Hekataios of Abdera) helped to create an enthusiasm to describe an *ethnos* in idealistic terms and to press native claims over and above the claims of the author's own *patria*. Not surprisingly this competitive spirit appeared at the same time as rival Hellenistic kingdoms established themselves. This created a double-edged field of competition: native vs. Hellenic and native vs. native.

In spite of the tendency attested in both Hekataios and Megasthenes to honor their new homeland, they remained indubitably Greek. Both the questions they asked and the form in which they wrote their answers bear the unmistakable imprint of Hellenism. One wonders what the priests who provided the answers in the first place thought of such presentations. Fortunately, we have some idea.

CHAPTER FOUR

THE ORIGINS OF APOLOGETIC HISTORIOGRAPHY

> We discovered these things because
> we were very eager to understand
> Phoenician culture and investigated
> a good deal of material beyond what
> is found in Greek authors, since that
> is contradictory and has been written
> by some more for the sake of ar-
> gumentation than for truth.
>
> Philo of Byblos in *PE* 1.9.27

While the imposition of Hellenism on the East was a political and cultural reality, it was not achieved without resistance.[1] The opposition assumed various forms depending upon the position of the conquered. Within a literary context one of the responses was the attempt to readdress the identity of the subdued ethnic group. The tendency in ethnography to measure Near Eastern cultures by Greek standards did not sit well with those who felt that they had been misrepresented and shortchanged. This was particularly true for the priests of the various cults who – because they were both the guardians of the sacred traditions and in positions of authority – were in a unique position to respond. At the same time, these priests could not avoid coming to grips with Hellenism: it is no accident that they wrote in Greek and were influenced by Greek literary forms. The result was the creation of a new literary genre which *challenged* and *identified* with Hellenism at the same time.

---

[1] The most important study of resistance is Samuel K. Eddy, *The King is Dead: Studies in Near Eastern Resistance to Hellenism 334-31 B.C.* (Lincoln: University of Nebraska Press, 1961).

BEROSSOS[2]

Life

The first indigenous author to present a native perspective was
Berossos.[3] Berossos was not a Greek, but ἀνὴρ βαβυλώνιος (TT 2,
8d).[4] He must have been born c. 350 B.C.E. since he was a contemporary of Alexander the Great (TT 1, 2; F 1) and lived well into
the next century. He was apparently trained as a scribe in the traditional Summerian and Akkadian classics since he became ἱερεὺς τοῦ
παρ' αὐτοῖς βήλου (T 2).[5] How familiar he was with Greek literature is a matter of dispute. Josephos wrote about him: γνώριμος δὲ
τοῖς περὶ παιδείαν ἀναστρεφομένοις (CA 1.129 = T 3).[6] A. von
Gutschmid thought that this meant he had received a Greek education. P. Schnabel has, however, correctly argued that it means he
was familiar to the Greeks as the subsequent clause suggests.[7] He
did, nonetheless, have some familiarity with Greek literature as we
will show. Stanley Burstein has taken this a step further by suggesting that he was a member of the Seleucid court.[8] While it may

---

[2] The most important works on Berossos are: *RE* s.v. "Berossos," by E.
Schwartz, 3: 309-316; Paul Schnabel, *Berossos und die babylonisch-hellenistische Literatur*
(Berlin: B.G. Teubner, 1923; reprint ed., Hildesheim: Georg Olms, 1968); G.
Komoróczy, "Berosos and the Mesopotamian Literature," *Acta Antiqua* 21 (1973):
125-152; Stanley Burstein, *The "Babyloniaca" of Berossus* (Malibu, California: Undena Publications, 1978); *KP*, s.v. "Beros(s)os," by W. Spoerri, 1: 1548, which includes a good bibliography; and Amélie Kuhrt, "Berossus' *Babyloniaka* and Seleucid
Rule in Babylonia," in *Hellenism in the East: The interaction of Greek and non-Greek civilizations from Syria to Central Asia after Alexander*, ed. Amélie Kuhrt and Susan Sherwin-
White (Berkeley/Los Angeles: University of California Press, 1987), pp. 32-56. For
the text see *FGrH* 680.
[3] His name has come down to us in multiple forms. The two major problems
for the Greek name are whether it should have one σ or two and where the accent
belongs. I have followed Schnabel, *Berossos und die babylonisch-hellenistische Literatur*,
pp. 3-5, in opting for the double σ. Komoróczy, "Berosos and the Mesopotamian
Literature," p. 125, has suggested that his name was *Bel-re'usu*, "Bel is his
shepherd."
[4] He is also called ἀνὴρ Χαλδαῖος μὲν τὸ γένος (TT 3, 7b) and virum Chaldai-
cum (T 4).
[5] Komoróczy, "Berosos and the Mesopotamian Literature," p. 125, suggests
that his training would have taken place in the temple of Marduk in the Esagila,
a scientific center of Hellenistic Mesopotamia.
[6] He was also called ἀνὴρ ἱκανώτατος (T 2) and omnis doctrinae peritissimum
(T 4).
[7] See the discussion in Schnabel, *Berossos und die babylonisch-hellenistische Literatur*,
p. 15. Cf. also the translation of H. St. J. Thackeray in the *LCL*: "My witness here
is Berosus, a Chaldaean by birth, but familiar in learned circles through his publication for Greek readers of works on Chaldaean astronomy and philosophy."
[8] Burstein, *The "Babyloniaca" of Berossus*, p. 5. He adduces three bases for his
conclusion: Berossos' ability in Greek, his familiarity with Greek conceptions of the
Babylonian past, and the dedication of his work to Antiochos I.

be going too far to see him as an official member of the court,[9] his recognition of the role astrologers played for Seleukos is sound.[10] Berossos represents one of the members of the higher echelon of the Orient who lived in two worlds at the same time. His commitment to the Greek world is evidenced not only by his own writings but by the tradition that he resided in Cos where he opened a school (T 5).[11] This must have come at the end of his life[12] and serves as an echo of what he had attempted to do with his written work earlier. In any case, he became famous enough in the larger world to have legends cluster about his name.[13]

Berossos' entree to fame is his βαβυλωνιακά. We can date his work with some certainty since he dedicated it to Antiochos I (324-261 B.C.E.) (TT 2, 4). Antiochos ruled the eastern portions of his father's domain from 293/292 and assumed the throne in 281 B.C.E. It is very likely that Berossos published his work at the outset of Antiochos' reign.[14] This makes him a contemporary of Megasthenes with the latter's Ἰνδικά preceding by about a decade.

Βαβυλωνιακά[15]

1. *Pseudo-Berossos?* The βαβυλωνιακά has not come down to us in

---

[9] He appears to have resided in Babylon. Would a member of the court have lived outside one of the main centers? A residence in Seleukeia or Antioch would make this hypothesis more reasonable to me.

[10] He cites Diodoros 2.31.2 and Appian, *Syriaca* 58. A specific instance of the role of astrologers with Antigonos and Seleukos is in Diodoros 19.55.1-9, especially 7-9.

[11] Kuhrt, "Berossus' *Babyloniaka* and Seleucid Rule in Babylonia," pp. 43-44, thinks this is a Greek creation of the first century B.C.E. It is defended as authentic by Schnabel, *Berossos und die babylonisch-hellenistische Literatur*, pp. 10-13 and Burstein, *The "Babyloniaca" of Berossus*, p. 5. The issue is largely bound up with the authenticity of the astrological fragments. (See below)

[12] Komoróczy, "Berosos and the Mesopotamian Literature," p. 126 n. 10, thinks it should be placed early c. 316 and that he later returned to Babylon. I think it is more reasonable to assume that he was already well-known before he started his school. This would place the event late in his life.

[13] He was credited with the discovery of the semi-circular sundial (T 5) and with fathering Σάββη or Σίβυλλα, the famous Babylonian sibyl (T 7). For details see Burstein, *The "Babyloniaca" of Berossus*, p. 5, n.3. The Athenians are said to have erected a statue in his honor for his astrological prophecies (T 6).

[14] Schnabel, *Berossos und die babylonisch-hellenistische Literatur*, pp. 8-10, places it at c. 281 as does Burstein, *The "Babyloniaca" of Berossus*, pp. 4 and 34.

[15] The work has come down to us under several different appellations which mainly alternate between a form related to Χαλδαϊκά (T T2, 7b, 8a, 8b, 8c;FF 7, 8, 11) or Βαβυλωνιακά (FF 1 and 2). I have followed Schnabel, *Berossos und die babylonisch-hellenistische Literatur*, p. 16, who points out that Βαβυλωνιακά is the title used by Alexander Polyhistor who was the only source to use Berossos directly and that Χαλδαῖος and Βαβυλώνιος would have meant two separate things to Berossos.

its entirety. The work was first abridged by Cornelius Alexander Polyhistor in the first century B.C.E. for his history of Babylon.[16] Polyhistor's condensed version has also perished, but did serve as the basis for the extracts made by Abydenos in the second century C.E.[17] In the fourth century Eusebios made a second abridgement for his *Chronicle*, using not Berossos but Polyhistor.[18] He also preserved the extracts of Abydenos. Although it is debatable, Josephos appears to have known Berossos' work directly.[19] While this state of affairs is at first distressing, we are fortunate that both Polyhistor and Eusebios appear to have worked on the basis of reduction rather than retelling. This allows us to formulate a fairly clear idea of Berossos' work.

The greatest problem which we face is the authenticity of the astrological fragments which have come down to us in Berossos' name. The primary issues are: Why have the fragments not come down to us through Polyhistor and how should we explain the presence of what appears to be a clear dependence upon Greek philosophy?[20] Jacoby's solution was to place these together under a

---

[16] *FGrH* 273. I will deal with Polyhistor in detail in chapter five. This work of Polyhistor's consisted of both an Assyrian and Babylonian history. Berossos was used for the Babylonian half. Burstein, *The "Babyloniaca" of Berossus*, p. 6, summarized his abridgement as follows: "For the Babylonian portion of his work Polyhistor relied almost entirely on Berossus, preserving the basic organization of his book but abridging it, possibly excluding strictly non-historical material such as Berossus' allegorical and astrological interpretation of creation and occasionally interpolating material on Babylon from other authors."

[17] On Abydenos see *FGrH* 685.

[18] On the *Chronicle* see Alden A. Mosshammer, *The "Chronicle" of Eusebius and Greek Chronographic Tradition* (Lewisburg: Bucknell Univeristy Press, 1979).

[19] See chapter six.

[20] The latter is particularly bound up with F 21 (= Seneca, *QNat* 3.29.1), which attributes the concept of the ἐκπύρωσις to Berossos. Seneca wrote: Berosos, qui Belum interpretatus est, ait ista cursu siderum fieri. Adeo quidem affirmat ut conflagrationi atque diluvio tempus assignet. Arsura enim terrena contendit, quandoque omnia sidera quae nunc diversos agunt cursus in Cancrum convenerint, sic sub eodem posita vestigio ut recta linea exire per orbes omnium possit; inundationem futuram, cum eadem siderum turba in Capricornum convenerit. Illic solstitium, hic bruma conficitur; magnae potentiae signa, quando in ipsa mutatione anni momenta sunt. The Stoics attributed their view of ἐκπύρωσις, the cyclical consumption of the world by fire, to Herakleitos. The problem with this is that they adopted Herakleitos as their authority on matters of physics. See *KRS*, p. 85. The earliest Greek witness of the Great Year is Plato, *Tim.* 39C-D.

hypothetical Pseudo-Berossos (FF 15-22).[21] This construct has not, however, gone unchallenged. Schnabel defended their authenticity by arguing that they have not come down to us through Polyhistor because Eusebios omitted them when he reduced Polyhistor.[22] Robert Drews entered the discussion by pointing out that Berossos' reputation depended upon his astrological expertise, a reputation which must have been built upon a written work. He also questioned whether the "Great Year" was derived from Greek philosophy.[23] The latter drew the ire of W.G. Lambert who contended that we do not have any Babylonian parallels to the "Great Year" as well as several other matters expressed in the fragment. We therefore should continue to consider Pseudo-Berossos a viable option.[24] S. Burstein has countered Lambert by pointing out that if Berossos were to successfully communicate Babylonian ideas to Greeks he would have to do it in terms that were intelligible to them, even quasi-philosophical terms.[25] Besides, we have ancient testimony which directly affirms that Berossos did write about astrological matters.[26] He therefore accepts them in his edition of Berossos.[27] Amélie Kuhrt has recently offered the most telling case against them by pointing out that the fragments have nothing distinctively Babylonian.[28]

While dogmatism is out of order, I can not see a substantial enough reason in this instance to discredit the ancient testimony about Berossos. Since his claim to fame in antiquity was primarily his astrological lore, it is reasonable to conclude that he did write some of it down.[29] It is not surprising that this section was excised

---

[21] For a summary of the development of Pseudo-Berossos in scholarship see Robert Drews, "The Babylonian Chronicles and Berossus," *Iraq* 37 (1975): 51-52.

[22] Schnabel, *Berossos und die babylonisch-hellenistische Literatur*, p. 19.

[23] Drews, "The Babylonian Chronicles and Berossus," p. 52.

[24] W.G. Lambert, "Berossus and Babylonian Eschatology," *Iraq* 38 (1976): 171-173.

[25] This point had already been made by Schnabel who maintained that even technical expressions did not in and of themselves necessitate Greek thought. *Berossos und die babylonisch-hellenistische Literatur*, pp. 182-184.

[26] Josephos, *CA* 1.128 (= T 3); Abydenos F 2b; and Hyginus, *Genealogiae*, 247.16, where his statement, Oannes qui in Chaldea de mari exisse dicitur astrologiam interpretatus est, must be a reference to Berossos. Cf. also TT 5 and 6.

[27] Burstein, The "Babyloniaca" of Berossus, pp. 31-32.

[28] "Berossus' Babyloniaka and Seleucid Rule in Babylonia," pp. 36-44.

[29] It would be possible to posit another work for these fragments written by the authentic Berossos. What weighs against this is the fact that we can place them

in the tradition.[30] We must also ask whether the technical terms are due to Berossos or the tradents. Even if we ascribe them to Berossos, it is possible as Burstein has already pointed out that it is simply a matter of accommodation. As we will see, in other instances he deliberately cast his material in Hellenistic terms.

2. *Content.* We may now reconstruct the contents of the work. We know that the Βαβυλωνιακά comprised three books (T 2). We are fortunate to have several fragments which expressly state the book from which they have been taken. The first fragment is from book one.[31] Berossos began with an autobiographical notice. He then offered a brief summary of the land of Babylon emphasizing its fertility. He opened his "history" proper by relating how the first humans lived like animals. Their primitive state changed when the fish-like creature, Oannes,[32] emerged from the Persian gulf to instruct them in the arts of civilization and to deliver a revelation of how the world and humanity were created. F 2 which recounts the feast of Sakaia in which the servants rule their masters is also attributed to book one. According to F 3 the second book listed the ten ante-diluvian kings.[33] The third book has two fragments: F 9 summarizes the reigns of Nabouchodonosoros, Eveilmaradouchos, Neriglisaros, Laborosoarchodos, Nabonnedos, and the fall of Babylon to Kyros; F 11 says that Artaxerxes, the son of Dareios, introduced idols.

We may now situate some of the other fragments on the basis of these points of reference. F 1 of Abydenos which relates the building of the walls of Babylon first by Bel and then by Nabouchodonosoros belongs to book one by its association with Bel's victory over Tiamat.[34] The second book has a good deal more. F 14, the lon-

---

nicely within the structure of the Βαβυλωνιακά and there is no solid testimony in antiquity for the existence of a separate book. Cf. T 1.

[30] Interestingly Mosshammer, *The "Chronicle" of Eusebius and Greek Chronographic Tradition*, p. 264, accepts them as authentic.

[31] Synkellos (preserving Eusebios) summarized the first book in this fragment: περιέχειν δὲ τὰς ἀναγραφὰς ἱστορίας περὶ τοῦ οὐρανοῦ καὶ θαλάσσης καὶ πρωτογονίας καὶ βασιλέων καὶ τῶν κατ' αὐτοὺς πράξεων. Schnabel, *Berossos und die babylonisch-hellenistische Literatur*, p. 21, astutely pointed out that Josephos dropped the final clause in CA 1.128.

[32] Oannes = *ummanu*, "Werkmeister." So Schnabel, *Berossos und die babylonisch-hellenistische Literatur*, p. 175.

[33] It is striking that Gen. 5 also lists ten ante-diluvian figures.

[34] See Schnabel, *Berossos und die babylonisch-hellenistische Literatur*, pp. 41-42 and Burstein, *The "Babyloniaca" of Berossus*, p. 17, n. 23.

gevity of the ante-diluvians, is most logically placed here. F 2 of
Abydenos, his list of ante-diluvian monarchs, and F 3 of Abydenos,
the flood, clearly belong to the second book. This is also true of F
4 which recounts the flood in association with the final ante-diluvian
figure, Xisuthros. FF 5 and 6 recall individuals after the flood, but
expressly linked to it and should therefore also be placed in book
two. F 6 of Abydenos mentions Nabouchodonosoros and his successors and is therefore part of book three. F 8 again deals with the same
figure. The Persian kings of F 10 must come after these fragments
in book three since the work clearly moves sequentially.

We now only have to decide where book two ends and book three
begins[35] and where to place the astronomical fragments (FF 13,
15-22) and F 12 in which Babylonian gods are equated with Greek.
The exact break between the second and third books is difficult, but
it is best to follow the lead of Schnabel and Burstein and place it between Nabonasaros and Phulos.[36] The location of the astrological
fragments is debated. Schnabel and Burstein place them in book one
since they would naturally follow the creation of the stars.[37] Robert
Drews, on the other hand, thought they should be placed at the end
of book three which otherwise summarily dispensed with the Neo-
Babylonian empire.[38] If Berossos had ended his account with the
Neo-Babylonian empire, Drews would have a case; however, his
account apparently extended down to Alexander.[39] It is best then to
place them in book one where they would most naturally follow the
account of the stars. I am also inclined to place F 12 there since it
deals with the gods.

I would thus reconstruct the Βαβυλωνιακά as follows:

---

[35] Polyhistor (F 3a) indicates that the kings appear in book two. This enables us
to easily demarcate book one from book two.
[36] Schnabel, *Berossos und die babylonisch-hellenistische Literatur*, pp. 22-26 and Burstein, *The "Babyloniaca" of Berossus*, pp. 22-23.
[37] Schnabel, *Berossos und die babylonisch-hellenistische Literatur*, pp. 17-22 and Burstein, *The "Babyloniaca" of Berossus*, pp. 15-17.
[38] Drews, "The Babylonian Chronicles and Berossus," p. 53: "If, like most, a
book of the *Babyloniaca* ran to c. 2000 lines, almost two thirds of the book remains
unaccounted for. I suggest that here, constituting about a quarter of the whole
work, was to be found the 'astronomy and philosophical doctrines of the Chaldeans,' the presentation of which secured for Berossus whatever reputation he did enjoy in the classical world."
[39] F 1 of Abydenos suggests this. It is reasonable to think that Polyhistor
dropped part of this section since his work concentrated on Babylon proper.

Book One: 1. Autobiographical Introduction
            2. The Land of Babylon
            3. Primitive Humanity
            4. Oannes establishes Civilization
            5. Oannes reveals Creation
            6. The Astrological Material
Book Two: 1. The Ten Ante-Diluvian Kings
            2. The Deluge
            3. The Kings Down to Nabonassaros
Book Three: 1. Assyrian Kings
            2. The Neo-Babylonian Kings
            3. The Persian Kings
            4. The Conquest of Alexander

Does this analysis permit us to place Berossos within the tradition which we have been tracing? I believe that it does. Berossos is aware of the ethnographic tradition as his inclusion of geography,[40] history, and his lone νόμος indicate.[41] Yet he clearly does not feel compelled to follow it as a canonical model. His text swallows up the land, νόμοι, and θαυμάσια in favor of history. This, however, can be somewhat misleading since he does not treat the story of his people with an even hand. Polyhistor—who rarely inserts an editorial comment—apparently could not refrain from making this observation about the second book: ". . . und in zweiten hat er die Könige, einen nach dem andern darstellend, beschreiben." He continues more specifically: "Der Könige Namen nur tut er sammelnd aufschichten, ihre etwaigen Taten jedoch erzählt er keineswegs genau, oder auch erachtet sie gar nicht einmal der Erwähnung würdig, wenn (nur) dabei die Zahl der Könige aufgestellt werde" (F 3a).[42] In fact, there are only two kings in the work which receive any detailed treatment: Senecherib (F 7) and Nabouchodonosoros (F 8). The bulk of the work appears to consist of the account of the creation, astrological material, the flood, and king lists.

Why these shifts? While it would be possible to argue that the need to describe the land was minimized since Antiochos I hardly needed

---

[40] So also Schnabel, *Berossos und die babylonisch-hellenistische Literatur*, p. 176, who points out that the Assyrians and Babylonians did have a world map; and Kuhrt, "Berossus' *Babyloniaka* and Seleucid Rule in Babylonia," p. 47.

[41] F 2.

[42] Cf. also F 10.

to be informed about the territory he had ruled for over ten years, this will not satisfactorily account for all of the changes in emphasis. The key is found in the opening statement of the work: "Berossos says . . . that he [translated] many (?) books which had been preserved with great care at Babylon and which dealt with a period of more than 150,000 years." We then get a summary of the contents: "These books contained the histories of heaven (and of earth) and sea and the first birth and the kings and their deeds."[43] Did he live up to his promise? There can be no doubt that he did.[44]

In some instances we can pinpoint the specific source and in others offer general parallels. Taking the text in its own order we may posit the following sources. Berossos begins with a description of humanity living like wild animals, a presentation which parallels Sumerian texts of the third and second millenia B.C.E.[45] The two great foci in cuneiform tradition are the theomachy and the deluge: the two main points of the first two books of Berossos. The revelation Oannes gives about creation so closely parallels the great epic, *Enuma elish*, that there can be no real doubt about its place as our *Vorlage*.[46] The flood story is not as straightforward. There is no

---

[43] Burstein's translation of F 1. Cf. also TT 3 and 4.

[44] The summaries of Schwartz, *RE*, s.v. "Berossos," 3: 310 and Schnabel, *Berossos und die babylonisch-hellenistische Literatur*, pp. 172-184, are now somewhat dated in particulars, but still recognize his use of native sources.

[45] Komoróczy, "Berosos and the Mesopotamian Literature," pp. 140-142, offers a number of examples. See also Jeffrey H. Tigay, *The Evolution of the Gilgamesh Epic* (Philadelphia: University of Pennsylvania Press, 1982), pp. 202-206. Both cite *The Dispute Between Cattle and Grain* or *Lahar and Ashnan*: "Mankind at that time (i.e., primordial times)/Knew not the eating of Bread,/Knew not the wearing of garments;/The people went around with skins on their bodies [Komoróczy: people went about with naked limbs]/They ate grass with their mouths like sheep,/Drank water from ditches." (Translation of Tigay, p. 203)

[46] A comparison of F 1 with *Enuma elish* reveals the following structural similarities:

Item	Enuma Elish	Berossos
The Monsters	1.133-143	F 1.6
Tiamat contains All	1.4	F 1.6
Splitting of Tiamat	4.135-140	F 1.7
Creation from Halves	4.141-5.166	F 1.7
Creation of Stars, Sun		
Moon, and Five Planets	5.1-44	F 1.9

Komoróczy, "Berosos and the Mesopotamian Literature," pp. 131-133, has shown that this is more than a general pattern. He has shown that the name of the woman, Omorka who is identified as *Thalath* (= Tiamat) in Berossos and which

question that Berossos knew the Mesopotamian flood-story[47]; the only issue is whether we can specify a particular version. At present it is possible to dismiss the *Gilgamesh Epic* as the source since the names of the two heroes are different and there are too many variations.[48] It is more likely that Berossos rehearsed a version similar to the *Epic of Ziusudra*.[49] The remainder of Berossos' text is primarily a king list. Whether the early section is from a Sumerian king list or the Neo-Babylonian chronicles—the latter now appears more likely—there is once again no reason to question Berossos' employment of cuneiform sources.[50] His use of such sources not only proves their existence at his date, but also matches the revival of cuneiform when the Seleukids came to power.[51]

This heavy use of native sources is combined with a criticism of Greek sources. Josephos tells us that in his third book Berossos

---

he derives from θάλασσα, is taken from 2.100ff., where the term *e-ma-ru-uk-ka*, a hapax legomenon which he derives from the Sumerian *a-ma-ru* or *a-ma-uru*, "flood," occurs. Berossos has offered a Greek equivalent of the Sumerian in an attempt to let the principle of the sea dominate. On the differences between the two accounts see Alexander Heidel, *The Babylonian Genesis: The Story of Creation*, 2nd ed. (Chicago: The University of Chicago Press, 1951), pp. 77-81. Heidel also concluded that *Enuma elish* was the primary source and thought Berossos may have employed some secondary cuneiform sources.

[47] This is widely recognized. E.g., Alexander Heidel, *The Gilgamesh Epic and Old Testament Parallels*, 2nd ed. (Chicago: University of Chicago Press, 1949), pp. 116-119 and Millard in W.G. Lambert and A.R. Millard, *Atra-Hasis: The Babylonian Story of the Flood* (Oxford: The Clarendon Press, 1969), pp. 136-137.

[48] The *Gilgamesh Epic* is dismissed by Schnabel, *Berossos und die babylonisch-hellenistische Literatur*, pp. 180-182; Komoróczy, "Berosos and the Mesopotamian Literature," pp. 133-135; Burstein, *The "Babyloniaca" of Berossus*, p. 8; and Tigay, *The Evolution of the Gilgamesh Epic*, p. 251.

[49] Berossos' Xisouthros is obviously a Grecized form of Ziusudra. There is a partial (the text has not been fully recovered) edition in translation in *ANET*, 1: 42-44.

[50] Komoróczy, "Berosos and the Mesopotamian Literature," p. 135, thought Berossos used a Sumerian king list. On the Sumerian king list see Thorkild Jacobsen, *The Sumerian King List*. The Oriental Institute of the University of Chicago Assyriological Studies 11 (Chicago: University of Chicago Press, 1939). Burstein, *The "Babyloniaca" of Berossus*, pp. 8-9, has more recently argued for the Neo-Babylonian chronicles. Drews, "The Babylonian Chronicles and Berossus," p. 54, also contends for the latter. He suggests the chronicles were drawn up for judicial astrology rather than extispicy and were "temporal charts showing the occurrence of certain types of phenomena which either directly express or else symptomize suffering or well-being in Babylon and its environs. These phenomena were not understood as being tied to each other in a causal chain, and apparently were all seen as direct results of divine decree," p. 45. See also 46-50.

[51] So R. Campbell Thompson, "The Influence of Babylonia," in *The Assyrian Empire*. CAH (Cambridge: University Press, 1970), 3: 245.

μέμφεται τοῖς Ἑλληνικοῖς συγγραφεῦσιν ὡς μάτην οἰομένοις ὑπὸ
Σεμιράμεως τῆς Ἀσσυρίας κτισθῆναι τὴν Βαβυλῶνα καὶ τὰ θαυμά-
σια κατασκευασθῆναι περὶ αὐτὴν ὑπ᾽ ἐκείνης ἔργα ψευδῶς γεγραφόσι
(CA 1.142 = F 8). We have no way of knowing which particular
sources Berossos knew,[52] but it is clear that while he had read
Greek accounts he is giving the native tradition, not a rehashed
Greek version.

3. *Form*. The result of this procedure was to create a new form of
writing, apologetic historiography proper. The basis of the writing
is ethnography, especially as it was altered by Hekataios (and to a
lesser extent Megasthenes). Yet it is new. We no longer have a
Greek attempting to assimilate native traditions within the framework of ethnography. On the other hand, there are no native works
which attempt to build a unified structure by placing the individual
bricks of their traditions into a single superstructure. It is this synthesis of native texts placed together within the general pattern of
ethnography which constitutes the nexus of apologetic historiography.

The marriage of native traditions and Greek ethnography did not
always produce a blissful union. The problem would always be the
dominance of one partner. What form does Berossos' Βαβυλωνιακά
take? That he presented his material in Greek dress is beyond question. The very fact that he wrote in Greek, poor as it was, establishes
this.[53] The influence runs deeper however. He opens with an autobiographical statement, a clear bow to Greek historiography.[54]
That he attempted to bring his material into contact with Greek concerns and conceptions is clear from his allegorical treatment of the

---

[52] The most likely candidate for this stricture is Ktesias who gave a detailed
description of Semiramis' building at Babylon. Cf. Diodoros 2.7.2-11. Herodotos
also mentioned some of her projects in 1.184.1. Burstein, *The "Babyloniaca" of
Berossus*, p. 28 n. 107, argued that since Berossos apparently ignored Herodotos'
ascription of the major monuments to Nitokris (1.185-187 [rather than Semira-
mis]), he did not know Herodotos. His argument is *e silentio* and not conclusive. We
can not prove his knowledge of Herodotos one way or the other. On *a priori* reasoning, I would be surprised if he did not have some acquaintance with the *pater
historiae*.
[53] On his Greek see Schnabel, *Berossos und die babylonisch-hellenistische Literatur*,
pp. 29-32.
[54] The practice is at least as old as Hekataios of Miletos who opened his
Genealogiai with an autobiographical declaration (F 1). The most famous examples
are Herodotos and Thukydides. Xenophon did not begin autobiographically.

creation through Tiamat,[55] the probable use of ἐκπύρωσις,[56] and his equation of Babylonian gods with Greek.[57] These concessions were not however determinative.[58] The Βαβυλωνιακά remains essentially a composite of native traditions and as such was unsavory to the Greek palate.

One of his most important omissions of Greek ethnography is the *apparent*—we must remember these are fragments—absence of *nomoi*. As we have seen, *nomoi* functioned to identify people for the Greeks. The question which an ethnography answers is who are these people. The removal of the key Herodotean answer is significant. The Babylonians are not defined as a group of people who practice certain things in contradistinction to other groups, but those who have continuity with and lay claim to a noble and illustrious heritage which Berossos has set forth. Perhaps this shift was essential in light of the reality of Greek political dominance and the infusion of Hellenism. He therefore turned away from a less than grandiose present to the past which glistened with pristine grandeur.

Is the *Babyloniaka* then a history?[59] As with Hekataios of Miletos, how we answer this depends upon how far we are willing to extend the scope of "history." If we mean the tradition which began with Herodotos and came down through Thukydides we must answer negatively. If, on the contrary, we mean the tradition which began with Hekataios of Miletos and came down through Herodotos and

---

[55] F 1. Heidel, *The Babylonian Genesis*, p. 79, made this important observation: "Here Berossus is obviously making a concession to certain Greek philosophers in order to render Babylonian speculation more acceptable to them, without implying, however, that he came upon this kind of interpretation through the study of Greek thought. On the contrary, the type of interpretation which Berossus here follows was doubtless known to all thinkers of Babylonia and Assyria. Every priest knew that Ti'amat was nothing but the dark primeval salt-water ocean personified, containing all the elements of which heaven and earth were afterward made, for up to the latest times of Babylonian-Assyrian history *tamtu* (a later development of *ti'amatu*, which when applied to the primeval female principle was shortened to *ti'amat*) was used as the regular designation for the sea or ocean."

[56] F 21. See above.

[57] F 12. Bel = Zeus; Sandes = Herakles; Anais = Aphrodite.

[58] Schwartz, *RE*, s.v. "Berossos," 3: 315-316, thought that Greek philosophy was a determining factor in the Βαβυλωνιακά. Although it is true that Berossos accents Babylonian wisdom, I do not see that he went nearly as far as Hekataios of Abdera or Megasthenes in allowing it to form the framework of his discussion.

[59] Drews, "The Babylonian Chronicles and Berossus," pp. 53-54 and Burstein, *The "Babyloniaca" of Berossus*, p. 7, both have expressed reservations about calling the *Babyloniaka* a "history."

Hekataios of Abdera, we may reply affirmatively. It is history in the sense that it preserves the records of a given civilization, not in the sense that it attempts to reconstruct events and thoughts buried within the records.

4. *Function.* What purpose did this new amalgamation serve? As we have already noted, Berossos dedicated his work to Antiochos I.[60] Schnabel thought that this was the priest's way of thanking Antiochos for his rebuilding of the temple of Marduk.[61] Schwartz saw a parallel between the work of Berossos and Manethon, suggesting both served political ends.[62] Murray argued that Berossos was commissioned by Antiochos to answer the claims of Hekataios.[63] Burstein has offered yet another possibility. Since Seleukos I had degraded Babylon by moving to Seleukeia, he proposed that Berossos saw an opportunity for promoting Babylon with the accession of the new king.[64]

In order to determine the purpose we must ask what the contents emphasized. The *Babyloniaka* should be considered a cultural history. When Oannes gave humanity the arts of civilization, it gave them everything there was: ἀπὸ δὲ τοῦ χρόνου ἐκείνου οὐδὲν ἄλλο περισσὸν εὑρεθῆναι (F 1.4).[65] Thus, rather than a Greek view of civilization which posited development through discoveries and firsts, Berossos claims that civilization is a result of revelation.[66]

---

[60] T 2 'Αντιόχῳ τῷ μετ' αὐτὸν τρίτῳ τὴν Χαλδαίων ἱστορίαν ἐν τρισὶ βιβλίοις κατατάξας. Cf. also T 4.

[61] Schnabel, *Berossos und die babylonisch-hellenistische Literatur*, pp. 7-8, esp. 8.

[62] Schwartz, *RE*, s.v. "Berossos," 3: 314.

[63] Murray, "Herodotus and Hellenistic Culture," p. 208. He has been followed by Kuhrt, "Berossus' *Babyloniaka* and Seleucid Rule in Babylonia," pp. 53-56.

[64] Burstein, *The "Babyloniaca" of Berossus*, pp. 5-6. He makes a very intriguing suggestion to explain the attention given to only two kings. Senecherib represented a king who like Seleukos had tried to destroy Babylon and had been assassinated by his sons while Nabouchodonosoros who had worked with the priests had enjoyed a long and glorious reign.

[65] W.G. Lambert, "Ancestors, Authors, and Canonicity," *Journal of Cuneiform Studies* 11 (1957): 9, thought that this statement implied a loose view of a Babylonian literary canon: "There is a Babylonian conception of canonicity which is implicit in the colophons just cited, and which is stated plainly by Berossus: that the sum of revealed knowledge was given once for all by the antediluvian sages."

[66] Burstein, *The "Babyloniaca" of Berossus*, p. 7, has done an excellent job in pointing out this difference. It is interesting to me that Genesis also begins with paradise and then works downwards. We could speak of de-evolution rather than evolution.

Further, this revelation was not given to the Greeks, nor to the Egyptians, nor to the Indians; it was given to the Babylonians. That it was given prior to the emergence of civilizations in other locales is buttressed by the insistence on the incredible antiquity of the revelation and Babylonian civilization. This explains at least some of the attention to chronological matters.[67]

Our assessment of the purpose of the *Babyloniaka* must take into account this cultural claim. Like Hekataios and Megasthenes, Berossos is defending a specific culture. Its dedication to Antiochos I conveys political concerns. The issue is what were they? Were they *to* or *for* Antiochos? Here we should recall the role which astrologers played for Antiochos. They gave him advice which was to serve his well-being. In this instance, it is most probable that Berossos dedicated his work at the accession of Antiochos or shortly thereafter, reminding his political ruler of the great prestige of Babylon and tacitly—but firmly—urging him to accord it the honor it deserved. At the same time, this was to the credit of Antiochos: he ruled the most ancient and glorious civilization known to man humanity. Here was the proof for all of the Greek world to see. The common element in this analysis is Berossos' native pride, i.e., his insistence on Babylon's greatness.

Significance

How did the *Babyloniaka* fare? Apparently not well. Although Josephos tells us that his works for Greeks brought him recognition in learned circles (*CA* 1.129), we know of only five Greek authors who used him directly.[68] Why? There does appear to have been interest on the part of Greeks in the native traditions of the Assyrians and Babylonians.[69] Besides the poor quality of his Greek and the insignificance of Babylon from a Greek perspective, the main reason

---

[67] It is interesting to note that in contrast to the *Gilgamesh Epic*, the flood story in Berossos has a specific date. The Sumerian flood story is too fragmentary to determine whether a specific date was offered.

[68] Kleitarchos, Pseudo-Eupolemos, Poseidonios, Polyhistor, and Juba. See Schnabel, *Berossos und die babylonisch-hellenistische Literatur*, pp. 28-29, and his chapters on each of these.

[69] We even have examples of Greek students trying to learn Sumerian and Akkadian. See, for example, Edmond Sollberger, "Graeco-Babyloniaca," *Iraq* 24 (1962): 63-72, who offers eight fragments of second and first century B.C.E. Greek students. At least eight other such fragments exist.

is likely the fact that Berossos did not extend his bridge far enough into the Greek world. That is to say that the *Babyloniaka* remained too true to Babylonian ideals and was consequently foreign to Greeks.[70]

Does the *Babyloniaka* respond to Hekataios?[71] There is no evidence to suggest that his work was a direct response. Antiochos did not commission it as a type of Seleucid repartee and there are no lines of dependence observable in the fragments. The emphasis on native sources and scorning of Greek accounts could as easily stem from his own response to Hellenism as from an awareness of Hekataios' work. On the other hand, the proximity of time and place make it possible that he knew Hekataios' *Aigyptiaka*. The observation that he served as a model for Manethon (T 10), does point to the possibility of exchange between the two rival kingdoms of the Seleukids and Ptolemies. Too much should not be made of this observation, however, since similarities in method and claims could have led to this conclusion without any actual literary dependence. *In nuce*, the evidence only allows us to state that while we may not posit a direct borrowing and exchange, as a priest of Bel, Berossos would not have been pleased with the claims of Egypt. It is to the latter that we must once again turn.

MANETHON[72]

Life

Manethon whose name probably means "pastor of horses"[73] was

---

[70] Burstein, The *"Babyloniaca"* of Berossus, pp. 9-10, has an excellent summary of this point.

[71] So Murray, "Herodotus and Hellenistic Culture," pp. 208-209, who only alludes to "the arrangement of his material and his explanations" fitting the pattern established by Hekataios.

[72] I have used *FGrH* 609. Cf. also W.G. Waddell, *Manetho*, LCL (Cambridge: Harvard University Press, 1980). General studies include: *RE*, s.v. "Manethon," by R. Laqueur, 14: 1060-1101; *EncJud*, s.v. "Manetho," by Menahem Stern, 11: 872-873; and *KP*, s.v. "Manethon," by Hans Wolfgang Helck, 3: 952-953. Doron Mendels has recently made a noteworthy contribution: "The Polemical Character of Manetho's *Aegyptiaca*," in *Purposes of History: Studies in Greek Historiography from the 4th to the 2nd Centuries B.C.* (*Proceedings of the International Colloquium Leuven, 24-26 May 1988*), ed. H. Verdin, G. Schepens, and E. De Keyser. Studia Hellenistica 30. (Lovanii, 1990), pp. 91-110.

[73] The Coptic form of his name would most likely have been ⲙⲁⲛⲉ-ϩⲧⲟ which J. Černý, *Coptic Etymological Dictionary* (Cambridge: Cambridge University

not a Greek. Μανεθὼν δ' ἦν τὸ γένος Αἰγύπτιος (T 7a).[74] He was a younger contemporary of Berossos who lived during the reigns of Ptolemy Soter (T 3) and Ptolemy Philadelphos (308-246 B.C.E.) (T 11a,b,c). Although there is some confusion among ancient tradents, he spent the early years of his life in Sebennytos on the west bank of the Damietta branch of the Nile.[75] One of the ancient traditions about Sebennytos is that Solon visited it and taught there.[76] Whether there is any basis to this or not, it is likely that Hellenism was strongly present in Sebennytos as Manethon grew up. Josephos would say of Manethon: ἀνὴρ τῆς Ἑλληνικῆς μετεσχηκὼς παιδείας (T 7a; cf. also 14a). Like Berossos Manethon became a priest, rising even to the level of ἀρχιερεύς (TT 1 [?], 11a,b). He most likely served in Heliopolis.[77] The only thing which we know he did is extremely important for our understanding of Manethon. Manethon along with Timotheos helped Ptolemy officially introduce the cult of Sarapis (TT 3, 4, 5).[78] Sarapis was a hybrid god whose cult was

---

Press, 1976), p. 84, interprets as "pastor of horses." (ⲙⲁⲛⲉ means "herdsman" and ⲉⲧⲟ "horse".) So also W.E. Crum, *A Coptic Dictionary* (Oxford: The Clarendon Press, 1939), p. 723a. The underlying form would then be *mjnjw-htrj* which Helck renders as "Pferdehirt" in *KP*, s.v. "Manethon," 3: 952. An alternative explanation is "Truth of Thoth." (ME is "truth.") On the confusion in the Greek forms of his name see the note in Jacoby, *FGrH* 609 T 1.

[74] Cf. also TT 6b, 9, 14b, and F 23.

[75] T 1 (= Suda) has him from Μένδης τῆς Αἰγύπτου. Mendes is only about seventeen miles from Sebennytos. Confusion could also have arisen between Ptolemy of Mendes, a priest at the time of Augustus who wrote a three volume Egyptian chronology, and Manethon. Finally, it is possible that the Suda intended to differentiate between two Manethons. See Waddell, *Manetho*, p. x-xi. T 2 (= Suda) has Διοσπόλεως τῆς Αἰγύπτου ἢ Σεβεννύτης. Again the two are close: only thirty miles separate them and the nomes are contiguous. Since Sebennytos was the seat of the thirtieth dynasty, it is possible that Manethon had some ties with Diospolis (= Tell el-Balamun) very early in his life. However, tradition clearly links him with Sebennytos (TT 3, 11a,b,c, and F 19). Sebennytos was ancient Tjeb-nuter, "city of the sacred calf," and modern Samannud.

[76] Proklos, *in Plat. Tim.* 1.101.

[77] R. Laqueur, *RE*, s.v. "Manethon," 14: 1061, argued this on the ground of the importance of Heliopolis as a center for priests and observed: "M. wußte infolgedessen unzweifelhaft von dem heiligen Baum in der großen Halle von Heliopolis, auf dem die Göttin Seschat, die Herrin der Schrift, die Beherrscherin des Bücherhauses Namen und Taten der Herrscher mit eigener Hand niederschrieb. Er hat also nicht anderes getan, als die Griechenwelt mitzuteilen, was die Göttin aufgezeichnet hatte. Aber er tat dies mit dem vollen Gefühl der Überlegenheit, die sich gegenüber dem von ihm bekampften Herodot auf die heiligen Urkunden der Ägypter berief."

[78] Waddell, *Manetho*, pp. xiii-xiv, has an excellent discussion of the evidence. The exact origins of Sarapis are a matter of debate. The most important ancient

designed to help merge Egyptian and Greek elements.[79] Paradoxically, the cult was never well accepted by native Egyptians but became the Egyptian god universally worshipped outside of Egypt.[80] The fact that Manethon helped to formulate the cult demonstrates that he wanted to find ways to merge the two worlds in which he lived.

Manethon's other effort at the same task was his writing. There are at least eight titles attributed to him in the fragments Jacoby collected.[81] Of these some are undoubtedly spurious[82] and others may not refer to separate works.[83] At present we simply can not say how many distinct works Manethon composed.[84] It is his *magnum opus*, however, that concerns us.

Αἰγυπτιακά

1. *Textual Problem.* The text of Manethon represents one of the

---

sources are Tacitus, *Hist.* 4.80-84; Plutarch, *Isis and Osiris* 361D-362B; and Clement of Alexandria, *Protr.* 4.48.1-6. The texts merely indicate that Sarapis came from some distant locale: Tacitus says that some think he came from Seleukeia while both Tacitus and Plutarch record the tradition that he was brought from Sinope by Ptolemy I. C. Bradford Welles, "The Discovery of Sarapis and the Foundation of Alexandria," *Historia* 11 (1962): 271-298, has argued that Alexander founded Alexandria on his return from Siwah on 25 Tybi (7 April 331) and that he found a temple of Osiris-Apis/Sarapis in Racotis, accepted the god, and then spread the cult on his travels. Even though the ancient testimony is unclear, it is probably due to the founders of the cult who wanted to shroud their god in a veil of mystery. I am for that reason unwilling to set it aside for an earlier date which involves a good number of difficulties.

[79] The name Sarapis is from Osorapis which is from Osiris and Apis. The Apis bull was thought to become an Osiris after its death and funeral in Memphis. The actual blending of elements consists of qualities of Greek gods and Osiris. On the attempt to use this to bring the two different races together, see A.D. Nock, *Conversion: The Old and the New in Religion from Alexander the Great to Augustine of Hippo* (Oxford: The Clarendon Press, 1933), pp. 37-41.

[80] On the spread of the Sarapis cult see Tran tam Tinh, "Sarapis and Isis," in *Jewish and Christian Self-Definition*, 3: 101-117.

[81] Ἱερὰ βίβλος (T 7); Τὰ Αἰγυπτιακά (FF 1-12); Τὰ πρὸς Ἡρόδοτον (F 13); Περὶ Ἀρχαισμοῦ καὶ Εὐσέβειας (F 14); Περὶ ἑορτῶν (F 15); Περὶ κατασκευῆς κύφιων (F 16); Φυσικῶν ἐπιτομή (F 17); βίβλος τῆς Σώθεος (F 25).

[82] Synkellos thought that the βίβλος τῆς Σώθεος was genuine, but it is not. It is based upon Josephos and Eusebios and is generally dated to the third century C.E. Cf. Waddell, *Manetho*, pp. 234-249 and especially n. 1 on pp. 234-235.

[83] The τὰ πρὸς Ἡρόδοτον (F 13) is generally thought to be part of the *Aigyptiaka*. How many of the others are is a matter of some debate. It is clear that Manethon wrote more than one title (T 9); the issue is how many.

[84] On the different titles see Laqueur, *RE*, s.v. "Manethon," 14: 1099-1101 and Waddell, *Manetho*, pp. xiv-xv.

greatest textual conundrums from antiquity.[85] We, of course, do not have a full copy of the original. What we have are two different traditions. Coming down one genealogical tree, we possess the fragments of Josephos who appears to have used the authentic Manethon.[86] Proceeding along a different course down to us is a summary of Manethon's chronological work in Sextus Julius Africanus and in two separate works of Eusebios.[87] Both Christian chronographers were interested in synchronizing Eastern chronologies with that of the biblical text, a task which made Manethon ideal. Their work has in turn vanished except in the Armenian recension of Eusebios' *Chronicle* and the Ἐκλογή Χρονογραφίας of Synkellos.[88] Synkellos, which simply denotes the office of George the Monk[89] who was an attendant of Tarasius the Patriarch of Constantinople from 784-806, used Africanus, Eusebios, an old Egyptian chronicle, and the Book of Sothis in his survey from Adam to Diokletian.

The difference between the two strands is immediately apparent on a first reading. The fragments in Josephos suggest that the work of Manethon had a full narrative, while the chronographers' reports would lead us to think that Manethon was himself a chronographer with only a skeleton frame for his history. Nor is the only difficulty the reconciling of the two major strands. Each individual tradition

---

[85] Laqueur, *RE*, s.v. "Manethon," 14: 1061, quoted Boeckhs whose assessment in 1845 is not much different from what can be offered today: ''. . . 'nie ein verwirrterer Gegenstand der Betrachtung als dieser M. vorgekommen' sei.''

[86] On Josephos' use of Manethon see Arnaldo Momigliano, "Intorno al *Contro Apione*," *Revista di Filologia e di Istruzione Classica* n.s. 9 (1931): 483-503 and Lucio Troiani, "Sui frammenti di Manetone nel primo libro del *Contra Apionem* de Flavio Giuseppe," *Studi Classici e Orientali* 24 (1975): 97-126. *Contra* Stern, *EncJud*, s.v. "Manetho," 11: 872, who thinks that Josephos only knew Manethon through the Hellenistic Jewish historians.

[87] On Africanus see Heinrich Gelzer, *Sextus Julius Africanus und die byzantinische Chronographie*, 2 vols. (Leipzig, 1898; reprint ed., New York: Burt Franklin, n.d.). Eusebios has two accounts: the *Chronicle* which has only come down to us in Armenian and the section of *PE* which we have via Synkellos. In Jacoby the fragments are F 2 (Africanus), F 3a (Eusebios, the *Chronicle*), and F 3b (Eusebios via Synkellos). On the *Chronicle* see, Mosshammer, *The "Chronicle" of Eusebius*.

[88] On Synkellos see *RE*, s.v. "Synkellos," by Richard Laqueur, II 4: 1388-1410 and *KP*, s.v. "Synkellos," by Hans Gartner, 5: 456. The title of his work is suggested by Parisinus 1711 and 167.13: κατὰ τὴν παροῦσαν χρονογραφίαν. Cf. also 152.1; 156.7; 160.4; and 617.7.

[89] So Laqueur, *RE*, s.v. "Synkellos," II 4: 1388: "Das Wort S. bezeichnet allgemein denjenigen, der mit einem anderen die Cella teilt, im speziellen wird es von Mönchen angewandt, welche Genossen hochstehender Geistlicher sind und zum Teil auch als deren Beichtväter fungierten."

is fraught with major problems since neither is without contradictions within itself. In Josephos there are two distinct traditions which he thinks Manethon related about the origins of the Jews.[90] It almost goes without saying that the names and numbers in the chronographers do not fully tally.[91]

The most important effort to solve this textual labyrinth is that of R. Laqueur.[92] Laqueur thought that Josephos did preserve excerpts from the original Manethon.[93] However, the original text of Manethon apparently circulated in several forms. Besides the authentic version a second version developed which contained both "eine rationalistische Kritik des echten M. . . . von einem Hellenisten"[94] and barbs made by Jews and Egyptians in their exchanges. At first Josephos used only the genuine Manethon; later however, he learned of the other material and incorporated it in *CA* 1.250ff. It is this additional material of which he is so critical. What is imperative for us is to realize "daß das Werk M.s bereits vor Josephus Gegenstand zahlreicher literarischer Auseinandersetzungen war." The situation with the Christian chronographers is likewise complex. Laqueur suggested that shortly after Manethon, an epitome was made of dynasties 1-31.[95] This epitome was in turn edited by Hellenistic Jews. Africanus found a copy of the original epitome which he employed, while Eusebios obtained a copy of the edited epitome.[96]

It is outside our purposes to enter fully into the discussion of the

---

[90] *CA* 1.74-92 (= F 8) is Josephos' account of the Hyksos whom he presents as migrating peacefully to Judea and founding Jerusalem (especially 88-90). *CA* 1. 223-253 (= F 10) relates the revolt of the lepers under their king Osarsephos and their expulsion to Syria.

[91] Jacoby, *FGrH*, 3c: 56-80, has provided a chart comparing all of the names, dates, and numbers of the rulers of Egypt via the major witnesses.

[92] *RE*, s.v. "Manethon," 14: 1064-1080 on Josephos and 1080-1089 for the Christian chronographers.

[93] *CA* 1.75-82, 84-90, 94-102a, 232-249, 251.

[94] *CA* 1. 254-261, 267-269, 271-274, 276-277, and possibly 102b-103.

[95] What impact did the epitomator have on the work? Laqueur made the following observation which is of importance: "Allerdings wird es dadurch fraglich, ob bei M. die Dynastien bereits die Rolle gespielt haben, die wir auf Grund der Epitome erschließen. . . . So ist das Material bei M. restlos vorhanden gewesen, nur hat sich bei ihm das chronologische Schema nicht so einseitig vorgedrängt wie bei dem Epitomator, der unter Verzicht auf den größten Teil des sonstigen Stoffes das Ganze auf die Dynastieübersicht hin orientierte, wobei er je einem Buch des M. einen Tomos entsprechen lieb." *RE, s.v.* "Manethon," 14: 1090.

[96] Laqueur is followed by Waddell, *Manetho*, pp. xv-xx.

text; however, the following observations are of crucial importance for our reconstruction of the general lines of Manethon. First, Josephos does appear to know and use the authentic Manethon although it is certainly possible that the text had been corrupted by later editing.[97] This means that we should not follow the lead of the chronographers in our assessment of the nature of Manethon's work, but that of Josephos, i.e., it is clearly more than a mere listing of the kings with their dates.[98] Second, it is best to posit an epitome from which Africanus and Eusebios both drew. The hand of the epitomator is evident in the addition of the thirty-first dynasty. F 12 indicates that the original text of Manethon ended with Nectanebo and the thirtieth dynasty,[99] a comment which is supported by the fact that there are no totals given in the thirty-first dynasty.[100] The extension of either nine (Africanus) or sixteen years (Eusebios) serves to mark the approximate date of the editor. The epitomator basically pared the text down from a narrative to a skeletal chronological frame, although it is also likely that Manethon himself at times engaged in a simple listing as did Berossos.[101]

We must also be careful not to attribute to Manethon a comment of Africanus or Eusebios. The former openly adds comments of his own to the epitome.[102] These, however, are few in number and are

---

[97] On Josephos' knowledge of Manethon see the discussion in chapter six. Josephos does indicate a shift ἐκ τῶν ἱερῶν γραμμάτων to τὰ μυθευόμενα καὶ λεγόμενα in CA 1.228-229 and 252-253. Gager, Moses in Graeco-Roman Paganism, p. 118 (see pp. 116-118), thought that the shift in 250 was substantial enough to posit a Pseudo-Manethon. He based this on the fact that Osarsiph is introduced in 238 without being equated with Moses, the names are spelled differently in 238 and 250 (where Osarsiph is equated with Moses), and λέγεται in 250 indicates a secondary comment. Stern, GLAJJ, 1: 64, rejects the Pseudo-Manethon hypothesis. On a very different level, Jean Yoyotte, "L'Egypt ancienne et les origines de l'antijudaïsme," Revue de l'Histoire des Religions 163 (1963): 133-143, argues that there is no need to posit intermediate interpolations between Manethon and Josephos since Egyptian antipathy towards foreigners is well established in Pharaonic Egypt. Cf. esp. p. 135.

[98] So also Laqueur, RE, s.v. "Manethon," 14: 1089.

[99] F 12: hic autem Nectanebus postremus fuit Aegyptiorum rex, a Manethone enarratur. . .

[100] Cf. Jacoby, FGrH, 3c: 62-63 n. 38 and Waddell, Manetho, pp. 184-185 n.1.

[101] It may be that the brief references which we have in the epitome reflect larger sections of text and that where there are no details in the epitome there were none in Manethon. There is, however, no reason why the editor might not have applied his scissors fully to some events in the original text.

[102] I would divide these into biblical and non-biblical additions. For the former the reference to Moses at the time of Amos (18th D.) is openly stated by Africanus

easily detectable. The two versions of Eusebios are more complex. The two are clearly related.[103] If we compare the Eusebion account with that of Africanus we find a number of additions,[104] some different details,[105] and a significant number of instances where conscious condensation has taken place.[106] *In nuce*, Eusebios gives fewer names but more information than Africanus.[107] Since the text of Eusebios is more openly edited, I have used the account of Africanus as my base, but have not excluded the additional information in Eusebios unless it is clearly secondary in nature.

2. *Content*. With these *caveats* in mind we may now offer a basic reconstruction of Manethon's text. T 8a tells us that Manethon "in drei Abschnitten verfasst hat die Geschichten von den Göttern und von den Göttersprosslingen und von den Totengeistern und von den sterblichen Königen."[108] That he in fact executed this in three books seems beyond question (T 8a,b; F 3a). The scope of his history thus covers Egypt from the beginning down to the end of Nectanebo in 341 B.C.E (T 8c,d,e).[109] We are even fortunate enough

---

to be his statement. The cross-references to the taking of Jerusalem by Neachao (26th D.) and the flight of the Jews to Egypt under Ouaphris (26th D.) when Jerusalem fell should also be attributed to Africanus. The verbatim repetition of these last two by Eusebios may indicate that Eusebios knew Africanus' work. I will discuss the non-biblical references below.

[103] Compare, for example, the wording for the second dynasty, the fourth through the sixth, and the ninth over against the account of Africanus.

[104] E.g., Memes (1st D.) goes on a campaign (F 3a and b), under Memphses (1st D.) many extraordinary events occurred (F 3a and b), he notes the physical size of Sesotris (12th D.) (F 3a and b), Armais (18th D.) is said to have ruled over the Argives (F 3a and b [Cf. also 3c and 6]), Ramesses (18th D.) is identified as Egyptos (F 3a, b, c), and Psammouthis (26th D.) is also known as Psametichos (F 3a, b, c).

[105] Thouoris (19th D.) is called Ἀλκάνδρας ἀνήρ by Africanus and "ein Mann sehnenarmig, mächtig" by Eusebios in F 3a.

[106] Examples include the omission of the 4th-6th and 9th kings of the second dynasty, the 3rd-8th in the third, the discussion of only Souphis in the 4th dynasty although Africanus lists eight and Eusebios says there are seventeen, the inclusion of only the 1st and 4th of 31 in the fifth (= sixth in Africanus who only has six rulers) dynasty, the reduction to Nitokris only in the sixth dynasty, the summary reduction of the last three kings of the twelfth dynasty, and the complete summary reduction of the fifteenth dynasty.

[107] Synkellos made the following observation about Eusebios' tendencies: σημειωτέον, ὁπόσον ὁ Εὐσέβιος Ἀφρικανοῦ λείπεται ἀκριβείας ἔν τε τῇ τῶν βασιλέων ποσότητι καὶ ταῖς τῶν ὀνομάτων ὑφαιρέσεσι καὶ τοῖς χρόνοις, σχεδὸν τὰ Ἀφρικανοῦ αὐταῖς λέξεσι γράφων (F 3b after the fifth dynasty).

[108] T 9 indicates a similar coverage, πᾶσαν . . . τὴν Αἰγυπτιακὴν ἱστορίαν . . . ἰδίως τε τὰ περὶ τῆς κατ' αὐτοὺς θεολογίας.

[109] M.B. Rowton, "Manetho's Date for Ramesses II," *Journal for Egyptian*

to have the book divisions in the epitome. We may therefore reconstruct the basic outline as follows:

Book One: 1. Gods (FF 3a, 4, 5)
             2. Demi-gods (FF 3a, 4)
             3. Spirits of the dead (F 3a)
             4. Dynasties 1-11 (FF 2, 3a, 3b)
Book Two: 1. Dynasties 12-19 (FF 2, 3a, 3b)
Book Three: 1. Dynasties 20-30 (FF 2, 3a, 3b, 3c)

As we have already indicated, most of the material is very brief in
our summaries. There is very little on the gods, demi-gods, and
spirits of the dead who ruled Egypt. The dynasties consist of either
a brief summary notice of the dynasty as a whole or lists of the kings
in the individual dynasty.[110] When the kings are listed, the list
principally consists of noting their length of reign. However, in
some instances details are also offered. The following chart denotes
their frequency.

	Length of Reign Only	Details
Book One	35	16
Book Two	27	8
Book Three	39	6
Totals	101	30

While the 3:1 ratio suggests that we are mainly looking at lists, the
number of details does support our contention that Manethon's
work was a narrative as the excerpts from Josephos imply. The most
common detail is significantly θαύματα.[111] Closely associated with

---

Archaeology 34 (1948): 58-59, pointed out that although the Persian conquest took
place in 343 B.C.E., Manethon assigns Nectanebo 18 years instead of 16. His sixteenth was in 343 since the Apis bull of 17 years which died in 329 was born in the
fourteenth year of Nectanebo and the epitomator gives nine and not eleven years
until the Greek conquest in 332.

[110] Eighteen of the dynasties have lists of rulers. Book one: 1, 2, 3, 4, 5, 6; book
two: 12, 15, 18, 19; book three: 21, 22, 23, 25, 26, 27, 29, 30. The remaining twelve
are merely summarized. Book one: 7, 8, 9, 10, 11; book two: 13, 14, 16, 17; book
three: 20, 24, 28.

[111] Book one: under Nephercheres (2nd D.) the Nile flowed with honey for
eleven days; the immense size of Sesochris (2nd D.) is noted; and the beauty and
nobility of Nitokris (6th D.) are duly recorded. In book two Amenophis (18th D.)
becomes a speaking stone and in book three under Bonchoris (23rd D.) a lamb
spoke. Cf. also Memphses (1st D.) under whom many extraordinary events were
said to have occurred according to Eusebios (F 3a and b).

this is the inclusion of the building projects of the numerous rulers.[112] Other information covers important political events which relate Egypt to the outside world,[113] the violent deaths of the kings,[114] and natural disasters.[115] There are occasional notices about the rulers themselves such as family relations,[116] writings by the king,[117] their age when it is highly unusual,[118] and the naming of a nome after the king.[119] *Nomoi* are conspicuously few.[120] There are several possible occasions when Manethon linked Egypt to Greece.[121] Other possible comments

---

[112] Athothis (1st D.), Ouenephes (1st D.), Souphis (4th D.), Nitokris (6th D.), and Lamares (12th D.).

[113] Under Necherophes (3rd D.) Libya revolted; Sesostris (12th D.) marched victoriously through Asia and Europe as far as Thrace; and under Kambyses (27th), the Persians took over. According to Eusebios (F 3a and b) Memes (1st D.) also went on a campaign.

[114] Menes (1st D.) by a hippo, Othoes (6th D.) by his bodyguard, Achthoes (9th D.) was consumed by a crocodile, and Ammanemes (12th D.) was assassinated by his eunuchs.

[115] These are recorded under Ouenephes (1st D.), Semempses (1st D.), and Boethos (2nd D.).

[116] Sesonchosis (12th D.), Skemiophris (12th D.), and Sebichos (25th D.).

[117] It can not be accidental that both Athothis (1st D.) and Tosorthros (3rd D.) were interested in medicine. Manethon himself had an interest in the subject (T 13).

[118] Phiops (6th D.) who began ruling when he was six and died when he was 100.

[119] Saites (15th D.).

[120] Under Kaiechos (2nd D.) the worship of Apis, Mneuis, and the Mendesian goat began. The right of women to rule was decided while Binothris (2nd D.) reigned. Finally, it is possible that Sabakon's (25th D.) burning of Bochchoris reflects a *nomos*. See Waddell, *Manetho*, pp. 166-167 n. 2.

[121] Osorcho (23rd D.) is called Herakles. Thrice rulers are connected with key events in the Greek world. Misphragmouthosis (18th D.) is linked with the flood of Deukalion. Thouoris (19th D.) is associated with the fall of Troy. This appears to be authentic since Manethon assigns it to 1198-1191. There were two basic dates for the fall of Troy which circulated in the Greek world: Timaios placed it at 1193 and Eratosthenes at 1183. The latter date became the standard figure. Rowton, "Manethon's Date for Ramesses II," p. 62, pointed out that the compiler would have most likely used the date of Eratosthenes rather than the earlier date. The third example is probably not authentic. Africanus connects Petoubates (23rd D.) with the celebration of the first Olympic festival. This is due not to Manethon but Africanus since only Africanus makes the association (made nowhere else in Manethon) and he is known to have employed the Olympiads for dating purposes. See Gelzer, *Sextus Julius Africanus*, pp. 167-169 and Mosshammer, *The "Chronicle" of Eusebius*, pp. 154-157. Eusebios also has a couple of references to the Greek world omitted by Africanus. He identifies Armais (28th D.) with Danaos and tells us that he fled from his brother Ramesses, whom he identifies as Aigyptos, to Greece where he ruled the Argives. This is seconded by F 6 in which both Danaos and Aigyptos are said to have ruled Egypt.

do not alter our basic impression.[122]

The most detailed section we have from Manethon is his treatment of the Hyksos (FF 2, 3a, 3b, 3c, 7, 8[123]).[124] The gist of Manethon's record is fairly clear: a group of foreign rulers successfully invaded Egypt,[125] took Memphis and then built a new capital, Auaris, in the eastern Nile delta (= Tell el-Dabaa) from which they ruled Egypt. The details of his story are opaque, however, as a result of the confused state of our witnesses. Although the epitome is extremely abbreviated, it now appears likely that it offers a more reliable restatement of the details it has than does Josephos.[126]

In any case, it is now transparent that Manethon's *Aigyptiaka* is a step removed from Berossos. We have no description of the land and very little attention devoted to νόμοι apart from religious considerations. The text is entirely consumed by historical reporting. The reason for this is also known. Josephos tells us in *CA* 1.73 (= T 7a) that Manethon γέγραφεν γὰρ Ἑλλάδι φωνῇ τὴν πάτριον ἱστορίαν ἔκ τε τῶν[127] ἱερῶν, ὥς φησιν αὐτός, μεταφράσας.[128] The principle championed by Hekataios of Abdera and also applied by Berossos has now been fully utilized: only native sources are proper material.[129]

---

[122] Eusebios also tells us that Psammouthis (26th D.) is Psametichos (F 3a,b,c) and F 3c adds that Bocchoris (24th D.) gave Egypt her laws or courts and that Nechao (26th D.) is also Nechepsos.

[123] On Josephos and the Hyksos and Jews see the bibliography and summaries in Louis H. Feldman, *Josephus and Modern Scholarship (1937-1980)* (Berlin/New York: Walter de Gruyter, 1984), pp. 157-161.

[124] On the Hyksos see John Van Seters, *The Hyksos* (New Haven/London: Yale University Press, 1966) and the recent summary of James M. Weinstein in *Harper's Bible Dictionary*, s.v. "Hyksos," p. 413.

[125] The Egyptians called them *Heqau khasut*, "rulers of foreign hill-countries." They were at least partially Semitic. In our fragments they are called ποιμένες.

[126] So Van Seters, *The Hyksos*, pp. 121-126 and Donald B. Redford, *History and Chronology of the Eighteenth Dynasty of Egypt: Seven Studies*. Near and Middle East Series 3 (University of Toronto Press, 1967), pp. 41-46, who points out that while Apophis is fourth in Josephos, he is sixth in Africanus. Since the second Kamose stela demonstrates that he was an enemy of Kamose at the beginning of the eighteenth dynasty, he must have reigned at the end of the seventeenth.

[127] There is a question about τε τῶν here. I have followed the text of Niese's *editio major*. Jacoby supplies γραμμάτων after ἱερῶν. Gutschmid suggested that τε τῶν should be δέλτων which is printed by Thackeray in the Loeb edition. In any case the sense is unaffected.

[128] Cf. also TT 7b,c and 9.

[129] On his possible sources see Laqueur, *RE*, s.v. "Manethon," 14: 1091-1099; Waddell, *Manetho*, pp. xx-xiv; and Helck, *KP*, 3: 952, who suggests that

When Hekataios and Berossos applied this principle they also attacked Greek authors who did not use native sources. Manethon is no exception. In particular, he singled out Herodotos. The statement from Josephos which we have just quoted continues: καὶ πολλὰ τὸν Ἡρόδοτον ἐλέγχει τῶν Αἰγυπτιακῶν ὑπ᾽ ἀγνοίας ἐψευσμένον. His criticism was extensive enough that he was credited with a book against Herodotos.[130] In the *Aigyptiaka* he mentions Herodotos twice. Manethon tells us that Herodotos called Menes (1st D.) Min.[131] A more pointed observation takes place in the fourth dynasty when Manethon tells us that Souphis erected the great pyramid, not Cheops as Herodotos says.[132] These specific references do not, however, exhaust Manethon's use of Herodotos. As we will see, Manethon may have known Herodotos' record of Sethos' campaign even though he does not mention him directly.[133] The principle which appears to have controlled Manethon's references is whether or not he is critiquing them. When he openly corrects Herodotos he mentions him; when, on the other hand, he follows the account of his Ionian predecessor, he adroitly omits his name. How extensive was his familiarity? O. Kimball Armayor has recently argued that Herodotos' account served as the foundation for Manethon.[134] While the similarities which he has adduced are

---

for the first four dynasties, Manethon used Datenliste (i.e., annals in which the most important events of the year were recorded); from the fifth dynasty on he employed king-lists; and he also used the historical reports which were available from the time of the Middle Kingdom.

[130] F 13 (= Eustanthius, *Hom. "Il."* 9. 480). Jacoby, *FGrH*, 3c: 98, treats this as a separate work. This is also accepted by Arnaldo Momigliano, "The Place of Herodotus in the History of Historiography," *History* 43 (1958)1: 13, which is reprinted in his *Studies in Historiography* (London: Weidenfeld and Nicolson, 1966), pp. 127-142. See p. 133. However see n. 256.

[131] Cf. Herodotos 2.4.2; 2.99.1-3. The mention of Herodotos is only recorded in Eusebios. Africanus has no notice.

[132] Cf. Herodotos 2.124-125. The reference to Herodotos here is recorded by both Africanus and Eusebios.

[133] F 9. See Herodotos 2.102-110. On Manethon's dependence see Lloyd, *Herodotus: Book II*, pp. 110-111.

[134] O. Kimball Armayor, "Herodotus' Influence on Manethon and the Implications for Egyptology," *The Classical Bulletin* 61 (1985): 7-11. Armayor goes so far as to claim that Manethon did not use native sources, but that his work is Greek in source and authority. This goes too far in my judgment. Manethon's work is too similar in its orientation to Berossos' and too different from Herodotos' to make this statement.

impressive, we need to ask if it is possible for Herodotos to have obtained his information from the priests as he claimed and whether the similarities might not be due to a common source, i.e., the native records. We may at least say that Manethon is aware of and reacting to Herodotos.

What about Manethon's other and more immediate predecessor, Hekataios? That both commented on the same matters is undeniable.[135] However, the relationship goes well beyond common topics. Manethon's account of Sesostris' campaign is indebted to Hekataios as the synopsis on pp. 129-131 will demonstrate.

A reading of these texts reveals the general agreement among the three authors. The major differences among them are as follows. Herodotos and Hekataios both record the presence of the inscription which Manethon omits. Hekataios has a couple of details which the other two do not: he alone mentions the Kykades and explains why the campaign terminated in Thrace. Manethon changes the order of the reason for the stelae by placing it prior to the specific forms whereas Herodotos and Hekataios interpret the meaning of the genitalia after mentioning them. Hekataios and Manethon provide some details which are not included in Herodotos: both mention the length of the campaign as nine years, both relate the extent of the march prior to their discussion of the stelae while Herodotos notes it afterwards, and they both include a specific reference to male genitals as well as female whereas Herodotos only alludes to the female.

What should we make of this? First, it is clear that Manethon knew and used Hekataios. Everything in Manethon has a counterpart in Hekataios. It appears that Manethon's version is simply a condensed recapitulation of Hekataios. This is reinforced by both their general agreements over against Herodotos and by verbal echoes. The latter is particularly sharp in the account of the stelae. Second, Hekataios knew and used Herodotos. Third, it is also likely that Manethon knew Herodotos. If we ask whether he knew him directly or only indirectly through Hekataios, the answer must be

---

[135] F 18 (= Eusebios, *P.E.* 3.2.6) records Manethon's connections between Egyptian and Greek gods. At the end of the passage, Eusebios astutely noted: γράφει δὲ καὶ τὰ περὶ τούτων πλατύτερον μὲν ὁ Μανεθῶς, ἐπιτετμημένως δὲ ὁ Διόδωρος ἐν τῇ προλεχθείσῃ αὐτοῦ γραφῇ . . . Cf. Diodoros 1.11-13. This section from Diodoros could stem from Poseidonios. Even if it does in its present form, it is likely that Hekataios had some similar treatment and that Diodoros has replaced it. F 19 offers different interpretations of Ἀμοῦν by Hekataios and Manethon.

Herodotos 2.102.3-103.1	Hekataios (D.S. 1.55.6-8)	Manethon F2
		Σέσωστρις ἔτη μη̄,
3 κατὰ τῶν ἱερῶν τὴν φάτιν στρατιὴν πολλὴν (τῶν) λαβὼν ἤλαυνε διὰ τῆς ἠπείρου,	6 Ὅμοιως δὲ καὶ τὴν λοιπὴν Ἀσίαν ἅπασαν ὑπήκοον ἐποιήσατο	ὃς ἅπασαν ἐχειρώσατο τὴν Ἀσίαν
πᾶν ἔθνος τὸ ἐμποδὼν καταστρεφόμενος.	(Cf. 10 συντελέσας τὴν στρατείαν ἐν ἔτεσιν ἐννέα) καὶ τῶν Κυκλάδων νήσων τὰς πλείους. διαβὰς δ᾽ εἰς τὴν Εὐρώπην καὶ διεξιὼν ἅπασαν τὴν Θρᾴκην ἐκινδύνευσεν ἀποβαλεῖν τὴν δύναμιν διὰ σπάνιν τροφῆς καὶ τόπων δυσχωρίας.	ἐν ἐνιαυτοῖς ἐννέα
	7 διόπερ ὅρια τῆς στρατείας ποιησάμενος ἐν τῇ Θρᾴκῃ, στήλας κατεσκεύασεν ἐν πολλοῖς τόποις τῶν ὑπ᾽ αὐτοῦ κατακτηθέντων.	καὶ τῆς Εὐρώπης τὰ μέχρι Θρᾴκης,
		πανταχόσε μνημόσυνα ἐγείρας
4 ὅτεοισι μὲν νῦν αὐτῶν ἀλκίμοισι ἐνετύγχανε καὶ δεινῶς γλιχομένοισι (περὶ) τῆς ἐλευθερίης, τούτοισι μὲν στήλας ἐνίστη ἐς τὰς χώρας		τῆς τῶν ἐθνῶν σχέσεως,

Herodotos 2.102.3-103.1	Hekataios (D.S. 1.55.6-8)	Manethon F2
διὰ γραμμάτων λεγούσας	αὗται δὲ τὴν ἐπιγραφὴν εἶχον Αἰγυπτίοις γράμμασι τοῖς ἱεροῖς λεγομένοις, Τήνδε τὴν χώραν ὅπλοις κατεστρέψατο τοῖς ἑαυτοῦ Βασιλεὺς Βασιλέων καὶ δεσπότης δεσποτῶν Σεσόωσις.	
τό τε ἑωυτοῦ οὔνομα καὶ τῆς πάτρης καὶ ὡς δυνάμι τῇ ἑωυτοῦ κατεστρέψατό σφεας·		
5 ὅτεων δὲ ἀμαχητὶ καὶ εὐπετέως παρέλαβε τὰς πόλιας, τούτοισι δὲ ἐνέγραφε ἐν τῇσι στήλῃσι κατὰ ταὐτὰ καὶ τοῖς ἀνδρηίοισι τῶν ἐθνέων γενομένοισι καὶ δὴ καὶ αἰδοῖα γυναικὸς προσενέγραφε, δῆλα βουλόμενος ποιέειν ὡς εἴησαν ἀνάλκιδες.	8 τὴν δὲ στήλην κατεσκεύασεν ἔχουσαν αἰδοῖον ἐν μὲν τοῖς μαχίμοις ἔθνεσιν ἀνδρός, ἐν δὲ τοῖς ἀγεννέσι καὶ δειλοῖς	ἐπὶ μὲν τοῖς γενναίοις ἀνδρῶν, ἐπὶ δὲ τοῖς ἀγεννέσι
	γυναικὸς	γυναικῶν μόρια ταῖς στήλαις ἐγχαράσσων . . . .
	ἀπὸ τοῦ κυριωτέρου μέρους τὴν διάθεσιν τῆς ἑκάστων ψυχῆς φανερωτάτην τοῖς ἐπιγινομένοις ἔσεσθαι νομίζων.	

Herodotos 2.102.3-103.1	Hekataios (D.S. 1.55.6-8)	Manethon F2
1 ταῦτα δὲ ποιέων διεξῆιε τὴν ἤπειρον, ἐς ὃ ἐκ τῆς Ἀσίης ἐς τὴν Εὐρώπην διαβὰς τούς τε Σκύθας κατεστρέψατο καὶ τοὺς Θρήικας. ἐς τούτους δέ μοι δοκέει καὶ προσώτατα ἀπικέσθαι ὁ Αἰγύπτιος στρατός. ἐν μὲν γὰρ τῇ τούτων χώρῃ φαίνονται σταθεῖσαι (αἱ) στῆλαι, τὸ δὲ προσωτέρω τούτων οὐκέτι.		

that he was acquainted with him directly. This is not evident in our text—which actually raises the other possibility—but must be the case based upon our observations above.

3. *Form*. It is difficult—if not impossible—to consider Manethon's work an ethnography. While he clearly stands in the tradition of Herodotos and Hekataios, he swerves so far from the former in form that we are clearly dealing with a second generation offspring. What we have is an expansion of the historical section of Herodotos and Hekataios based upon native sources.

The form which this takes is somewhat symmetrical. As we have seen in our reconstruction, there are three books—a feature which may directly echo Berossos. Interestingly, there are three groups of mythical rulers (gods, demigods, and the spirits of the dead) prior to the rehearsal of the dynasties which are subdivided into three books. Synkellos suggests that the analogy goes further: he says that there were thirty dynasties of gods, demigods, and spirits of the dead.[136] If that is so, then Manethon attempted to offer a balance between the prehistorical figures and the historical. The most important structural device which he employed for the kings is that he appears to have grouped them into dynasties (T 10), a device which is still with us.[137] The fact that the thirty dynasties are somewhat arbitrary, may be due to his structural procedure.

Manethon deviates from native Egyptian material most in his comments on the gods. Here we find Greek names standing side-by-side with Egyptian indicating that his role in the establishment of the cult of Sarapis was not the only occasion in which he attempted to merge native and foreign religious traditions. The same effort appears in his identification of the five planets with Egyptian appellations (F 5).

---

[136] See F 2 in Waddell, *Manetho*, p. 10: Μετὰ δὲ ταῦτα καὶ περὶ ἐθνῶν Αἰγυπτιακῶν πέντε ἐν τριάκοντα δυναστείαις ἱστορεῖ τῶν λεγομένων παρ' αὐτοῖς θεῶν καὶ ἡμιθέων καὶ νεκύων καὶ θνητῶν . . . I must admit that I am somewhat bothered by the fact that the thirty are not as apparent in the fragments as the thirty dynasties of human rulers are.

[137] Manethon's divisions are not always accurate; however, his system is too entrenched to be displaced. So James Henry Breasted, *A History of Egypt: From the Earliest Times to the Persian Conquest*, 2nd ed. (New York: Charles Scribner's Sons, 1909), pp. 13-14, who is echoed by Sir Alan Gardiner, *Egypt of the Pharaohs* (London/Oxford/New York: Oxford University Press, 1961), p. 46. Gardiner provides a king list including Manethon, the king lists, and monuments on pp. 429-453.

The consequences of these shifts should not be overlooked. Why did Manethon not relate an Egyptian theogony and cosmogony? Berossos certainly did.[138] The emphasis in the text is squarely on historical Egypt. Was this due to a rationalistic perspective on the part of Manethon or is it simply due to his effort to present the royal traditions which had been of interest since the days of Hekataios of Miletos?

4. *Function*. In order to answer this, we need to examine how the text functions. Synkellos captured the overwhelming impression τοῦ τε Βηρώσσου καὶ τοῦ Μανεθῶ τὸ ἴδιον ἔθνος θελόντων δοξάσαι τοῦ μὲν τῶν Χαλδαίων, τοῦ δὲ τὸ τῶν Αἰγυπτίων (T 11c. Cf. also 11d). Manethon glorified his homeland by stressing its antiquity (FF 3a and 4). Nor was the emphasis innocent. Even the otherwise dull scribe who worked from Africanus in composing the *Excerpta Latina Barbari* saw this as he began recounting Manethon's history: Egyptiorum regnum invenimus vetustissimum omnium regnorum (F 4). So Manethon notes some significant discoveries—although not with the thoroughness of other writers.[139] As with Hekataios, Megasthenes, and Berossos, he manages to make it evident that Greece is dependent upon his *patria*.[140] The key to proving this for Manethon lay in the great antiquity of Egypt, an antiquity which could be demonstrated in her royal records. For this reason he accentuated them.

Why should he feel the need for doing this? Synkellos preserves a tradition which suggests that Manethon dedicated his work to Ptolemy Philadelphos.[141] This would match the pattern which had developed with Hekataios, Megasthenes, and Berossos. Was Manethon answering Berossos?[142] Once again we encounter the same set

---

[138] For examples of Egyptian texts relating creation see *ANET*, 1: 3-10.

[139] Hephaistos discovered fire (F 3a) and Tosorthros discovered the art of building [Note: There is a problem here. On the text see the emendation of Sethe in Waddell, *Manetho*, p. 40 and n. 4 on p. 41.]. Cf. also Bocchoris (24th D.) who Aegyptiis iura constitiut (F 3c = Book of Sothis).

[140] So Armais (18th D.) settles Argos (F 3a). Nor does Manethon miss the opportunity of locating Greek heroes first in Egypt, e.g., Danaos (F 6. Cf. also F 9).

[141] TT 11 and 12. There are some problems with the authenticity of the details in these statements since they are linked with the book of Sothis. The letter in 12 is spurious. The issue is whether it preserves some facts. On Ptolemy see *RE*, s.v. "Ptolemaios II. Philadelphos," by Hans Volkmann, 23: 1645-1666.

[142] That the two are related has been argued by Laqueur, *RE*, s.v. "Manethon," 14: 1063-1064 and Waddell, *Manetho*, pp. viii and x. Synkellos thought that Manethon wrote after Berossos (T 11b. Cf. also 11c). Based on the placement after

of circumstances as we had with Hekataios and Berossos. The only evidence for a historical connection is indirect: their geographical and chronological proximity and general methodology. This makes a connection a possibility but does not establish it. What the works do prove is the competitive milieu in which both authors lived. It is not necessary to argue that Manethon was commissioned to make his claims for Egypt, since his own native pride is a sufficient motive.

Significance

Manethon thus stands as another representative of the indigenous response to Hellenism. His work is more significant for this than for its value as a source of Egyptian history.[143] With him the movement from Greek ethnography and its form to native traditions has been completed. Later authors will follow his lead and dispense with what does not easily fit into their own material. He is also a witness of the inter-rivalry which developed among the indigenous peoples themselves.

In fact, it is for the latter that Manethon is principally remembered today. In *CA* 1.223-253 (= F 10) Josephos relates what he claims is the Egyptian gossip about the origins of the Jews as told by Manethon. The story runs as follows: Amenophis, the Egyptian ruler, had a desire to see the gods. His namesake advised him to remove all the lepers and ill of the land (230-233). He therefore consigned them to the quarries, but so feared the wrath of the gods for this injustice that he committed suicide (234-236). After a period of time, the lepers requested the former Hyksos city of Auaris which they were given (237). With their own city, they also appointed their own leader, Osarsephos (238) who established anti-Egyptian laws (240) and made preparations for a revolt against the Egyptians (240-245). When the Egyptians realized what had taken place, they fled to Ethiopia (246-247). Left to themselves the lepers behaved abominably (248-250). Finally, the Egyptians staged a return under Amenophis and Rampses and expelled the lepers to Syria (251).

While some of the details have likely been embellished with the

---

Berossos, Murray suggested that Manethon may have mentioned Berossos in his text. "Herodotus and Hellenistic Culture," p. 209.

[143] Gardiner, *Egypt of the Pharaohs*, pp. 46-47, 61-62, has pointed out that Manethon can not be relied upon too heavily. He was attacked for falsehoods in antiquity (TT 10 and 11).

passing of time and the handing on of the tradition, it is clear that
Manethon had a less than savory opinion of the residents of Syria.
Although I am reluctant to apply the term anti-Semite to Manethon,[144] the material which first circulated under his name would
later come to be used by those whose vituperation may be so
labeled.[145] Nor would his calumnies go unnoticed by those whom
he inveighed against.

SUMMARY

The principal informants for ethnographers were native priests. In
the earlier period of ethnography, the travelers returned to the West
and delivered their accounts far from their sources. Following the
conquests of Alexander, the Greeks came to stay and wrote their accounts in their adopted countries. The proximity of the priests and
their ability to understand the accounts as they became Hellenized
provoked responses. The first two of these which have come down
to us are the *Babyloniaka* of Berossos and the *Aigyptiaka* of Manethon.
That these two priests offered indigenous corrections to the presentations of their respective peoples in the Greek ethnographic tradition is clear from their strictures on Greek authors, their rejection
of the methods of Greek ethnographic investigation, and their defensive posture towards the Greeks. The key element in their presentations was their own native records which provided both a different
methodological stance and proof of their antiquity. Combining
these in chronological sequence they created complete stories of their
illustrious cultures. Their accounts were as new to their own cultures
as they were to the Greeks.

Paradoxically, the new form of historiography also identified with

---

[144] On the problems associated with the term see J.N. Sevenster, *The Roots of Pagan Anti-Semitism in the Ancient World.* NovTSup 41 (Leiden: E.J. Brill, 1975), pp. 1-4. Perhaps the best definition is that of M. Simon cited on pp. 4-5: "une attitude fondamentalement et systématiquement hostile aux Juifs, fondée par surcroît sur des mauvaises raisons, sur des calomnies, sur une image incomplète, partiale ou fausse de la réalité."

[145] On the issue of Manethon and anti-Semitism see *ibid.*, pp. 184-188 and John G. Gager, *The Origins of Anti-Semitism: Attitudes Toward Judaism in Pagan and Christian Antiquity* (New York/Oxford: Oxford University Press, 1983), pp. 42-43. A convenient collection of pagan texts which relate the origins of the Jews may be found in Molly Whittaker, *Jews & Christians: Graeco-Roman Views.* Cambridge Commentaries on Writings of the Jewish & Christian World 200 BC to AD 200 6 (Cambridge: Cambridge University Press, 1984), pp. 35-55.

Hellenism. The fact that these writers "translated" their texts into Greek demonstrates a recognition and acceptance of Hellenism. Even though their records dictated the contents of what they wrote, their indebtedness to ethnography is evident: they continued to tell the story of a specific people (content), using some of the same categories (form), in an attempt to replace faulty understandings of who they were by tendering a self-definition (function).

The tension this created between nationalism and Hellenism was solved by claiming that the Greeks were their heirs and debtors. It was at this point that the issue of anteriority and/or antiquity entered the arena. Both Berossos and Manethon placed their civilizations in the remotest past, making them either explicitly or implicitly the mother of culture. In this way they both maintained pride in their native culture and opened themselves up to Hellenism.

It was this marriage of Hellenism and native Near Eastern traditions which gave birth to a new genre, apologetic historiography.

CHAPTER FIVE

THE HELLENISTIC JEWISH HISTORIANS

"For what is Plato except Moses
speaking in Attic?"
Numenios[1]

The largest literary corpus which we have that reflects the attempt
of an ethnic group to present its own story within the Hellenistic
world is Jewish.[2] Jewish contacts with Greeks go back well beyond
the Hellenistic world itself.[3] The Hebrew Bible appears to begin
referring to the Greeks in late seventh century and exilic texts.[4] The

---

[1] Cited first by Clement, *Strom.* 1.22.150.4. Cf. also Eusebios, *PE* 9.6.9 and
11.10.14. All references to Clement are from Otto Stählin, Ludwig Früchtel, and
Ursula Treu, eds. *Clemens Alexandrinus*, 3 vols. GCS (Berlin: Akademie Verlag,
1985 and 1970), vols. 2-3. References to Eusebios are from Karl Mras, ed. *Die
Praeparatio Evangelica*, 2 vols. GCS (Berlin: Akademie Verlag, 1982-1983. On the
saying see Gager, *Moses and Greco-Roman Paganism*, pp. 66-69.
[2] There are certainly other examples. One of the most significant is Quintus
Fabius Pictor (*FGrH* 809) who wrote the first history of Rome in Greek tracing Roman history from its alleged connections to Aeneas down to the Punic wars of his
own time. That he wanted to justify and glorify Rome is clear from the strictures
of Polybios 1.14; 3.9.1-5. Arnaldo Momigliano, *Alien Wisdom*, p. 92, classifies him
with Berossos and Manethon. Fornara, *The Nature of History in Ancient Greece and
Rome*, pp. 39-41, questions this by pointing out the differences in basic orientation,
i.e., Fabius' work was primarily oriented to the present (a large part deals with the
Punic wars), whereas the priests from the Orient were primarily oriented to the
past. The difference—in my opinion—is more apparent than real. All belong to the
same genre (Fabius' work also gave consideration to Rome's origins). The
common ground is that they all presented their own accounts because each—to borrow the words of Fornara about Fabius—"was proud of his people and desired to
parade its greatness before the international community." *Ibid.*, p. 41. The audience of the Roman is not as certain as that of the priests: it could have been addressed to Romans. The difference in audience would not, however, preclude its
presence in apologetic historiography as I argue in this chapter. Pilhofer, *Presbyteron .
Kreitton*, pp. 84-90, emphasizes the apologetic nature of his work.
[3] Cf. Momigliano, *Alien Wisdom*, pp. 74-81, for a summary of the evidence
from both Jewish and Greek perspectives.
[4] There are two terms for Greeks in the Hebrew bible: יָוָן is found 11t. in Gen.
10:2,4; Is. 66:19; Ez. 27:13,19; Zech. 9:13; Dn. 8:21; 10:20; 11:2 and I Chr. 1:5,7.
כִּתִּים appears in Gen. 10:4; Num. 24:24; Isa. 23:1,12; Jer. 2:10; Ezek. 27:6; Dan.
11:30 and I Chr. 1:7. We should also mention the important gentilic יְוָנִי in Joel
4:6. The earliest evidence therefore consists of Gen. 10:2,4; Num. 24:24; Jer. 2:10;
and Ezek. 27:13,19. The other texts are either clearly post-exilic or arguably so.

priestly author of the Pentateuch mentions the Greeks in his impressive ethnographic account which we have come to call "the Table
of Nations." Among the sons of Japheth listed in Gen. 10:2 we find
יון whose sons are in turn given in v. 4 as אלישה תרשיש כתים
ודדנים. While all four of these names refer to cities or islands in the
Aegean and Mediterranean area, the most significant is כתים.
Originally the word referred to a colony of Tyre on Cyprus which
is כת in the Phoenician inscriptions and Κιτιον in Greek.[5] Here it
may refer to either the city or by metonymy the entire island.[6] In
either case, the term יון must refer to the Ionians in general and
כתים to a particular group. Where the priestly author derived his information is open to debate, but it is clear that he knew of the
Greeks.[7]

One incontestable source of contact between Greeks and Jews was
trading. Ezek. 27:13 and 19 refer to יון as a trading partner of
Tyre.[8] There was enough contact that Jeremiah could challenge a

---

[5] Cf. H. Donner and W. Röllig, *Kanaanäische und aramäische Inschriften*, 4th ed.
3 vols. (Wiesbaden: Otto Harrassowitz, 1962-1979), n. 46.5-6, ם, צר אם לכת/,
"Tyre, the mother of Kition," and 49.13, (3rd century inscription from stairway
of Osiris temple in Abydos, Egypt, which contains graffiti of travelers who wanted
Osiris' help in death) אנכי עבראשמן בן שלם הכתי, "I am *'bd'smn*, son of *slm*, the
Kitionite."

[6] The difficulty in being precise is that אלישה is equivalent to *alasia* of the
Amarna letters which refers to Cyprus. Efforts by recent commentators to avoid a
tautology include E.A. Speiser, *Genesis*. AB 1 (Garden City, New York: Doubleday
& Company, Inc., 1964), p. 66, who argued that Elishah denoted the island and
Kittim the city; Claus Westermann, *Genesis 1-11: A Commentary*, trans. by John J.
Scullion (Minneapolis: Augsburg Publishing House, 1984), p. 507, who considers
Kittim and Rhodanim to be appended "here from another context because it filled
out the table in this place;" and Gordon J. Wenham, *Genesis 1-15*. Word Biblical
Commentary 1 (Waco, Texas: Word Books, 1987), pp. 218-219, who suggests that
Elishah is a town on Crete and Kittim Cyprus.

[7] Robert H. Pfeiffer, "Hebrews and Greeks Before Alexander," *JBL* 56
(1937): 94, thought a Greek source provided the information since the Assyrians
and Babylonians did not know the children of Javan and there is an anti-Phoenician
bias in v. 15. Gerhard von Rad, *Genesis: A Commentary*, rev. ed. trans. by John H.
Marks. OTL (Philadelphia: The Westminster Press, 1972), p. 141, believed some
map, perhaps a neo-Babylonian world map, underlay the priestly work.

[8] The chapter may well be composite of a lament and a prose section (vs. 12-24)
as Walter Zimmerli, *Ezekiel*, 2 vols. trans. by Ronald E. Clements and James D.
Martin. Hermeneia (Philadelphia: Fortress Press, 1979-1983), 2:53-56, suggests.
It should still be regarded as exilic, however. Zimmerli dates the prose between
587-571 B.C.E. It is worth pointing out that the LXX reads Ἑλλάς in v.13 and
the Vulgate *Graecia* in vs. 13 and 19.

Judean audience to "cross over to the אִיֵּי כִתִּיִּם" and expect them to understand his reference. (Jer. 2:10) Nor are we limited to these few biblical statements.[9] Archaeologists have been finding Greek items in various sites throughout Israel for some time now: Greek coins struck in the fifth century at Gaza, Greek ware at Shechem (6th-5th centuries), and even Greek ware in fifth century Mizpah.[10] These may well indicate commercial ties. There is, however, some new evidence which suggests that contacts extended beyond commercial transactions. In the sixties, Greek ware was found at two small fortresses: Mezad Hashavyahu on the coast between Ashdod and Joppa[11] and Tel Malhata located to the SE of Arad.[12] A key which possibly explains the Greek ware in these fortresses was uncovered at Arad.[13] Among the ostraca Yohanan Aharoni found

---

[9] The texts which have been cited are the only sure literary references from the seventh and sixth centuries B.C.E. The theory of A. Marmorstein, "A Greek Lyric and a Hebrew Prophet," *JQR* 37 (1946-47): 167-173, that Alkaios, a Lesbian Lyric poet of the sixth century B.C.E. knew Isa. 5:1-6 is not convincing. The only common element is the vineyard owner's expectation that his vine would produce good grapes and the vine's production of wild or sour grapes. Such a general pattern which is common to viticulture is insufficient to establish literary dependence.

[10] Cf. D. Winton Thomas, ed., *Archaeology and Old Testament Study: Jubilee Volume of the Society for Old Testament Study 1917-1967* (Oxford: The Clarendon Press, 1967). See the articles by T.C. Mitchell, "Philistia," p. 417; G.E. Wright, "Shechem," p. 367; and D. Diringer, "Mizpah," p. 330. Summaries of the evidence for early contacts are in Salo Wittmayer Baron, *To the Beginning of the Christian Era*, 2nd ed. A Social and Religious History of the Jews 1 (Philadelphia: the Jewish Publication Society of America, 1952), pp. 183-184 and Morton Smith, *Palestinian Parties and Politics That Shaped the Old Testament* (New York/London: Columbia University Press, 1974), pp. 57-62.

[11] J. Naveh, "The Excavations at Mesad Hashavyahu: Preliminary Report," *IEJ* 12 (1962): 96-97, who dated the pottery to 630-600 B.C.E. based on the Middle Wild Goat style. He preferred to explain the presence of Greek pottery as due to Greek mercenaries in the service of Egypt since Herodotos tells us they served there (2.152,154). He did note, however, that there are "no remains whatever . . . which could point to Egyptian control of the fortress" (p. 99, n. 16). John Strange, "The Inheritance of Dan," *ST* 20 (1966): 136-139, more plausibly argued that the fortress served Josiah since there were no Egyptian interests to protect, but there are obvious ones for Judea.

[12] Cf. W.J. Dever, "Tel Malhata," *IEJ* 17 (1967): 273, who first reported the Greek pottery here at the end of the Iron age, i.e., 7th-6th centuries B.C.E.

[13] Cf. Y. Aharoni's reports: "Hebrew Ostraca from Tel Arad," *IEJ* 16 (1966): 1-7, esp. 1-5; "The Use of Hieratic Numerals in Hebrew Ostraca and the Shekel Weights," *BASOR* 184 (1966): 14-16; "Arad: Its Inscriptions and Temple," *BA* 31 (1968): 13-15; *The Archaeology of the Land of Israel: From the Prehistoric Beginnings to the End of the First Temple Period*, trans. by Anson F. Rainey (Philadelphia: The Westminster Press, 1978), p. 264; and his *Arad Inscriptions*, trans. by Judith Ben-Or (Jerusalem: The Israel Exploration Society, 1981).

there, he discovered seventeen letters in one room which were addressed to Eliashib, son of Eshyahu, which instructed him to provide
rations. In ten of these כתים are mentioned: nine times as recipients
and once as a messenger carrying provisions.[14] Who are the כתים?
While it would be possible to see them as merchants, the small
amounts suggest that the כתים are receiving rations for traveling
not business. Aharoni suggested they were "Greek or Cypriot
mercenaries serving in the Judean army, perhaps especially in garri-
sons of the more remote fortresses."[15] Apparently, Arad served as
a supply depot. The mercenaries who were stationed at fortresses
such as Mezad Hashavyahu and Tel Malhata sometimes stopped at
Arad with orders for supplies while en route to another fortress. It
is, therefore, possible that Greeks served as mercenaries in the army
of Josiah.

Yet all of these contacts hardly prepared the Jews for Alexander.
It is one thing to trade with someone or to have them serve at remote
outposts; it is an entirely different matter to have them as masters.
True, the Jews knew servitude to the Assyrians, Babylonians, and
Persians (and Egyptians) before the Macedonians; yet all of these
were Oriental cultures—Greek clearly was not. While the significance of Hellenism might not have appeared to be all that great
at first, it eventually affected Judaism more than any of her preceding conquerors.[16]

The Greeks apparently knew very little about the Jews prior to
Alexander. As we have already seen, the standard perception among
Greek intellectuals such as Hekataios of Abdera and Megasthenes
at the beginning of the Hellenistic age was that the Jews were
philosophers. Such naive generalizations rapidly give way as shoulders rub on a daily basis. The door thus stood ajar for the Jews to
define themselves within the new world. That all were not anxious

---

[14] *Ibid.*, nos. 1,2,4,5(?),7,8,10,11,14, for the Kittim as recipients and n. 17, for
the Kitti as a messenger.

[15] *Ibid.*, pp. 12-13. Aharoni has been followed by Benedikt Otzen, "Noch Einmal das Wort *TRKB* auf einem Arad-Ostracon," *VT* 20 (1970): 242; André
Lemaire, *Inscriptions Hébraïques. Tome I: Les Ostraca: Introduction, Traduction, Commentaire* (Paris: Les Éditions du Cerf, 1977), pp. 159-161; and John Bright, *A History
of Israel*, 3rd ed. (Philadelphia: The Westminster Press, 1981), p. 322, n. 33.

[16] The most significant works detailing the interaction of Jews with Greeks are
Tcherikover, *Hellenistic Civilization and the Jews*; Samuel K. Eddy, *The King is Dead*,
pp. 183-256, who saw four types of resistance to Hellenism: the passive use of
legends which venerated ancient heroes, militant wars of religion, messianism, and

to walk through this door is quite obvious.[17] On the other hand, there were a good number who gladly entered a new and larger world. It is to four representatives of the latter that we now turn.[18]

The Textual Problem

Our knowledge of Jewish historical works written in Greek in the third and second centuries B.C.E. is largely—if not completely—fragmentary.[19] Quotations from Hellenistic Jewish authors have come down to us in Eusebios,[20] Clement,[21] and Josephos.[22] All three of these derived their information from the work of the first century B.C.E. Roman savant, Alexander Polyhistor. Since the bulk of our information comes from Eusebios who in turn copied from Polyhistor, we must begin by ascertaining the extent to which they altered the works they preserved.

---

proselytism (see pp. 335-339); Hengel, *Judaism and Hellenism*; and Elias J. Bickerman, *The Jews in the Greek Age* (Cambridge/London: Harvard University Press, 1988).

[17] It is interesting to note that in some Jewish circles the Hebrew terms for Greeks became synonyms for Israel's enemies. For example, OT texts which were composed in the Hellenistic period, Zech. 9:13; Dn. 8:21; 10:20; 11:2, all use יון to denote the Greeks as Israel's enemies as the translators of both the LXX and Vulgate correctly understood. (Note also the use in 4QpNah 1.2 where מלך יון refers to the Seleucids.) The extension of the term כתים to refer to an enemy of Israel without reference to Greeks is attested by Dan. 11:30 and 1QpHab. The LXX and Vulgate render the former by 'Ρωμαῖοι and *Romani* respectively. In three instances the LXX adds a reference to the Greeks as enemies of Israel: Isa. 9:11 "Ελληνας for ופלשתים; Jer. 26:16 (46:16 MT) where the translators substituted 'Ελληνικῆς for an equivalent of the Hebrew feminine participle יונה (= be violent, oppressive) in the phrase "because of the oppressive sword" (it is possible that they read the gentilic היוניה); and Jer. 27:16 (50:16 MT) where the same phrase appears.

[18] I have chosen Demetrios, Artapanos, Pseudo-Eupolemos, and Eupolemos for two reasons. First, the material which has come down to us from them is the most substantial which we have from incontestably Jewish or Samaritan sources. Second, they represent a cross-section of Egypt (Demetrios and Artapanos) and Palestine (Pseudo-Eupolemos and Eupolemos).

[19] The major exception would be II Maccabees which epitomized the five-volume history of Jason of Cyrene (presumably written in Greek). II Maccabees was written prior to 63 B.C.E. when Pompey annexed Judea since Rome is viewed in positive terms. It was probably composed in the first part of the first century B.C.E. and belongs to a different literary genre of historiography since it covers a period of only twenty or so years, 180-161 B.C.E.

[20] *PE* 9.17-39.

[21] *Strom.* 1.21.130; 1.21.141; 1.23.153-156.

[22] *AJ* 1.240. Cf. also *CA* 1.218. Josephos' relationship to Polyhistor will be discussed in the next chapter.

Eusebios

Eusebios quotes extensively from Polyhistor in the ninth book of his *Praeparatio Evangelica*. The two issues which we must raise are: how accurately has he quoted his sources and how fully. J. Freudenthal addressed the first of these and demonstrated that Eusebios carefully copied his sources.[23] In fact, there are only six occasions in which we know that Eusebios incorrectly referred to a work in the entire *PE*.[24] In terms of the wording of the quotations, Freudenthal has shown that deviations—which appear to be few—are only minor matters which do not affect the meaning of the text.[25] The second issue is more difficult. We know that Eusebios condensed Polyhistor since in five instances he breaks off a quote with an editorial comment which makes it clear that he has omitted some of his *Vorlage*.[26] What we do not know is how much he elided. The fact that there are forty-five pages in Mras' edition of Eusebios which are directly attributable to Polyhistor leads me to conclude that Eusebios has preserved the bulk of his predecessor.

Eusebios openly states the contents of his ninth book in his preface (ch. 1). He is going to present witnesses to the piety and history of the Jewish people.[27] He clearly marks the structure of this

---

[23] In spite of its age, Freudenthal's work has not been superseded on this matter. *Alexander Polyhistor und die von ihm erhaltenen Reste judäischer und samaritanischer Geschichtswerke*. Hellenistische Studien, Heft 1 & 2 (Breslau: H. Skutsch, 1875), pp. 3-16. André Pelletier, *Lettre d'Aristée à Philocrate*. Sources Chrétiennes 89 (Paris: Les Éditions du Cerf, 1962), pp. 22-41, has established Eusebios' reliability for his transmission of the Letter of Aristeas in *PE* 8.2-5; 9.38.

[24] Listed by Mras, *Praeparatio Evangelica*, 1:LV.

[25] Freudenthal, *Alexander Polyhistor*, p. 9, distinguishes between texts Eusebios condenses himself where he is more liable to make mistakes and those which he simply selects and reproduces. Of the latter his conclusion still stands, p. 11: "Wo er blosse Abschriften liefert, da verändert er seine Vorlagen fast nie oder doch nur in unbedeutendem Maasse, und auch die tiefgreifenden Veränderungen, welche er in verschwindend wenigen Fällen . . . sich erlaubt hat, sind nicht tendenziöser Art und lassen den Sinn und den Gesammtgehalt der Quellen fast gänzlich unversehrt." He has been followed by Denis, *Introduction aux Pseudépigraphes Grecs d'Ancien Testament*, pp. 242-244; Walter, *JSHRZ*, 1:93 and Mras, *Praeparatio Evagelica*, 1:LV-LVIII. This would appear to justify Eusebios' initial introduction of Polyhistor: ἱστορεῖ κατὰ λέξιν τὸν τρόπον. (9.17.1)

[26] *PE* 9.19.4: οἷς μεθ' ἕτερα ἐπιφέρει λέγων; 9.29.12: τούτοις ἐπάγει, μετά τινα τὰ μεταξὺ αὐτῷ εἰρημένα, λέγων; 9.29.14: πάλιν μεθ' ἕτερα ἐπιλέγει; 9.29.15: καὶ πάλιν μετ' ὀλίγα; 9.29.16: καὶ μετὰ βραχέα.

[27] *PE* 9.1.2: πρῶτα δὲ τὰ πρῶτα παραθήσομαι, δεικνὺς ὅσοι τῶν Ἑλληνικῶν συγγραφέων ἐπ' ὀνόματος Ἰουδαίων τε καὶ Ἑβραίων τῆς τε παρ' αὐτοῖς τὸ παλαιὸν ἀσκουμένης φιλοσοφίας καὶ τῆς ἀνέκαθεν τῶν προπατόρων αὐτῶν ἱστορίας ἐμνημόνευσαν.

book with editorial notices. He opens with a group of citations from Greeks testifying to the high caliber of ancient Jewish philosophy (chs. 2-10).[28] Beginning with 9.10.6 he collects authors who have commented on the history of Israel.[29] He arranges his excerpts around major events, people, or locales. He begins with the flood (chs. 11-12), the longevity of the ante-diluvians (ch. 13), the tower of Babel (chs. 14-15), and then Abraham (chs. 16-20).[30] He next follows a biographical scheme including Jacob (chs. 21-22),[31] Joseph (chs. 23-24),[32] Job (ch. 25),[33] and Moses (chs. 26-29).[34] The subsequent section does not have an editorial note, but is a unit devoted primarily to Jerusalem (chs. 30-38). He finally discusses the fall of Jerusalem in prophecy (ch. 39) and in history (ch. 40-41).[35] He concludes with a final reference from Josephos (ch. 42).[36]

The range of the quotations was so impressive to Joseph Scaliger that he called the *PE* "divini commentarii."[37] We should not, however, be led to the conclusion that Eusebios knew all of the sources he cited firsthand. He tended to rely upon more recent compilers rather than the original authors.[38] Apparently the library at Caesarea where Eusebios served as bishop from c. 315 until his

---

[28] *PE* 9.1.3: ἄρξεται δέ μοι ὁ λόγος ἀπὸ τοῦ τῶν ἀνδρῶν βίου, ὡς ἂν μάθοις ὅτι μὴ ἐκτὸς σώφρονος λογισμοῦ τὴν τῶν δηλουμένων φιλοσοφίαν τῆς Ἑλλήνων προτετιμήκαμεν.

[29] *PE* 9.10.6: Περὶ μὲν οὖν τῆς Ἰουδαίων τε καὶ Ἑβραίων προσηγορίας τῆς τε παρ' αὐτοῖς πάλαι διαπρεπούσης εὐσεβείας τε καὶ φιλοσοφίας ἐκκείσθω ταῦτα. περὶ δὲ τῆς πατρίου αὐτῶν ἱστορίας θέα ὁπόσοι συνεφώνησαν.

[30] Each of these four is marked by a reference to Moses' treatment of the subject: 9.10.7; 9.13.1; 9.14.1; 9.16.1.

[31] *PE* 9.20.4-21.1: Τὰ μὲν οὖν περὶ τοῦ Ἀβραὰμ ὡς ἐν ὀλίγοις τοσαῦτα παρακείσθω. Ἀπίωμεν δὲ πάλιν ἐπὶ τὸν Πολυΐστορα.

[32] *PE* 9.22.11: Τούτοις καὶ τὰ ἑξῆς περὶ τοῦ Ἰωσὴφ ἐκ τῆς αὐτῆς τοῦ Πολυΐστορος γραφῆς ἐπισυνήφθω.

[33] *PE* 9.24.1: καὶ τὰ ἑξῆς. ταῦτα καὶ περὶ τοῦ Ἰωσήφ. Ἄκουε δὲ οἷα καὶ περὶ τοῦ Ἰὼβ ὁ αὐτὸς ἱστορεῖ.

[34] *PE* 9.25.4: Τοσαῦτα καὶ περὶ τούτον ὁ Πολυΐστωρ. Καὶ περὶ Μωσέως δὲ ὁ αὐτὸς πλεῖστα παρατίθεται, ὧν καὶ αὐτῶν ἐπακοῦσαι ἄξιον.

[35] *PE* 9.39.1: Ἐπὶ τούτοις καὶ τῆς Ἱερεμίου προφητείας τοῦ Πολυΐστορος μνήμην πεποιημένου . . .; and 9.40.1: Τούτοις ἐπισυνάψαι ἀναγκαῖον καὶ τὰ περὶ τῆς Ἰουδαίων αἰχμαλωσίας τῆς ὑπὸ Ναβουχοδονόσορ γεγενημένης.

[36] *PE* 9.42.1: Ταῦτα μὲν οὖν ἡμῖν αὐτάρκως περὶ τῶνδε. προσκείσθω δὲ ἐπὶ πᾶσι καὶ τὰ ἀπὸ τῆς Ἰουδαίων Ἀρχαιότητος Ἰωσήπου . . .

[37] Cited by Edwin Hamilton Gifford, ed. and trans. *Eusebius: Preparation for the Gospel*, 2 vols. (Oxford: the Clarendon Press, 1903; reprint ed., Grand Rapids: Baker Book House, 1981), 1:xvi.

[38] Freudenthal, *Alexander Polyhistor*, p. 7 and Pelletier, *Lettre d'Aristée à Philocrate*, p. 40.

death c. 340 C.E. had an impressive collection of compilations including that of Alexander Polyhistor whom Eusebios explicitly cites
as his source for chs. 17-19, 21-37, and 39.[39]

Alexander Polyhistor[40]

1. *Life*. We know very little about the life of Alexander Cornelius
Polyhistor. He was born around the final decade of the second century B.C.E. in Miletos.[41] He was brought to Rome as a slave c. 82
B.C.E. after Sulla's eastern campaign and sold to Cornelius Lentu-
lus whom he served as a *paidagōgos* and from whom he received the
name Cornelius (T 1). He was granted his freedom[42] and eventually established himself as a significant figure in Ciceronian Rome.[43]
His most noted pupil was Iulius Hyginus (T 3) who was brought to
Rome in the mid-forties[44] and later became head of the Palatine
library founded by Augustus. Polyhistor died in a fire at Laurentum
in the mid-thirties (T 1). This means that Polyhistor's *floruit* should
be placed between 80 and the forties or perhaps even the thirties.[45]

---

[39] He mentions Polyhistor by name in *PE* 9.17.1; 19.4; 20.2; 21.1,19; 22.11;
37.3; 39.1.

[40] Cf. *FGrH* 273; *RE*, s.v. "Alexandros," by E. Schwartz, 1:1449-1452; and
KP, s.v. "Alexandros," by Walther Sontheimer, 1:252, for Polyhistor in general.
For his Περὶ Ἰουδαίων see also Freudenthal, *Alexander Polyhistor*, pp. 16-35; Denis,
Introduction aux Pseudépigraphes Grecs d'Ancien Testament, pp. 244-248; Wacholder, *Eu-
polemus*, pp. 44-52; Conzelmann, *Heiden-Juden-Christen*, pp. 69-72; John Strugnell,
"General Introduction with a Note on Alexander Polyhistor," in *OTP*, 2:777-778;
and Schürer, *The History of the Jewish People in the Age of Jesus Christ*, 3:510-513.

[41] T 1: Ἀλέξανδρος ὁ Μιλήσιος. All other identifications should be rejected. So
Freudenthal, *Alexander Polyhistor*, p. 204 and Jacoby, *FGrH*, 3a:250.

[42] T 1: εἶτα ἠλευθερώθη. T 2: quem Lucius Sulla civitate donavit. The first
(Suda) implies that Cornelius released him. The second clearly states that it was
Sulla. The latter appears to be correct. Cf. Jacoby, *FGrH*, 3a:248-249.

[43] Cf. Jacoby, *FGrH*, 3a:248: "Obwohl wir infolgedessen über seine Beziehungen zu den römischen Gelehrten kaum noch etwa wissen, muss er im geistigen Leben der ciceronischen Zeit eine gewisse Rolle gespielt haben." This claim is substantiated by the statements of Suetonius (T 3), quem propter antiquitatis notitiam
Polyhistorem multi, quidam Historiam vocabant, and Eusebios (T 7b = *PE*
9.17.1), πολύνους ὢν καὶ πολυμαθὴς ἀνήρ, τοῖς τε μὴ πάρεργον τὸν ἀπὸ παιδείας καρ-
πὸν πεποιημένοις Ἕλλησι γνωριμώτατος.

[44] There is a discrepancy in the tradition about whether he was brought from
Spain or Alexandria. In either case, he began studying with Polyhistor in the
forties.

[45] So G.F. Unger, "Die Bluthzeit des Alexander Polyhistor," *Philologus* 47
(1888): 176-183 and Jacoby, *FGrH*, 3a:249; *contra* Schwartz, *RE*, s.v. "Alexandros," 1:1449, who places it from 70-60.

2. *Works*. We have twenty-five titles of Polyhistor's preserved for us: a large number, but probably not all which circulated under his name.[46] While the titles suggest a broad range of interests such as philosophy,[47] wonders,[48] philology,[49] and geography,[50] his major area of concern appears to be ethnographic.[51] In fact, as Felix Jacoby pointed out, the works we know about are principally oriented toward the East.[52]

The large number of works which he produced leads us to believe that he was a compiler rather than a critical thinker. This is confirmed by the fragments themselves which are a series of loosely connected fragments accompanied by the authors' names and the titles but without critical comments.[53] He thus stands within the tradition of compilers represented by figures such as Agatharchides of Knidos (late second century to early first century B.C.E.)[54] and Juba of Mauretania (first century B.C.E. to c. 23 C.E.).[55]

The fact that eleven of the twenty-five titles deal with regions affected by the eastern campaigns of Pompey in 66-62 B.C.E., leads me to believe that a major function of Polyhistor's works was to inform Roman society about their new subjects—although this is speculative.[56] I do not mean that his works were political hand-

---

[46] Suda (T 1) states: οὗτος συνέγραψε βίβλους ἀριθμοῦ κρείττους. Jacoby, *FGrH*, 3a:250, pointed out that a significant number of his works are mentioned only once and that only in passing.

[47] ΦΙΛΟΣΟΦΩΝ ΔΙΑΔΟΧΑΙ and ΠΕΡΙ ΠΥΘΑΓΟΡΙΚΩΝ ΣΥΜΒΟΛΩΝ.

[48] ΘΑΥΜΑΣΙΩΝ ΣΥΝΑΓΩΓΩΝ and ΠΕΡΙ ΤΟΥ ΕΝ ΔΕΛΦΟΙΣ ΧΡΗΣΤΗΡΙΟΥ.

[49] ΚΟΡΙΝΝΗΣ ΥΠΟΜΝΗΜΑΤΑ.

[50] ΠΕΡΙ ΤΩΝ ΠΑΡ' ΑΛΚΜΑΝΙ ΤΟΠΙΚΩΣ ΕΙΡΗΜΕΝΩΝ.

[51] Nineteen of the twenty-five titles are ethnographic treatments.

[52] *FGrH*, 3a:250. Sixteen of the titles deal with countries from the East and only three with the West. It is particularly significant that eight of the sixteen deal with Asia Minor. The titles for the West: De Illyrico tractu, ΙΤΑΛΙΚΑ, ΠΕΡΙ ΡΩΜΗΣ; East: ΑΙΓΥΠΤΙΑΚΑ, ΙΝΔΙΚΑ, ΠΕΡΙ ΙΟΥΔΑΙΩΝ, ΚΡΗΤΙΚΑ, ΠΕΡΙ ΚΥΠΡΟΥ, ΛΙΒΥΚΑ, ΠΕΡΙ ΣΥΡΙΑΣ, and ΧΑΛΔΑΙΚΑ; Asia Minor: ΠΕΡΙ ΒΙΘΥΝΙΑΣ, ΠΕΡΙ ΕΥΞΕΙΝΟΥ ΠΟΝΤΟΥ, ΠΕΡΙ ΚΑΡΙΑΣ, ΠΕΡΙ ΚΙΛΙΚΙΑΣ, ΛΥΚΙΑΚΑ, ΛΥΚΙΑΣ ΠΕΡΙΠΛΟΥΣ, ΠΕΡΙ ΠΑΦΛΑΓΟΝΙΑΣ, and ΣΥΝΑΓΩΓΗ ΤΩΝ ΠΕΡΙ ΦΡΥΓΙΑΣ.

[53] The best test can be made on Eusebios, *PE* 9.17-39, since this is the most extensive text we have. That he was a simple compiler has become *opinio communis*. E.g., Schwartz, *RE*, s.v. "Alexandros," 1:1449 and Sontheimer, *KP*, s.v. "Alexandros," 1:252.

[54] *FGrH* 86.

[55] *FGrH* 275.

[56] The eleven are the eight which deal with Asia Minor plus his volumes on the Jews, Syria, and Crete. On Pompey's additions to Rome see H.A. Ormerod and M. Cary, "Rome and the East," *CAH*, 9:350-396, especially 392-396 and the

books, but that they helped to satisfy the curiosity of Romans about people with whom they now had a political relationship.[57] The extent of his works suggests that he saw himself as a second Hekataios of Miletos who wanted to present the new world to his contemporaries.[58] His other ethnographic works should also be seen within the framework of Rome's expansion and the interest it created about other peoples and regions.

3. Περὶ Ἰουδαίων. The most significant of his works in many ways is his Περὶ Ἰουδαίων.[59] In the portion which Eusebios has preserved for us, there are twenty-six quotations: seventeen from Jews, four from Greeks, four which are anonymous, and one from a Samaritan (although one Jewish quote should be moved to this category).[60] Whether or not Polyhistor used a previous collection or gathered these sources himself is difficult to determine.[61] Since there are no traces of an earlier editorial hand,[62] it is best to conclude that he compiled them himself.

---

facing map. Others who have seen a connection between Pompey's conquests and Polyhistor's writings include Jacoby, *FGrH*, 3a:256-257; Fornara, *The Nature of History in Ancient Greece and Rome*, p. 191; Walter, *JSHRZ*, 1:93; and Harold W. Attridge, "Historiography," in *Jewish Writings of the Second Temple Period*, ed. Michael E. Stone. CRINT (Philadelphia: Fortress Press, 1984), p. 161. Cf. also Schwartz, *RE*, s.v. "Alexandros," 1:1452 and Denis, *Introduction aux Pseudépigraphes Grecs d'Ancien Testament*, p. 245, both of whom emphasize his role in informing Roman society.

[57] Wacholder, *Eupolemus*, p. 51, plays with the idea that they were "handbooks that served as a background for the Roman occupation forces." Jacoby, *FGrH*, 3a:256-257, emphasized their practical orientation.

[58] I do not mean to imply that he envisioned the totality of his ethnographic works as a world *periēgēsis*. Freudenthal, *Alexander Polyhistor*, p. 19 and Jacoby, *FGrH*, 3a:251-252, have both pointed out that there is no evidence for a single unified work. It is, however, true that his works constitute a comprehensive introduction to the new east.

[59] On its authenticity see Schürer, *The History of the Jewish People in the Age of Jesus Christ*, 3:511-512.

[60] I have omitted chs. 20 and 38 which do not appear to be from this work. On the incorrect attribution see below under Pseudo-Eupolemos. The authors are Jews: Demetrios, Artapanos, Eupolemos, Aristeas (all prose), and Philo, Ezekiel (both poetry); Greeks: Molon, Timochares, the author of a work on Syria (Xenophon of Lampsakos or Timochares?), and Theophilos; Samaritan: Theodotos (although he may be Jewish).

[61] Freudenthal, *Alexander Polyhistor*, pp. 102-103, thought that he used a work which consisted of different sentiments between Jews and Samaritans. Denis, *Introduction aux Pseudépigraphes Grecs d'Ancien Testament*, pp. 245-246, conjectured that he used a previous work "réunis en Égypte sur l'ordre d'un Ptolémée, peut-être Ptolemée VII Évergète II Physcon (145-116) . . ."

[62] The only possible traces would be the references to the Bible discussed below.

We have seen that Eusebios carefully structured his book. In the case of the material from Polyhistor, he apparently followed the order of his predecessor. This can be established by comparing the order of material in the one running section of Clement with that of Eusebios as the chart below indicates.

Author Cited	Clement	Eusebios
Eupolemos	1.23.153.4	9.26.1
Artapanos	1.23.154.2-3	9.27.23-25
Ezekiel	1.23.155.1-156.2	9.28.2-3

Since both Clement and Eusebios used Polyhistor independently,[63] the agreement in order suggests that each found it in their common *Vorlage*.[64] We can, therefore, be secure in stating that Polyhistor's volume began with Abraham and continued in chronological order down to the fall of Jerusalem.[65] Whether it continued on down to Pompey's annexation of Syria—as both the genre and the current political situation would seem to suggest—can not be proved.[66]

Upon what basis did Polyhistor structure his work? One intriguing possibility is that he knew the LXX and ordered his sources in the same sequence which he found there.[67] There are three passages in which the savant appears to mention the Bible.[68] The first of these is *PE* 9.20.3 which reproduces Josephos *AJ* 1.239 and may come from Polyhistor's Λιβυκά rather than his Περὶ Ἰουδαίων.[69]

---

[63] Clement can not have used Eusebios. The additional material from Polyhistor in Eusebios shows that he did not depend upon Clement.

[64] So also Denis, *Introduction aux Pseudépigraphes Grecs d'Ancien Testament*, pp. 246-248 and Schürer, *The History of the Jewish People in the Age of Jesus Christ*, 3:510-511.

[65] Eusebios introduces Polyhistor for the first time with these words (*PE* 9.17.1): ὃς ἐν τῇ Περὶ Ἰουδαίων συντάξει τὰ κατὰ τὸν Ἀβραὰμ τοῦτον ἱστορεῖ . . . The final citation is Jeremiah's prophecy about the fall of Jerusalem, 9.39.

[66] Wacholder, *Eupolemus*, pp. 49-51, argues that it does.

[67] Those who contend that Polyhistor knew the LXX include Freudenthal, *Alexander Polyhistor*, pp. 29-30 and Wacholder, *Eupolemus*, pp. 49-50, who goes so far as to say: "Alexander Polyhistor not only displays a mastery of biblical history, but he also uses it as the basis for his works on the Jews." His knowledge of the Bible is questioned by Schwartz, *RE*, s.v. "Alexandros," 1:1451; Jacoby, *FGrH*, 3a:253; and Conzelmann, *Heiden-Juden-Christen*, pp. 53-54.

[68] The appeal to *PE* 9.39 and 10.10.7 are not significant. The first which shows awareness of Jeremiah and the fall of Jerusalem is probably a quotation from Eupolemos and the latter which alludes to the antiquity of the Jews is too general.

[69] Κλεόδημος δέ φησιν ὁ προφήτης, ὁ καὶ Μαλχᾶς, ἱστορῶν τὰ περὶ Ἰουδαίων, καθὼς καὶ Μωσῆς ἱστόρηκεν ὁ νομοθέτης αὐτῶν. On the issue of which work this stems from see the discussion in the next chapter.

The second and third both appear in connection with quotations from Demetrios.[70] One major difficulty in accepting these statements at face value is that Polyhistor is also credited with having reported that a Hebrew woman named Mōsō is the author of the Jewish law[71] and that Juda and Idumea are the children of Semiramis.[72] While this could simply be uncritical reporting of a anti-Jewish sources, it forces us to pause. Given the fact that we do not have a known citation of the LXX by a pagan until the celebrated passage of Pseudo-Longinos in the first century C.E.,[73] it is problematic to credit him with such knowledge. I would prefer to attribute the references to a general knowledge based upon oral reports or a consensus of his sources rather than a detailed reading of the LXX.[74] The basis for his chronological structure would then be the sources themselves which follow a common pattern. That he was not locked into their sequence entirely is suggested by the fact that chs. 30-38 should be considered an ethnographic section on Jerusalem. He thus moves in an ethnographic pattern of early history and then geography.[75]

The date in which Polyhistor wrote is disputed. The *terminus a quo*

---

[70] *PE* 9.29.1: Δημήτριος δὲ περὶ τῆς ἀναιρέσεως τοῦ Αἰγυπτίου καὶ τῆς διαφορᾶς τῆς πρὸς τὸν μηνύσαντα τὸν τελευτήσαντα ὁμοίως τῷ τὴν ἱερὰν βίβλον γράψαντι ἱστόρησε; 9.29.15: Ἐκεῖθεν ἦλθον ἡμέρας τρεῖς, ὡς αὐτός τε ὁ Δημήτριος λέγει καὶ συμφώνως τούτῳ ἡ ἱερὰ βίβλος.

[71] *FGrH* 273, F 70: Ἀλέξανδρος ὁ Μιλήσιος . . . καὶ περὶ Ῥώμης βιβλία ε'. ἐν τούτοις λέγει ὡς γύνη γέγονεν Ἑβραία Μώσω, ἧς ἐστι σύγγραμμα ὁ παρ' Ἑβραίοις νόμος.

[72] *FGrH* 273, F 121. Cf. also Stern, *GLAJJ*, 1:164. Plutarch, *De Iside et Osiride* 363C, relates the tradition that Hierosolumos and Judaios are the sons of Typhon in a text which associates ass-worship with the Jews.

[73] *De subl.* 9.9. For the text and commentary see Stern, *GLAJJ*, 1:361-365. Gager, *Moses in Greco-Roman Paganism*, pp. 56-63, also has a good summary of the major arguments about whether the author was a Hellenized Jew or a pagan with Jewish proclivities. The other texts which pre-date Christian influence on pagans are Hekataios of Abdera (Diodoros 40.3.6) and Okellos Lukanos, *De Universi Natura*, 45-46, which may well date from the second century B.C.E. The difficulty with the latter is that the reference is too general. For the text see Stern, *GLAJJ*, 1:131-133. Hekataios' citation is complicated by the fact that there is no direct biblical parallel—although the quote is given in *oratio recta*—and that he does not betray any direct awareness of the biblical text elsewhere.

[74] It is, of course, possible that Polyhistor checked these references himself—although I question this. Another possibility would be to see the work of a Jewish editor who made a collection of Jewish (and Samaritan?) authors which served as the basis for Polyhistor's own work.

[75] It is interesting to remember that Hekataios of Abdera also moved immediately from Moses to Jerusalem (Diodoros 40.3.3).

is the most recent author whom Polyhistor cites. This is Apollonios Molon,[76] the famous rhetor who visited Rome in 81 B.C.E.[77] and later taught both Cicero[78] and Caesar in Rhodes.[79] The *terminus ad quem* is more difficult since the last datable reference is controversial. In a fragment of Eupolemos preserved by Clement there is a clear chronological addition by an editorial hand.[80] Unfortunately, the MS tradition is patently corrupt, a circumstance which has spawned a number of proposed emendations.[81] L reads: ἀπὸ δὲ τοῦ χρόνου τούτου ἄχρι τῶν ἐν ῾Ρώμῃ ὑπάτων Γαίου Δομετιανοῦ Κασιανοῦ. The suggestion which stays closest to the MS tradition itself is that of Freudenthal who proposed: ἀπὸ δὲ τοῦ χρόνου τούτου ἄχρι τῶν ἐν ῾Ρώμῃ ὑπάτων Γναίου Δομετίου καὶ ᾽Ασινίου συναθροίζεται ἔτη ἑκατὸν εἴκοσι.[82] The one hundred and twenty years are to be counted from the previous reference to the fifth year of the reign of Demetrios Soter I (162-150 B.C.E.), thus 158/157 B.C.E. Freudenthal's emendation makes the year 40 the *terminus ad quem* since this was the year Gnaeus Domitius and Gaius Asinius Pollio served as consuls. Although the computation does not fit exactly, it is close enough to be credible.[83]

The question now arises: Whose hand is behind this addition? Freudenthal thought it was Clement's who added the reference because this was the year of Herod's accession to the kingship of Judea.[84] While this is possible, it is strained: Was the accession of

---

[76] *PE* 9.19.1-3.

[77] Cicero, *Brutus*, 307 and 312. The timing of the reference in 307 may be a mistake (Cicero places him there in 87). The second reference is correct. The date is secured by the reference to Sulla's dictatorship.

[78] Cicero, *Brutus*, 316; Plutarch, *Cicero*, 4.4-5.

[79] Plutarch, *Caesar*, 3.1.

[80] *Strom.* 1.21.141.5.

[81] Cf. the *apparatus criticus* of Holladay, *Fragments from Hellenistic Jewish Authors*, p. 134 and pp. 155-156, n. 121.

[82] *Alexander Polyhistor*, p. 214. This was first suggested by C.G.A. Kuhlmey, *Eupolemi Fragmenta prolegomenis et commentario instructa* (Berlin, 1840); cited by Wacholder, *Eupolemus*, p. 42 and Walter, *JSHRZ*, 1:108, n. b. His proposal has been printed in the editions of Albert-Marie Denis, *Fragmenta pseudepigraphorum quae supersunt Graeca una cum historicorum et autorum Judaeorum hellenistarum fragmentis* (published with M. Black, *Apocalypsis Henochi Graece*). PVTG 3 (Leiden: E.J. Brill, 1970), p. 186; Holladay, *Fragments from Hellenistic Jewish Authors*, p. 134. It has also been translated by the last two major translations: Walter, *JSHRZ*, 1:108 and Fallon, *OTP*, 2:872.

[83] Apparently the error lies in the understanding of the date of Demetrios.

[84] *Alexander Polyhistor*, p. 214. This is based upon Josephos, *AJ* 14.389: καὶ ὁ μὲν οὕτως τὴν βασιλείαν παραλαμβάνει, τυχὼν αὐτῆς ἐπὶ τῆς ἑκατοστῆς καὶ ὀγδοηκοστῆς

Herod that significant for Clement? A. Gutschmid accepted the basic emendation but thought there must have been a chronographer behind the addition and so added "by Cassianus," a second century gnostic and chronographer whom Clement had already mentioned.[85] Yet this still hardly explains why the consuls of the year 40 B.C.E. were added. It must have been someone living in 40 B.C.E. who recognized a system of dating by consuls. Ben Zion Wacholder thought this was Ptolemy of Mendes, an Egyptian priest who wrote a chronology of Egypt.[86] Even this proposal seems unduly complicated: it presupposes an early circulation of Polyhistor's work in Egypt and Ptolemy's acquaintance with Polyhistor. The simplest solution is that Polyhistor added this chronographic note.[87] Since we know that he was active in Rome at this time, there is no reason to discredit the suggestion. In fact, the addition of Judea as a client state under the kingship of Herod would make a suitable occasion for the publication of his work.[88]

As we pointed out, Polyhistor was a compiler. Can we determine how carefully he has preserved the excerpts of the Hellenistic Jewish authors he cites? Since we do not have any original fragments to which we may compare our fragments, our analysis must be based entirely on Polyhistor's work in Eusebios. On three occasions, Polyhistor indicates that he has selectively chosen the passages he has copied.[89] All three of these texts deal with poetic works. It is obvious

---

καὶ τετάρτης ὀλυμπιάδος, ὑπατεύοντος Γναίου Δομετίου Καλβίνου τὸ δεύτερον καὶ Γαΐου Ἀσινίου Πωλίωνος. Freudenthal has been followed by Denis, *Introduction aux Pseudépigraphes Grecs d'Ancien Testament*, p. 254 and Conzelmann, *Heiden-Juden-Christen*, p. 144.

[85] A. Gutschmid, *Kleine Schriften*, 5 vols. ed. by F. Ruhl (Leipzig: B.G. Teubner, 1889-1894), 2:192. Clement mentions him in *Stromata* 1.21.101.2 which is cited by Eusebios, *PE* 10.12.1. The latter mentions him again in *HE* 6.13.7.

[86] Wacholder, "Biblical Chronology in the Hellenistic World Chronicles," *HTR* 61 (1968): 471 and *Eupolemus*, pp. 40-44. He has been followed by Walter, *JSHRZ*, 1:94, n. 4. On Ptolemy see *FGrH* 611 and Stern, *GLAJJ*, 1:379-381.

[87] So Wilhelm Bousset and Hugo Gressmann, *Die Religion des Judentums im Späthellenistischen Zeitalter*, 4th ed. Handbuch zum Neuen Testament 21 (Tübingen: J.C.B. Mohr (Paul Siebeck), 1966), p. 20 and F. Fallon, "Eupolemus," in *OTP*, 2:861-862.

[88] I can not accept Freudenthal's suggestion that the Περὶ Ἰουδαίων was an excursus of Polyhistor's Περὶ Συρίας. The amount of material is too large for an excursus. Cf. *Alexander Polyhistor*, pp. 34-35.

[89] Cf. Eusebios, *PE* 9.20.1: καὶ τὰ ἑξῆς. οἷς μετ' ὀλίγα ἐπιφέρει; 9.28.3: τούτοις μεθ' ἕτερα ἐπιλέγει; 9.37.2: οἷς πάλιν ὑποβὰς περὶ τῆς πληρώσεως ἐπιλέγει.

on a first perusal that in the case of poetic texts, Polyhistor has simply reproduced select passages between which he has interspersed summaries or brief introductions. When we examine the prose texts we find them all in *oratio obliqua*. Here he has apparently shortened the texts as he reported them.

How did such selectivity and abbreviating affect the texts? There is no evident bias in Polyhistor's procedure:[90] he cites authors from not only divergent, but hostile traditions.[91] Further, while he turns the original *oratio recta* into *oratio obliqua*, he still manages to preserve some of the flavor and style of each author. The area where Polyhistor is most vulnerable is in accidental errors. Some of the texts are corrupt. There is no doubt that indolent scribes have created some of these conundrums; others, however, must be due to Polyhistor.[92]

---

[90] So also Freudenthal, *Alexander Polyhistor*, p. 24, 28; Jacoby, *FGrH*, 3a:251,255; Strugnell, *OTP*, 2:778.

[91] Josephos, *CA* 2.236,255,258,295, makes it very clear that Apollonios Molon whom Polyhistor cites (*PE* 9.19.1-3) was hostile to the Jews in his work.

[92] A clear example of this is the listing of Jacob's children in the fragment of Demetrios in *PE* 9.21.1-19, where the problem recurs throughout the fragment. In 9.21.3-5, Demetrios provides the year and month of the birth of each of Jacob's twelve children. (The biblical text lying behind this is Gen. 29:31-30:24) There are, however, two major problems: one, Zilpah is Leah's handmaid not Rachel's as in 3 (both the biblical text and section 4 of Demetrios affirm this); two, according to the calculations of 9.21.5, Leah would have to give birth to Zebulun and Dinah at the same time—even though there is no hint of them being twins! In 9.21.8, Dan is entirely omitted in the listing and again in 9.21.17-18 along with Issachar. The common problem in all three lists is the place or omission of Dan, the first child of Bilhah, Leah's handmaid. It is very unlikely that all of this confusion is due to Demetrios since he is extremely careful in all of his calculations. (Although note the deliberate omission of Dan in Rev. 7:5-8 by the later Christian apocalyptist.) The most likely source of the problem is Polyhistor since we would not expect a scribal error to pervade the entire fragment. Nor is the mistake inexplicable. Demetrios listed the births of the children of Jacob in ten month intervals. (For a ten month period see also the Wisdom of Solomon 7:1-2; *contra* II Macc. 7:27 where nine months is given.) Since he has a seven year period to work with less the four months which are left over at the end, he has 80 months in which four women must have twelve children. This means that he has eight ten month periods which necessitates doubling up on four occasions. In the present text, Demetrios has doubled up Naphtali/Gad and Asher/Issachar. It is also clear that the current Zebulun/Dinah combination indicates a third place where Demetrios doubled up. Assuming that Demetrios followed the biblical text, he must have doubled Judah/Dan (Bilhah had Naphtali after Dan) and Dinah/Joseph. This gives us the following scheme:

Date	Child	Date	Child
8/10	Reuben	10/6	Levi
9/8	Simeon	11/4	Judah and Dan

He apparently read his sources with some care but did not study them. We may, therefore, conclude that Polyhistor transmitted his texts faithfully, but not with the care of a critical scholar.

With these caveats in mind we may now turn to the historians themselves.[93]

Date	Child	Date	Child
12/2	Naphtali and Gad	13/10	Zebulun
12/12	Asher and Issachar	14/8	Dinah and Joseph

Polyhistor must have fallen victim to homoeoteleuton in 9.21.3. I would reconstruct the text as παιδίσκην [Βαλλάν, τῷ αὐτῷ χρόνῳ ᾧ καὶ Λείαν συλλαβεῖν Ἰούδαν, καὶ τεκεῖν τῷ ἑνδεκάτῳ ἔτει μηνὶ τετάρτῳ υἱὸν ὃν Ῥαχὴλ καλέσαι Δάν, καὶ Λείαν δοῦναι τῷ Ἰακὼβ τὴν ἑαυτης παιδίσκην] Ζελφάν. This omission explains why Dan is not mentioned in the other two lists. Since Polyhistor omitted Dan in the initial list, he must have dropped him from the other two (9.21.8, 17-18). 9.21.5 should then drop the reference to Dan and read instead: τεκεῖν [θυγατέρα Δείναν, καὶ Ῥαχὴλ λαβεῖν ἐν γαστρὶ καὶ τεκεῖν τῷ αὐτῷ χρόνῳ,] τῷ τεσσαρεσκαιδεκάτῳ ἔτει . . . A scribe must have added the reference to Dan in our MSS in an attempt to introduce him back into the list. (If Polyhistor did this, it could be used as evidence that he did know the LXX.) In 9.21.8, we should then insert [Δὰν ἐτῶν ἐννέα μηνῶν ὀκτώ] immediately after Judah and allow Dinah to stand as she does (*contra* Mras). The third list is more difficult since the ages do not tally with those of the first list and Dan and Issachar are omitted. The reinsertion of the two names is not difficult: Issachar was likely elided by parablepsis caused again by homoeoteleuton (Asher and Issachar were the same age). The confusion in ages most likely stems from scribal errors with the numbers. On other attempts to reconstruct the text see Freudenthal, *Alexander Polyhistor*, pp. 54-56 and Walter, *JSHRZ*, 3:285, n.c and 288, nn. to section 17, who thinks that the omission of Dan occurred before Polyhistor.

[93] I have used the text of Holladay, *Fragments from Hellenistic Jewish Authors* for the following. Works which cover these authors as a whole are Freudenthal, *Alexander Polyhistor* which in spite of its age remains of fundamental importance; Attridge, "Historiography," in *CRINT*, 157-184 and his more recent "Jewish Historiography," in *Early Judaism and Its Modern Interpreters*, ed. Robert A. Kraft and George W.E. Nickelsburg. The Bible and Its Modern Interpreters (Atlanta: Scholars Press, 1986), pp. 311-343; Robert Doran, "The Jewish Hellenistic Historians Before Josephus," in *Rise and Decline of the Roman World*, ed. Wolfgang Haase. ANRW II 20.1 (Berlin/New York: Walter de Gruyter, 1987), pp. 246-297; Nikolaus Walter, "Jüdisch-hellenistische Literatur vor Philon von Alexandrien (unter Ausschluß der Historiker)," in *ibid*, pp. 67-120; and D. Mendels, "'Creative History' in the Hellenistic Near East in the Third and Second Centuries BCE: The Jewish Case," pp. 13-20.

DEMETRIOS[94]

Life

The only information which we have about Demetrios is what we can glean from the fragments themselves.[95] There is only one statement which offers any biographical clues. In a fragment preserved by Clement, Demetrios appears to provide his own *floruit*: ἀφ' οὗ δὲ αἱ φυλαὶ αἱ δέκα ἐκ Σαμαρείας αἰχμάλωτοι γεγόνασιν ἕως Πτολεμαίου τετάρτου ἔτη πεντακόσια ἑβδομήκοντα τρία μῆνας ἐννέα.[96] Working on the assumption that Demetrios brought his chronology down to his own time, he lived and wrote during the reign of Ptolemy IV Philopator (221-205 B.C.E.).[97] This is supported by the simple style of his writing which we would expect at an early date. The statement also implies that Demetrios lived within the realm of the Ptolemaic kingdom. While this could be Palestine, Cyrene, or Egypt itself, the latter is the most probable since Demetrios shows a thorough knowledge of both the LXX and different forms of Greek literature.[98] This,

---

[94] The most important works on Demetrios are: Freudenthal, *Alexander Polyhistor*, pp. 35-82; Peter Dalbert, *Die Theologie der hellenistisch-jüdischen Missions-Literatur unter Ausschluß von Philo und Josephus*. TF 4 (Hamburg-Volksdorf: Herbert Reich, 1954), pp. 27-32; Denis, *Introduction aux Pseudépigraphes Grecs d'Ancient Testament*, pp. 248-251; Fraser, *Ptolemaic Alexandria*, 1:510, 690-694; Walter, *JSHRZ*, 3:280-292; E.J. Bickerman, "The Jewish Historian Demetrios," in *Christianity, Judaism and Other Greco-Roman Cults: Studies for Morton Smith at Sixty*, ed. Jacob Neusner. SJLA 12 (Leiden: E.J. Brill, 1975), pp. 72-84; Conzelmann, *Heiden-Juden-Christen*, pp. 141-142; Carl R. Holladay, "Demetrius the Chronographer as Historian and Apologist," in *Christian Teaching: Studies in Honor of Lemoine G. Lewis* (Abilene, Texas: Abilene Christian University, 1981), pp. 117-129 and his *Fragments from Hellenistic Jewish Authors*, pp. 51-91; John J. Collins, *Between Athens and Jerusalem: Jewish Identity in the Hellenistic Diaspora* (New York: Crossroad, 1983), pp. 27-30; Attridge, "Historiography," pp. 161-162; J. Hanson, "Demetrius," in *OTP*, 2: 843-854; and Schürer, *The History of the Jewish People in the Age of Jesus Christ*, 3:513-517.

[95] The only *testimonium* is Josephos *CA* 1.218 which I will discuss in the next chapter.

[96] F 6 = Clement, *Stromata* 1.21.141.2.

[97] Freudenthal, *Alexander Polyhistor*, pp. 57-62, argued that this should be Ptolemy III Euergetes (246-241 B.C.E.) in an effort to bring the dating of the fragment into conformity with our current dating of the fall of Samaria. There are, however, difficulties with his view which has not been adopted by any of the works I have consulted. See especially, Bickerman, "The Jewish Historian Demetrius," pp. 80-84.

[98] The only two dissenting voices to an Egyptian provenance are Wacholder, *Eupolemus*, pp. 280-282, who thinks he may have lived in Palestine and Schürer,

in turn, suggests Alexandria as a specific location.

We, unfortunately, do not know a great deal about the Jews in Alexandria during the reign of Philopator.[99] The major trend which Polybios notes about Philopator's reign is an upsurge of Egyptian nationalism. This was due to his use of Egyptians in the army when he defeated Antiochos III at Raphia in 217 B.C.E.[100] The role which the native troops played stimulated a sense of national pride which led to rebellions at home.[101] Thus in spite of his victory, his own maladroitness in governing and his newly created problems spelled the beginning of the end of Ptolemaic greatness.[102] The position of the Jews in his kingdom is not clear. III Maccabees reports an attempt by Philopator to exterminate a good number of Jews in Egypt (2:25-7:23) after he was miraculously prevented from entering the most holy place of the Jerusalem temple (1:6-2:24) following his victory at Raphia (1:1-5).[103] In spite of its legendary embellishments, the text probably points to a strained relationship between Philopator and the Jewish populace.[104] Demetrios thus lived in an age when weaknesses were beginning to appear in Ptolemaic power, when native Egyptian forces were exerting themselves, and when Jews found themselves in a more

---

The History of the Jewish People in the Age of Jesus Christ, 3:516, who sees no reason to limit the option to Egypt. On his relationship to the LXX and Greek literature see below.

[99] Our principle literary source for Philopator is Polybios 5.34.1-87.8; 107.1-3. For a current summary see Fraser, *Ptolemaic Alexandria*, 1:75-86, which covers the years 215-145 B.C.E.

[100] Polybios 5.65.5,9, mentions the inclusion of Egyptians.

[101] Polybios, 5.107.1-3.

[102] Polybios 5.34.1-11, is scathing in its reproach of his conduct.

[103] On III Maccabees see Cyril W. Emmet, "The Third Book of Maccabees," in *The Apocrypha and Pseudepigrapha of the Old Testament in English*, 2 vols., ed. R.H. Charles (Oxford: The Clarendon Press, 1913), 1:155-173 (Hereafter abbreviated *APOT*); M. Hadas, *The Third and Fourth book of Maccabees*. JAL (New York: Harper, 1953); and H. Anderson, "3 Maccabees," in *OTP*, 2:509-529.

[104] A major problem in the historicity of the persecution is that Josephos preserves the same story only places it in the time of Ptolemy Physcon (= Ptolemy VII (VIII) Euergetes II (145-117 B.C.E.) in *CA* 2.53-55. In this instance it is likely that III Maccabees preserves some kernel of truth since the description of Raphia follows the basic lines of Polybios and the picture of Philopator matches what we know of him elsewhere. See the commentaries in the previous note for details. On the specific issue of Jewish rights under Philopator see Aryeh Kasher, *The Jews in Hellenistic and Roman Egypt: The Struggle for Equal Rights* (Tübingen: J.C.B. Mohr (Paul Siebeck, 1985), pp. 211-232.

hostile environment than what they had previously known.

Work

1. *Content.* There are four fragments which have come down to us bearing the name of Demetrios.[105] In addition to these four, Freudenthal thought that two of the anonymous fragments in Eusebios belonged to Demetrios.[106] In the case of the second of these (*PE* 9.29.16), he is surely correct since it closely follows a fragment attributed to Demetrios[107] and the style and type of material is exactly what we find in the four known fragments.[108] On the other hand, I am unconvinced about the first of these. The strongest arguments for authenticity are the style of the writing, its dependence upon the LXX, and our inability to find another Hellenistic Jewish author to whom we may attribute it. Against its authenticity stand the very imprecise temporal introduction which flies in the face of all that we know about Demetrios[109] and the content of the fragment: it is simple narrative.[110] For these reasons—primarily the general temporal reference, I am reluctant to accept it and will not use it in my analysis.[111]

F 2, the longest of the remains, selectively retells the lives of Jacob and Joseph from the time Jacob fled to Haran until the Israelites entered Egypt with a very heavy emphasis on the precise ages of all the principals. It concludes with a chronological summary of what the author considered epoch-making events and a chronological

---

[105] Eusebios, *PE* 9.21.1-19; 9.29.1-3; 9.29.15; and Clement, *Strom.* 1.21.141.1-2.

[106] Eusebios, *PE* 9.19.4 and 9.29.16 in *Alexander Polyhistor*, p. 36.

[107] Eusebios, *PE* 9.29.15. There are two brief quotations from Ezekiel between the two fragments.

[108] The form of a *quaestio* on a difficult text (in this instance from the LXX specifically) is common to Demetrios. See under Form below.

[109] μετ' οὐ πολὺν δὲ χρόνον is unmatched by any other temporal reference in the undisputed fragments.

[110] The closest parallel would be F 4 (= *PE* 9.29.15), which however, has a specific temporal reference. Since we only have four fragments it would be dubious to dismiss this fragment on only this ground.

[111] The fragment was accepted as authentic by Denis, *Fragmenta pseudepigraphorum quae supersunt Graeca*, p. 175 and Holladay, *Fragments from Hellenistic Jewish Authors*, p. 80, n. 1. It is questioned by Jacoby, *FGrH* 722, who prints it separately under the heading "Ohne Autornamen;" Walter, *JSHRZ*, 3:280, n. 1; and J. Hanson, *OTP*, 2:848, n. a. Doran, "The Jewish Hellenistic Historians Before Josephus," pp. 249-250, questions the authenticity of both anonymous fragments.

genealogy of Moses. F 3 explains how Zipporah was a descendent of Abraham through Keturah and how the generations of Moses and Zipporah neatly align themselves. The fourth fragment simply and briefly recounts the oases of Marah and Elim. F 5 is in the form of a *quaestio et solutio* and explains how the Israelites obtained their weapons since they left Egypt unarmed. The sixth and final fragment offers a chronological summary of three major dates: the interval between the captivity of Samaria and Jerusalem (128 years and six months), the time from the fall of Samaria until the reign of Philopator (573 years and nine months), and the elapsed span between the fall of Jerusalem and the time of Philopator (338 years and three months).

The only remnant of a title is that preserved by Clement who mentioned Demetrios' Περὶ τῶν ἐν τῇ ᾿Ιουδαίᾳ βασιλέων (F 6).[112] The question immediately arises: Does this refer to all of the above fragments or only to some of them? Is it, in fact, a title or merely a sectional heading within a larger work? While the latter is a possibility, Clement cites it as a work and there is not a sufficient reason for doubting the reference.[113] It is more difficult to decide whether the fragments of Eusebios also fall underneath this title. Why did Clement preserve the title and Eusebios drop it if it headed the work of Demetrios in Polyhistor?[114] Clement is obviously citing a later section or another work which appeared later in Polyhistor. Further, is it appropriate to head a work which deals not only with Moses, but also the patriarchs with such a heading? There is not a problem in calling Moses a king.[115] If the title is for the patriarchs as well,

---

[112] This is commonly assumed to be the title. So Dalbert, *Die Theologie der hellenistisch-jüdischen Missions-Literatur*, p. 27; Fraser, *Ptolemaic Alexandria*, 1:691; Conzelmann, *Heiden-Juden-Christen*, p. 141; Hanson, *OTP*, 2:843; and Schürer, *The History of the Jewish People in the Age of Jesus Christ*, 3:513. It is worth pointing out that the same title is assigned to the *opus* of Eupolemos. (See below)

[113] Clement also cites Polyhistor's Περὶ ᾿Ιουδαίων in *Strom.* 1.21.130.3 and Artapanos' Περὶ ᾿Ιουδαίων in 1.23.154.2. Although the accuracy of the latter could be questioned, it is evident that Clement means the whole work and not just a section by the title.

[114] This appears to be the decisive reason why Walter, *JSHRZ*, 3:280, rejects the title for all of the fragments.

[115] Philo called Moses a king in *Vit. Mos.* 2.292 and Justus of Tiberias wrote a history of Judean kings from Moses until Herod Agrippa II entitled ᾿Ιουδαίων βασιλέων οἱ ἐν τοῖς στέμμασιν. Cf. *FGrH* 734 T 2. On Moses as king see Wayne A. Meeks, "Moses as God and King," in *Religions in Antiquity: Festschrift E.R. Goodenough*, ed. Jacob Neusner. Studies in the History of Religion 14 (Leiden: E.J. Brill, 1968), pp. 354-359.

they must have served as an introduction of sorts. Since we lack any evidence which ties the fragments together, we can only affirm that Demetrios consistently dealt with chronological matters.

This leads us to ask about the scope of his work(s). If the chronological points of reference are reliable indicators—and they appear to be given the nature of his work—then we may conclude that the work(s) encompassed history from Adam until Philopator.[116]

What remains of such a work(s) is scanty at best. Does it accurately reflect the contents of what once must have been a much more extensive work(s)? Several factors lead me to believe that it does. First, the fragments are different from the other material in Polyhistor's work. Why would a first century B.C.E. editor choose such bland chronological and exegetical samples if the work were a running narrative with mere side excurses into chronological and exegetical matters? Second, F 2 provides a lengthy excerpt covering a long period of time and a broad range of events. There is no evidence that Polyhistor excised significant sections from this fragment. We may confidently assume, then, that our fragments do represent Demetrios' work.[117]

2. *Form.* We are now in a position to examine the form which Demetrios' work took. It is immediately apparent that Demetrios is retelling select events from the biblical text as the following chart will demonstrate.[118]

Content	LXX	DEMETRIOS
Jacob flees to Haran	Gen.27:41-28:5	F 2.1
Ages of Isaac and Jacob		F 2.2
Jacob marries Leah & Rachel	29:15-28	F 2.3a
Jacob's children w/birthdate	29:31-30:24	F 2.3b-5
Total years in Haran		F 2.6
Jacob wrestles an angel	32:23-33	F 2.7
Ages of children in Shechem		F 2.8
Ages of principals when Dinah defiled	34:1-33	F 2.9
Vision at Bethel	35:9-15	F 2.10a
Birth of Benjamin	35:16-21	F 2.10b
Return to Isaac	35:27	F 2.11a

---

[116] Adam is one of the points of reference in F 2 (= *PE* 9.29.18) and Philopator in F 6.

[117] Cf. also Freudenthal, *Alexander Polyhistor*, pp. 79-80.

[118] For the sake of convenience I will cite the fragment and then the section from either Eusebios or Clement so that the text may be located quickly.

Content	LXX	DEMETRIOS
Ages of patriarchs when Joseph sold	(37,39)	F 2.11b
Summary of Joseph's rise	40:1-41:52	F 2.12
Why Joseph did not quickly send for his family		F 2.13
Why Joseph gave Benjamin more		F 2.14-15
Total years in Canaan		F 2.16
Ages of patriarchs when they entered Egypt		F 2.17
Chronological summary		F 2.18
Chronological genealogy of Moses	(Ex. 6:16-20)	F 2.19
Zipporah, Abraham's descendant		F 3.1-3
Marah and Elim	15:22-27	F 4.15
How the Israelites obtained their weapons		F 5.16
Chronological summary		F 6.1-3

The relationship of Demetrios to the biblical text is not fully disclosed by this chart. What is not apparent is that virtually everything he discusses has a biblical base. Further, Demetrios is easily the most sober of all the Hellenistic Jewish authors in his retelling of the text. He does not create new episodes or even recast them in a contemporary light. He simply uses the text as it stands for his own purposes.[119]

The first question which we must raise is which biblical text did Demetrios use? There can be no doubt that he knew and used the LXX.[120] This is obvious from the spelling of names and places,[121] verbal echoes,[122] and his agreement with the LXX when it diverges

---

[119] Freudenthal, *Alexander Polyhistor*, pp. 37-40, emphasized his fidelity to the biblical text. I am not aware of any dissenting judgments on this point.

[120] This was established by Freudenthal, *Alexander Polyhistor*, pp. 40-44, 48-51.

[121] Of the forty-four personal names in our fragments, only twelve vary from the LXX: Ρουβιν or Ρουβηλ instead of Ρουβην, Νεφθαλειμ instead of Νεφθαλι (Lucian has Νεφθαλειμ), Δεινα in place of Δινα, Ασενεθ for Ασεννεθ, Κλαθ for Κααθ, Μωσης for Μωυσης (Lucian has Μωσης), Ιοθωρ for Ιοθορ, Οβαβ for Ιωβαβ, Ιεζαν instead of Ιεξαν, Δαδαν for Δαιδαν, Ισααρ in the place of Ισσααρ, and Ιωχαβετ for Ιωχαβεδ. Of the nineteen place names, there are only three deviations: Χαφραθα for χαβραθα, Ελειμ instead of Αιλιμ, and Ιεροσολυμων in place of Ιερουσαλημ. (I am uncertain whether the dative Μαμβρι should decline in the nominative as the LXX Μαμβρη or not. Cf. F 2 (*PE* 9.21.11))

[122] In F 2.4 that Leah obtained rights to Jacob ἀντὶ τῶν μήλων τῶν

from the MT. The last is particularly evident in his chronological system,[123] his genealogical treatment of Zipporah,[124] as well as in minor instances.[125] It is much more difficult to determine whether or not Demetrios knew Hebrew.[126] The only example which I have been able to find where Demetrios follows the lead of MT over against the LXX is in the age of Kohath. MT and Demetrios say that he lived 133 years, while the LXX only claims 130.[127] While this is too slim to establish his knowledge of Hebrew, it does at least make the point that simply because Demetrios used the LXX, such usage does not preclude knowledge of the Hebrew text. As we will see, Demetrios had good reasons for preferring the LXX.

μανδραγόρου. The Hebrew of Gen. 30:14,15,16 reads דוּדָאִים which the LXX renders μῆλα μανδραγόρου in v. 14. (μανδραγορῶν in vs. 15 and 16) Demetrios appears to echo this. A more explicit example is in section 7 of the same fragment which recounts Jacob's wrestling with the angel (Gen. 32:23-33). The following are clear echoes: παλαῖσαι of ἐπάλαιεν (v. 25), καὶ ἄψασθαι τοῦ πλάτους τοῦ μηροῦ τοῦ Ἰακώβ of καὶ ἥψατο τοῦ πλάτους τοῦ μηροῦ αὐτοῦ (v. 26), τὸν δὲ ναρκήσαντα of ἐνάρκησεν (v. 26) and ὃ ἐνάρκησεν (v. 33), and ἐπισκάζειν of ἐπέσκαζεν (v. 32).

[123] See below under purpose for specifics. One notable example is F 2.16 and 18 where Demetrios computes the time of the patriarchs in Canaan at 215 years. This is in agreement with the LXX (and SP) rendering of Ex. 12:40 where the 430 years which the MT assigns to the time in Egypt is made to include both the time of the patriarchs in Canaan as well as the Israelites in Egypt. The Vulgate, Peshitta, and Targum Onqelos all follow MT.

[124] The LXX of Gen. 25:3 varies notably from MT. Most significantly for Demetrios the LXX includes Ragouel in its account. The MT completely omits any mention of him. Demetrios' genealogical exegesis of Zipporah as a descendant of Abraham through Keturah stands upon the LXX.

[125] There are two examples of this. F 2.10 recounts Gen. 35:16. MT reads ויהי עוד כברת הארץ לבוא אפרתה which literally means "and while there was still some distance to go to Ephrath." The LXX translators apparently did not fully understand the expression and so transliterated it: ἐγένετο δὲ ἡνίκα ἤγγισεν χαβραθα εἰς γῆν ἐλθεῖν Εφραθα. In Demetrios the phrase is ἐκεῖθεν δὲ ἐλθεῖν εἰς Χαφραθα. While it would be possible to argue that Demetrios was as puzzled as the LXX translators over the phrase, it is more reasonable to conclude that he took the transliterated form as a place name. (It is also possible that Demetrios left the transliterated form as it appeared and that Polyhistor made the mistake—although I think less likely.) The second instance is F 2.15 (Gen. 45:22) where MT reads שלש מאות כסף. which the LXX and Demetrios both give as τριακοσίους χρυσοῦς.

[126] Freudenthal, *Alexander Polyhistor*, pp. 65, 77; Walter, *JSHRZ*, 3:281-282; and Holladay, *Fragments from Hellenistic Jewish Authors*, p. 52, contend that he only knew the LXX. Wacholder, *Eupolemus*, pp. 281-282 and Schürer, *The History of the Jewish People in the Age of Jesus Christ*, 3:516, allow for the possibility of his knowing Hebrew.

[127] Ex. 6:18 and F 2.19. It is also worth pointing out that in F 2.19, Demetrios says that Amram died at 136. MT of Ex. 6:20 has 137 and the LXX 132. Could Demetrios have originally written ρλζ (= 137) which a scribe has corrupted to ρλς (= 136)?

The major thrust of Demetrios' record is chronological.[128] He
has meticulously provided dates for as many events as the hints in
the biblical text would allow.[129] Yet he has done more. He has sys-
tematized his chronology by establishing major events into which all
other events may be subsumed. The major events are: Adam, the
flood, the call of Abraham, the entrance into Egypt, the fall of
Samaria, the fall of Jerusalem, and the reign of Philopator.[130] We
are undoubtedly missing some such as the exodus, but we have a
clear impression of how he worked. A second feature of his system
is that he cross-references dates of biblical events.[131] What is missing is a reference to an outside event in the Greek world.[132] Only
the reign of Philopator is mentioned. Demetrios evidently wrote a
biblical chronology.

The second most dominant concern of Demetrios appears in the
form of ἀπορίαι καὶ λύσεις. On four occasions we have a question
(sometimes explicit and sometimes implicit) followed by an answer:
Why did Joseph wait so long before sending for his family (F 2.13)?
Why did Joseph give Benjamin so much more than the others (F
2.14)?[133] How could Moses have married a foreign woman (F 3.3)?

---

[128] The only non-chronological matters are those dealt with below under *quaestiones* and the one *nomos*.

[129] There are only thirteen texts which provide the immediate information
which Demetrios utilized: F 2.3 = Gen. 29:20, Jacob was with Laban seven years
before he married; F 2.6 = Gen. 31:41, Jacob worked for Laban six years and remained with him a total of twenty; F 2.11 = Gen. 37:2, Joseph was seventeen when
he was sold; F 2.11 = Gen. 41:46, Joseph rose to power when he was thirty; F 2.11
= Gen. 35:28, Isaac died at 180; F 2.12 = Gen. 41:47, Joseph ruled for seven
years; F 2.13 = Gen. 45:6, Joseph received his family after two years of famine;
F 2.17 = Gen. 47:9, Jacob came to Egypt when he was 130; F 2.19 = Gen. 47:28,
Jacob died at 147; F 2.19 = Ex. 6:16, Levi died at 137; F 2.19 = Gen. 50:26,
Joseph died at 110; F 2.19 = Ex. 6:18, Kohath died at 133; F 3.2 = Gen. 21:5,
Abraham fathered Isaac at 100. All other chronological references are based upon
deductions from texts and Demetrios' systematic chronological approach.

[130] The first four are dealt with in F 2.18 and the last three in F 6.1-2.

[131] F 2.11, Isaac's death is linked to Joseph's entrance into Egypt; F 2.19,
Kohath is born in the year Jacob died; F 6.1, the time between the captivities of
Samaria and Jerusalem is given.

[132] This is similar to Jubilees.

[133] Doran, ''The Jewish Hellenistic Historians Before Josephus,'' pp. 249-250,
argues this is not a *quaestio* but an example of midrashic exegesis. I do not concur
since the text explicitly casts it into the form of a question used in Hellenistic exegesis. On the form in both traditions see Saul Lieberman, *Hellenism in Jewish Palestine:
Studies in the Literary Transmission Beliefs and Manners of Palestine in the I Century B.C.E. -
IV Century C.E.*. Texts and Studies of the Jewish Theological Seminary of America
18 (New York: The Jewish Theological Seminary, 1950), p. 48.

Where did the Israelites obtain their weapons (F 5)? This is a clear use of a technique which had become famous through the Homeric questions and indicates Greek influence.[134] On the other hand, the questions which are raised are not those which would concern a Greek who knew nothing about the biblical text, but a Jew whose own careful reading of the text had generated perplexities which needed attention.

The only other forms which appear in these fragments are an aetiological explanation of a νόμος and a very brief narrative.[135] It is worth noting that Demetrios did attach his own name to his work—a practice in keeping with the exigencies of writing in Greek.[136]

If we try to imagine what form the whole work took, we should not think of a well-connected narrative. It followed the course of biblical history primarily in an effort to establish a chronology. Perhaps we should remember the work of Demetrios' contemporary, Eratosthenes (c. 275-194B.C.E.), who succeeded Apollonios Rhodios as the head of the Alexandrian library.[137] Eratosthenes wrote a Χρονογραφίαι which represents the first scientific attempt to fix the dates of major events.[138] The scope of his work extends from the fall of Troy to the death of Alexander (F 1). It is interesting that it, like Demetrios, chooses major events as chronological keys. In form it was more of a chronological listing (F 1) with some attention to cultural matters (F 3) if our fragments are representative. It seems

---

[134] See RAC, s.v. "Erotapokriseis," by Heinrich Dörrie and Hermann Dörries, 6:342-370, esp. 342-345. Examples of the form include Duris of Samos' Ὁμηρικὰ ζητήματα (c. 340-260 B.C.E.) and Porphery's later work of the same name. Fraser, Ptolemaic Alexandria, 1:693, has emphasized Demetrios' debt to Hellenism in this regard as well as in his critical approach. Cf. also Hengel, "Anonymität, Pseudepigraphie und 'Literarische Fälschung' in der jüdisch-hellenistischen Literatur," p. 236.

[135] F 2.7 and F 4 respectively.

[136] So Bickerman, "The Jewish Historian Demetrius," p. 72.

[137] Fraser, Ptolemaic Alexandria, 1:693-694, pointed out the general similarity between the two. On Eratosthenes see FGrH 241, esp. FF 1-3 and Fraser's discussion on 1:456-457.

[138] Greek historians prior to Eratosthenes had used various chronological systems: Herodotos used the reigns of Persian and Lydian kings; Thukydides the years of the war; and Timaios introduced the Olympiads as a system. Hellanikos of Mytilene (FGrH 4), who established a chronological frame through the Argive priestesses, and Hippias of Elis (FGrH 6), who collected and listed the victors of the Olympic games, are significant forerunners of Eratosthenes. (They are both fifth century figures.) Eratosthenes' contribution was to eliminate the mythical period (i.e., the period prior to the Trojan war) and establish a systematic guide.

more than coincidental that Demetrios should attempt to work out a biblical chronological system in Alexandria at the same time Eratosthenes laid the basis for the chronology of the Greek world.

3. *Function*. This naturally leads us to ask what function or purpose Demetrios' text(s) served. The major issue which has been raised in previous research is whether the fragments are apologetic and if so, in what sense? Peter Dalbert contended that they were apologetic in the sense that the fragments both defend the biblical text and were composed with missionary goals.[139] Others have denied that the fragments have any apologetic tendencies.[140] Still others prefer to speak of an implicit apology which attempts to answer questions and address problems within the Jewish community.[141] We must address three areas of concern in order to answer this question.

First, what can we deduce about the audience of Demetrios? Although there is no unanimity, I can not see how these fragments could have been addressed to any but the Jewish community.[142] The fragments presuppose some knowledge of the biblical text and a keen interest in its details. As we have already seen, the issues which are directly raised by the *quaestiones et solutiones* are those of the

---

[139] *Die Theologie der hellenistisch-jüdischen Missions-Literatur*, p. 29. Cf. also Hadas, *Hellenistic Culture*, pp. 94-95 and Hengel, *Judaism and Hellenism*, 1:69.

[140] So Victor Tcherikover, "Jewish Apologetic Literature Reconsidered," *Eos* 48 (1956): 179; Fraser, *Ptolemaic Alexandria*, 1:713 and 715, who contends that Demetrios is academic and that apologetic literature proper only arose in the second century B.C.E. when the Jews were important enough and racial tension between Egyptians and Greeks gave birth to Egyptian hostility; and Conzelmann, *Heiden-Juden-Christen*, p. 141.

[141] Denis, *Introduction aux Pseudépigraphes Grecs d'Ancien Testament*, p. 251; Walter, *JSHRZ*, 3:282; and Hanson, *OTP*, 2:845.

[142] Those who argue for a pagan audience include Dalbert, *Die Theologie der hellenistisch-jüdischen Missions-Literatur*, p.31, who bases his position on the explanation of the abstention from the *nervus ischiadicus*. The aetiological aspect of the passage would, however, suit a Jewish audience just as well. He has been followed by Hadas, *Hellenistic Culture*, p. 95 and Denis, *Introduction aux Pseudépigraphes Grecs d'Ancien Testament*, p. 251. A Jewish audience is presumed by Freudenthal, *Alexander Polyhistor*, p.81; Tcherikover, "Jewish Apologetic Literature Reconsidered," pp. 28-29; Eddy, *The King is Dead*, p. 195; Fraser, *Ptolemaic Alexandria*, 1:693; Wacholder, *Eupolemus*, pp. 281-282, who interestingly turns Dalbert's argument around by contending that since the abstention referred to the sons of Israel, the passage was addressed to Jews, and his article in *EncJud*, s.v. "Demetrius," 5:1491; Bickerman, "The Jewish Historian Demetrius," pp. 72-73; Collins, *Between Athens and Jerusalem*, p. 29; Hanson, *OTP*, 2:845; and Schürer, *The History of the Jewish People in the Age of Jesus Christ*, 3:515-516.

believing community not the outside world. The real world audience of the autograph text should thus be considered Jewish.

Second, does the text answer charges leveled against the Jewish people? Several have thought that Demetrios was responding to the attack of Manethon.[143] The problem with this view is that there is simply no evidence for it in our fragments.[144] The most that can be said is that both Manethon and Demetrios utilize chronology to establish the antiquity of their own people. (See below) It would certainly be going beyond the evidence to argue that Demetrios directly responded to Manethon. On the other hand, the *quaestiones* do betray an interest in defending the biblical text through solving some of the difficulties it poses.[145] If we are correct in positing a Jewish audience, then the defense must be to Jews who through Hellenization have begun to ask probing questions about the text and who have heard some of the claims of other peoples.[146] Like his compatriots, Demetrios had developed a critical sense, but he mingled it with piety in his ancestral faith.

Third, what function does the chronology play? Was this an academic exercise or is there a major issue at stake here?[147] In a summary of Clement's work, Eusebios lists the different authors whom Clement mentioned including Ἰωσήπου τε καὶ Δημητρίου καὶ Εὐπολέμου, Ἰουδαίων συγγραφέων, ὡς ἂν τούτων ἁπάντων ἐγγράφως πρεσβύτερον τῆς παρ' Ἕλλησιν ἀρχαιογονίας Μωυσέα τε καὶ τὸ Ἰουδαίων γένος ἀποδειξάντων.[148] There can be no doubt that establishing antiquity was a major concern for cultural and national claims in antiquity. In Plato's *Timaeus*, an Egyptian priest taunts Solon with the charge: Ἕλληνες ἀεὶ παῖδές ἐστε, γέρων δὲ Ἕλλην οὐκ ἔστιν.[149] This was an oriental defense mechanism against

---

[143] E.g., Eddy, *The King is Dead*, p. 195 and Fraser, *Ptolemaic Alexandria*, 1:693-694 (possibly). Cf. also Denis, *Introduction aux Pseudépigraphes Grecs d'Ancien Testament*, p. 251, who allows for the possibility of his response to Greek historians.

[144] Freudenthal, *Alexander Polyhistor*, p. 81, offers a *non licet* while Schürer, *The History of the Jewish People in the Age of Jesus Christ*, 3:516, denies there is any polemic against any foreign people.

[145] Freudenthal, *Alexander Polyhistor*, p. 44, pointed out Demetrios' interest in defending the biblical text.

[146] So also Collins, *Between Athens and Jerusalem*, p. 29 and Walter, *JSHRZ*, 3:282.

[147] There does not appear to be anything apologetic about Eratosthenes work which shows that this was a viable genre.

[148] Eusebios, *HE* 6.13.7.

[149] *Timaeus* 22B. See 21E-23C. Cf. also Pseudo-Plato, *Epinomis* 987D-988A.

Hellenism. Josephos offers the clearest statement of its *raison d'être*: ἀμέλει πειρῶνται τὰ παρ' αὑτοῖς ἕκαστοι πρὸς τὸ ἀρχαιότατον ἀνάγειν, ἵνα μὴ μιμεῖσθαι δόξωσιν ἑτέρους, ἀλλ' αὐτοὶ τοῦ ζῆν νομίμως ἄλλοις ὑφηγήσασθαι.[150]

The flip side of the attempt to date one's own people back as far as possible was to downgrade the dates of other peoples. An outstanding example of this is the effort by authors hostile to Judaism to move the date of the exodus down in time.[151] Manethon is the first author to give the exodus a date in Egyptian history. His date is complicated by the fact that he appears to offer two separate versions: the first identifies the Jews with the Hyksos of the fifteenth and sixteenth dynasties and the second more scurrilous tradition locates them in the eighteenth under Amenophis.[152] Chaeremon (first century C.E.) follows Manethon's second version.[153] The eighteenth dynasty was opted for by Ptolemy of Mendes (first century B.C.E.) and one tradition associated with Apion (first century C.E.) who both placed it under Amosis, a contemporary of the Argive king Inachos.[154] This was apparently still too early for Apion himself who synchronized the exodus with the seventh Olympiad.[155] Whether Apion drew upon Lysimachos (second-first century B.C.E.?) directly or only upon the same tradition is hard to say. The latter, however, is very close to Apion when he states that the expulsion of the lepers took place under Bocchoris of the twenty-fourth dynasty.[156] This diversity of dates led Josephos to comment about

---

Kastor of Rhodes (*FGrH* 250) wrote a Χρονικά in which he offered synchronistic tables of Oriental, Greek, and Roman kings in an effort to give the West parity with the East.

[150] *CA* 2.152. Cf. also Diodoros 1.9.3.

[151] That this was a deliberate procedure is recognized by Wacholder, "Biblical Chronology in the Hellenistic World Chronicles," pp. 477-481 and Gager, *Moses in Greco-Roman Paganism*, pp. 114-115, n. 4. Josephos railed against such dates in *CA* 2.15-19.

[152] The first account is preserved by Josephos in *CA* 1.75-90 and the second in 1.227-253. The first account seems to equate the Hyksos with the Jews in 1.89-90 where they are credited with settling in Syria and founding Jerusalem. On the accounts see Stern, *GLAJJ*, 1:62-86, especially 62-65.

[153] Cf. Josephos, *CA* 1.288-292. For text with commentary see Stern, *GLAJJ*, 1:417-421.

[154] This was Ahmose I, Egypt's liberator from the Hyksos. On Ptolemy see Stern, *GLAJJ*, 1:379-381, and for Apion, 1:389-416, especially 392 (= Eusebios, *PE* 10.10.16).

[155] Josephos, *CA* 2.17. This appears to be Apion's own position.

[156] Cf. Josephos, *CA* 1.304-311 and 2.16. Stern, *GLAJJ*, 1:382-388, provides texts and commentary.

Apollonios Molon's dating in disgust: Μόλων δὲ καὶ ἄλλοι τινές ὡς αὐτοῖς ἔδοξεν.[157]

The Jewish community was fully aware of this line of argumentation. The beginnings of Jewish efforts to consciously date Israel in the remote past go back to the LXX. A quick glance at the dates offered in the genealogies of Gen. 5 and 11 makes this clear. In Gen. 5 the ages of the ante-diluvian figures are essentially the same for their total life-span, but radically different for the age when they beget their sons. The result is that the span from Adam to the flood in the MT is 1656 years, while in the LXX it is 2242 years.[158] The same phenomenon takes place in Gen. 11:10-26 where the LXX adds one generation and in six of the nine names found in MT adds 100 years to the age of the post-diluvian figure before he begets a son. The result of these and other alterations is that from the birth of Shem to the death of Terah the MT gives 2996 years, the LXX 4080. If we total the years from Adam until Abraham, we get 1948 years in MT and 3314 in the LXX.[159]

Does Demetrios' work participate in this debate? Demetrios incontestably follows the LXX.[160] It is clearly the text of preference (or possibly the only text) for him. Is there any reason why he would prefer the LXX apart from the fact that he wrote in Greek?[161] The fact that the *solutiones* in the fragments evidence a concern to defend

---

[157] *CA* 2.16.

[158] Wacholder, "Biblical Chronology in the Hellenistic World Chronicles," p. 453, gives 2264 for the LXX. He must be assuming that the LXX should credit Methuselah with 187 years instead of 167 before the birth of his son. MT has 187. Cf. Gen. 5:25. I presume that the other two years come from Gen. 11:10 where we are told that Shem was 100 years old two years after the flood which means that he was born 98 years before it or in the 502nd year of Noah. It is a mistake, however, to count these two years prior to the flood.

[159] I have added in the two years mentioned in Gen. 11:10.

[160] In F 2.18, he gives the time from Adam until the entrance into Egypt as 3624 years. This is based upon: 3334 years from Adam to Abraham (the genealogies of Gen. 5 [including reading 187 instead of 167 in Gen. 5:25] and 11), Abraham's age of 100 when he begat Isaac (F 3.2 = Gen. 21:5), Isaac's age of 60 when he begat Jacob (F 2.11), and the age of Jacob when he entered Egypt, 130 (F 2.17 = Gen. 47:9).

[161] Wacholder, "Biblical Chronology in the Hellenistic World Chronicles," p. 456 n. 15 and 457 n. 19 and *EncJud*, s.v. "Demetrius," 5:1491, suggested that Demetrios was one of the translators of the LXX. He argued that since Demetrios explains the reasoning behind the numbers of the LXX he must be the originator rather than the follower of the scheme. The greatest difficulties with this are the tradition that the LXX began under Ptolemy Philadelphos and our proof that Demetrios knew Hebrew is scanty.

the text make it likely that we should see his chronological efforts in the same light. Demetrios lived in an age when Egyptian nationalism was on the upswing. He lived in a city where the foundations of Greek chronology had just been laid and where the competing claims of antiquity for various cultures were undoubtedly heard. It is reasonable—although not ineluctable—to conclude that in such a milieu a work which systematically worked out biblical chronology did so in an effort to help the Jewish community establish its own antiquity.[162]

Significance

To what genre should we assign these fragments? Some have called them a chronology,[163] others history,[164] and still others exegesis.[165] The difficulty arises from weighing the different aspects of the fragments. If we consider them from the standpoint of form alone, I would call Demetrios an exegetical chronographer. On the other hand, if we consider the purpose of the fragments, it is natural to call him a historian in the same sense that we do Berossos and Manethon. After all they have a great deal in common: they all use native traditions to establish the antiquity of their own people. The major differences are in form and audience. The variation in form should not be overdrawn: Demetrios more freely shaped his native documents in forms that were current in his day than the others did. The form is, nonetheless, built upon and firmly anchored in his native documents. Demetrios thus stands as a witness to the diversity in which native authors attempted to carve out their self-identity in the new world of Hellenism.

---

[162] So also Ben Zion Wacholder, "How Long Did Abram Stay in Egypt? (A Study in Hellenistic, Qumran, and Rabbinic Chronography)," *HUCA* 35 (1964): 51-52; Hengel, "Anonymität, Pseudepigraphie und 'Literarische Fälschung' in der jüdisch-hellenistischen Literatur," pp. 235-236 and *Judaism and Hellenism*, 1:69; Bickerman, "The Jewish Historian Demetrios," pp. 76-80; and *RAC*, s.v. "Erfinder II," by K. Thraede, 5:1243.

[163] So Freudenthal, *Alexander Polyhistor*, p. 37 (his heading for Demetrios on p. 35 is "Demetrios, der Chronograph"), who also emphasized his exegetical concerns on pp. 65-77; Dalbert, *Die Theologie der hellenistisch-jüdischen Missions-Literatur*, p. 28; and Hanson, *OTP*, 2:843, who has the same heading as Freudenthal.

[164] Fraser, *Ptolemaic Alexandria*, 1:690.

[165] Walter, *JSHRZ*, 3:280-292, where he is placed together with Aristobulos and Aristeas as an example of a Jewish exegete and again in "Jüdisch-hellenistische Literatur vor Philon von Alexandrien," p. 78.

Demetrios is very important for our understanding of Judaism at the end of the third century. He is the first Jewish author whom we know wrote in Greek, as well as the first to cite the LXX. The elaborate chronological system and the ἀπορίαι καὶ λύσεις point to the existence of a Jewish school of exegesis at this early date.[166] He thus stands at the head of Jewish chronography which again surfaces in the second century in the sectarian works of the Genesis Apocryphon and Jubilees and then later in the more normative Seder Olam Rabbah (c. 150 C.E.). He is also the first Jewish author who attempted to define Judaism within the context of the Hellenistic world. We now turn to his successors.

ARTAPANOS[167]

Life

We have no ancient *testimonia* for Artapanos and must deduce what we can from his fragments to form a conception of his *Sitz im Leben*. Artapanos is a Persian name.[168] While earlier scholars thought he was a pagan because of the apparent acceptance of non-Jewish views, his open patriotism on behalf of the Jewish people demands that we regard him as a Jew.[169] Freudenthal attempted to resolve

---

[166] The formulaic use of διὰ τί (F 2.14) and πῶς (F 5.16) point in this direction. So also Wacholder, "Biblical Chronology in the Hellenistic World Chronicles," p. 454 and *Eupolemus*, p.99; Denis, *Introduction aux Pseudépigraphes Grecs d'Ancien Testament*, p. 251; Attridge, "Historiography," p. 162; and Hanson, *OTP*, 2:844.

[167] The most important works on Artapanos include: Freudenthal, *Alexander Polyhistor*, pp. 143-174; *RE*, s.v. "Artapanos," by Eduard Schwartz, 2:1306; Dalbert, *Die Theologie der hellenistisch-jüdischen Missions-Literatur*, pp. 42-52; K.I. Merentites, Ὁ Ἰουδαῖος Λόγιος Ἀρταπανὸς καὶ τὸ Ἔργον Αὐτοῦ (Athens, 1961); John Collins and Bill Poehlmann, "Artapanus," Unpublished Paper from NT Seminar 201 (Harvard University, 1970); Denis, *Introduction aux Pseudépigraphes Grecs d'Ancien Testament*, pp. 255-257; Fraser, *Ptolemaic Alexandria*, 1:704-706, 714; Walter, *JSHRZ*, 1:121-136; Conzelmann, *Heiden-Juden-Christen*, pp. 149-152; Holladay, *Fragments from Hellenistic Jewish Authors*, pp. 189-243; Collins, *Between Athens and Jerusalem*, pp. 32-38 and his "Artapanus," in *OTP*, 2:889-903; Attridge, "Historiography," pp. 166-168; Schürer, *The History of the Jewish People in the Age of Jesus Christ*, 3:521-525; Droge, *Homer or Moses?*, pp. 25-35; and Pilhofer, *Presbyteron Kreitton*, pp. 156-159.

[168] Fraser, *Ptolemaic Alexandria*, 2:985, n. 199, has an excellent summary of what we know about the name itself.

[169] His Jewish ethnicity was established by Freudenthal, *Alexander Polyhistor*, pp. 143-153. Carl R. Holladay, *"Theios Aner" in Hellenistic-Judaism: A Critique of the Use of This Category in New Testament Christology*. SBLDS 40 (Missoula, Montana: Scholars Press, 1977), pp. 201-204, has a good summary of earlier views. I am unaware of any contemporary work which regards Artapanos as a pagan. The shift has come because of the realization that Judaism was not monolithic in the Hellenistic period.

the tension between the open syncretism and obvious nationalism by suggesting that the name was a *nom de plume* used by a patriotic Jew who spoke as if he were an Egyptian priest.[170] He then went on to identify this Jew with Pseudo-Aristeas and also credited him with the work which has commonly passed under the name of Pseudo-Hekataios.[171] The greatest problem with this view is that Pseudo-Aristeas is openly critical of Egyptian cults: a view diametrically opposed to that of Artapanos.[172] Dalbert correctly rejected Freudenthal's identification, but still thought that the work was a *Trugschrift*.[173] There is, however, no reason to question the authenticity of the name since there is no known reason for a forger to use it. We may, therefore, consider Artapanos to be the name of the Jewish author—probably of mixed descent—who wrote our fragments.[174]

The *termini* for Artapanos' dates are his dependence on the LXX and Polyhistor's use of his work, i.e., c. 250-40 B.C.E. Attempts to be more specific have placed him in all three centuries.[175] The

---

[170] *Alexander Polyhistor*, pp. 143-153.

[171] *Ibid.*, pp. 162-169. On Pseudo-Hekataios see our comments in chapter three.

[172] *Letter of Aristeas*, 138-139.

[173] *Die Theologie der hellenistisch-jüdischen Missions-Literatur*, p. 44.

[174] So also Denis, *Introduction aux Pseudépigraphes Grecs d'Ancien Testament*, pp. 256-257; Fraser, *Ptolemaic Alexandria*, 1:704 and 2:985, n. 199; Hengel, "Anonymität, Pseudepigraphie und 'Literarische Fälschung' in der jüdisch-hellenistischen Literatur," pp. 239-240; Walter, *JSHRZ*, 1:123-124 and 124, n. 13; Holladay, *Fragments from Hellenistic Jewish Authors*, p. 189; and Schürer, *The History of the Jewish People in the Age of Jesus Christ*, 3:522-523.

[175] Third century during the reign of Ptolemy IV Philopator and therefore a contemporary of Demetrios: Denis, *Introduction aux Pseudépigraphes Grecs d'Ancien Testament*, p. 257 and Collins, *Between Athens and Jerusalem*, pp. 32-33, 38 and *OTP*, 2:890-891, who argues that the enigmatic passages of F 3.20, 24-26, refer to Philopator's attempt to impose the worship of Dionysos on the Jews, elephantiasis (F 3.20) was first discovered in the third century and the reference would make more sense if the discovery were new, and the inclusion of Egyptians in Pharaoh's army (F 3.77) first occurred when Philopator prepared for Raphia. He openly acknowledges the tentative nature of these arguments. Early second century: Wacholder, "Biblical Chronology in the Hellenistic World Chronicles," pp. 460-461 and *Eupolemus*, p. 106, n. 40, who likewise pointed out the discovery of elephantiasis and argued that the open syncretism pointed to a period before the Maccabean revolt. Mid-second century: Conzelmann, *Heiden-Juden-Christen*, p. 149 and Holladay, *Fragments from Hellenistic Jewish Authors*, p. 190, both see a reference to the temple of Onias at Leontopolis in F 2.4 where the Jews built a temple at Heliopolis (Leontopolis was in the Heliopolite nome). Second century: Dalbert, *Die Theologie der hellenistisch-jüdischen Missions-Literatur*, p. 44. First century: Walter, *JSHRZ*, 1:125 and "Jüdisch-hellenistische Literatur vor Philon von Alexandrien," p. 98, who places him c. 100 and Isidore Levy, *La Légende de Pythagore de Grèce en Palestine* (Paris: Bibliothèque de l'École de Hautes Études, 1927), p. 138, who

difficulty is that there are no decisive factors which allow us to specify a date. The most that can be safely said is that he wrote long enough before Polyhistor for his work to circulate and pass into the hands of the collector.

Since all of the fragments deal with Egypt, an Egyptian provenance is unquestioned. One immediately thinks of Alexandria since so much Hellenistic Jewish literature emanated from there.[176] It is, however, by no means the only possibility.[177] Leontopolis and Memphis have also been proposed.[178] A major reason for placing Artapanos outside Alexandria is that our fragments differ from the Alexandrian corpus in being more popular in orientation. This, however, would not necessarily disqualify an Alexandrian provenance, but does say something about the social level of our author.[179] On the whole, it is best to simply affirm that he wrote in Egypt.[180]

Work

1. *Content*. We have three fragments attributed to Artapanos in the *Praeparatio Evangelica*.[181] The third has a partial parallel in the *Stromata* of Clement.[182]

---

places him between 75 and 50 since he thought Artapanos was dependent upon Pseudo-Hekataios. Schürer, *The History of the Jewish People in the Age of Jesus Christ*, 3:523-525, rejects all attempts to be specific as speculative.

[176] Walter, *JSHRZ*, 1:124-125 and Attridge, "Historiography," p. 168.

[177] For the evidence of Jewish settlements throughout Egypt see Schürer, *The History of the Jewish People in the Age of Jesus Christ*, 3:38-60.

[178] Leontopolis: Hengel, "Anonymität, Pseudepigraphie und 'Literarische Fälschung' in der jüdisch-hellenistischen Literatur," p. 239 and Holladay, "*Theios Aner*", p. 217. Memphis: Fraser, *Ptolemaic Alexandria*, 1:706, who wrote: "He is familiar with the native life of Egypt and the purely priestly traditions, and it is most natural to see in him not a member of the influential Jewish circles around Philometor or a later Ptolemy, but . . . as a Jew of mixed descent, possibly resident in another centre such as Memphis, where the residence of Jews from an early date exacerbated a problem which was still only nascent in the capital."

[179] Artapanos' literary connections point to a lower social level than that of Demetrios or Aristeas. So Martin Braun, *History and Romance in Graeco-Oriental Literature* (Oxford: Basil Blackwell, 1938), pp. 3ff., esp. 26-31; Fraser, *Ptolemaic Alexandria*, 1:706; and Holladay, "*Theios Aner*", pp. 212-214.

[180] So also Holladay, *Fragments from Hellenistic Jewish Authors*, p. 190 and Collins, *Between Athens and Jerusalem*, p. 33 and *OTP*, 2:891.

[181] *PE* 9.18.1; 23.1-4; 27.1-37.

[182] *Stromata* 1.23.154.2-3. There are six variations between the two accounts. One, in Clement's editorial introduction he first states that Moses was thrown into prison and then gives the reason while in Eusebios Moses is thrown into prison after

The first fragment explains that the "Hermiouth" were first called Hebrews at the time of Abraham who came to Egypt where he taught Pharaoh astrology.[183] After twenty years he returned to Syria, but some of his company remained.

F 2 recounts the career of Joseph in Egypt. Joseph astutely foresaw the antipathy of his brothers and persuaded some Arabs to take him to Egypt. After having become acquainted with Pharaoh, he became the financial administrator of the country—a role he fulfilled well by land reforms and the invention of measures. He also raised a family which was supplemented by the arrival of his father and brothers. Here in Egypt the Hermiouth built temples and Joseph enjoyed unrivaled power.[184]

The adult life of Moses in Egypt comprises the third and longest fragment. The fragment naturally falls into two halves: the first half (1-20) narrates the struggle between Chenephres and Moses; the second half (21-37) retells Moses' role in the exodus.[185] The fragment opens with a reference to a new king's, Palmanothes', persecution of the Jews. In the course of time the king gave his daughter, Merris, in marriage to Chenephres, ruler of one of Egypt's regions. Since

---

he has told Pharaoh why he has come (2 vs. 22-23). Two, during the night the prison doors open κατὰ βούλεσιν τοῦ θεοῦ in Clement (2) and αὐτομάτως in Eusebios (23). The last four deviations are details omitted in Clement but found in Eusebios: the reference to the dead or sleeping guards and their shattered weapons at the prison (23), the open doors of the palace (23), the sleeping bodyguards (24), and the manner in which Pharaoh asked Moses to tell him the name of God, διαχλευάσαντα αὐτόν (24). Eusebios' version stands closer to Polyhistor than Clement's which is an obvious condensation. The effect of Clement's reductions is the toning down of the miraculous.

[183] Gerard Mussies, "The Interpretatio Judaica of Thot-Hermes," in *Studies in Egyptian Religion: Dedicated to Professor Jan Zandee*, edited by M. Heerma van Voss, D.J. Hoens, G. Mussies, D. van der Plas, and H. te Velde. Studies in the History of Religions 43 (Leiden: E.J. Brill, 1982), p. 112, has plausibly suggested that "Hermiouth" means something like "men of Judah." The *erm-* could be a variant of Coptic ⲣⲙ, the construct of ⲣⲱⲙⲉ, "man."

[184] Walter, *JSHRZ*, 1:128, n. 4c, thinks that the final clause, παραθέσθαι καὶ τῆς Αἰγύπτου δεσπότην γενέσθαι, belongs to Demetrios F 2.2. This is perhaps too radical. I think it is preferable to see a promotion in Joseph's position from διοικητής (finance minister or treasurer in 2) to δεσπότης in 4.

[185] David Lenz Tiede, *The Charismatic Figure as Miracle Worker*. SBLDS 1 (Missoula, Montana: The Society of Biblical Literature, 1972), p. 164, pointed out the differences between the two halves: the first is the conflict between the two men; the second introduces God, the conflict is now between Jews and Egyptians, and miracles and magic become common. Holladay, *"Theios Aner"*, pp. 219-220, noticed that the first half made no attempt to retell the biblical text while the second essentially summarized Ex. 2:23-16:36.

she was barren she adopted a Jewish child named Moses by the
Hebrews and Mousaios by the Greeks. At this point the conflict begins. The struggle moves through two plots as Chenephres schemes
to eliminate Moses. Each follows the same basic pattern as the following chart will show:

Event	First Plot	Second Plot
Moses' accomplishments		
and fame	4-6	12
Plot	7	13-14
Failure	8-9	15-18
Moses' subsequent success	10	21-37

The first plot arose after Moses invented numerous machines and
established Egyptian religion. Chenephres was moved with jealousy
and tried to kill Moses by sending him on a campaign against Ethiopia with a band of farmers for an army. Contrary to his expectations, Moses returned triumphant. Back at Memphis, Moses again
contributed to Egyptian religion by euhemeristically pointing out
the value of the ox. Dejected but not defeated, Chenephres attempted to have Moses assassinated by Chanethothes while they were
burying Merris. The plot failed when Moses overpowered
Chanethothes and fled to Arabia. This now opens up the second half
of the fragment: just as Moses enjoyed his success in the first half
by defeating the Ethiopians, he will now enjoy success in the second
half by leading the Israelites from Egypt. After a miraculous theophany, Moses decided to return to Egypt. When he arrived, the
king arrested him. Following a miraculous escape he performed a
series of signs and led the people from Egypt.

There are two titles preserved in the fragments: 'Ιουδαϊκά (F 1.1)
and Περὶ 'Ιουδαίων (FF 2.1; 3.1; 3b.2). Do we have two separate
works or one in which case one or both of the titles given are subtitles
or secondary?[186] It is worth pointing out that both Eusebios and
Clement attest the title Περὶ 'Ιουδαίων. Of more significance,
however, is the fact that we appear to have the basic structure of a

---

[186] Two separate works: Denis, *Introduction aux Pseudépigraphes Grecs d'Acien
Testament*, p. 255. One work: Jacoby, *FGrH* 726; Fraser, *Ptolemaic Alexandria*, 1:704;
Holladay, *Fragments from Hellenistic Jewish Authors*, p. 189; Collins, *OTP*, 2:889;
Schürer, *The History of the Jewish People in the Age of Jesus Christ*, 3:521, all of whom
prefer Περὶ 'Ιουδαίων as the title. Walter, *JSHRZ*, 1:121, suggested that both were
added by Polyhistor who did not have a title in the exemplar from which he worked.

single work preserved within our fragments. The three fragments which we have all relate the careers of Israel's most illustrious ancestors in Egypt. It appears that Artapanos only dealt with the history of Israel in Egypt.[187] We can go farther than this, however, and suggest that we have the basic structure of Artapanos' work represented in the fragments. This is supported by the transitional introductions of FF 2 and 3. F 2 begins with a reference to Artapanos' statement that τῷ 'Αβραὰμ 'Ιωσὴφ ἀπόγονον γενέσθαι, υἱὸν δὲ 'Ιακώβου. The emphasis is not on Joseph's relationship to Jacob, but to Abraham. I suggest that Artapanos omitted Isaac and Jacob from his account—except for incidental references—because they were not significant figures in Israel's history in Egypt. F 3 opens with a statement which is probably corrupt: 'Αβραὰμ τελευτήσαντος καὶ τοῦ υἱοῦ αὐτοῦ Μεμψασθενώθ, ὁμοίως δὲ καὶ τοῦ βασιλέως τῶν Αἰγυπτίων, τὴν δυναστείαν παραλαβεῖν τὸν υἱὸν αὐτοῦ Παλμανώθην. As the text stands we have a parallel between Abraham and his son and the king of Egypt and his son. There are two problems with the text: who is Mempsasthenoth and why is the name of the king omitted? The statement is evidently based upon Ex. 1:6 and 8, where we are informed of Joseph's death and the coming to power of another king who did not know him. Freudenthal suggested that Mempsasthenoth was the name of the king and not of Abraham's son.[188] In addition, he thought that Polyhistor incorrectly wrote Abraham in the place of Jacob.[189] Most recently Collins has identified Abraham with Joseph (mistake made by Polyhistor) and Mempsasthenoth with his son.[190] I would suggest Abraham means Abraham and that Mempsasthenoth was the name of the king of Egypt.[191] It was mistakenly transferred by either Polyhistor or a

---

[187] So also Freudenthal, *Alexander Polyhistor*, p. 150; Fraser, *Ptolemaic Alexandria*, 1:706; and Walter, *JSHRZ*, 1:121-122.

[188] *Alexander Polyhistor*, p. 217. He has been followed by Jacoby, *FGrH* 726, F 3; and Walter, *JSHRZ*, 1:128-129. Freudenthal correctly—in my opinion—pointed out that the confusion arose due to the similarity in names (see below).

[189] He has been seconded here by Holladay, *Fragments from Hellenistic Jewish Authors*, p. 230, nn. 31 and 32, who bases this on the fact that Jacob and Joseph were just discussed. Cf. Eusebios, *PE* 9.21-24.

[190] *OTP*, 2:898, nn. The strength of identifying Μεμψασθενώθ with a son of Joseph is the similarity of the second half to Joseph's wife, 'Ασενέθ (F 2.3). He also recognizes the possibility of Abraham = Jacob (due to error) and Mempsasthenoth = Joseph (based on Gen. 41:45).

[191] I find no merit in the suggestion of Wallace Nelson Stearns, *Fragments from Graeco-Jewish Writers* (Chicago: The University of Chicago Press, 1908), p. 53, that

scribe when he omitted Psonthomphanech (= Joseph, Gen. 41:45) which has the same number of syllables—as Freudenthal correctly observed.[192] There is, however, no mistake in calling Joseph Abraham's son since υἱός can mean descendant as well as immediate male progeny.[193] If this analysis is correct, then F 3 opens with a reference back to Abraham (F 1) and Joseph (F 2). It thus establishes one work for Artapanos which probably circulated under the name Περὶ Ἰουδαίων.

These comments also help us to determine the scope of Artapanos' work. It began with Abraham and continued on down through the wilderness wanderings relating only the events which involved Egypt. If our fragments preserve any sense of proportion, then Abraham was dealt with briefly, Joseph more in detail as the vizier of Egypt, and Moses was the central figure. The work was thus biographically cast and appropriately concluded with a description of Moses.[194]

2. *Form.* The form which these fragments took is partially due to the sources which Artapanos utilized. The most obvious of these is the biblical text. The following chart indicates the passages where F 3 has some relationship to the biblical text.

Event	*LXX* (Ex.)	*Artapanos*
Palmanothes comes to power	1:8	1
Jews mistreated	1:9-11	2
Merris adopts Moses	2:1-10	3
Moses as *Kulturbringer*		4-5
Moses' popularity		6
The Ethiopian campaign		7-10
Chenephres' second plot		11-14
Moses & Chanethothes bury Merris		15-16
Moses flees Memphis		17

Mempsasthenoth is Isaac. This is biblically correct, but does not offer any help here.

[192] These names must have been as foreign to Greek speaking scribes as they are to us.

[193] The LXX which Artapanos used (see below) has a number of examples of υἱός as "grandson," e.g., Gen. 32:1; 45:10. F 2.1 does, as we have seen, recognize that Jacob was Joseph's immediate father.

[194] This is an expansion of Deut. 34:7. There is no evidence that Artapanos dealt with Sinai. Given what we have in our fragments, the wilderness must have been summarily introduced as a way of finishing the exodus story. Ending with a physical description gives the work a biographical flair.

Event	LXX (Ex.)	Artapanos
Moses kills Chanethothes	2:11-12	18
Moses arrives in Arabia	2:13-21	19
Chenephres dies	2:23	20
The call of Moses	3:1-4:17	21
Moses returns to Egypt	4:27-28; 5:1-4	22
Moses imprisoned & the divine name		23-26
Rod turns into snake	7:10	27
Nile floods	7:20-21	28
Pharaoh petitions Moses		29
Priests perform signs	7:11-12,22	30
Winged creatures	8:20-24?	31
Frogs, locusts, flees	8:1-2;10:12-15 8:12-15(MT 16-19)	32a
Rod honored		32b
Hail and earthquakes	9:23-25; Ps. 76:19(MT 77:18)	33
Exodus	11:31-32,35-36; 13:17-22	34
Alternate versions		35
The event at the Sea	14:15-31	36-37a
Forty years in wilderness	16:4-36	37b
Description of Moses	Deut. 34:7	37c

Like Demetrios, Artapanos made use of the LXX.[195] This can be shown by the proper names[196] and by verbal echoes.[197] The only

---

[195] Freudenthal, *Alexander Polyhistor*, pp. 152,216; Dalbert, *Die Theologie der hellenistisch-jüdischen Missions-Literatur*, p. 43; Denis, *Introduction aux Pseudépigraphes Grecs d'Ancien Testament*, p. 257; Conzelmann, *Heiden-Juden-Christen*, p. 149; Holladay, *Fragments from Hellenistic Jewish Authors*, p. 192; and Collins, *Between Athens and Jerusalem*, p. 32 and *OTP*, 2:894.

[196] Of the twenty proper names in Artapanos six agree with the LXX (Αβρααμ (however in F 1 it is Αβρααμος), Ιωσηφ, Ισραηλ, Ισαακ, Ααρων, and Απις in F 3.12 which does not have a parallel in Ex., but does appear in the same form in Jer. 26:15), five vary, and nine have no parallel. The variations include Φαρεθωθης for Φαραω, Ιακωβος for Ιακωβ, Ασενεθ in stead of Ασεννεθ, Μωυσος (dominant form in fragments) in place of Μωυσης, and Ραηουηλος for Ραγουηλ. It should be noted that the basic distinction is that in Artapanos the names assume a fully declinable form instead of the indeclinable transliterations of the LXX. The same pattern holds true for place names. Of the eleven which occur, four agree with the LXX (Αιγυπτος, Ηλιοπολις, Μεμφις (occurs in Hos. 9:6; Ezek. 30:13, 15, 16 *et alii*), and most significantly, η Ερυθρα θαλασσα), two are anachronistic (Συρια for ἐν γῇ Χανααν (F 1 = Gen. 13:12) and Αραβια for ἐν γῇ Μαδιαμ (F 3.17, 34 = Ex. 2:15)—both names appear in the same form elsewhere in the LXX), and five have no biblical parallel (Σαις, Αθως, Ερμοπολιτης, Ερμου πολις, Μεροη).

[197] In F 3.28 ἐποζέσαι echoes Ex. 7:18,21 and F 3.30 διά τινων μαγγάνων καὶ

indication that Artapanos knew Hebrew is in F 1 where he says
καλεῖσθαι δὲ αὐτοὺς Ἑβραίους ἀπὸ ᾽Αβραάμου. This is likely dependent upon the Hebrew text of Gen. 14:13.[198] The difficulty is that
we do not know whether Artapanos had read the text himself or
whether he simply drew upon an oral tradition which was based
upon this text.

In his use of the biblical text, Artapanos represents the obverse of
Demetrios: instead of drawing from the biblical material, Artapanos
uses the text as a point of departure to tell his stories. He not only
adds to it as the preceding chart shows, but modifies or even con-
tradicts the biblical text—seemingly at will.[199]

How should we explain this freedom with his traditions? Do we
have a menagerie of assorted sources or a creative author?[200] If Artapanos used sources, are they literary or oral?[201] How did his
sources affect the shape of his work and do they tell us anything
about its nature?

In order to answer these questions, we must recognize the common mold into which each of the three major characters are cast:
they are all *Kulturbringer*. Abraham teaches Pharaoh astronomy,
Joseph is both a great land reformer and the discoverer of measures,

---

ἐπαοιδῶν recalls Ex. 7:11 (οἱ ἐπαοιδοὶ τῶν Αἰγυπτίων) and δράκοντα Ex. 7:12
(δράκοντες; v. 10 δράκων).

[198] MT: וינגד לאברם העברי; LXX: ἀπήγγειλεν Αβραμ τῷ περάτῃ.

[199] I count five deviations from the biblical text for F 1 (Jews named Hermiouth, Pharethothes as a proper name, Abraham taught Pharethothes astrology,
Abraham remained in Egypt twenty years, and many of his family remained in
Egypt) and eight for F 2 (Joseph envied for virtue rather than as favorite, Joseph
asks the Arabs to take him to Egypt, Arab is anachronistic, Joseph as a land reformer, his discovery of measures, the love of the Egyptians for Joseph, the Israelites settled in Heliopolis and Sais, and they built temples in Athos and Heliopolis).
It is fair to say that there are more disagreements than agreements.

[200] Holladay, "*Theios Aner*", p. 217: "Far from being a creative piece of work,
it merely assembles traditions and legends indiscriminately." Schwartz, *RE*, s.v.
"Artapanos," 2:1306, also thinks that the work depended upon sources, but cautions against deciding whether a particular point is a tradition or the creation of Artapanos.

[201] Those who contend for written sources include Walter, *JSHRZ*, 1:124, who
thinks he used Hellenistic accounts of Egypt. Those who specifically argue for dependence upon Hekataios include: Levy, *La Légende de Pythagore de Grèce en Palestine*,
pp. 206-210; Denis, *Introduction aux Pseudépigraphes Grecs d'Ancien Testament*, pp.
256-257; Collins and Poehlmann, "Artapanus," p. 45 and Collins *Between Athens
and Jerusalem*, p. 54, n. 48 and *OTP*, 2:894. Dalbert, *Die Theologie der hellenistisch-
jüdischen Missions-Literatur*, p. 43 and Holladay, *Fragments from Hellenistic Jewish
Authors*, p. 192, opt for oral traditions. Conzelmann, *Heiden-Juden-Christen*, p. 152,
thinks that source criticism in Artapanos is a waste of time ("aussichtslos").

and Moses is the founder of Egyptian civilization. Together the fragments trace the glory and grandeur of Egyptian civilization to the Jews. Yet they do this in a way which is very different from how Berossos and Manethon each made their respective claims. The latter relied upon native documentation for their claims and eschewed foreign reports. Artapanos boldly goes well beyond his traditions. Why?

Besides the works of *literati* who both knew and critiqued Greek oeuvres, indigenous people also had legends which glorified national heroes on a popular level.[202] Plutarch mentions some of the most prominent: καίτοι μεγάλαι μὲν ὑμνοῦνται πράξεις ἐν Ἀσσυρίοις Σεμιράμιος, μεγάλαι δὲ Σεσώστριος ἐν Αἰγύπτῳ· Φρύγες δὲ μέχρι νῦν τὰ λαμπρὰ καὶ θαυμαστὰ τῶν ἔργων Μανικὰ καλοῦσι, explaining, διὰ τὸ Μάνην τινὰ τῶν πάλαι βασιλέων ἀγαθὸν ἄνδρα καὶ δυνατὸν γενέσθαι παρ' αὐτοῖς, ὃν ἔνιοι Μάσδην καλοῦσι.[203] These heroes allowed conquered people to point to their past greatness as a way of compensating for their present servitude. The most significant of these for our purposes are Semiramis of Assyria[204] and Sesoosis (Sesostris) of Egypt.[205] Each was championed as a national hero and was even set over against the other in a form of national rivalry.[206]

---

[202] Braun, *History and Romance*, pp. 3-4, was the first to make this distinction.

[203] Plutarch, *De Iside et Osiride*, 360B. He goes on to mention Kyros and Alexander.

[204] Diodoros 2.4.1-20.5, preserves the Semiramis material most fully. As it stands the Diodoron version relates Semiramis' birth (2.4.1-6), marriage to Onnes and then Ninos (2.5.1-6.10), building projects (2.7.1-12.3), and campaigns (2.13.1-20.2), to which an alternate version is appended (2.20.3-5). For an analysis of the legend see Braun, *History and Romance*, pp. 6-13, who sees an evolution of two steps: the first when the legend arose as a result of Persian domination and the second in response to the conquests of Alexander. Eddy, *The King is Dead*, pp. 121-125, distinguishes three stages of development: the anti-Persian (attested in Herodotos), Semiramis the conqueror (attested in Ktesias), and the Hellenistic legend which is built on the model of Alexander (source is Kleitarchos).

[205] Legend preserved in Diodoros 1.53.1-58.5. As the text stands it describes Sesoosis' upbringing (1.53.2-4), campaigns (1.53.5-55.12), building program (1.56.1-57.8), greatness over other kings (1.58.1-2), death and legacy (1.58.3-4). For an analysis see Braun, *History and Romance*, pp. 13-18 and Eddy, *The King is Dead*, pp. 280-282.

[206] In the case of Sesoosis explicit claims are made: he conquered more than Alexander (1.55.3), was greater than Dareios (1.58.4) or any native Egyptian king (1.55.10; 58.3). The competition between the two is expressed through legends of conquest: Semiramis conquered Egypt (1.56.5; 2.14.3; 2.16.1); Sesoosis vanquished Babylon (1.56.3; cf. also 1.55.2).

A reading of Artapanos against this background quickly shows that he is working with this type of material.[207] For example, I find five parallels between Sesoosis and Moses.

Deed	Sesoosis (DS)	Moses
Divided Egypt into 36 nomes	1.54.3	F 3.4
Ethiopian campaign	1.55.1	F 3.7-10
Honored the gods	1.56.2	F 3.4
Plot against his life on return from campaign	1.57.6-8	F 3.11-18
Organized military	1.94.4 (54.5)	F 3.4,8

I do not mean to imply that Artapanos only worked with the biblical texts and our known popular legends, but that the latter both comprise and illustrate the grist of his mill. A couple of examples will suffice.

One of the areas of knowledge to which many ancient people laid claim was astronomy. Babylonians, Egyptians, and Greeks all protested that their ancestors were the first to unlock the secrets of the heavens.[208] Nor should we think that this was an argument which only found a forum among the intelligentsia of the Hellenistic world. One of Semiramis' great buildings was a temple of Bel (= Zeus) in which the Chaldeans accurately observed the stars.[209] It is, therefore—in spite of the biblical text—not shocking to find a Jew claiming that Abraham was responsible for teaching ἀστρολογιά to

---

[207] This has been argued by Braun, *History and Romance*, pp. 17-18; Tiede, *The Charismatic Figure as Miracle Worker*, pp. 153-160; Holladay, *"Theios Aner"*, pp. 210-212; and Doran, "The Jewish Hellenistic Historians Before Josephus," pp. 259-260, 263. Tiede and Holladay stress the connection between Sesoosis and Moses, although Tiede leaves the question of dependence open, p. 160.

[208] Babylonians: Herodotos 2.109.3 (time divisions); Didoros 2.30.1-31.10 (31.9, they had practiced astrology for 473,000 years before Alexander crossed the Hellespont); 19.55.8 (many myriads of years); and 2.29.2 & 17.112.2, where it is their claim to fame; Diogenes Laertios 1.1. Egyptians: Herodotos 2.82.1-2; Diodoros 1.9.6; 1.16.1 (Hermes, the servant of Osiris discovered it); 1.50.1 (Thebans); 1.69.5; 1.98.3-4; and 1.28 & 1.81.3-6, where it is said to have gone from Egypt to Chaldea; Diogenes Laertios 1.11. Greeks (Atlas was commonly said to have given astronomy to the Greeks): Diodoros 3.60.2; 4.27.5; and 3.57.1-2 (Aktis taught the Egyptians astrology); 5.67.1 (Hyperion).

[209] Diodoros 2.9.4: καὶ τοὺς Χαλδαίους ἐν αὐτῷ (i.e., ἱερῷ—GES) τὰς τῶν ἄστρων πεποιῆσθαι παρατηρήσεις, ἀκριβῶς θεωρουμένων τῶν τ' ἀνατολῶν καὶ δύσεων διὰ τὸ τοῦ κατασκευάσματος ὕψος. The text does not make any explicit claims about the origins of astronomy; yet the inclusion of its careful practice within this context makes it a claim for national pride.

the Egyptians (F 1). Artapanos has simply entered the race for national glory and registered Abraham as his first entrant.[210]

This tendency is most fully developed in the presentation of
Moses. Moses is introduced by his Jewish name Μώϋσος as well as
by his Greek designation Μουσαῖος (F 3.3). This is not merely a case
of accommodation to an alternate spelling—although the spelling
suggested the identification,[211] but a cultural claim as the next
statement demonstrates: Moses was the teacher of Orpheus (F 3.4).
Mousaios was commonly associated with Orpheus in antiquity, but
always as a disciple or son: never as a teacher.[212] The Egyptian
claim was that Orpheus had visited Egypt and there learned his rites
which he then introduced to Greece.[213] By inverting the normal
order of succession, Artapanos has cleverly made Greece dependent
upon Moses.[214]

He then proceeds to offer a catalogue of the "discoveries" of
Moses: καὶ γὰρ πλοῖα καὶ μηχανὰς πρὸς τὰς λιθοθεσίας καὶ τὰ
Αἰγύπτια ὅπλα καὶ τὰ ὄργανα τὰ ὑδρευτικὰ[215] καὶ πολεμικὰ καὶ τὴν

---

[210] Isa. 47:13 pronounces judgment on Babylonian astrologers. Jewish attitudes towards astrology varied in documents of this time period. Positive: I En.
72-82, esp. 75:3; II En. 21:6; 30:3-7; Treatise of Shem; 4Q Cryptic. Negative: I
En. 8:3 (taught to humanity by one of the watchers); Sib. Or. 3.220-236 (Jews in
Ur refuse astronomy); Jub. 12:16-18 (Abraham turns from astronomy at the direction of God!). Cf. James H. Charlesworth, "Jewish Astrology in the Talmud,
Pseudepigrapha, the Dead Sea Scrolls, and Early Palestinian Synagogues," HTR
70 (1977): 183-200. Charlesworth correctly observed that Artapanos does not advocate astrology as much as he makes a cultural claim, p. 190. So also Wacholder,
"How Long Did Abram Stay in Egypt?," pp. 44, 53-56.

[211] The only other attested instance of this spelling for Moses is in the case of
the second century C.E. Pythagorean philosopher, Numenios of Apamea, who
probably wrote it as a simple orthographic adjustment. See PE 9.8.1-2.

[212] The two are associated in Aristophanes, Ra. 1032-1034; Plato, Rep. 364E;
Diodoros 1.96.2; Tatian, Cohort. ad Graec. in PE 10.11.27. Mousaios is presented
as his son in DS 4.25.1 (otherwise he is considered the son of Eumolpos as in Diogenes Laertios 1.3) or disciple in Clement, Stromata 1.21.131.1; Tatian, Cohort. ad
Graec. in PE 10.11.30.

[213] That Orpheus visited Egypt see Diodoros 1.69.4; 4.25.3. In 1.23.2-8 and
1.96.4 it is affirmed that he brought his rites to Greece from Egypt. On Orphism
see Guthrie, The Greeks and Their Gods, pp. 307-332 and the literature cited there.

[214] Robert McL. Wilson, "Jewish Literary Propaganda," in Paganisme,
Judaisme, Christianisme: Influences et affrontements dans le monde antique (Mélanges offerts
à Marcel Simon), ed. André Benoit, Marc Philonenko, and Cyrille Vogel (Paris: E.
de Boccard, 1978), p. 62, suggests this identification was the product of Orphic
literature which presented Judaism in Orphic-Stoic dress and links this movement
with the Sibylline oracles.

[215] It is worth noting that in the description of the hanging gardens in the

φιλοσοφίαν[216] ἐξευρεῖν (F 3.4).[217] He credits Moses with the establishment of Egyptian religion (F 3.4)[218] and brings his opening portrait of Moses to a close by telling us that the priests called him Ἑρμῆν, διὰ τὴν τῶν ἱερῶν γραμμάτων ἑρμηνείαν (F 3.6).[219] It is interesting to note that in the account of Hermes—who is Osiris' most honored servant—in Diodoros, the same pattern is encountered: a catalogue of inventions followed by the bestowal of the name Hermes.[220] While there is not enough similarity in the catalogues to posit direct dependence, it is very clear that Artapanos asserts for Moses what the Egyptians and Greeks did for Thot-Hermes.[221]

Semiramis legend (not attributed to Semiramis by Diodoros), τῶν ὑδάτων ὄργανα are explicitly mentioned. See 2.10.6.

[216] The origin of philosophy was a matter of great dispute. Cf. Diogenes Laertios 1.3: λανθάνουσι δ' αὐτοὺς τὰ τῶν Ἑλλήνων κατορθώματα ἀφ' ὧν μὴ ὅτι γε φιλοσοφία, ἀλλὰ καὶ γένος ἀνθρώπων ἦρξε, βαρβάροις προσάπτοντες. Diogenes' prologue is an attempt to prove that philosophy had its origins among the Greeks.

[217] On the whole issue of discoveries see RAC, s.v. "Erfinder II," by K. Thraede, 5:1191-1278, esp. 1242-1245 and his subsequent article, "Das Lob des Erfinders: Bemerkungen zur Analyse der Heuremata-Kataloge," Rheinisches Museum für Philologie 105 (1962): 158-186. Thraede points out that the Jews used Abraham to claim superiority over other Orientals and Moses over the Greeks. Both strands are present in Artapanos. Cf. RAC, 5:1243-1244. For Jewish traditions hostile to discoveries see I En. 7-8; 69; Sib. Or. 1.91-96, where the "watchers" reveal or discover inventions.

[218] This has been the source of a great deal of confusion, especially among earlier scholars. The issue is how could a Jew have the founder of the Jewish nation establish the illicit cults of Egypt? Answers have ranged from denying Artapanos was a Jew (see above under life); the presentation is qualified euhemeristically (see F 3.12): Dalbert, Die Theologie der hellenistisch-jüdischen Missions-Literatur, 46 and Collins, Between Athens and Jerusalem, p. 35; or qualified by distancing phrases, Tiede, The Charismatic Figure as Miracle Worker, pp. 161-162 and Holladay, "Theios Aner", pp. 229-231; it is a standard apologetic reverse answering Egyptian accusations: Donna Runnals, "Moses' Ethiopian Campaign," JSJ 14 (1983): 145; it is apologetically necessitated if Moses is to be the founder of Egyptian culture: Walter, JSHRZ, 1:123 and Schürer, The History of the Jewish People in the Age of Jesus Christ, 3:523. If we consider the overall thrust of the fragments, I do not see how we can avoid concluding that the establishment of animal cults was only one cultural accomplishment among many.

[219] In this fragment Moses also teaches the Ethiopians and Egyptian priests circumcision (10), suggests the ox as an animal cult (12), names the river and city where he buried Merris Meroe (Cf. Diodoros 1.33.1; Strabon 17.1.5; Pseudo-Kallisthenes 3.18, for other figures who found Meroe), and is responsible for the flooding of the Nile (28).

[220] Diodoros 1.16.1 offers the catalogue and 1.16.2 the name: καὶ τοὺς Ἕλληνας διδάξαι τοῦτον τὰ περὶ τὴν ἑρμηνείαν, ὑπὲρ ὧν Ἑρμῆν αὐτὸν ὠνομάσθαι. This account is patently designed to give Egypt precedence over Greece.

[221] On Moses as Thot-Hermes see Mussies, "The Interpretatio Judaica of

The major difference is that Artapanos treats Thot-Hermes euhemeristically, i.e., he is the mortal Moses.

This laudatory introduction serves to set the stage for the conflict
between Chenephres and Moses. Chenephres' first effort to do away
with Moses is to send him on a campaign to Ethiopia.[222] What lies
beneath this story? Freudenthal argued that it was based upon an actual campaign undertaken by a certain Messu.[223] This, however,
requires that both Artapanos and his audience knew of this governor
and flies in the face of Artapanos' propensity for legends. If Artapanos' version originally had the account of Moses marrying the
Ethiopian princess as does that of Josephos, then a haggadic development of Num. 12:1 could explain its origins.[224] There is,
however, a simpler explanation. Semiramis and Sesoosis are both
said to have conquered Ethiopia.[225] If Moses is to compete in the
international arena with other legends, then he too must be a military victor.[226]

The second plot against Moses terminates in Moses' slaying of his
would-be-assassin. In this instance, there appears to be a biblical
base for the story, Ex. 2:11-15 (especially 11-12). Yet the account
is scarcely recognizable. Why? The biblical account leaves Moses
open to the charge of murder. In Artapanos he kills his assailant in
self-defense. Moses is thus exonerated from all possible charges of
misconduct.[227]

Thot-Hermes,'' pp. 89-120. For the later rivalry between Moses and Thot-Hermes
see Gager, *Moses in Greco-Roman Paganism*, p. 149.

[222] Besides the general works already cited see Isodore Levy, ''Moïse en
Éthiope,'' *REJ* 53 (1907): 201-211; Daniel Jeremy Silver, ''Moses and the Hungry
Birds,'' *JQR* 64 (1973-1974): 123-153; Tessa Rajak, ''Moses in Ethiopia: Legend
and Literature,'' *JJS* 29 (1978): 111-122; A. Shinan, ''Moses and the Ethiopian
Woman,'' *Scripta Hierosolymitana* 27 (1978): 66-78; Sebastian Brock, ''Some Syriac
Legends concerning Moses,'' *JJS* 33 (1982): 237-255; and Runnals, ''Moses'
Ethiopian Campaign,'' pp. 135-156. I will discuss the origins in the next chapter.

[223] *Alexander Polyhistor*, pp. 155-156.

[224] So Holladay, *Fragments from Hellenistic Jewish Authors*, p. 235, n. 56.

[225] Diodoros 2.14.4 and 1.55.1 respectively. Kambyses failed in his attempt to
conquer ''the long-lived Ethiopians.'' See Herodotos 3.17-25.

[226] Levy, ''Moïse en Éthiope,'' pp. 208-209 and Rajak, ''Moses in Ethiopia,''
pp. 115-116, think that the legend was inspired by that of Sesostris (Sesoosis). Shinan, ''Moses and the Ethiopian Woman,'' pp. 68-69, sees an underlying myth
''concerning an ancient Egyptian hero, almost certainly the god Thoth.'' Collins,
OTP, 2:899, n. m, suggests legendary conquests of Ethiopia as well as Num. 12:1
prompted the account.

[227] The slaying of the Egyptian was a delicate story for Hellenistic Jewish ex-
egetes. Philo, *Mos.* 1.43-44, transforms the account into the execution of justice

The second half of the Moses fragment is much closer to the biblical text. The major difference is the inclusion of the imprisonment scene (23-26). A miraculous release from prison is a common theme in ancient literature.[228] The incorporation of this episode serves both to enhance the miraculous power of God which is brought to the fore by the sacred name[229] and to underscore Moses' status as the hero of the story.[230] It is fully in keeping with the greater interest in the miraculous which runs through the second half of the fragment.[231]

We may now return to our queries. It does appear that Artapanos worked with more than Scripture and his imagination. The primary type of non-biblical material which surfaces in his fragments is drawn from the hero stories of different nationalities. Whether Artapanos read Hekataios or learned about these figures orally is impossible to determine. The acceptance of this material has significantly altered his presentations of Abraham, Joseph, and Moses from what they are in the biblical record: Abraham's life is not tied to the promises; Joseph no longer illustrates God's control of history; and Moses is never presented as the law-giver. What are they? Dieter Georgi and others have argued that Moses is cast as a θεῖος

---

against a murderous overseer. Josephos avoids it altogether by omitting it. In his version Moses flees when he learns of a plot against his life and does not kill anyone. *AJ* 2.254-257.

[228] The most famous accounts are that of Dionysios in Euripides, *Bacchae* 434-641 and Apollonios of Tyana in Philostratos, *VA* 8.30 (cf. also 7.38). J. Jeremias, *TDNT*, s.v. θύρα, 3:175-176, claims that the use of a door in such escapes is limited to Dionysios and the lives of divine men. Cf. however, Holladay, "*Theios Aner*", pp 205-209, who points out that in Artapanos it is the power of God which is emphasized in this episode not that of Moses.

[229] On the ineffability of the sacred name note the translation of the tetragrammaton by κύριος in the LXX and the qere, עֲרֹנָי. On the relationship of the two see *TDNT*, s.v. κύριος, by Gottfried Quell, 3:1059,1061. See also Philo, *Mos.* 2.114 and Josephos, *AJ* 2.276. For the later connections between Moses and the divine name see Gager, *Moses in Greco-Roman Paganism*, pp. 142-144.

[230] Whether Artapanos invented the account (so Fraser, *Ptolemaic Alexandria*, 1:705) or simply appropriated a tradition, the form and function of this episode remain the same. Holladay, "*Theios Aner*", pp. 205-209, leaves the issue of source open.

[231] E.g., in 21 when God calls Moses, there is no burning bush: the fire simply issues from the ground. Cf. also Aristobulos in Eusebios *PE* 8.10.15 (= F 2.15 in *OTP*). The same tendency re-emerges in 37 when Artapanos states that the Egyptians were overcome by both water and fire. I am inclined to think that this inclination is dramatically motivated rather than theologically.

ἀνήρ.[232] This, however, separates Moses from the other two heroes and fails to consider the nature of the material which constitutes the record.[233] It is more accurate to see them as national heroes along the same lines as Semiramis and Sesoosis (Sesostris).[234]

3. *Function*. Why write an account of Jewish activities in Egypt claiming that they are the fount of Egyptian civilization? There can be no doubt that Artapanos wrote *ad maiorem Iudaeorum gloriam*.[235] The question is why? Is Artapanos reacting to anti-Jewish slander? It is instructive to read Artapanos in light of the accusations which appear in Manethon's account of the Jews in *CA* 1.227-253.[236] The following chart will elucidate the possible exchange.

CA	Charge	F 3	Rebuttal
1. 229,233	Jews were lepers	20	First to die from elephantiasis was Chenephres.
2. 239,244, 246,249	Moses opposed Egyptian cults	4,12	Moses established cults
3. 246-247	Amenophis fled to Ethiopia from Hyksos	7-10	Moses conquered Ethiopia
4. 250	Moses was Egyptian	3	Moses was adopted
5. 250,279	Moses was a leper	37	Moses was physically impressive

---

[232] Dieter Georgi, *The Opponents of Paul in Second Corinthians* (Philadelphia: Fortress Press, 1986), pp. 124-126.

[233] Georgi's analysis was correctly challenged by Tiede, *The Charismatic Figure as Miracle Worker*, pp. 146-177 and Holladay, "*Theios Aner*," pp. 199-232. It is interesting that Moses became as well-known in the pagan world as he did. Apparently the early attempts to present him were successful. For Moses in apologetic literature see Gager, *Moses in Greco-Roman Paganism*, pp. 77-78. Cf. also Jean Pépin, "Le 'Challenge' Homère-Moise aux Premiers Siècles Chrétiens," *Revue des Sciences Religieuses* (1955): 105-122.

[234] So also Walter, *JSHRZ*, 1:122; Collins, *Between Athens and Jerusalem*, p. 36; and Holladay, *Fragments from Hellenistic Jewish Authors*, p. 192.

[235] This has been emphasized by Hengel, "Anonymität, Pseudepigraphie und 'Literarische Fälschung' in der jüdisch-hellenistischen Literatur," p. 241 and Holladay, "*Theios Aner*", p. 231.

[236] This does not appear to be as valid for the more positive account in *CA* 1.73-92, where Manethon deals with the Hyksos. The basic charges here are that the Hyksos invaded (75) and burned the cities and razed the temples (76). In F 2.4, Artapanos says that the Hermiouth built the temples in Athos and Heliopolis. The charge of invasion does not appear to have a counterpart. In F 3.19, Moses refuses Raguel's suggestion to invade Egypt, but apparently changes his mind after the divine voice charged him with such a mission (21-22).

Is this correspondence coincidental or intentional? We have already seen that the claim that Moses established the cults is part of the presentation of Moses as a *Kulturbringer*. This would not, however, exclude the possibility that a second motive lurked beneath the asseveration. The Ethiopian campaign likewise has more credence as part of the stock-in-trade of national hero material. It, however, could also serve double duty. The description of Moses' physical appearance may simply be a nice biographical touch and has a biblical base as does his adoption. The strongest case can be made with regard to the charge of leprosy. This was a charge which had a wide circulation as its continual reappearance demonstrates.[237] What is more impressive than any single correspondence, however, is the way that each charge of Manethon has an echo in Artapanos. It is this general pattern which leads me to see an effort by Artapanos to answer some of the charges leveled against Jews. Whether he knew Manethon directly or only the popular gossip which followed him is difficult to say. On the whole, I prefer to see some awareness of Manethon although the connection must be considered tenuous on the basis of our present evidence.[238]

Who constituted the reading audience of these fragments? Were they Greeks, Jews, or both?[239] Perhaps here we should distinguish between two levels of audience. On the one hand, the glorification

---

[237] Cf. Lysimachos (second or first century B.C.E.?) in Josephos, *CA* 1.304-311; Pompeius Trogus (first century B.C.E.-first century C.E.) quoted by Iustinus, *Historiae Philippicae*, 36 (= Stern, *GLAJJ*, 1:334-342); Chaeremon (first century C.E.) *apud* Josephos, *CA* 1.288-292; and Nikarchos (first century C.E.) in *GLAJJ*, 1:532-533. Cf. also Tacitus, *Historiae*, 5.3. Philo, *Mos.* 1.39, is aware of this accusation as well as Ezekiel, *Exagoge*, 129-131, where Moses puts his hand into his bosom and it becomes white like snow but nothing is said about leprosy.

[238] Those who either argue for or allow for a possible connection include Freudenthal, *Alexander Polyhistor*, p. 162; Braun, *History and Romance*, pp. 26-31; Fraser, *Ptolemaic Alexandria*, 1:704-706; Walter, *JSHRZ*, 1:125; Holladay, "*Theios Aner*", pp. 213-214; and Collins, *Between Athens and Jerusalem*, pp. 33-34 and *OTP*, 2:892,894. Tiede, *The Charismatic Figure as Miracle Worker*, pp. 174-175, thinks that Artapanos is responding to charges on a popular level rather than a literary figure such as Manethon. The difficulty with this is that there is a point by point parallel. Undoubtedly, Artapanos is also answering popular gossip or counter-claims.

[239] Pagan: Freudenthal, *Alexander Polyhistor*, p. 144; *The Jewish Encyclopedia*, s.v. "Artapanus," by Louis Ginzburg, 2:145; Runnals, "Moses' Ethiopian Campaign," pp. 136-137, who thinks of the "Ptolemaic ruling class and the Greeks of Egypt." Jewish: Tiede, *The Charismatic Figure as Miracle Worker*, p. 176 and Walter, "Jüdisch-hellenistische Literatur vor Philon von Alexandrien," p. 99. Both: Collins, *Between Athens and Jerusalem*, p. 36 and *OTP*, 2:892.

of Israel and the rebuttal of anti-Jewish charges has an outward slant. Thus the fragments presume an imaginary audience which consists of outsiders. On the other hand, there is no evidence that Greeks read works written by nationals except for collectors like Polyhistor. The real world audience of the work is therefore Jews. The Jews who read this would have to deal with the fragments' imaginary audience in the real world.

The oeuvre served to give the Jews a sense of their own identity in Ptolemaic Egypt. This identity was different from previous conceptions. After all, they no longer lived in their homeland where they constituted the majority, but found themselves in the position of a subgroup within a much larger culture. Their locus was not in the temple nor in the law, but in their national consciousness and sense of superiority.[240] They could, therefore, think of themselves not merely in terms of their own traditions, but could use those traditions in competition with those of others to locate themselves within the larger world of Hellenism.[241]

Significance

How should we view such a work? Virtually all contemporary assessments of it attach the term "romance" to it.[242] We need to be careful, however, about how we define romance. Romance in the

---

[240] So Collins, *Between Athens and Jerusalem*, p. 36.

[241] Such a broad perspective does not always win applause. Ginzberg, *The Jewish Encyclopedia*, s.v. "Artapanos," 2:145 wrote: "Artapanus evidently belonged to that narrow-minded circle of Hellenizing Jews that were unable to grasp what was truly great in Judaism, and therefore, in their mistaken apologetic zeal . . .set about glorifying Judaism to the outer world by inventing all manner of fables concerning the Jews."

[242] Denis, *Introduction aux Pseudépigraphes Grecs d'Ancien Testament*, p. 256: "roman biblique;" Collins and Poehlman, "Artapanus," pp. 41-44,50: "a national and religious romance;" Hengel, "Anonymität, Pseudepigraphie, und 'Literarische Fälschung' in der jüdisch-hellenistischen Literatur," p. 239: "die romanhafte, aretalogische Mosebiographie;" Holladay, "*Theios Aner*", p. 215: "national romantic history" and in *Fragments of Hellenistic Jewish Authors*, pp. 190-191: "popular romance literature" which should be read as "popular religious propaganda;" Walter, *JSHRZ*, 1:121: "Mose-Roman" and "Jüdisch-hellenistische Literatur vor Philon von Alexandrien," p. 99: "eine erste jüdisch-hellenistische 'Personal-Biographie' romanhafter Art;" Conzelmann, *Heiden-Juden-Christen*, p. 149: "eine Art historischer Roman;" Attridge, "Historiography," p. 168 wrote: ". . .the work had closer ties to popular romance than to serious historiography and that its aim was as much to entertain as to instruct;" and *OTP*, 2:889, places Artapanos under the heading of "Romance."

sense of novel is not an appropriate designation for Artapanos. The extant novels which we have differ greatly from Artapanos: they are heavily erotic, are personal in their orientation, and are designed to entertain rather than make claims on behalf of the author's own ethnic group.[243] On the other hand, there is a great deal to be said for using the adjectival form of the word. Without addressing the issue of the origin of the novel itself, it is clear that it has ties to both national legends and to historiography.[244] The latter is discernible in the continuous prose narrative common to both.[245] At the same

---

[243] Extant Greek novels: Chariton of Aphrodisias, *Erotic Tales About Chaereas and Kallirhoe* (first century B.C.E.? or c. 125 C.E.); Xenophon of Ephesus, *Ephesiaka* (c. 200 C.E.); Heliodoros of Emesa, *Aethiopika* (c. 225 or 350-400 C.E.); Longos, *Daphnis and Chloe* (c. 150-250 C.E.); and Achilles Tatios of Alexandria, *Leukippe and Klitophon* (c. 300 C.E.?). Latin: Petronius, *Satyricon* (66 C.E.); Lucian, *Metamorphoses*; and Apuleius, *Golden Ass* (c. 180 C.E.). The Greek material has recently appeared in an important collection, B.P. Reardon, ed., *Collected Ancient Greek Novels*, (Berkeley/Los Angeles/London: University of California Press, 1989). Novels did not have a name in antiquity probably because they were not considered true literature by the literators. So Thomas Hägg, *The Novel in Antiquity* (Oxford: Basil Blackwell, 1983), pp. 3-4 and N. Holzberg, *Der antike Roman: Eine Einführung* (München: Artemis, 1986), p. 15. Ben Edwin Perry, *The Ancient Romances: A Literary-Historical Account of Their Origins*. Sather Classical Lectures 37 (Berkeley/Los Angeles: University of California Press, 1967), pp. 44-45, offers the following definition: ". . .an extended narrative published apart by itself which relates—primarily or wholly for the sake of entertainment or spiritual edification, and for its own sake as a story, rather than for the purpose of instruction in history, science, or philosophical theory—the adventures or experiences of one or more individuals in their private capacities and from the viewpoint of their private interests and emotions." Cf. also Holzberg, *Der antike Roman*, p. 33.
[244] The Ninus romance is a good example of the connection between national legends and later novels. Novels often used national heroes as their subjects. The two most important works on the origins of the novel are Erwin Rhode, *Der griechische Roman und seine Vorläufer*, 2nd ed. (Leipzig: Breitkopf und Hartil, 1900; 4th ed., Hildesheim: Georg Olms, 1960) and Perry, *The Ancient Romances*. The basic argument is whether novels developed (Rhode) or were invented (Perry): evolution versus creation. The more recent work of Graham Anderson, *Ancient Fiction: The Novel in the Graeco-Roman World* (Totowa, New Jersey: Barnes & Noble Books, 1984), pp. 1-24, which attempts to link the origins of novels to ancient Near Eastern materials is much less illuminating.
[245] On the connection between history and the novel see Perry, *The Ancient Romances*, pp. 36-39,55,66-69; Hägg, *The Novel in Antiquity*, p. 112; B.P. Reardon, "The Greek Novel," *Phoenix* 23 (1969): 295; and Holzberg, *Der antike Roman*, pp. 43-46. Hägg and Reardon credit history with having more influence on the form of the novel than any preceding genre. It is interesting that some of the novelists gave their works the same names that an ethnographer or apologetic historian would have given his, e.g., *Ephesiaka* and *Aethiopika*. A good example of ethnographic carry-over can be seen in Heliodoros' *Aethiopika*. So 2.27.3-28.5 presents Egyptian customs and a discussion on the sources of the Nile; 3.14.1-4 links Homer to Thebes; 10.5.1-2 is a description of Meroe (!); 10.26.1-27.4 lists gifts from differ-

time, it resembles both epic and drama—before the novel fiction was always in poetry—in its creativity. If our analysis is correct, Artapanos shares these qualities.

If it is not a full-fledged romance, then how does it relate to the national legends it incorporates? Is it parallel to them or does it simply draw from them? I am inclined to think the latter for three reasons. First, it is broader than a simple collection of competitive legends. It tells the story of a people in Egypt—even if Moses is the towering figure in that story. For all of its creative recasting, it remains a selective rewriting of Israel's sacred traditions. Second, it serves not only to compete in the larger world, but to offer a new self-definition for the inside community. Third, national legends were primarily oral material—although some were obviously recorded. Artapanos marks a shift from oral to written and must be viewed in literary terms. The work thus stands between national legends and the novel as we know it.[246]

I would therefore call it romantic national history.[247] By history I mean that it presents the accounts of a group of people as the story of that people—however fanciful some of the episodes are. What makes it history rather than romance is its purpose. It, therefore, stands within the same general tradition as Berossos and Manethon. In some respects, it reverts back to the pattern of Hekataios who used both Greek and Egyptian material for his *Aigyptiaka*. It does not, however, present its story within the mold of ethnography as Hekataios did, but within the framework of native traditions: both old and new.

Artapanos stands as a witness that we can not expect mere repetition of form or substance—even within the same general tradition. Creativity as well as continuity must always be given its due.

---

ent countries representing what is unusual about each (e.g., 26.2: Troglodytes bring gold dug by ants). Cf. Héliodore, *Les Éthiopiques*, 3 vols. ed. and trans. R.M. Rattenbury, T.W. Lumb, and J. Maillon (Paris: Societé d'Édition 'Les Belles Lettres,' 1960). Moses Hadas, *An Ethiopian Romance* (Ann Arbor: The University of Michigan, 1957), p. ix, goes too far when he says: "In effect the book is a glorification of a dark-skinned race and an obscure sect."

[246] The work of Pseudo-Kallisthenes is similar in several respects. It is not, however, identical. Hägg, *The Novel in Antiquity*, pp. 115-117, classifies it as a biography.

[247] Collins, *Between Athens and Jerusalem*, p. 33 and *OTP*, 2:891-892, calls it "competitive historiography," an apt phrase.

PSEUDO-EUPOLEMOS[248]

Identity

As Eusebios has preserved Polyhistor's work, it opens with a quotation attributed to Eupolemos, followed by an excerpt from Artapanos, and then an anonymous extract which has a striking resemblance to the first citation.[249] Freudenthal saw the connection between the first and third fragments and argued that both came from an anonymous Samaritan author.[250] While he has been seconded by a majority of scholars, there has been and continues to be a significant minority who question his analysis.[251] We must begin our investigation by determining whether or not the first fragment is the work of Eupolemos or of some other author, and if so, if anything can be said about the writer's identity.

The strongest argument against Polyhistor's ascription is the

---

[248] The most significant studies on this anonymous author are: Freudenthal, *Alexander Polyhistor*, pp. 82-103; Ben Zion Wacholder, "Pseudo-Eupolemus' Two Greek Fragments on the Life of Abraham," *HUCA* 34 (1963): 83-113; N. Walter, "Zu Pseudo-Eupolemos," *Klio* 43-45 (1965): 282-290 and his later edition with notes in *JSHRZ*, 1:137-143; Denis, *Introduction aux Pseudépigraphes Grecs d'Ancien Testament*, pp. 261-262 and his later article, "L'Historien anonyme d'Eusèbe (Praep. Ev. 9,17-18) et la Crise des Macchabées," *JSJ* 8 (1977): 42-49; Hengel, *Judaism and Hellenism*, pp. 88-92; Conzelmann, *Heiden-Juden-Christen*, pp. 145-148; Collins, *Between Athens and Jerusalem*, pp. 38-39; Holladay, *Fragments from Hellenistic Jewish Authors*, pp. 157-187; Attridge, "Historiography," pp. 135-136; R. Doran, "Pseudo-Eupolemos," in *OTP*, 2:873-882; Schürer, *The History of the Jewish People in the Age of Jesus Christ*, 3:528-531; Droge, *Homer or Moses?*, pp. 19-25; and Pilhofer, *Presbyteron Kreitton*, pp. 148-153.

[249] *PE* 9.17.2-9 (Eupolemos); 9.18.1 (Artapanos); 9.18.2 (ἐν δὲ ἀδεσπότοις).

[250] *Alexander Polyhistor*, pp. 82-91.

[251] Those who see a Pseudo-Eupolemos include: Jacoby, *FGrH* 724; Wacholder, "Pseudo-Eupolemos," p. 84; Denis, *Introduction aux Pseudépigraphes Grecs d'Ancien Testament*, pp. 252, 261 and "L'Historien anonyme d'Eusèbe," p. 45; Hengel, *Judaism and Hellenism*, p. 88; Walter, *JSHRZ*, 1:137; Conzelmann, *Heiden-Juden-Christen*, p. 145; Collins, *Between Athens and Jerusalem*, p. 38; Holladay, *Fragments from Hellenistic Jewish Authors*, pp. 158-159; Attridge, "Historiography," p. 165; John R. Bartlett, *Jews in the Hellenistic World: Josephus, Aristeas, the Sibylline Oracles, Eupolemus.* Cambridge Commentaries on Writings of the Jewish and Christian World 200 BC to AD 200 1.1 (Cambridge: Cambridge University Press, 1985), p. 56; Schürer, *The History of the Jewish People in the Age of Jesus Christ*, 3:529. Those who are willing to let the attribution stand include: Bousset and Gressmann, *Die Religion des Judentums*, p. 21, n. 2; Tarn and Griffith, *Hellenistic Civilization*, p. 234; Vermes, *Scripture and Tradition in Judaism*, pp. 80-81, 81 n. 1, 97 n. 2, 101 n. 1, who cites it as from Eupolemos (although see p. 81 n. 1); Fergus Millar, "The Background to the Maccabean Revolution: Reflections on Martin Hengel's 'Judaism and Hellenism,'" *JJS* 29 (1978): 6 n. 12; Strugnell, *OTP*, 2:777 n. 2; Doran, *OTP*, 2:873-876, who has the fullest discussion; and it is questioned in Schürer, *The History of the Jewish People in the Age of Jesus Christ*, 3:517.

reference to ἱερὸν Ἀργαριζίν, ὃ εἶναι μεθερμηνευόμενον ὄρος ὑψίστου (F 1.5).[252] Could a Jew with the known and open ties Eupolemos had to the Jerusalem temple have written this? The tension is particularly acute since the location of the respective temples was the focal point of contention between Jews and Samaritans.[253] I can not see how a Jew with ties to the Hasmoneans and the cleansing of the Jerusalem temple could have written this without some qualification.[254]

This is reinforced by the identification of Salem with Gerizim which underlies the reference. Gen. 14:18 says that Melchizedek was king of Salem. Our author understands this to be Gerizim, the sacred mount of the Samaritans. While there is a possible basis for this in the LXX of Gen. 33:18, Jewish tradition consistently identifies Salem with Jerusalem.[255] Our suspicions are reinforced when

---

[252] In II Macc. 6:2 the temple is called ἱερὸν Διὸς Ξενίου and in Josephos, AJ 12.261 ἱερὸν Διὸς Ἑλληνίου.

[253] Jn. 4:20-22 reflects this altercation from a later date. The temple was built under Sanballat III, a contemporary of Alexander the Great. (Josephos, AJ 11.322-324) It is well known that the Samaritans altered their Scriptures in order to sanction their claim. The most significant changes are their addition of the tenth commandment (they count nine and ten in MT as nine) after Ex. 20:17 and Deut. 5:18 which specifies Gerizim as the temple mount; the 21t. יבחר is changed to בחר in Deut. (12:5, 11, 14, 18, 21, 26; 14:23, 24, 25; 15:20; 16:2, 6, 7, 11, 15, 16; 17:8, 10; 18:6; 26:2; 31:11) to show that God had already chosen the site of the temple; and similar changes such as the insertion of מול שכם in Deut. 11:30 to note the tie between Shechem and Gerizim and the replacement of עיבל with הר גרזים in Deut. 27:4. On the origin of SP and its relationship to Samaritan history see James D. Purvis, The Samaritan Pentateuch and the Origin of the Samaritan Sect. HSM 2 (Cambridge: Harvard University Press, 1968), pp. 16-118. On the tenth commandment see Moses Gaster, The Samaritans: Their History, Doctrines and Literature (London: Oxford University Press, 1925), pp. 42, 185-190 and John Bowman, Samaritan Documents Relating to their History, Religion and Life. Pittsburgh Original Texts and Translation Series 2 (Pittsburgh: The Pickwick Press, 1977), pp. 9-26, who provides inscriptions and texts. For the Samaritans' theological conceptions of Gerizim see James Alan Montgomery, The Samaritans: The Earliest Jewish Sect (Their History, Theology and Literature) (1907; reprint ed. with an introduction by Abraham S. Halkin, New York: Ktav Publishing House, Inc., 1968), pp. 234-239; John Macdonald, The Theology of the Samaritans (London: SCM press Ltd, 1964), pp. 327-333; and Reinhard Plummer, The Samaritans. Iconography of Religions (Leiden: E.J. Brill, 1987), pp. 8-10.

[254] Doran, OTP, 2:875, points out that the derivation is based upon Gen. 14:18. While this is true, the issue which remains is whether a Jew would make such a connection at a time when relations between Jews and Samaritans were strained.

[255] MT has ויבא יעקב עיר שלם שכם which the LXX renders by καὶ ἦλθεν Ιακωβ εἰς Σαλημ πόλιν Σικιμων. Interestingly SP has שלום for שלם. This is also found in Targum Onqelos ("and Jacob came to the city of Shechem which is in the land of

the fragment goes on to affirm that Abraham received gifts from Melchizedek (F 1.6). While the biblical text is somewhat ambiguous and this could be a reference to the bread and wine of v. 18, it more likely refers to the final clause of v. 20 which received more attention. Jewish interpretations from this period have Abraham give Melchizedek a tithe.[256] It is in Samaritan texts that we encounter the reverse.[257]

A third hint that the author was not the Jew Eupolemos is the consistent designation of Canaan as "Phoenicia."[258] Why? There are two possible explanations. The LXX and Philo of Byblos each attest the connection between Canaan and Phoenicia.[259] The use could therefore be taken as a stylistic anachronism. On the other hand, the Samaritans claimed to be Sidonians.[260] It could, therefore, reflect a Samaritan perspective of Canaan. If we attempt to explain the reason for such a usage in isolation from the preceding two points, we have an inadequate basis for a decision. However, viewed in light of the other evidence, the Samaritan orientation suggested by this usage should be weighed.[261]

The final bit of evidence we have is the difference in breadth

---

Canaan in peace"—my translation) as well as the Peshitta (identical to the targum). For details on the traditions see Wacholder, "Pseudo-Eupolemus' Two Greek Fragments on Abraham," p. 107, who points out that while Jewish tradition recognized two Salems, it "maintains unanimously that Salem is to be equated with Jerusalem."

[256] Both the MT and LXX of Gen. 14:20b (see 18-20) are ambiguous about who gave the מעשר (δεκάτην) to whom. The *terminus technicus* suggested to Jewish writers that Abraham paid a tithe to Melchizedek. So 1QapGen 22.17; Jub. 13:25-27; Josephos, *AJ* 1.181. Cf. however, Gen. Rabbah 43 for a possible Jewish version of this view.

[257] Cf. S. Lowry, *The Principles of Samaritan Bible Exegesis.* Studia Post-Biblica 28 (Leiden: E.J. Brill, 1977), pp. 41, 320. Cf. also Moses Gaster, *The Asatir: The Samaritan Book of the "Secrets of Moses"* (London: The Royal Asiatic Society, 1927), pp. 9-27.

[258] 3t. in F 1.4.

[259] LXX renders כנען by φοίνικες (Josh. 5:12) and φοινίκη (Ex. 16:35); כנענים by φοίνικες (Jb. 40:30) and כנעני by φοινίκη (Josh. 5:1). Philo (*PE* 1.10.39) wrote: Εἰσίριος . . . ἀδελφὸς Χνᾶ τοῦ πρώτου μετονομασθέντος Φοίνικος.

[260] Josephos, *AJ* 11.344 and 12.260.

[261] I agree with Doran, *OTP*, 2:874-875, that the obvious preference for Phoenicia over Egypt does not disqualify Eupolemos. *Contra* Holladay, *Fragments from Hellenistic Jewish Authors*, p. 181 n. 13. This, however, sidesteps the issue which was stated forcefully by Wacholder, "Pseudo-Eupolemus' Two Greek Fragments," p. 104: ". . .the implication that the Lord promised Phoenicia, and not Canaan, to Abraham's descendants would probably have been offensive to one believing that the divine promise referred to Jerusalem."

between this fragment and those of Eupolemos. As we will see this fragment freely combines pagan and biblical myths in a sweeping manner. Eupolemos may refer to non-biblical events, but there are no combinations such as we have here.[262]

Together these data are convincing. We should therefore consider *PE* 9.17.2-9 to be the work of an anonymous Samaritan author.

Life

We know nothing about the personal life of this author.[263] We can, however, make some deductions about his date and locale based upon the fragments. Virtually all research places the work in the second century B.C.E.[264] The *terminus ad quem* is the omission of the destruction of the temple at Shechem by John Hyrcanos in 129/128 B.C.E.[265] It would be possible to push this back even farther if an air-tight case could be made for the use of Pseudo-Eupolemos by the author of the third Sibylline Oracle around the middle of the century.[266] The *terminus a quo* is furnished by the author's use of the LXX. (See below) A more specific date is suggested by the preference for Phoenicia at the expense of Egypt. (See below) This probably reflects a political tie to the Seleucids at a time when they and

---

[262] This was forcefully stated by Hengel, *Judaism and Hellenism*, p. 95. Doran, *OTP*, 2:875, countered Hengel by arguing that while Solomon was anchored in history, the Genesis text was "ripe for connections with other accounts of origins." It is true that Eupolemos also made cultural claims for Jewish ancestors which went well beyond the text. Where they differ is in their mind-set. Eupolemos is simply not as open as is this author.

[263] Wacholder, "Pseudo-Eupolemus' Two Greek Fragments on Abraham," p. 104, thought that he was "either a descendant of the Greek settlers or a Hellenized Phoenician." In *Eupolemus*, p. 289, he suggested that he was a priest based upon the parallel careers of Berossos, Manethon, Eupolemos, and Josephos and the shift in the order of Melchizedek's role from king and priest in the biblical text to priest and king in F 1.6.

[264] So Jacoby, *FGrH* 724 (places a question mark after II); Wacholder, "Pseudo-Eupolemus' Two Greek Fragments on the Life of Abraham," pp. 85-87 (200-167 B.C.E.) and "Biblical Chronology in the Hellenistic World Chronicles," p. 458 (c. 200 B.C.E.); Denis, *Introduction aux Pseudépigraphes Grecs d'Ancien Testament*, pp. 46-47 (200-165 B.C.E.); Hengel, *Judaism and Hellenism*, p. 88 (200-167 B.C.E.); Walter, *JSHRZ*, 1:140 (200-150 B.C.E.); Holladay, *Fragments from Hellenistic Jewish Authors*, pp. 159-160 (200-150 B.C.E.); Attridge, "Historiography," p. 166 (early second century); Schürer, *The History of the Jewish People in the Age of Jesus Christ*, 3:530 (before 129 B.C.E.).

[265] Josephos, *AJ* 13.254-256.

[266] Cf. Sib. Or. 3.97-161.

the Ptolemies vied for control of Coele-Syria, i.e., the early part of the second century.[267]

The locale is more difficult to pinpoint. Syria-Phoenicia-Palestine comes to mind first.[268] There were also Samaritan communities in Egypt.[269] However, the strong preference for Phoenicia over against Egypt in the fragments makes it likely that the author lived somewhere within the Seleucid empire.

Work

1. *Content.* As we observed, the third excerpt in Polyhistor is very similar to the first. We now need to address the issue of how the two relate.[270] It is strange that Polyhistor ascribed the first to Eupolemos but not the third. Or perhaps we should ask how *PE* 9.17.2-9 came to circulate under Eupolemos' name, but *PE* 9.18.2 did not. The fragments are very similar. Taking the order from the third (= F 2 in Holladay) and supplying the section number from the first fragment we find the following common elements: Abraham traced his genealogy to the giants (3); one of the giants was Belos (9); the giants built a tower in Babylon (2); Abraham learned astrology in Babylon (3)[271]; he first went to Phoenicia where he instructed the Phoenicians (4-5) and then to Egypt (6-8). Both have the same basic events in the same general order.

There are, however, some significant differences. Again following the order of F 2 we find that the outcome of the giants is very different. In F 2 they are destroyed, while in F 1.3 they are scattered

---

[267] I am unable to see why the Maccabean revolt would preclude the universalism of this Samaritan as Wacholder, ''Pseudo-Eupolemus' Two Greek Fragments on Abraham,'' pp. 86-87, argues.

[268] Favored by Freudenthal, *Alexander Polyhistor*, p. 99; Denis, *Introduction aux Pseudépigraphes Grecs d'Ancien Testament*, p. 262; Hengel, *Judaism and Hellenism*, p. 88; Conzelmann, *Heiden-Juden-Christen*, p. 147; Holladay, *Fragments from Hellenistic Jewish Authors*, p. 157.

[269] For these settlements see Schürer, *The History of the Jewish People in the Age of Jesus Christ*, 3:59-60. Those who think that the anonymous Samaritan may have lived in either Palestine or Egypt include Walter, *JSHRZ*, 1:139-140; Collins, *Between Athens and Jerusalem*, p. 38; Schürer, *op cit.*, 3:529-530. Attridge, ''Historiography,'' p. 166, says either Palestine or the diaspora.

[270] Conzelmann, *Heiden-Juden-Christen*, pp. 145-146, has a helpful discussion.

[271] The fragment is not fully consistent here. In 3 we read: ὃν δὴ καὶ τὴν ἀστρολογίαν καὶ Χαλδαϊκὴν εὑρεῖν. However in 8 we find: Φάμενον Βαβυλωνίους ταῦτα καὶ αὐτὸν εὑρηκέναι, τὴν δὲ εὕρεσιν αὐτῶν εἰς Ἐνὼχ ἀναπέμπειν, καὶ τοῦτον εὑρηκέναι πρῶτον τὴν ἀστρολογίαν, οὐκ Αἰγυπτίους. Perhaps we should understand 8 as an amplification of 3.

throughout the earth. The agent of their retribution is significantly different in the two accounts: F 2 ὑπὸ τῶν θεῶν vs. F 1.3 ὑπὸ τῆς τοῦ θεοῦ ἐνεργείας. Third, in F 2, Belos manages to escape this punishment and builds the tower in Babylon; in F 1.2 the giants are dispersed after they build the tower.

How are we to explain these phenomena? Freudenthal thought that F 2 was a summary of F 1 written by Polyhistor who misplaced an anonymous fragment (our F 1) among the writings of Eupolemos. When he could not locate the fragment (F 1) he composed a summary and appropriately attributed it to an anonymous author (F 2).[272] Yet if Polyhistor knew the contents of F 1 well enough to compose F 2 from memory, why could he not recognize it as the misplaced fragment when he saw it? Walter offered another solution. He thought that F 2 comprised two separate sections. The first half consists of Babylonian material about the giants collected by Polyhistor which he then united with a condensation of F 1.4 and 6b (the second half).[273] The problem here is that this presupposes a degree of editorial work on the part of Polyhistor which is not paralleled in the rest of the work. Part of the difficulty may be more apparent than real. Freudenthal himself pointed out that F 2 could deal with the flood and F 1 with the events after the flood.[274] While this would solve some of the differences, it would also imply that F 2 contains information which F 1 does not and would eliminate the hypothesis that F 2 is merely a resume of F 1. Likewise, it would still fail to explain the shift from the monotheism of F 1 to the polytheism of F 2. R. Doran has most recently cut the Gordian knot by attributing F 1 to Eupolemos and F 2 to Polyhistor.[275]

We are thus left to decide whether the fragments stem from a common source, or if the second is an editorial synopsis of the first by another hand, or if they come from two entirely different authors. The similarity of the two rules out the last mentioned option in my opinion: not only do they deal with the same basic events but they

---

[272] *Alexander Polyhistor*, p. 91.

[273] Walter, *JSHRZ*, 1:137-138 n.4, 143 n. on 18.

[274] *Alexander Polyhistor*, p. 92. So also Holladay, *Fragments from Hellenistic Jewish Authors*, p. 187 n.45. *Contra* Conzelmann, *Heiden-Juden-Christen*, p. 146 and apparently Doran, *OTP*, 2:874.

[275] *OTP*, 2:873-874, 878. Cf. also his "The Jewish Hellenistic Historians Before Josephus," pp. 270-274. As I have argued above, I can not accept Eupolemos' authorship for the first fragment.

share a common perspective. Is the second a later summary? The differences between the two rule this out unless a second *Vorlage* is presupposed which supplied the additional information.[276] Although it remains problematic, I propose the following explanation. Both fragments originally stem from the work of a now anonymous Samaritan who dealt with the giants in connection with both the flood (F 2) and subsequent events (FF 1 and 2). The connection with Gerizim and the temple there formed a nice counterbalance to the work of Eupolemos who emphasized the Jerusalem temple. At some point prior to Polyhistor an excerpt was made (F 1) and became associated with the work of Eupolemos. Polyhistor thus cited it correctly as he found it. He also found the original work from which he independently extracted F 2.

F 1.2 appears to preserve a title for this work, Περὶ 'Ιουδαίων τῆς 'Ασσυρίας. There is, however, a problem: a Samaritan author would not write a Περὶ 'Ιουδαίων[277] and it is difficult to imagine how 'Ασσυρία relates to Abraham. It is better to see 'Ασσυρίας in connection with the subsequent πόλιν and to regard Περὶ 'Ιουδαίων as the heading supplied by Alexander Polyhistor.[278] We are then left without a specific title.

Combining the two fragments, we can reconstruct the basic contours of the story as follows.[279] God decided to punish the impiety of the giants who lived in Babylonia through a deluge (F 2). One of these, however, Belos (= Noah), escaped and settled in Babylon where he built a tower (FF 2 and 1.2). Again God brought judgment and destroyed the tower scattering the giants (F 1.3). Ten (or thirteen) generations later, a descendant of these giants named Abraham was born in Camarine (= Ur, FF 2 and 1.3). Abraham was an outstanding intellect who learned astrology from Enoch (= Atlas) in Chaldea (FF 2 and 1.3,8,9). In obedience to the directive of God, Abraham went to Phoenicia where he taught the Phoenicians astrology (FF 2 and 1.4). When the Armenians invaded Phoenicia

---

[276] It is worth observing that Polyhistor did say ἐν δὲ ἀδεσπότοις. *PE* 9.18.2.
[277] 'Ιουδαῖος does not appear in the fragments.
[278] First proposed by Freudenthal, *Alexander Polyhistor*, pp. 89, 207, and followed by Wacholder, "Pseudo-Eupolemus' Two Greek Fragments on Abraham," pp. 84-85 and Holladay, *Fragments from Hellenistic Jewish Authors*, p. 159.
[279] My reconstruction does not take into account the distinct possibility that the author presented more than one version of an event. I am only trying to establish the basic lines at this point.

and carried off his nephew, Abraham led a successful mission to reclaim Lot and the enemies' families (F 1.4-5). After being honored at Gerizim by Melchizedek (F 1.5-6), Abraham journeyed to Egypt. (FF 2 and 1.6) When he informed the king that Sarah was his sister, the king took her as his wife. Unable to have intercourse with her, he summoned his diviners who informed him of the deception (F 1.6-7). With his wife restored, Abraham taught the priests of Heliopolis a number of new things including the science of astrology (F 1.6-8). Pseudo-Eupolemos stressed the significance of these events through a genealogical tree (F 1.9) which looks like this:

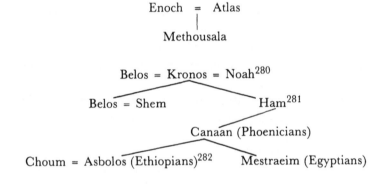

Enoch = Atlas
|
Methousala

Belos = Kronos = Noah[280]

Belos = Shem   Ham[281]

Canaan (Phoenicians)

Choum = Asbolos (Ethiopians)[282]   Mestraeim (Egyptians)

---

[280] Wacholder, "Pseudo-Eupolemus' Two Greek Fragments on Abraham," pp. 89-90, identifies Belos of F 2 with Nimrod on the basis that "Babel means Bel came; as Scripture says that Nimrod founded Babylon, Nimrod must be a variant of Belus" (p. 90). He equates Belos in F 1 with Noah and the second Belos with Shem (p. 94). He does not solve how Belos = Nimrod of F 2 fits into this tree. I prefer the equation with Noah in F 2 since he is said to have survived the flood. Hengel, *Judaism and Hellenism*, 2:60 n. 244, explains the identification "because the anonymous Samaritan identifies the γίγαντες of Gen. 6:4 and the γίγας of 10:9." Holladay, *Fragments from Hellenistic Jewish Authors*, p. 187 n. 46, also thinks this is Noah. The connection of Belos (= Noah) with the tower of Babel in F 2 is due to Pseudo-Eupolemos' effort to connect *Belos* with *Babel* (= Bel came). *Ibid.*, n. 47.

[281] This follows the emendation of Χαναav to Χαμ first suggested by Bochard and accepted by Freudenthal, *Alexander Polyhistor*, p. 208; Jacoby, *FGrH* 724 (3c:679); and Walter, *JSHRZ*, 1:142. It serves to bring the text into conformity with Gen. 10:6. The troublesome phrase in F 1.9, τοῦτον δὲ τὸν Χαναὰν γεννῆσαι τὸν πατέρα τῶν Φοινίκων, can also be translated in various ways. The translation upon which the emendation is based is: "this Canaan begot the father of the Phoenicians." Holladay, *Fragments from Hellenistic Jewish Authors*, p. 175, renders it: "this Belus fathered Canaan, the father of the Phoenicians," understanding the clause in apposition to the preceding phrase. Doran, *OTP*, 2:881 n. u, offers another possibility: "this person begot Canaan, the father of the Phoenicians."

[282] In Gen. 10:6 Χους is the brother of Χαναav.

2. *Form.* The form which this account took varies from what we have examined so far. This is largely due to the use of various sources which the following chart will help to locate. In the chart on pp. 196-199 I have listed only the major sources. I have indicated where there is a contradiction between Pseudo-Eupolemos and the source by placing the reference in italics.

It is certain that Pseudo-Eupolemos used the LXX.[283] This is clear from both the names,[284] verbal echoes,[285] and interpretations which depend upon the LXX rather than the Hebrew text.[286] As with the other Hellenistic Jewish authors, knowledge of Hebrew is harder to ascertain.[287] There are two lines of evidence in this case. First, on two occasions, Pseudo-Eupolemos offers explicit etymological explanations.[288] Second, there are three instances where the fragments ultimately depend upon the Hebrew: the connection between the tower and Babylon,[289] placing Abraham in the tenth

---

[283] Freudenthal, *Alexander Polyhistor*, pp. 98-99; Wacholder, ''Pseudo-Eupolemus' Two Greek Fragments on Abraham,'' p. 87; Denis, *Introduction aux Pseudépigraphes Grecs d'Ancien Testament*, p. 262 and "L'Historien anonyme d'Eusèbe," p. 46; Hengel, *Judaism and Hellenism*, p. 89; Walter, *JSHRZ*, 1:138; Conzelmann, *Heiden-Juden-Christen*, p. 147; Collins, *Between Athens and Jerusalem*, pp. 38-39; Holladay, *Fragments from Hellenistic Jewish Authors*, p. 157; Attridge, "Historiography," p. 165; and Schürer, *The History of the Jewish People in the Age of Jesus Christ*, 3:530.

[284] Six of the seven biblical names in the fragments all agree with the LXX: Αβρααμ (although note that in F 2 it is Αβραμος), Μελχισεδεκ, Χανααν, Χους, Ενωχ, and Μαθουσαλα. The only variation is Μεστραειμ (F 1.9) for Μεσραιμ (Gen. 10:6).

[285] There may be echoes on two occasions: διασπαρῆναι for διέσπειρεν (F 1.3 = Gen. 11:8,9) and the use of ὕψιστος in F 1.5 = Gen. 14:18 (see also vv. 19, 20, 22).

[286] According to Pseudo-Eupolemos, the γίγαντας founded Babylon (F 1.2). This rests upon Gen. 10:8-10 where Nimrod—credited with the founding of Babylon—is called גבר (v.8) and גבר ציד (v.9 *bis*) by the Hebrew and γίγας (v.8) and γίγας κυνηγός (v. 9 *bis*) by the LXX. F 1.3 says that Οὐρίη is interpreted as Χαλδαίων πόλιν which may recall the LXX's rendition of בעוא כשדים (Gen. 11:28, 31) into ἐν τῇ χώρᾳ τῶν Χαλδαίων.

[287] Those who think he knew Hebrew include Wacholder, ''Pseudo-Eupolemus' Two Greek Fragments on Abraham,'' p. 88; Hengel, *Judaism and Hellenism*, p. 89; and Holladay, *Fragments from Hellenistic Jewish Authors*, p. 157. Walter, *JSHRZ*, 1:139, has questioned this and Schürer, *The History of the Jewish People in the Age of Jesus Christ*, 3:530, is uncertain.

[288] F 1.3 connects Οὐρίη to Χαλδαίων πόλιν. (Did he read עיר כשדם? F 1.5 derives 'Αργαριζίν from ὄρος ὑψίστου (= הר גריזים).

[289] FF 1.2 and 2. Note that in Gen. 11:9 the LXX omits the crucial reference to Babel. MT: על כן קרא שמה בבל כי שם בלל יהוה שפת כל הארץ. LXX: διὰ τοῦτο ἐκλήθη τὸ ὄνομα αὐτῆς Σύγχυσις, ὅτι ἐκεῖ συνέχεεν κύριος τὰ χείλη πάσης τῆς γῆς.

Possible Sources for Pseudo-Eupolemos
Parallels F 1 (*PE* 9.17.1-9)

Event	Pseudo-Eupolemos	Gen. Biblical text	Jewish authors	Pagan authors
Babylon founded by giants who survived flood.	2	10:10 (LXX)		
Giants build a tower God destroys	2-3	11:1-9	Jub. 10:26	Abydenos (Eus. *PE* 9.14.2)
Birth of Abraham in 10th generation	3	11:10-26 (MT)		Berossos (Jos. *AJ* 1.158)
Abraham's greatness	3		Jub. 10:16-17	Berossos (Jos. *AJ* 1.158)
Abraham teaches Phoenicians astronomy	4			
Abraham rescues Lot	4-6	14:1-24		
Armenians defeat Phoenicians	4	14:1-12	1QapGn. 21.23-22.1	
Abraham rescues Lot	4	14:13-15	1QapGn. 22.1-13	
Also captures children and wives of Armenians	4	*14:16*	1QapGn. 22.11	
Ambassadors approach Abraham	5	*14:17*	*1QapGn. 22.18*	

Possible Sources for Pseudo-Eupolemos
Parallels F 1 (*PE* 9.17.1-9)

Event	Pseudo-Eupolemos	Gen. Biblical text	Jewish authors	Pagan authors
Abraham returns booty	5	14:21-24	1QapGn. 22.18-26	
Guest near Argarizin	5	*14:17*	1QapGn. 22.13-14	
Received gifts from Melchizedek	6	*14:18-20*	*1QapGn. 22.17*	
Abraham in Egypt	6-8	12:10-20	Jub. 13:10-15	
Famine	6	12:10	1QapGn. 19.10	
Abraham and all his house go to Egypt	6	12:20		
King takes his wife whom Abraham claims as sister	6	12:11-15	1QapGn. 20.2-10	
King can not have sexual relations with her	7		1QapGn. 20.15, 17	
King and house suffer	7	12:17	1QapGn. 20.16-18	

Possible Sources for Pseudo-Eupolemos
Parallels F 1 (*PE* 9.17.1-9)

Event	Pseudo-Eupolemos	Gen. Biblical text	Jewish authors	Pagan authors
King summons diviners	7		1QapGn. 20.19-20	
They inform him woman is not a widow	7		1QapGn. 20.21-26	
King returns her to Abraham	7	12:18-19	1QapGn. 20.27-28	
Abraham lives in Heliopolis	8			
Instructs Egyptians	8		Artapanos F 1	
Enoch first discovered astrology	8		Jub. 4:17-19 I En. 72-82	
Babylonian claim	9			
Greek claim	9			
Methuselah revealed everything through angels	9		1QapGn. 2.19-21 Cf. Jub. 4:21 (Enoch) I En. 65:14; 81:5; 82:1; 83:1; 85:2; 91:1; 107:3; II En. 1:10	

Possible Sources for Pseudo-Eupolemos
Parallels F 2 (*PE* 9.18.2)

Event	Pseudo-Eupolemos	Gen. Biblical text	Jewish authors	Pagan authors
Abraham traced lineage to giants	2			
The gods destroyed the giants in Babylonia	2	6:1-8:22		
Bel built tower in Babylon	2	10:10		Berossos (*FGrH* 685 F 1)
Abraham learned astrology	2			
Taught Phoenicians	2	Gen. 12:1-9		
Went to Egypt	2	Gen. 12:10-20		

generation,[290] and the mention of Ur.[291] The greatest problem is in determining whether a particular exegetical position rests upon the text or upon an oral tradition. While the evidence is, therefore, somewhat ambiguous I think that we should credit Pseudo-Eupolemos with a knowledge of Hebrew.

Even the most cursory reading of these fragments reveals that while they retell the biblical text, they do so in a most creative way. Some of the divergences are also attested in Jewish works of this period, particularly I Enoch, the Genesis Apocryphon, and Jubilees. In particular there are several instances where Pseudo-Eupolemos and the Genesis Apocryphon[292] agree over against the biblical text: both employ the method of using anachronistic names,[293] both add the detail that Abraham captured the goods of the invaders as well as their plunder,[294] both insist that the king of Egypt could not have sexual relations with Sarah,[295] both have the king summon diviners when he and his house are smitten,[296] and both trace the revelation of heavenly secrets from Enoch through Methuselah.[297] On the other side of the ledger there are some notable differences: 1QapGn follows the sequence of biblical events, Pseudo-Eupolemos does not[298]; on three occasions 1QapGn remains true to the biblical text and Pseudo-Eupolemos does not[299];

---

[290] The LXX adds one generation to the genealogy of Gen. 11:10-26 which should result in placing Abraham in the eleventh generation. It is possible that Pseudo-Eupolemos did not count Shem. In any case this tradition is complicated by the relationship to Berossos. (See below)

[291] Gen. 11:28, 31: בעור כשדים which the LXX gives as ἐν τῇ χώρᾳ τῶν Χαλδαίων. Pseudo-Eupolemos apparently knows both.

[292] For 1QapGn. I have used the text of Joseph A. Fitzmyer, *The Genesis Apocryphon of Qumran Cave 1: A Commentary*, 2nd ed. Biblica et Orientalia 18A (Rome: Biblical Institute Press, 1971).

[293] F 1.4 and 1QapGn. 21.23. Only the method is shared; the names are not even though they are describing the same event.

[294] They do differ in detail, however: F 1.4: καὶ τῶν πολεμίων αἰχμαλωτίσαι τέκνα καὶ γυναῖκας; 1QapGn. 22.11 וכול סבתהון.

[295] F 1.7 and 1QapGn. 20.15, 17, 30.

[296] F 1.7 and 1QapGn. 20.19-20. Once again the details vary: In Pseudo-Eupolemos they tell the king Sarah is not a widow and in 1QapGn they are unable to cure him.

[297] F 1.9 and 1QapGn. 2.19-21.

[298] Pseudo-Eupolemos reverses Gen. 12:10-20 and 14:1-24, 1QapGn. does not.

[299] One, F 1.5 has ambassadors (πρέσβεων) meet Abraham after his victory; 1QapGn. follows Gen. 14:17 in having the king of Sodom meet him. Two, F 1.6 has Abraham receive gifts from Melchizedek; 1QapGn. 22.17 has Abraham pay Melchizedek a tithe. Three, in F 1.6 Abraham claims Sarah as his sister; in

and finally and very significantly, they disagree about where Abraham met with the people of Canaan after his victory.[300] The most likely explanation of these data is that Pseudo-Eupolemos knew Palestinian exegetical traditions in the first half of the second century B.C.E. and incorporated them—as did his Jewish counterparts—into his œuvre.[301] I am inclined to think that he knew these through oral sources since the presentation of what is common to these works varies as much as it does.[302]

Our Samaritan knew more than Palestinian traditions. In F 1.9 he expressly cites Babylonian and Greek claims.[303] This is substantiated by an analysis of the fragments. Most importantly it is possible that our author had read Berossos. The strongest case for dependence is the description of Abraham which I have set out in parallel columns.

BEROSSOS (AJ 1.158)	PSEUDO-EUPOLEMOS (PE 9.17.3)
μετὰ τὸν κατακλυσμὸν δεκάτῃ γενεᾷ παρὰ Χαλδαίοις	δεκάτῃ δὲ γενεᾷ, φησίν, ἐν πόλει τῆς Βαβυλωνίας Καμαρίνῃ ἥν τινας λέγειν πόλιν Οὐρίην

1QapGn. 20.2-10 (= Gen. 12:11-15) Sarah lies about their relationship. (It should be noted that in Gen. 12:18 Pharaoh asks Abraham why he lied about the matter.)

[300] Gen. 14:17 says that the king of Sodom met him אל עמק שוה הוא עמק המלך which the LXX renders by εἰς τὴν κοιλάδα τὴν Σαυη (τοῦτο ἦν τὸ πέδιον βασιλέως). Without noting a change of locale it then introduces Melchizedek. F 1.5 omits any locale in connection with the ambassadors but says that Abraham was entertained ὑπὸ πόλεως ἱερὸν 'Αργαριζίν, ὃ εἶναι μεθερμηνευόμενον ὄρος ὑψίστου. 1QapGn. 22.12-14 also plays with the text, but says that the king of Sodom came לשלם היא ירושלם. It goes on to explain that Abraham was encamped בעמק שוא והוא עמק מלכא בקעת בית כרמא where Melchizedek went out to meet him.

[301] Vermes, *Scripture and Tradition in Judaism*, pp. 123-124, deduced from the similarities that "the literature of Hellenistic Judaism was built upon Palestinian foundations" (p. 124). Wacholder, "Pseudo-Eupolemus' Two Greek Fragments on Abraham," p. 109 (see 109-112), more correctly argued "that Genesis Apocryphon and Pseudo-Eupolemus were products of Palestinian scholarship."

[302] *Contra* Wacholder, "Pseudo-Eupolemus' Two Greek Fragments on Abraham," pp. 97-98, who argues for literary familiarity based upon "the author's wide acquaintance with the contemporary literature" (p. 97). Contacts with Jubilees and I Enoch are much less striking. The composite I Enoch is an apocalypse and radically different in its orientation. Jubilees also may be considered apocalyptic, although with some qualification. See John J. Collins, *The Apocalyptic Imagination: An Introduction to the Jewish Matrix of Christianity* (New York: Crossroad, 1984), pp. 1-32, especially p. 4.

[303] F 1.9: Βαβυλωνίους γὰρ λέγειν; ὑπὸ τῶν 'Ελλήνων λέγεσθαι; "Ελληνας δὲ λέγειν.

Berossos (AJ 1.158)	Pseudo-Eupolemos (PE 9.17.3)
	(εἶναι δὲ μεθερμηνευομένην Χαλδαίων πόλιν), (ἢ) ἐν τρισκαιδεκάτῃ γενέσθαι Ἀβραὰμ γενεᾷ,
τις ἦν δίκαιος ἀνὴρ καὶ μέγας	εὐγενείᾳ καὶ σοφίᾳ πάντας ὑπερβεβηκότα,
καὶ τὰ οὐράνια ἔμπειρος.	ὃν δὴ καὶ τὴν ἀστρολογίαν καὶ Χαλδαϊκὴν εὑρεῖν . . .

What is so striking about this comparison is how each item in Berossos has a complement in Pseudo-Eupolemos: the flood (*PE* 9.17.2), the tenth generation, his greatness, and his astrological acuteness. On the other hand, the individual elements within this pattern vary in specifics with the exception of the second. The question then becomes whether the general pattern is strong enough to posit dependence. On the whole I am inclined to think that it does.[304] It is also probable that the construction of the tower by Belos in F 2 stems from Berossos.[305]

Greek influence is not quite as obvious. In F 1.9 there are three specific claims made in the name of Greeks: Belos = Kronos; Choum = Asbolos; and Atlas discovered astrology. The third is—as we have already seen—a popular claim made by Greeks. The second is likely only an identification made by Pseudo-Eupolemos who intends for the reader merely to recognize the Greek name.[306] The first is much more important. According to Pseudo-Eupolemos,

---

[304] Those who also posit dependence include Freudenthal, *Alexander Polyhistor*, pp. 93-94; Schnabel, *Berossos und die babylonisch-hellenistische Literatur*, pp. 28, 67-69, 246, who has the fullest argument for dependence on pp. 67-69 (his argument on Choum = Asbolos = Somasbelos in Berossos is not valid as the works of Wacholder and Doran have pointed out); Wacholder, ''Pseudo-Eupolemus' Two Greek Fragments on Abraham,'' pp. 92, 95, 101-102; Hengel, *Judaism and Hellenism*, p. 88; Walter, *JSHRZ*, 1:139; Collins, *Between Athens and Jerusalem*, p. 39; and Holladay, *Fragments from Hellenistic Jewish Authors*, p. 159. Those who have challenged dependence are Conzelmann, *Heiden-Juden-Christen*, p. 146 and Doran, *OTP*, 2:877.

[305] *FGrH* 680 F 1.7,9, Bel is the creator of the world. However, in Abydenos who is dependent upon Berossos, Bel both creates the world and founds Babylon (*FGrH* 685 F 1).

[306] Asbolos is mentioned in Hesiod, *Sc.* 185. Wacholder, ''Pseudo-Eupolemos' Two Greek Fragments on Abraham,'' p. 95, very plausibly suggested that Asbolos was a perfect choice to identify with Ethiopia since the word means ''soot'' and is therefore suitable for the dark-skinned Ethiopians.

Belos (= Kronos) founded Babylon and built the tower (F 2). Since F 1 tells us that the giants built the tower, we should probably assume that Belos and the giants were associated in some way.[307] How? In a passage redolent of Pseudo-Eupolemos, the third Sibylline Oracle describes the fall of the tower and then goes on to associate it with the struggle between Zeus and Kronos who led the Titans by paraphrasing Hesiod's *Theogony*.[308] The author of the Sibylline was apparently interested in showing how both accounts pointed out that the tower/Titan episode was the beginning of numerous kingdoms and war.[309] Did the author make this connection for the first time or was it in a *Vorlage*? The fact that Belos (= Kronos) is connected with the tower in Pseudo-Eupolemos makes us wonder. Kastor of Rhodes (first century B.C.E.) also attests to a mixture of Oriental and Greek myths in a description of the conflict between Belos and the Titans.[310] Wacholder argued that these connections came from an earlier source and that consequently Pseudo-Eupolemos must have fused Berossos and Hesiod by claiming that the tower builders were giants led by Belos, the Greek Kronos.[311] But why would Pseudo-Eupolemos make this connection in the first place? Hesiod related the myth about how Kronos castrated his father Ouranos with the sickle his mother had formed. When Ouranos' blood spilled upon the ground, Gaia received it and from this union came μεγάλους τε Γίγαντας.[312] I suggest that it is the common mention of the giants in both the LXX and Hesiod that led Pseudo-Eupolemos to make a connection, especially since the giants

---

[307] F 2 tells us that Belos was one of the giants, but there may be more of a link than just this.

[308] Sib. Or. 3.97-161. There are several points of contact which can not be explained by reference to the biblical text. The tower is destroyed (F 1.3 and 3.96-98, 105) not deserted (Gen. 11:8). The next biblical event cited is the tenth generation which is linked to Ur of the Chaldeans (F 1.3 and 3.108-109, 218-219). This is followed by a reference to astrology: in F 1.3, 8; F 2, Abraham learns astrology; in 3.220-233, astrology is denounced and it is affirmed that the race of righteous persons there do not practice it. Is this common order coincidental?

[309] Note the concluding refrains in 3.105-107 and 154-155.

[310] *FGrH* 250 F 1. This is the struggle between Zeus and Kronos in Hesiod.

[311] Wacholder, "Pseudo-Eupolemus' Two Greek Fragments on Abraham," pp. 90-93. He has been followed by Hengel, *Judaism and Hellenism*, 1:89; 2:60 n. 246 and Holladay, *Fragments from Hellenistic Jewish Authors*, p. 161 n. 7. For later equations of Babel with the Titans see Pfeiffer, "Hebrews and Greeks Before Alexander," p. 98.

[312] *Theog.* 147ff., especially 176-186.

were principally known for their battle against the gods. Thus Kronos, the leader of Titans, became associated with the γίγας of Gen. 10:8-10 who founded Babylon and consequently with Belos, Berossos' founder of Babylon.[313]

Our fragments are then an account of Abraham, tracing his lineage back to the giants and presenting his journey from Mesopotamia to Phoenicia and finally to Egypt. The individual episodes have been molded by a mixture of biblical, Palestianian, Babylonian, and Greek elements.

3. *Function.* Why write such an account? Is this just a syncretistic mishmash of sources?[314] Not at all.[315] The identification of Babylonian and Greek gods with biblical characters constituted "demythologizing euhemerism"—to use Hengel's apt phrase.[316] The function of the extra biblical material is to confirm the text of Genesis. The identifications show that other traditions can be accepted as long as they fit within the framework of the biblical record. After all, it is the biblical text which structures the work.

The selection of the material in our remaining fragments is illuminating. Every incident in these fragments presents Abraham in relation to foreigners with the exception of his ancestry to the giants. The work thus has a universal perspective. We do not read about Abraham's call in connection with the promise (as in Gen. 12:1-3), but only to go to Phoenicia where we are told he taught astrology (F 1.4)! The fragments are free from nationalism in this respect. At the same time, Abraham always emerges as the hero: he teaches the Phoenicians, defeats the Armenians, is honored by the Phoenicians in the person of Melchizedek, and instructs the Egyptians.

This is not to say that the fragments lack any national tendencies. As a matter of fact, they are rather pronounced. There is a very evi-

---

[313] Gutschmid, *Kleine Schriften*, 2:575-576, argued that Pseudo-Eupolemos also used Ktesias.

[314] So Freudenthal, *Alexander Polyhistor*, p. 96.

[315] Others have also objected to the term syncretistic. Walter, *JSHRZ*, 1:139, thought that the identifications were not syncretistic "sondern vielmehr das echt hellenistische Bestreben, die Einheit der Menschheit in ihrer Frühzeit durch Gleichsetzung ihrer alten Überlieferungen aufzuweisen." Collins, *Between Athens and Jerusalem*, p. 42, also protested on the grounds that Pseudo-Eupolemos maintained a sense of identity and even superiority.

[316] *Judaism and Hellenism*, p. 88. Cf. also his "Anonymität, Pseudepigraphie und 'Literarische Fälschung' in der jüdisch-hellenistischen Literatur," p. 237. Note as well Wacholder, "Pseudo-Eupolemus' Two Greek Fragments on Abraham," pp. 94, 99.

dent bias against Egypt in cultural history.[317] Astrology is placed first not in Egypt, but in Babylon. Even worse, it is not taught in Egypt until it has been disseminated in Phoenicia. This perhaps explains why Pseudo-Eupolemos reversed the order of events as he did: he held Gen. 12:10-20 (Abraham's journey to Egypt) until after Gen. 14 (the war with the Armenians) to keep Abraham in Phoenicia for a longer period before he went down into Egypt.[318] His journey into Egypt is the last event in the fragments. This is undoubtedly the same reason why the genealogy in F 1.9 alters the biblical order: Chous is now the son of Canaan instead of his brother as in Gen. 10:6. The reason is that Canaan is the father of the Phoenicians; Chous the father of the Ethiopians and brother of Mestraeim, the father of the Egyptians.[319] Once again Egypt has taken last place. This consistent *Tendenz* implies that our author is politically pro-Seleucid and anti-Ptolemaic.

Are the fragments anti-Jewish?[320] They are pro-Samaritan and absolutely silent about Jews. They are not openly biased as against Egypt. They are also not warm as they are towards Phoenicia. Their silence hardly amounts to a commendation, but neither should we interpret it as a condemnation. Jews are simply not significant in these fragments.

Given these tendencies, what purpose could these fragments have served? In the first half of the second century B.C.E., the Samaritans accepted Hellenization without the struggle which characterised their counterparts to the south.[321] There are several reasons

---

[317] So also Wacholder, "Pseudo-Eupolemus' Two Greek Fragments on Abraham," p. 87; Denis, *Introduction aux Pseudépigraphes Grecs d'Ancien Testament*, p. 246; Walter, *JSHRZ*, 1:138; Holladay, *Fragments from Hellenistic Jewish Authors*, p. 159; Attridge, "Historiography," p. 166; and Schürer, *The History of the Jewish People in the Age of Jesus Christ*, 3:529. Doran, *OTP*, 2:875, denies that this has any political overtones. He thinks that it is a matter of cultural history. Is our author an academe who simply engages in intellectual jousts?!

[318] Wacholder, "Pseudo-Eupolemus' Two Greek Fragments on Abraham," p. 108.

[319] In Gen. 10:6 Mesraim is the brother of Chous.

[320] So Freudenthal, *Alexander Polyhistor*, p. 89 and Denis, *Introduction aux Pseudépigraphes Grecs d'Ancien Testament*, p. 262.

[321] See Josephos, *AJ* 11.344 and 12.257-264; II Macc. 6:2. For a commentary on the longer Josephos text see Jonathan A. Goldstein, *II Maccabees*. AB 41A (Garden City, New York: Doubleday & Company, Inc., 1983), pp. 523-539. The greatest single difference between Jews and Samaritans appears to be that the latter did not have a revolutionary core which violently opposed Hellenization.

for this: Samaria had a Greek city, Samaria, and could regularly observe the practice of pagan cults. Judea had neither. Our author represents the avant-garde among the Samaritans. The fragments show how a Samaritan could remain loyal to the Torah and at the same time accept other traditions by subordinating them to her/his own.[322] They thus serve to carve out a niche for Samaritans in the Seleucid world. Babylonian and Greek gods are simply humans in their own traditions. Culturally speaking, their own ancestor, Abraham, served as the *Kulturbringer* to both Phoenicia and Egypt. There is, therefore, no need to fear the new culture: it must simply be assimilated into existing structures.[323] At the same time, this stance would show the Antiochenes that τοῖς Ἑλληνικοῖς ἔθεσιν αἱροῦνται χρώμενοι ζῆν.[324]

Significance

Does such a work stand within the tradition of Berossos and Manethon? The use of native traditions in an effort to provide a self-definition in a new and larger world suggests that it does. The unabashed cultural claim stands squarely within this form of writing.[325] The open acceptance of other traditions does not negate this since they are utilized in a subordinate role.

Pseudo-Eupolemos takes his rightful place as a Samaritan representative of early Hellenistic writing to be followed by other Hellenistic Samaritan authors.[326]

---

[322] So also Hengel, "Anonymität, Pseudepigraphie und 'Literarische Fälschung' in der jüdisch-hellenistischen Literatur," pp. 237-238 and *Judaism and Hellenism*, p. 91.

[323] Cf. the conclusion of Denis, "L'Historien anonyme d'Eusèbe," p. 149: "L'hellénisme de la Lettre d'Aristée est de langue et de culture. Pour le Siracide, il est philosophique; aux yeux des Macchabées, il est moral et religieux. Notre historien veut l'introduire par l'histoire et la science."

[324] Josephos, *AJ* 12.263. I think that the audience must have been the Samaritans themselves since the fragments are so heavily anti-Ptolemaic and pro-Seleucid. Had they been directed to the Seleucids, I would have expected them to try to win a better position for the Samaritans rather than the Seleucids.

[325] So also Schürer, *The History of the Jewish People in the Age of Jesus Christ*, 3:529.

[326] Two disputed possibilities are Theodotos and Kleodamos Malchos. On Theodotos see *PE* 9.22.1-11. The debate is over whether Theodotos is Samaritan or Jewish. For Kleodemos Malchos see Holladay, *Fragments from Hellenistic Jewish Authors*, pp. 245-259. He has been identified as a Samaritan, a Jew, and a pagan.

EUPOLEMOS[327]

Life[328]

Eupolemos ("good at war") is an unusual name.[329] Although Josephos says that he was a Greek, Eusebios is much more accurate when he takes him for a Jew since it is all but impossible to attribute the fragments in his name to an individual of any other ethnicity.[330] I Macc. 8:17 informs us that Judas chose τὸν Εὐπόλεμον υἱὸν Ἰωαννου τοῦ Ακκως as well as Jason the son of Eleazar to go to Rome on an embassy. Several factors make an identification of our author with this Eupolemos all but certain.[331] First, the unusual name associated with an ambassador and an author from the same time period naturally leads us to think of one leading individual.[332] Second, this ambassador was a priest; our fragments focus on the temple. Third, both have ties to the Hasmoneans: the ambassador as a representative and the author's political perspective.

We therefore can be reasonably certain that Eupolemos was from the distinguished Hakkoz family. This family had served in the

---

[327] The major studies on Eupolemos in the last one hundred years are Freudenthal, *Alexander Polyhistor*, pp. 105-130; Adolf Schlatter, "Eupolemus als Chronolog und seine Beziehungen zu Josephus und Manetho," *Theologische Studien und Kritiken* 4 (1891): 633-703; *RE*, s.v. "Eupolemos," by Felix Jacoby, 6:1227-1229; Dalbert, *Die Theologie der hellenistisch-jüdischen Missions-Literatur*, pp. 35-42; J. Giblet, "Eupolème et l'Historiographie du Judaïsme Hellénistique," *ETL* 39 (1963): 539-554; Denis, *Introduction aux Pseudépigraphes Grecs d'Ancien Testament*, pp. 252-255; Hengel, *Judaism and Hellenism*, pp. 92-95; Wacholder, *Eupolemus* and his article in *EncJud*, s.v. "Eupolemus," 6:964-965; Walter, *JSHRZ*, 1:93-108; Conzelmann, *Heiden-Juden-Christen*, pp. 143-144; Collins, *Between Athens and Jerusalem*, pp. 40-42; Holladay, *Fragments from Hellenistic Jewish Authors*, pp. 93-156; Attridge, "Historiography," pp. 162-165; F. Fallon, "Eupolemus," in *OTP*, 2:861-872; Schürer, *The History of the Jewish People in the Age of Jesus Christ*, 3:517-521; and Droge, *Homer or Moses?*, pp. 13-19; and Pilhofer, *Presbyteron Kreitton*, pp. 153-156.
[328] The best discussion of his life is that of Wacholder, *Eupolemus*, pp. 7-21.
[329] The name is Greek. According to Wacholder, *Eupolemus*, p. 4, there is no other Jew in antiquity attested by this name.
[330] Josephos, *CA* 1.216; Eusebios, *HE* 6.13.7.
[331] S. Krauss in *The Jewish Encyclopedia*, s.v. "Eupolemus," 5:269, denied this identification. N. Turner in *IDB*, s.v. "Eupolemus," 2:181, speaks of the identification only as a possibility. All the other works listed as major studies make the connection.
[332] The mission took place in 161 B.C.E. On its date see Goldstein, *I Maccabees*, pp. 358-359, who places it between 10 March and 11 November 161 B.C.E., since those dates mark the *termini* of the Mediterranean sailing season. Eupolemos the author can be dated independently by the reference in F 5 to 158/157 B.C.E. (See below)

Solomonic temple (I Chron. 24:10), but when they returned from exile were unable to establish their genealogy and were temporarily excluded from service (Ez. 2:59-63; Neh. 7:61-65). According to Neh. 3:4 and 21, the genealogy of the family at that time moved from Hakkoz to Uriah to Meremoth who served as the temple treasurer (Ez. 8:33). We even have a sherd bearing the stamp of a seal impression which N. Avigad has identified with this Uriah.[333] Eupolemos should thus be seen as a scion of an illustrious priestly family.

His father lived up to this tradition when he obtained royal concessions from Antiochos III after the latter had annexed Judea.[334] He may also have represented the Jews along with Absalom before Lysias in 164 B.C.E. (II Macc. 11:17), although I prefer to think of this as another John.[335] In any event, Eupolemos came from a politically active priestly family.

He must have been born during the latter part of the third century B.C.E.,[336] and have either been infirm or deceased in 143 B.C.E. when another delegation was sent to Rome since he was not a part of it.[337] These dates may also serve to mark the limits of his written work. Fortunately, F 5 provides a specific year for his *opus* although it is complicated by an error. Eupolemos summarizes all the years

---

[333] N. Avigad, "A New Class of *Yehud* Stamps," *IEJ* 7 (1957): 146-153, especially 149-150.

[334] II Macc. 4:11. Antiochos defeated Skopas, Ptolemy's general at Paneion near the headwaters of the Jordan in 198 B.C.E. Polybios 16.18; Josephos, *AJ* 12.132. The concessions were probably those of *AJ* 12.138-146.

[335] John was a very common name. What bothers me about identifying this John with the John of 4:11 is that the John of 4:11 must have been a mature man c. 198 B.C.E. Would he still have been active thirty-four years later? On the other hand, the known ambassadorial roles of this family could be used as support for another John of the same family.

[336] Based upon the age of his father as ambassador to Antiochos III at the beginning of the second century. So also Wacholder, *Eupolemos*, p. 12, who thinks his birth was prior to the last decade.

[337] I Macc. 12:16. During the second and first centuries the Jews tended to use the same individuals or members of the same family for diplomatic missions. So II Macc. 4:11 and I Macc. 8:17. Again note the link with Jason in I Macc. 8:17 and 12:16 (father and son?). (Cf. also Josephos, *AJ* 13.260 where a Diodoros, the son of Jason, represented John Hyrkanos at Rome and 14.146 where Alexander, the son of Jason, served the Jews before the Roman senate at the time of Hyrkanos and Antipater.) The same ambassadors who served Jonathan (I Macc. 12:16) later went to Rome on behalf of Simon (I Macc. 14:22, 24). That Eupolemos was out of the diplomatic service at the time of Jonathan is also held by Wacholder, *Eupolemus*, pp. 20-21 and Bartlett, *Jews in the Hellenistic World*, pp. 58-59.

from Adam ἄχρι τοῦ πέμπου ἔτους Δημητρίου βασιλείας Πτολεμαίου τὸ δωδέκατον βασιλεύοντος Αἰγύπτου as 5149. The difficulty is that we can not fully synchronize the dates of a Seleucid and Ptolemaic ruler with these years. Freudenthal persuasively argued that the Demetrios was Demetrios I Soter (162-150).[338] This would make his fifth year 158/157 B.C.E. This is very close to the twelfth year of Ptolemy VIII Euergetes II Physcon who began ruling in 170 B.C.E. Ptolemy's twelfth year would be 159/158. Unfortunately, Ptolemy was not ruling Egypt at the time, but Cyrene.[339] It is doubtful that a diplomat would make such an error. It is more likely that Alexander Polyhistor has added the reference to Ptolemy just as he did the Roman consuls later in this fragment.[340] We therefore should date Eupolemos' work at 158/157 B.C.E.

Eupolemos was a Palestinian aristocrat who lived through one of the Jewish nation's greatest crises.[341] The data we have collected about his life suggest that he was a moderate in his outlook. He was certainly not an Antiochene or Judas would never have asked him to serve as an ambassador. At the same time, he was not entirely opposed to Hellenism: he bore a Greek name, wrote in Greek—however poorly,[342] presumably conversed in Greek in his ambassadorial role, and knew some Greek literature as we will see. He thus stood somewhere between the radical Hellenists and the Hasidim. How close he was to the Hasmoneans can only be determined by examing his writings.

---

[338] *Alexander Polyhistor*, pp. 213-214. The only other option would be Demetrios II Nikator (145-140/139 B.C.E.) who as Freudenthal pointed out did not begin to rule in the seventh year of a Ptolemy. Besides Freudenthal's arguments, he is ruled out if Eupolemos died before 140.

[339] He ruled Egypt jointly with Ptolemy VI Philometor from 170-164, alone in 164-163, was king in Cyrene from 163-145, and then Egypt again in 145-116.

[340] This was first suggested by Gutschmid, *Kleine Schriften*, 2:191, who, however, attributes the additions to Clement of Alexandria who in turn depended upon Julius Cassianus. Others who see a secondary hand in the mention of Ptolemy include Jacoby, *FGrH* 724; Wacholder, *Eupolemus*, pp. 41-42; Walter, *JSHRZ*, 1:107; and Fallon, *OTP*, 2:863, 871-872 n. c. Cf. also Schürer, *The History of the Jewish People in the Age of Jesus Christ*, 3:519-520, who thinks it is either a gloss or a corruption.

[341] Giblet's attempt to locate Eupolemos as a refugee in Egypt instead of Palestine must be considered forced. Cf. "Eupolème et l'Historiographie du Judaïsme Hellénistique," pp. 546-547, 552.

[342] Jacoby, *RE*, s.v. "Eupolemus," 6:1229, excoriated his style: "Sein Stil ist miserabel, der Wortschatz dürftig, der Satzbau plump. Alles verrät den nur oberflächlich vom griechischen Geiste berührten Juden, der denn auch neben der LXX fleißig den hebraischen Urtext benutzt."

Work

Since Eupolemos served as an envoy for Judas, is explicitly mentioned in both I and II Maccabees, and is a known historian, there
has been a great deal of speculation that he is one of the sources for
I and II Maccabees.[343] While there is some merit to these
proposals, it is impossible to prove what material came from Eupolemos. For this reason I will only deal with the fragments which have
come to us in his name.

1. *Content.* There are eight fragments in Clement and Eusebios
which bear Eupolemos' name. We have seen that one of these is erroneous. Of the remaining seven, Clement and Eusebios have
preserved parallel accounts in two instances.[344] We then have five
fragments with which to work.[345] There is, however, a difficulty
with F 4 (= *PE* 9.39.1-5): Eupolemos is not mentioned by Polyhistor in his comments. This led Jacoby to place this fragment last under the heading "Ohne Autornamen" in his edition.[346] The MSS
do, nonetheless, all contain the heading of Eusebios: Εὐπολέμου
περὶ Ἰερεμίου τοῦ προφήτου ὁμοίως.[347] Walter thought Eusebios
shortened Polyhistor's introductory comments including the reference to Eupolemos and then supplied the name in his heading.[348] It
is also possible that Eusebios supplied the title on his own based
upon what he knew of Eupolemos' work (via Polyhistor)—although
this would require a great deal of Eusebios. What is certain is that
Eusebios thought that it came from Eupolemos and the internal evi-

---

[343] Wacholder, *Eupolemus*, pp. 27-40, attributes the first part of I Macc. 8 (vs.
1-6) to him and thinks that all of the chapter rests upon his history (pp. 35-36). He
also thinks that the references to foreign affairs in the Acts of Judah go back to Eupolemos (pp. 37-38). In II Macc. he contends that 1:18b-2:15 preserve "a lost, if
embellished, fragment of Eupolemus" (p. 40) and that chs 3-5 depend upon him.
Goldstein, *II Maccabees*, pp. 37-41, 48, tentatively supplies Eupolemos' name for
the author of the Common Source for I and II Maccabees. (He calls it a "plausible
guess.") Bartlett, *Jews in the Hellenistic World*, p. 58, is more guarded and only com-
mits Eupolemos to "a hand in the composition of the letter (i.e., II Macc.
1:10-2:18)," although he mentions the other theories. The most important work
on the sources of I and II Maccabees is Klaus-Dietrich Schunck, *Die Quellen des I.
und II. Makkabäerbuches*, Diss. Greifswald (Halle (Salle): Niemeyer, 1954).

[344] F 1 = *Strom.* 1.23.153.4; *PE* 9.25.4-26.1 and F 2 = *Strom.* 1.21.130.3; *PE*
9.30.1-34.18.

[345] Of the remaining three two are from Eusebios (F 3 = *PE* 9.34.20 and F 4
= *PE* 9.39.1-5) and one from Clement (F 5 = *Strom.* 1.21.141.4-5).

[346] *FGrH* 723 F 5.

[347] ION. B also except it lacks ὁμοίως.

[348] *JSHRZ*, 1:93.

dence of the fragment supports him in both its phraseology and contents.[349] There are some indications that Polyhistor erred while
condensing the text.[350] The major places are the following. In F 2.2
the phrase μετὰ δὲ ταῦτα moves us from Joshua to Samuel with no
mention of the judges![351] Yet in F 2.8, we read that David delivered
the kingdom to Solomon in the presence of Eli. The substitution of
Eli for Zadok, however, is more likely due to Eupolemos.[352] F 2.3
states that David is Saul's son which again can be understood as a
revisionist change by Eupolemos.[353] A more telling example is the
name of the angel who commanded David not to build the temple
himself, Διάναθαν which originally must surely have been διὰ
Νάθαν. (F 2.6)[354] We must therefore be careful in attributing all
difficulties to Eupolemos himself. Some are much more explicable
as the mistakes of a pagan who did not know the biblical text. We

---

[349] So also Freudenthal, *Alexander Polyhistor*, pp. 208-209, who supplies verbal
parallels with the undisputed fragments; Holladay, *Fragments from Hellenistic Jewish
Authors*, p. 100 n. 9, who argues from the title; Bartlett, *Jews in the Hellenistic World*,
p. 70, who argues from both the title and the internal evidence; Schürer, *The History
of the Jewish People in the Age of Jesus Christ*, 3:518, who accepts it on internal grounds.
The interests in prophecy and the temple are of great concern in the uncontested
fragments.
[350] The most important discussions of this are Freudenthal, *Alexander Polyhistor*,
pp. 120-123 and Wacholder, *Eupolemus*, pp. 129-131.
[351] Μετὰ δὲ ταῦτα appears only here in Polyhistor. Those who think this is Polyhistor's error are Freudenthal, *Alexander Polyhistor*, p. 121; Wacholder, *Eupolemus*,
p. 129, who wavers between omission through Polyhistor or a chronological summary by Eupolemos, although he inclines to the former; Walter, *JSHRZ*, 2:99 n.
2a; Bartlett, *Jews in the Hellenistic World*, pp. 61-62; Fallon, *OTP*, 2:866 n. e.
[352] Freudenthal, *Alexander Polyhistor*, p. 121, attributes this to Polyhistor.
Walter, *JSHRZ*, 1:101 n. 8c, also thinks that it is Polyhistor's error, but asks:
"Hatte Eupolemos geschrieben 'Abjathar, der letzte Priester aus dem Geschlecht
Elis' oder Zadok genannt . . .?" Wacholder, *Eupolemus*, pp. 131, 151-155, however,
thinks that this was a deliberate deviation by Eupolemos who mentioned Eli in an
effort to whitewash Solomon's bloodletting of the Eleazarites who sided against him
(cf. I Kgs. 2:26-27) and to slight the Zadokites of his own day who had cooperated
with the Syrians. He has been seconded by Bartlett, *Jews in the Hellenistic World*, p.
66 and Fallon, *OTP*, 2:867 n. u.
[353] Polyhistor's error: Walter, *JSHRZ*, 1:99 n. 3aa; Holladay, *Fragments from
Hellenistic Jewish Authors*, p. 139 n. 19; Fallon, *OTP*, 2:866 n. g; and Doran, "The
Jewish Hellenistic Historians Before Josephus," p. 266. Eupolemos' deliberate effort to eliminate the throne succession narrative or to redeem Saul's reputation:
Wacholder, *Eupolemus*, p. 130 and Bartlett, *Jews in the Hellenistic World*, p. 62 respectively.
[354] Freudenthal, *Alexander Polyhistor*, p. 121, followed by Wacholder, *Eupolemus*,
pp. 141-143 (hesitatingly); Walter, *JSHRZ*, 1:100 n. 6aa; Holladay, *Fragments from
Hellenistic Jewish Authors*, p. 141 n. 29; Bartlett, *Jews in the Hellenistic World*, p. 65
(without attributing it to Polyhistor); and Fallon, *OTP*, 2:866 n. p.

must also realize that Polyhistor abbreviated the text to a significant degree.

Clement and Eusebios each preserve a different title for Eupolemos: Clement has Περὶ τῶν ἐν τῇ Ἰουδαίᾳ βασιλέων (F 1 = *Stromata* 1.23.153.4) while Eusebios gives Περὶ τῆς Ἠλίου προφητείας in F 2 = *PE* 9.30.1. Freudenthal pointed out that the title in Eusebios has nothing at all to do with the fragment which follows, while that of Clement fits the contents of the fragments nicely. He accordingly discarded Περὶ τῆς Ἠλίου as an error and considered Περὶ τῶν ἐν τῇ Ἰουδαίᾳ βασιλέων to be the correct title. He left open the matter of whether the title was a heading for a subsection or an error of Polyhistor.[355] Jacoby sought to resolve the issue of the title's origin by suggesting that a book number had fallen out between ἐν and πρὸ Ἠλει.[356] While most subsequent studies have concurred with Freudenthal,[357] J. Giblet and Wacholder have maintained that there were two independent works since both titles are attested and there is no satisfactory way—in their opinion—of reconciling them.[358] Bartlett and Doran profess agnosticism on the title.[359]

Here it would be helpful to note the scope of the work. The fragments themselves cover events from Moses (F 1) to the fall of Jerusalem (F 4). The fifth fragment, however, gives a chronological summary from Adam until the fifth year of Ptolemy. Presumably this is only a recapitulation of what was a more extensive chronological treatment. Since Eupolemos provides dates within his work,[360] he must have dealt with chronology throughout the history.[361] This

---

[355] *Alexander Polyhistor*, p. 208.

[356] *FGrH* 723 F 2. See apparatus.

[357] Stearns, *Fragments from Graeco-Jewish Writers*, p. 29; Dalbert, *Die Theologie der hellenistisch-jüdischen Missions-Literatur*, p. 36; Denis, *Introduction aux Pseudépigraphes Grecs d'Ancien Testament*, pp. 252-253, who attributes the error to Polyhistor; Hengel, *Judaism and Hellenism*, p. 92; Walter, *JSHRZ*, 1:93 n. 1, ascribes it "auf einem ungeklarten Irrtum;" Conzelmann, *Heiden-Juden-Christen*, p. 143; Holladay, *Fragments from Hellenistic Jewish Authors*, p. 93; Fallon, *OTP*, 2:861; and Schürer, *The History of the Jewish People in the Age of Jesus Christ*, 3:517.

[358] Giblet, "Eupolème et l'Historiographie du Judaïsme Hellénistique," pp. 540-541 and Wacholder, *Eupolemus*, pp. 21-26. Attridge, "Historiography," p. 163, also considers two independent works possible, although he assigns all of the five remaining fragments to the work on kings.

[359] Bartlett, *Jews in the Hellenistic World*, p. 57 and Doran, "The Jewish Hellenistic Historians Before Josephus," p. 264.

[360] F 2 (30.1, 2, 8; 34.4) and F 3.

[361] Walter, *JSHRZ*, 1:95, leaves open the question whether the chronology was a section or extended throughout the history.

implies that the scope extended from Adam until 158/157. The statement in F 5 reflects a summary statement of Eupolemos, probably towards the end of the œuvre.

All five of our fragments fit nicely within this framework. It is reasonable to assume that they stem from a single work. What was the title? Freudenthal was correct in pointing out the suitability of Περὶ τῶν ἐν τῇ 'Ιουδαίᾳ βασιλέων. How do we then explain Περὶ τῆς 'Ηλίου προφητείας? Most likely it was a section heading which Polyhistor inadvertently gave as a title.

We may now offer a tentative reconstruction of the work. Eupolemos began with a summary treatment of the early period ranging from Adam to Samuel. Some of this material was probably only sketched chronologically with bare notes of biographical identifications.[362] In other instances, Eupolemos made Jewish cultural claims in the persons of her ancestors.[363] Apparently the early leaders were considered prophets not kings.[364] The history of the kings proper as well as the bulk of his narrative—if the proportion of the fragments is any indication—began with Saul and concentrated in particular on David and Solomon and the temple (FF 2 and 3). He proceeded on to the fall of Jerusalem concentrating on the kings of Judah[365] and prophets.[366] He must have then provided some coverage of the events down to his own time. If he authored the Common Source of I and II Maccabees, it is possible that it constituted the final section.[367] This must, however, remain conjectural.

---

[362] As F 2 (30.1-2).

[363] E.g., F 1. Did he make some claims for Abraham? This might also be another reason why the fragment belonging to Pseudo-Eupolemos was attached to Eupolemos.

[364] It is interesting to note the shift in vocabulary in the summary of early Jewish history given in F 2 (30.1-2). Eupolemos says Moses προφητεῦσαι, Joshua [προφητεῦσαι—this is grammatically understood from the previous statement about Moses], and then leaps to Samuel with μετὰ δὲ ταῦτα προφήτην γενέσθαι Σαμουήλ. All three of the early leaders of the Jews are prophets. The language shifts, however, when we come to Saul: εἶτα τῇ τοῦ θεοῦ βουλήσει ὑπὸ Σαμουήλ Σαοῦλον βασιλέα αἱρεθῆναι. So also Walter, JSHRZ, 1:94.

[365] The title suggests this.

[366] F 4. It should be noted that Jeremiah's prophecy is related to the reign of a king and deals with a terminal point in the history of Judah.

[367] It is interesting that the Common Source ended at either the death of Judas (161 B.C.E.) or the death of Alkimos the high priest (159 B.C.E.), dates which are very close to the writing of our work. Goldstein, II Maccabees, p. 48, dates the Common Source between mid-159 and 132 B.C.E.

THE HELLENISTIC JEWISH HISTORIANS

214

2. *Form.* Like Demetrios, Artapanos, and Pseudo-Eupolemos, Eupolemos structured his narrative on the basis of the biblical text. He undoubtedly knew both the LXX and the Hebrew text.[368] His use of the LXX is evident in proper names,[369] verbal echoes,[370] and instances where the LXX differs from the Hebrew text.[371] His dependence on the Hebrew appears in the name Souron,[372] places where he follows the Hebrew over against the LXX,[373] and the

---

[368] Primary use of the LXX with reference to the Hebrew: Freudenthal, *Alexander Polyhistor*, pp. 108-109, 119-120, 126; Dalbert, *Die Theologie der hellenistisch-jüdischen Missions-Literatur*, p. 37; Walter, *JSHRZ*, 1:95; and Conzelmann, *Heiden-Juden-Christen*, p. 144. Use of both without emphasis stated: Denis, *Introduction aux Pseudépigraphes Grecs d'Ancien Testament*, p. 254; Hengel, *Judaism and Hellenism*, p. 92; Holladay, *Fragments from Hellenistic Jewish Authors*, pp. 95, 101 n. 15; Fallon, *OTP*, 2:862-863; and Schürer, *The History of the Jewish People in the Age of Jesus Christ*, 3:519. Wacholder, *Eupolemus*, pp. 243-254, notes that while Eupolemos used the LXX for the Pentateuch and Joshua, it is not as evident in the case of Chronicles and Kings. Here-according to Wacholder—he depended entirely upon the Hebrew.

[369] Of the sixteen proper names, seven agree (Μωυσης/Μωσης, Σολομων, Ιησους, Ναυη, Σαμουηλ, Ηλει, and Ναβουχοδονοσορ), seven disagree (Δαβιδ for Δαυιδ, Υπερωων for Χιραμ, Σαουλος for Σαουλ, Σουρων for Χιραμ, Ιερεμιος instead of Ιερεμιας, and Ιωναχειμ in place of Ιωακειμ), and two have no parallel (Ουαφρης and Αστιβαρης). Among the disagreements it should be noted that Υπερωων may be an effort to solve a difficult text, II Chron. 2:12. Σαουλος and Ιερεμιος simply offer declinable forms. The other variations are noteworthy. Note also the place names: four agree (ἡ ἐρυθρὰ θάλασσα, Ἰερουσαλήμ/Ἰεροσόλυμα, Σηλώ, and Τύρος), two disagree (Ἐλάνος as an anachronism for Αιλαθ and Σιλος for Σηλω [he does give the LXX form in *PE* 9.34.14]), and one has no parallel (Οὐφρῆς νῆσος).

[370] Cf II Par. 2:11-15; III Kgdms. 5:21-23 and F 2 (34.1-3). The correspondence is noteworthy but not convincing in and of itself.

[371] In F. 2 (30.8) Solomon comes to power ὄντι ἐτῶν ιβ'. I Kgs. 2:12 has no equivalent in Hebrew; the LXX reads υἱὸς ἐτῶν δώδεκα. The second example is the connection between Jeremiah and Ἰωναχείμ. F 4 appears to stretch Jeremiah's relationship to Ἰωναχείμ to both יהויקים (609-598) and יהויכין (598-597). This is probably due to the fact that the LXX transliterates both Hebrew names by Ἰωναχείμ.

[372] Eupolemos: Σούρων; MT: חורם, חירום, and חירם; LXX: Χιράμ or Χειράμ; Herodotos (7.98): Σιρωμος.

[373] F 2 (34.5) describes the interior walls of the temple: ξυλῶσαι ἔσωθεν κεδρίνοις ξύλοις καὶ κυπαρισσίνοις. This is based upon I Kgs. 6:15 which in Hebrew reads: "he built the interior walls of the house with boards of cedar (בצלעות ארזים) . . . and covered the floor of the house with boards of cypress (בצלעות ברושים)." The LXX renders the two woods by διὰ ξύλων κεδρίνων and ἐν πλευραῖς πευκίναις (III Kgdms. 6:15). The substitution of pine for cypress is not followed by Eupolemos who goes back to the Hebrew. A second instance takes place in F 2 (34.6) where Eupolemos informs us that the two pillars were made of bronze. Only MT specifies their material (I Kgs. 7:15 vs. III Kgdms. 7:3).

technical temple terminology of the Hebrew text which the LXX transliterates but which Eupolemos translates.[374]

We can even be more specific about his text. Eupolemos tended to prefer Chronicles to Kings.[375] On at least eight occasions Eupolemos follows Chronicles over against Kings.[376] This should not be construed to mean that Eupolemos neglects Kings: when Kings adds a detail that Chronicles omits or offers a version which suits Eupolemos better, he opts for it.[377] Eupolemos thus has a

---

[374] Given by Freudenthal, *Alexander Polyhistor*, pp. 119-120 and Wacholder, *Eupolemus*, p. 252 (in a convenient chart).

[375] Freudenthal, *Alexander Polyhistor*, pp. 106, 119; Jacoby in *RE*, s.v. "Eupolemos," 6:1229; Dalbert, *Die Theologie der hellenistisch-jüdischen Missions-Literatur*, p. 36 n. 28; Giblet, "Eupolème et l'Historiographie du Judaïsme Hellénistique," p. 547; Denis, *Introduction aux Pseudépigraphes Grecs d'Ancien Testament*, p. 254; Wacholder, *Eupolemus*, pp. 147-149; Walter, *JSHRZ*, 1:95; and Holladay, *Fragments from Hellenistic Jewish Authors*, p. 95.

[376] All of these are in F 2: one, only Chronicles explicitly identifies the location of the altar with the threshing floor of Ornan the Jebusite (I Chron. 22:1; II Chron. 3:1; F 2 [30.5]); two, while both Kings and Chronicles mention David's wars as a reason for the prohibition of his building the temple, only Chronicles adds the reference to blood (I Chron. 28:3; F 2 [30.5] vs. I Kgs. 5:3); three, Chronicles alone records David's preparations for the temple (I Chron. 22:2-5, 14-16; 28:1-29:19 [especially 29:2-9]; F 2 [30.6]); four, the presence of the heads of the tribes and David's gifts to Solomon at his coronation are only supplied by Chronicles (I Chron. 29; F 2 [30.8]); five, the letter of Souron to Solomon follows II Chron. 2:11-15 rather than I Kgs. 5 (III Kgdms. 5:21-23) in dealing with the chief architect rather than with wood (F 2 [34.2]); six, only II Chron. 2:16 makes note of Joppa as the port where the wood would be brought (F 2 [34.4]; cf. I Kgs. 5:9); seven, the speaker's platform of F 2 (34.10) is only supported by II Chron. 6:13; eight, the description of the altar is located in II Chron. 4:1 (F 2 [34.10]; cf. also I Kgs. 8:22 and III Kgdms. 8:22, 31, 54, 64 where it is presumed but not described). It is also possible that the incorrect statement in F 2 (34.2) that the chief architect's mother was from the tribe of David is due to confusion over the reading of II Chron. 2:13 where she is traced from Dan. (Confusion between ΔΑΔ and ΔΑΝ would be relatively easy.) In I Kgs. 7:13 (III Kgdms. 7:2) he is said to be of the tribe of Naphtali. Finally, if Eupolemos formed Σούρων from the Hebrew form חורם, it should be noted that this form of his name only appears in Chronicles (I Chron. 14:1 Q; II Chron. 2:2, 10, 11; 8:2, 18; 9:21); Kings has either חירם (I Kgs. 5:15, 16, 21, 22, 25, 26; 9:11, 12, 14, 27; 10:11, 22; cf. also II Sam. 5:11) or חירום (I Kgs. 5:24, 32).

[377] Only I Kgdms. 2:12 (LXX) gives Solomon's age at his accession (F 2. [30.8]); the 160,000 workers in F 2 (34.4) must come from a computation based on I Kgs. 5:27-32 (10,000 + 70,000 = 80,000) and not on II Chron. 2:17-18 which omits the 10,000 (at one time, 30,000 total) conscripted Israelites (Was this omission politically motivated?); the covering of the walls with two types of wood depends upon I Kgs. 6:15 and not II Chron. 3:5 where only one wood is stipulated (F 2 [34.5]); Eupolemos says that the doors of the temple were covered with wood (F 2 [34.8]), a detail only mentioned in I Kgs. 6:31, 33-34—although the types of

harmonizing tendency with priority given to Chronicles.

This also helps us to understand why David and Solomon serve as the foci of his work. If I am correct in stating that the earlier period was only sketched, we have a rough parallel with the structure of the Chronicler's history who begins with genealogies as a way of summarizing (I Chron. 1-9)—even if they serve a different purpose than Eupolemos' pre-king period—then goes on to give a great deal of attention to David (I Chron. 10-29) and Solomon (II Chron. 1-9), and finally rehearses the story of Judah through her kings (II Chron. 10-36).

Up until this point we have emphasized Eupolemos' dependence on the biblical text. Yet the first impression one has in reading him is how different his version of Jewish history is from the biblical record.[378] He freely supplements and alters it. The nature of his additions is varied: he tells us that Moses was the first wise man and presents him as a *Kulturbringer*[379]; like so many historians of the Hellenistic world, he includes documents and chronological notices[380]; more like other Jewish texts, he offers haggadic stories[381]; and finally he may be said to embellish the temple in his description.[382] His alterations are along the same lines: he changes

---

wood do not entirely agree; the fortification of Jerusalem described in F 2 (34.12) only echoes I Kgs. 3:1; 9:15.

[378] Wacholder, *Eupolemus*, pp. 243-246, has a chart summarizing Eupolemos' relationship to the biblical text.

[379] F 1.

[380] For documents see F 2 (31.1-34.3). The correspondence between Solomon and Souron has a biblical base (I Kgs. 5:8-9; II Chron. 2:3-16); the correspondence between Solomon and Ouaphres has been created on this model. His chronological additions are in FF 3 and 5.

[381] David's involvement with the temple preparations is heightened by his request for the location of the altar of the temple (F 2 [30.5]) and his construction of ships in Elana to ferry gold from the island of Ophir (F 2 [30.7]). Solomon's involvement with the temple is likewise increased when he personally goes to bring the trees (F 2 [34.4]) which David had already felled (F 2 [34.4])! His magnanimity is heightened through his gifts to the workers (F 2 [34.17]) and to Ouaphres, the king of Egypt (F 2 [34.17]). The same pattern appears in F 4 when Jeremiah is imprisoned to be burned. (Could this reflect a common *topos* of this time? Cf. Dan. 3:1-30; II Macc. 7:1-6) Nebuchadnezzar only makes plans to attack Jerusalem *after* hearing Jeremiah's prophecies (F 4.4). He enlists the aid of Astibares, the Median king (F 4.4) and then his numbered army (F 4.5) conquers the territory leading up to Jerusalem (F 4.5) before taking the city itself. When Jerusalem falls, Jeremiah rescues the ark and the tablets. (This again must have been an item of discussion in this time—and later as well. Cf. II Macc. 2:1-8)

[382] E.g., note the description of how the outer courses of the temple were constructed (F 2 [34.5]; all further references are to F 2), the guilding of the temple's

the conquests of David from the biblical record to fit a more contemporary setting,[383] recasts the correspondence between Solomon and Souron into the mold of Hellenistic epistolography,[384] and consistently alters the dimensions of items for the temple.[385] Other variations follow this same pattern. The most conspicuous omission in what is preserved is the elimination of a great deal about the temple.

Unlike Artapanos and Pseudo-Eupolemos, there is no evidence that non-Jewish sources have affected the form of his narrative. He does apparently know Ktesias and possibly—although this is far

---

interior (34.5), the construction of the ceiling and roof (34.6), the pillars covered with gold (34.6), the weight of the lampstands at ten talents (34.7), the addition of seventy gold lamps (34.8), the silver to the doors (34.8), the north portico (34.9), the location of the sea (34.9), the scarecrow (34.11), the added features to Jerusalem's walls (34.12), the additional items brought from the tabernacle (34.14-15), and the grand total of precious metals (34.16).

[383] F 2 (30.3-4). He presents David's military conquests in three campaigns. First: the Syrians (II Kgdms. 8:5-6 [= I Chron. 18:5-6]; 10:1-19 [= I Chron. 19:1-19]), the Assyrians, and the Phoenicians. Second: the Idumaeans (II Kgdms. 8:13-14; III Kgdms. 11:15-17; I Chron. 18:11-13), the Ammonites (II Kgdms. 8:12 [= I Chron. 18:11]; 10:1-19 [= I Chron. 19:1-19]; 11:1-27; 12:26-31 [= I Chron. 20:1-3]), the Moabites (II Kgdms. 8:1-2 [= I Chron. 18:2], 12), the Itureans, the Nabataeans, and the Nabdaeans. Third: Souron [= Hiram] (vs. III Kgdms. 5:15). Eupolemos is clearly not intent on reproducing the biblical text as his additions indicate. This is established even more powerfully by his omission of David's greatest military achievement: the subjugation of the Philistines, II Kgdms. 5:17-25. He is also openly anachronistic in the use of Kommagene and the Nabataeans who were not even in the area until the sixth-fourth centuries B.C.E. His clear contradiction of the biblical text in the case of the final campaign probably indicates anti-Seleucid views. (Freudenthal, *Alexander Polyhistor*, p. 115, thought the inclusion of Tyre was due to the influence of Ps. 83 (82):8. This is possible but still does not explain the reasons for the selection of the nations mentioned. The same text also mentions the Philistines which Eupolemos glides over.) For details see Wacholder, *Eupolemus*, pp. 131-139 and Holladay, *Fragments from Hellenistic Jewish Authors*, p. 140 n. 20.

[384] Note especially the epistolary greeting in F 2 (34.1). Freudenthal, *Alexander Polyhistor*, pp. 110-112, suggested that the correspondence was based upon that of Aristeas.

[385] On four occasions he increases the dimensions (All references are to F 2): the temple width is 60 cubits (34.2) vs. 20 in I Kgs. 6:2; II Chron. 3:4; the laver is 20x20x5 cubits (34.9) vs. the circular shape in I Kgs. 7:23-26 and II Chron. 4:2-6 where it has a diameter of 10, a circumference of 30, and a height of 5; the altar is 25x20x12 (34.10) vs. 20x20x10 (II Chron. 4:1); and the number and weight of shields are greater in F 3 than in either the MT or LXX of I Kgs. 10:16-17; II Chron. 9:15-16. Three times he diminishes the numbers: the circumference of the pillars is 10 cubits (34.7) vs. 12 (MT) or 14 (LXX in III Kgdms. 7:3); the platform is only 2 cubits high (34.10) rather than 3 (II Chron. 6:13); and the number of sacrifices Solomon offered at the dedication is more realistic at 2000 sheep and 3500 cattle (34.16) vs. 120,000 sheep and 22,000 cattle (I Kgs. 8:63; II Chron. 7:5).

from certain—Herodotos.[386] Other alleged instances of dependence on other pagan authors should be taken *cum grano salis*: there
is simply not enough evidence to support them.[387]

It is better to see Eupolemos as a revisionist who uses the biblical
text for his own purposes. It is his own agenda which best explains
the form his narrative took. It is fair to say that Eupolemos is a
Hellenistic redaction of Chronicles in much the same way Chronicles revises Kings.[388]

3. *Function*. What was his agenda? The two foci of his revision are
his cultural claims and the temple. The former assumes two primary
forms in his work. One, he presents Moses as the first wise man who
first gave the Jews the alphabet which then was transmitted to the
Phoenicians and finally to Greece. He was also the first lawgiver (F
1).[389] The threefold repetition of πρῶτον which I have duplicated
here should not be missed. Eupolemos is boldly affirming that

---

[386] His awareness of Ktesias explains the reference to Ἀστιβάρης in F 4.4. Ktesias had already created this king of the Medes. Cf. Diodoros 2.34.6, where his
name is spelled Ἀστιβάρας. That Eupolemos drew upon Herodotos is more
difficult to establish. Possible points of contact are: F 1, the alphabet came from
Phoenicia (= Herodotos 5.58.1-2); F 2 (30.4), Σούρων was formed under the influence of Σιρωμος in Herodotos 7.98; the golden pillar of F 2 (34.18) is mentioned
in Herodotos 2.44.1-2; and the grand total of 300,000 troops which Nebuchadnezzar mustered equals the army of Mardonios after Salamis (Herodotos 8.113.3;
9.32.2). The problem with the first and third points is that they were topics of discussion in the Hellenistic world. (On the golden pillar see also Theophilos in *PE*
9.34.19) In regard to Souron, if the name were closer the argument would be
stronger; as it stands it is more likely that Eupolemos formed it on the basis of the
Hebrew. The fourth point is an interesting coincidence but may be no more than
that, especially since Eupolemos does not give the grand total (and if he did how
would the chariots figure into the total?) and Herodotos does not give the two numbers of 120,000 and 180,000. The evidence is too slim to claim dependence with
any note of certainty in my judgment. Those who favor dependence on Ktesias
include: Freudenthal, *Alexander Polyhistor*, p. 118. On Ktesias and Herodotos:
Wacholder, *Eupolemus*, pp. 231-234 (Ktesias), 164, 234-235 (Herodotos); Walter,
JSHRZ, 1:95; Holladay, *Fragments from Hellenistic Jewish Authors*, pp. 95, 101 n. 16;
Schürer, *The History of the Jewish People in the Age of Jesus Christ*, 3:517.

[387] Wacholder, *Eupolemus*, pp. 85-87, contended that the presentation of Moses
depended upon Hekataios of Abdera. This is too simplistic: the issues of the origin
of culture became stock arguments in the Hellenistic world. Other possibilities in
his judgment include Euhemeros of Messene's *Sacred Scripture* as the source for the
island Ouphre in F 2 (30.7) (pp. 149-150) and Menander of Ephesos for the pillar
in F 2 (34.18) (p. 219). He has a summary statement on pp. 255-256.

[388] He is freer with his text than the Chronicler. On this parallel see
Wacholder, *Eupolemus*, pp. 171-172, 249.

[389] On Moses as a wise man see Tiede, *The Charismatic Figure as Miracle Worker*,
pp. 138-140.

Moses and not an Oriental or Hellenic god/hero was the first benefactor of civilization. Both the origin of the alphabet[390] and the question of who the first lawgiver was were matters of dispute.[391] That Eupolemos was entering this forensic is beyond question. He reaffirms this by his chronological computations. According to F 5, 5149 years had elapsed since Adam and 2580 since the time of the exodus. This means that the exodus took place in 2738 B.C.E. or 2569 *anno mundi*. The antiquity of this number has bothered a good many scholars and the text has frequently been emended by dropping the διο from διοχίλια, thus giving us 1738 B.C.E. or 3569 *anno mundi*.[392] The former is closer to MT and the latter to the LXX and Demetrios.[393] Although the emendation makes Eupolemos more palatable to us, the fact that the other number is defensible from the biblical text leads me to accept it.[394] In either case the exodus extends back well beyond the range of Manethon or those who followed his lead. The point of both his presentation of Moses and his chronology is that civilization began with the Jews, not with the Phoenicians or the Greeks.

This same sense of superiority manifests itself in the correspondence of Solomon. Solomon writes to the kings of Phoenicia and Egypt as *primus inter pares*. The letters and the willingness of both kingdoms to help in the construction of the temple is a clear sign that they recognized the prestige of Solomon. Why did Eupolemos create

---

[390] Egypt: Hekataios of Miletos F 24 (Nenci = *FGrH* 1 F 20), where it is linked to Danaos; Plato, *Phdr.* 274C-D (the Egyptian god Theuth); Diodoros 1.16.1, where Hermes is credited with its discovery and 1.69.5, where it is simply presented as an Egyptian claim. Phoenicia: Herodotos 5.58.1-2; Philo of Byblos *PE* 1.10.14, where it is assigned to Misor; Diodoros 3.67.1 (Kadmos brought it from Phoenicia). Greeks also had their claimants, e.g., Aeschylos, *PV* 460; Diodoros 5.57.3-5, where the Greeks are credited with its invention, but lost the skill of writing through the flood. Syrians: Diodoros 5.74.1, which offers a sense of the debate.

[391] See Diodoros 1.94.1-2.

[392] This was first suggested by H.F. Clinton in 1824 and has been taken seriously enough to appear as a conjectural deletion in every major edition of Eupolemos in the last one hundred years: Freudenthal, *Alexander Polyhistor* (1875); Jacoby, *FGrH* (1958); Denis, *Fragmenta Pseudepigraphorum quae supersunt Graeca* (1970); Holladay, *Fragments from Hellenistic Jewish Authors* (1983); and Stählin, *Clemens Alexandrinus* (1985). It was accepted and translated by Walter, *JSHRZ*, 1:108 (cf. also p. 95 n.7).

[393] MT places the exodus at 2668 *anno mundi*; the LXX has it at 3819 and Demetrios at 3839.

[394] Defended by Wacholder, *Eupolemus*, pp. 111-113 and Fallon, *OTP*, 2:872 n. e.

the Egyptian correspondence? Was this part of the cultural debate
or are there other reasons?

As we have seen, David's campaigns are anachronistic in their
specifics and can be construed to reflect Maccabean expansion policies.[395] It is very important to note that while David makes an alli-
ance with Egypt, he conquers and extorts tribute from Souron (F 2
[30.4]). In fact, Eupolemos singles out the Phoenicians by twice
mentioning that David defeated them. Why? As a revisonist, Eupolemos expressed his own political convictions: he is anti-Seleucid.
He thus stands in direct opposition to Pseudo-Eupolemos who favored the Seleucids. The correspondence represents the two powers
who had a direct impact on the destiny of Judea. The message of the
correspondence is that Judea is a power with whom one has to
reckon.[396]

The largest bulk of the fragments deals with the temple.[397] This
likely represents the original emphasis as well since Polyhistor does
not have any known proclivity in this regard. Why so much attention? Was this simply a matter of piety?[398] Or should we explain it
as due to his priestly background?[399] While both of these answers
are true, they are also limited. Eupolemos' temple is not the temple
of Solomon nor can I believe that this glorious structure is a description of the temple of his day: it is too idealistic.[400] It is more vision-
ary like that of Ezekiel.[401] What was the vision? One of the greatest
moments in Eupolemos' life as a patriotic priest has to have been the

---

[395] F 2 (30.3-4). Judas' first forays into foreign territories were to rescue fellow
Jews, I Macc. 5:9-54; II Macc. 12:10-31; Josephos, *AJ* 12.330-349. Later,
however, he appears to have engaged in an expansion policy, I Macc. 6:65-68;
Josephos, *AJ* 12.353. The specific connection between the Idumeans of F 2 (30.3)
and the descendants of Esau in I Macc. 5:65 should not be overlooked.

[396] Cf. also Hengel, "Anonymität, Pseudepigraphie und 'Literarische Fälschung' in der jüdisch-hellenistischen Literatur," p. 239. Compare Josephos'
apologetic appeals to the alleged correspondence between Solomon and Hiram in
AJ 8. 50-56, esp. 55-56 and *CA* 1.111.

[397] Wacholder, *Eupolemus*, p. 174, estimates that one-fourth of the fragments
describe the temple proper and that if we include the preparations and dedication,
the temple occupies four-fifths of our fragments.

[398] Dalbert, *Die Theologie der hellenistisch-jüdischen Missions-Literatur*, p. 42.

[399] Giblet, "Eupolème et l'Historiographie du Judaïsme Hellénistique," p.
553 and Holladay, *Fragments from Hellenistic Jewish Authors*, p. 95. Cf. also
Wacholder, *Eupolemus*, p. 139.

[400] The second temple was apparently less glorious than the first. (Hag.
1:15-2:9, ET 2:1-9) It had subsequently been plundered by Antiochos IV (I Macc.
1:20-24). *In nuce*, it simply was not in a state of repairs to fulfill this description.

[401] Wacholder, *Eupolemus*, p. 201, considers it "a futuristic Temple."

cleansing of the temple on the 25 Kislev, 164 B.C.E.[402] The temple served as the rallying point for the revolt. Judas had thought enough of Eupolemos to choose him for the negotiations with Rome, an unambiguous statement about where Eupolemos stood in the revolt. Eupolemos therefore had historical and personal reasons for concentrating his attention on the temple. As in the revolt, it serves as the rallying point for his work.[403]

Eupolemos' history served the fledgling Maccabean movement by holding out its glorious past. To whom did Eupolemos address such a nationalistic work?[404] The fact that a Palestinian Jew composed it in Greek and made the cultural claims he did, could be construed as having been directed to a pagan audience. As an ambassador, Eupolemos must have been sensitive to the international scene. On the other hand, would a Greek wade through the description of the temple? While the historical temple was of interest from an ethnographic standpoint, the revisionist picture of Eupolemos is more suited for a Jewish audience. On the whole, I prefer to think that Jews were the primary readers of his work. This would not exclude the hope of a pagan reader, but does recognize *de facto* that the audience was predominantly Jewish.[405]

This means that rather than functioning as a missionary tract, the *Concerning the Kings in Judea* helped the Jewish community of the mid-second century B.C.E. to form a new self-identity.[406] Interestingly, the definition offered is not loyalty to the law nor is it apocalyptic in outlook.[407] For Eupolemos, Jewish identity is centered in the

---

[402] I Macc. 4:36-59; II Macc. 10:1-8; Josephos, *AJ* 12.316-326.

[403] So also Walter, *JSHRZ*, 1:96. I can not agree with the suggestion of Mendels, " 'Creative History' in the Hellenistic Near East," p. 17, that it gave more legitimacy to the temple of Jerusalem than to the temple of Onias in Leontopolis. The description could have served that purpose, but there is nothing in the fragments to indicate a sectional rift between the two groups.

[404] Pagan: Freudenthal, *Alexander Polyhistor*, p 127 and Giblet, "Eupolème et l'Historiographie du Judaïsme Hellénistique," pp. 547, 552. Jewish: Walter, *JSHRZ*, 1:97. Both: Holladay, *Fragments from Hellenistic Jewish Authors*, p. 97 (primarily addressed to Jews but read by pagans) and Fallon, *OTP*, 2:863 (designed for Greeks but read more by Jews). Unclear: Bartlett, *Jews in the Hellenistic World*, p. 59.

[405] Some pagans read it as Polyhistor proves both personally and by including it in his work for a Roman audience.

[406] Conzelmann, *Heiden-Juden-Christen*, p. 144 and Collins, *Between Athens and Jerusalem*, p. 42.

[407] Eupolemos only mentions the law within the context of "firsts," not as a litmus test for loyalty.

primacy of the Jewish nation and the focal point for this nationalism is the temple. Eupolemos does not, however, have a parochial perspective. The Jews are part of a larger community. They can no longer define themselves in isolation, but must locate themselves within the Hellenistic world.[408]

Significance

This encomiastic work stands within the tradition we have been tracing. It shares the same content (native traditions), form (cultural claims and a eulogistic stance), and purpose (to provide a new self-definition) with the works of the other Near Eastern priests we have examined.[409] It is a surprising work from one close to the Maccabean revolt and reminds us of the diversity of views within that circle. While it is not hard to imagine what an individual like the "Teacher of Righteousness" would have said about such a work, it would be interesting to know what Eupolemos' fellow priests thought.

SUMMARY

We began this chapter by noting that the first impression of the Jews which the Greeks recorded was that they were philosophers. The contacts, however, had been negligible and there was a need for the Jews to locate themselves within the Hellenistic world. The momentous step of translating their own native Scriptures into Greek helped their own community, but had no impact on Greeks assessments of the Jews—nor was it undertaken with that it mind.[410] If Jews were to impress Greeks, they would have to do it on Greek terms.[411]

---

[408] He dates his work to the fifth year of Demetrios, not to a Jewish ruler. For the development of Jewish chronological systems see Wacholder, "Biblical Chronology in the Hellenistic World Chronicles," and the revision of that article in *Eupolemus*, pp. 97-128. He distinguishes three stages: one, the reconciliation of biblical data (Demetrios); two, the fusion of biblical and Greek myth (Pseudo-Eupolemos and Artapanos); three, the fusion of the bible with the world chronicle (Eupolemos). It should be noted that Demetrios also dates himself to a foreign ruler.

[409] So also Holladay, *Fragments from Hellenistic Jewish Authors*, p. 95; Attridge, "Historiography," p. 163; and Mendels, "'Creative History' in the Hellenistic Near East," p. 17.

[410] On the origins of the LXX see S. Jellicoe, *The Septuagint and Modern Study* (Oxford: Oxford University Press, 1968). Bickerman, *The Jews in the Greek World*, pp. 101-105, moves against the consensus by arguing that the LXX was for pagans. He compares it to the work of Berossos and Manethon.

[411] Momigliano, *Alien Wisdom*, pp. 90-92.

The four authors whom we have considered undertook the task of restating their history in terms which were heavily influenced by Hellenism. In some ways, their works are a refutation of the notion that the LXX was designed for pagans, or at least a witness of its failure. I have argued that these four œuvres all stand within the same literary tradition. This is supported by our model for genre analysis. They all share the same basic content: they retell their own story. They all go about this in the same general way: they retell their native traditions in an extended prose narrative—an outline in the case of Demetrios—written in Greek (form). While they vary in their fidelity to the Bible—Demetrios uses it carefully for chronological purposes, Eupolemos revises it, and Artapanos and Pseudo-Eupolemos weave other traditions into its framework—they all use it as their basic point of reference. The specific devices they utilize to shape their individual versions cover a wide range: chronology (Demetrios and Eupolemos), *quaestio et solutio* (Demetrios), national legends (Artapanos), euhemerism (Artapanos and Pseudo-Eupolemos), and the motif of *Kulturbringer* (Artapanos, Pseudo-Eupolemos, and Eupolemos). Regardless of the specific conventions, they all self-consciously use Greek literary modes for their *Geschichten*.[412] What gives them a sense of unity in this diversity is that they all wrote *ad maiorem Iudaeorum gloriam*. They are national historians—tout-à-fait—who claim the superiority of the Jewish nation over both other Oriental people and Greeks.[413]

Why did they write such histories? Clement and Eusebios preserved them because they saw in them apologists of an earlier era. Is their judgment sound? In the nineteenth and early twentieth centuries, their lead was commonly followed.[414] It was clear that the works—at times anyway—answered charges made against the Jews.[415] This suggested additionally, that the audience must be

[412] Holladay, *Fragments from Hellenistic Jewish Authors*, p. 1.
[413] Freudenthal, *Alexander Polyhistor*, p. 105 and Hengel, "Anonymität, Pseudepigraphie und 'Literarische Fälschung' in der jüdisch-hellenistischen Literatur," p. 244. On Hellenistic historiography as a whole along these lines see R.A. Oden, "Philo of Byblos and Hellenistic Historiography," pp. 115-126.
[414] On Jewish apologetics generally see M. Friedländer, "La Propagande Religieuse des Juifs Grecs avant l'ère Chrétienne," *REJ* 30 (1895): 161-181 and George Isaac Matthews, "The Jewish Apologetics to the Grecian World in the Apocryphal and Pseudepigraphal Literature" (Ph.D. dissertation, The University of Chicago, 1914).
[415] Freudenthal, *Alexander Polyhistor*, pp. 197-198, emphasized this.

pagan. A further implication was inferred from this: the works were missionary.[416] In 1956, Victor Tcherikover published an essay which challenged this view, claiming that the literature served internal Jewish needs. In his judgment, apologetic literature proper did not develop until 30 B.C.E.-66 C.E. during the course of the Jewish struggle for emancipation.[417] Since that time, scholars have begun to speak about them as being apologetic but not missionary[418] or indirectly apologetic.[419]

Since the shift in perspectives has arisen over the issue of audience, a summary of our findings is in order. In the case of Demetrios, the evidence clearly points to a Jewish audience. The evidence for the other three is not as perspicuous. The fragments self-consciously engage the Hellenistic world. The question is: Do they do this to answer charges or to reassure those who have heard the charges? I think it is both. The fragments presuppose an international audience in which their cultural claims can be made. We should remember that, after all, they have come down to us through a pagan and not through Jewish channels. At the same time, the real audience were the authors' compatriots. For all of their acceptance of Hellenism, they remain indubitably Jewish. This coupled with the poor literary quality of a work like Eupolemos consigns them to an audience of initiates.[420] Much like Philo of Alexandria, the audience must have been Jewish, but there was always an eye turned out to the larger world.

This dual audience helps us to understand the function of the fragments in a new light. The works served to give the Jewish people a

---

[416] Matthews, "The Jewish Apologetic to the Grecian World in the Apocryphal and Pseudepigraphal Literature," p. 27. This has been argued most forcefully by Dalbert, *Die Theologie der hellenistisch-jüdischen Missions-Literatur* and Georgi, *The Opponents of Paul in Second Corinthians*, pp. 83-151.

[417] "Jewish Apologetic Literature Reconsidered," pp. 169-193. On the time of development see p. 189.

[418] E.g., Attridge, "Jewish Historiography," p. 312.

[419] Schürer, *The History of the Jewish People in the Age of Jesus Christ*, 3:509,594,609. Note in particular p. 609: "Much of this apologetic, though not all, was directed towards strengthening the confidence of a Jewish audience in their own heritage, and it is doubtful whether a gentile audience was ever intended to read it." Others who have posited a Jewish audience include: Baron, *A Social and Religious History of the Jews*, 1:196; Eddy, *The King is Dead*, p. 233; and Hengel, *Judaism and Hellenism*, p. 70. Momigliano, *Alien Wisdom*, pp. 92-93, continues to argue for a pagan audience.

[420] On their literary worth see Freudenthal, *Alexander Polyhistor*, p. 1.

new identity in a new world.[421] The crucial issue was how could they remain Jewish and at the same time accept Hellenism. The key to their answer was their national solidarity.[422] On the one hand, they had an ancient and illustrious past which offered them a sense of who they were. On the other, the new and superior—at least it must have appeared that way to most—culture in which they lived was not superior at all. Their own ancestors were *Kulturbringer*. This allowed them to identify with Hellenism and yet maintain a superior posture. *In nuce*, their ancestry was more noble than that of any other people—Oriental or Occidental.[423] They could proudly take their place as a vanquished people knowing that their past had been greater than that of any other nation. As for the present, the rabbis expressed it best: "May the beauty of Japheth dwell in the tents of Shem."[424]

---

[421] The most important work along these lines is that of Collins, *Between Athens and Jerusalem*, p. 51.

[422] Conzelmann, *Heiden-Juden-Christen*, p. 130: "Das Bewußtsein, das erwählte Volk zu sein, ist die Basis *aller* Apologetik."

[423] Claiming an illustrious past as a means of buttressing a present self-image is a long-standing device. Cf. the conclusion to an article in the *Southern Literary Messenger* 30 (June 1860): 401-409: "The Southern people come of that race . . . recognized as Cavaliers . . . directly descended from the Norman Barons of William the Conqueror (the Yankees were Anglo-Saxons—GES), a race distinguished in its earliest history for its warlike and fearless character, a race in all times since renowned for its gallantry, chivalry, honor, gentleness, and intellect." Quoted in James M. McPherson, *Battle Cry of Freedom: The Civil War Era*. The Oxford History of the United States 6 (New York/Oxford: Oxford University Press, 1988), p. 197.

[424] Bab. Talmud *Megillah* 9b.

CHAPTER SIX

THE *ANTIQUITATES JUDAICAE* OF JOSEPHOS

> I surrender to the Romans willingly
> and live; but I testify that I go not as
> a traitor, but as your servant.
>
> *BJ* 3.354

As Eusebios summarizes Clement's references in his *Stromateis*, he says that Clement μνημονεύει τε . . . ἔτι μὴν Φίλωνος καὶ 'Αριστοβούλου 'Ιωσήπου τε καὶ Δημητρίου καὶ Εὐπολέμου, 'Ιουδαίων συγγραφέων. He then gives the reason for their inclusion: ὡς ἂν τούτων ἀπάντων ἐγγράφως πρεσβύτερον τῆς παρ' "Ελλησιν ἀρχαιογονίας Μωυσέα τε καὶ τὸ 'Ιουδαίων γένος ἀποδειξάντων.[1] Jerome made a very similar observation when he enumerated Clement's sources: Nec non de Iudaeis Aristobulum quendam et Demetrium et Eupolemum, scriptores adversum gentes, refert, qui in similitudinem Iosephi ἀρχαιολογίαν Moysi et Iudaicae gentes adseruerint.[2] While the ancient scholar clearly needs some chronological help, he recognized the common ground which exists between Josephos and the Hellenistic Jewish historians.

Surprisingly, modern scholars have paid scant attention to the genre of the *Antiquitates*.[3] At the beginning of this century, Bene-

---

[1] *HE* 6.13.7.

[2] *De viris illus.* 38.

[3] The literature on Josephos is enormous. The standard bibliographies are Heinz Schreckenberg, *Bibliographie zu Flavius Josephus.* ALGHJ 1 (Leiden: E.J. Brill, 1968); his later *Bibliographie zu Flavius Josephus: Supplementband mit Gesamtregister.* ALGHJ 14 (Leiden: E.J. Brill, 1979); and Loius H. Feldman, *Josephus and Modern Scholarship (1937-1980)* (Berlin/New York: Walter de Gruyter, 1984). I have used the edition of H. St. J. Thackeray, Ralph Marcus, and Louis Feldman, *Josephus*, 10 vols. LCL (Cambridge: Harvard University Press, 1926-1965) in consultation with that of Benedictus Niese, *Flavii Iosephi Opera*, 7 vols. (Berlin: Weidmann, 1887-1889; reprint ed., 1955). All word statistics depend upon Karl Heinrich Rengstorf, *A Complete Concordance to Flavius Josephus*, 4 vols. with 2 Supplements (Leiden: E.J. Brill, 1973-1986). General treatments of Josephus published in this century are: *ERE*, s.v. "Josephus," by Benedictus Niese, 7:569-579 (a careful summary which is still worth reading); *RE*, s.v. "Josephus," by G. Hölscher, 9:1934-2000 (represents a classic statement of the nineteenth century approach to Josephos with an overdue emphasis on source criticism); Richard Laquer, *Der*

dictus Niese echoed Eusebios and Jerome by affirming that Josephos followed the Hellenistic Jewish historians.[4] Interestingly, scholars who have studied the Hellenistic Jewish historians have frequently voiced the same opinion, but those who have studied Josephos have failed to address it.[5]

A little over two decades later, Martin Braun drew his distinction between Oriental literature produced by the higher levels of society and that which was produced by the lower. He placed Josephos

---

jüdische Historiker Flavius Josephus (Giessen: Munchow, 1920; reprint ed., Darmstadt, 1970) (although his specific reconstruction of Josephos' life is no longer followed in detail, his interpretation of Josephos' writings in light of his life remains an indispensable part of Josephan studies); H. St. John Thackeray, *Josephus: The Man and the Historian* (New York, 1929; reprint ed. with an introduction by Samuel Sandmel, New York: Ktav Publishing House, Inc., 1967) (for years the standard introduction on Josephos which remains valuable although his famous assistant theory is no longer widely held); *KP*, s.v. "Iosephos," by Berndt Schaller, 2:1440-1444 (too brief to be of great help); *EncJud*, s.v. "Josephus Flavius," by Abraham Schalit, 10:251-265 (summary of a lifetime of research by an Israeli scholar); Shaye J.D. Cohen, *Josephus in Galilee and Rome: His 'Vita' and Development as a Historian.* Columbia Studies in the Classical Tradition 8 (Leiden: E.J. Brill, 1979) (penetrating study of the relationship between *BJ* and *V* and how Josephos developed as a historian); Tessa Rajak, *Josephus: The Historian and His Society* (Philadelphia: Fortress Press, 1983) (excellent analysis of Josephos and the revolt from a social perspective, but too apologetic for Josephos); Harold W. Attridge, "Josephus and His Works," in *Jewish Writings of the Second Temple Period*, edited by Michael Stone. CRINT (Philadelphia: Fortress Press, 1984), pp. 185-232 (balanced overview); L.H. Feldman, "Flavius Josephus Revisited: the Man, His Writings, and his Significance," in *Religion* (*Hellenistisches Judentums in römischer Zeit: Philon und Josephus*) ANRW II 21.2 (Berlin/New York: Walter de Gruyter, 1984), pp. 763-862 (primarily a summary of recent work rather than a critical essay); Villalba I. Varneda, *The Historical Method of Flavius Josephus.* ALGHJ 19 (Leiden: E.J. Brill, 1986) (excellent collection of the Josephan material but fails to synthesize the material critically and does not engage contemporary scholarship); Per Bilde, *Flavius Josephus between Jerusalem and Rome: His Life, his Works, and their Importance.* JSPSup 2 (Sheffield: Sheffield Academic Press, 1988) (an attempt to offer a new Thackeray: excellent summaries of contemporary work with an overall argument for the unity of the Josephan corpus).

[4] *ERE*, s.v. "Josephus," 7:572, 573.

[5] So Holladay, *Fragments from Hellenistic Jewish Authors*, pp. 2, 97 and Schürer, *The History of the Jewish People in the Age of Jesus Christ*, 3:509. In a qualified sense: Wacholder, *Eupolemus*, pp. 304-305, who thinks that Justus of Tiberias is closer to them than Josephos who was influenced by their tradition without knowing them directly (pp. 52-53 n. 107); and Collins, *Between Athens and Jerusalem*, pp. 49-50, who points to the assimilation to Hellenistic models as the common ground. Walter, *JSHRZ*, 1:97, argued that Eupolemos was a forerunner to Josephos. With somewhat different concerns, Arthur Droge, *Homer or Moses?*, pp. 35-47, has provided an important assessment of Josephos' treatment of culture in the same tradition as the Hellenistic Jewish historians. Pilhofer, *Presbyteron Kreitton*, pp. 193-206, treats *CA* but not *AJ*.

along with Berossos and Manethon in the former and Artapanos in the latter.[6] Interestingly, in the two full-length articles which have subsequently attempted to locate Josephos in a specific historiographical tradition, Paul Collomp and Tessa Rajak have both stressed his ties to Oriental over against Occidental historiography as a result of his insistence upon native sources.[7]

The unambiguous Hellenistic tendencies have not, however, gone unnoticed. Harold Attridge who thought that the *Antiquitates* belonged to "antiquarian rhetorical historiography" and Louis Feldman who did not believe there was any parallel to Josephos' "extended apologetic," have emphasized his similarities with Dionysios of Halikarnassos.[8] Pere Villalba Varneda contends that he is closest to Polybios[9] while Shaye Cohen maintains that he belongs to the Greek tradition without offering a specific placement.[10]

Moving in a different direction, Per Bilde has acknowledged Josephos' indebtedness to Thukydides and Polybios, but thinks that "he is to be related closer to Old Testament and Jewish tradition than to Hellenistic literature and historiography."[11]

There is clearly no *opinio communis* to which one may appeal. The reason for so much diversity is that there are different elements

---

[6] *History and Romance in Graeco-Oriental Literature*, pp. 4-5.

[7] Paul Collomp, "La Place de Josèphe dans la Technique de l' Historiographie Hellénistique," *Études historiques de la Facultie des Lettres de Strasbourg* 106: *Mélanges* 1945,3. *Études Historiques* (Paris, 1947): 81-92 and Tessa Rajak, "Josephus and the 'Archaeology' of the Jews," *JJS* 33 (1982): 465-477. Rajak places him in line with Hekataios, Berossos, and Manethon, but not the Hellenistic Jewish historians who did not share his "broad objectives" (p. 474). Cf. also Elias Bickermann, "*Origenes Gentium*," *Classical Philology* 47 (1952): 74-74, who without commenting on the genre of *AJ* pointed out that Hekataios, Berossos, Manethon, Artapanos, and Josephos shared a common "ethnological method."

[8] Harold Attridge, *The Interpretation of Biblical History in the 'Antiquitates Judaicae' of Flavius Josephus*. HDR 7 (Missoula, Montana: Scholars Press, 1976), pp. 43-60, who also places Livy in this category; Louis Feldman, "Josephus' Portrait of Saul," *HUCA* 53 (1982): 46-52 and "Hellenizations in Josephus' *Jewish Antiquities*: The Portrait of Abraham," in *Josephus, Judaism, and Christianity*, ed. by Louis H. Feldman and Gohei Hata (Detroit: Wayne State University Press, 1987), p. 150. On Josephos' relationship to Dionysios see under Form.

[9] *The Historical Method of Flavius Josephus*, p. 256.

[10] *Josephus in Galilee and Rome*, pp. 24-33, especially p. 27. Cohen argues that on the basis of formulae and method "Josephus stands squarely in the Greek tradition," p. 31. He does, however, recognize that the emphasis on native sources could mark the work as an *ethnika* similar to that of other Hellenized Orientals such as Berossos and Manethon as well as Greeks like Ktesias and Hekataios of Abdera.

[11] *Flavius Josephus between Jerusalem and Rome*, pp. 202-206.

within the text itself. What has happened is that some have appealed to one group of tendencies while others have given more weight to an alternate set. The purpose of this chapter is to locate the *Antiquitates* within a specific tradition through genre analysis.

LIFE

We have a great deal of information about the life of Josephos— relatively speaking. Most of it is in the *Vita*, although there is also a significant amount of material in *Bellum Judaicum*. I will follow the *Vita* in my analysis as long as there is concord with the other works.

Events

'Ιώσηπος[12] was born into one of the priestly families of Jerusalem[13] between 14 September 37, and 17 March 38 C.E..[14] He grew up in

---

[12] His name was 'Ιώσηπος which is also written 'Ιώσηππος, 'Ιώσιππος, or more rarely 'Ιώσιπος. Christians later altered it to 'Ιώσηφος on the basis of 'Ιωσήφ. In Latin it is Iosepus, Ioseppus, Iosippus. Cf. Italian Giuseppe. Iosephus is first attested in the ninth century from which our English Josephus is derived. On his name see Niese, *Flavii Iosephi Opera*, 1:V n. 1 and *ERE*, s.v. "Josephus," 7:569.

[13] He offers a genealogy in *V* 1-2, where he claims that he is a member of one of the twenty-four priestly families (Note also *BJ* 1.3; 3.352; *AJ* 15.419 (?); *V* 198; *CA* 1.54) and has ties to the Hasmoneans (he also claims Hasmonean descent in *AJ* 16.187). There are two major problems with his genealogy: one, he claims ties to the Hasmoneans through his maternal side and then proceeds to trace his genealogy through his father; two, there are missing generations in his genealogical tree. His Hasmonean descent is considered bogus by Hölscher, *RE*, s.v. "Josephus," 9:1935 and Cohen, *Josephus in Galilee and Rome*, p. 108 n. 33, who objects that Josephos made no such claims in *BJ*. (Did he intentionally omit such a connection because of the associations of the Hasmoneans with Jewish independence?) His claim is accepted by Thackeray, *Josephus: The Man and the Historian*, p. 6; Max Radin, "The Pedigree of Josephus," *Classical Philology* 24 (1929): 193-194; Rajak, *Josephus*, pp. 15-16, who points out that the name Matthias reflects the family consciousness of this connection; Bartlett, *Jews in the Hellenistic World*, p. 72; Schürer, *The History of the Jewish People in the Age of Jesus Christ*, 1:44; and Bilde, *Flavius Josephus between Jerusalem and Rome*, p. 28. Possible solutions to the missing generations are: textual confusion on the part of both Josephos and scribes: Radin, "The Pedigree of Josephus," pp. 194-196 and Schürer, *The History of the Jewish People in the Age of Jesus Christ*, 1:46 n. 3; Josephos omitted two or so generations: Joachim Jeremias, *Jerusalem in the Time of Jesus: An Investigation into Economic and Social Conditions during the New Testament Period*, trans. by F.H. and C.H. Cave (Philadelphia: Fortress Press, 1969), p. 214 n. 212 and Rajak, *Josephus*, pp. 16-17.

[14] *V* 5 tells us he was born in the first year of Caligula which ended 18 March 38. *AJ* 20.267 informs us that Josephos was 56 in the thirteenth year of Domitian (14 September 93-13 September 94 C.E.). He was therefore born between the beginning of Domitian's accession date and the end of Caligula's year.

Jerusalem where he was probably educated by his parents in his early years.[15] Josephos describes this process with the same measure of modesty that characterizes his self-assessment throughout his writings: he presents himself as a child prodigy.[16] Although his self-adulation is clearly beyond the bounds of reality,[17] what it does tell us is important: Josephos received a Jewish education.[18] How much Greek this involved is a matter of dispute, but he must have at least acquired a rudimentary level of proficiency.[19] He, therefore, stands in the same social tradition as Berossos, Manethon, and Eupolemos and should be considered unus ex nobilibus as Suetonius says.[20]

As he entered adulthood, Josephos claims that he consciously identified himself with the Pharisees after having investigated the other two main Jewish sects and living with an ascetic for three years.[21] It is difficult to know exactly what to make of his account. Not only are there problems with the story as it stands,[22] but

---

[15] *BJ* 1.3.

[16] *V* 9.

[17] His description is a Hellenistic commonplace. Child prodigies were a *topos* in Hellenistic literature. Cf. Lk. 2:41-50; Plutarch, *Alex.* 5.1; Philostratos, *Vit. Apoll.* 1.7. His emphasis on memory was a celebrated component of Jewish education. Cf. Mishnah, *'Abot* 2.8, where Rabbi Eliezer ben Hyrkanos who also grew up in pre-70 Jerusalem is lauded: he is "like a plastered cistern which loses not a drop." b. *Hag.* 9b: "He who had repeated a chapter 100 times is not to be compared with him who has repeated it 101 times." This was, however, by no means only praised in Jewish circles. Philostratos, *Vita Apol.* 1.7, praises Apollonios in these words: Προϊὼν δὲ ἐς ἡλικίαν, ἐν ᾗ γράμματα, μνήμης τε ἰσχὺν ἐδήλου καὶ μελέτης κράτος.

[18] *AJ* 20.264; *CA* 1.54. This makes the claim of Samuel Belkin, *The Alexandrian Halakah in the Apologetic Literature of the First Century C.E.* (Philadelphia: The Jewish Publication Society, 1936), p. 8, that Josephos "had a very limited knowledge of Jewish theology and law" suspect. It is much more accurate to see the halakic and haggadic knowledge he betrays in *AJ* and *CA* as stemming from this period.

[19] He was sent on an embassy to Rome at age 26 as we will see. This presupposes some ability to communicate in the *lingua franca* of the Roman world. On the Greek he acquired in Palestine see J.N. Sevenster, *Do You Know Greek? (How Much Greek could the first Jewish Christians have known?)*. NovTSup 19 (Leiden: E.J. Brill, 1968), pp. 61-76.

[20] *Vesp.* 8.5.6. Cf. also *BJ* 5.419. For descriptions of Jerusalem and the aristocracy of this time see Jeremias, *Jerusalem in the Time of Jesus*, pp. 96-99 and Rajak, *Josephus*, pp. 17-26.

[21] *Vita* 9-12.

[22] There are two major problems. First, Josephos only allows three years for all of his investigations, most of which was spent with Bannous. This appears too short a time span, e.g., the probationary period at Qumran was two years. 1QS 6.13-23. Cf. also *BJ* 2.137-138, where instead of the two year sequence of 1QS, Josephos describes a sequence of an initial year of exploratory attachment followed by two

Josephos' own attitude toward the Pharisees changed from *BJ* to *AJ* causing us to wonder if this is anachronistic.[23] When he was twenty-six, Josephos made his first trip to Rome where he successfully procured the release of some priests Felix had arrested through the help of Poppaea who showered him with gifts.[24]

When he arrived in Judea, he found the country in a state of open revolt. He tried to dissuade the people from their revolutionary course, but was unsuccessful. After Cestius was unexpectedly defeated in his retreat from Jerusalem, Josephos and other aristocrats who remained in Jerusalem joined the revolution.[25] At this point we encounter a major problem. The accounts in *Vita* and *Bellum Judaicum* vary widely in their portrait of Josephos' activities in Galilee.[26] In *BJ*, Josephos is appointed general of both Galilees and acquits himself bravely. In *Vita* he goes to Galilee as a member of a commission of three priests to try to calm the waters and to wait

---

years of associate membership. At best Josephos' language is misleading. Second, searching for the best philosophy was a common *topos*. Nikolaos, *FGrH* 90 F 132; Galen, *De aff. dign.* 8; Justin Martyr, *Dial. with Trypho* 8; Apollonios, in Philostratos, *Vita Apol.* 1.7. Augustine did move through numerous stages. Cf. his *Confessions*.

[23] Rajak, *Josephus*, pp. 34-39, defends the account. Hölscher, *RE*, s.v. ''Josephus,'' 9:1936 and Cohen, *Josephus in Galilee and Rome*, pp. 106-107; Attridge, ''Josephus and His Works,'' p. 186, do not accept the account as it stands. For a detailed study see Steve Mason, *Flavius Josephus on the Pharisees: A Composition-Critical Study*. SPB 39 (Leiden: E.J. Brill, 1991).

[24] *Vita* 13-16. Feldman, ''Flavius Josephus Revisited,'' p. 782, thinks that the gifts were because ''Josephus promised to try to defuse the revolution that was starting in Judaea.'' There is no basis for this whatsoever. The gifts were from Poppaea, not Nero, and were probably personal. Had they been otherwise, Josephos would certainly have mentioned it since he is anxious to defend his hesitancy in the war in *Vita*. Poppaea is said to have intervened on the Jews' behalf when they sent an embassy defending the wall they built in the temple which blocked Agrippa II's view of the temple. See *AJ* 20.195, where she is called a θεοσεβής. She is also mentioned at 20.252.

[25] The basis for this paragraph is the agreement between *BJ* and *V*. Compare the following: Josephos urges the Jews not to revolt (17-19) with the advice of the chief priests (*BJ* 2.316, 320) and Agrippa's speech (*BJ* 2.345-404); Josephos hides in the temple (20) with the struggle between the aristocracy and the rebels (*BJ* 2.411-429); the insurgents take Antonia (20 with *BJ* 2.430-432); Menahem is slain (21 with *BJ* 2.433-448); the chief priests and Josephos outwardly align themselves with the war party but hope for a quick victory by Cestius (21-23 has no parallel in *BJ*); Cestius defeated (24 with *BJ* 2.499-555); reprisals against Jews in Syria (25 with *BJ* 2.457-465, 477-486), Scythopolis (26 with *BJ* 2.466-476), and Damascus (27 with *BJ* 2.487-498); and the position of the Jewish leaders after the defeat of Cestius (28 with *BJ* 2.562).

[26] The most important discussion of this problem is that of Shaye J.D. Cohen, *Josephus in Galilee and Rome*.

and see what the Romans will do.[27] Setting aside the literary
problems, the major historical issue is: Was Josephos an ardent supporter of the revolt or did he go to Galilee as a pro-Roman advocate
in Jewish clothing? What we may say is that his background and activities prior to the war suggest that he was a moderate who wanted
peace. He clearly did not align himself with the pro-war party. At
the same time, he did actively fight the Romans in Galilee, especially at Jotapata.[28] To put it simply, Josephos found himself between
Skylla and Charybdis: he could not go as far as Agrippa II and remain loyal to Rome and yet, he could not identify with the revolutionaries he despised. Forced to choose, he sided with the latter
openly but maintained some contact with the former.[29] The tension
appeared in his policies, however, and became the basis of the disputes he faced in Galilee. It is this same tension which resurfaces in
various ways in the works which he later wrote.[30]

At the fall of Jotapata, Josephos ingloriously surrendered to the
Romans and upon entering the Roman camp delivered his famous
oracle proclaiming Vespasian to be the future emperor.[31] He

---

[27] The most famous inconsistency is the commission of Josephos. Compare *V*
28-29 with *BJ* 2.562-571. Rajak, *Josephus*, pp. 156-158, has attempted to resolve the
discrepancy by arguing that these texts refer to two separate events: Josephos first
went on a pacific mission (*V* 28); when he arrived and realized the nature of the
situation, he wrote back to the Sanhedrin (*V* 62); they wrote back commissioning
him as general (*V* 135, 176, 230, 250, and *BJ* 2.562-571, which collapses this
process into his official appointment). While this is plausible, we must recognize
that the two works leave very different impressions on the reader.

[28] *BJ* 3.141-288. This is what constitutes the decisive point for Cohen, *Josephus
in Galilee and Rome*, p. 204. He thinks that Josephos' activities at Jotapata are not
those "of a man who was only pretending to be anti-Roman."

[29] See in particular *V* 126-148 for his continuing ties to Agrippa II.

[30] The most important discussions on Josephos in Galilee are Cohen, *Josephus
in Galilee and Rome*, pp. 181-231 and Rajak, *Josephus*, pp. 144-173.

[31] *BJ* 3.340-408. I see no reason to question the historicity of Josephos' prophecy at this point. It is fully in keeping with the political climate of the times, was
recorded in a work presented to Vespasian, and was mentioned by a number of pagan authors. Suetonius, *Vesp.* 8.6; Cassius Dio 65.1.4; Appian in Zonaras 11.16.
It is also worth remembering that Yohanan ben Zakkai is said to have made a similar prophecy after being smuggled out of Jerusalem in a coffin. There are four versions of Yohanan's escape and prophecy. For the texts and analysis see Jacob Neusner, *A Life of Yohanan Ben Zakkai*, 2nd ed. SPB 6 (Leiden: E.J. Brill, 1970),
pp. 157-166 and the more recent article of Anthony J. Saldarini, "Johanan ben
Zakkai's Escape from Jerusalem. Origen and Development of a Rabbinic Story,"
JSJ 6 (1975): 189-204, who maintains that the legend is designed to explain the
founding of the school at Jamnia. I can not follow Abraham Schalit, "Die
Erhebung Vespasians nach Flavius Josephus, Talmud und Midrasch. Zur

remained a special prisoner for two years.[32] After the army acclaimed Vespasian emperor in Caesarea and the East hailed him in Alexandria,[33] Vespasian recalled Josephos' prophecy and at the urging of Titus had Josephos' chains ceremoniously broken with an axe giving him a full pardon.[34] In the spring of 70 he returned to Jerusalem with Titus where he encouraged the Jews to surrender.[35]

When Jerusalem finally succumbed to the incessant assaults of the Romans, Titus magnanimously gave Josephos the right to take whatever he wanted. Josephos took some sacred books and requested the liberation of all of his friends and acquaintances whom he could find.[36] Titus also rewarded him with a grant of land near the coast, since Jerusalem was to be the home of a Roman garrison.[37] Josephos sailed with Titus sometime around the spring of 71 C.E., and must have seen with his own eyes the triumph celebrated by Vespasian and Titus. Vespasian showed him every courtesy including providing him with a house (the residence he occupied prior to becoming emperor), a pension, and Roman citizenship.[38] Jewish antipathy for Josephos was understandably rife in this period: he found himself the target of numerous accusations, but was acquitted by Vespasian.[39] His position continued unaltered under Titus who likewise dismissed all charges leveled against his former prisoner.[40]

Geschichte einer messianischen Prophetie," in *Politische Geschichte (Kaisergeschichte)*, ed. by Hildegard Temporini. ANRW 2.2 (Berlin/New York: Walter de Gruyter, 1975), pp. 208-327, esp. 297-300 and *EncJud*, s.v. "Josephus Flavius," 10:253, who argued that this prophecy should be placed at a later date between Galba's death (15 January 69 C.E.) and the acclamation of Vespasian as emperor in Alexandria (1 July 69 C.E.). Suetonius, *Vesp.* 8.6, appears to place the event at Carmel, but precision on this matter should not be pressed in his account. For a thorough review of Schalit see H.R. Moehring, 'Joseph ben Matthia and Flavius Josephus: the Jewish Prophet and Roman Historian," in ANRW II.2:917-944.

[32] *BJ* 3.408; *V* 414; *CA* 1.48.
[33] *BJ* 4.592-604 and 616-621 respectively.
[34] *BJ* 4.622-629; *CA* 1.48.
[35] *BJ* 5.114, Titus appealed for terms through him; 5.261, he is near enough to the wall that his companion, Nikanor, is struck with an arrow; 5.325-330, he sees through a Jewish ruse at the wall; 5.361, Titus commissions him to speak to the Jews; 5.362-419, his first speech; 5.541-547, he is struck by a stone and thought dead, but recovers; 6.94, 96-111, second speech; 6.118-120, appeals with other refugees; 6.124-129, serves as Titus' translator; 6.365, continues his appeals.
[36] *V* 417-421.
[37] *V* 422.
[38] *V* 422-423.
[39] *BJ* 7.437-453 (especially 447-450); *V* 424-425.
[40] On Josephos and Titus see Zvi Yavetz, "Reflections on Titus and Josephus," *GRBS* 16 (1975): 411-432.

During the reign of Vespasian Josephos began his literary career. His first effort was an account of the war written in Aramaic and addressed to the Parthians, Babylonians, the remote tribes of Arabia, his fellow Jews on the other side of the Euphrates, and the Adiabenes.[41] Between 75 and 79,[42] he published a Greek version covering the same basic material which we know as *Bellum Judaicum*.[43]

Circumstances under Domitian are not as certain, although Josephos' picture remains the same. He claims that Domitian not only punished his never-ending accusers, but gave him tax exempt status on his property in Judea. Beyond this, Domitian continually showed kindness.[44] Josephos published his *Antiquitates Judaicae* in the thirteenth year of Domitian when he was 56 years of age (= between 14 September 93 and 13 September 94 C.E.).[45] Within a presumably short period of time, he composed an appendix to it, i.e., the *Vita*.[46] Some time after that he issued the last

---

[41] *BJ* 1.1, 3.

[42] The last mentioned event is the construction of the Temple of Pax (*BJ* 7.158) which was completed in 75 C.E. (Cassius Dio 65.15). The *terminus ad quem* is the death of Vespasian, since Josephos presented a copy of the work to him (*V* 359 and 361; *CA* 1.50).

[43] The Greek is apparently not simply a translation from a Semitic original, but a fresh work based on the Aramaic. So Gohei Hata, "Is the Greek Version of Josephus' *Jewish War* a Translation or a Rewriting of the First Version?" *JQR* 66 (1975-76): 89-108. Some have suggested that the work underwent several stages. In particular, the seventh book may represent a later addition to 1-6: Thackeray, *Josephus: The Man and the Historian*, p. 35, 105; Cohen, *Josephus in Galilee and Rome*, pp. 84-90; Attridge, "Josephus and His Works," pp. 192-193; and Seth Schwartz, "The Composition and Publication of Josephus's *Bellum Judaicum* Book 7," *HTR* 79 (1986): 373-386, who in contrast to the others does not view book seven as a unity, but a work of three stages: the Ur-book in 79-81 C.E., a Domitianic edition in 82-83, and a final rendition under Trajan.

[44] *V* 429-430.

[45] *AJ* 20.267.

[46] Josephos makes this unmistakably clear. He ends *AJ* with the note (20.266): ἴσως δ᾽ οὐκ ἂν ἐπίφθονον ἐγένοιτο οὐδὲ σκαιὸν τοῖς πολλοῖς φανήσεται καὶ περὶ γένους τοὐμοῦ καὶ περὶ τῶν κατὰ τὸν βίον πράξεων βραχέα διεξελθεῖν ἕως ἔχω ζῶντας ἢ τοὺς ἐλέγχοντας ἢ τοὺς μαρτυρήσοντας. His proposal is then to treat his pedigree and life events. He opens *V* with Ἐμοὶ δὲ γένος ἐστὶν οὐκ ἄσημον. (Note the repetition of γένος, the beginning with δέ, and the lack of a preface in general which we find in the other three works of Josephos.) He then recounts his life—primarily his activities in Galilee prior to the arrival of Vespasian—and concludes with σοὶ δ᾽ ἀποδεδωκώς, κράτιστε ἀνδρῶν Ἐπαφρόδιτε, τὴν πᾶσαν τῆς ἀρχαιολογίας ἀναγραφὴν ἐπὶ τοῦ παρόντος ἐνταῦθα καταπαύω τὸν λόγον (430). The external evidence also supports this conclusion. Eusebios quotes a passage from *Vita* (361-364) which he says Josephos appended to the end of the *Antiquitates* (*HE* 3.10.8-11). In fact, all of the manuscripts which Niese consulted except one have the *Vita* attached to the

work which has come down to us from him, the *Contra Apionem*.

Josephos hinted that he was planning other works in the future throughout the *Antiquitates*. Whether these passages refer to the *Vita* and *Contra Apionem* or to works which he simply never completed is difficult to determine.[47] For our purposes it is sufficient to note that the *Antiquitates* was written in Rome in association with the highest literary circles of the empire. Eusebios tells us that Josephos was the ἐπιδοξότατος Jew of his day among both his compatriots—infamous would be more correct in this case—and Romans. The latter honored him with a statue and deposited his works in the library of Rome.[48]

His Self-Understanding

For centuries the name Josephos has carried the same connotation in Jewish quarters that Benedict Arnold has in American circles. How did such an individual understand himself? More specifically, how could Josephos write an apologetic work on behalf of the Jewish people while living on a Roman pension which had been awarded to him for his service against the revolt?

Fortunately Josephos was not reticent about talking about himself. The key to his self-understanding is his description of his surrender at Jotapata. At the fall of Jotapata, Josephos hid in a cave along with forty other notables from the city.[49] Following the dis-

---

Antiquitates. See *Flavii Iosephi Opera*, 1:V-VI. The *Vita* may have been issued in a second edition of *AJ* (contrast 20.266 with 267 and compare 259 with 267), although this is debatable. On the second edition theory see Laquer, *Der jüdische Historiker Flavius Josephus*, pp. 1-6, who formulated it and David A. Barish, "The Autobiography of Josephus and the Hypothesis of a Second Edition of his *Antiquities*," *HTR* 71 (1978): 61-75, for a summary of the arguments against it.

[47] Hans Petersen, "Real and Alleged Projects of Josephus," *American Journal of Philology* 79 (1958): 274, argued that we have every work of Josephos. More recent controversy has focused on the work on customs hinted at in 20.268. Petersen contended that it is included in *CA*, pp. 263-265. David Altshuler, "The Treatise ΠΕΡΙ ΕΘΩΝ ΚΑΙ ΑΙΤΙΩΝ 'On Customs and Causes' by Flavius Josephus," *JQR* 69 (1978): 226-232, maintained that it is incorporated in a revised edition of Josephos in which 3.224-286 and 4.67-75 were included. Those who think that it was simply never completed include: Geza Vermes, "A Summary of the Law by Flavius Josephus," *NovT* 24 (1982): 290 and Schürer, *The History of the Jewish People in the Age of Jesus Christ*, 1:56. The latter has a good summary of all of the possible works on pp. 55-57.

[48] *HE* 3.9.2.

[49] *BJ* 3.340-408, records Josephos' capture. He says that he found the pit which provided access to the cave δαιμονίῳ τινὶ συνεργίᾳ χρησάμενος (341). Given

covery of the cave, he began to recall his dreams δι' ὧν ὁ θεὸς τάς τε μελλούσας αὐτῷ συμφορὰς προεσήμανεν 'Ιουδαίων καὶ τὰ περὶ τοὺς 'Ρωμαίων βασιλεῖς ἐσόμενα.[50] With these in mind he began to reflect on the meaning of the prophecies of the ἱερῶν βίβλων. He then offered a silent prayer. He began by observing the present circumstances of his nation: ἐπειδὴ τὸ 'Ιουδαίων φῦλον κλάσαι δοκεῖ σοι τῷ κτίσαντι, μετέβη δὲ πρὸς 'Ρωμαίους ἡ τύχη πᾶσα; and then passed on to his own: καὶ τὴν ἐμὴν ψυχὴν ἐπελέξω τὰ μέλλοντα εἰπεῖν. In recognition of God's election of the Romans and his own prophetic role he announced his decision: δίδωμι μὲν 'Ρωμαίοις τὰς χεῖρας ἑκὼν καὶ ζῶ, adding, μαρτύρομαι δὲ ὡς οὐ προδότης, ἀλλὰ σὸς ἄπειμι διάκονος.[51] His companions would not, however, let him surrender which was tantamount to treason. They suggested that he commit suicide. After a long theoretical discourse against suicide, Josephos found himself surrounded by enraged compatriots. Never at a loss, he proposed that they draw lots and slay one another in turn. When this was accepted, Josephos found himself and one other left.[52] He persuaded his fellow—one presumes easily—to forego their pact and surrender to the Romans alive.

Why did Josephos record what appears to be a self-condemnation? The narrative must be apologetic in some way. Is it enough to see this as a self-defense against accusations of treachery on his part? I find the account too damning for that: silence would have been the better part of valour.[53] The explanation lies in the contrast between the two terms at the end of his prayer. Josephos did not see himself as a προδότης, but as σὸς διάκονος. What he meant by this is specified in his earlier statement: τὴν ἐμὴν ψυχὴν ἐπελέξω τὰ μέλλοντα εἰπεῖν. Josephos thus understood the critical step of his life not to be

---

Josephos' capacity for survival I think this was a cave that he and the other city leaders had preselected. He does tell us that the cave had provisions for some time (342)!

[50] *BJ* 3.351.

[51] *BJ* 3.354.

[52] He inserts εἴτε ὑπὸ τύχης χρὴ λέγειν, εἴτε ὑπὸ θεοῦ προνοίας. *BJ* 3. 391. I can not take this seriously. The Slavonic reads instead: "he counted the numbers with cunning and thereby misled them all." Cited by Thackeray, *Josephus: The Man and the Historian*, p. 14. Cf. Hölscher, *RE*, s.v. "Josephus," 9:1938, "durch einen Betrug."

[53] Rajak, *Josephus*, pp. 171-172, argued this. For the reaction in Jerusalem see 3.432-442.

an act of treason, but obedience to God's call to the prophetic office.[54]

Josephos immediately donned the prophetic mantle by announcing his prophetic status (ἐγὼ δ᾽ ἄγγελος ἥκω σοι μειζόνων) and Vespasian's future rise to the imperial throne.[55] Although Vespasian was skeptical—he has by no means been the last—he questioned some of the other prisoners and found a number of Josephos' forecasts about Jotapata to be true. Our initial reaction to this account is that of Vespasian: Josephos wanted to save his neck and *mirabile dictu* happened to be lucky.

Josephos, however, continues to present himself in a prophetic role. When he appeared before the walls of Jerusalem, he compared his situation to that of Jeremiah.[56] He like the priest/prophet of the earlier fall of Jerusalem urged surrender. The difference was that Zedekiah was more lenient to Jeremiah than they were to him.[57] He is therefore not a traitor, but the true patriot who stood before the walls of Jerusalem as Jeremiah *redivivus*.[58]

---

[54] That this episode was understood by Josephos to be a call to the prophetic office has been emphasized by Martin Braun, "The Prophet Who Became a Historian," *The Listener* 56 (1956): 56; F.F. Bruce, "Josephus and Daniel," *Annual of the Swedish Theological Institute* 4 (1965): 159; Marianus de Jonge, "Josephus und die Zukunftserwartungen seines Volkes," in *Josephus-Studien: Untersuchungen zu Josephus, dem antiken Judentum und dem Neuen Testament*, ed. by Otto Betz, Klaus Haacker, and Martin Hengel (Göttingen: Vandenhoeck & Ruprecht, 1974), pp. 205-206; Helgo Lindner, *Die Geschichtsauffassung des Flavius Josephus im Bellum Judaicum: Gleichzeitig ein Betrag zur Quellenfrage*. AGJU 12 (Leiden: E.J. Brill, 1972), p. 56; David M. Rhoades, *Israel in Revolution: 6-74 C.E.: A Political History Based on the Writings of Josephus* (Philadelphia: Fortress Press, 1976), pp. 8-11; H.R. Moehring, "Joseph ben Matthia and Flavius Josephus," pp. 864-944; Attridge, "Josephus and His Works," p. 192; and Bilde, *Flavius Josephus between Jerusalem and Rome*, p. 52, and the bibliography cited there.

[55] *BJ* 3.399-408, especially 399-402. *BJ* 6.312-313, appears to give the Vespasian oracle a Messianic interpretation.

[56] *BJ* 5.391-393.

[57] Josephos claims that the rebels detested him, but that the people were willing to listen, especially the upper class. Cf. *BJ* 5.420, 547; 6.112-114. The revolutionaries imprisoned Josephos' parents in their zeal to prevent any betrayal. See *BJ* 5.533 (father) and 544 (mother).

[58] He does not explicitly identify himself with Jeremiah the prophet in this text, but with their common circumstances. His claim to the prophetic office and his extended interest in Jeremiah in *AJ* suggests, however, that he saw himself as a second Jeremiah. So also Braun, "The Prophet Who Became a Historian," p. 56; De Jonge, "Josephus und die Zukunftserwartungen seines Volkes," pp. 206-207; Reinhold Mayer and Christa Moller, "Josephus—Politiker und Prophet," in

We now must ask how seriously we should take these texts. The historicity of the Vespasian oracle suggests that at the time of Josephos' surrender at Jotapata, he saw himself as a prophet. The account of his decision to surrender doubtless contains a great deal of anachronistic rationalizing from a historical standpoint—how could it be otherwise? More importantly, it states Josephos' self-understanding at the time when he lived in Rome: he was God's servant.

This has important repercussions for our understanding of *AJ*. In an important argument in *CA*, Josephos makes an explicit connection between prophecy and the writing of history. For Josephos, the authors of scripture were Moses and the prophets.[59] He thus like the Rabbis considered the books after the Torah to be prophetic. The difficulty with Jewish records for the period of time after the canonical books of prophetic history is that the succession of prophets has not remained intact.[60] This connection leads us to ask whether Josephos saw himself within the line of OT prophets-historians. Although he never openly calls himself a προφήτης, the texts we have examined indicate that he understood himself to be one. It is his prophetic status that allows him to write a definitive history of the Jewish people.[61] His work thus has direct ties to the OT tradition of historiography in the sense that it is prophetic history, i.e., history written by a prophet.

Relation to Rome

A second major issue which has important implications for our understanding of *AJ* is the issue of Josephos' relation to the Flavian dynasty. Did Josephos' relationship change from good rapport with

---

Josephus-Studien, p. 284; Cohen, *Josephus in Galilee and Rome*, p. 232; David Daube, "Typology in Josephus," *JJS* 31 (1980): 20, 26-27, 33; and Bilde, *Flavius Josephus between Jerusalem and Rome*, pp. 55-56, 191. Lindner, *Die Geschichtsauffassung des Flavius Josephus im Bellum Judaicum*, p. 73 n. 2, warns against using this parallel to form our judgment of Josephus since Jeremiah had no Jotapata.

[59] *CA* 1.37, states that only prophets write scripture. It goes without saying that the legislator wrote scripture (*CA* 1.40).

[60] *CA* 1.41.

[61] So also Joseph Blenkinsopp, "Prophecy and Priesthood in Josephus," *JJS* 25 (1974): 241; Daube, "Typology in Josephus," p. 35; D.E. Aune, "The Use of ΠΡΟΦΗΤΗΣ in Josephus," *JBL* 101 (1982): 421; and Louis H. Feldman, "Prophets and Prophecy in Josephus," in *Society of Biblical Literature 1988 Seminar Papers*, ed. David J. Lull (Atlanta: Scholars Press, 1988), pp. 424-441, esp. 431-433. Feldman provides an overview of the concept of prophecy in Josephus.

Vespasian and Titus to a strained relation under Domitian and is that alteration evident in his works?

We must begin by asking whether Vespasian and Titus had any official connections with the writing of *BJ*. There are two related issues. First, were the different versions—the Aramaic version in particular—officially commissioned works or unofficial tomes written with the approval of the emperor?[62] According to Suetonius, Vespasian did support and reward persons of letters.[63] Since Josephos was on Vespasian's payroll and living in Vespasian's former residence, it is tempting to think of him as a supported writer: Was the stipend only for his role in the war or was more expected? A connection with Titus is explicitly made in *Vita* 363, where Josephos tells us that Titus ἐκ μόνων αὐτῶν ἐβουλήθη τὴν γνῶσιν τοῖς ἀνθρώποις παραδοῦναι τῶν πράξεων, ὥστε χαράξας τῇ ἑαυτοῦ χειρὶ τὰ βιβλία δημοσιῶσαι προσέταξεν. Finally, we should remember that Josephos began writing while in the Roman camp.[64] While these factors fall short of proof of a commission they do point out the close tie between Josephos and the emperors. Second, how much difference would it make if *BJ* were only sanctioned rather than commissioned by the emperor? There is a distinction; nonetheless, the connection with the Flavians must be given its due.[65]

The evidence for a change from his early period in Rome to the later is twofold. First, Josephos dedicated his last three works—all issued in the nineties—to the same individual, Epaphroditos.[66]

---

[62] Official works: Laquer, *Der jüdische Historiker Flavius Josephus*, p. 126 and Thackeray, *Josephus: The Man and the Historian*, p. 27. Unofficial: Rajak, *Josephus*, pp. 174-184. She treats the issue of patronage specifically on pp. 185-222.

[63] *Vesp.* 8.18: Primus e fisco Latinis Graecisque rhetoribus annua centena constituit; praestantis poetas, nec non et artifices . . . insigni congiario magnaque mercede donavit.

[64] *CA* 1.49.

[65] Rajak, *Josephus*, pp. 185-222, downplays this connection in order to maintain Josephos' nationalism. She, however, overplays the distinction between writing under contract and writing under pecuniary obligation (pp. 196-197). She dismisses the statement of Suetonius by pointing out that historians are not mentioned—a correct observation, but an argument from silence (p. 197).

[66] *AJ* 1.8; *V* 430; *CA* 1.1; 2.1, 296. The Epaphroditos in question may be one of two persons. He could be either Nero's freedman and secretary who later served Domitian but was executed by him for helping Nero to commit suicide (Suetonius, *Dom.* 8.4; Cassius Dio 67.14.4-5) or Marcus Mettius Epaphroditus. The latter was first the slave and then the teacher of the Alexandrian scholar Archias. He was freed by the governor of Egypt, M. Mettius, and came to Rome where he amassed a library of 30,000 works. He died in the reign of Trajan at the age of 75. (See Suda,

Why the shift in dedication away from the emperor? Is the dedication to Epaphroditos an indication that Josephos has fallen from imperial favor? The last three works of Josephos are unquestionably much more openly apologetic on behalf of the Jews than was *Bellum Judaicum*. Richard Laquer attempted to write a biography of Josephos based upon the shifts detectable within his writings. He thought that a definite break between Josephos and Domitian had transpired and that in his later life Josephos wanted to reinstate himself with his fellow Jews—a thesis which has by no means gone unchallenged.[67] The question has a direct bearing on the function of the *Antiquitates*. Since it requires an analysis of the texts themselves we must register a *sub judice* at this point of our discussion and return to the debate in our conclusions.

THE *ANTIQUITATES JUDAICAE*

Historiographical Tradition

In order to understand *AJ* we need to examine Josephos' own historiographical conceptions.[68] We must begin with a comment which Josephos made at the end of his literary career. In *CA* 1.53-56, the apologist defends the veracity of his historical works by asserting that there are only two acceptable methods of acquiring accurate

---

s.v. "Epaphroditus") The importance of deciding which of the two it is lies in the dating of Josephos' works. If it is the former, then *AJ*, *V*, and *CA* all had to be completed by 95 when Domitian removed his secretary. This seems to put a severe strain on time. *V* gives the impression of being written quickly, but *CA* is a very careful and deliberate work. I therefore prefer to think of the latter. Nero's freedman: Niese, *Flavii Iosephi Opera*, 5:III and *ERE*, s.v. "Josephus," 7:570-571. The bibliophile: Laquer, *Der jüdische Historiker Flavius Josephus*, pp. 23-36; Thackeray, *Josephus: The Man and the Historian*, p. 53 and *Josephus*, 4:x-xi; Richards, "The Composition of Josephus' *Antiquities*," p. 37; Rajak, *Josephus*, pp. 223-224; Attridge, "Josephus and His Works," p. 187. Not possible to determine: Cohen, *Josephus in Galilee and Rome*, p. 174 n. 230 and Schürer, *The History of the Jewish People in the Age of Jesus Christ*, 1:48 n. 9.

[67] *Der jüdische Historiker Flavius Josephus*, p. 260. The controversy is over whether Josephos underwent a personal shift later in his life or whether there is continuity throughout. The major representatives in the current debate are Cohen, *Josephos in Galilee and Rome*, pp. 232-242, who sees a shift vs. Rajak, *Josephus*, pp. 223-229 and Bilde, *Flavius Josephus between Jerusalem and Rome*, pp. 173-206, who contend for continuity.

[68] The most important historiographical statements in the Josephan corpus are: *BJ* 1.1-30; 7.454-455; *AJ* 1.1-26; 14.1-3; 16.183-187; 20.154-157, 259-266; *CA* 1.6-56. Cf. also his polemical remarks in *AJ* 1.121; 8.253, 260-262; 12.358-359.

knowledge in historical writing: ἢ παρηκολουθηκότα τοῖς γεγονόσιν ἢ παρὰ τῶν εἰδότων πυνθανόμενον (53). The *Antiquitates* is an example of the first since it is a translation (54), and *Bellum Judaicum* a representative of the second since he was an eye-witness (55). This implies that the two works belong to two different historiographical traditions: a conclusion which the programmatic statements of each work bear out.[69]

Bellum Judaicum opens with the claim that the war of the Jews against the Romans πόλεμον συστάντα μέγιστον οὐ μόνον τῶν καθ' ἡμᾶς, σχεδὸν δὲ καὶ ὧν ἀκοῇ παρειλήφαμεν ἢ πόλεων πρὸς πόλεις ἢ ἐθνῶν ἔθνεσι συρραγέντων which immediately brings to mind the opening of Thukydides.[70] He criticizes all previous accounts as being rhetorical works with no accuracy—whether they were written by armchair generals or actual participants (2). He then presents his credentials as a participant in the war (3). He returns to his own qualifications and mission in a polemic against Greek historians who write about events of the distant past rather than of the present as he is doing (13-16). He thinks: τό γε μὴν μνήμη τὰ [μὴ] προϊστορηθέντα διδόναι καὶ τὰ τῶν ἰδίων χρόνων τοῖς μεθ' ἑαυτὸν συνιστάνειν ἐπαίνου καὶ μαρτυρίας ἄξιον (15). The Greeks, he claims, are long-winded in judicial settings and short on truthfulness in history (16). It is hard not to hear echoes of Polybios in such statements.[71] If any doubts linger about where Josephos places himself, they are removed by the final sentence of the work: καὶ πῶς μὲν ἡρμήνευται, τοῖς ἀναγνωσομένοις κρίνειν ἀπολελείφθω, περὶ τῆς

---

[69] Recognized by Attridge, *The Interpretation of Biblical History in the 'Antiquitates Judaicae' of Flavius Josephus*, pp. 44-53. It is a great weakness of Varneda, *The Historical Method of Flavius Josephus*, that he does not recognize this point.

[70] Cf. also 4. Thukydides 1.1: Θουκυδίδης Ἀθηναῖος ξυνέγραψε τὸν πόλεμον . . . ἐλπίσας μέγαν τε ἔσεσθαι καὶ ἀξιολογώτατον τῶν προγεγενημένων. The claim to write on the greatest war does not in itself establish knowledge of Thukydides since selecting a great topic was a commonplace. (See below under the discussion on Dionysios of Halikarnassos.) It should, however, be weighed with the other similarities.

[71] Cf. the famous statement of Polybios in 9.2.1-7, where he pits his own utilitarian history of the present course of events over against authors who write περὶ τὰς γενεαλογίας καὶ μύθους καὶ περὶ τὰς ἀποικίας, ἔτι δὲ συγγενείας καὶ κτίσεις (1). Both Josephos and Polybios consider efforts to write antiquities a matter of rehashing history. *BJ* 1.15 and Polybios 9.2.2. It is also worth recalling Thukydides 1.21, which—as we have already observed—pits the unreliable ancient stories of the logographers over against Thukydides' record of the contemporary war.

ἀληθείας δὲ οὐκ ἂν ὀκνήσαιμι θαρρῶν λέγειν, ὅτι μόνης ταύτης παρὰ πᾶσαν τὴν ἀναγραφὴν ἐστοχασάμην (7.455). The nicely balanced contrast (μὲν . . . δέ) between rhetoric and truthfulness is unmistakable. While I would not credit Josephos with the objectivity (measured relatively of course) of Thukydides or Polybios, he has pitched his tent in their camp.[72]

When we turn to the *Antiquitates*, we find a different set of presuppositions. Josephos now undertakes ἀρχαιολογεῖν μὲν δὴ τὰ Ἰουδαίων—a task he considered out of place (ἄκαιρον) and superfluous (ἄλλως περιττόν) in *BJ* since it had already been accomplished and he presumably did not want to violate his own castigation of rewritten history.[73] Nor is Josephos oblivious to the fact that he is shifting traditions. He opens his prologue by reflecting on the different motives for historical writing: the display of their verbal skills and the glory which comes from its recognition, flattery, overwhelming experiences of life which compel an account, and the correction of general ignorance for common profit (1-3). He wrote *Bellum* as a result of the third of these (4).

He now has in mind a different work stemming from the fourth motive (5-9). ταύτην δὲ τὴν ἐνεστῶσαν ἐγκεχείρισμαι πραγματείαν νομίζων ἅπασι φανεῖσθαι τοῖς Ἕλλησιν ἀξίαν σπουδῆς (5). He claims that he had already considered this task when writing *Bellum*, but since the extent was so expansive put it off and made a separate volume of his account of the war (6-7a). This recalls his ἄκαιρον in *BJ* 1.17, but hardly does justice to ἄλλως περιττόν and his criticism of the writers of antiquity. He conveniently omits all mention of that in order to maintain harmony within his corpus. He justifies his present effort by the instigation of his patron, Epaphroditos (7b-9). Josephos says he yielded to his goadings because he knew Epaphroditos was an ardent supporter of any who could produce χρήσιμον ἢ καλόν τι and was ashamed to think that he would prefer idleness rather than τῷ περὶ τὰ κάλλιστα χαίρειν πόνῳ (9a).

His concern was whether his ancestors had been willing to communicate their traditions and whether Greeks were willing to listen

---

[72] It is interesting to note that all three were soldier-statesmen who later turned to historical writing. Shutt, *Studies in Josephus*, pp. 102-106, has a brief discussion of the possible stylistic connections between Polybios and Josephos.

[73] *BJ* 1.17-18.

to them (9b). This was resolved by the LXX which formed a basis for his own more complete translation (10-13).

There is a lesson for those who will read the history: God blesses those who keep his laws, whereas those who wander from them find their possibilities impossible (14).[74] The readers should then concentrate on God and by their own reflection determine whether the Jewish lawgiver provides an accurate portrayal of the nature and power of God by keeping his account of God free from all the unseemly mythology in the works of others (πάσης καθαρὸν τὸν περὶ αὐτοῦ φυλάξας λόγον τῆς παρ' ἄλλοις ἀσχήμονος μυθολογίας, 15). He has done this in spite of the fact that he lived over two thousand years ago (16)! The reader can be assured that she/he will have this opportunity since this work is an accurate translation of the scriptures (17).

Since so much hinges on Moses, a few more comments on him are in order (18-26). Moses advocated a theory of natural law. Humans must begin by reflecting on God, the perfection of virtue, and then follow the model they have seen (18-20). In contrast to other legislators, Moses begins with God rather than myths (μῦθοι) since he wants us to participate in this perfect virtue (21-23). It is, then, from the standpoint of reason that the readers should examine his work.[75] If concepts require further elaboration, the reader will find it in a future work by the author. (24-25) For now, we must proceed with the narrative (26).

Josephos' presuppositions again surface in his preface to Book 14. He says that a history about the hoary past must have τὸ τῆς ἀπαγγελίας κάλλος so that the readers μετὰ χάριτός τινος καὶ ἡδονῆς τὴν ἐμπειρίαν παραλαμβάνοιεν. More than anything else, however, the

---

[74] ἄπορα μὲν γίνεται τὰ πόριμα which is an allusion to Aeschylos, *PV* 904: ἄπορα πόριμος. Thackeray, *Josephus*, 4:8-9 n. a, pointed out the play off of Aeschylos.

[75] It is hard not to think of Philo's *De opificio mundi*, especially 1-3, when reading this section of the preface. Both contrast Moses and other legislators and credit him with a theory of natural law by beginning with creation. Josephos mentions Philo in *AJ* 18.259-260, in connection with the Alexandrian delegation before Caligula. He tells us four things about Philo: he was the head of the delegation, highly honored, the brother of Alexander the alabarch, and ὧν καὶ φιλοσοφίας οὐκ ἄπειρος (259). All that can be said about the preface to *AJ* is that Josephos and Philo share a common perspective. On the larger issue of whether or not Josephos had read Philo see Feldman, *Josephus and Modern Scholarship*, pp. 410-418, for the literature.

main objective must be ἀκριβείας.[76] The same dual emphasis on style and reliability steps forward in the conclusion where Josephos humbly tells us that he is uniquely qualified for the writing of this work since he has combined the best of Judaism and Hellenism: he is the leading Jewish scholar of his day and is fully conversant with the Greek language—except for pronunciation—and literature. Jews do not consider γλαφυρότητι λέξεων τὸν λόγον ἐπικομψεύοντας wise, but those who know τὰ νόμιμα σαφῶς and can interpret the sacred scriptures. The former is clearly characteristic of the Greeks in Jewish thinking. It is his accurate knowledge of the Jewish material and his grace of expression which makes his work what it is.

These comments would lead us to believe that Josephos has given equivalent weight to both his own Oriental tradition and the Greek. But does he? On five different occasions in *AJ* Josephos engages other historians polemically. In 1.121, he charges Greek historians with having altered the names of the nations in an effort to prove that these nations were their descendants. He corrects Herodotos in 8.253, 260-262, and Polybios in 12.358-359. He charges Nikolaos of Damascus with obsequiousness in 16.183-187, while protesting his own objectivity. He has a similar polemic in 20.154-157, where he again pits his aim of truth alone over against other writers on Nero who have been carried away by either favor or hatred. Is it accidental that all of these authors are Occidental?

The answer to this is given in *Contra Apionem* 1.6-56. In this long prefatory digression Josephos argues that πάτριός ἐστιν ἡ περὶ τῶν παλαιῶν ἀναγραφὴ τοῖς βαρβάροις μᾶλλον ἢ τοῖς "Ελλησι.[77] He pleads his case by first attacking the Greeks (6-27). There are two major problems with Greek historiography as Josephos sees it: one, it is a recent development (6-14); two, it is untrustworthy since there is so much contradictory testimony. He elaborates on the latter by pointing out that the Greek proclivity to argumentation among themselves is well known (15-18). The reasons why they can not agree are: they do not have any official records (19-23) and they are more concerned with style than truth (24-25).[78] *In nuce*, ὅλως δὲ τὸ πάντων ἐναντιώτατον ἱστορίᾳ πράττοντες διατελοῦσι (26a). Over

---

[76] *AJ* 14.2-3.
[77] *CA* 1.58. For the entire argument see 1.6-56.
[78] *CA* 1.24: οἱ γὰρ ἐπὶ τὸ γράφειν ὁρμήσαντες οὐ περὶ τὴν ἀλήθειαν ἐσπούδασαν . . . λόγων δὲ δύναμιν ἐπεδείκνυντο.

against the Occidental tradition, the Oriental nations, and the Jews above all others (28-46), keep accurate records (28-29). The Jews have their priests as guardians of the records (30-36) which are clearly defined in twenty-two books (37-41). Jewish esteem for these scriptures is so high that they are willing to die for them (42-43), a ludicrous proposition for Greeks (44-46)![79]

Josephos' programmatic statements make it clear that he considers *BJ* and *AJ* to belong to two different historiographical traditions. The two share a common concern, however: the pursuit of truth in contrast to the rhetorical menu of standard Greek historiography. In terms of *AJ*, his *magnum opus* stands in a Near Eastern tradition of historiography which emphasizes native traditions. In a broad way, Josephos has defined apologetic historiography for us. The question now becomes how he perceived it and what his procedures can tell us about the genre.

Content

Josephus entitled his *magnum opus* Ἰουδαϊκὴ Ἀρχαιολογία. There can be no doubt about this since he refers to it as his ἀρχαιολογία throughout the corpus.[80] What he meant by the term can be seen from the two texts where he does not use it in a titular sense. In *AJ* 1.5, he explains why the Greek world will find his πραγματεία to be of interest: μέλλει γὰρ περιέξειν ἅπασαν τὴν παρ' ἡμῖν ἀρχαιολογίαν καὶ [τὴν] διάταξιν τοῦ πολιτεύματος. In this text the term denotes Jewish history with an accent on ancient history. The same meaning is even more evident in *CA* 1.3-4. The apologist promises to διδάξαι δὲ πάντας ὅσοι τἀληθὲς εἰδέναι βούλονται περὶ τῆς ἡμετέρας ἀρχαιότητος (3). In order to do this, he will produce the most credible witnesses in the Greek world περὶ πάσης ἀρχαιολογίας (4). The juxtaposition of ἀρχαιότης and ἀρχαιολογία makes it clear that the word refers to antiquity as the Latin translation of the title admirably expresses.

Of more importance is to note the instances where Josephos refers to the works of other authors under the same heading. In *AJ* 1.93-95,

---

[79] On Josephos' relationship to the Greeks see Christoph Schaublin, "Josephus und die Griechen," *Hermes* 110 (1982): 316-341, especially 320-323 for his historiographical views.

[80] *AJ* 20.259, 267; *V* 430; *CA* 1.1, 2 (where the word may simply mean antiquity but clearly refers to what Josephos has written about it), 54, 127; 2.136, 287.

he buttresses the biblical account of the deluge by claiming that πάντες οἱ τὰς βαρβαρικὰς ἱστορίας ἀναγεγραφότες have mentioned it. He begins his list with Berossos who wrote about it που (93). He next mentions Hieronymos the Egyptian ὁ τὴν ἀρχαιολογίαν τὴν Φοινικικὴν συγγραψάμενος.[81] He concludes this list with Mnaseas and Nikolaos of Damascus (94).[82] The other occasion follows almost immediately. After defending the longevity of the ante-diluvians with his own rationales, Josephos says: μαρτυροῦσι δέ μου τῷ λόγῳ πάντες οἱ παρ' Ἕλλησι καὶ βαρβάροις συγγραψάμενοι τὰς ἀρχαιολογίας (107). He then enumerates them: Μανέθων ὁ τὴν Αἰγυπτίων ποιησάμενος ἀναγραφήν, Βηρωσὸς ὁ τὰ Χαλδαϊκὰ συναγαγών. He goes on to include Mochos,[83] Hestiaios,[84] and the Egyptian Hieronymos, οἱ τὰ Φοινικικὰ συγγραψάμενοι (107). He then gives a second list of those who agree with the unusually long lives of the ante-diluvians[85]: Hesiod, Hekataios, Hellanikos, Akousilaos,[86] and finally ends by throwing in Ephoros[87] and Nikolaos (108). Josephos does not make a distinction between Orientals and Greeks in the writing of ἀρχαιολογίαι in these texts. It is significant, however, to note that pride of place is clearly given to Manethon, Berossos, and the Phoenician authors. He thus aligns himself with the tradition of writing the ancient history of a given nation.

Josephos describes the scope of the *Antiquitates* in his conclusion: ἀπὸ πρώτης γενέσεως ἀνθρώπου . . . μέχρι ἔτους δωδεκάτου τῆς Νέρωνος ἡγεμονίας.[88] In his prefaces to both *AJ* and *CA* he computes this span to be five thousand years.[89] In his summary he gives us an idea of how he perceived the contents of *AJ*. In the first place it embraced τῶν ἡμῖν συμβεβηκότων τοῖς Ἰουδαίοις κατά τε τὴν Αἴγυπτον καὶ Συρίαν καὶ Παλαιστίνην (20.259). This indicates the material covering their origin and settlement through the early cen-

---

[81] *FGrH* 787.

[82] *FGrH* 90. On Nikolaos see Ben Zion Wacholder, *Nicolaus of Damascus.* University of California Publications in History 75 (Berkeley/Los Angeles: University of California Press, 1962).

[83] *FGrH* 784.

[84] *FGrH* 786.

[85] He introduces it with συμφωνοῦσι τοῖς ὑπ' ἐμοῦ λεγομένοις.

[86] *FGrH* 2. Cf. also *CA* 1.13.

[87] *FGrH* 70, who wrote a universal history in thirty books which extended from the return of the Heracleidae to 341 B.C.E.

[88] *AJ* 20.259.

[89] *AJ* 1.13; *CA* 1.1.

turies of the monarchy. He then adds: ὅσα τε πεπόνθαμεν ὑπὸ Ἀσσυρίων τε καὶ Βαβυλωνίων, τίνα τε Πέρσαι καὶ Μακεδόνες δεινὰ διατεθείκασιν ἡμᾶς, καὶ μετ' ἐκείνους Ῥωμαῖοι (20.260). The contrast between the participle, συμβεβηκότων, and the verb, πεπόνθαμεν, is striking. Why focus on suffering for the latter part of his history? I think that it is more than an appeal to the reader for sympathy. The early part of Israel's history is the story of an independent nation; the latter portion relates Israel as a subject nation. Her greatest glory lay in the remote past even as that of other Oriental peoples. The second item which Josephos chooses to emphasize is τὴν τῶν ἀρχιερέων ἀναγραφὴν τῶν ἐν δισχιλίοις ἔτεσι γενομένων and τὴν περὶ τοὺς βασιλεῖς διαδοχήν τε καὶ ἀγωγήν . . . (261). The inclusion of the high priests suggests that this is more than a mere rehearsal.[90] In *CA* Josephos argues that the Jews have carefully preserved their records—in contrast to the Greeks. One of the proofs which he offers for this is that the priests have scrupulously kept them. This is confirmed by the fact that there are genealogical records for the high priests for two thousand years: from Aaron to the war.[91] The inclusion of the high priests is therefore a guarantee of the veracity of the record as well as a claim to antiquity. What is interesting about this summary is that it indicates Josephos used the same scope, creation to his own time period, as did Berossos, Manethon, and the Hellenistic Jewish historians.

The historian tells us that he accomplished this tour de force in twenty books and sixty thousand lines.[92] This implies that Josephos himself is responsible for the book divisions: a fact which is substan-

---

[90] *AJ* 20.224-251, does give a summary of the high priests from Aaron to Phanasos whom the revolutionary party appointed during the war. According to Josephos there were eighty-three high priests. He regularly reports the appointments of high priests in his narrative as well.

[91] *CA* 1.30-36, especially 36. For the two thousand year period see also *AJ* 1.16; 20.227.

[92] *AJ* 20.267. Louis Feldman, *Josephus*, 10:141 n. d; "Josephus' Portrait of Saul," *HUCA* 53 (1952): 97 n. 94; and "Josephus as a Biblical Interpreter: The 'Aqedah," *JQR* 75 (1985): 252 n. 108, has computed the lines in Niese's edition to be c. 44,250. (In the Loeb edition Feldman calculated Niese's sections to have an average of eight lines while in his later articles he estimates six. The number of lines is given in the articles and is based upon the figure of six; eight = 59,000.) Josephos' lines must have been shorter. Cf. also Thackeray, *Josephus: The Man and the Historian*, p. 73, (following Rendel Harris) who points out that one of the reasons for the stichometry was to determine the pay of the scribes.

tiated by internal references within *AJ*.[93] Five of these references
constitute prefaces to the book they introduce: the first two being
summaries of the previous book,[94] the middle two being both a
summary of the preceding book and a preview of the present
book,[95] and the last being only a connecting link.[96] Interestingly
three of these appear in sequential books.[97] There is not always an
evident rationale for the relationship between content and book division. Apparently Josephos imposed his book divisions on his narrative rather than fitting his narrative into the book divisions.[98]
Perhaps the individual book divisions were due to the practical concern of the length of a scroll.

Did Josephos offer any additional structure to his mammoth
work? Henry St. J. Thackeray pointed out that the work falls into
two equal halves: 1-10, culminating with the exile, and 11-20, which
bring the story on down to the outbreak of the war. This is supported
by the fact that the biblical text is the primary source for the first half
and other material for the second.[99] Harold Attridge gave more
precision to this analysis by subdividing the second half into three
units: 11-13 (a continuation of Jewish history through Alexandra
Salome), 14-17 (the rise and fall of the Herodian kingdom), and
18-20 (which does not have a distinct focus).[100] Per Bilde has more
recently followed the same basic pattern, but has refined it even
more. He suggests that the key is the temple: the first was destroyed
in 10 and the second temple's destruction is anticipated in 20. He
subdivides the first half into two equal parts: 1-5, the founding of
Israel; 6-10, the evolution and fall of Israel. Following Attridge, he

---

[93] *AJ* 4.74; 8.1; 13.1; 14.1-3; 15.1; 20.1.
[94] *AJ* 8.1; 13.1.
[95] *AJ* 14.1; 15.1.
[96] *AJ* 20.1.
[97] *AJ* 13.1; 14.1; 15.1. I must confess that I am not certain what to make of
this or if anything should be made of it. Hölscher, *RE*, s.v. "Josephus," 9:1950,
attributed this to a new source. The greatest problem with this is that Josephos uses
I Maccabees in both books twelve and thirteen.
[98] Josephos clearly does not feel compelled to make his books conform to the
biblical divisions. *AJ* 1 = Gen. 1:1-35:29; 2 = Gen. 36:1-Ex. 15:21 (2.1-3 = Gen.
25:29-34); 3 = Ex. 15:22-Num. 14:38; 4 = Num. 14:39-Deut. 34; 5 = Josh. 1:1-I
Sam. 4:22; 6 = I Sam. 5:1-31:13; 7 = II Sam. 1:1-I Kgs. 2:11; 8 = I Kgs.
2:12-22:40; 9 = I Kgs. 22:51 (actually II Chron. 19:1)-II Kgs. 17:28; 10 = II Kgs.
18:12-Dan. 8; 11 = I Esdr. 2:1-Esth. 10:3. Some of these come close to forming
distinct units as we will see below.
[99] *Josephus: The Man and the Historian*, p. 58 and *Josephus*, 4:xi-xii.
[100] "Josephus and his Works," pp. 211-213.

offers the following schema for the second half: 11-13 (the re-establishment of Israel), 14-17 (the first phase of the second fall: the Herodians), 18-20 (the second phase of the second fall: Roman rule).[101]

There is a great deal of merit to these analyses, especially since the first half is essentially a paraphrase of the biblical text and the second relies on other sources. It is, however, important to note Josephos' own assessment of history. In *CA* 1.39-41, he describes the canon of Jewish scriptures within the framework of history. According to his understanding, there are three basic time periods: the five books of Moses encompassing a period of almost three thousand years (39), from the death of Moses to Artaxerxes I during which the prophets chronicled the events of their time in thirteen books—the other four books of the canon are mentioned at this point as containing hymns to God and advice for life (40), and from Artaxerxes until the time of writing. This final period also has its recorded history, but these records have not been deemed equal to their predecessors διὰ τὸ μὴ γενέσθαι τὴν τῶν προφητῶν ἀκριβῆ διαδοχήν (41). If we apply this schematization of history to Josephos' own work we obtain the following result: 1-4, from creation until the death of Moses[102]; 5-11, from the death of Moses until Artaxerxes[103]; 12-20, from Artaxerxes until the beginning of the war.

We are now in a position to recapitulate the material. Josephos opens with his programmatic proem (1.1-26). The first book recounts pre-Abrahamic and patriarchal stories by combining a large number of quotations from pagan sources with the biblical text as a way of buttressing the credibility of the narrative.[104] The second

---

[101] *Flavius Josephus between Jerusalem and Rome*, pp. 89-92.

[102] It is significant that 4 ends with the death of Moses and 5 begins with Joshua. Josephos appears to be tipping us to his own conception here.

[103] The division in *AJ* is not as neat here as it was between 4 and 5. Josephos finishes retelling Esther at 11.296. The book goes on, however, to relate the Alexander material. This could be due to a number of factors: Josephos did not utilize this threefold division in his own work; he associated Alexander with the fall of Persia; or he had to add the material in order to fill out his scroll properly.

[104] *AJ* 1.93-95: Berossos, Hieronymos the Egyptian, Mnaseas, and Nikolaos of Damascus; 107-108: Manethon, Berossos, Mochos, Hestiaios, Hieronymos the Egyptian, Hesiod, Hekataios, Hellanikos, Akousilaos, Ephoros, and Nikolaos of Damascus; 118-119: Sibyl, Hestiaios; 158-160: Berossos, Nikolaos of Damascus; 240-241: Kleodamos also called Malchos through Polyhistor. It is interesting to note the distribution of these citations. The next example comes in 7.101-103, where he again appeals to Nikolaos (although note the parallel drawn with

book continues the story with a focus on Egypt: it begins with the
sale of Joseph into Egypt and concludes with the event at the sea.[105]
Josephos lavishes particular attention on Joseph and the early years
of Moses. The third book presents Israel in the wilderness up until
and including the time of their disobedience. It concentrates on the
tabernacle (102-187) and the laws (222-286). Like the biblical text,
the fourth book does not concentrate on the wilderness (9-10,
11-66), but on events in Trans-Jordan. (76-195) It again offers a
summary of the laws (67-75, 199-301). and concludes with an encomium on Moses which forms a nice *inclusio* with the final element
of the preface (1.18-26).

The second unit (5-11) opens with the conquest of the land and
continues on down to the capture of the ark by the Philistines. One
of the most interesting features of this book is that Josephos places
the appendices to Judges prior to the history of the judges[106] and relates the story of Ruth immediately after that of Sampson. The sixth
book could be called the book of Saul even as the seventh the book
of David. At the point of David, a reader who is familiar with the
biblical text realizes that Josephos has woven Chronicles and Kings
together. The eighth through the tenth books retell the history of the
kings of Israel and Judah highlighting the temple (8.63-98), the fall
of Israel (9.277-287), and Judah (10). Besides relating the Elijah-
Elisha cycle as we would expect, Josephos has included references
to the literary prophets within his text.[107] The most striking of these
is his reference to and use of Jeremiah in book ten—an interest
which is more than literary.[108] The eleventh book narrates the same

---

Alexander in 2.347-348). Later examples again are more scattered: 8.144-149:
Menander, Dios; 8.157: Herodotos; 8.253, 260-262: Herodotos is cited but corrected (!) by Josephos; 8.324: Menander; 9.282-287: Menander; 10.18-20:
Herodotos, Berossos; 10.34b: Berossos; 10.219-228: Berossos, Megasthenes, Diokles. Josephos continues to cite pagan authors in the last section of *AJ*, but the significance changes. (See under Form) Cf. 12.5-6: Agatharchides of Cnidos;
12.135-137a: Polybios; 12.358-359: where he attacks Polybios' account of Antiochos' death; 13.251: Nikolaos of Damascus; 13.287: Strabon; 13.319: Strabon;
14.35-36: Strabon; 14.68: Strabon, Nikolaos of Damascus, Livy; 14.112-118:
Strabon; 14.138-139: Strabon; 15.9b-10: Strabon.

[105] *AJ* 2.1-6, deal with Esau. This is, however, only a minor treatment and
really does not detract from the focus of the book.

[106] *AJ* 5.136-174 = Judg. 19:1-21:24; *AJ* 5.175-178 = Judg. 18:1-31; *AJ*
5.179ff. = Judg. 3:7ff.

[107] *AJ* 9.208-214, Jonah; 9.239-242, Nahum; 10.35, Isaiah and the twelve.

[108] *AJ* 10.78b-80, 88-95 (cf. Jer. 26:1-26; 36:1-26), 102-107, 110-115 (Cf. Jer.
37:5-15), 117-130 (Cf. Jer. 38:1-28), 141, 156-180 (Cf. Jer. 40:1-43:13). Josephos'

material as I Esdras, Nehemiah, Esther, and the Alexander legend.

The third and final section of Josephos' tome may be subdivided into three sections: 12-13, 14-17, and 18-20. The key to this is the Herodian material which forms a discernible block in 14-17.[109] The twelfth book opens by recounting the origin of the LXX as it is told in the Letter of Aristeas (12-118).[110] He continues by informing his audience of the privileges the Jewish nation enjoyed under the Syrians (119-128) and Antiochos III in particular (137b-153). He returns to his narrative by relating the Tobiad romance (154-236). At this juncture he begins to parallel I Maccabees. The Hasmoneans form the basis for the remainder of book twelve and for all of thirteen, welding the two books into one unit: the revolt under Mattathias (12.240-285), Judas (12.286-434), Jonathan (13.1-193), Simon (13.194-229), John Hyrkanos (13.230-300), Aristobulos (13.301-319), Alexander Jannaeus (13.320-407), and Alexandra Salome (13.408-432). Interspersed within this general framework is a significant body of material on the Seleucids as well as two asides on Jewish matters: the temple of Onias at Leontopolis (13.62-73) and a very brief account of the three Jewish philosophies (13.171-173).

Books 14-17 present the history of Herod to us: 14, his rise to power (from the death of Salome until he took Jerusalem in 37 B.C.E.); 15, the consolidation of his power and the opposition to him (37 B.C.E. to the completion of the temple); 16, Antipater vs. Aristobulos and Alexander culminating in the deaths of the later two; 17, the effective end of the Herodian dynasty in Judea: the deaths of Antipater, Herod, and the banishment of Archelaos. Within this lengthy description Josephos has included a great deal of Roman history as well. More importantly, he has inserted blocks of *acta* which demonstrate Jewish privileges in the past.[111]

---

interest could be due to the sizeable amount of historical material in Jeremiah; however, most of it is about the prophet. The only other prophet who receives this much attention is Daniel whose book is retold at the end of ten.

[109] Book 14 begins with the most extensive preface of any of the books in *AJ* with the exception of the first. See 14.1-3.

[110] *AJ* 12.1-11, set the stage for this account. It should be noted that Josephos has chosen to begin the third and final phase of history with an account of the model for his own work, at the same basic point that the canonical material has run out. While the event naturally falls into this time period, it may be more than coincidence that the task of translation begins at the point that the twenty-two books end.

[111] *AJ* 14.145-155, 185-267 (188-264 proper), 306-323; 16.160-178. See also the later collections at 19.278-291; 20.10-14.

The final section, 18-20, illustrates the building tension between the Jews and their overlords. Rulers again serve as focal points within the text. This is particularly true of Herod Agrippa I who serves as a link-pin for 18.143-19.352, even if some of the material is only indirectly related, e.g., Caligula.[112] The remaining material continues to portray the growing hostility with one major exception: the conversion of the royal house of Adiabene (20.17-96). The work ends with a formal conclusion(s) (20.259-266, 267-268).

Form

1. *A Translation.* In his preface Josephos claims that his work is a translation of the Hebrew writings.[113] This is an important concern to the historian who repeatedly mentions scripture as the source for

---

[112] *AJ* 18.256, the two periods of his rule; 18.257-260, the Alexandrian delegation; 18.261-309, his image and the temple in Jerusalem; 19.1-14, his intolerable madness; 19.15-16, justification for the account of his assassination; 19.17-200, his assassination; 20.201-211, summary. Th. Mommsen, "Cornelius Tacitus und Cluvius Rufus," *Hermes* 4 (1870): 322-324, suggested that Josephos was dependent upon M. Cluvius Rufus for his account of Gaius' assassination.

[113] In *AJ* 1.5 and *CA* 1.54, he uses the verb μεθερμηνεύω. In AJ 10.218 he employs μεταφράζω. The former regularly denotes the process of translation whether of an entire document, e.g., Eccles. prologue (only occurrence in the LXX), or of individual words, e.g., Diodoros 1.11.2; Dionysios of Hal. *AR* 4.76.2; and 8t. in the NT. (In each of the examples given where it renders a single word, it appears in a passive participle [except Acts 13:8, where it is finite].) Josephos uses it a total of 10t.: to note the translation of a word (*BJ* 4.11; 5.151; *AJ* 1.52; 8.142; *CA* 1.167), the LXX (*AJ* 12.20, 48), and Manethon's translation (*CA* 1.228). The latter carries the notion of paraphrase or restating the same concept in different words without necessarily meaning to restate them in a different language, e.g., Dionys. of Hal. *De Thuc.* 45. Interestingly, the cognate noun, μετάφρασις, occurs in II Ma. 2:31 (only occurrence of the word group in the LXX) where the writer defends the condensation of Jason of Cyrene's five volume work into a shorter narrative, τὸ δὲ σύντομον τῆς λέξεως μεταδιώκειν καὶ τὸ ἐξεργαστικὸν τῆς πραγματείας παραιτεῖσθαι τῷ τὴν μετάφρασιν ποιουμένῳ συγχωρητέον. It can also carry the notion of translating, e.g., Plutarch, *Cat. Mai.* 19.3 and *Cic.* 40.2. Josephos uses it 4t.: the translation of Menander of Ephesus (*FGrH* 783) who rendered Phoenician records into Greek (*AJ* 8.144; 9.283) and Manethon (*CA* 1.73). Josephos does not appear to make a formal distinction between the two since he uses μεταφράζω in 10.218 to summarize his claim of 1.5 where he employed μεθερμηνεύω. He also uses μεταβάλλω in 1.10; 12.14, 15, to mark the translation from Hebrew into Greek in the LXX. (Note also *BJ* 1.3 [where it denotes the translation of the Aramaic *War* into the Greek] and 17 [where it marks the work of the Greeks who rendered former Jewish accounts of their antiquities into Greek]). It should be noted that in every instance where Josephos speaks of translating a document, it is always a native document which is being rendered into Greek.

his work.[114] He presents the LXX as a model in 1.10-13. Like his own work, the LXX is an attempt to present the writings of the Hebrews in Greek. The problem with the previous effort is that "those who were sent to Alexandria to interpret delivered only the parts relating to the Law" (12). In reality, "the things presented in the sacred scriptures are myriad, since the history of five thousand years is contained within them" (13). Shortly afterwards he asserts that his account will set forth τὰ . . . ἀκριβῆ τῶν ἐν ταῖς ἀναγραφαῖς and will do this κατὰ τὴν οἰκείαν τάξιν. He then promises that he οὐδὲν προσθεὶς οὐδ' αὖ παραλιπών.[115] These statements cause us to ask what Josephos means by such pronouncements. Even the briefest reading of his "translation" of the biblical text itself reveals that this promise has not been kept—at least not *au pied de la lettre*. More than this, the final division of the work (Books 12-20) is not even based on the twenty-two books of Jewish scripture as he himself acknowledges.[116] Further, Josephos himself admits an omission on at least one occasion.[117] It is clear then that Josephos is using a traditional statement which he does not fully honor. Where did he find this statement and why did he make it?

Paradoxically the claim that he neither added nor omitted anything became a *cause célèbre* for earlier scholarship to attack Josephos—a view which has not entirely died today.[118] Even if the truthfulness of the claim is a sham, this hardly explains why Josephos would make such an assertion. There are several possible traditions from which Josephos might have drawn the last phrase, οὐδὲν προσθεὶς οὐδ' αὖ παραλιπών. It is part of the biblical text itself.[119] It is also used in Greek historiography.[120] He could, there-

---

[114] *AJ* 1.5, 17, 26; 10.218; 20.261; *CA* 1.1, 54, 127.

[115] *AJ* 1.17. See also 4.196; 10.218; 14.1 where the same claim is made. In 20.261 he asserts that he has fulfilled his pledge of 1.17. In other texts he protests that he is giving exact reporting: 2.347; 9.208, 214; 20.260, 261.

[116] *CA* 1.38-41.

[117] *AJ* 9.242, where he tells his readers that he is going to omit some of what Jonah preached to the Ninevites so that he will not seem ὀχληρός.

[118] E.g., H. Paul Kingdom, "The Origins of the Zealots," *NTS* 19 (1972-1973): 78 (see 77-78), thought that where Josephos departed from the text "he must have relied upon his mainly non-Jewish readers not referring to the biblical texts."

[119] Deut. 4:2: לא תספו על הדבר אשר אנכי מצוה אתכם ולא גרעו ממנו; Deut. 13:1: לא תסף עליו ולא תגרע ממנו.

[120] Dionysios of Halikarnassos, *De Thukydide* 5, 8; Lucian, *Hist. Conscr.* 47. Those who see it as a simple historiographical commonplace are Attridge, *The*

fore, have simply appropriated it and used it as a means of adding respectability to his work. There are, however, other possibilities. W.C. van Unnik argued that in Hellenistic circles this was not simply a rhetorical phrase, but that it was used to claim that the sources had been transmitted truthfully.[121] His point has been countered by several who have observed that it is not only attested in Greek tradition; it is well known in rabbinic literature.[122] Louis Feldman has made yet another proposal. In an earlier article, Feldman argued that "what is written" included both the written scripture and "the Jewish tradition of interpretation . . . which was regarded as an integral part of that tradition."[123] More recently he has honed his view and suggested that while the source which Josephos did not alter is both written and oral tradition, this phrase is bound to Josephos' understanding of what it means to translate. According to Feldman, Josephos understood the process of translation to be more than "mechanical . . . it involved interpretation, amplification, and explanation in the broadest sense."[124] He based his argument on the fact that Josephos used the LXX as a model and it is interpretative. Finally, Tessa Rajak noted that the claim of translation was

---

Interpretation of Biblical History in the 'Antiquitates Judaicae' of Flavius Josephus, pp. 58-60 and Cohen, *Josephus in Galilee and Rome*, pp. 27-29.

[121] *Flavius Josephus als historischer Schriftsteller*. Franz Delitzsch Vorlesungen, neue Folge (Heidelberg: Lambert Schneider, 1978), pp. 26-40. See also his earlier article, "De la règle Μήτε προσθεῖναι μήτε ἀφελεῖν dans l'histoire du canon," *VC* 3 (1949): 1-36, especially 17-18. He has been followed by Vermes, "A Summary of the Law by Flavius Josephus," p. 290.

[122] It has been explained on this basis by David Goldenberg, "Josephus Flavius or Joseph ben Mattithiah," *JQR* 70 (1979): 180-181 and H. W. Basser, "Josephus as Exegete," *Journal of the American Oriental Society* 107 (1987): 24-25 n. 23.

[123] "Hellenizations in Josephus' Portrayal of Man's Decline," in *Religions in Antiquity: Festschrift E.R. Goodenough*, ed. by Jacob Neusner. Studies in the History of Religions 14 (Leiden: E.J. Brill, 1968), p. 338 (see 336-339). Compare the comment of Georgi, *The Opponents of Paul in Second Corinthians*, p. 140: "All this points to a characteristic freedom on the part of the Apologists with respect to the text and its limits, and the simplest explanation for this nonchalance may be that it was nurtured by the confidence in the power of the letter, which precisely because of its fixed character was capable of transcending itself. The respect for scripture seems to have produced the proliferous tradition, but in that process scripture became a part of the tradition, with tradition towering over everything. Josephus's work shows how in this way one was easily capable of reaching into and including the present."

[124] "Hellenizations in Josephus' *Jewish Antiquities*: The Portrait of Abraham," p. 134 (see 133-134), 151 n. 2. This has also been argued by Bilde, *Flavius Josephus between Jerusalem and Rome*, pp. 95-97.

common to Hekataios, Berossos, and Manethon. She, therefore, argued that Josephos used it to align himself with the Oriental tradition.[125]

What is surprising in this debate is that Josephos' own use of the phrase in other texts has been neglected. In *AJ* 12.108-109, he reports the success of the LXX translation. After it was decided that the LXX should not be altered,[126] the community ordered that εἴ τις ἢ περισσόν τι προσγεγραμμένον ὁρᾷ τῷ νόμῳ ἢ λεῖπον, he should make it known. He uses the exact wording in a second text. As he presents Jewish veneration of their scriptures he says: τοσούτου γὰρ αἰῶνος ἤδη παρῳχηκότος οὔτε προσθεῖναί τις οὐδὲν οὔτε ἀφελεῖν αὐτῶν οὔτε μεταθεῖναι τετόλμηκεν.[127] In both of these cases the phrase is used to guarantee the reliability of the biblical text. It now seems clear that it has the same significance in the prologue.

What is more important is to recognize that this claim helps us to locate Josephos. Rajak was right in pointing out that it is apologetic historiography which insists upon the translation of native sources. This is buttressed by the fact that Berossos, Manethon, and Josephos—as well as Eupolemos—were priests and accordingly custodians of the traditions, a point Josephos does not fail to make himself.[128] However, previous authors had simply insisted upon the tradition without making the claims of accuracy which Josephos does.[129] Why does he add them? I think it has to do with how Josephos saw his work. The use of the phrase suggests that *AJ* is in the same line as the Hebrew scriptures and the LXX. How is this? Josephos' status as a prophet-historian allowed him to present the Hebrew writings in an interpreted form and to write the part of Jewish history which had hitherto lacked recognition. This phrase is his way of marking his history out as *the* history of the Jews for Greeks. *In nuce*, what we have is a definitive *translation* of scripture, not replacing the Hebrew scriptures themselves but on equal footing with the LXX and actually displacing it.[130]

---

[125] "Josephus and the 'Archaeology' of the Jews," pp. 47-49.

[126] καὶ διαμεῖναι ταῦθ', ὡς ἔχει, καὶ μὴ μετακινεῖν αὐτά.

[127] *CA* 1.42.

[128] *CA* 1.54: his priestly ancestry is why he knows the books so well.

[129] Diodoros 1.69.7 (Hekataios); *FGrH* 680 F 1 (Berossos); *CA* 1.73 (Manethon).

[130] We should remember that Philo claimed inspiration for the translators of the LXX in these words: καθάπερ ἐνθουσιῶντες προεφήτευον οὐκ ἄλλα ἄλλοι, τὰ δ' αὐτὰ πάντες ὀνόματα καὶ ῥήματα, ὥσπερ ὑποβολέως ἑκάστοις ἀοράτως ἐνηχοῦντος.

Josephos claims that his πραγματείαν is ἐκ τῶν Ἑβραϊκῶν μεθηρμηνευμένην γραμμάτων.[131] This, however, is misleading.[132] While Josephos may well have consulted a Semitic text,[133] especially for the Torah, in his later books he utilized a Greek text.[134] In fact, we can even identify the form of this text in places as proto-Lucianic.[135] Whether or not he used an Aramaic targum is very difficult to decide. For our purposes, we may simply recognize that, like Eupolemos before him, our priest knew both the Hebrew and Greek forms of the OT. The fact that we have difficulty determining the specific form of text is a witness to the extent he rewrote it.

2. *Major Influences*. The LXX did offer Josephos a precedent and even the basic structure for the first two divisions of his work. It does not, however, constitute a formal parallel for Josephos' creative retelling of Jewish history. The literal word-for-word rendering of the LXX does not address Josephos' concept of what it meant to

---

Mos. 2.37. Feldman, "Prophets and Prophecy in Josephus," p. 433, argues that Josephos recognized a distinction between biblical and later prophets: only the former could write canonical works.

[131] *AJ* 1.5. He also implies that it is from Hebrew into Greek in 10.218.

[132] Efforts to establish which text Josephos employed have proved frustrating in many ways. Hölscher, *RE*, s.v. "Josephus," 9:1953, actually asked—in all seriousness—if Josephos even consulted the biblical text! He thought that *AJ* 1-11 stemmed from "der jüdischen Gelehrtenschule von Alexandreia," 9:1959. This however, is due to Hölscher's assessment of Josephos as an author: he is only a compiler—a view which is impossible to sustain. The most likely assessment of his text was stated by Heinrich Bloch, *Die Quellen des Flavius Josephus* (Leipzig: B.G. Teubner, 1879; reprint ed., Wiesbaden: Dr. Martin Sandig OHG, 1968), pp. 8-22, who maintained that Jospehos primarily used a Greek text, but knew and referred to the Hebrew text. He also pointed out that the LXX served as a more natural source for Josephos since it had already rendered the Hebrew text into Greek (p. 18). So also Niese, *ERE*, s.v. "Josephus," 7:572-573; Schalit, *EncJud*, s.v. "Josephus Flavius," 10:258; Attridge, "Josephus and His Works," p. 211; and Schürer, *The History of the Jewish People in the Age of Jesus Christ*, 1:48-49. Thackeray, *Josephus: The Man and the Historian*, pp. 75-99, offered the following analysis. Pentateuch: Semitic text (LXX slight); Joshua, Judges, Ruth: Semitic text with a targum for Judges; Samuel on: Greek of the Lucianic type.

[133] *V* 418, Josephos says that he took some of the sacred books from Jerusalem when it fell. His Hebrew etymologies indicate his knowledge of Hebrew and of the terms in the Hebrew text. E.g., 1.33, 34, 36, 333; 2.278; 5.121, 200, 201, 323, 336; 6.22, 302; 7.67. He sometimes offers a Hebrew term for items, e.g., 3.134, 159, 291; 9.290.

[134] Good examples of this are his use of I Esdras in 11.3-157 and the additions to Esther in 11.229-241, 273-283.

[135] Eugene Charles Ulrich, Jr., *The Qumran Text of Samuel and Josephus*. HSM 19 (Missoula, Montana: Scholars Press, 1978), p. 259, for his conclusion.

translate. What other sources of influence helped shape *AJ* or did he write *a novo*?

a. *Rewritten Scripture*. Josephos was by no means the first Palestinian to retell the scriptures.[136] By his day, the effort was several centuries old. Three of the most significant efforts which we now have are Jubilees, the Genesis Apocryphon, and the *Liber Antiquitatum Biblicarum* of Pseudo-Philo. The first two were composed during the second century B.C.E. and are related literarily, although the issue of priority is still debatable.[137] Jubilees was originally composed in Hebrew and consists of a retelling of Gen. 1-Ex. 14, 24.[138] Ostensibly a revelation granted to Moses on Mount Sinai by an "angel of the Presence" it retells the biblical text with numerous *halakhic* additions. The work especially emphasizes the solar calender and sexual purity. 1QapGn. is one of the seven scrolls taken from cave one of Qumran in 1947. The columns which have been preserved well enough to be published retell events from Gen. 6-15. What is surprising about the document is that it is relatively free from theological tendencies; the Aramaic scroll rather creates a continuous narrative which develops the story through non-biblical additions.[139] The *Liber Antiquitatum Biblicarum* was originally composed in Hebrew and is only extant in Latin.[140] While the chronicle recounts events from Adam until the death of Saul, it does so in a highly selective way with the exception of Judges where it only omits the first three chapters. Unlike Jubilees, it omits *halakhic* matters; and more like 1QapGn. it interweaves legendary material into the biblical

---

[136] For surveys of this material with bibliographies see George W.E. Nickelsburg, *Jewish Literature Between the Bible and the Mishnah: A Historical and Literary Introduction* (Philadelphia: Fortress Press, 1981), pp. 73-80 and 231-275 and his "The Bible Rewritten and Expanded," in *Jewish Writings of the Second Temple Period*, pp. 89-156; and Schürer, *The History of the Jewish People in the Age of Jesus Christ*, 3:308-341.

[137] Nahman Avigad and Yigael Yadin, eds., *A Genesis Apocryphon: A Scroll from the Wilderness of Judea* (Jerusalem: Magnes Press, 1956), pp. 21, 38, argued in the *editio princeps* for the priority of 1QapGn. Fitzmyer, *The Genesis Apocryphon of Qumran Cave 1*, p. 16, argued the reverse. Both have been seconded by a significant number of studies. H. Lignée, "L'Apocryphe de la Genèse," in *Les Textes de Qumran*, ed., J. Cargomignac, E. Cothenet, and H. Lignée (Paris: Letouzey et anè, 1963), p. 217, cut the Gordian knot by claiming they came from a common milieu.

[138] For a critical edition of the Ethiopic see James C. Vanderkam, *The Book of Jubilees: A Critical Text*, 2 vols. CSCO 510-511 (Louvain: E. Peeters, 1989).

[139] E.g., the description of Sarah's beauty in 20.2-8 is surprising in a document from Qumran and underscores the unusual nature of this particular scroll.

[140] The standard text is Daniel J. Harrington, *Les Antiquités Bibliques*, 2 vols. SC 229-230. (Paris: Éditions du Cerf, 1976).

text. It appears to have been written in the last part of the first century C.E. and in some ways represents a Palestinian counterpart
to Josephos' *Antiquitates*. What these three works share is the inter-
weaving of interpretation and biblical text. They and others which
are similar all belong to the category of rewritten scripture or narrative midrash.[141]

The significance of these works for Josephos is twofold. First, they
attest to some of the same exegetical traditions in *AJ* and demonstrate that Josephos was aware of Palestinian exegetical traditions.[142] Second, Josephos' methodology in retelling the scripture
was influenced by his predecessors in his homeland. As a Jerusalem
youth, he must have learned to interweave scripture and interpretation. At the same time, the differences between Josephos and these
works are immense. The fact that they were composed in Aramaic
and Hebrew indicates their audience; they can in no way be considered parallels to the "translation" of Josephos. Further, these
works are all selective in the biblical traditions they relate; Josephos
attempted to tell the whole story of Israel. More importantly yet,
their open hostility to Hellenism is at direct odds with Josephos' insistence upon it.[143] They thus helped to mold some of his understanding of the traditions and how to retell them, but can not be considered to belong to the same genre.

b. *Hekataios, Berossos, and Manethon.* We now need to examine how
Josephos fits within the Oriental tradition into which he placed him-

---

[141] So G. Vermes, *Scripture and Tradition in Judaism*, p. 124. Fitzmyer, *The Genesis Apocryphon of Qumran Cave 1*, pp. 6-14, esp. 10-11, emphasizes the unique nature
of 1QapGn. rather than calling it midrash.

[142] Examples from Jubilees and 1QapGn. include the settling of the ark on one
of the mountains of Ararat (Jub. 5:28; 1QapGn. 10.12; *AJ* 1.90 [MT and LXX
have "mountains"]); Noah atoned for the land (Jub. 6:2; 1QapGn. 10.13; *AJ*
1.98); and Noah drank with his children (Jub. 7:6; 1QapGn. 12.16; *AJ* 1.92).
Parallels with Pseudo-Philo have been collected by Louis H. Feldman in M.R.
James, *The Biblical Antiquities of Philo*, 2nd ed. with an introduction by Louis H.
Feldman. The Library of Biblical Studies (New York: Ktav Publishing House,
Inc., 1971), pp. LVIII-LXVI and *Josephus and Modern Scholarship*, pp. 419. On
Josephos' knowledge of oral tradition see 15.425. The most ambitious project com-
paring Josephos' exegetical treatments with those of the later rabbis is S. Rap-
paport, *Agada und Exegese bei Flavius Josephus* (Wien, 1930).

[143] E.g., Jub. 15:23-32, where the law of circumcision is stated in strongly nationalistic terms and 25:1-3, where Rebecca urges Jacob not to marry a Canaanite
in an addition to the biblical text; *LAB* 5:9, where Tamar decides to have intercourse with Israel rather than a Gentile (*contra* Gen. 38); 45:7, where the concubine
of the Benjamite of Judg. 19 is abused until she dies because she had formerly lain
with an Amalekite! 1QapGn. does not have the same open hostility.

self. That Josephos knew the founders of that tradition is beyond question. In fact, it is interesting to note that Josephos is a major source for the preservation of these very authors: Hekataios of Abdera, Berossos, and Manethon. The issues are: In what form did Josephos know these authors and what implications does that have for his own historical work?

We have already seen that Josephos attributes an entire work on the Jews to Hekataios.[144] He mentions him in *AJ* in 12.38, where he is dependent upon the report in Pseudo-Aristeas 31. For our purposes it is more important to know if he was familiar with the Αἰγυπτιακά. There are two very intriguing passages which suggest that he was. Twice Josephos recasts a biblical episode into the form of a colonization movement. The first instance is when God commands the post-diluvians to send out colonies (στέλλειν ἀποικίας, 1.110) to avoid friction and cultivate the earth. When they refuse, he again counsels them to colonize (αὐτοῖς συνεβούλευσε ποιεῖσθαι τὴν ἀποικίαν, 1.111). In open defiance they remain together and build a tower to escape a possible second deluge. God responds by making them speak different languages and dispersing them. As they went they founded colonies everywhere (τὰς ἀποικίας ποιησάμενοι πανταχοῦ, 1.120). The result was that "every continent was filled with them both in the interior and on the seaboard" (1.120). The second occasion is when Abraham sent away his sons through Keturah; not to distance them from Isaac as the biblical text suggests, but to establish colonies.[145] Why these transformations? The significance of the colonization movement is seen in the polemical epilogue to the first example: some of these people still retain their original names, but others have been altered by the Greeks who want to claim that they have descended from them (1.121). This immediately recalls the colonization section of Hekataios which must have comprised a significant portion of the original work.[146] While Josephos' transformation of these biblical episodes can not be claimed as proof that he knew Hekataios' Αἰγυπτιακά firsthand, the fact that he knew Hekataios' work and the close similarity makes us

---

[144] *AJ* 1.159, where he refers to a work on Abraham; *CA* 1.183; 214. Cf. 183-204; 2.43 for the work and our discussion in chapter three. He mentions Hekataios by name in *CA* 1.183, 186, 190, 204, 213, 214; 2.43.

[145] Gen. 25:5-6. *AJ* 1.139: Abraham ἀποικιῶν στόλους μηχανᾶται; 1.255: οἱ γὰρ ἐκ τῆς Κατούρας εἰς τὰς ἀποικίας ἐξεληλύθεισαν.

[146] Diodoros 1.28.1-29.6. See chapter three.

wonder.[147] At any rate we may affirm that he was aware of the type of cultural claims made by Hekataios and countered them with asseverations of his own.

We should point out that Josephos does mention Megasthenes.[148] The difficulty with the reference is that it is so brief that he may have only known him via an intermediate source. This becomes more certain when we realize that Megasthenes is included in a cluster of minor authors who are only mentioned, not as a sole reference which he quotes.[149] Almost all doubt is removed when we realize that Abydenos also quotes the same passage.[150] We must ask whether it is more likely that two authors would quote the same text from a single author or if they would draw from a common source which had already selected the quotation in a compilation. The latter seems more likely.

One of the most important authors—if the number of citations is any indicator of value—for Josephos was Berossos.[151] He underscored Berossos' reliability in these terms: ὁ ταῖς ἀρχαιοτάταις ἐπακολουθῶν ἀναγραφαῖς.[152] It hardly seems coincidental that Josephos also uses ἀναγραφή to refer to the records he translated.[153] Did the Jewish historian know the Babylonian chronicler directly[154] or indirectly through the Χαλδαϊκά of Alexander Polyhistor?[155]

---

[147] If Josephos only knew Pseudo-Hekataios, the force of this argument is reduced.

[148] *AJ* 10.227 repeated in *CA* 1.144. Josephos says that Megasthenes reported a campaign of Nebuchadnezzar in Libya and Iberia in the fourth book of his work.

[149] *AJ* 10.219-226, Berossos; 227, Megasthenes; 228, Diokles and Philostratos.

[150] *FGrH* 715 F 1b. The passage is preserved by Eusebios in his *Chronicle*. The church father openly identifies his source as Abydenos.

[151] The two authors to whom Josephos refers most frequently are Nikolaos of Damascus and Strabon who both served as sources for material in the final third of the work, especially Nikolaos. After them, comes Berossos who is cited more than any other author in the first two sections of *AJ* (Books 1-11): 1.93, 107ₓ 158; 10.20, 34b, 219-226. Josephos also quotes from him extensively in *Contra Apionem* 1.129-153. He mentions him by name in 129, 130, 134, 143, 145. Note also the textual gloss at 134.

[152] *CA* 1.130.

[153] *AJ* 1.17. He does not use a single phrase to describe the sacred records of the Jews when he speaks of them as his source: τὰ Ἑβραϊκὰ γράμματα, *AJ* 1.5; αἱ ἱεραὶ βίβλοι, *AJ* 1.26; 20.261; *CA* 1.1; οἱ ἀρχαῖοι βίβλιοι, *AJ* 10.218; τὰ ἱερὰ γράμματα, *CA* 1.54, 127.

[154] Freudenthal, *Alexander Polyhistor*, pp. 26-27; Schalit, *EncJud*, s.v. "Josephus Flavius," 10:258.

[155] Schwartz, *RE*, s.v. "Berossos," 315, through Polyhistor or Juba; Schnabel, *Berossos und die babylonisch-hellenistische Literatur*, pp. 166-167; Bickerman, "The Jewish Historian Demetrios," p. 77; Lambert, "Berossus and Babylonian Eschatology," p. 171.

That Josephos knew the Χαλδαϊκά of Polyhistor seems to be secured through his citation of the third Sibyl via Polyhistor.[156] The question is whether or not Josephos also knew the Βαβυλωνιακά of Berossos. He cites him as a main reference, not as a secondary source to which he only alludes.[157] The impression that he is citing directly is heightened by the fact that in the three texts where there is an actual quotation it is in *oratio recta* not *oratio obliqua* as we would expect from Polyhistor.[158] This is reinforced by the fact that in his *Chronicle* Eusebios quotes from both Polyhistor and Josephos for the same account of Berossos. Why if Josephos only reproduces Polyhistor?[159] Finally, Josephos knows of the Great Year.[160] Where did he learn about it? It is natural to think of Berossos, although he is by no means the only source from whom Josephos may have learned about it: he could have picked it up via Stoic philosophy.[161] Josephos' acquaintance with Berossos, however, makes him the leading candidate. The significance of this is that Polyhistor did not preserve the astronomical material of Berossos. Josephos therefore either learned of this directly from Berossos or through another intermediary. Although the evidence can be argued either way, I am inclined to think that Josephos knew Berossos directly.

The final major founder of apologetic historiography is Manethon. We have already seen that Josephos considered him the author of an ἀρχαιολογία since he ὁ τὴν Αἰγυπτίων ποιησάμενος ἀναγραφήν.[162] In *Contra Apionem* he is even more explicit about the

---

[156] *AJ* 1.118. Given Josephos' use of the plural "gods" rather than the singular in the text of the Sibyl, it appears likely that he is quoting from a pagan source. Since the third Sibylline oracle (97-161, 162-195, 196-294, 545-656, 657-808) dates from the second century B.C.E. (J.J. Collins, *OTP*, 1:354-355), a pagan between the mid-second century and the end of the first century combined the third Sibyl with the tower of Babel. The most likely candidate is Polyhistor. This has been proven by Bloch, *Die Quellen des Flavius Josephus*, pp. 54-55, who set the quotation of Josephos beside the original form and the quote from Polyhistor in Synkellos.
[157] He appears as the first author cited in *AJ* 1.93, 158; 10.219-226. He stands at the head of the list of authors with Manethon in 1.107. He comes after Herodotos in 10.20, where there appears to be a break in the textual tradition and his quote has fallen out. He is the sole reference in 10.34b.
[158] Although Schnabel, *Berossos und die babylonisch-hellenistische Literatur*, pp. 69-72, 166-167, pointed out that Josephos did turn the indirect speech of Polyhistor's quotation of the Sibyl back into direct speech.
[159] This was the decisive factor for Freudenthal, *Alexander Polyhistor*, p. 27.
[160] *AJ* 1.70, 106.
[161] On Berossos see *FGrH* 680 F21 (= Seneca, *QNat* 3.29.1) and our discussion in chapter four.
[162] *AJ* 1.107.

262 THE *ANTIQUITATES JUDAICAE* OF JOSEPHOS

nature of his work: γέγραφε γὰρ Ἑλλάδι φωνῇ τὴν πάτριον ἱστορίαν ἐκ δέλτων ἱερῶν, ὥς φησιν αὐτός, μεταφράσας.[163] Josephos has Manethon's account in mind on at least two occasions in *AJ* where he does not name him. This is evident from the parallels in *CA* where he explicitly cites him. In 2.177 he apologizes for giving the names of Jacob's sons but feels compelled to do so in order to counter the charge that the Jews are not Mesopotamians but Egyptians.[164] The related charge that they were lepers is refuted in 3.265-268 in much the same terms as it is in *CA* 1.279-287.[165] As these examples indicate, the real case for Josephos' knowledge of Manethon is in *CA* not *AJ*. Here there are two major blocks of material: 1.73-105 and 1.227-253.[166] The first deals with the Hyksos and the second with the band of lepers. Given the amount of material involved and the prominence Josephos gives it, I see no reason to think that the Jewish historian depended upon a digest in this instance. It is much more likely that he had read Manethon—perhaps in an edited form—himself.[167]

It thus seems likely that Josephos knew Manethon directly and probably also Berossos. He knew Polyhistor's Χαλδαϊκά as his citation of the third Sibyl and knowledge of Megasthenes establish. He was aware of the work of Hekataios and thought it significant enough to engage it polemically. This raises the issue of the significance of these authors for the *Antiquitates*, i.e., how did apologetic historiography affect the shaping of *AJ*?

It began at the most fundamental level. Theoretically, *AJ* shares the same framework which governed the writing of Berossos' *Babyloniaka* and Manethon's *Aigyptiaka*. Each author saw himself as a member of a misrepresented subgroup within the larger world. As

---

[163] *CA* 1.73. Cf. also 1.228: ὁ τὴν Αἰγυπτιακὴν ἱστορίαν ἐκ τῶν ἱερῶν γραμμάτων μεθερμηνεύειν ὑπεσχημένος.

[164] *CA* 1.223-226, states the charge. Josephos prefers to sidestep this accusation by turning the tables on his source. In 1.104, 229, 252-253, 278, he argues that Manethon provides the evidence that the Jews are not Egyptians by his account of the Hyksos (75). He does not deal with this issue from the standpoint of the second less savory version.

[165] Both texts claim that it is absurd to charge Moses with leprosy in light of the legislation he gave on it. See Lev. 13-14; Num. 12:10-15.

[166] He is mentioned by name in 1.73, 74, 87, 91, 93, 103, 104, 105, 228, 251, 252, 270, 278, 287, 288, 296, 300; 2.1, 16.

[167] The text of Manethon is fraught with difficulties. See the discussion in chapter four.

custodians of the groups' traditions (priests), they undertook the task of setting their own story out before the Hellenistic world. This meant insisting upon native records as the source for the history.[168] The scope of the presentation was also clear within the tradition: he would tell Israel's story from the beginning of its records until a point approximately contemporaneous with his own, a task which was broader than a retelling of his own scriptures—as it was for each of the writers within the tradition. Embraced within this scope was an insistence upon the antiquity of the group, a claim intended to win respect. It also meant "translating" them from their original language into Greek. The task of "translating" was not simply to offer a literal rendition of the native sources into Greek, but to Hellenize them. It is at this point that Josephos towers over the founders of apologetic historiography. Yet it would be unfair to compare them on this matter since Josephos had the advantage of writing after not only Berossos and Manethon, but authors within his own ethnic group who had written within the tradition.

   c. *The Hellenistic Jewish Historians.* These authors were the Hellenistic Jewish historians. We must now ask what—if any—role they played in the formation and nature of *AJ*. First we must determine whether Josephos knew them and if so, in what form? Once again, the most contradictory opinions have been offered: Josephos did not know them,[169] he knew them through Alexander Polyhistor,[170] he and they stem from a common Hellenistic Jewish tradition,[171] and he knew them directly.[172]

---

[168] Rajak, "Josephus and the 'Archaeology' of the Jews," pp. 473-474, pointed out that Josephos differed here. Berossos and Manethon had to select and compile from their native records; for Josephos the scriptures had already done this. He did not chose among documents, but among events within documents.

[169] Wacholder, *Eupolemus*, pp. 52-53 n. 107, who as noted in n. 5 above does think that the tradition influenced Josephos. He does not explain how Josephos can be ignorant of the historians and stand under the influence of the tradition.

[170] Freudenthal, *Alexander Polyhistor*, pp. 34, 182, 183, 184, 187-188; Emil Schürer, *The Literature of the Jewish People in the Time of Jesus*, reprint ed., edited with an intro. by Nahum N. Glatzer (New York: Schocken Books, 1972), p. 197; Jacoby, *FGrH*, 3b:257 (occasional use); Denis, *Introduction aux Pseudépigraphes Grecs d'Ancien Testament*, p. 246; and Attridge, "Josephus and His Works," p. 211 (very hesitatingly).

[171] Hölscher, *RE*, s.v. "Josephus," 9:1963-1964.

[172] Bloch, *Die Quellen des Flavius Josephus*, pp. 53, 55-56. N. Walter, "Zur Überlieferung einiger Reste früher jüdisch-hellenistischer Literatur bei Josephus, Clemens, und Euseb.," in *Studia Patristica* 7. TU 92 (Berlin: Akademie Verlag, 1966), p. 316, argues that Josephos did not know Polyhistor and leaves open the issue of whether or not he knew individual historians directly.

Josephos alludes to or mentions the tradition on three different occasions.[173] In *BJ* 1.17, he explains why he thought it redundant to write an ἀρχαιολογία: ἐπειδήπερ καὶ Ἰουδαίων πολλοὶ πρὸ ἐμοῦ τὰ τῶν προγόνων συνετάξαντο μετ' ἀκριβείας καί τινες Ἑλλήνων ἐκεῖνα τῇ πατρίῳ φωνῇ μεταβαλόντες οὐ πολὺ τῆς ἀληθείας διήμαρτον. Here Josephos acknowledges the presence of numerous Jewish treatments of the past although—according to him—they were written in a native language and *translated* into Greek. He again alludes to these Jewish authors in *CA* 1.41 where he tells us that the third time period (Artaxerxes-the present) has been recorded in detail. The Greek translators he has in mind are actually specified in *CA* 1.218: ὁ μέντοι Φαληρεὺς Δημήτριος καὶ Φίλων ὁ πρεσβύτερος καὶ Εὐπόλεμος οὐ πολὺ τῆς ἀληθείας διήμαρτον· οἷς συγγιγνώσκειν ἄξιον. He then explains why they are excused: οὐ γὰρ ἐνῆν αὐτοῖς μετὰ πάσης ἀκριβείας τοῖς ἡμετέροις γράμμασι παρακολουθεῖν. It is likely that the Demetrios of this passage is not Demetrios of Phalerum as stated, but the Hellenistic Jewish historian. It is striking that Josephos considers these "Greeks" to have translated Jewish records.

Yet how can Josephos say that Demetrios, Philo the elder, and Eupolemos are Greeks?! One obvious possibility is that Josephos only knew these authors at a distance through some intermediary, i.e., Alexander Polyhistor.[174] He may have assumed that they were Greeks since they wrote in Greek. After all, Greeks had written about Jews.[175] On the other hand, Josephos is loathe to betray sources which served as a model and may be intentionally misleading us in order to present himself as the *primus* to write a Jewish ἀρχαιολογία in Greek.[176] He is certainly not above such mendacity. Ben Zion Wacholder has added yet a third option: Josephos did not consider them Greeks, but criticized them for failing to use the

---

[173] It is possible to interpret *AJ* 20.265 to also allude to these. The difficulty is in knowing whether the training which only two or three Jews have successfully completed is the mastery of both Greek and Jewish wisdom or only the latter. Even if it is the former, Josephos gives us no indication of whom he might be thinking. (Philo?)

[174] Rajak, "Josephus and the 'Archaeology' of the Jews," p. 474, thinks that this is proof that Josephos did not know the Hellenistic Jewish historians. She does not, however, address the issue of whether he knew them through Polyhistor.

[175] So, for example, Teukros of Kyzikos, *FGrH* 274, wrote a six volume Ἰουδαϊκὴ ἱστορία in the first century B.C.E.

[176] So Bartlett, *Jews in the Hellenistic World*, p. 56 and Schürer, *The History of the Jewish People in the Age of Jesus Christ*, 3:519.

Hebrew text.[177] This will not stand scrutiny. Josephos has just told us that a good number of Greeks have mentioned the Jews (215). He has then given a list (216) and now proceeds to comment on the accuracy of the different Greek historians: most have strayed wide of the mark (217), but these are exceptional (218). We are thus left to decide whether Josephos was ignorant or mendacious. We can only answer this by examining Josephos' relationship to the fragments.

Our examination will deal with possible points of contact between Josephos and the Hellenistic Jewish historians. It will concentrate on those points in which Josephos and the earlier writer agree and which diverge from the biblical text. Disagreements—which are extensive in every case involving material not exclusively preserved by Josephos—will be noted only where they constitute a weighty counterpart to significant agreements.

i. *Demetrios*. Among the fragments of Demetrios there are three possible points of contact. The first occurs in the third fragment where Demetrios is summarizing the career of Moses. Speaking of Moses and Zipporah he wrote:

Demetrios F 3	Josephos *AJ* 2.257
κατοικεῖν δὲ αὐτοὺς	
Μαδιὰμ πόλιν,	εἴς τε πόλιν Μαδιανὴν
	ἀφικόμενος πρὸς μὲν τῇ
	Ἐρυθρᾷ θαλάσσῃ κειμένην
ἣν ἀπὸ ἑνὸς	ἐπώνυμον δ' ἑνὸς
τῶν 'Αβραὰμ	τῶν 'Αβράμῳ
παίδων ὀνομασθῆναι	γενομένων ἐκ Καταούρας
	υἱῶν

Here it is possible that both Demetrios and Josephos, or his source, have made a similar deduction independently since the LXX's Μαδιαμ (= MT מדין) represents both a son of Keturah and the land of Moses' exile.[178]

The second instance is the account of how the Israelites received their weapons when leaving Egypt. The MT of Ex. 13:18 says: וחמשים עלי בני ישראל מארץ מצרים which the LXX renders as: πέμπτῃ δὲ γενεᾷ ἀνέβησαν οἱ υἱοῖ Ισραηλ ἐκ γῆς Αἰγύπτου. The problem is how are we to understand חמשים? The term appears to

---

[177] *Eupolemus*, p. 3.
[178] Gen. 25:2; Ex. 2:15.

denote something like "in battle array"[179] and was so understood by Targum Onqelos, the Peshitta, and the Vulgate.[180] The translators of the LXX, however, associated it with חמש, "five," and offered their interpretation accordingly. With the LXX before him, Demetrios had to raise the question of how the Israelites obtained their weapons. He ingenuously concluded: φαίνεται οὖν τοὺς μὴ κατακλυσθέντας τοῖς ἐκείνων ὅπλοις χρήσασθαι.[181] Josephos follows this same tradition. In *AJ* 2.321 he describes the Egyptians' thoughts of easy victory since the Israelites ἀνόπλων τε ὄντων. The Israelites themselves are aware of their plight: ὅπλων τε σπανίζοντες εἰ καὶ μάχεσθαι δόξειεν αὐτοῖς.[182] In 2.349 he relates the washing ashore of the Egyptians' weapons and Moses' deduction that God's providence had supplied them ὅπως μηδὲ ὅπλων ὦσιν ἄποροι; a thought he repeats in 4.44 when he states that God ὁ γυμνοῖς οὖσι τὴν ἐξ ὅπλων ἀσφαλείαν χαρισάμενος. Here we have a clear-cut case of a common exegetical tradition. The major difference is that Demetrios cast his into the form of a *quaestio et solutio*, whereas Josephos wrote a narrative.[183] The tradition, however, is not limited to Demetrios and Josephos: it is also attested in the *Exagoge* of Ezekiel[184] and the Wisdom of Solomon.[185] What may responsibly be said is that Josephos knew the tradition which is first attested in Demetrios.[186]

The third and final point is a chronological note. In the second

---

[179] E.g., Francis Brown, S.R. Driver, and Charles Briggs, *A Hebrew and English Lexicon of the Old Testament* (Oxford: Clarendon Press, 1906), s.v. חמש and Ludwig Koehler and Walter Baumgartner, *Lexicon in Veteris Testamenti Libros*, 2nd ed. (Leiden: E.J. Brill, 1958), s.v. חמש.

[180] Onqelos reads: ומזרזין סליקו בני ישראל מארעא דמצרים; the Peshitta: ܡܙܝܢܝ ; the Vulgate: armati.

[181] F 5.

[182] *AJ* 2.326.

[183] Freudenthal, *Alexander Polyhistor*, p. 46, thought that this constituted a major shift in perspective: "Die Vergleichung mit Josephus, der wohl aus Demetrios dieselbe Antwort, aber als historisches Factum mitteilt (Ant. II 16, 6), zeigt auch hier die bescheidene Zurückhaltung unseres Chronisten gegenüber der unberechtigten Sicherheit des jüngeren Geschichtschreibers."

[184] *Exagoge* 210: αὐτοὶ δ' ἄνοπλοι πάντες εἰς μάχην χέρας. The *Exagoge* should be dated to the second half of the second century B.C.E. See Howard J. Jacobson, *The 'Exagoge' of Ezekiel* (Cambridge: Cambridge University Press, 1983), pp. 5-13.

[185] Sap. 10:20: διὰ τοῦτο δίκαιοι ἐσύκευσαν ἀσεβεῖς. For details see David Winston, *The Wisdom of Solomon*. AB 43 (Garden City, New York: Doubleday & Company, Inc., 1979), pp. 221-222.

[186] Freudenthal, *Alexander Polyhistor*, p. 46, argued for dependence here.

fragment, Demetrios indicated that 215 years elapsed from the call of Abraham until the descent into Egypt—a deduction which divides the 430 years of Ex. 12:40-41 into two equal halves and thus estimates the Egyptian sojourn at 215 years. Josephos also calculates the time from Abraham's entrance into Canaan until Jacob's entrance into Egypt at 215 years.[187] He does this at the point in his narrative where he is summarizing Ex. 12:40. We have already noted that the LXX and SP both add "in Canaan" to the text of Ex. 12:40 and make the 430 years the time from Abraham until the exodus. It is therefore possible that Demetrios and Josephos both made independent deductions from the LXX. There are, however, two other factors which must be weighed. One, this statement of Josephos is at odds with his earlier one that the Israelites endured hardship in Egypt 400 years.[188] This conflict suggests that Josephos did not have his own chronological system fully worked out and employed other sources in his narrative.[189] Two, it is interesting that in a statement which is giving the length of time in Egypt, Josephos gives the wrong half: instead of stating that the Israelites remained in Egypt for 215 of the 430 years, he says that the patriarchal period lasted 215 years. Why? Is it in his source?[190]

Freudenthal also thought he found a second example of concurrence in the time between captivities. Demetrios counted 128 years and six months between the carrying away of Israel and the exile of Judah.[191] Josephos computed 130 years, six months, and ten days[192]: figures which Freudenthal argued he could harmonize.[193] There are, nonetheless, two problems: one, we do not have verbal agreement; and two, both figures could well be deduced from the biblical text independently.

Did Josephos know Demetrios?[194] He certainly knew some of the

---

[187] *AJ* 2.318.

[188] *AJ* 2.204.

[189] It is, of course, also possible that Josephos was simply sloppy and did not bother to harmonize his own calculations made at different times in his narrative.

[190] I. Broydé, *The Jewish Encyclopedia*, s.v. "Demetrius," 4:513, thought that Josephos used Demetrios' chronological system. One major difficulty here is that Josephos' chronology itself is problematic.

[191] F 6.1.

[192] *AJ* 10.185.

[193] *Alexander Polyhistor*, pp. 59-61, especially the note on 61.

[194] Knowledge of Demetrios: Freudenthal, *Alexander Polyhistor*, pp. 63, 77; Denis, *Introduction aux Pseudépigraphes Grecs d'Ancien Testament*, p. 249, who allows for

exegetical traditions which are first attested in the latter.

ii. *Artapanos*. There are more points of contacts with Artapanos than with any other historian. In the Abraham fragment (F 1), Artapanos calls the king of Egypt Φαρεώθης; Josephos dubs him Φαραώθης.[195] This is significant because the LXX has Φαραω. Abraham's mission in Egypt is similar. Artapanos claims that Abraham τὴν ἀστρολογίαν αὐτόν (the king—GES) διδάξαι; Josephos says that he τήν τε ἀριθμητικὴν αὐτοῖς χαρίζεται καὶ τὰ περὶ ἀστρονομίαν παραδίδωσι.[196] This was a tradition shared by several different authors as we have already seen.[197] Abraham's connection to astrology actually became one of the main items known by later pagans about Abraham.[198] It must have been fairly widespread. The other idiosyncratic features of the first fragment have no parallel in Josephos.[199]

The second fragment (Joseph) illustrates the relationship more fully. Josephos appears to follow Artapanos when he has Joseph go down into Egypt through the agency of he Arabs.[200] However, a major difference emerges in their handling of this tradition: Artapanos has Joseph willingly go down, whereas Josephos remains truer to the biblical text by having him sold. After Joseph has come to power, both authors whitewash his land policies. Again they do it in divergent ways: in Artapanos Joseph is a land reformer,[201]

---

direct knowledge "peut-être". No knowledge: Wacholder, *EncJud*, s.v. "Demetrius," 5:1491.

[195] This is the standard form in Josephos who also employs Φαραώνης, Φαραών, and Φαραώ.

[196] *AJ* 1.167. Feldman, "Hellenizations in Josephus' *Jewish Antiquities*: The Portrait of Abraham," p. 139, thinks that Josephos "has elevated Abraham's stature by having him teach the Egyptian philosophers and scientists" rather than the king. Cf. also his earlier "Abraham the Greek Philosopher in Josephus," *TAPA* 99 (1968): 154.

[197] Pseudo-Eupolemos F 1.8 and F 2.

[198] Vettius Valens, *Anthologiae* 2.29 (second century C.E.) in Stern, *GLAJJ*, 2:173-175; Firmicus Maternus, *Mathesis*, IV, Prooemium 5; 17.2, 5; 18.1 (first half of fourth century C.E.) in Stern, *GLAJJ*, 2:492-494; Julian, *Contra Galilaeos*, 356C (331-363 C.E.) in Stern, *GLAJJ*, 2:502-572; *Scriptores Historiae Augustae*, Alexander Severus, 29:2 (end of fourth century C.E.) in Stern, *GLAJJ*, 2:631. On Abraham among pagans see Jeffrey Siker, "Abraham in Graeco-Roman Paganism," *JSJ* 18 (1987): 188-208, especially 193-197.

[199] Josephos omits the etymological explanation of the Jews as Hermiouth (cf. *AJ* 1.146, where they are named Hebrews after Heber), the time of Abraham's stay as twenty years, and the permanency of some of Abraham's descendants in Egypt.

[200] F 2.1; *AJ* 2.32. Both trace the Arabs to Abraham. Cf. Gen. 37:25.

[201] F 2.2.

while in Josephos he is motivated by knowledge of the impending drought.[202] Our first impression is that Josephos has not wandered as far from the biblical text. Then we read that he returned the land to the original owners once the crisis had passed![203] A third parallel is more impressive. I have set out the texts which describe where the Israelites settled in Egypt in a chart:

Locale	Text
ἐν γῇ Ραμεσση	Gen. 46:11, LXX
ἐν τῇ Ἡλίου πόλει καὶ Σάει	Artapanos 2.3
ἐν Ἡλίου πόλει	Josephos *AJ* 2.188

The most important fragment is the third (Moses). The same type of pattern which we witnessed in fragment two reappears here. Both toy with the theme of Egyptian persecution, but in different ways: Artapanos says that the Jews were forced to wear linen as a means of marking them out for harassment, while Josephos simply expands the building tasks.[204] Both add the detail that Pharaoh's daughter was barren,[205] an exegetical tradition also attested by Philo.[206] The most important expansion which the two share in common is the Ethiopian campaign. Since it has provoked so much discussion, I have set the two accounts out in a synoptic fashion (pp. 270-276).

The initial impression a reading of this synopsis makes is that we have one story told in two very different ways. The structure of the stories is essentially the same. After the Ethiopians have successfully invaded Egypt, the Egyptians appointed Moses general of a retaliatory incursion in the hope that he would be slain. Contrary to their expectations, Moses was successful. His victory, however, only led to envy and a plot against his life. When Moses learned of this assassination, he fled.

Once we have recognized the same literary plot, the differences demand attention. In the first place there are no verbal parallels. Not only that, but almost all of the episodes differ. These begin with the cast of characters. In Artapanos the struggle is between Moses and Chenephres (3.7); in Josephos the conflict is between the Egyptian scribes (243) and the king (255-256) on the one hand and Moses

[202] *AJ* 2.88.
[203] *AJ* 2.191-192.
[204] F 3.20; *AJ* 2.203.
[205] F 3.3; *AJ* 2.232.
[206] *Mos.* 1.13.

The Ethiopian Campaign

Artapanos 3.7-18	Josephos AJ 2.239-256
7 τὸν δὲ Χενεφρῆν ὁρῶντα τὴν ἀρετὴν τοῦ Μωῦσου φθονῆσαι αὐτῷ καὶ ζητεῖν αὐτὸν ἐπ' εὐλόγῳ αἰτίᾳ τινὶ ἀνελεῖν.	Cf. 255

Josephos AJ 2.239-256 (continued)

239 Αἰθίοπες, πρόσοικοι δ' εἰσὶ τοῖς Αἰγυπτίοις,
ἐμβαλόντες εἰς χώραν αὐτῶν
ἔφερον καὶ ἦγον τὰ τῶν Αἰγυπτίων.
οἱ δ' ὑπ' ὀργῆς στρατεύουσιν ἐπ' αὐτοὺς
ἀμυνούμενοι τῆς καταφρονήσεως,
καὶ τῇ μάχῃ κρατηθέντες οἱ μὲν αὐτῶν ἔπεσον
οἱ δ' αἰσχρῶς εἰς τὴν οἰκείαν διεσώθησαν φυγόντες.

Artapanos

καὶ δή ποτε τῶν Αἰθιόπων ἐπιστρατευσαμένων τῇ Αἰγύπτῳ

240 ἐπηκολούθησαν δὲ διώκοντες Αἰθίοπες
καὶ μαλακίας ὑπολαβόντες τὸ μὴ κρατεῖν ἁπάσης τῆς Αἰγύπτου
τῆς χώρας
ἐπὶ πλεῖον ἥπτοντο
καὶ γευσάμενοι τῶν ἀγαθῶν οὐκέτ' αὐτῶν ἀπείχοντο,
ὡς δὲ τὰ γειτνιῶντα μέρη πρῶτον αὐτοῖς ἐπερχομένων
οὐκ ἐτόλμων ἀντιστρατεύειν,
προὔβησαν ἄχρι Μέμφεως καὶ τῆς θαλάσσης
οὐδεμίας τῶν πόλεων ἀντέχειν δυνηθείσης.

241 τῷ δὲ κακῷ πιεζόμενοι πρὸς χρησμοὺς Αἰγύπτιοι καὶ μαντείας
τρέπονται·

τὸν Χενεφρῆν ὑπολαβόντα εὑρηκέναι καιρὸν εὔθετον
πέμψαι τὸν Μωῦσον ἐπ' αὐτοὺς στρατηγὸν μετὰ δυνάμεως·

συμβουλεύσαντος δ' αὐτοῖς τοῦ θεοῦ συμμάχῳ χρήσασθαι τῷ
Ἑβραίῳ
κελεύει ὁ Βασιλεὺς τὴν θυγατέρα
παρασχεῖν τὸν Μωυσῆν στρατηγὸν αὐτῷ γενησόμενον.

242 ἡ δὲ ὅρκους ποιησαμένῳ, ὥστε μηδὲν διαθεῖναι κακόν,
παραδίδωσιν ἀντὶ μεγάλης μὲν εὐεργεσίας κρίνουσα τὴν συμ-
μαχίαν
κακίζουσα δὲ τοὺς ἱερέας,

The Ethiopian Campaign

Artapanos 3.7-18	Josephos *AJ* 2.239-256
	εἰ κτεῖναι προαγορεύσαντες αὐτὸν ὡς πολέμιον οὐκ ἠδοῦτο νῦν χρῄζοντες αὐτοῦ τῆς ἐπικουρίας.
	243 Μουσῆς δὲ ὑπό τε τῆς Θερμούθιδος παρακληθεὶς καὶ ὑπὸ τοῦ βασιλέως ἡδέως προσδέχεται τὸ ἔργον. ἔχαιρον δ' οἱ ἱερογραμματεῖς ἀμφοτέρων τῶν ἐθνῶν, Αἰγυπτίων μὲν ὡς τοὺς τε πολεμίους τῇ ἐκείνου κρατήσοντες ἀρετῇ καὶ τὸν Μουσῆν ταὐτῷ δόλῳ κατεργασόμενοι, οἱ δὲ τῶν Ἑβραίων ὡς φυγεῖν αὐτοῖς ἐσομένου τοὺς Αἰγυπτίους διὰ τὸ Μουσῆν αὐτοῖς στρατηγεῖν.
τὸ δὲ τῶν γεωργῶν αὐτῷ συστῆσαι πλῆθος, ὑπολαβόντα ῥᾳδίως αὐτὸν διὰ τὴν τῶν στρατιωτῶν ἀσθένειαν ὑπὸ τῶν πολεμίων ἀναιρεθήσεσθαι.	244 ὁ δὲ φθάσας πρὶν ἢ καὶ πυθέσθαι τοὺς πολεμίους τὴν ἔφοδον αὐτοῦ τὸν στρατὸν ἀναλαβὼν ἦγεν οὐ διὰ τοῦ ποταμοῦ ποιησάμενος τὴν ἐλασίαν, ἀλλὰ διὰ γῆς. ἔνθα τῆς αὐτοῦ συνέσεως θαυμαστὴν ἐπίδειξιν ἐποιήσατο· 245 τῆς γὰρ γῆς ὁπόσης χαλεπῆς ὁδευθῆναι διὰ πλῆθος ἑρπετῶν, παμφορωτάτη γάρ ἐστι τούτων, ὡς καὶ τὰ παρ' ἄλλοις οὐκ ὄντα μόνη τρέφειν δυνάμει τε καὶ κακίᾳ καὶ τῷ τῆς ὄψεως ἀσυνήθει διαφέροντα, τινὰ δ' αὐτῶν ἐστι καὶ πετεινὰ ὡς λανθάνοντα μὲν ἀπὸ γῆς κακουργεῖν καὶ μὴ προϊδομένους ἀδικεῖν ὑπερπετῆ γενόμενα, νοεῖ πρὸς ἀσφάλειαν καὶ ἀβλαβῆ πορείαν τοῦ στρατεύματος στρατήγημα θαυμαστόν· 246 πλέγματα γὰρ ἐμφερῆ κιβωτοῖς ἐκ βίβλου κατασκευάσας

The Ethiopian Campaign

Artapanos 3.7-18	Josephos *AJ* 2.239-256
Cf. 9	καὶ πληρώσας ἴβεων ἐκόμιζε. πολεμιώτατον δ' ἐστὶν ὄφεσι τοῦτο τὸ ζῷον· φεύγουσί τε γὰρ ἐπερχομένας καὶ ἐφιστάμενοι καθάπερ ὑπ' ἐλάφων ἁρπαζόμενοι καταπίνονται· χειροήθεις δ' εἰσὶν αἱ ἴβεις καὶ πρὸς μόνον τὸ τῶν ὄφεων γένος ἄγριοι.
	247 καὶ περὶ μὲν τούτων παρίημι νῦν γράφειν οὐκ ἀγνοοῦτον τῶν Ἑλλήνων τῆς ἴβιδος τὸ εἶδος. ὡς οὖν εἰς τὴν γῆν ἐνέβαλε τὴν θηριοτρόφον, ταύταις ἀπεμάχετο τὴν τῶν ἑρπετῶν φύσιν ἐπαφεὶς αὐτοῖς καὶ προπολεμούσαις χρώμενος. τοῦτον οὖν ὁδεύσας τὸν τρόπον οὐδὲ προμαθοῦσι παρῆν τοῖς Αἰθίοψι,
8 τὸν δὲ Μώϋσον ἐλθόντα ἐπὶ τὸν Ἑρμοπολίτην ὀνομαζόμενον νομόν, ἔχοντα περὶ δέκα μυριάδας γεωργῶν, αὐτοῦ καταστατοπεδεῦσαι· πέμψαι δὲ στρατηγοὺς τοὺς προκαθεδουμένους τῆς χώρας, οὓς δὴ πλεονεκτεῖν ἐπιφανῶς κατὰ τὰς μάχας·	248 καὶ συμβαλὼν αὐτοῖς κρατεῖ τῇ μάχῃ καὶ τῶν ἐλπίδων, ἃς εἶχον ἐπὶ τοὺς Αἰγυπτίους, ἀφαιρεῖται τάς τε πόλεις αὐτῶν ἐπῄει καταστρεφόμενος, καὶ φόνος πολὺς τῶν Αἰθιόπων ἐπράττετο.
λέγειν δὲ φησιν Ἡλιουπολίτας γενέσθαι τὸν πόλεμον τοῦτον ἔτη δέκα.	καὶ τῆς διὰ Μωυσῆν εὐπραγίας γευσάμενον τὸ τῶν Αἰγυπτίων στράτευμα πονεῖν οὐκ ἔκαμνεν, ὡς περὶ ἀνδραποδισμοῦ καὶ παντελοῦς ἀναστάσεως τὸν κίνδυνον εἶναι τοῖς Αἰθίοψι· 249 καὶ τέλος συνελαθέντες εἰς Σαβὰν πόλιν βασίλειον οὖσαν τῆς Αἰθιοπίας,

The Ethiopian Campaign

Artapanos 3.7-18	Josephos *AJ* 2.239-256

ἦν ὕστερον Καμβύσης Μερόην ἐπωνόμασεν
ἀδελφῆς ἰδίας τοῦτο καλουμένης, ἐπολιορκοῦντο.
ἦν δὲ δυσπολιόρκητον σφόδρα τὸ χωρίον
τοῦ τε Νείλου περιέχοντος αὐτὴν καὶ κυκλουμένου
ποταμῶν τε ἄλλων Ἀστάπου καὶ Ἀσταβόρα
δύσμαχον τοῖς πειρομένοις διαβαίνειν τὸ ῥεῦμα ποιούντων·

250 ἡ γὰρ πόλις ἐντὸς οὖσα νῆσος οἰκεῖται
τεῖχούς τε αὐτῇ καρτεροῦ περιηγμένου
καὶ πρὸς μὲν τοὺς πολεμίους πρόβλημα τοὺς ποταμοὺς ἔχουσα
χώματά τε μεγάλα μεταξὺ τοῦ τείχους,
ὥστε ἀνεπίκλυστον εἶναι βιαιότερον ὑπὸ πλήθώρας φερομένων,
ἅπερ καὶ τοῖς περαιωσαμένοις τοὺς ποταμοὺς
ἄπορον ἐποίει τῆς πόλεως τὴν ἅλωσιν.

251 ψέροντι τοίνυν ἀηδῶς τῷ Μωυσεῖ τὴν τοῦ στρατεύματος ἀργίαν,
εἰς χεῖρας γὰρ οὐκ ἐτόλμων ἀπαντᾶν οἱ πολέμιοι,
συνέτυχέ τι τοιοῦτον.

252 Θάρβις θυγάτηρ ἦν τοῦ Αἰθιόπων βασιλέως.
αὕτη τὸν Μωυσὴν πλησίον τοῖς τείχεσι προσάγοντα τὴν στρατιὰν
καὶ μαχόμενον γενναίως ἀποσκοποῦσα
καὶ τῆς ἐπινοίας τῶν ἐγχειρήσεων θαυμάζουσα,
καὶ τοῖς τε Αἰγυπτίοις αἴτιον ἀπεγνωκόσιν ἤδη τὴν ἐλευθερίαν
τῆς εὐπραγίας ὑπολαμβάνουσα
καὶ τοῖς Αἰθίοψιν αὐχοῦσιν
ἐπὶ τοῖς κατ' αὐτῶν κατορθουμένος τοῦ περὶ τῶν ἐσχάτων
κινδύνου,
εἰς ἔρωτα δεινὸν ὤλισθεν αὐτοῦ
καὶ περιόντος τοῦ πάθους πέμπει πρὸς αὐτὸν τῶν οἰκετῶν τοὺς
πιστοτάτους
διαλεγομένη περὶ γάμου.

The Ethiopian Campaign

Artapanos 3. 7-18	Josephos AJ 2.239-256
	253 προσδεξαμένου δὲ τὸν λόγον ἐπὶ τῷ παραδοῦναι τὴν πόλιν καὶ ποιησαμένου πίστεις ἐνόρκους ἦ μὴν ἄξεσθαι γυναῖκα καὶ κρατήσαντα τῆς πόλεως μὴ παραβήσεσθαι τὰς συνθήκας, φθάνει τὸ ἔργον τοὺς λόγους. καὶ μετὰ τὴν ἀναίρεσιν τῶν Αἰθιόπων εὐχαριστήσας τῷ θεῷ συνετέλει τὸν γάμον Μωυσῆς
9 τοὺς οὖν περὶ τὸν Μώϋσον διὰ τὸ μέγεθος τῆς στρατιᾶς πόλιν ἐν τούτῳ κτίσαι τῷ τόνῳ καὶ τὴν ἶβιν ἐν αὐτῇ καθιερῶσαι, διὰ τὸ ταύτην τὰ βλάπτοντα ζῷα τοὺς ἀνθρώπους ἀναιρεῖν· προσαγορεῦσαι δὲ αὐτὴν Ἑρμοῦ πόλιν.	Cf. 246-247
10 οὕτω δὴ τοὺς Αἰθίοπας, καίπερ ὄντας πολεμίους, στέρξαι τὸν Μώϋσον ὥστε καὶ τὴν περιτομὴν τῶν αἰδοίων παρ' ἐκείνου μαθεῖν· οὐ μόνον δὲ τούτους, ἀλλὰ καὶ τοὺς ἱερεῖς ἅπαντας.	
	καὶ τοὺς Αἰγυπτίους ἀπήγαγεν εἰς τὴν ἑαυτῶν
	254 οἱ δ' ἐξ ὧν ἐσώζοντο ὑπὸ Μωυσέος μῖσος ἐκ τούτων πρὸς αὐτὸν ἀνελάμβανον καὶ θερμότερον ἅπτεσθαι τῶν κατ' αὐτοῦ βουλευμάτων ἠξίουν, ὑπονοοῦντες μὲν μὴ διὰ τὴν εὐπραγίαν νεωτερίσειε κατὰ τὴν Αἴγυπτον, διδάσκοντες δὲ τὸν βασιλέα περὶ τῆς σφαγῆς.
	255 ὁ δὲ καὶ καθ' αὑτὸν μὲν εἶχε τὴν τοῦ πράγματος ἔπινοιαν ὑπό τε φθόνου τῆς Μωυσέος στρατηγίας καὶ ὑπὸ δέους ταπεινώσεως,
11 τὸν δὲ Χενεφρῆν λυθέντος τοῦ πολέμου λόγῳ μὲν αὐτὸν ἀποδέξασθαι ἔργῳ δὲ ἐπιβουλεύειν. Cf. 13	
παρελόμενον γοῦν αὐτοῦ τοὺς ὄχλους τοὺς μὲν ἐπὶ τὰ ὅρια τῆς Αἰθιοπίας πέμψαι προφυλακῆς χάριν,	

The Ethiopian Campaign

Artapanos 3.7-18	Josephos *AJ* 2.239-256
τοῖς δὲ προστάξαι τὸν ἐν Διὸς πόλει ναὸν ἐξ ὀπτῆς πλίνθου κατεσκευασμένον καθαιρεῖν, ἕτερον δὲ λίθινον κατασκευάσαι τὸ πλησίον ὄρος λατομήσαντας· τάξαι δὲ ἐπὶ τῆς οἰκοδομίας ἐπιστάτην Ναχέρωτα. 12 τὸν δὲ ἐλθόντα μετὰ Μωύσου εἰς Μέμφιν πυθέσθαι παρ' αὐτοῦ εἴ τι ἄλλο ἐστὶν εὔχρηστον τοῖς ἀνθρώποις· τὸν δὲ φάναι γένος τῶν βοῶν, διὰ τὸ τὴν γῆν ὑπὸ τούτων ἀροῦσθαι· τὸν δὲ Χενεφρῆν, προσαγορεύσαντα ταῦρον Ἄπιν, κελεῦσαι ἱερὸν αὐτοῦ τοὺς ὄχλους καθιδρύσασθαι καὶ τὰ ζῷα τὰ καθιερωθέντα ὑπὸ τοῦ Μωύσου κελεύειν ἐκεῖ φέροντας θάπτειν, κατακρύπτειν θέλοντα τὰ τοῦ Μωύσου ἐπινοήματα. 13 ἀποξενωσάντων δὲ αὐτῶν τῶν Αἰγυπτίων ὁρκωμοτῆσαι τοὺς φίλους μὴ ἐξαγγεῖλαι τῷ Μωύσῳ τὴν ἐπισυνισταμένην αὐτῷ ἐπιβουλὴν καὶ προβαλέσθαι τοὺς ἀναιρήσοντας αὐτόν. 14 μηδενὸς δ' ὑπακούσαντος ὀνειδίσαι τὸν Χενεφρῆν Χανεθόθην, τὸν μάλιστα προσαγορεύομενον ὑπ' αὐτοῦ. τὸν δὲ ὀνειδισθέντα ὑποσχέσθαι τὴν ἐπίθεσιν, λαβόντα καιρόν. 15 ὑπὸ δὲ τοῦτον τὸν καιρὸν τῆς Μέρριδος τελευτησάσης ὑποσχέσθαι τὸν Χενεφρῆν τῷ τε Μωύσῳ καὶ τῷ Χανεθόθη τὸ σῶμα διακομίσαντας, εἰς τοὺς ὑπὲρ Αἴγυπτον τόπους θάψαι, ὑπολαβόντα τὸν Μωύσον ὑπὸ τοῦ Χανεθόθου ἀναιρεθήσεσθαι. 16 πορευομένου δὲ αὐτῶν τὴν ἐπιβουλὴν τῷ Μωύσῳ τῶν συνειδότων ἐξαγγεῖλαί τινα· τὸν δὲ φυλάσσοντα αὐτὸν τὴν μὲν Μέρριν θάψαι, τὸν δὲ ποταμὸν καὶ τὴν ἐν ἐκείνῳ πόλιν Μερόην προσαγορεῦσαι·	ἐπειχθεὶς δ' ὑπὸ τῶν ἱερογραμματέων οἷός τε ἦν ἐγχειρεῖν τῇ Μωυσέος ἀναιρέσει. 256 φθάσας δὲ τὴν ἐπιβουλὴν καταμαθεῖν . . .

The Ethiopian Campaign

Artapanos 3.7-18	Josephos *AJ* 2.239-256
τιμᾶσθαι δὲ τὴν Μέρριν ταύτην ὑπὸ τῶν ἐγχωρίων οὐκ ἐλαχίστως ἢ τὴν Ἶσιν. 17 Ἀάρωνα δὲ τὸν τοῦ Μωΰσου ἀδελφὸν τὰ περὶ τὴν ἐπιβουλὴν ἐπιγνόντα συμβουλεῦσαι τῷ ἀδελφῷ φυγεῖν εἰς τὴν Ἀραβίαν· τὸν δὲ πεισθέντα, ἀπὸ Μέμφεως τὸν Νεῖλον διαπλεύσαντα ἀπαλλάσσεσθαι εἰς τὴν Ἀραβίαν. 18 τὸν δὲ Χανεθώθην πυθόμενον τοῦ Μωΰσου τὴν φυγὴν ἐνεδρεύειν ὡς ἀναιρήσοντα· ἰδόντα δὲ ἐρχόμενον σπάσασθαι τὴν μάχαιραν ἐπ' αὐτόν, τὸν δὲ Μωῦσον προκαταταχήσαντα τήν τε χεῖρα κατασχεῖν αὐτοῦ καὶ σπασάμενον τὸ ξίφος φονεῦσαι τὸν Χανεθώθην·	

on the other. The stories accordingly move along different lines. This is seen in the motive for the campaign: in Artapanos the Ethiopian invasion is only an excuse for Artapanos to send Moses off on what he considers a suicide mission (3.7), while in Josephos it is a divine oracle which instructs the Egyptians to appeal to Moses for help in their dire straits (241). Josephos therefore had to give an extended account of the Ethiopian invasion (239-240), whereas Artapanos only had to mention it (3.7). In Artapanos Moses leads a ragtag army (3.7); in Josephos he leads an army of both Egyptians and Hebrews (242-243). The differences become even more pronounced in the actual campaign. The account in Artapanos focuses on the camp of Moses in the nome of Hermopolis where Moses and his army won every battle (3.8). The military aspect, however, is relatively unimportant: Moses founded the city of Hermopolis, established the cult of the ibis, and taught the Ethiopians and Egyptian priests circumcision (9-10). The reverse is true in Josephos. Moses uses the ibises to cross the desert (244-247a). What is an animal cult in Artapanos is a proof of sagacity in Josephos. The campaign in Ethiopia is related and culminates in Moses' marriage to Tharbis and the surrender of the Ethiopians' last stronghold (248-253). Moses' return provokes a second plot by Chenephres in Artapanos which is matched by a plot in Josephos. Again, however, the entire structure varies. In Artapanos Chenephres tries to slay Moses through Chanethothes (14-15); in Josephos, the matter is compressed into a relatively few lines: Moses' success sparks suspicions of revolution and a plot by the king (254-256). There is no mention about the dismissal of the army (3.11), the animal cults Moses established (3.12), the burial of Merris (16),[207] or the slaying of Chanethothes (17-18). This does not mean that Josephos was insensitive to the slaying of the Egyptian in Ex. 2:11-12: he handles it by omitting it. The only items the two accounts have in common are the revelation of the plot to Moses and his flight.

How should we explain their relationship? There have been three major theories: Josephos' account is entirely independent,[208] it is

---

[207] In Artapanos, Moses names the city where he buried Merris, Meroe (F 3.16). In *AJ* 2.249, Saba, the city Moses took by marrying Tharbis, is named Meroe by Kambyses after his sister.

[208] So Niese in *ERE*, s.v., "Josephus," 7:573 and Thackeray, *Josephus*, 4:269 n.b., who thought that the Alexandrian community developed the legend in an attempt to explain Num. 12:1.

dependent upon Artapanos,[209] or both have drawn from a common source.[210] Can we say anything definite in light of the obvious difficulties which earlier works reflect? Josephos does know the story told by Artapanos: the structural similarity demands this. The dissimilarities, on the other hand, make it all but certain in my opinion that Josephos knew the story in a form other than what Polyhistor preserved of Artapanos. This is demanded by not only the additions in Josephos,[211] but more importantly by the changes in the basic framework of the story. As we will see, Josephos rewrites his sources freely, but generally leaves the structure intact.[212] Was this other source Artapanos' original version, a tradition from which Artapanos' also drew, or an intermediate source? While it is tempting to think of Artapanos' original version, there is a major problem. Polyhistor has certainly abbreviated the account which could explain the extra material in Josephos. Polyhistor would not, however, have altered the basic story line. This leaves us to conclude that Josephos did or found it already changed in a source. I have indicated that on methodological grounds the latter is more likely. We are now left to decide between a common tradition or an intermediate source. It has proven extremely difficult to posit a suitable intermediate source. The view which best explains the relationship is that

---

[209] Freudenthal, *Alexander Polyhistor*, pp. 170-171, 174, who contended that Josephos had a revised version of Artapanos before him; Bloch, *Die Quellen des Flavius Josephus*, pp. 60-62; Heinemann in *RE*, s.v. "Moses," 16:372-374, who first suggested that Josephos deliberately deviated from Artapanos; Collins and Poehlmann, "Artapanus," pp. 45-47 and Collins, *OTP*, 2:895; Fraser, *Ptolemaic Alexandria*, 2:984 n. 188, who like Heinemann thought Josephos was engaged in a polemic against Artapanos; Walter, *JSHRZ*, 1:130 n. 7b; Holladay, *Fragments from Hellenistic Jewish Authors*, p. 235 n. 56; and possibly Feldman, "*Josephus, Judaism, and Christianity*," p. 36 (introduction).

[210] Levy, "Moïse en Éthiope," pp. 203, 210-211, who suggested Pseudo-Hekataios was the common source; Braun, *History and Romance in Graeco-Oriental Literature*, pp. 99-102, who maintained that Artapanos eliminated the Tharbis material; Wacholder, *Nicolaus of Damascus*, p. 58, who posited Nikolaos of Damascus as the source (critiqued by Gager, *Moses in Greco-Roman Paganism*, p. 21); Abraham Schalit in *EncJud*, s.v. "Artapanus," 3:646; Rajak, "Moses in Ethiopia," pp. 120-122, who attributes it to oral tradition; and Runnals, "Moses' Ethiopian Campaign," p. 147, who attempts to show how each shaped the tradition.

[211] Josephos could have added material from other sources and welded them into a unified narrative. He weaves Num. 22:1-24:25; 31:16; 25:1-18 into a single flowing account in *AJ* 4.100-155.

[212] See under *Ars Narrandi* below. It is, of course, possible that Josephos freely wrote this story; I simply think it more reasonable to postulate a different source given Josephos' known tendencies.

each Jewish author drew from a common tradition. The presence of so much material in later writings attests to the interest in the early years of Moses. The differences are then due to the way that Artapanos and Josephos have reshaped the legend for their own purposes. This does not preclude Josephos' knowledge of Artapanos' version; it does, however, indicate that he preferred a different form.

The contacts continue for Moses' career. Artapanos' connection between the divine name and the miraculous appears to be echoed in Josephos, although in a very different way.[213] Artapanos and Josephos both have Pharaoh promise or concede to let the Israelites depart after the water has turned to blood—a point not attested in the biblical tradition.[214] They each display some concern over the despoiling of the Egyptians (Ex. 12:36). The most significant phrases are:

MT	וינצלו את מצרים
LXX	καὶ ἐσκύλευσαν τοὺς Αἰγυπτίους
Art. 3.34	τοὺς δὲ χρησαμένους παρὰ τῶν Αἰγυπτίων πολ-λὰ μὲν ἐκπώματα, οὐκ ὀλίγον δὲ ἱματισμὸν ἄλ-λην τε παμπληθῆ γάζαν . . .
Jos. *AJ* 2.314	δώροις τε τοὺς Ἑβραίους ἐτίμων, οἱ μὲν ὑπὲρ τοῦ τάχιον ἐξελθεῖν, οἱ δὲ καὶ κατὰ γειτνιακὴν πρὸς αὐτοὺς συνήθειαν.

The borrowing of Artapanos and the honoring in Josephos clearly tone down the note of despoiling in the biblical text.[215] Once again we are dealing with an exegetical tradition which is by no means limited to these two authors.[216]

---

[213] F 3.24-26, where the power of the name is manifest by the collapse of Pharaoh and the death of the scoffer; *AJ* 2.275-276, where the name is associated with the miracles God gave Moses to authenticate his mandate before Pharaoh. The connection in Josephos is not as apparent, but does seem to be present since he inserts the revelation of the divine name into the narrative on the miracles. On this issue see Tiede, *The Charismatic Figure as Miracle Worker*, pp. 229-230 n. 227.

[214] F 3.28-29; *AJ* 2.295; Ex. 7:22-25.

[215] So Holladay, '*Theios Aner*' *in Hellenistic Judaism*, p. 213 n. 89 and *Fragments from Hellenistic Jewish Authors*, p. 242 n. 113. *Contra* Tiede, *The Charismatic Figure as Miracle Worker*, p. 175, who argued that Artapanos does not show any sensitivity to this issue. While Artapanos is not as insistent as Josephos, his language does soften the biblical statements.

[216] Ezekiel, *Exagoge*, 162-166: ὅταν δὲ μέλλητ' ἀποτρέχειν, δώσω χάριν/λαῷ, γυνή τε παρὰ γυναικὸς λήμψεται/ σκεύη κόσμον τε πάνθ', ὃν ἄνθρωπος φέρει,/ χρυσόν τε καὶ ἄργυρόν τε καὶ στόλας, ἵνα/ [ἀνθ'] ὧν ἔπραξαν μισθὸν ἀποδῶσιν βροτοῖς.

The similarities continue on into the exodus proper. Each narrative informs us that the Israelites arrived at the Red Sea in three days.[217] Each betrays a proclivity to rationalize the event at the sea.[218] They both claim that the Egyptians were destroyed by more than water; although as we have come to expect, the specifics vary.[219] Finally, Josephos preserves a tradition about manna (Ex. 16:14) which is attested in Artapanos:

MT   כפר

LXX   ὡσεὶ κόριον λευκόν

Art. 3.37   χιόνι παραπλήσιον τὴν χρόαν

Jos. *AJ* 3.27 τοῦ πλήθους ἀγνοοῦτος καὶ νομίζοντος νίφεσθαι

Are these correspondences enough to posit literary dependence? The quantity suggests they are. The issue is: In what form did Josephos know Artapanos? Was it direct or indirect through Polyhistor?[220] The differences should be attributed to other sources—as in the case of the Ethiopian campaign—and Josephos' own creative rewriting of the biblical text.

iii. *Pseudo-Eupolemos.* The two fragments of Pseudo-Eupolemos likewise have some points of contact with Josephos. The Samaritan in common with the later Jewish historian, emphasizes the mental capacities of Abraham.[221] They accentuate this by assigning astrological lore to Abraham.[222] Together with Artapanos they have Abraham instruct the Egyptians in this science.[223] Yet they are each careful to assign the discovery of astronomy to Enoch.[224]

---

[217] F 3.34; *AJ* 2.315. Both use τριταῖος. It is possible that both derived this independently from Ex. 13-14, although there is nothing in the biblical narrative which immediately suggests a journey of three days.

[218] F 3.35, where he offers the accounts of the Memphians (Moses knew the tides) and Heliopolitans (the Egyptians rushed down on the Jews); *AJ* 2.347-348, where Josephos mentions the account of Alexander's crossing of the Pamphylian Sea as a possible parallel and concludes with his non-committal phrase.

[219] F 3.37, fire and flood annihilate them; *AJ* 2.343-344, all nature fights against them.

[220] Those who think that Josephos knew Artapanos directly include: Freudenthal, *Alexander Polyhistor*, pp. 169-174, especially 170-171 (directly or through Jewish redaction); Denis, *Introduction aux Pseudépigraphes Grecs d'Ancien Testament*, p. 257; Walter, *JSHRZ*, 1:121; Holladay, *Fragments from Hellenistic Jewish Authors*, p. 192; Collins, *OTP*, 2:894-895.

[221] F 1.3; *AJ* 1.154, 157.

[222] F 1.3; *AJ* 1.156.

[223] F 1.8, astrology and other things; *AJ* 1.167-168, arithmetic and astronomy.

[224] F 1.8; *AJ* 1.69.

More importantly, Pseudo-Eupolemos and Josephos both elaborate
on Abraham's role as an instructor who interacted with the Egyptians.[225] On an entirely different note is the fact that in *BJ* 1.63,
Josephos has the same form as Pseudo-Eupolemos for הר ארגריזים (=
ὄρος Γαριζιν in LXX), 'Αργαριζίν.[226]

May we posit any literary influence based upon these data? One
major problem is the issue of whether or not Josephos would use a
Samaritan author.[227] If Josephos knew the ethnic identity of the
author he probably would not. However, if he were ignorant of the
author's ethnicity, there is no reason why he might not have used
such a work. This would necessitate second-hand knowledge. It does
not, however, answer the original question. The widespread connection of Abraham with astrology makes it impossible to affirm
direct dependence. We must simply recognize that in this instance
the evidence is too scanty to allow for a definite verdict.

iv. *Eupolemos*. The first fragment of Eupolemos is a panegyric on
Moses: Moses was the first σόφος who delivered the alphabet to the
Jews and gave the first code of laws. There are no direct equivalents
in Josephos, but the general perception of Moses is the same.[228]

The second fragment concentrates on the temple.[229] There are
only two noteworthy points. First, both describe a scarecrow in the
temple which was designed to scare off the birds—although
Josephos' description is in *BJ*.[230] This may be due to a practical
concern which was shared and should not be pressed too hard.[231]

---

[225] F 1.8, with the priests; *AJ* 1.166, with the Egyptians. Bousset and Gressmann, *Die Religion des Judentums im späthellenistischen Zeitalter*, p. 74 n. 1, thought that
this established dependence. Wacholder, "Abraham the Greek Philosopher," pp.
155-156, has argued that the portrayal of Abraham "as a scientist with an interna-
tionalist scholarly outlook" is a common bond between Josephos and Pseudo-
Eupolemos.

[226] F 1.5.

[227] This is the objection of Gaster, *The Asatir*, p. 67.

[228] *AJ* 1.18-26 praises Moses as a legislator as we have seen. *CA* 2.154 openly
claims that Moses is the first law-giver. Josephos also states that the Greeks were
late in receiving the alphabet (*CA* 1.10-11).

[229] Besides the points discussed in the text, it is worth noting that in the opening
summary there are two approximate similarities. Eupolemos says that Joshua
pitched the tabernacle ἐν Σιλοῖ. (F 2 [30.1]) The LXX has Σηλω. Josephos has
Σιλοῦς and Σιλώ. Eupolemos also states that Saul reigned twenty-one years (F 2
[30.2]); Josephos twenty (*AJ* 10.143). On this see Bloch, *Die Quellen des Flavius
Josephus*, pp. 58-59, who argues for dependence.

[230] F 2 (34.11); *BJ* 5.224.

[231] So also Wacholder, *Eupolemus*, pp. 198-199, who attributes it to their priestly background.

Second, they have approximate but not identical etymologies for Ἱεροσόλυμα: Eupolemos connects it with ἱερὸν Σολομῶνος, whereas Josephos connects the second half with the Homeric Σόλυμα.[232] Otherwise, the differences between the descriptions of the temple are enormous.

There is nothing in the third and fourth fragments which would hint of dependence. The fifth fragment affords the most important evidence. Adolf Schlatter has shown that the figure of 1580 years for the time from the exodus to c. 158/157 B.C.E. agrees with the calculations of Josephos in *AJ* 20.224-238.[233] The greatest problem is that this requires the conjectural deletion of διο from διοχίλια, a deletion I am reluctant to admit.

The evidence for Eupolemos like Pseudo-Eupolemos is thin. There is no reason to think that Josephos independently knew Eupolemos.

Summary. We are now ready to return to our initial question. Did Josephos know the Hellenistic Jewish historians and if so in what form? The evidence for direct knowledge is too scant with the exception of Artapanos. Here we encounter the greatest number of similarities. This might indicate that Josephos knew Artapanos directly.

There is, however, another possibility. Josephos certainly knew the work of Alexander Polyhistor. We have already seen that he was familiar with his Χαλδαϊκά. On one occasion Josephos quotes Polyhistor directly.[234] What is especially important about this quote is that Eusebios also gives it in PE 9.20.2-4. At first glance this would imply that Josephos knew Polyhistor's Περὶ Ἰουδαίων. There is, however, a complicating factor. Eusebios breaks his normal pattern

---

[232] F 2 [34.13]; *AJ* 7.67 and *CA* 1.174. Josephos apparently knew Homer first-hand. He mentions him several times in *CA* including 1.12 which was made famous by Wolf in his *Prolegomena* to Homer. Cf. also 2.14, 155, 256.

[233] "Eupolemus als Chronolog und seine Beziehungen zu Josephus und Manetho," pp. 633-703. A summary is offered in the introduction on pp. 633-635. His conclusion is stated on p. 697 where he argues that Josephos knew Eupolemos through Polyhistor. The principal data are: from exodus to temple = 612 years (230), from the temple to exile = 467 years, 6 months, and ten days (232), 70 years for the exile (233), from the return to Eupator = 414 years (234), the priesthood of Onias (Menelaos) = 10 years (*AJ* 12.385), the priesthood of Jakimos = 3 years (237). Since Alkimos (= Jakimos) died c. 160 B.C.E. another three years should be added which brings the total to 1580.

[234] *AJ* 1.239-241, citing Kleodamos Malchos via Polyhistor.

of citing Polyhistor at this point and quotes directly from Josephos. Why? Wasn't it in the Περὶ 'Ιουδαίων Eusebios had before him? Freudenthal suggested that Eusebios simply wanted to add another name to his repertory of authors, especially a Jewish one.[235] A. von Gutschmid thought that it was from a different work of Polyhistor's, his Λιβυκά[236]—a suggestion that has won the approval of most scholars.[237] This makes perfectly good sense since the fragment deals with Libya and should be accepted.

Did Josephos know Polyhistor's Περὶ 'Ιουδαίων? Several factors suggest that he did. In the first place, he explicitly names three of the authors preserved by Polyhistor in his Περὶ 'Ιουδαίων, i.e., Demetrios, Philo the elder, and Eupolemos.[238] How did he know these authors? There is no evidence for his direct use of the two we have examined and we know of no other collection of them. Second, Clement cites both the names and texts from all three of these authors in a single passage. Since there is no doubt that he was following Polyhistor, it is only reasonable to conclude that Josephos was as well.[239] Third, the large number of points of agreement with Demetrios, Artapanos, and Pseudo-Eupolemos suggest that Josephos was aware of a body of traditions corresponding to those preserved by Polyhistor. The simplest explanation is that he knew these authors through Polyhistor. Our conclusion makes perfectly good sense since Josephos was living in Rome and writing on Jewish history. If Polyhistor's work had any circulation in the latter half of the first century C.E., Josephos must have known it.

This also could help us to understand how he can call them Greeks: he only knows them second-hand. On the other hand, Josephos does not name any Jewish sources apart from the scriptures. He clearly does not want to distract from his accomplishment—it is not accidental that the texts where he does speak of

---

[235] *Alexander Polyhistor*, p. 15.

[236] *Kleine Schriften*, 2:182.

[237] Walter, "Zur Überlieferung einiger Reste früher jüdisch-hellenistischer Literatur bei Josephus, Clemens, und Euseb.," p. 316 and *JSHRZ*, 1:115; Denis, *Introduction aux Pseudépigraphes Grecs d'Ancien Testament*, p. 260; Holladay, *Fragments from Hellenistic Jewish Authors*, p. 245; R. Doran, "Cleodamus Malchus," in *OTP*, 2:883-884.

[238] *CA* 1.218.

[239] *Strom.* 1.21.141.1-5. This connection was pointed out by Feldman, *Josephus and Modern Scholarship*, p. 401.

Jewish historians of a similar stripe are in *BJ* and *CA*.[240] The most likely explanation of his comments is that he knew they were Jews, but did not want to acknowledge them. It may be that the popular conception in Rome was that they were Greeks, a perception Josephos willingly exploited for his own purposes.

There is, however, one major objection to this conclusion. Why does Josephos fail to mention Polyhistor with but one exception? Polyhistor is noticably absent in his roll call of Greek witnesses to Jewish antiquity.[241] Was this due to ignorance or was it deliberate?[242] Freudenthal thought that because Polyhistor was a secondary compiler Josephos chose not to mention him.[243] I would like to suggest another possibility. Josephos did not name Polyhistor because he did not want to detract from the prestige of his own work as the definitive history on Jews.

What significance did these authors have for Josephos? Since he only knew them in a secondary form, they were not primary literary models. They did, however, exert an influence on both the contents and the methodology of *AJ*. Like the authors of rewritten scripture within Palestine, they provided specific interpretations of texts for him. More importantly, they demonstrated how the Jewish scriptures could be effectively "translated." It was here, not in the LXX, that Josephos learned how to communicate the Jewish story in Greek: not only verbally but also conceptually. They moved beyond Berossos and Manethon in their openness to Hellenism and showed Josephos what could be done with native traditions—even his own. As a corollary, they suggested ways in which Judaism could be redefined in Hellenistic terms. The *Antiquitates* is thus not a unique work standing like a solitary tree against the horizon of the Greco-Roman world, but like a redwood in a stand of pines.

d. *Dionysios of Halikarnassos*. While the Hellenistic Jewish historians provided insight into how Josephos could proceed in a general way, they were too limited and dated to give Josephos the historiographical guidance he needed to successfully Hellenize his tradi-

---

[240] *BJ* 1.17; *CA* 1.41.

[241] *CA* 1.161-218.

[242] Walter, "Zur Überlieferung einiger Reste früher jüdisch-hellenistischer Literatur bei Josephus, Clemens, und Euseb.," pp. 317-318, regarded this as decisive evidence that Josephos did not know Polyhistor's *On the Jews*.

[243] *Alexander Polyhistor*, pp. 33-34. Cf. also the similar view of Feldman, *Josephus and Modern Scholarship*, p. 401.

tions within the framework of the end of the first century. His task required a contemporary model of Hellenistic historiography which he could adapt for his own purposes.

Josephos found that model in "antiquarian rhetorical historiography." There is a striking correspondence between the basic structure of Josephos' work and the *magnum opus* of Dionysios of Halikarnassos. Their titles have an identical formation, Ῥωμαϊκὴ Ἀρχαιολογία and Ἰουδαϊκὴ Ἀρχαιολογία, and they both consist of twenty books. These obvious points of contact have led scholars to look for other areas of contact such as shared *topoi* and formulae,[244] verbal contacts,[245] and programmatic similarities.[246] The discussion these arguments have provoked has failed to establish a unified perspective about whether Dionysios served as a model.[247] The

---

[244] Thackeray, *Josephus: The Man and the Historian*, pp. 56-58 and *Josephus*, 4:ix-x. Thackeray argued that both dealt with antiquities, that Josephos owed his description of the death of Moses (*AJ* 4.326) to the deaths of the founding fathers in Dionysios (Aeneas, 1.64.4-5; Romulus, 2.56.2). and that the formula indicating a non-committal stance to the miraculous was due to Dionysios' influence. Cf. 1.48.1 (κρινέτω δὲ ὡς ἕκαστος τῶν ἀκουόντων βούλεται), 48.4; 2.40.3, 70.5; 7.66.5; and *AJ* 1.108 (ὡς ἂν ἑκάστοις ᾖ φίλον, οὕτω σκοπείτωσαν); 2.348; 3.81 (Note the language here: καὶ περὶ μὲν τούτων ὡς βούλεται φρονείτω ἕκαστος τῶν ἐντευξομένων), 268, 322; 4.158; 8.262; 10.281; 17.354; 19.108; and *BJ* 5.257. It should be pointed out that this was a historiographical commonplace. It appears in Herodotos 3.122.1: πάρεστι δὲ πείθεσθαι ὀκοτέρῃ τις βούλεται αὐτέων. Cf. Lucian, *Hist. Conscr.* 60: Καὶ μὴν καὶ μῦθος εἴ τις παρεμπέσοι, λεκτέος μέν, οὐ μὴν πιστωτέος πάντως, ἀλλ' ἐν μέσῳ θετέος τοῖς ὅπως ἂν ἐθέλωσιν εἰκάσουσι περὶ αὐτοῦ· σὺ δ' ἀκίνδυνος καὶ πρὸς οὐδέτερον ἐπιρρεπέστερος.

[245] Shutt, *Studies in Josephus*, pp. 92-101. David Ladoceur has overturned Shutt's arguments in "Studies in the Language and Historiography of Flavius Josephus," (Ph.D. dissertation, Brown University, 1976) and his later article which summarizes his work, "The Language of Josephus," *JSJ* 14 (1983): 18-38.

[246] Attridge, *The Interpretation of Biblical History in the 'Antiquitates Judaicae' of Flavius Josephus*, pp. 43-60.

[247] Those who think Josephos used Dionysios as a model (besides Thackeray, Shutt, and Attridge) include: F.J. Foakes Jackson, *Josephus and the Jews: The Religion and History of the Jews as Explained by Flavius Josephus* (1930; reprint ed., Grand Rapids: Baker Book House, 1977), pp. 247-248; Richards, "The Composition of Josephus' *Antiquities*," p. 36; Bickerman, "*Origenes Gentium*," pp. 68, 70-71 (similar methodology); Schalit, *EncJud*, s.v. "Josephus Flavius," 10:257; Feldman, "Josephus' Portrait of Saul," pp. 51-52 and "Hellenizations in Josephus' *Jewish Antiquities*: The Portrait of Abraham," p. 134; Bartlett, *Jews in the Hellenistic World*, p. 85; and Schürer, *The History of the Jewish People in the Age of Jesus Christ*, 1:48. Those who do not think that Dionysios served as a model or that he served as a foil are: Collomp, "La Place de Josèphe dans la Technique de l'Historiographie Hellénistique," pp. 86-92; Daube, "Typology in Josephus," pp. 35-36; Rajak, "Josephus and the 'Archaeology' of the Jews," pp. 466-472; Bilde, *Flavius Josephus between Jerusalem and Rome*, pp. 92, 202-203.

issue is not whether Josephos knew Dionysios' work—that is incontrovertible in my judgment—but whether he used it as a blueprint for his own work.[248]

Dionysios[249] came to Rome c. 30 B.C.E.[250] According to his own testimony he spent twenty-two years learning Latin and studying Roman writings.[251] After this preparation, he published his *magnum opus* in 7 B.C.E.[252] Throughout his years of teaching rhetoric in Rome, Dionysios also composed a number of shorter essays and letters which we have come to know as the *Scripta Rhetorica*. Since he presents his theories within these,[253] I will begin by briefly summarizing his comments here and then look at how he actually executed his theory in the *Antiquitates Romanae*.

The touchstone for Dionysios' views of history is his assessment of Thukydides. He first contrasts him with Lysias in *De Demonsthene*,[254] then more fully with Herodotos in his *Epistula ad Pompeium*, and finally devoted a full essay to him, *De Thucydide*.[255] Dionysios divides his comments into subject matter and style.[256] In his *Epistula*, he offers five tasks κατὰ τὸν πραγματικὸν τόπον: the choice of the subject, the beginning and ending, the decision on what to include, the distribution of the material, and the historian's own outlook. Using these criteria, he praises Herodotos and censures Thukydides. After all, Herodotos wrote of the conflict between Greeks and barbarians while Thukydides relates a war which is

---

[248] David L. Balch, "Two Apologetic Encomia: Dionysius on Rome and Josephus on the Jews," *JSJ* 13 (1982): 102-122, has shown that they both use the same form of encomium. Cf. *AR* 1.9-2.29 and *CA* 2.145-295. This does not establish contact in and of itself, but it certainly strengthens our impression.

[249] On Dionysios see *RE*, s.v. "Dionysios von Halikarnassos," by E. Schwartz, 5:934-961 (for *AR*) and *KP*, s.v. "Dionysios von Halikarnassos," by Michael von Albrecht, 3:70-71.

[250] *AR* 1.7.2.

[251] *AR* 1.7.2.

[252] *AR* 1.3.4.

[253] On Dionysios' comments in his rhetorical works see Kenneth S. Sacks, "Historiography in the Rhetorical Works of Dionysios of Halicarnassus," *Athenaeum* 61 (1983): 65-87.

[254] *Dem.* 2. He compares their differences to the opposite ranges of the musical scale in a series of seven contrasts.

[255] The order of the individual works in the *scripta rhetorica* is not secure. I have followed the basic order given by Stephen Usher, *Dionysius of Halicarnassus: The Critical Essays*, 2 vols. LCL (Cambridge: Harvard University Press, 1974 [vol. 1]), 1:xxii-xxvii.

[256] *Pomp.* 3; *De Thuc.* 2.

better forgotten. This is compounded by Thukydides' beginning and ending which do not praise Athens, but criticize her. Again, Herodotos praises what is good and blames what is not; Thukydides is negative. Dionysios then goes on to present ten criteria κατὰ τὸν λεκτικόν (style).[257] By opting for Herodotos over against Thukydides, Dionysios has consciously aligned himself with the rhetorical school at which Polybios railed. For Dionysios the historian *par excellence* is Theopompos who brought to light not only what is obvious, ἀλλ' ἐξετάζειν καὶ τὰς ἀφανεῖς αἰτίας τῶν πράξεων καὶ τῶν πραξάντων αὐτὰς καὶ τὰ πάθη τῆς ψυχῆς ... καὶ πάντα ἐκκαλύπτειν τὰ μυστήρια τῆς τε δοκούσης ἀρετῆς καὶ τῆς ἀγνοουμένης κακίας.[258] While his critique is somewhat mitigated in *De Thucydide*, he remains openly critical of the Athenian.[259]

The preface to the *Antiquitates Romanae* demonstrates that Dionysios has implemented his views. He begins by arguing that methodologically speaking there are two essential requirements for a historian: he/she must select a subject which is καλὰς καὶ μεγαλοπρεπεῖς καὶ πολλὴν ὠφέλειαν τοῖς ἀναγνωσομένοις φερούσας (1.1.2) and

---

[257] The first three are primary features and the last seven secondary in Dionysios' system. 1. Purity ἡ καθαρὰ τοῖς ὀνόμασι καὶ τὸν Ἑλληνικὸν χαρακτῆρα σώζουσα διάλεκτος; 2. [missing]; 3. conciseness, τρίτον ἔχει χώραν ἡ καλουμένη συντομία; 4. vividness, ἐνάργεια (πρώτη μὲν τῶν ἐπιθέτων ἀρετῶν); 5. imitation, [τῶν] ἠθῶν τε καὶ παθῶν μίμησις; 6. impressiveness, αἱ τὸ μέγα καὶ θαυμαστὸν ἐκφαίνουσαι τῆς κατασκευῆς ἀρεταί; 7. force, αἱ τὴν ἰσχὺν καὶ τὸν τόνον καὶ τὰς ὁμοιοτρόπους δυνάμεις τῆς φράσεως ἀρεταὶ περιέχουσαι ...; 8. pleasure, ἡδονὴν δὲ καὶ πειθὼ καὶ τρέψιν καὶ τὰς ὁμοιογενεῖς ἀρετάς ... ; 9. naturalness and brilliance, κατὰ φύσιν ... τὸ δεινόν; 10. appropriateness, πασῶν ἐν λόγοις ἀρετῶν ἡ κυριωτάτη τὸ πρέπον.

[258] *Pomp.* 4. It is not surprising that Polybios attacked Theopompos savagely in 8.9-11. On Theopompos see *FGrH* 115. I, therefore, can not agree with Clemence Schultz, "Dionysius of Halicarnassus and his audience," in *Past Perspectives: Studies in Greek and Roman Historical Writing*, ed. I.S. Moxon, J.D. Smart, and A.J. Woodman (Cambridge: Cambridge University Press, 1986), p. 125, who thinks that Dionysios stands in the Thukydidean-Polybion tradition.

[259] The literary critic discusses Thukydides subject matter (5-20) in relationship to his predecessors (5-8), arrangement (9-12), and proportion (13-20). Here he does not censure Thukydides for his decision to write about a single contemporary war, but approves his commitment to truth. This does not mean, however, that Thukydides' predecessors were wrong to include myths, only that such were inappropriate for Thukydides' purposes. Thukydides is much more open to blame for his arrangements (alternating summers and winters [9] and his beginning and conclusion [10-12]) and sense of proportion (battles [13-15], speeches [16-18], and introduction [19-20]). He again offers examples of praise and blame for Thukydides' style. He concludes by answering Thukydides' defenders (50-51) and holding out his own hero Demosthenes who incorporated Thukydides' assets and avoided his liabilities (52-53). Cf. also *Din.* 8.

equip themself with the requisite skills (1.1-4). Dionysios maintains
that he has selected a worthy subject since it is obvious that Roman
rule has surpassed any empire—barbarian or Greek—which has
exercised dominion (1.2.1-3.6). The reason (1.4.1-6.5) that Dionysios has selected the early period of Rome's history for his subject
is that the Greeks are ignorant of Rome's origins (4.1-3; 6.1-2).[260]
He therefore wants to dispel the erroneous views currently held by
showing that the earliest inhabitants of Rome were actually Greeks
(5.1-4).[261] In this way he hopes that his readers can form an accurate impression of Rome so that they will not be disgusted with
their current subjection especially when they learn of the examples
of Roman virtue which neither Greeks nor barbarians can match
(6.3-5).[262] The readers, therefore, have a right to know his sources
over which he has labored for twenty-two years (1.7.1-4). The oral
reports are from the most distinguished Romans and the written
from the histories which the Romans themselves praise.[263] The
scope of his life's work begins ἀπὸ τῶν παλαιοτάτων μύθων . . . and
continues on down to the first Punic War (265 B.C.E.) (1.8.1-4). He
warns his readers that the form which his work takes is different from
what they are accustomed to seeing. His is ἐξ ἁπάσης ἰδέας μικτὸν
ἐναγωνίου τε καὶ θεωρητικῆς καὶ διηγηματικῆς. In this way both
those who want to pursue serious topics as well as those who simply
want to find entertainment can profit (8.3).

We may now address the issue of a possible relationship. The rhetorical works of Dionysios contain a sustained polemic against
Thukydides as a model, the very model Josephos chose for *Bellum*

---

[260] Schwartz, *RE*, s.v. "Dionysios von Halikarnassos," 5:934, argued that the
selection of a theme in antiquity showed that this belongs to the school of rhetorical
historiography according to which "die Redekunst nicht bloß als ein Kunstmittel
neben anderen gilt, sondern umgekehrt der historische Stoff nichts weiter ist als ein
Objekt, an welchem diese Kunst gezeigt und dokumentiert wird gewissermassen
das Thema einer μελέτη grossen Stils. D. will im Grunde in seinem Geschichtswerke ein παράδειγμα des Classicismus liefern."

[261] This is the thrust of the entire first book. He again argues it in 7.70.1-73.5.

[262] Dionysios thus addresses himself explicitly to a Greek audience. H. Hill,
"Dionysius of Halicarnassus," *JRS* 51 (1961): 88-93, has argued that Dionysios
was also addressing a Roman audience and that he countered the prevalent account
of Rome's origins with his own in order to win a more respectable position for
Greeks in Roman eyes. So also Schultze, "Dionysius of Halicarnassus and his audience," pp. 133-141, esp. 138-141.

[263] On the issue of sources see Alfred Klotz, "Zu den Quellen der Archaiologia
des Dionysios von Halikarnassos," *Rheinisches Museum für Philologie* 87 (1938):
32-50.

Judaicum. This tension dissipates when we turn to the *magna opera*. It is very clear that the prefaces of the *Antiquitates Romanae* and the *Antiquitates Judaicae* have a great deal in common: they both justify the selection of their subject,[264] address themselves to the Greek world in an effort to remove ignorance and prejudice against a particular people,[265] cast their histories in a moralizing narrative,[266] criticize their predecessors,[267] emphasize their sources,[268] share a similar but not identical scope,[269] and both seek to inform in a pleasant style.[270] There is even some agreement in small details concerning subject matter.[271] Again, just as Dionysios had prepared himself, so had Josephos.[272] These historiographical agreements indicate that Josephos knew the rhetorical-historiographical tradition in which Dionysios wrote if not Dionysios' own work.

There is, on the other hand, a glaring difference. Dionysios wrote as a Greek to other Greeks trying to persuade them to accept the Romans because in reality they were Greeks! This line of argumentation was anathema to an Oriental. The equivalent for Josephos would be for him to have written the *Antiquitates* to the Greeks in an effort to persuade them that the Jews were acceptable since they were in reality long-lost Greeks!! This stands the *Antiquitates* on its head.

How should we explain Josephos' ambivalent relationship to Dionysios? The claim which runs throughout all of Josephos' works is that his main aim is truth. For him this means either an eye-witness account in the Thukydidean-Polybion tradition or the apologetic claim to follow native sources. At the same time, when he "translated" his native sources into Greek he had to make them intelligible to Greeks. Another literal translation was both doomed

---

[264] *AR* 1.2.1-3.6; *AJ* 1.5.
[265] *AR* 1.4.1-6.5; *AJ* 1.5, 9.
[266] *AR* 1.5.3; 6.4; *AJ* 1.14, 19-23.
[267] *AR* 1.6.1-2; *AJ* 1.12-13. This was a common motif. As we have already seen, we can trace it all the way back to Hekataios of Miletos, F 1.
[268] *AR* 1.7.1-4; *AJ* 1.5, 17, 26. It is interesting that Dionysios claims to have used Roman sources in his preface. At the end of Book One, he informs us that he has read many Greek and Roman works about Roman origins. As we have already seen, Josephos' insistence upon native traditions belongs to Oriental works.
[269] *AR* 1.8.1; *AJ* 1.5, 13.
[270] *AR* 1.8.3; *AJ* 1.9; 14.2-3.
[271] *AR* 1.8.2; *AJ* 1.5, 13.
[272] *AR* 1.7.2; *AJ* 20.263.

to failure and contrary to Josephos' historical instincts. He there-fore needed a model of how to write an 'Αρχαιολογία in Greek. Dionysios—or the historiographical tradition he represents—served that role admirably.[273] Josephos thus exploited Dionysios or the school he represents formally—just as the Hellenistic Jewish histori-ans had utilized different Hellenistic traditions—but maintained his distance when he was forced to declare his own allegiances. In this case he was an Oriental with a reliable rather than contradictory historical record.[274]

3. *Ars Narrandi.* Specifically how did Josephos shape his narra-tive?[275] He is explicit about his own procedure in at least one pas-sage. In 4.197, he explains that he is guilty of one innovation: he has sytematically collected the laws which Moses left σποράδην. He con-sistently follows this principle of grouping non-narrative material into blocks within his narrative.

The narrative of Josephos has several outstanding patterns which run throughout. First of all, Josephos has written a unified narra-tive. Even where the collection of biblical texts offered a fairly coher-ent line, there were gaps and inconsistencies which Josephos had to address. This means that he sometimes rearranges the order of events and brings together data from various places. So he in-troduces the literary prophets in his narrative where he thinks it ap-propriate and interweaves Kings and Chronicles in a single thread. Second, Josephos has a definite proclivity towards the individual as the focal point or centrum of his narrative.[276] Third, Josephos has

---

[273] Attridge, *The Interpretation of Biblical History in the 'Antiquitates Judaicae' of Flavius Josephus*, p. 56, suggests that rather than moving from content to form, Josephos moved from form to content, i.e., he became aware of "the possibilities of historical literature as they were defined by historical rhetoricians like Di-onysius." I prefer the former since Josephos aligns himself with the Oriental tradi-tion, although it must be recognized that we can not trace the actual course of Josephos' development as a historian from *BJ* to *AJ*.

[274] Note that while Josephos eschews all myths, Dionysios is more sanguine about their possible use. *AR* 1.8.1 (where he openly declares he will begin with them); 2.20.2 (where he cautions against Greek myths); *AJ* 1.15, 16, 22.

[275] The most important formal treatment of how Josephos writes is Varneda, *The Historical Method of Josephus*, pp. 64-241. Naomi G. Cohen, "Josephus and Scripture: Is Josephus' Treatment of the Scriptural Narrative Similar Throughout the *Antiquities* I-XI?" *JQR* 54 (1963-1964): 311-332, argued that 1-5 are more freely retold than 6-11.

[276] Varneda, *The Historical Method of Flavius Josephus*, pp. 24-39, 69-88. The character studies of Louis Feldman are based upon this insight, i.e., Feldman has studied the major characters in an effort to understand Josephos' agenda since they constitute the epicenter of his work. (See below)

a flair for the dramatic. This is brought to the fore by his novelistic tendencies[277] which are especially evident in his psychological comments[278] and the increased erotic element.[279] Fourth, Josephos thoroughly rewrites his sources with an eye to improving the style of the narrative.[280]

a. *Omissions.* If we compare Josephos' text to the biblical record he retells, we soon realize that he has omitted a number of episodes. Some of these may be due to the exigencies of his narrative[281]; others, however, are clearly dropped intentionally. While he is not fully consistent, he omits a good deal of the biblical text which is potentially embarrassing. Gone are the stories of Isaac's lie about Rebekah,[282] Jacob's selective breeding of Laban's herd,[283] Judah and Tamar,[284] Moses' slaying of the Egyptian,[285] Zipporah's indignant circumcision of her son,[286] the golden calf,[287] the complaint of Miriam and Aaron,[288] Moses' sin at Meribah,[289] the fiery serpents,[290] and David's eating the bread of presence.[291] If there

---

[277] Cf. Martin Braun, *Griechischer Roman und hellenistische Geschichtschreibung.* Frankfurter Studien zur Religion und Kultur der Antike (Frankfurt: Vittorio Klostermann, 1934) and Horst R. Moehring, "Novelistic Elements in the Writings of Josephus," (Ph.D. dissertation, University of Chicago, 1957).

[278] E.g., 7.31, 36, 284-285, comments on Joab's motives; 16.150-159, is basically a psychoanalysis of Herod the Great.

[279] E.g., 2.39-59, Potiphar's wife; 2.252-253, Moses and Tharbis; 5.136-137, explains that the Levite's wife (concubine in the biblical text [Judg. 19:1]) was an outstanding beauty. He was passionately in love with her, but she did not return the sentiment. This created arguments which led her to leave him to return to her parents. 5.276-277, Manoches (= Manoah) was married to a woman of surpassing beauty whom he loved to the point of insane jealousy.

[280] Bilde, *Flavius Josephus between Jerusalem and Rome,* p. 98, stressed Josephos' philological polishing.

[281] E.g., He leaves out Tola in his account of the judges, Judg. 10:1-2.

[282] Gen. 26:6-11. Josephos does relate the two occasions when Abraham lied about Sarah. However, in both instances, Abraham does not lie but merely acts like he is her brother. 1.162, 207.

[283] Gen. 30:35-43, especially 37-43.

[284] Gen. 38.

[285] Ex. 2:11-15.

[286] Ex. 4:24-26.

[287] Ex. 32.

[288] Num. 12. According to the biblical text, Miriam became leprous. Such an admission was unsuitable in a work which was engaged against the charge that the Israelites were lepers.

[289] Num. 20:2-13.

[290] Num. 21:4-9.

[291] I Sam. 21:3-6 are omitted from vs. 1-9 when he relates the incident in 6.242-244.

were only a couple of incidents like these which had been shelved by
Josephos, we might not pay particular attention. However, these examples show that Josephos wants to portray Israel in the very best
possible light.[292]

There are also some thematic omissions which run throughout the
tome. Betsy Amaru pointed out that Josephos consistently deletes
the land theology of the biblical text.[293] He does this by omitting
covenant scenes, reinterpreting other covenant scenes to stress the
greatness of Israel's numbers rather than the land, and presenting
land acquistion in the form of predictions rather than divine
promises. One reason for this is that Josephos is dedicated to the diaspora as well as his *patria*. A classic statement of his view is given
in the speech of Balaam: "You will acquire the land to which he has
sent you; it will always be subject to your children. The earth and
sea will be filled with their fame and you will be able to supply the
world in each land with residents from your race."[294] There is,
however, a second and more important *raison d'être*. In the words of
Amaru, Josephos "did not want the land to be a focal point, as it
was for Davidic messianism, with all its revolutionary implications."[295]

The avoidance of an emphasis on the land because of messianic
concerns fits into the larger tendency to suppress eschatology.
Messiahs are revolutionaries and are therefore to be avoided. Even
Nathan's oracle to David which stands at the core of royal theology
in the OT is stripped of any messianic overtones.[296] This does not
mean that Josephos does not have an eschatology: he does. This becomes obvious in his handling of Daniel's interpretation of
Nebuchadnezzar's dream. Josephos refuses to interpret the meaning of the stone because "I did not think it was proper to relate this
since I am obligated to narrate what is over and done not what is yet
to be."[297] This implies that Rome is not the eternal city and there
is yet a future for Israel—a thought which is supported by the

---

[292] So also Feldman, "Josephus' Portrait of Saul," pp. 53-54.

[293] Betsy Halpern Amaru, "Land Theology in Josephus' *Jewish Antiquities*,"
JQR 71 (1980): 201-229.

[294] *AJ* 4.115.

[295] *Op cit.*, p. 229.

[296] *AJ* 7.90-93. Cf. II Sam. 7:1-17.

[297] *AJ* 10.210. He refers any inquiring reader to the book of Daniel for more information.

Balaam oracle in Josephos.[298] Josephos thus appears to have a national hope, but he keeps it under lock and key with but a few exceptions.[299] The same reserve also characterizes the Hellenistic Jewish historians and Philo.[300]

b. *Alterations*. The same pattern also emerges when we view the text from the perspective of alterations. When Josephos retells the unseemly story about the Benjamites' lust for the Levite stranger he has them demand not the Levite as the biblical text, but his wife![301] Saul's demand for 100 foreskins of the Philistines in exchange for the hand of Michal in marriage now becomes 600 heads.[302] Again, Saul does not fall upon his own sword but is slain by an Amalekite youth.[303]

Josephos also tinkers with the text in an effort to solve problems which the narrative itself raises. So, for example, the age-old question of where Cain and Abel got their wives is solved by the daughters which Adam and Eve also had.[304] The same difficulty pre-

---

[298] *AJ* 4.114-117, where the nation will fill the entire world. In 125 Josephos states: ἐξ ὧν ἁπάντων λαβόντων τέλος ὁποῖον ἐκεῖνος προεῖπε τεκμήραιτ' ἄν τις, ὅ τι καὶ ἔσοιτο πρὸς τὸ μέλλον.

[299] On Josephos' eschatology see Marianus de Jonge, "Josephus und die Zukunftserwartungen seines Volkes," pp. 205-219; Ulrich Fischer, *Eschatologie und Jenseitserwartung im hellenistischen Diasporajudentum.* BZNW 44 (Berlin/New York: Walter de Gruyter, 1978), pp. 157-183, note also pp. 144-156; Amaru, "Land Theology in Josephus' *Jewish Antiquities*," p. 225; Bilde, *Flavius Josephus between Jerusalem and Rome*, pp. 187-189. The key texts in *BJ* are 3.350-354, 400-402 (prophecy about Vespasian); 6.312-313 (a messianic interpretation applied to the previous prophecy [*contra* De Jonge who argues that this does not associate Vespasian with the messiah, p. 209]; 5.367 (*Tyche* and authority *now* reside with Rome).

[300] The key treatise in Philo is *On Rewards and Punishments*. Philo may have thought of a Messiah, but he was very careful to avoid tying the Messiah to the Davidic house. Cf. Henry Austryn Wolfson, *Philo: Foundations of Religious Philosophy in Judaism, Christianity, and Islam*, 2 vols. (Cambridge: Harvard University Press, 1947), 2:395-426, especially 413-415 and David Winston, *Logos and Mystical Theology in Philo of Alexandria* (Cincinnati: Hebrew Union College Press, 1985), pp. 55-58.

[301] Judg. 19:22; *AJ* 5.143-146.

[302] I Sam. 18:25; *AJ* 6.197.

[303] I Sam. 31:4; *AJ* 6.371. Josephos has simply taken the claim of the Amalekite youth II Sam. 1:9-10 and made it his narrative in order to avoid the charge of suicide. That he is worried about such a charge is evident from the explanation given for the request to the Amalekite: διὰ τὸ μὴ ταῖς χερσὶν αὐτὸν τοῦτο δύνασθαι ποιῆσαι. Feldman thinks that Josephos refused to raise the issue of suicide here because he was too conscience-stricken about his own debacle at Jotapata. "Josephus' Portrait of Saul," pp. 91-92.

[304] *AJ* 1.52. Cf. also Jub. 4:1, 8, 9.

sented by the biblical text re-emerges when God banishes Cain as
a wanderer on the earth. Cain protested that whoever found him
would slay him. Josephos alters this to a fear of wild beasts thus
relieving himself of explaining who these other people were.[305] For
every reader of scripture who wondered how Jacob could mistake
Leah for Rachel on their wedding night Josephos has the answer:
Jacob was drunk and it was dark.[306] Rachel did not steal the ter-
aphim because she reverenced them in any way, but to have some
bargaining power with Laban if necessary.[307] The significance of
alterations such as these is that they show us that Josephos like other
Jewish interpreters was concerned with explaining the difficulties of
the text.

Josephos also works with the text on the positive side of the ledger.
One of the most interesting shifts in Josephos away from the
Hellenistic Jewish historians is the diminished role of *Kulturbringer*.
In fact, the most extensive section Josephos has on inventions is his
commentary on Cain and his descendants in which inventions are
presented in a negative light.[308] He balances this with the descendants of Seth who σοφίαν τε τὴν περὶ τὰ οὐράνια καὶ τὴν τούτων
διακόσμησιν ἐπενόησαν.[309] Later on he presents Abraham, Joseph,
and Moses in terms similar to those of the Hellenistic Jewish historians as we have seen.[310] We could explain the Cain narrative as an
aberration since Josephos wants to portray Cain and his descendants
negatively and the inventions of his descendants are in the text.
However, if this were the case, I would not have expected him to
have added the inventions of Cain and would have expected him to
add more claims in a positive light later. I think it is rather a matter
of relative unimportance to the later Jewish historian. Cultural
claims are part of Josephos' apology, but not like they were for the
Hellenistic Jewish historians. He has chosen to make his case along
somewhat different lines.

---

[305] Gen. 4:14; *AJ* 1.59. Cf. also Thomas W. Franxman, *Genesis and the Jewish
Antiquities of Flavius Josephus*. Biblica et Orientalia 35 (Rome: Biblical Institute
Press, 1979), p. 70. Philo, *QG* 1.74 has the same tradition.

[306] Gen. 29:23; *AJ* 1.301.

[307] Gen. 31:34-35; *AJ* 1.311.

[308] Gen. 4:16-22; *AJ* 1.60-64.

[309] *AJ* 1.69.

[310] *AJ* 1.155-157, 166-168, Abraham the first monotheist who taught the Egyptians; 2.192, Joseph the land reformer; 4.328-329, Moses the greatest intellect.

We have already noted that individuals form epicenters for the narrative. It is therefore not surprising that Josephos has lavished a great deal of care on the major characters in his narrative. Over the last twenty-five years Louis Feldman has studied these characters and shown that Josephos consistently recasts his figures into categories of the Hellenistic world. So, for example, Abraham is a philosopher.[311]

c. *Additions.* There are two groups of major additions to the narrative of Josephos. In the first two sections of the *Antiquitates* where Josephos is retelling scripture he buttresses the realibility of his text by quoting from pagan authors who confirm the account. In the final unit he continues to quote from pagan sources only now they are more likely the sources from which he is working.[312]

In the final division of the *Antiquitates* Josephos inserts a large number of *Acta* which state Jewish privileges decreed by various powers.[313] Whether or not these decrees are historically accurate, their inclusion by Josephos is significant.

4. *Theological Controls.* The overarching theological control which binds all of this material together is providence as Harold Attridge has shown.[314] The term πρόνοια itself occurs 120 times: 63 times referring to human activity and 57 to divine. Interestingly the distri-

---

[311] See his "Abraham the Greek Philosopher," pp. 143-156; "Hellenizations in Josephus' Version of Esther (Ant. Jud. 11.185-295)," *TAPA* 11 (1970): 143-170; "Josephus as an Apologist to the Greco-Roman World: His Portrait of Solomon," in *Aspects of Religious Propaganda in Judaism and Early Christianity*, ed. by Elisabeth Schlüssler-Fiorenza. University of Notre Dame Center for the Study of Judaism and Christianity in Antiquity 2 (Notre Dame: University of Notre Dame Press, 1976), pp. 69-98; "Josephus' Portrait of Saul," pp. 45-99; "Hellenizations in Josephus' *Jewish Antiquities*: The Portrait of Abraham," pp. 133-153; "Josephus' Version of Samson," *JSJ* 19 (1988): 171-214. Besides these specific character studies see also his "Hellenizations in Josephus' Portrayal of Man's Decline," pp. 333-353; "Josephus as a Biblical Interpreter: The '*Aqedah*,'" pp. 212-252. There are also now two essays on Josephos' presentation of women which have reached the same conclusion: James L. Bailey, "Josephus' Portrayal of the Matriarchs," in *Josephus, Judaism, and Christianity*, pp. 154-179 and Betsy Halpern Amaru, "Portraits of Biblical Women in Josephus' *Antiquities*," *JSJ* 39 (1988): 143-170.
[312] This is particularly true of Nikolaos of Damascus and Strabon. Nikolaos is a major source for Josephos and Strabon a secondary source. On Nikolaos see Shutt, *Studies in Josephus*, pp. 79-92 and Wacholder, *Nicolaus of Damascus*, pp. 4-6, 52-64. On Strabon see Shutt, pp. 106-109.
[313] *AJ* 14.145-155, 188-264 (see 185-267), 306-323; 16.162-173 (see 160-178); 19.278-291; 20.10-14.
[314] *The Interpretation of Biblical History in the 'Antiquitates Judaicae' of Flavius Josephus.*

bution of the term is uneven. When πρόνοια refers to God in *AJ*, it occurs 44 times in the first eleven books and only 13 times in the last nine. Why? The term clusters around three major events: the exodus,[315] Balaam's blessing,[316] and Daniel and his companions.[317] The recipients of God's providence are Israel and her illustrious heroes.[318] The emphasis is clearly on the connection between God and Israel in her past. Is the failure to underscore God's care of Israel in the post-exilic period simply accidental or is it intentional? Josephos expressly states that providence is conditional. The best example is in Moses' farewell address: "God who has ruled over you up until now . . . will not at this present time cease his πρόνοιαν, but as long as you want to have him as protector, by remaining in the pursuit of virtue, you will enjoy his attentive care."[319] Providence is thus tied to virtue.[320] In *AJ* the characters who exemplify virtue are the heroes of Israel's past. The connection is therefore made on this basis.

This helps us to understand the moralizing tendency of the *Antiquitates*. Josephos stated in the prologue that the main lesson his readers could expect from his work was that those who keep God's laws are blessed beyond belief, while those who depart find that their suffering corresponds to their disobedience—a point Josephos makes repeatedly in his narrative.[321] God' providence acts as a judge on the conduct of humans and nations.[322] It also serves as a

---

[315] *AJ* 2.330, 332, 336, 349. The text is dealt with by Attridge, *op cit.*, pp. 76-78.

[316] *AJ* 4.114, 117, 128, 157. Cf. Attridge, *op cit.*, pp. 96-98.

[317] *AJ* 10.214, 260, 278, 280.

[318] Adam, 1.46; Jacob, 1.283; 2.8; Abraham and Isaac, 1.346; Joseph, 2.60; Jacob's offspring, 2.174; Moses, 2.219, 236; Israel, 2.230, 332, 336, 349; 3.38, 99; 4.114, 117, 128, 185, 239, 316; 5.107; 7.95; 11.169; Samson, 5.277, 312; David, 7.338; Solomon, 7.385; Daniel's relatives, 10.214; Daniel, 10.260. In the final section the following are recipients: Alexander, 13.80; Jonathan, 13.163; Joseph, 14.391; Herod, 14.462; Agrippa I, 18.197; Petronius, 18.309; Izates, 20.18, 91. There are three pagans in this list: Alexander of Syria, Petronius, and Izates. The reasons for their inclusion are transparent: Alexander graciously received Jonathan, Petronius refused to profane the temple, and Izates became a convert to Judaism.

[319] *AJ* 4.185. Cf. Attridge, *The Interpretation of Biblical History in the 'Antiquitates Judaicae' of Flavius Josephus*, pp. 90-92, for a treatment of the text.

[320] See also 1.346; 11.169; 18.309.

[321] *AJ* 1.14. Josephos repeats the principle throughout the *Antiquitates*. E.g., 1.20, 23, 72; 6.307; 7.93; 17.60; 19.16. Josephos frequently adds moralizing comments of his own, e.g., 13.152, 310.

[322] Note the definition of providence given by Attridge, *op cit.*, p. 107: "This

sign of hope for those who will learn from the *exempla* of Israel's past. Josephos has successfully welded the retributive theology of the Deuteronomistic history with the concept of providence as it was used in Hellenistic historiography.[323]

Summary. The *Antiquitates* is a flowing narrative which like the accounts of the Hellenistic Jewish historians was written *ad maiorem Iudaeorum gloriam*. Not only are difficulties either removed or transmuted, but material is added which is expressly calculated to add to the prestige of Israel. At the same time, the material is Hellenized both in language and in substance. This bi-polar stance, i.e., an apology to Hellenism through the glorification of the Jewish past and the Hellenization of Israel's traditions, appears to be the dominant hermeneutical device through which the historian shaped his *magnum opus*. His moralizing tendency helped to hold it all together by incorporating Deuteronomistic theology in the form of "providence" drawn from Hellenistic historiography.

Function

How did this amalgam of Jewish tradition clothed in Hellenistic dress function? We may begin by ascertaining how Josephos thought it should. At the outset he declared that he had undertaken the work with the hope that the Greek world would take it seriously.[324] He specified what he had in mind when he wrote *Contra Apionem*: "I believe that in my writing of the *Antiquitates* . . . I have made perfectly clear to any who read it that the Jewish race is most ancient, is originally of pure stock, and how it settled the land which we now possess."[325] The first claim reverberates the statement in the prologue of *AJ* that the histcry embraces a span of five thousand years.[326] That this was more than an idle claim made in both the prologues of *AJ* and *CA* is evident by Josephos' concern to date the

---

providence consists primarily in the rewarding of virtue and punishing of vice. The history of Israel is seen to be a collection of miraculous and prophetical evidence for the truth of that belief."

[323] Providence was a mainstay of Stoicism. It is tempting to think that Josephos has borrowed his concept from the Stoa. Josephos does not, however, evidence any technical knowledge of Stoic philosophy. It is better to agree with Attridge that Josephos is following Hellenistic historiography. *Op cit.*, pp. 154-165.

[324] *AJ* 1.5.

[325] *CA* 1.1.

[326] *AJ* 1.13; *CA* 1.1.

high priests in *AJ*. It unquestionably places the *Antiquitates* in the debate over origins and the pervasive assumption that the oldest is the best.[327] The second and third claims are a rejoinder to any who would cast aspersions on Jewish origins. That there were various theories circulating is clear from the six options which Tacitus lists.[328] Josephos continued to ascribe an apologetic role to the *Antiquitates* in the repeated references back to it in *Contra Apionem*.[329] He thus makes it clear that what is implicit in the *Antiquitates* is explicit in *Contra Apionem*. Measured by this standard, *Contra Apionem* is a witness to the failure of the *Antiquitates*.

It is fair to say then that Josephos saw *AJ* in an apologetic context. His statements, however, hardly do justice to the wide-ranging body of material in *AJ*. Can we do any more justice to it by examining the hints he gives us in *AJ* itself?

1. *A Greek Audience*. The ancient penman tells us that he is writing to Greeks.[330] The text of *AJ* supports this address. Josephos presupposes a Hellenistic audience which does not know the Hebrew language,[331] months,[332] system of measures,[333] or customs and structure of Jewish life.[334] Although some of these could be true of a Hellenized Jew, some are so basic that the imagined readership can not have had any significant Jewish training or knowledge.

The relationship between Jews and the populace of the Roman empire seems to have been strained in a significant number of locales. There are repeated references in *AJ* to the disdain felt by

---

[327] *CA* 2.152, makes this explicit.

[328] *Hist.* 5.2.1-3.2: exiles from Crete, excess population of Egypt who made their way out under the leadership of Hierosolymus and Iuda, Ethiopians who were forced to flee, Assyrian refugees, originally the Homeric Solymi, and a band of plague-stricken Egyptian exiles who were led by Moses. The fact that Tacitus devotes as much space to the final option as he does to the first five indicates that it is his preference even though he does not proffer his opinion explicitly. For the text with translation and commentary see Stern, *GLAJJ*, 2:1-93.

[329] *CA* 1.1-5, 127; 2.136, 287.

[330] *AJ* 1.5, 9b, 12; 16.174; 20.262.

[331] E.g., *AJ* 1.34, 36, 117, 146, 258, 284, 305, 333; 2.278; 3.32, 134, 151, 152, 153, 156, 157, 159, 163, 166, 172, 195, 252, 282, 291; 4.73; 5.121 (where he explains the meaning of *adoni*), 200, 201, 323, 336; 6.22, 302; 7.10, 67; 8.95; 9.290; 10.243, 244; 11.329; 13.188. Note especially 1.129 where he explains to the Greeks that he has Hellenized the names.

[332] E.g., *AJ* 8.100; 11.109; 12.248, 319, 412.

[333] E.g., *AJ* 3.142, 144, 234, 321; 15.314.

[334] E.g., *AJ* 17.200 (seven days of mourning); 17.213 and 20.106 (unleavend bread served at Passover); 20.216 (Levites a Jewish tribe).

communities against the Jews.[335] The first revolt helped to exacer-
bate the situation in places, Antioch and Alexandria being the prime
examples.[336] Nor was the animosity limited to political struggles:
according to Josephos, some of the accounts of the war were composed out of a vindictive spirit.[337] In spite of the reprisals which
were to be expected, Vespasian and Titus allowed the Jews of the
diaspora to maintain their ancestral way of life.[338] There was,
however, one major exception: the *fiscus Judaicus*. Funds that were
formally sent to the temple in Jerusalem were now placed in the
coffers of the Capitoline temple.[339]

Circumstances apparently remained stable until the reign of
Domitian. Exactly what happened under Vespasian's younger son
is a matter of dispute. Suetonius tells us: Praetor ceteros Iudaicus
fiscus acerbissime actus est; ad quem deferebantur, qui vel inprofessi Iudaicam viverent vitam vel dissimulata origine imposita genti
tributa non pependissent. He then recalls a personal experience: In-
terfuisse me adulescentulum memini, cum a procuratore frequentis-
simorque consilio inspiceretur nonagenarius senex, an circumsectus
esset.[340] This passage occurs within the context of Suetonius'
description of Domitian's need to raise revenue. One way in which
this was done was to seize property on the basis of an accusation.[341]
His statement about the Jews is an example of how people were subject to such calumny. This is confirmed by Nerva's measures which
reversed Domitian's policy of permitting individuls to accuse a Jew
of ἀσεβείας or the Jewish way of life.[342] What does Suetonius mean

---

[335] *AJ* 12.120, 121, 125-126; 13.104, 195, 200; 14.213, 242, 245; 16.27-28,
45-47, 58, 160, 170; 18.371; 19.278; 20.173-178, 183-184. It should be noted that
most of these references occur within the context of the *Acta*.

[336] Antioch: *BJ* 7.46-62, 100-111; *AJ* 12.121. Alexandria: *AJ* 12.121. On the
whole issue see E. Mary Smallwood, *The Jews Under Roman Rule*. SJLA 20 (Leiden:
E.J. Brill, 1976), pp. 356-388, especially 356-368.

[337] *BJ* 1.2, 6.

[338] *AJ* 12.121-124. This is confirmed by Cassius Dio 65.7.2.

[339] *BJ* 7.218; Cassius Dio 65.7.2. Cf. Smallwood, *op cit.*, pp. 371-376 for
details.

[340] *Dom.* 8.12.2.

[341] *Dom.* 8.12.1: Bona vivorum ac mortuorum usque quaque quolibet et
accusatore et crimine corripiebantur.

[342] Cassius Dio 68.1.2, who is describing those who made false accusations under Domitian. Some of the coins Nerva struck read: fisci Judaici calumnia sublata.
H. Mattingly, ed. *Coins of the Roman Empire in the British Museum*, (1923-), 3:15, 17,
19; cited by E. Mary Smallwood, "Domitian's Attitude toward the Jews and Judaism," *Classical Philology* 51 (1956): 4 and *The Jews Under Roman Rule*, p. 378. Cf.
also Eusebios, *HE* 3.20.8.

when he says that the *fiscus Judaicus* was enacted acerbissime? The text suggests that it was levied against two groups other than practicing Jews: the inprofessi and those who had concealed their circumcision through epispasm. The latter is certainly the intent of dissimulata origine as the memory of the trial he relates shows. The inprofessi must be Jewish adherents who practiced Judaism as a lifestyle, but were not circumcised.

A second passage which is linked to this is the account of Domitian's execution of the consul, Flavius Clemens, and the banishing of his wife, Flavia Domitilla, both of whom were his relatives.[343] Dio tells us that they were charged with ἔγκλημα ἀθεότητος, an accusation which was frequently made against those who began practicing Judaism.[344] Some were condemned while others lost their property. Apparently either adherence or conversion to Judaism by a Roman was grounds for prosecution, although in the case of Clemens and Domitilla it might have been their proximity to the throne that bothered Domitian.[345] Dio goes on to relate the execution of Glabrio who was similarly accused, although the main cause— ostensibly anyway—for Domitian's ire was that he fought with beasts.[346]

Our other evidence is much less trustworthy. Eusebios, following Hegesippos (second century C.E.), claims that after the destruction of Jerusalem, Vespasian ordered a search for all Davidides in an attempt to exterminate the royal family: a charge which issued in another Jewish catastrophe.[347] He repeats the story under Domitian only omits any reference to a persecution.[348] How much credence we can give this story is difficult to determine. There is a natural sense of plausibility in trying to remove any messianic claimants. On the other hand, the fact that the account only comes down to us through Christians raises serious doubts: it looks like persecution against the Messiah has been read back into history. On

---

[343] Cassius Dio 67.14.1-3.

[344] Smallwood, "Domitian's Attitude toward the Jews and Judaism," pp. 5-6, argues that this involved a refusal to participate in the emperor's cult.

[345] Suetonius, *Dom.* 8.15.1., says that Domitian executed Clemens ex tenuissima suspicione. He mentions this in the same sentence that he tells us Domitian had appointed Clemens' sons as his heirs.

[346] 67.14.3: κατηγορηθέντα τά τε ἄλλα καὶ οἷα οἱ πολλοὶ καὶ ὅτι καὶ θηρίοις ἐμάχετο. . . .

[347] *HE* 3.12.

[348] *HE* 3.19.

the whole, I think that a Domitianic order to remove all Jewish leaders with messianic (understand revolutionary) connections has grown into a legend of persecution against members of Jesus' own family.[349]

Such episodes can hardly have inspired confidence within Domitian's Jewish subjects.[350] Was he hostile to the Jews or are these texts simply Jewish examples of the extremes to which he went?[351] While these texts offer no evidence for any official action against the Jews, they do point out a sneering animus which must have characterized the way Domitian viewed Jews.

Nor was he alone. Tacitus has preserved the most extensive description of Jews which we have in Latin literature.[352] His sentiments undoubtedly express the opinion of the upper levels of Roman society at the beginning of the second century C.E. He is most open in his section on customs. He tersely gave voice to his feelings in the sentence: Profana illic omnia quae apud nos sacra, rursum concessa apud illos quae nobis incesta.[353] He undoubtedly would have agreed with the famous complaint of his contemporary, Juvenal: iam pridem Syrus in Tiberim defluxit Orontes.[354] The satirist does not specify Jews in this slur, but he unquestionably would have included them as his specific comments about them demonstrate. In the fourteenth satire he digs his barbs into Jewish sons who learn to despise Roman customs and laws in favor of their own.[355]

---

[349] Note that in Eusebios the order to execute the royal family resulted in the trial of the grandsons of Judas, Jesus' brother, *HE* 3.20.1-6.

[350] Smallwood, "Domitian's Attitude toward Jews and Judaism," p. 10 and *The Jews Under Roman Rule*, pp. 382-383, discusses the Jewish texts which relate to Domitian. There was some concern among Jews. She explains Sib. Or. 12.124-142, which has a very favorable image of Domitian, as provincial in perspective rather than from the higher levels of Jewish society. See "Domitian's Attitude toward the Jews and Judaism," p. 11.

[351] Hostile: Smallwood, *op cit.* (both article and book); M.P. Charlesworth, "The Flavian Dynasty," in *CAH*, 11:42; Michael Grant, *The Jews in the Roman World* (Dorset Press, 1984), pp. 224-227. No particular hostility: Harry J. Leon, *The Jews of Ancient Rome* (Philadelphia: The Jewish Publication Society of America, 1960), pp. 33-36.

[352] *Hist.* 5.2-13. See Stern, *GLAJJ*, 2:1-93.

[353] *Hist.* 5.4.1.

[354] *Sat.* 3.62.

[355] *Sat.* 14.96-102: Quidam sorti metuentem sabbata patrem/ nil praeter nubes et caeli numen adornat,/ nec distare putant humana carne suillam,/ qua pater abstinuit, mox et praeputia ponunt;/ Romanas autem soliti contemnere leges/ Iudaicum ediscunt et servant ac metuunt ius,/ tradidit arcano quodcumque volumine Moyses. For all of his statements on Jews see Stern, *GLAJJ*, 2:94-107.

Quintillian also could not resist a jab: "founders of cities are open
to blame for producing a race pernicious to others, like the founder
of the Jewish superstition."[356] A survey of the literature as a whole
reveals more complaints than compliments.[357]

We may now summarize the situation at the end of the first century. Scattered throughout the empire were locales where the relationship between Jews and the locale populace was strained, if not
hostile. Along with this there was an attitude of disdain freely expressed by the intelligentsia. Traditionally the Jews had been able
to depend upon Rome for support—support which had continued in
spite of the revolt. With Domitian also came a sense of uneasiness.
Was the official backing of the government weakening?

Josephos addressed the *Antiquitates* to the Greek world at large in
the hope of winning respectability for his nation. He must have had
in mind litterateurs like his patron whom he hoped to impress and
who would in turn have influence on others. The act of writing the
Antiquitates implied discontent with what was available. In Rome this
meant the Περὶ Ἰουδαίων of Alexander Polyhistor. At its broadest
level *AJ* should be seen as a replacement for Polyhistor. It presented
Israel's glorious past to the Greek world from an insider who could
give an accurate account in the place of the slanderous stories which
were in circulation.

2. *A Roman Audience*. The evidence we have just considered naturally leads us to ask whether or not *AJ* specifically addressed Rome?
Early in this century Shirley Jackson Case argued that *AJ* was addressed to the Roman government.[358] Case contended that *AJ*
reflected growing tensions between Domitian and the Jewish people.
The evidence which he cited are the *Acta*, the changed picture of
Herod, and the parallelism between Gaius and Domitian. His point
was that the potential oppressor should take warning from the les-
sons of history.

---

[356] 3.7.21: qualis est primus Iudaicae superstitionis auctor.

[357] Jerry L. Daniel, "Anti-Semitism in the Hellenistic-Roman Period," *JBL*
98 (1979): 45-65, concluded: "A survey of the comments about Jews in the
Hellenistic-Roman literature shows that they were almost universally disliked, or
at least viewed with an amused contempt." We should, however, remember the
social position of the writers whose comments we have preserved. The *locus* of opposition was Alexandria where feelings ran deep. Besides the collection of Stern, Molly Whittaker, *Jews and Christians: Graeco-Roman Views*, pp. 16-130, has the most important texts in translation.

[358] "Josephus' Anticipation of a Domitianic Persecution," *JBL* 44 (1925):
10-20.

In his analysis, Case touched·upon the two crucial pieces of evidence which bear on the political concerns of *AJ*: the *Acta* and the presentation of rulers in relationship to the Jewish people. Josephos is very forthright in stating why he has included the *Acta*. He says that he has included these documents in his work for the Greeks "showing them that in the past we were granted all respect and were not prevented from practicing any of our ancestral customs by the rulers, but actually had their cooperation . . ." He explains that he has cited them so frequently in an effort "to reconcile the nations and to remove the causes for hatred which have become deeply engrained in senseless people among both us and them."[359] The repetition of this point along with the *acta* make it clear that Josephos is concerned about Jewish rights.[360] Overtly then the *acta* address Greeks throughout the diaspora in an effort to persuade them to allow Jews to practice their ancestral customs.[361] The summary statements also indicate that Josephos is not pleading for any specific rights as much as he is respectability and acceptance on a general basis. Attitudes rather than individual cases are at the heart of his appeal.[362]

The second way in which Josephos expresses his political concerns is through the presentation of rulers. On one side of the ledger, he consistently presents rulers as being tolerant of Jews and Judaism. In an important recent study, Shaye J.D. Cohen has analyzed the concept of tolerant monarchs and dignitaries.[363] He has shown that

---

[359] *AJ* 16.174-175, see 174-178.

[360] Cf. also *AJ* 12.122; 14.185-189, 267, 323; and 20.183-184, where Josephos attributes the outbreak of war in Caesarea to the revocation of Jewish rights.

[361] Bilde, *Flavius Josephus between Jerusalem and Rome*, pp. 220-221, also thinks that Josephos included the *acta* from antiquarian motives.

[362] The literature on these *acta* is large. Two important recent studies which argue opposing views are H. R. Moehring, "The Acta Pro Judaeis in the *Antiquities* of Flavius Josephus," in *Christianity, Judaism and other Greco-Roman Cults: Studies for Morton Smith at Sixty*, ed. by Jacob Neusner. SJLA 12 (Leiden: E.J. Brill, 1975), pp. 124-158, who questions their authenticity and Tessa Rajak, "Was There a Roman Charter for the Jews?" *JRS* 74 (1984): 107-123, who defends their authenticity. There is also no agreement on whether or not Josephos collected these or found them in an existing collection. Josephos collected: Rajak, p. 121. Previous collection by Nikolaos of Damascus: Niese, *ERE*, s.v. "Josephus," 7:10:575; Attridge, "Josephus and His Works," p. 226. Previous collection by cities: Schalit, *EncJud*, s.v. "Josephus Flavius," 10:261. Whether or not the *acta* are genuine, their function is the same.

[363] "Respect for Judaism by Gentiles According to Josephus," *HTR* 80 (1987): 412-415. I have slightly modified his analysis.

Gentile rulers not only guarantee Jewish rights, but honor the temple and God through assistance in its construction or actually worshipping in it.[364] Potentates recognize that God protects and punishes Israel[365] and appoints rulers.[366] These are proof that Gentiles have respected Jews in the past and serve as *exempla* for the present. On the other side, when rulers have attempted to injure or destroy Jewish practices, they have met with calamity.[367]

Does *AJ* address Rome? There is no substantial evidence to presuppose a Domitianic persecution of the Jews. The erosion of Roman support was, however, a matter of real concern: its loss would mean open and violent confrontations in centers like Alexandria and Antioch with no recourse for the Jews to a neutral party.[368] Consequently, I prefer to think that Rome was included but not exclusively.[369]

So far we have argued that *AJ* was designed to win respectability with the Greco-Roman world. Was it intended to do more? That is to say, was it missionary?[370] One line of approach in answering this

---

[364] Assistance in construction: 11.31-32, 58, 78, 97-103 (Kyros and Dareios); 11.123-130 (Xerxes who "held the Jews in the highest esteem," 120); 12.138-141 (Antiochos III). Worshipped in the temple: 11.336 (Alexander the Great). Sent sacrifices: 12.50 (Ptolemy Philadelphos); 13.55 (Demetrios); 13.242-243 (Antiochos Sidetes); 14.488 (Sossios).

[365] *AJ* 8.379; 9.16, 87; 10.7.

[366] *AJ* 10.139 (Nebuchadnezzar); 11.3-4 (Kyros); 11.31, 58 (Dareios); 11.279 (Artaxerxes); 12.25, 47 (Ptolemy Philadelphos); 12.357-359 (Anitochos IV Epiphanes).

[367] The clearest cases are Antiochos IV Epiphanes (12.357-359 [cf. also I Macc. 6:8-13]) and Gaius (18.306; 19.16; cf. also 18.260, 297). Cohen, "Respect for Judaism by Gentiles According to Josephus," p. 415, emphasizes a different aspect: "The only rulers who oppressed the Jews were those whose madness and/or wickedness were generally admitted (Cambyses, Antiochus IV Epiphanes, Cleopatra, Nero, and various procurators of Judea)."

[368] Grant, *The Jews in the Roman World*, p. 222, thinks that one of Josephos' major concerns is "the obliteration of the traditional Roman sympathy, or even neutrality, towards the Jews as a whole" following the revolt.

[369] Cf. also Bilde, *Flavius Josephus between Jerusalem and Rome*, pp. 102-103, who envisions two audiences: the neutral non-Jewish public and the influential, including perhaps the Romans. There are a couple of hints in the text that indicate the audience is not primarily Roman. 18.195 mentions a bird which "the Romans call βουβῶνα (bubo, owl) and more importantly 19.24 explains that chariot races are a favorite pastime of the Romans.

[370] Feldman, *Josephus, Judaism, and Christianity*, p. 42, thinks that it is missionary and appeals to the law about loan-free interest as an attraction to proselytes. Bilde, *Flavius Josephus between Jerusalem and Rome*, pp. 120-121, also calls it missionary, but bases this on the statements in *Contra Apionem* about proselytism.

question is to consider the examples of conversion in *AJ*.[371] What is surprising is that only the conversion of the royal house of Adiabene can be considered in a positive light.[372] Yet even it could have been included because of the historical ties they had with the Jews[373] or because of the satisfaction it would have given a Roman audience when they read that part of the Persian empire had converted away from their ancestral gods.[374]

This picture changes when we come to *Contra Apionem*. Josephos now openly revels in the fact that Gentiles have converted to Judaism. He even surreptitiously extends an invitation on two occasions.[375] Why the shift? Cohen thought that Josephos followed an Alexandrian source in *CA*.[376] Even if he did—and this is debatable—he still chose to make the claim. Did his position shift? I can not accept this since there is so much continuity between *AJ* and *CA*. I think it more likely that the shift is one of argumentation rather than substance. Missionary activity was a sensitive issue. More than one pagan author hurled abuse at the Jews for doing such and under Domitian proselytes were liable to a charge of *maiestas* as

---

[371] The most important treatment of this issue is Cohen, "Respect for Judaism by Gentiles According to Josephus." He draws a distinction between adherence and conversion (Following Nock, *Conversion*, pp. 6-7): "the crucial distinction between 'adherence' and 'conversion' is that the latter entails the exclusive acceptance of a new theological or philosophical system, while the former does not. In 'conversion' the new replaces the old, in 'adherence' the new is added to the old" (p. 410). He argues that 'adherence' is viewed positively in *AJ* (3.217, 318-319; 14.110; 20.34, 41, 195) and conversion negatively (pp. 421-422). On this basis he concludes that *AJ* is non-missionary (pp. 423-424).

[372] *AJ* 20.17-96. Contrast the instances in which Gentiles were compelled to convert when their homeland was conquered (13.257-258 and 15.254-255; 13.318); Gentiles wanted to marry Jewish women (16.225; 20.139 [cf. also 19.355]; 20.145-146); Gentiles who fear Jewish reprisals as a result of Artaxerxes' decree (11.285); and a Roman matron, Fulvia (18.82).

[373] *BJ* 4.147, 567; 6.356-357.

[374] *AJ* 20.70-71, Izates counseled against a campaign against Rome due to Jewish ties. Schalit, *EncJud*, s.v. "Josephus Flavius," 10:261-262, thought it was included as a result of the role they played in the war. H. Lawrence Schiffman, "The Conversion of the Royal House of Adiabene in Josephus and Rabbinic Sources," in *Josephus, Judaism, and Christianity*, pp. 307-308, argued that it was both historically relevant and answered the charge that Jews hated Greeks: they welcomed proselytes. Cohen, *op cit.*, p. 425 and Feldman, *Josephus, Judaism, and Christianity*, p. 52, both contend that it is directly tied to the fact that Parthia was Rome's traditional enemy.

[375] *CA* 2.209-210, 261. In 2.123 he tells us that many Greeks have converted and in 2.281-286 that many have imitated or followed Jewish laws.

[376] "Respect for Judaism by Gentiles According to Josephus," pp. 425-427.

we have seen.[377] I think that *AJ* omitted mention of proselytism as a result of these circumstances. In *CA* Josephos chose to take a different line of approach. The shift might well be due to the date: after Domitian Josephos felt free to make the claim.[378]

This, however, still does not mean that *AJ* is missionary. The reason Josephos gives for the documents in particular and *AJ* as a whole should stand in my opinion: he wanted to win respect for the Jews.[379] This does not mean that he would despise a convert. On the contrary, I think he would welcome one. The purpose of *AJ*, however, was not to win them.

3. *A Jewish Audience.* When Josephos explained his method of collecting the laws systematically, he apologized to any of his Jewish readers who might take offense.[380] Nor is this the only time that he takes note of potential Jewish readers. He counsels his readers not to examine the ages of the ante-diluvians at their deaths, but at the time when they begat their first son.[381] This presupposes that his readers will consult the biblical text—hardly a fair assumption for a pagan audience.[382] Such statements along with the exegetical concerns of the text have led an increasing number of scholars to speak of a Jewish audience as well as a Greek readership.[383] Some have even gone so far as to say that Josephos' works were primarily addressed to Jews in the diaspora.[384] This is going too far, but

---

[377] Horace, *Sat.* 1.4.139-143; Tacitus, *Hist.* 5.5.2. On the well known expulsion under Tiberius see Suetonius, *Tib.* 3.36; Tacitus, *Ann.* 2.85.4; Cassius Dio 57.18.5a.

[378] I am, of course, presupposing that *CA* postdated Domitian. This is likely in my opinion since *AJ* was first published in 93-94 and then came out in a second edition with the *Vita* sometime later, presumably within a few years. *CA* is a carefully written document. If Josephos' rate of production in the past is any indication of how he continued to work, then *CA* would have come after Domitian's death on 18 September 96.

[379] So also Niese, *ERE*, s.v. "Josephus," 7:572, 576; Schalit, *EncJud*, s.v. "Josephus Flavius," 10:257; Schürer, *The History of the Jewish People in the Age of Jesus Christ*, 3:545.

[380] *AJ* 4.197.

[381] *AJ* 1.88.

[382] It could presuppose a scholarly audience although I think the explanation given is more likely.

[383] Feldman, "Josephus' Portrait of Saul," pp. 45-46 and "Hellenizations in Josephus' *Jewish Antiquities*: The Portrait of Abraham," pp. 134-135; Bartlett, *Jews in the Hellenistic World*, p. 75; Bilde, *Flavius Josephus between Jerusalem and Rome*, pp. 121-122, 205; Amaru, "Portraits of Biblical Women in Josephus' *Antiquities*," p. 139 n. 1.

[384] Elvira Migliario, "Per l'Interpretazione dell'Autobiografia di Flavio Giuseppe," *Athenaeum* 59 (1981): 92, 96, 136. Cf. also Rajak, *Josephus*, p. 178.

does recognize a component which must be addressed.

One of the well known shifts from *BJ* to *AJ* is the more positive treatment of the Pharisees—although this is not entirely consistent. Recently several have attempted to explain this change as due to Josephos' willingness to represent the rabbis in Rome.[385] Certainly his insistence on keeping the law and his exegetical traditions offer some support for this. At the same time it is difficult to imagine the Rabbis welcoming Josephos to a discussion at Jamnia! Their silence about him indicates he was a *persona non grata*. More than that, Josephos' message is significantly different from that offered in Palestine.[386]

The Jewish people responded to the destruction of Jerusalem and the temple in at least three ways. First, in continuity with earlier traditions there were several apocalyptic efforts to come to grips with the collapse of the Jewish center. From Palestine we have 4 Ezra, 2 Baruch, and the Apocalypse of Abraham. We also have 3 Baruch which may come from Egypt.[387] The second response was that of the rabbis who successfully laid the basis for Judaism as a "book" religion.[388] The third response is that of Josephos. The *Antiquitates Judaicae* served the Jewish community by offering a definition of Judaism. Like the rabbis, Josephos found the touchstone to be the law.[389] This is clear from the prologue where he makes the keeping

---

[385] Morton Smith, "Palestinian Judaism in the First Century," in *Israel: Its Role in Civilization*, ed. by Moshe Davis (New York: Harper & Brothers, 1956), pp. 74-77, who thought that the popular support the Pharisees enjoyed in *AJ* was a recommendation by Josephos to the Roman government to accept them as the new leaders in Palestine; Ellis Rivkin, *The Shaping of Jewish History: A Radical New Interpretation* (New York: Charles Scribner's Sons, 1971), p. 88, who goes so far as to suggest that Josephos was responsible for Vespasian's treatment of Yohanan ben Zakkai; Jacob Neusner, *From Politics to Piety: The Emergence of Pharisaic Judaism* (Englewood Cliffs, New Jersey: Prentice-Hall Inc., 1973), pp. 45-66, especially 64-65 where he follows the lead of Smith; Cohen, *Josephus in Galilee and Rome*, pp. 237-238; Attridge, "Josephus and His Works," pp. 210, 226-227.

[386] Basser, "Josephus as Exegete," p. 30, thinks that Josephos is more of an exegete like the rabbis than a historian. I do not think this is a satisfactory explanation of books 1-11 and entirely disregards 12-20. From the other end the rabbis wrote nothing even remotely similar to the *Antiquitates*.

[387] They are treated as a group in Collins, *The Apocalyptic Imagination*, pp. 155-186, 198-201.

[388] On this period see the recent work of Shaye J.D. Cohen, *From the Maccabees to the Mishnah*. Library of Early Christianity (Philadelphia: The Westminster Press, 1987), pp. 214-231.

[389] So also Rivkin, *The Shaping of Jewish History*, pp. 54-57.

308 THE *ANTIQUITATES JUDAICAE* OF JOSEPHOS

of the law the criterion for God's providential care.[390] It is also the reason why in *Contra Apionem* he gave his justly famous presentation of the law.[391] Being a Jew means fidelity to the law. If Josephos shared the same basic definition, then why is he so different from the rabbis? The answer is that his version of the law varies. Rather than living in comparative isolation from the Greco-Roman world, Josephos presents a Judaism that interacts with that world. For Josephos the issue is not Judaism or Hellenism, but Judaism in Hellenism. He recasts Jewish history in these terms hoping to reconcile both Greeks to Jews and Jews to Greeks.[392]

SIGNIFICANCE

Our analysis has shown that the *Antiquitates* is a complex work which has connections to multiple traditions and serves more than a single need. Is there anything which unites what appear to be disparate elements? I think there is. At its core the *Antiquitates* offers a self-definition of Judaism in historical terms. It presented Judaism to the Greek world in a bid to overturn misconceptions and to establish a more favorable image. It presented Judaism to the Roman world with the hope that the favorable status Judaism had enjoyed would continue unabated. Finally it presented Judaism to the Jews themselves in the form Josephos thought would best serve as the basis for a reconstructed Judaism.

Josephos consciously placed himself and his work in the category of Oriental historiography, i.e., apologetic historiography. His task demanded this: he defined the Jewish people on the basis of their own records rather than through Hellenistic misconceptions. Yet at the same time, he recognized that the success of his work depended upon its presentation in terms understandable to the Greek world.

---

[390] *AJ* 1.14. It is emphasized by his panegyric on Moses and the reasonableness of his legislation in 18-26.

[391] *CA* 2.125-295.

[392] That Josephos wanted to reconcile Jews to Greeks is also defended by Migliario, "Per l'Interpretazione dell'Autobiografia di Flavio Giuseppe," p. 136; Bartlett, *Jews in the Hellenistic World*, p. 75; and Bilde, *Flavius Josephus between Jerusalem and Rome*, p. 122. I have not dealt with the thesis of André Paul, "Flavius Josephus' 'Antiquities of the Jews': An Anti-Christian Manifesto," *NTS* 31 (1985): 473-480, here because I do not think a case can be made for it. Paul argues that *AJ* was written in direct response to Christianity. I do not think that Christians were significant enough at this point to warrant a work like the *Antiquitates* and find too much material which has no bearing on the issue.

Fortunately for Josephos, there was a rich Jewish tradition which had preceded him. Following this lead, he exploited Dionysios of Halikarnassos or the school of antiquarian rhetorical historiography which he represents. *AR* was after all a Greek ἀρχαιολογία. Jerome was thus not entirely wrong when he called Josephos Graecus Livius.[393]

What sets Josephos apart is not only the comprehensive coverage of his work and the skill with which he executed it, but his own unique version of Israel's past. It is his concept of Hellenized-Judaism which he hoped would reconcile the antagonistic elements of his world and establish a place for the Jewish nation in the new world after the revolt. That he took his task seriously is beyond all doubt: he was writing sacred history, an—*the* by his claim—accurate translation of Jewish scriptures.

The validity of his definition for first century Jews was largely bound up with the circumstances of his own life. His acceptance of Rome and Hellenism requires us to ask about his patriotism in *AJ* and *CA*. We are thus once again led to ask: Did Josephos undergo a major shift or did he remain the same? Another way of putting the same question is to ask whether or not there is a sense of unity in the Josephan corpus.[394] Some have pointed out that in *AJ* 1.6, Josephos informs us that he conceived *AJ* before writing *BJ*.[395] This, however, is belied by the preface to *BJ* where he rejected such a task as we have seen.[396] The real issue of unity is the relationship between *BJ* and *AJ*.

It is senseless to argue that the two have identical viewpoints. The differences in perspective in the material which the two share in common is too well known to require argumentation.[397] The *Bellum* clearly has a pro-Roman slant that the *Antiquitates* lacks. In the former, providence is on Rome's side; in the latter, it is connected to Israel.[398] This is connected to the contemporary perspective of

---

[393] *Epist.* 22.35.8. Cf. also Cassiodorus, *Institutiones* 1.17.1 Ioseppus, paene secundus Livius.

[394] E.g., Conzelmann, *Heiden-Juden-Christen*, p. 189: "Eine Apologie für das jüdische Volk ist sein gesamtes Werk."

[395] Thackeray, *Josephus: The Man and the Historian*, pp. 52-53; Petersen, "Real and Alleged Literary Projects of Josephus," pp. 265-266; Bilde, *Flavius Josephus between Jerusalem and Rome*, p. 80.

[396] So Niese, *ERE*, s.v. "Josephus," 7:572.

[397] The most famous case is that of Herod.

[398] Note *BJ* 3.144; 4.366, 622; 7.82, 318. On two occasions it is used with respect to Jewish individuals, 3.28; 4.219.

BJ as opposed to the antiquarian viewpoint of *AJ* which champions Jewish antiquity.

On the other hand, there is a direct line of continuity. Josephos opens *BJ* with a criticism of other accounts because they disparage the Jews.[399] He wants to correct these by demonstrating the greatness of the Jews as opponents.[400] At the same time, he goes out of his way to stress that it was not the Jewish people as a whole who started the war, but a group of revolutionary fanatics.[401] The blame for the war should not then be placed on the shoulders of the Jewish nation but on the radicals who fanned the flames of sedition—a charge he will make again in *AJ*.[402] In this sense *BJ* is nationalistic.[403] It is a negative posture in contrast to the positive stance of *AJ*, but it is the same stand. The message to the Jews is likewise similar to that of *AJ*: survival will not come through subsequent revolts, but through accomodation with Rome.[404]

Did Josephos change his viewpoint? From an external perspective it is hard to answer this in anything but the affirmative. If, however, we were to ask Josephos himself he would just as certainly respond negatively. He wrote: "May I never live in such a way as a captive that I reject my own people or forget my ancestral traditions."[405] The *Antiquitates* was his memorial.

---

[399] *BJ* 1.2, 7.

[400] *BJ* 1.8.

[401] *BJ* 1.4, 10, 11, 27. The *locus classicus* for the innocence of the populace is 4.397. The best treatment of Josephos and the rebels is that of Rajak, *Josephus*, pp. 78-143.

[402] *AJ* 20.166, where he contrasts the *sicarii* with the Jewish people: διὰ τοῦτ' οἶμαι καὶ τὸν θεὸν μισήσαντα τὴν ἀσέβειαν αὐτῶν ἀποστραφῆναι μὲν ἡμῶν τὴν πόλιν.

[403] So William Reuben Farmer, *Maccabees, Zealots, and Josephus: An Inquiry into Jewish Nationalism in the Greco-Roman Period* (New York: Columbia University Press, 1956), pp. 17-20 and Solomon Zeitlin, "A Survey of Jewish Historiography: From the Biblical Books to the *Sefer Ha-kab-balah* with Special Emphasis on Josephus," *JQR* 59 (1968-1969): 179-180, 182.

[404] The key texts on the warning against any further sedition are *BJ* 1.4-5; 2.388-389; 3.108.

[405] *BJ* 6.107.

CHAPTER SEVEN

LUKE-ACTS[1]

Quid ergo Athenis et Hierosolymis?
Tertullian, *De Praescriptione* 7.9

In 109 (110) C.E. Trajan appointed the urbane and reliable nephew
of the celebrated Roman scientist Pliny *legatus* of Bithynia-Pontus.[2]
Pliny the Younger arrived in Bithynia on 17 September 111.[3] In
the course of his tour through the province, Pliny found himself

---

[1] The literature on Luke-Acts is almost limitless. A recent bibliographic guide
to the gospel is Martin Rese, "Das Lukas-Evangelium. Ein Forschungsbericht,"
in *Religion* (*Vorkonstantinisches Christentum: Leben und Umwelt Jesu; Neues Testament
[Kanonische Schriften und Apokryphen]*, Forts.) ANRW II 25.3 (Berlin/New York:
Walter de Gruyter, 1985), pp. 2258-2328. On Acts see Paul F. Stuehrenberg, "The
Study of Acts before the Reformation: A Bibliographic Introduction," *NovT* 29
(1987): 100-136; A.J. Mattill and M.B. Mattill, *A Classified Bibliography of Literature
on the Acts of the Apostles*. NTTS 7 (Leiden: E.J. Brill, 1966) and the more recent up-
date of W.E. Mills, *A Bibliography of the Periodical Literature on the Acts of the Apostles
1962-1984*. NovTSup 58 (Leiden: E.J. Brill, 1986); W. Ward Gasque, *A History
of the Criticism of the Acts of the Apostles* his recent, "A Fruitful Field: Recent Study
of the Acts of the Apostles," *Interpretation* 42 (1988): 117-131 (note the bibliographies on p. 118 n. 2), and his brief summary of commentaries, "Recent Commentaries on the Acts of the Apostles," *Themelios* 14 (1988): 21-23; Eckhard Plümacher,
"Acta-Forschung 1974-1982," *TRu* 48 (1983): 1-56; 49 (1984): 105-169; Ferdinand Hahn, "Der gegenwärtige Stand der Erforschung der Apostelgeschichte:
Kommentare und Aufsatzbände 1980-1985," *TRev* 82 (1986): 178-190. On Luke-
Acts as a whole see Earl Richard, "Luke-Writer, Theologian, Historian: Research
and Orientation of the 1970's," *BTB* 13 (1983): 3-15 and G. Wagner, ed., *An
Exegetical Bibliography of the New Testament* (Macon, GA: Mercer University Press,
1985), vol. 2: *Luke and Acts*. On Luke as a theologian see F. Bovon, *Luke the
Theologian: Thirty-Three Years of Research (1950-1983)*, trans. K. McKinney. Princeton Theological Monograph Series 12 (Allison Park, PA: Pickwick Publications,
1987).

[2] He is called *legatus* in an inscription conveniently printed and translated in Pliny, *Letters and Panegyricus*, 2 vols., trans. by Betty Radice. LCL (Cambridge: Harvard University Press, 1969), 2:550-551. According to the agreement of Augustus
and the senate in 27 B.C.E., Bithynia and Pontus were senatorial provinces. Cf.
Cassius Dio 53.12.1-9, especially 4. The tenth book of Pliny's *Epistulae* is devoted
to his correspondence with Trajan when he was governor of Bithynia-Pontus.

[3] *Ep.* 10.17b.

trying cases of people who were accused as *Christiani*.[4] Uncertain of
legal precedents, he proceeded to try them *cognitio extra ordinam*. The
number of cases soon swelled to the point that he began trying to discover what he could about Christians. After he tortured two deaco-
nesses (*ministrae*) he could only write: Nihil aliud inveni quam super-
stitionem pravam et immodicam.[5] He decided to write to Trajan
because so many people were involved: Neque civitates tantum, sed
vicos etiam atque agros superstitionis istius contagio pervagata est;
quae videtur sisti et corrigi posse.[6] Pliny's letter indicates that there
was no official policy against this new *superstitio*. Trajan full-
heartedly approved of his procedure.[7]

Pliny's contemporary, Tacitus, shared a similar opinion. He explained that Nero punished the *Christiani* in an effort to squelch the
rumor that he was responsible for the fire of Rome.[8] In spite of
their innocence as incendiaries, Tacitus clearly thought that they
received their just desserts as practioners of what he called an *exitiabi-
lis superstitio*. The historian was seconded by another contemporary,
Suetonius, who *en passant* mentioned the persecution of Christians
under Nero: afflicti suppliciis Christiani, genus hominum superstitionis novae ac maleficae.[9]

It is clear that at the beginning of the second century, the upper
strata of Roman society considered Christianity another one of those
pernicious cults which had made its way west. Tacitus complained
about its penetration into Rome quo cuncta undique atrocia aut
pudenda confluunt celebranturque.[10] For high-standing Romans,
Christianity was a *superstitio*.

If this is how Romans saw Christians, we should ask how Christians viewed Romans, and in particular the Roman government.
Significantly, not all early Christians shared the same perspective.

---

[4] Pliny's dealings with Christians are recorded in *Ep.* 10.96. Trajan's reply is
letter 97.

[5] *Ep.* 10.96.8.

[6] *Ep.* 10.96.9.

[7] On Pliny and Christians see Robert L. Wilken, *The Christians as the Romans
Saw Them* (New Haven/London: Yale University Press, 1984), pp. 1-30.

[8] *Ann.* 15.44.

[9] *Nero* 6.16.2. Cf. also *Claudius* 5.25.4, where he mentions the expulsion of the
Jews from Rome under Claudius: Iudaeos impulsore Chresto assidue tumultuantis
Roma expulit. It is debatable whether this refers to Christian missionary activity
or local Jewish disturbances.

[10] *Ann.* 15.44.

The earliest recorded view is that of Paul who wrote his letter to the Romans during Nero's initial *quinquennium*. Paul believed governments were ordained by God and that Christians should pay their taxes.[11] Several decades later (c. 75 C.E.), the author of First Peter wrote to Christians in Asia Minor and again urged submission.[12] Both authors wrote within the context of Christian paranesis and reflect a concern to avoid giving offense to Rome. The Apocalypse (c. 90-95 C.E.) offers a very different view of imperial power: Rome is now the enemy of God and her downfall only awaits its destined fulfillment. The framework of these comments has moved from epistolary exhortation to apocalyptic consolation. There is a third alternative in the New Testament, that of Luke-Acts. Since there is a direct connection—in my opinion—between the genre of Luke-Acts and its view of Rome we must first determine its literary position.

PREVIOUS RESEARCH

Ancient Views

Although the early church ascribed both Luke and Acts to the same author, the two books circulated independently.[13] The former came to be associated with the three other gospels. The first author to refer to the writings which describe Jesus' life and death under this heading is Justin Martyr (c. 100-c. 165 C.E.). In his first *Apology* Justin recounts the institution of the Eucharist by writing: Οἱ γὰρ ἀπόστολοι ἐν τοῖς γενομένοις ὑπ' αὐτῶν ἀπομνημονεύμασιν, ἃ καλεῖται εὐαγγέλια . . .[14] Justin's own term for the gospels is ἀπομνημονεύματα, "memoirs," the significance of which is debated.[15] By the end of the second century individual gospels were

---

[11] Rom. 13:1-7. It should be noted that Paul does not mention Rome specifically. Within the social context of his letter Rome is undoubtedly included.

[12] I Peter 2:13-17. The Christians the author addressed were undergoing some persecution, although I think it was social pressure rather than physical violence. See I Peter 3:13-17; 4:12-16. The most important treatment of this situation is that of John H. Elliott, *A Home for the Homeless: A Sociological Exegesis of I Peter* (Philadelphia: Fortress Press, 1981). Compare also the *Sitz im Leben* of the readers of Hebrews (10:32-34; 12:4).

[13] There is not a single manuscript which unites the two to my knowledge.

[14] *I Apol.* 66. Cf. also *Dial.* 10.2; 100.1.

[15] *E.g.*, *I Apol.* 66.3; 67.3 [cf. also 33.5]; and in *Dial.* 100-107, where he uses the ἀπομνημονεύματα τῶν ἀποστόλων to interpret Psa. 21. For a contemporary

designated as εὐαγγέλια along with the name of the supposed author. Thus the *Canon Muratorianus* (later half of the second century) designates our gospel: Tertium evagelii librum secundum Lucam.[16] P75 (175-225 C.E.), our oldest extant manuscript of the gospel, has Εὐαγγέλιον κατὰ Λοῦκαν as its heading.

There was apparently no set name for the book we have come to call Acts in the second century.[17] The *Canon Muratorianus* has: Acta autem omnium apostolorum sub uno libro scripta sunt.[18] An old independent prologue (the so-called "anti-Marcionite" prologue) to the gospel which also stems from the second century designates it as Πράξεις ᾿Αποστόλων in the Greek version and Actus Apostolorum in the Latin.[19] This secondary title is apparently an attempt to connect Acts with Πράξεις literature. Earlier examples include the accounts of Alexander by Kallistenes, Aristotle's nephew,[20] and Anaximenes of Lampsakos (c. 380-320 B.C.E.)[21] along with Sosylos' Περὶ ᾿Αννίβου πράξεων (*floruit* late third century B.C.E.).[22] The *res gestae* in Latin literature appear to be Roman equivalents. Although Peter and Paul are presented as heroes there are some major difficulties with this classification. Our work deals with more

---

summary of interpretations of Justin's usages see H. Koester, "From the Kerygma-Gospel to Written Gospels," *NTS* 35 (1989): 377-380. Koester argues that Marcion first used the term εὐαγγέλιον as a technical expression for a written document, pp. 375-377. For a full discussion of the term in the early period see Koester's *Ancient Christian Gospels: Their History and Development* (London: SCM Press Ltd/ Philadelphia: Trinity Press International), pp. 1-48.

[16] *Canon Muratorianus* 2. The second century dating of *Canon Muratorianus* has been challenged by Albert C. Sundberg, Jr., "Canon Muratori: A Fourth Century List, *HTR* 66 (1973): 1-41. Even if Sundberg were correct, the evidence of P75 secures my point. The patristic texts relating to the gospels are conveniently printed in Kurt Aland, ed., *Synopsis Quattuor Evangeliorum: Locis parallelis evangeliorum apocryphorum et patrum adhibitis*, 11th ed. (Stuttgart: Deutsche Bibelstiftung, 1976), pp. 531-548. Hereafter *SQE*.

[17] See Gerhard Schneider, *Die Apostelgeschichte*, 2 vols. HTKNT (Freiburg/ Basel/Wien: Herder, 1980-1982), 1:74.

[18] *Canon Muratorianus* 34-35. Patristic texts on Acts have been collected and printed with an English translation in F.J. Foakes Jackson and K. Lake, gen. eds., *The Beginnings of Christianity*, 5 vols. (London: Macmillan, 1920-1923; reprint ed., Grand Rapids: Baker Book House, 1979), 2:209-245. Hereafter abbreviated *Beginnings*.

[19] *SQE*, p. 533.

[20] *FGrH* 124 T 26.

[21] *FGrH* 72. See esp. the comment of Diogenes Laertios 2.3. Strabon 17.1.43, grouped the authors of the life of Alexander together as οἱ τὰς ᾿Αλεξάνδρου πράξεις ἀναγράψαντες.

[22] *FGrH* 176. Polybios considered his work more gossip than history (3.20.5).

than one hero and is actually more about God's actions in history
than about the accomplishments of the heroes. I know of no modern
scholar who takes this title as a serious designation of the literary
genre of the book.[23] The significance of the title for us is that it indicates the early church saw Acts as a historical work.[24]

Modern Critical Assessments

As in the early church, the predominant tendency in modern
scholarship has been to consider Luke and Acts separately. At the
very end of the period of liberalism, Clyde Weber Votaw published
an essay in which he argued that the gospels were Christian examples of biography.[25] Although his work was soon eclipsed by Neo-
Orthodoxy it has become important in more recent assessments.

During the heyday of liberalism, Franz Overbeck made the suggestion that the gospels were a unique contribution from Christianity.[26] Following World War I the concept that the gospels were *sui
generis* became almost a canonical tenet in *Formgeschichte*: all three of
the founding fathers argued for it vigorously.[27] This conclusion was

---

[23] For specific criticisms see Schneider, *Die Apostelgeschichte*, 1:74-75 (title only
appropriate for apocryphal Acts); Klaus Berger, "Hellenistische Gattungen im
Neuen Testament," in *Religion* (*Vorkonstantinisches Christentum: Leben und Umwelt
Jesu; Neues Testament, Forts [Kanonische Schriften und Apokryphen]*). ANRW II 25.2
(Berlin/New York: Walter de Gruyter, 1984), p. 1279 (*Praxeis* literature only deals
with one individual and has very loose connections between episodes); Rudolf
Pesch, *Die Apostelgeschichte*, 2 vols. EKKNT (Zürich/Einsiedeln/Köln: Benziger
Verlag and Neukirchener Verlag, 1986), 1:23 (fits neither the content nor the intention of Acts); and D. E. Aune, *The New Testament in Its Literary Environment*, p. 78
("*Praxeis* is a nontechnical, descriptive term").
[24] So also Eckhard Plümacher in *RESup*, s.v. "Lukas als griechischer Historiker," 14:262.
[25] "The Gospels and Contemporary Biographies," *American Journal of Theology*
19 (1915): 45-73; reprinted as *The Gospels and Contemporary Biographies in the Greco-
Roman World*. Facet Books/Biblical Series 27 (Philadelphia: Fortress Press, 1970).
[26] "Über die Anfänge der patristischen Literatur," *Historische Zeitschrift* 48
(1882): 417-472; reprinted as *Über die Anfänge der patristischen Literatur* (Darmstadt:
Wissenschaftliche Buchgesellschaft, 1966), pp. 36-37.
[27] Martin Dibelius, *Die Formgeschichte des Evangeliums*, 6th ed. (Tübingen:
J.C.B. Mohr, 1971) and his "The Structure and Literary Character of the
Gospels," *HTR* 20 (1927): 161-162, where Dibelius argues that the gospels were
created for missionary preaching; K.L. Schmidt, "Die Stellung der Evangelien in
der allgemeinen Literaturgeschichte," in EYXAPIΣTHPION: *Festschrift H. Gunkel*,
ed. H. Schmidt (Göttingen: Vandenhoeck und Ruprecht, 1923), pp. 50-140; and
Rudolf Bultmann in *RGG*, s.v. "Evangelien," 2:418-422.

directly linked to the collapse of the quest for the historical Jesus and
the emergence of dialectical theology in which a direct encounter
with the Word of God was thought possible through the kerygma.
From a literary perspective the gospels were *Kleinliteratur*. Now that
Neo-Orthodoxy has waned and all but vanished except within some
evangelical circles, this view has found fewer and fewer advocates
although it has not disappeared entirely.[28]

The search for parallels to the gospels never entirely ceased.
Moses Hadas and Morton Smith repeatedly argued that the gospels
are aretalogies presenting Jesus as a *theios aner*.[29] There are, however, several grave difficulties with this position. In the first place,
it is highly dubious that Jesus is presented as a *theios aner* in the
gospels.[30] Second, the existence of aretalogies as a distinct genre is
questionable.[31]

The displacement of form criticism by redaction criticism as the
leading hermeneutical tool for understanding the gospels accented
the role of the author and again kindled interest in parallels. While
recent research has considered a large number of possible precursors
for the gospels ranging from various Hellenistic forms to indigenous

---

[28] J. Arthur Baird, "Genre Analysis as a Method of Historical Criticism," in
Society of Biblical Literature Proceedings 1972 (Missoula, Montana: Scholars Press,
1972), pp. 400, 411, who prefers to call the gospels a "pseudo-genre" or "collective
genre." Two recent studies emanating from evangelical authors which summarize
preceding discussions and argue for this view are Robert H. Gundry, "Recent Investigations into the Literary Genre 'Gospel,'" in *New Dimensions in New Testament
Study*, edited by Richard N. Longenecker and Merrill C. Tenney (Grand Rapids:
Zondervan Publishing House, 1974), pp. 97-114, who does consider Luke-Acts
historical writing (p. 109) and does not consider the gospels to be a formal genre
since they have no predecessors (p. 114); and Robert Guelich, "The Gospel
Genre," in *Das Evangelium und die Evangelien: Vorträge vom Tübinger Symposium 1982*,
edited by Peter Stuhlmacher (Tübingen: J.C.B. Mohr (Paul Siebeck), 1983), pp.
183-219, who does consider them to be a unique genre.

[29] Hadas, *Hellenistic Culture*, p. 177; Moses Hadas and Morton Smith, *Heroes
and Gods: Spiritual Biographies in Antiquity*. Religious Perspectives 13 (New York:
Harper & Row, Publishers, 1965), pp. 101-104, 161-195, where they print excerpts
from the gospel of Luke as an example of this literary category; and Morton Smith,
"Prolegomena to a Discussion of Aretalogies, Divine Men, the Gospels and Jesus," *JBL* 90 (1971): 174-199, who argues that the gospels are aretalogies on the
basis of their content (pp. 195-199), especially the miracle stories. He suggests that
a collection of miracle stories covering the period from Jesus' baptism to his trans-
figuration lies behind the first half of Mark (p. 197).

[30] Tiede, *The Charismatic Figure as Miracle Worker* and Holladay, "*Theios Aner*" in
Hellenistic Judaism.

[31] Howard C. Kee, "Aretalogy and Gospel," *JBL* 92 (1973): 402-422.

Christian materials,[32] the trend appears to be angling back to Votaw and considering the gospels as some form of biographical writing.[33]

Cursory as this glance is, it indicates a fundamental problem which has tended to cloud gospel studies, i.e., consideration of the synoptics as a group rather than each gospel as a unit. This is particularly acute with Luke since it also has clear ties to Acts. Regardless of a final conclusion, the relationship with Acts must be explained.[34]

The same situation holds true for Acts. The dominant conception has been and remains that it belongs to the *Gattung* of history.[35] In the past it has been common simply to view Acts as a historical work without locating it in any specific tradition.[36] Some have demon-

---

[32] Howard Clark Kee, *Community of the New Age: Studies in Mark's Gospel* (Philadelphia: The Westminster Press, 1977), pp. 14-49, esp.17-30, has a pointed overview of the theories.

[33] So John Drury, *Tradition and Design in Luke's Gospel: A Study in Early Christian Historiography* (London: Darton, Longman & Todd, 1976), pp. 27-32; Charles H. Talbert, *What is a Gospel? The Genre of the Canonical Gospels* (Philadelphia: Fortress Press, 1977), his "Biographies of Philosophers and Rulers as Instruments of Religious Propaganda in Mediterannean Antiquity," in *Religion (Heidentum: Römische Religion, Allgemeines)*, ed. Wolfgang Haase. ANRW II 16.2 (Berlin/New York: Walter de Gruyter, 1978), pp. 1619-1651, and his most recent "Once Again: Gospel Genre," *Semeia* 43 (1988): 53-73 [and the following rejoinder by David P. Moessner, "And Once Again, What Sort of 'Essence?:' A Response to Charles Talbert," pp. 75-84, who argues that Luke is history]; Philip L. Schuler, *A Genre for the Gospels: The Biographical Character of Matthew* (Philadelphia: Fortress Press, 1982), who classified Matthew as an *encomium biography*; Albrecht Dihle, "Die Evangelien und die biographische Tradition der Antike," *ZTK* 80 (1983): 33-49; Berger, "Hellenistische Gattungen im Neuen Testament," pp. 1231-1264 and his later *Formgeschichte des Neuen Testaments* (Heidelberg: Quelle & Meyer, 1984), pp. 346-356, especially 347 where he follows Schuler; Detlev Dormeyer, "Evangelium als literarische Gattung und als theologischer Begriff. Tendenzen und Aufgaben der Evangelienforschung im 20. Jahrhundert, mit einer Untersuchung des Markusevangeliums in seinem Verhältnis zur antiken Biographie," ANRW II 25.2: 1581-1601; and Aune, *The New Testament in Its Literary Environment*, pp. 17-76, who classifies the gospels as a subtype of Greco-Roman biography.

[34] One sign of how pervasive the tendency to consider them separately has been is to scan commentaries on the two and look for a major work on Luke-Acts. I realize there are physical limitations which authors and publishers confront, but the absence of a major sustained commentary on the two is telling.

[35] So W. Ward Gasque, "A Fruitful Field," pp. 119, 129.

[36] Haenchen, *The Acts of the Apostles*, pp. 98-103; C.K. Barrett, *Luke the Theologian in Recent Study* (London: Epworth Press, 1961), p. 9; Momigliano, "Greek Historiography," p. 20; C.J. Hemer, "Luke the Historian," *BJRL* 60 (1977-1978): 29-34; and F.F. Bruce, "The Acts of the Apostles: Historical Record or Theological Reconstruction?" in ANRW II. 25.3:2569-2603.

strated the ties of Acts to Hellenistic historiography generally.[37] The most important effort along these lines was that of W.C. van Unnik who based upon the preface, speeches, and emphasis on autopsy, considered Acts as a historical work and then compared it to the rules of historiography in Dionysios of Halikarnassos' *Epistula ad Pompeium* and Lucian's *Quomodo historia conscribenda sit* and effectively demonstrated its congruence.[38]

More recently some have tried to specify the type of history or the category of historical writing. Hans Conzelmann thought Acts was a "historical monograph."[39] Klaus Berger has taken this a step further by arguing that Acts is a special type of historical monograph, i.e., apologetic history. He thinks that the closest analogues are I-III Maccabees, the Hellenistic-Jewish historians, and Josephos.[40] John

---

[37] Cadbury, "The Greek and Jewish Traditions of Writing History," in *Beginnings*, 2: 7-29, who astutely observed that as in Josephos both Greek and Jewish traditions are present; Dibelius, "The First Christian Historian," in *Studies in the Acts of the Apostles*, pp. 123-137; Étienne Trocmé, *Le 'Livre des Actes' et l'histoire*. Études d'Histoire et de Philosophie Religieuses. (Paris: Presses Universitaires de France, 1957), pp. 76-121; Hanneliese Steichele, *Vergleich der Apostelgeschichte mit der antiken Geschichtsschreibung: Eine Studie zur Erzählkunst in der Apostelgeschichte* (München: Hanneliese Steichele, 1971), who only argues that Acts shares three narrative techniques with Greek historiography (selection of the most important events for the theme, rhetorical and poetical formulation of the material, and the placement of the events in a flowing narrative); and Paul Vielhauer, *Geschichte der urchristlichen Literatur: Einleitung in das Neue Testament, die Apokryphen und die Apostolischen Väter* (Berlin/New York: Walter de Gruyter, 1975), pp. 399-400, who pointed out that the recognition of connections, the supra-historical speeches, and the emphasis on important figures marks Acts out as history but believes that like the Gospels it has no literary parallel.

[38] "Luke's Second Book and the Rules of Hellenistic Historiography," in *Les Actes des Apôtres: Tradition, rédaction, théologie*, ed. Jacob Kremer. BETL 48 (Leuven: University Press, 1979), pp. 37-60. His ten rules are: (1) the selection of a noble subject; (2) one that is profitable to the reader; (3) the historian must be independent; (4) the beginning and end must be appropriate; (5) collection of material; (6) proper selection of what to include and exclude; (7) disposition and order so that the narrative is clear; (8) vividness; (9) moderation in topographical information; (10) suitability in speeches.

[39] *Acts of the Apostles*, trans. by James Limburg, A. Thomas Kraabel, and Donald H. Juel. Hermeneia (Philadelphia: Fortress Press, 1987), p. xl; Eckhard Plümacher, "Die Apostelgeschichte als historische Monographie," in *Les Actes des Apôtres: Tradition, rédaction, théologie*, pp. 457-466 (the most important statement of this position) and *RESup*, s.v. "Lukas als griechischer Historiker," 14:262-263; Martin Hengel, *Acts and the History of Earliest Christianity*, pp. 14, 36-37, who does not think that Acts should be separated from Luke (p. 37); Schneider, *Die Apostelgeschichte*, 1:122; Earl Richard, "Luke—Writer, Theologian, Historian," p. 10; and Rudolf Pesch, *Die Apostelgeschichte*, 1:23.

[40] "Hellenistische Gattungen im Neuen Testament," pp. 1275, 1281; and *Formgeschichte des Neuen Testament*, pp. 359-360.

Drury and Daryl Schmidt have respectively argued that Luke and Acts are Jewish rather than Hellenistic.[41] In an important recent treatment David Aune has labelled Luke-Acts "general history" as opposed to monographs or antiquarian history.[42]

There have, however, been some important exceptions to the dominant perspective. One of the most persuasive attempts to classify Luke-Acts (not just Acts) is the work of Charles Talbert.[43] Talbert analyzed the patterns of the lives in Diogenes Laertios and concluded that they followed a threefold sequence: life of the founder, a narrative about the disciples and successors who formed a type of religious community, and a summary of the doctrine or teaching.[44] He argued that these lives were designed to define the specific way of life for each school.[45] He then argued that Luke-Acts followed this in content, form (i.e., the specific sequence of founder followed by successors), and function (both define the specific way).[46] The most helpful aspect of Talbert's analysis is that it attempts to explain Luke-Acts. There are, however, some serious difficulties. First, the narrative unity of Luke-Acts is far greater than the sequential lives of the individual figures of the philosophic schools in Diogenes.[47]

---

[41] Drury, *Tradition and Design in Luke's Gospel*, pp. 3-8 (p. 8: "Luke is Jewish in the story-telling tradition of the books of Genesis, Judges, Samuel and Kings and the tales in the Apocrypha, a tradition still alive in Josephus' grand historical *midrash*, *The Jewish Antiquities*, and in *Joseph and Asenath*."); Daryl Schmidt, "The Historiography of Acts: Deuteronomistic or Hellenistic?" in *Society of Biblical Literature 1985 Seminar Papers*, edited by Kent Harold Richards (Atlanta: Scholars Press, 1985), pp. 417-427. David Balch, "Acts as Hellenistic Historiography," *ibid.*, pp. 429-432, wrote a response to Schmidt.

[42] *The New Testament in Its Literary Environment*, pp. 77-157, especially pp. 77, 88-89. David L. Balch, "Comments on the Genre and a Political Theme of Luke-Acts: A Preliminary Comparison of Two Hellenistic Historians," in *Society of Biblical Literature 1989 Seminar Papers*, ed. David J. Lull (Atlanta: Scholars Press, 1989), pp. 343-361, has followed Aune's classification and attempted to refine it by comparing Luke-Acts with Dionysios of Halikarnassos.

[43] *Literary Patterns, Theological Themes and the Genre of Luke-Acts*. SBLMS 20 (Missoula, Montana: Scholars Press, 1974) and *Reading Luke: A Literary and Theological Commentary on the Third Gospel* (New York: Crossroad, 1982), pp. 2-6. Cf. also David L. Barr and Judith L. Wentling, "The Conventions of Classical Biography and the Genre of Luke-Acts: A Preliminary Study," in *Luke-Acts: New Perspectives from the Society of Biblical Literature Seminar*, edited by Charles H. Talbert (New York: Crossroad, 1984), pp. 63-88, who do not consider Luke-Acts to be a biography, but that the readers would have heard it with some of the same expectations as a biography.

[44] *Ibid.*, pp. 125-129.

[45] *Ibid.*, p. 128.

[46] *Ibid.*, pp. 129-134, especially 129-130.

[47] *Ibid.*, p. 133, Talbert sought to meet this objection by arguing that Luke-Acts and Diogenes worked from a common pattern and implemented it differently.

Second, Diogenes is concerned with who studied with whom rather than the validity of each philosopher's views. Luke-Acts is concerned with legitimacy as we will see.

Another recent alternative is that Acts is a romance.[48] The most important advocate of this view is Richard Pervo who based upon the presence of elements of adventure common to Acts and novels considers Acts a "historical novel."[49] It is to Pervo's credit that he has pointed out the entertaining nature of Acts more comprehensively than any of his predecessors. Once again, however, there are some serious drawbacks. First, the presence of dramatic elements in Acts is not a sufficient basis to classify Acts as a novel since it was common among historians as well.[50] One wonders against whom Polybios would have railed had Pervo's method been recognized in antiquity. Second, he must draw a sharp line between the gospel and Acts since we have some idea of how the author worked in the former by comparing it to his sources, Mark and Q.[51] (See below) I do not believe the two can be severed. Finally, was Acts intended to entertain or to inform in an entertaining way?

Summary

The arguments for locating Acts within the stream of historiography are persuasive for me. The speeches and the agreements in methodology with Hellenistic historians are most plausibly explained in this tradition. This, however, raises two questions. First, how do

---

In my opinion Luke-Acts tells the story of a people, not a loose-knit collection of stories about individual figures in a school of thought.

[48] Stephen P. Schierling and Marla J. Schierling, "The Influence of the Ancient Romances on *Acts of the Apostles*," *The Classical Bulletin* 54 (1978): 81-88, noted the similarities between Acts and the romances without classifying it as such. Cf. also Holzberg, *Der antike Roman*, pp. 28-29. Susan Praeder, "Luke-Acts and the Ancient Novel," *Society of Biblical Literature 1981 Seminar Papers*, edited by Kent Richards (Chico: Scholars Press, 1981), pp. 269-292, developed a "narrative paradigm" for genre classification and categorized Luke-Acts as a novel.

[49] *Profit with Delight: The Literary Genre of the Acts of the Apostles* (Philadelphia: Fortress Press, 1987), esp. pp. 12-85 (where he demonstrates the entertaining nature of Acts), 122, 135 (for his formal classification). He thinks the closest analogue is Artapanos, pp. 118-119.

[50] He attempts to head off this objection by broadening the concept of genre to include "more overtly historical and didactic works." *Ibid.*, p. 103. Cf. also p. 114, where he offers a list (incomplete!) of more than fifty works which he considers novels.

[51] *Ibid.*, p. 4, he recognized this.

Luke and Acts relate? Second, if they are a unit, Luke-Acts, what historiographical tradition most influenced their conception and formation?[52] Since one of the elements which addresses their possible unity is common authorship we will first turn to the writer.

LIFE

Identity

The third gospel and the book of Acts are both anonymous.[53] In spite of this there is a unanimous tradition in the early church that Luke wrote both volumes. The immediate question is: Was this tradition handed down apart from the text or is it based upon inferences made from the text itself? The first thing that strikes an investigator is the absence of the tradition in the first half of the second century. Papias (c. 60-130 C.E.), the bishop of Hierapolis and disciple of the elder John, provided information on both Mark and Matthew, but not on Luke.[54] When Marcion formulated his canon of scripture he used an edited version of Luke's gospel and rejected the other three. Interestingly, his single gospel appeared anonymously.[55]

It is not until the latter half of the second century that we have any testimony about the authorship of these works. There are three major witnesses to the tradition at this time. The first is the old independent prologue to Luke.[56] The preface names Luke as the author of both works and provides the following biographical data: he was a Syrian from Antioch (cf. Acts 11:28 D and the Western

---

[52] A first draft of the argument of this chapter appeared as "Luke-Acts and Apologetic Historiography," in *Society of Biblical Literature 1989 Seminar Papers*, pp. 326-342.

[53] Dibelius, *Studies in the Acts of the Apostles*, p. 104, thought that the works reached the book market and therefore had the name of the author on them. This, however, is doubtful. (See under Function)

[54] His work, Λογίων Κυριακῶν Ἐξηγήσεις, in five books has only come down to us through Irenaeus and Eusebios. On the gospels see Eusebios, *HE* 3.39.15-16. On Papias see Josef Kürzinger, *Papias von Hierapolis und die Evangelien des Neuen Testaments: Gesammelte Aufsätze, Neuausgabe und Übersetzung der Fragmente, Kommentierte Bibliographie* (Regensburg: Friedrich Pustet, 1983) and Ulrich H.J. Körtner, *Papias von Hierapolis: Ein Beitrag zur Geschichte des frühen Christentums*. FRLANT 133 (Göttingen: Vandenhoeck & Ruprecht, 1983).

[55] Tertullian, *Adv. Marc.* 4.2.3: Contra Marcion evangelio, scilicet suo, nullum adscribit auctorem, quasi non licuerit illi titulum quoque adfingere, cui nefas non fuit ipsum corpus evertere.

[56] *SQE*, 532-533.

witnesses[57]), a physician (cf. Col. 4:14), a companion of Paul who was with him μέχρις τοῦ μαρτυρίου αὐτοῦ (cf. Phlm. 24; II Tim. 4:11), and a bachelor who died in Boeotia at the ripe old age of 84.[58] The preface goes on to tell us that he composed the gospel in Achaia after Matthew and Mark had already written their works. The second source is Irenaeus (c. 130-c. 200) who openly demonstrates his dependence on the biblical text by citing two of the "we" passages from Acts (Acts 16:10-17; 20:5-15) along with II Tim. 4:10-11 and Col. 4:14.[59] The final source is the *Canon Muratorianus* which names Luke as the author of the third gospel. Luke is that physician (Col. 4:14)[60] whom Paul took with him as a companion (Acts 16:10-17; 20:5-15; 21:1-18; 27:1-28:16). He did not see the Lord himself (Lk. 1:2), but wrote on the basis of report (Lk. 1:3).[61] The same canon goes on to state that Luke wrote Acts based upon his own experiences since he omits both the death of Peter and Paul's release from prison.[62]

It thus appears that the tradition from the second century is primarily drawn from inferences made from the biblical text. The most impressive apparent exception is the name of the author, Luke. Yet even this could be deduced from the biblical text: the "we" pas-

---

[57] The relationship between the Western reading here and the tradition has been debated. James Hardy Ropes, *Beginnings*, 3:108, thought that the reading was derived from the tradition. Cadbury, *Beginnings*, 2:248, argued the opposite. T.W. Manson, "The Life of Jesus: A Survey of the Available Material. (3) The Work of St. Luke," *BJRL* 28 (1944): 388, contended that both were independently derived from the "fact" that Luke was an Antiochene Christian. In reality, the most plausible explanation for the appearance of the "we" in the Western text is the subsequent identification of the author with the Lukios of 13:1. So Haenchen, *The Acts of the Apostles*, p. 374 n. 7; Conzelmann, *Acts of the Apostles*, p. 90; and Schneider, *Die Apostelgeschichte*, 2:96.

[58] Note that this is the same age as the prophetess Anna in Lk. 2:37.

[59] *Adv. haeres.* 3.14.1 (*SQE*, 536).

[60] William Kirk Hobart, *The Medical Language of St. Luke: A Proof from Internal Evidence that 'the Gospel According to St. Luke' and 'the Acts of the Apostles' were Written by the Same Person, and that the Writer was a Medical Man*. Dublin University Press Series (Dublin: Hodges, Figgis, & Co., 1882), attempted to prove that the author of Luke-Acts was a physician through vocabulary studies. This, however, has been decisively answered by Henry J. Cadbury who demonstrated the presence of the same terms in educated Hellenistic writers generally. Cf. *The Style and Literary Method of St. Luke*. HTS 6 (Cambridge: Harvard University Press, 1920; reprint ed., New York: Kraus Reprint Co., 1969), pp. 39-72; "Lexical Notes on Luke-Acts: II. Recent Arguments for Medical Language," *JBL* 45 (1926): 190-206; and "V. Luke and the Horse-Doctors," *JBL* 52 (1933): 55-65.

[61] *SQE*, 538.

[62] Ll. 34-39 conveniently in *Beginnings*, 2:210.

sages furnishing the clue that the author was Paul's companion and Paul's letters providing possible names which were narrowed down by reference back to Acts. There was a clear motive for doing this: all books considered canonical had to be either apostolic or associated with an apostle.[63] The other incidental details which have no biblical counterpart are insignificant and reflect the tendency to offer biographical information on authors. Since subsequent tradition is essentially a recapitulation of the earlier material, there is no need to consider it independently. It is, therefore, difficult to give much credence to the tradition other than to note the fact that it is unanimous.[64] This, however, deserves attention since the name of Luke is not such an obvious deduction that all of the early sources would necessarily draw it independently.

We are thus thrown back onto the text itself. The first issue which we must address is whether the text supports a common authorship of the two works. The connection between the two is obvious from the prefaces of each (Lk. 1:1-4; Acts 1:1-3) with the common dedication to Theophilos and the reference in Acts back to τὸν πρῶτον λόγον (1:1).[65] The relationship is further cemented by the recapitulation of Lk. 24:36-53 in Acts 1:1-13. The final witness is the style which characterizes both books.[66] While there are some variations

---

[63] Tertullian, *Adv. Marc.* 4.2.1-5 (*SQE*, 540). Cf. also Clement of Alexandria, *Adumbrationes* (*ad I Petr. 5:13*) (*SQE*, 539). It is this fact which makes Origen's comments about the authorship of Hebrews so memorable. *Apud* Eusebios, *HE* 6.25.11-14.

[64] So also Cadbury, *Beginnings*, 2:250-264; Haenchen, *The Acts of the Apostles*, pp. 1-14; Schneider, *Die Apostelgeschichte*, 1:108-111; Pesch, *Die Apostelgeschichte*, 1:26-27. *Contra* Joseph A. Fitzmyer, *The Gospel According to Luke*, 2 vols. AB 28 and 28A (Garden City, New York: Doubleday & Company, Inc., 1981-1985), 1:37-41 and his more recent *Luke the Theologian: Aspects of His Teaching* (New York/Mahweh: Paulist Press, 1989), pp. 1-26.

[65] Πρῶτος here is used in place of πρότερος as is common in Hellenistic Greek and should not be pressed to presuppose a third volume was planned. The author follows the same convention in 7:12 and 12:10. See F. Blass and A. Debrunner, *A Greek Grammar of the New Testament and Other Early Christian Literature*, trans. and revised by Robert W. Funk (Chicago/London: The University of Chicago Press, 1961), 62. Josephos uses πρότερος in *CA* 2.1.

[66] This has been challenged on two occasions to my knowledge. Albert C. Clark, *The Acts of the Apostles: A Critical Edition with Introduction and Notes on Selected Passages* (Oxford: The Clarendon Press, 1933), pp. 393-408, denied a common authorship on linguistic grounds. His strongest arguments in my opinion were the frequencies of particles: τε (Lk. 8t; Acts 158t. including variants); μεν (Lk. 11t.; Acts 51t.). He was answered effectively by Wilfred L. Knox, *The Acts of the Apostles* (Cambridge: The University Press, 1948), pp. 1-15, who pointed out that the frequency of μεν even varies in Acts (1:5-12:25 = 16t. vs. 13:1-28:31 = 31t.). The

in style between the two books there is nothing which would prohibit common authorship and a great deal to commend it.

Are there any hints in either of the two about the author's identity? There are two occasions where the author of Luke-Acts uses the first person. The first is the prologue (Lk. 1:1-4). Luke opens his preface with a causal clause: Ἐπειδήπερ πολλοὶ ἐπεχείρησαν ἀνατάξασθαι διήγησιν περὶ τῶν πεπληροφορημένων ἐν ἡμῖν πραγμάτων, καθὼς παρέδοσαν ἡμῖν οἱ ἀπ᾽ ἀρχῆς αὐτόπται καὶ ὑπηρέται γενόμενοι τοῦ λόγου. . . (Vv. 1-2) The repetition of ἡμῖν is significant. In the first instance the author identifies himself as a Christian who stands in continuity with the events he is going to describe. In the second instance the term is narrowed by setting οἱ ἀπ᾽ ἀρχῆς αὐτόπται καὶ ὑπηρέται γενόμενοι τοῦ λόγου apart. This distinction helps us to see that there are three different groups in these verses: (1) the eyewitnesses, (2) the "many" previous accounts, and (3) the author and the audience of Luke. Nor can these three groups be understood to be contemporaries.[67] The "eyewitnesses" παρέδοσαν, a *terminus technicus* for the handing on of a tradition.[68] The accounts of the "many" had to have circulated for some time in order for our author to refer to them and expect the readers to relate to them. The author is thus clearly situated in the third generation of Christians in the first century.

The second group of texts are the famous "we" passages in Acts upon which the early church built its case (16:10-17; 20:5-15; 21:1-18; 27:1-28:16).[69] It must be acknowledged that the force of

---

controversy has recently re-emerged in the articles of A.W. Argyle, "The Greek of Luke and Acts," *NTS* 20 (1973-1974): 441-445, who argues against common authorship on the basis of different preferences for words in Luke and Acts. He has been answered by B.E. Beck, "The Common Authorship of Luke and Acts," *NTS* 23 (1976-1977): 346-352, who pointed out that not all of Argyle's pairs are synonyms, more attention needs to be paid to sources, and the fact that synonyms commonly appear in Luke and Acts as well as Luke-Acts. The ghost, however, has not entirely been laid to rest. J. Dawsey, "The Literary Unity of Luke-Acts: Questions of Style—A Task for Literary Critics," *NTS* 35 (1989): 48-66, has called for a new investigation of the whole matter. Full monographs which analyze Lukan style include: Cadbury, *The Style and Literary Method of Luke* and Joachim Jeremias, *Die Sprache des Lukasevangeliums: Redaktion und Tradition im Nicht-Markusstoff des dritten Evangeliums. Kritisch-exegetischer Kommentar über das Neue Testament* (Göttingen: Vandenhoeck & Ruprecht, 1980).

[67] So also Richard J. Dillon, "Previewing Luke's Project from His Prologue (Luke 1:1-4)," *CBQ* 43 (1981): 210.

[68] E.g., I Cor. 11:23; 15:3; Jude 3 where it refers to the passing on of Christian traditions.

[69] I can not except the view of patristic commentators and Cadbury that the

these texts is to claim that the author was present. The issue is whether he in fact was. There are three major problems with the claim. First, the author shows no awareness of Paul's letters.[70] Second, the record of Paul's activities in Acts is at odds with Paul's own statements in his letters.[71] Third, the theology of Acts is different from that of Paul.[72] Can we attribute a work encumbered with these difficulties to a traveling companion of Paul?

Martin Dibelius attempted to explain the "we" passages as references to an itinerary which Luke employed. He thought that Luke inserted the "we" references to those sections where he was personally present.[73] This, however, still leaves us with the problem of the association of Luke with Paul. W.G. Kümmel attempted to solve this by suggesting that an unknown author copied the itinerary and left the "we" in the narrative.[74] Ernst Haenchen, who early on agreed with Dibelius, changed his mind and discarded the itinerary and argued that the "we" statements were insertions made at the level of redaction either to provide historical verification for a crucial step in the Pauline mission (16) or to involve the reader in the narrative (20-21; 27-28).[75] A major difficulty with this position is that

---

first person plural in the preface of Lk. 1:1-4, conveys the meaning of the author's presence (see below).

[70] John Knox, "Acts and the Pauline Letter Corpus," in *Studies in Luke-Acts*, pp. 279-287, has argued that Luke intentionally omitted Paul's letters because of their "schismatic associations." While the author attempted to present a unified church, it remains inconceivable to me that he would have omitted the Pauline corpus if he saw in Paul a legitimate heir of Jesus.

[71] E.g., compare Gal. 1:13-2:14 with Acts 9:19-30; 11:27-30 and 12:25; 15:1-12; 18:22; and compare I Thess. 3:1-6 with Acts 17:13-16; 18:1, 5. These differences extend to the presentation of Paul: in his letters he presents himself as an apostle; in Acts he is a missionary (he is only called an apostle in Acts 14:4, 14, where it means a representative sent out from the church in Antioch). Ernst Haenchen, "The Book of Acts as Source Material for the History of Early Christianity," in *Studies in Luke-Acts*, edited by Leander E. Keck and J. Louis Martyn (reprint ed., Philadelphia: Fortress Press, 1980), pp. 258-278, states the difficulties forcefully. For an overview of the different approaches see A.J. Mattill, Jr. "The Value of Acts as a Source for the Study of Paul," in *Perspectives on Luke-Acts*, ed. Charles H. Talbert. Perspectives in Religious Studies/Special Studies Series 5 (Danville, VA: Association of Baptist Professors of Religion, 1978), pp. 76-98.

[72] Cf. the famous essay of Philipp Vielhauer, "On the 'Paulinism' of Acts," in *Studies in Luke-Acts*, pp. 33-50. The theological differences appear to be the straw that broke the back of the traditional view in contemporary thinking.

[73] *Studies in the Acts of the Apostles*, pp. 104-108, 196-206.

[74] Werner Georg Kümmel, *Introduction to the New Testament*, revised ed., trans. Howard Clark Kee (Nashville: Abingdon Press, 1975), pp. 177-185.

[75] *The Acts of the Apostles*, pp. 85-90 and "Das 'Wir' in der Apostelgeschichte und das Itinerar," *ZTK* 58 (1961): 329-366, especially 366. Cf. also Vernon

some of the stopping places included are insignificant. The "we" passages appear so unobtrusively that the most natural way to read them is still the quiet presence of the author or a source.[76]

What should we make of the tradition and the biblical text? The basic tension is between the tradition and the "we" texts on the one hand and the conflict between Acts and the Pauline corpus on the other. Joseph Fitzmyer proposed a mediating solution by pointing out that the "we" texts do not make the author an inseparable companion of Paul, but only an occasional traveling companion.[77] This still leaves us with the difficulty of explaining how Luke could be so ignorant of Paul: the "we" sections require more than mere acquaintance—as Fitzmyer has argued.

I would like to propose another solution. My suggestion must be considered tentative, but I believe that it does justice to the facts as we know them. We are on *terra firma* to recognize that Paul had a companion named Luke.[78] We also know that this Luke came to be associated with the authorship of Luke-Acts on the basis of the "we" passages from Acts. It is *possible* that Luke, Paul's companion, is the source for the "we" passages in Acts and perhaps for more of the material in Acts 13-28.[79] This Luke would be a second generation Christian. (Paul must be considered a first generation Christian.) Towards the end of the first century (see below) a third generation Christian—who had not accompanied Paul—using Luke as his authority for the latter half of Acts composed Luke-Acts.[80] It is impossible to say whether the author knew Luke personally or had a written source, although the unanimity of the tradition suggests a strong (and therefore personal) connection between the author and Paul's traveling companion. In either case, the "we" texts served

---

Robbins, "By Land and by Sea: The We-Passages and Ancient Sea Voyages," in *Perspectives on Luke-Acts*, pp. 215-242 and Schneider, *Die Apostelgeschichte*, 1:89-95, esp. 94-95.

[76] Conzelmann, *Acts of the Apostles*, p. xl: "The only certainty is that by using 'we' the author attempts to convey the impression of an eyewitness account."

[77] *The Gospel According to Luke*, 1:47-51.

[78] Phlm. 24; Col. 4:14 (which could be authentic); and II Tim. 4:11 (deutero-Pauline).

[79] It is widely known that the "we" passages form something of a unit: 16:10-17 (from Troas to Philippi); 20:5-15 (from Philippi to Miletos); 21:1-18 (from Miletos to Caesarea/Jerusalem); 27:1-28:16 (from Caesarea to Rome).

[80] I have retained masculine gender in the use of pronouns for the author since the author uses the masculine form of the participle in the self-reference in Lk. 1:3, παρηκολουθηκότι not παρηκολουθηκυῖα.

as an indication that the narrative was based upon an eyewitness account. In this way the third gospel and Acts came to be associated with the apostle's companion.[81]

Ethnicity

Traditionally, the author of Luke-Acts has been considered a Gentile.[82] The arguments are largely based on internal evidence such as the absence of Semitic expressions, the omission of Jewish concerns in the gospel, and the sensitivity to Gentile Christianity. These, however, are arguments about the intended audience rather than the author.[83] Some have tried to extend this to conclude that the author was a Greek. This is generally buttressed by either Col. 4:10-11, 14, or the quality of the Greek. The former may or may not tell us something about Paul's traveling companion, but offers no help for the author. The latter would prove Philo and Josephos to be Greeks! Joseph Fitzmyer has more recently advanced the thesis that he was a Syrian, an *incola* of Antioch of Pisidia.[84] The difficulty with Fitzmyer's view is that it depends upon the very dubious ecclesial tradition.[85] The second view is that the author was Jewish.[86] The major arguments for this position are the author's thorough

---

[81] It is possible that Marcion chose Luke on the basis of some connection with Paul rather than only on the basis of its content.

[82] Kümmel, *Introduction to the New Testament*, p. 149, went so far as to say: "The only thing that can be said with certaintly about the author, on the basis of Lk, is that he was a Gentile Christian."

[83] Fitzmyer, *The Gospel According to Luke*, 1:45. Fitzmyer provides a good overview of the positions and arguments in 1:41-47.

[84] *Ibid.*, 1:44-47.

[85] There is a real interest in Antioch evidenced in Acts. Fitzmyer seems to assume this confirms the tradition (*Ibid.*, pp. 46-47). I prefer to think it is the basis for it. He makes his case, however, on the tradition: the old prologue, Eusebios, *HE* 3.4.6; and Jerome, *De vir. ill.* 7.

[86] Recent representatives of this position among commentators are W.F. Albright in Johannes Munck, *The Acts of the Apostles*, rev. by W.F. Albright and C.S. Mann. AB 31 (Garden City, New York: Doubleday & Company, Inc., 1967), pp. 264-267 and E. Earle Ellis, *The Gospel of Luke, rev. ed.* NCB (Greenwood, S.C.: Attic Press, Inc., 1974), pp. 51-53. Marilyn Salmon, "Insider or Outsider? Luke's Relationship with Judaism," in *Luke-Acts and the Jewish People: Eight Critical Perspectives*, ed. Joseph B. Tyson (Minneapolis: Augsburg Publishing House, 1988), pp. 76-82, esp. 79-80, has recently stated the case for Jewish identity by noting that the author distinguishes among groups of Jews (outsiders tend not to concern themselves with such distinctions), devotes a great deal of attention to Torah observance, is interested in the *Gentile* (a Jewish perspective) mission, and presents Christianity as a *hairesis* (the same as a Jewish sect).

knowledge of the LXX, the accurate reflection of Judaism in the infancy narrative, and the concern for the Jewish people throughout
the work.[87] Apart from the arguments above, the major objection
to this view is Acts 1:19, where the author refers to Aramaic as τῇ
ἰδίᾳ διαλέκτῳ αὐτῶν.[88] This could, however, be written from the
readers' perspective rather than the author's.[89]

Can we reach a decision? The determining factor in my opinion
is the author's mastery of the OT. The intimate acquaintance evidenced in Luke and Acts was acquired over a period of years. A close
connection with the synagogue seems unavoidable, especially given
the author's knowledge of Hellenistic Judaism. (See below) He,
therefore, must have either been a God-fearer of long-standing[90] or
a Jew. It is clear that our author has received a Hellenistic education
as his style and techniques demonstrate.[91] The only certain thing

---

[87] Mention might also be made of the tradition in Epiphanios, *Panarion* 51.11,
that the author was one of the seventy-two disciples.

[88] The author is clearly speaking *in propria persona* rather than from the historical
standpoint. The only other text which would mitigate against Jewish authorship is
Acts 28:2, 4, where the narrator refers to οἱ βάρβαροι. Adolf von Harnack, *Luke the
Physician: The Author of the Third Gospel and the Acts of the Apostles*, trans. J.R. Wilkinson, 2nd ed. Crown Theological Library (New York: G.P. Putnam's Sons, 1909),
p. 13 n. 1, considered this decisive evidence that the author was a Greek. Josephos,
however, uses the term to refer to non-Hellenes, e.g., *CA* 1.58, 116, 161.

[89] It is also possible that a Hellenistic Jew who knew only Greek might refer to
Aramaic in this way. This would especially hold true if a Jewish Christian made
a distinction between Christians and Jews who had not converted.

[90] On οἱ φοβούμενοι τὸν θεόν see Acts 10:2, 22, 35; 13:16, 26. Σεβόμενοι is
used in 13:43, 50; 17:4, 17, to denote a group. It is used in the singular in 16:14
and 18:7 to describe the piety of Lydia and Titius Justus respectively. Josephos also
testifies to the existence of Gentiles who formed an attachment to Jews without becoming proselytes, *BJ* 2.461-463; 7.45; *AJ* 14.110; *CA* 2.282. Cf. the discussion of
Kirsopp Lake, *Beginnings*, 5:74-96, especially 84-88. Their existence has been recently challenged by A.T. Kraabel, "The Disappearance of the 'God-Fearers,'"
Numen 28 (1981): 113-126 and his more recent "Greeks, Jews, and Lutherans in
the Middle Half of Acts," *HTR* 79 (1986): 147-157, but unsuccessfully in my opinion. His views have generated a good deal of discussion. See in particular John G.
Gager, "Jews, Gentiles, and Synagogues in the Book of Acts," *HTR* 79 (1986):
91-99 and the more popular debate in *BAR* 12 (1986) among Robert S. MacLennan
and A. Thomas Kraabel, "The God-Fearers—A Literary and Theological Invention," pp. 46-53, 64; Robert F. Tannenbaum, "Jews and God-Fearers in the Holy
City of Aphrodite," pp. 54-57; and Louis Feldman, "The Omnipresence of the
God-Fearers," pp. 58-63.

[91] On the quality of the Greek of Luke-Acts see Jerome, *Comment. on Isaiah* 3.6;
Epistula 20.4; *De viris illustribus* 7 (Graeci sermonis non ignarus fuit). Cadbury, *The
Style and Literary Method of Luke*, pp. 1-39, compared Luke's vocabulary to that of
the Atticists. The capacity of the author is best demonstrated by Acts 27 where he

which we may affirm about the locale in which he wrote is that it was not Palestine.[92] We may say that he wrote in a Hellenistic city in the Eastern half of the empire.[93]

Date

We now need to address the issue of when Luke-Acts was composed. While there is still some debate, there is a general consensus that Luke-Acts was written between 80-90 C.E.[94] The *termini* are as fol-

---

reaches one of the literary peaks of the NT. On the author's knowledge of Hellenistic techniques see below under Form.

[92] The author transforms Palestinian details into Hellenistic concepts. E.g., he alters the composition of the roof of Mk. 2:4 which men can dig through (hence probably beams covered with reeds or weeds and clay typical of Palestinian roofs) to a tiled roof characteristic of Hellenistic houses in the eastern Mediterranean (Lk. 5:19). For details see Fitzmyer, *The Gospel According to Luke*, 1:582. His knowledge of Palestinian geography is also suspect. Cf. Conzelmann, *The Theology of St. Luke*, pp. 68-71 on Luke 17:11. Note also Lk. 4:44.

[93] A strong case can be made for Antioch as a specific locale. Years ago Harnack, *Luke the Physician*, pp. 20-24, made a case for Antioch on the basis of internal evidence. The difficulty is determining what the author knew independently from his sources. The author's connections to the East are obvious: it is the entire setting for his account. Asia Minor is also a candidate since it was home to numerous Pauline traditions, e.g., the Pastorals and the *Acts of Paul*.

[94] A survey of recent commentaries reveals the following results. (For the sake of brevity I have listed only the most significant commentaries for each position.) *C. 62 C.E.* (the end of the narrative): F.F. Bruce, *The Acts of the Apostles* (Grand Rapids: Wm. B. Eerdmans Publishing Co., 1951), pp. 10-14 and his *Commentary on the Book of the Acts*. NICNT (Grand Rapids: Wm. B. Eerdmans Publishing Company, 1954), pp. 22-23 (Bruce appears to have changed his mind since in "The Acts of the Apostles: Historical Record or Theological Reconstruction?" p. 2599, he dates it to 66-74) and a large number of evangelical commentaries; *Prior to 70*: Johannes Munck, *The Acts of the Apostles*, pp. XLVI-LIV and I. Howard Marshall, *The Acts of the Apostles*. Tyndale New Testament Commentaries (Grand Rapids: Wm. B. Eerdmans Publishing Co., 1980), pp. 46-48. *C. 70*: I. Howard Marshall, *The Gospel of Luke: A Commentary on the Greek Text*. NIGTC (Grand Rapids: Wm. B. Eerdmans Publishing Co., 1978), pp. 33-35. 70-80: Alfred Plummer, *The Gospel According to S. Luke*, 5th ed. ICC (Edinburgh: T. & T. Clark, 1901), pp. xxix-xxxiii; Josef Ernst, *Das Evangelium nach Lukas*. RNT (Pustet: Regensburg, 1977), pp. 32-33. *80-90*: John Martin Creed, *The Gospel According to St. Luke* (London: Macmillan & Co. Ltd., 1930), p. xxiii (Luke); Conzelmann, *Acts of the Apostles*, p. xxxiii (80-100); Gerhard Schneider, *Das Evangelium nach Lukas*, 2 vols. Ökumenischer Taschenbuch-Kommentar zum Neuen Testament 3.1-2 (Würzburg: Gerd Mohn, 1977), 1:34 and *Die Apostelgeschichte*, 1:118-121; Fitzmyer, *The Gospel According to Luke*, 1:57; Eduard Schweizer, *The Good News According to Luke*, trans. by David E. Green (Atlanta: John Knox Press, 1984), p. 6; Pesch, *Die Apostelgeschichte*, 1:28; and Frederick W. Danker, *Jesus and the New Age: A Commentary on St. Luke's Gospel*, rev. ed. (Philadelphia: Fortress Press, 1988),

lows. *Terminus a quo*: the third gospel uses the gospel of Mark which was composed c. 65-75. *Terminus ante quem*: Luke-Acts betrays no awareness of the Pauline corpus.[95] Another factor which should be considered is that Luke-Acts presents Christianity as a movement within the Roman empire. This means that there is a historical consciousness of Christianity, i.e., Christianity has a past which can be viewed and understood in relation to time and the world at large.[96] How soon such an awareness can develop is a relative phenomenon. I would, however, prefer to place Luke-Acts towards 90 or perhaps even during the early 90's. It must have been written prior to the *Sitz im Leben* of the Apocalypse since the perspective of the Roman government and of Christians within the empire is so different.[97]

Summary. Our author was an Eastern Christian who had close ties with Judaism if he was not in fact a Jew himself. As we will see, this background had a profound influence on the writing of Luke and Acts. It also gave him the same perspective as the other authors within the tradition we have traced: he belonged to an Oriental subgroup within the Greco-Roman world. Yet he also had a different perspective since he now belonged to a movement which was recent rather than ancient—or was it?

---

pp. 17-18 (75-85). There are also some who want to date Acts in the *second century*: J.C. O'Neill, *The Theology of Acts in its Historical Setting*, 2nd ed. (London: S.P.C.K., 1970), pp. 1-53 (115-130); Knox, "Acts and the Pauline Letter Corpus," p. 286 (125); John T. Townsend, "The Date of Luke-Acts," in *Luke-Acts: New Perspectives from the Society of Biblical Literature Seminar*, pp. 47-62.

[95] The exact date of the formation of the Pauline corpus is a matter of dispute. However, it appears to have been in the 90's or shortly thereafter. The basic evidence is Clement's (c. 96) knowledge of both Romans (I Clem. 35.5-6 = Rom. 1:29-32) and I Cor. (I Clem. 47.1-3 = I Cor. 1:11-13) and Ignatius' (c. 35-107) knowledge of I Corinthians (*Eph.* 12.2 = I Cor. 15:32; 16:8). Early references to an actual collection come in the second century: Polycarp, 3.2 (c. 69-155); II Pet. 3:15-16. The first known collection is that of Marcion c. 140 C.E. See C. Leslie Mitton, *The Formation of the Pauline Corpus of Letters* (London: The Epworth Press, 1955) and Jack Finegan, "The Original Form of the Pauline Collection," *HTR* 49 (1956): 85-103.

[96] The fact that Mark and Matthew have no sequels indicates the unique perspective of the third gospel.

[97] Early Christian tradition links the Apocalypse with Domitian. Cf. Irenaeus, *Adv. Haer.* 5.30.3. Domitian is considered the first persecutor of Christians after Nero. E.g., Melito (d. c. 190) in Eusebios, *HE* 4.26.9. See, however, Adela Yarbro Collins, *Crisis and Catharsis: The Power of the Apocalypse* (Philadelphia: The Westminster Press, 1984), pp. 69-73, 84-140, for a critical assessment of this tradition and an alternative reconstruction.

LUKE-ACTS

Unity

The first issue which we must address is whether or not Luke and Acts form a unit or whether they comprise two separate works loosely joined together. There can be no question that the two books are related, the question is how: Was Acts an afterthought or were the gospel and Acts conceived as a single work and subsequently separated in the formation of the Christian canon?

Henry Cadbury is largely responsible for the modern designation Luke-Acts.[98] Cadbury argued that the primary preface of Luke which is followed by the secondary preface in Acts was patterned on the widely known custom of dividing long works into separate books with prefaces to each. From this he concluded: "The Book of Acts is no afterthought."[99] Cadbury accordingly argued that the preface in Lk. 1:1-4 was designed to serve both books.[100] While this has not gone unchallenged,[101] an important point in the ensuing debate has been understated. The literary character of Lk. 1:1-4 and Acts 1:1-3(2) are different. Why? Is the preface in Acts designed to stand as an independent and major preface or is it by nature a secondary preface which presupposes an earlier prooemium? The reference back to the "former book" and summary of its contents are the clear signs of a secondary preface.[102] This means that Acts is not an

---

[98] E.g., *The Making of Luke-Acts* (New York: Macmillan Company, 1927; reprint ed., London: S.P.C.K., 1961), pp. 8-11.

[99] *Beginnings*, 2:491-492.

[100] *Ibid.*, p. 492, where he argued that it might have even been written after both works were complete. W.C. van Unnik, "Opmerkingen over het doel van Lucas' Geschiedwerk (Luc. 1.4)," *Nederlands Theologisch Tijdschrift* 9,6 (1955): 323-331; reprinted as "Remarks on the Purpose of Luke's Historical Writing (Luke I 1-4)," in *Sparsa Collecta: The Collected Essays of W.C. van Unnik* (Leiden: E.J. Brill, 1973), 1:8, has argued the obverse of this: Acts 1:1 should be understood as part of a connected work, not a new beginning.

[101] Among those who object to understanding Lk. 1:1-4 as a preface to both books are Schuyler Brown, "The Prologues of Luke-Acts in Their Relation to the Purpose of the Author," in *Society of Biblical Literature 1975 Seminar Papers*, 2 vols. edited by George MacRae (Missoula, Montana: Scholars Press, 1975), 2:2 and Schneider, *Die Apostelgeschichte*, 1:81. Cf. also Schweizer, *The Good News According to Luke*, p. 11, who thinks the author had both books in mind from the outset but did not write Lk. 1:1-4 as a prologue to both.

[102] We have already examined Josephos' practice in the preceding chapter. An excellent representative of the technique of writing introductory prefaces which

independent treatise but continues Luke. The two must, therefore, be viewed as a unit.[103]

Unsurprisingly the books constitute one continuous narrative. This is not only evident from the overlapping between Luke 24 and Acts 1, but from the geographical structure of the narrative. Luke opens and closes in Jerusalem. Acts opens in Jerusalem and closes in Rome. The position of Jerusalem is thus of critical importance for the author. In the gospel it is the *telos* of Jesus' journey; in Acts it is the beginning point of the journey of the church. It is the geographical centrum of the whole story.[104]

Nor is the unity of the narrative only obvious in such broad sweeping terms. Charles H. Talbert has shown that there are a number of architectonic parallels between Luke and Acts.[105] Although some of Talbert's parallels tend to be overdrawn, the basic congruence between the gospel and Acts is indisputable. The most striking of these is the journey motif which culminates in the arrest and trials of the chief characters. It also seems to be more than mere accident that both books begin the narrative proper with outpourings of the Holy Spirit.[106] Even more promising is the work of Robert Tannehill who has demonstrated the *narrative* unity of Luke-Acts through literary criticism. Tannehill argues that there is a unified plot "because there is a unifying purpose of God behind the events which are nar-

---

provide summaries of the preceding books and introduce the next is Diodoros Sikelos 2.1.1-3; 3.1.1-3; 4.1.1-7 (esp. 5-6); 11.1.1; 12.1.1-2.2 (esp. 2.1-2); 13.1.1-3; 14.1.1-2.4 (esp. 2.3-4); 15.1.1-6 (esp. 6); 16.1.1-2; 17.1.1-2; 18.1.1-6 (esp. 5-6); 19.1.1-10 (esp. 9-10); 20.1.1-2.3 (esp. 2.3). On Diodoros' prefaces generally see Kenneth S. Sacks, "The Lesser Prooemia of Diodorus Siculus," *Hermes* 110 (1982): 434-443, who places them in three groups: introductory (bks. 1, 37), moral or didactic questions pertaining to the books they introduce (12, 13, 14, 18, 19, 21, 25, 26, 32), and historiographical (4, 5, 15, 16, 17, 20). On primary prologues see Donald Earl, "Prologue-form in Ancient Historiography," in *Von den Anfängen Roms bis zum Ausgang der Republik.* ANRW I 1.2 (Berlin/New York: Walter de Gruyter, 1972), pp. 842-856.

[103] Conzelmann, *Acts of the Apostles*, p. 4, contends the reverse: the presence of the prooem in Acts excludes the unity of Luke-Acts. This would only be true if the prologue in Acts were a primary unit.

[104] Fitzmyer, *The Gospel According to Luke*, 1:164-168, has an excellent discussion of the significance of Jerusalem.

[105] *Literary Patterns, Theological Themes and the Genre of Luke-Acts*, pp. 16-18.

[106] Lk. 3:22; Acts 2:1-4.

rated.''[107] The purpose is the salvation of all humanity according to Tannehill.

Closely connected with the narrative unity of Luke-Acts are the efforts to write a theology of Luke-Acts.[108] What recent works have in common is the recognition that a common theology runs throughout Luke and Acts.

It is undeniable that the two books are bound by inseparable cords. Yet it would be possible to argue that Acts was written after Luke and built upon it rather than that both came from the same plan, i.e., Acts is a sequel rather than an integral part. Are there any indications within the text that Acts was already in mind when the author wrote Luke? I think there are.

First, each of the three synoptic gospels conclude with a reference to the final commission Jesus gave the disciples.[109] A comparison of the accounts reveals the special concerns of each author. What is particularly striking about the setting of the Lukan formulation is the connection he makes between the commission and the fulfillment of prophecy (v. 45). After Jesus explained to the disciples that it was necessary (δεῖ) for everything written about him in scripture to be fulfilled (v. 44), he opened the minds of the disciples so that they could understand the scriptures (v. 45). He then stated that γέγραπται (1) παθεῖν τὸν χρίστον (2) καὶ ἀναστῆναι ἐκ νεκρῶν τῇ τρίτῃ ἡμέρᾳ (3) καὶ κηρυχθῆναι ἐπὶ τῷ ὀνόματι αὐτοῦ μετάνοιαν εἰς ἄφεσιν ἁμαρτιῶν εἰς πάντα τὰ ἔθνη (vs. 46-47). The first two dependent clauses summarize the preceding narrative and are designed to help the disciples and readers understand the significance of what took place. The final dependent clause is Luke's version of the commission.[110] This is unquestionably a Lukan summary of the OT

---

[107] *The Narrative Unity of Luke-Acts: A Literary Interpretation*, 2 vols. Foundations and Facets (Philadelphia: Fortress Press, 1986-1990), 1:2.

[108] E.g., H. Flender, *Luke the Theologian of Redemptive History*, trans. R. Fuller and I. Fuller (Philadelphia: Fortress Press, 1967); I. Howard Marshall, *Luke: Historian and Theologian* (Grand Rapids: Zondervan Publishing House, 1970); Eric Franklin, *Christ the Lord: A Study in the Purpose and Theology of Luke-Acts* (Philadelphia: Westminster Press, 1975); Fitzmyer, *The Gospel According to Luke*, 1:143-270; and Robert F. O'Toole, *The Unity of Luke's Theology: An Analysis of Luke-Acts*. Good News Studies 9 (Wilmington, DE: Michael Glazier, 1984).

[109] Mk. 16:15-16 (non-Markan addition); Matt. 28:18-20; Luke 24:44-49.

[110] In Matthew the emphasis is on teaching and making disciples: πορευθέντες οὖν μαθητεύσατε πάντα τὰ ἔθνη, βαπτίζοντες αὐτοὺς εἰς τὸ ὄνομα τοῦ πατρὸς καὶ τοῦ

since there are no specific OT texts to which one can appeal.[111]

Why the connection between fulfillment and the commission? The author opened the prologue with the statement that many had undertaken to write a narrative περὶ τῶν πεπληροφορημένων ἐν ἡμῖν πραγμάτων. It is of crucial importance to understand the meaning of the participle πεπληροφορημένων. Cadbury argued that the participle simply meant "accomplished."[112] While this is possible, it violates the significance of the ἡμῖν. The inclusion of the "us" must be to link the church of the author's day with the events of the past. If we render the participle "accomplished" we leave everything in the realm of *bruta facta* and the "us" is superfluous. A second possibility is to understand it in the sense of "fully assured."[113] This, however, makes no sense in the context, i.e., how does "be assured" apply to πραγμάτων? A third option is to take πληροφορέω as a synonym for πληρόω and understand it to mean "fulfilled."[114] This yields the best sense and fits in nicely with the continued emphasis on the fulfillment of scripture in the narrative.[115] The events the author narrates are thus understood to be fulfillments of OT prophecy.

In his programmatic statement in Lk. 24:44-49, the author pro-

---

υἱοῦ καὶ τοῦ ἁγίου πνεύματος, διδάσκοντες αὐτοὺς τηρεῖν πάντα ὅσα ἐνετειλάμην ὑμῖν (28:19-20). I understand the present participles, βαπτίζοντες and διδάσκοντες, to explain the imperative μαθητεύσατε. In the addition to Mark it is simply κηρύξατε τὸ εὐαγγέλιον (16:15).

[111] There are some texts to which one could appeal for each individual element: on suffering cf. Ps. 22; Isa. 53; on the resurrection, Ps. 16; on preaching to the nations, Isa. 42:6; 49:6. These and other texts to which one could appeal, however, are not precise equivalents and must be interpreted Christologically to function in the NT. Since there are neither Jewish parallels—neither canonical nor non-canonical—nor was the specific formulation in a previous Christian source, Lukan composition should be posited here.

[112] *Beginnings*, 2:496. Cf. also Brown, "The Prologues of Luke-Acts in Their Relation to the Purpose of the Author," p. 3. The verb is used with this sense in II Tim. 4:5, 17.

[113] It is so used in Rom. 4:21; 14:5; Col. 4:12.

[114] *TDNT*, s.v. πληγοφορέω by G. Delling, 6:310; Schneider, *Das Evangelium nach Lukas*, 1:38; Marshall, *The Gospel of Luke*, p. 41; Dillon, "Previewing Luke's Project from His Prologue (Luke 1:1-4)," pp. 211-214; Fitzmyer, *The Gospel According to Luke*, 1:293; and Heinz Schürmann, *Das Lukasevangelium. Erster Teil*, 3rd ed. HTKNT 3 (Freiburg/Basel/ Wien: Herder, 1984), p. 5.

[115] Note the use of πληρόω in this sense in Luke 4:21; 24:44; Acts 1:16; 3:18; 13:27.

vides the fullest statement on what he considers these events to
be.[116] They are not only the events tied to Jesus' life, but the
proclamation of the significance of those events. This could be understood of the writing of the gospel, except for the fact that the
author continues the commission with the statement: ἀρξάμενοι ἀπὸ
'Ιερουσαλὴν ὑμεῖς μάρτυρες τούτων· καὶ [ἰδοὺ] ἐγὼ ἀποστέλλω τὴν
ἐπαγγελίαν τοῦ πατρός μου ἐφ' ὑμᾶς· ὑμεῖς δὲ καθίσατε ἐν τῇ πόλει
ἕως οὗ ἐνδύσησθε ἐξ ὕψους δύναμιν (vs. 47-49). Why this continuation? Why not simply end with the commission as the gospel of Matthew? This is unquestionably an entree into Acts as the deliberate
echoes of this text in the early chapters of Acts prove.[117] Acts is not
then a secondary extension of Luke, but part of the full scheme of
the "things which have been fulfilled among us."[118]

We therefore have an *inclusio* in the gospel of Luke accenting the
fulfillment of scripture in the narrative. The second half of this *inclusio* is designed to lead us into Acts even as the wording of Acts is
designed to help us recall the ending of Luke.

The second text which indicates that Acts was already planned at
the writing of the gospel is Acts 6:14. One of the accusations which
was leveled against Stephen was the charge filed against Jesus in
Mark 14:58 but omitted in the Lukan passion narrative. Why did
Luke omit the saying where it occurred in his sources and transfer
it here? The dominical logion which must have been something like
ἐγὼ καταλύσω τὸν ναὸν τοῦτον in the pre-Markan tradition was
problematic for the evangelists.[119] The third evangelist's decision

---

[116] Note the echo of πληροφορέω (1:1) by πληρόω in 24:44.

[117] Beginning in Jerusalem: Acts 1:8; the apostles as witnesses: Acts 1:8, 22;
2:32; 3:15; 5:32; 10:39; 13:31; 22:15; 26:16; the promise of the Father: Acts 1:4;
the command to wait in Jerusalem: Acts 1:4; power from on high: Acts 1:8; 2:1-4,
33. Tannehill, *The Narrative Unity of Luke-Acts*, 1:293-298, has an excellent discussion of how this text prepares the reader for Acts.

[118] It could be argued that Lk. 24:47-49 are an authorial interpolation retroac-
tively placed back into Lk. to provide a bridge to Acts. (If Lk. were still in the
author's possession before Acts was released.) There are, however, two points
which make this highly unlikely. First, the emphasis on going to the nations does
not appear here for the first time in Lk., but is part of a major theme. Second, this
is the commission scene in Lk. It is hard to imagine the gospel without it. (An interpolation would have to replace a previous commission.) *In nuce*, the acceptance of
Lk. 24:47-49 as part of the original gospel has far fewer difficulties than any other
explanation.

[119] Mk. 14:58 casts it in terms of χειροποίητον vs. ἀχειροποίητον (at the redactional level); Matthew alters Mark to τὸν ναὸν τοῦ θεοῦ (26:61), thus setting up an
identification with the temple of God and the Son of God (v. 63); a step the fourth

to omit it could be due to the embarrassment such a statement would cause in the trial of Jesus, especially in light of the politically sensitive handling of the trial in Luke. Why then did he incorporate it in Acts 6-7? It is here that our evangelist has his anti-temple polemic. He therefore placed the saying where it was appropriate for his narrative rather than where it had served his predecessor. Was this decision already made when the passion narrative of the gospel was written? It is possible to answer negatively and to argue that it was too offensive in the context of Christ's trial to include. Since the evangelist wrote the Stephen narrative with Jesus' trial in mind, the saying would naturally have come to him.[120] There are, however, two difficulties with this response. First, the other evangelists found ways of incorporating it; why not our author? Second, the tendency of the third evangelist to place items in a logical context argues for an intentional delay. I conclude that the author had Acts 6-7 in mind when he wrote the passion narrative in the gospel.

We have now established the unity of Luke-Acts.[121] We need, however, to account for some of the differences which exist between the two documents. If an individual sits down and reads Luke and then immediately turns to Acts, she/he is struck by the variation in the flow of the narrative. The gospel is still largely a collection of pericopae while Acts flows in longer and more sustained waves of narrative. If the reader knows Acts before reading the gospel, she/he wants to ask where the speeches have gone. The obvious answer is tied to *Vorlage*: the gospel remained close to Mark; since Acts had no predecessors, the author was much freer to wield his own literary skills.[122]

Other problems are somewhat more difficult. We have already

---

evangelist makes explicit in his allegorization of the temple as the body of Jesus (Jn. 2:21). On the dominical logion and its redaction in the gospel of Mark see John R. Donahue, *Are You the Christ? The Trial Narrative in the Gospel of Mark*. SBLDS 10 (Missoula, Montana: Society of Biblical Literature, 1973), pp. 103-138, especially 104-113. On Matthew's redaction see Robert H. Gundry, *Matthew: A Commentary on His Literary and Theological Art* (Grand Rapids: Wm. B. Eerdmans Publishing Co., 1982), pp. 542-543.

[120] Compare Acts 7:56 with Luke 22:69; Acts 7:59 with Luke 23:46; Acts 7:60 with the spurious reading in Luke 23:34.

[121] The are also instances of glances back in Acts. Compare 4:7 with Lk. 20:2 and 4:11 with Lk. 20:17-18. The author expects the reader of Acts to have read Luke.

[122] So Dibelius, *Studies in the Acts of the Apostles*, pp. 103, 148, 155.

alluded to some of the stylistic shifts. There is also at least one change in content. The impression a reader of Luke 24 has is that Jesus ascended on the same day as his resurrection.[123] When we come to Acts 1:3, however, we are told that he appeared to the disciples over a period of forty days. The forty days of the disciples' instruction in Acts 1:3 correspond to the forty days of Jesus' own preparation in Luke 4:2.[124] These incongruities suggest that not everything had been worked out in advance.

We may now attempt to offer a plausible reconstruction of the sequence of events which explains the relationship between Luke and Acts. What follows is only a hypothesis. Authors in antiquity—as today—were encouraged to make outlines of their work before actually writing out the episodes within them.[125] I would like to suggest that our author followed this procedure. There are two lines of evidence for this. First, we have already seen that there are some architectonic parallels between Luke and Acts. While this could be explained by positing Luke as a model for Acts, it is more reasonable to think that the connections were considered in outline form in advance. Second, the two works adhere to the principle of keeping the subject matter separated into appropriate books. Thus Jesus is the subject of the gospel and the story of the church constitutes the material of Acts. There is also a certain amount of symmetry to each: they both cover a period of roughly 30-35 years and are roughly the same length.[126] The division of a work into separate books appears to have started with Ephoros (c. 405-330 B.C.E.).[127] It was the practice of Hellenistic historians such as Diodoros Sikelos to

---

[123] Cf. also *Barnabas* 15.9.

[124] Pointed out by Pesch, *Die Apostelgeschichte*, 1:62.

[125] Aristotle, *Poet.* 17.5-8; Lucian, *Hist. conscr.* 48: καὶ ἐπειδὰν ἀθροίσῃ ἅπαντα ἢ τὰ πλεῖστα, πρῶτα μὲν ὑπόμνημά τι συνυφαινέτω αὐτῶν καὶ σῶμα ποιείτω ἀκαλλὲς ἔτι καὶ ἀδιάρθρωτον· εἶτα ἐπιθεὶς τὴν τάξιν ἐπαγέτω τὸ κάλλος καὶ χρωννύτω τῇ λέξει καὶ σχηματιζέτω καὶ ῥυθμιζέτω.

[126] Robert Morgenthaler, *Statistik des Neutestamentlichen Wortschatzes*, 3rd ed. (Zürich: Gotthelf, 1982), p. 166, gives the following figures for the number of words in each book: Luke, 19,404; Acts, 18,374.

[127] On Ephoros see Robert Drews, "Ephorus and History Written κατὰ γένος," *American Journal of Philology* 84 (1963): 244-255 and "Ephorus' κατὰ γένος History Revisited," *Hermes* 104 (1976): 497-498, who argues that Ephoros invented the division of subject matter into books and that he grouped his material into the major geographical areas of the world. Diodoros misunderstood κατὰ γένος to mean according to subject matter. Cf. 5.1.4. Sacks, "The Lesser Prooemia of Diodorus Siculus," p. 441 n. 23, follows Drews and provides a bibliography.

group their material into books according to subject matter.[128]
Every author knows that it is much easier to balance two separate
works successfully when working from an outline.[129]

The first stage in the writing of Luke-Acts was—on this
account—the drawing up of the outline. At this point the determination to write the account in two books along with the basic contours
of each was made. Since the author had a structure which he adopted
from Mark for the gospel (see below), it is reasonable to assume that
it was planned first and that Acts followed and was modeled on it to
the extent that the material and aims of the work would allow. This
explains why there are basic agreements in pattern between the two.
Other decisions such as where to place the temple charge were also
made at this time. The outline was not for circulation but only for
the author's use in composing.[130] Once the outline was completed
and the sequence of events planned, he proceeded to write the actual
books. I think it likely that he "published" Luke and Acts separately.[131] This is to say that when he finished Luke he submitted it
to the church.[132] He then returned to work on Acts which he com-

---

[128] See his comments in 5.1.4 and 16.1.1-2. So, for example, Diodoros groups
his material into the following: 1, Egypt; 2, Assyria in Asia, Chaldeans, Arabia,
Skythia, the Amazons, and the Hyperboreans; 3, the Ethiopians, Libyans, and At-
lantians; 4, the Greeks; 5, the islands.

[129] I do not intend for this suggestion to parallel the Proto-Luke hypothesis
since I am proposing an outline for Luke-Acts not a draft for Luke. I prefer to see
Mark as the base for Luke rather than Q and L. (See below) On Proto-Luke see
Burnett Hillman Streeter, *The Four Gospels: A Study of Origins* (*Treating of the
Manuscript Tradition, Sources, Authorship, & Dates*) (London: Macmillan & Co., Ltd,
1956), pp. 199-222.

[130] A parallel to this would be Josephos' outline of the events of the Jewish war.
Cf. *CA* 1.47-50. Laquer, *Der jüdische Historiker Flavius Josephus*, pp. 56-128, esp.
96-128, and Cohen, *Josephus in Galilee and Rome*, pp. 67-83, have persuasively argued that Josephos had an outline (Laquer: "Rechenschaftsbericht").

[131] We have an example of such a procedure attested in Dionysios of Halikarnassos, *AR* 7.70.2.

[132] Raymond J. Starr, "The Circulation of Literary Texts in the Roman
World," *CQ* 37 (1987): 213-223, outlined the basic process of circulation for a
work. After the work or sections were completed (not the outline) the author circulated it among friends. At this stage the work remained in the author's control. The
second stage was reached when the work began to circulate among strangers. An
author made it available through gift copies, copies made after recitations, deposit-
ing it in the public library, or by encouraging his friends to make it known. There
was also the book market. The difficulty with attempting to apply Roman literary
practices to Luke-Acts is the peculiar nature of the author's relationships. While
it seems probable that he would have had friends read parts to get a reaction, the
final copy was destined for church(es). Josephos appears to have sent Herod Agrippa II parts of his *Bellum* while he was writing it. Cf. *V* 361-367.

pleted some time later. When Acts was complete, it was also submitted to the church. In this way, books that were a single work began their circulation independently. Luke naturally became associated with the *tetraevangelium* and Acts went its own separate way. This seems more reasonable than to assume that a second century Christian severed the two.

This conclusion carries three important implications. First, it mandates placing Luke and Acts in a single genre. Second, the recognition of Acts as a historical oeuvre and the primary and secondary prefaces so common in Hellenistic historiography require that we consider not just Acts but Luke-Acts a historical work. Third, the preface in Lk. 1:1-4, serves as the primary preface for both works rather than for Luke alone and offers the author's programmatic statements for them.

Programmatic Statement[133]

The author began his work with one of the most polished sentences in the NT.[134] It consists of four nicely balanced clauses which may be grouped into two units: vs. 1-2 and 3-4. Each clause in the first subdivision is answered by the corresponding clause in the second: the predecessors of v. 1 are echoed by the author's present effort in v. 3 and the reliability of the tradition in v. 2 is matched by the purpose of the present work in v. 4. The structure implies that the corresponding pairs will elucidate one another.

---

[133] The literature on the Lukan preface is large. For the most significant older material see the bibliography in Fitzmyer, *The Gospel According to Luke*, 1:301-302. Recent work which treats the preface as a whole includes: Brown, "The Prologues of Luke-Acts in Their Relation to the Purpose of the Author,"; Vernon K. Robbins, "Prefaces in Greco-Roman Biography and Luke-Acts," in *Society of Biblical Literature 1978 Seminar Papers*, edited by Paul Achtemeier (Missoula, Montana: Scholars Press, 1978), pp. 193-207; Richard J. Dillon, "Previewing Luke's Project from His Prologue," pp. 205-227; E. Güttgemanns, "In welchem Sinne ist Lukas 'Historiker'? Die Beziehungen von Luk 1,1-4 und Papias zur antiken Rhetorik," *LingBib* 54 (1983): 9-26; F. Siegert, "Lukas—ein Historiker, d.h. ein Rhetor? Freundschaftliche Entgegnung auf Erhardt Güttgemanns," *LingBib* 55 (1984): 57-60; Terrance Callan, "The Preface of Luke-Acts and Historiography," *NTS* 31 (1985): 576-581; Loveday Alexander, "Luke's Preface in the Context of Greek Preface Writing," *NovT* 28 (1986): 48-74.

[134] Note the obvious effort to utilize literary forms: Ἐπειδήπερ is a hapax legomenon in the NT and LXX; πληροφορέω is probably an elevated synonymn for πληρόω; παρέδοσαν appears in this form only here in the NT (normally the aorist indicative uses κ. See *BDF* 95.1).

Before we examine these clauses, we need to clarify the nature of the vocabulary of the prologue. Traditionally the preface has been a determining factor in locating Luke and Acts within the context of Hellenistic historiography.[135] It certainly has the vocabulary of a historical preface and easily fits within this frame of reference.[136] In recent years there have been several challenges to this. Vernon K. Robbins examined prefaces to "didactic biographies" and demonstrated how the vocabulary of Luke 1:1-4 is paralleled in them.[137] Erhardt Güttgemanns thought that he found five (possibly eight) *termini technici* from rhetoric in the preface and concluded that while Luke is a historical work, it is rhetorical and unconcerned about *bruta facta*.[138] More recently, Loveday Alexander has compared the preface to those of scientific texts in the Hellenistic world and concluded that it is closest to the "label and address" prefaces common in scientific writings.[139] The Achilles heel of Alexander's proposal is that the preface must relate to the text in a meaningful way—even if it is detachable.[140] What these articles have demonstrated is that there was a common stock of terms used for prose prefaces in the Hellenistic world which transcended the boundaries of a single

---

[135] The most recent treatment of the preface from this perspective is Callan, "The Preface of Luke-Acts and Historiography," who thinks that the closest analogies are Josephos' *BJ* and Sallust's *On the Conspiracy of Cataline*.

[136] Note the advice of Lucian, *Hist. conscr.*, 52-54, on prefaces: the historian is to make two points in his preface. S/he is to show the audience that what s/he has to say is useful to them and briefly outline it for them. If we examine the preface in Luke 1:1-4 we may note that the author states its usefulness or personal importance to Theophilos (v. 4) and alludes to the contents through the reference to his predecessors and the apostolic tradition (vs. 1-2). The latter must, however, be considered inadequate by Lucian's guidelines. The preface meets the requirement of proportion set out in 23 and 55. Note also the strictures on the excessive length of Thukydides preface by Dionysios, *De Thuc.* 19-20.

[137] "Prefaces in Greco-Roman Biography and Luke-Acts," pp. 194-198.

[138] "In welchem Sinne ist Lukas 'Historiker'?", pp. 9-26. He has been answered by Siegert, "Lukas—ein Historiker, d.h. ein Rhetor?," pp. 57-60.

[139] "Luke's Preface in the Context of Greek Preface-Writing." Alexander argues that scientific prefaces (and Luke 1:1-4) are: 1. detachable; 2. written from the first person to the second; 3. share a common vocabulary. See pp. 57-60 and 72-74 for examples. According to Alexander there is not a single match, but Luke 1:1-4 bears a family resemblance to these prefaces. The closest match for vocabulary is Diokles' *Letter to Antigonos*, 7: σὺ δὲ πεισθεὶς τοῖς ὑφ' ἡμῶν λεγομένοις παρακολουθήσεις τῇ ἀκριβείᾳ τῇ περὶ αὐτῶν.

[140] The suggestion that these scientific texts are school texts which contain the written deposit of the craft tradition hardly explains the relationship between the preface of Luke and the narrative which follows. The function may be the same (i.e., defining the tradition), but the form is not.

genre.[141] Since I have placed Luke-Acts into the category of historiography on larger grounds, I will compare the statement with others in Hellenistic historiography.[142] What is important is not the simple presence (or absence) of terminology within a tradition, but how the terms function.

The Author and his Predecessors. The work opens with the recognition that πολλοὶ ἐπεχείρησαν ἀνατάξασθαι διήγησιν. We must begin by asking who the predecessors were and what our author's attitude toward them was. The *communis opinio* holds that the πολλοί include Q, Mark, and L. Although this analysis of the synoptic problem has been challenged in recent years, I remain convinced that it is the best solution and use a modified two-source theory here.[143]

How did the evangelist view these sources? The verb ἐπιχειρέω was used by Hellenistic historians to denote both undertaking the task of writing a history[144] and of undertaking the task unsuccessfully.[145] How does it function in our text?

Since the days of Origen the verb ἐπεχείρησαν has been understood by some to have a pejorative connotation.[146] The word only occurs three times in the NT—all in Luke-Acts—and in the other

[141] Plummer, *The Gospel According to S. Luke*, pp. 5-6, compared Luke 1:1-4 to Dioskorides Περὶ ὕλης ἰατρικῆς.

[142] It is at least worth pointing out that the author uses πράγματα in v. 1 to denote what his predecessors and he by extension recorded. This is regularly used by historians to mark their subject matter: Polybios 1.3.9; Dionysios of Halikarnassos 1.1.3; 8.4; Josephos *AJ* 1.26; Lucian, *Hist conscr.* 47, 55; Cassius Dio 1.2.

[143] The most important challenges have been William R. Farmer, *The Synoptic Problem: A Critical Analysis* (New York: The Macmillan Company, 1964) and Hans-Herbert Stoldt, *History and Criticism of the Marcan Hypothesis*, trans. Donald L. Niewyk with an introduction by William R. Farmer (Macon, GA: Mercer University Press, 1980). Joseph A. Fitzmyer, "The Priority of Mark and the 'Q' Source in Luke," in *Jesus and Man's Hope*. Perspective Books (Pittsburgh: Pittsburgh Theological Seminary, 1970, 1:131-170; reprinted in Fitzmyer, *To Advance the Gospel: New Testament Studies* (New York: Crossroad, 1981), pp. 3-40, has answered Farmer. The decisive factors in my opinion are the apparent acceptance of the Markan order in Matthew and Luke and the way in which each of the last two evangelists reduce and improve Mark.

[144] Both Polybios (2.37.4; 3.1.4) and Dionysios of Halikarnassos (1.7.3) use it to refer to their own works. They also used it to refer to others, e.g., Polybios 12.28.3.

[145] E.g., Josephos, *V* 40, 338, of Justus of Tiberias.

[146] *Homilia in Lucam 1* (*SQE*, 540-541). Origen contrasted the four canonical gospels with all other gospels and understood ἐπεχείρησαν as *conati sunt*. Cf. also Eusebios *HE* 3.24.15 and more recently Fitzmyer, *The Gospel According to Luke*, 1:291-292.

two it certainly bears this sense.[147] On the other side of the ledger some have appealed to the ἔδοξε κἀμοί of v. 3 to argue that the predecessors were models for the author.[148]

To answer this question we need to compare what the author says about his own work versus what he says about his predecessors. They ἐπεχείρησαν ἀνατάξασθαι διήγησιν (v. 1) and he has thought καθεξῆς σοι γράψαι (v. 3). Are these parallel[149] or is there a difference?[150] Ἀνατάσσομαι can mean either to "repeat in proper order" or to "draw up, compile."[151] How was it used here? The answer lies in what the author calls their works, διήγησις. The term occurs from Plato on and simply means a narrative whether written or oral.[152] Although it was not exclusive to historiography, it regularly appears to mark a historical narrative.[153] Here it implies that there was some order in his predecessors' works. With regard to his own effort the author used the adverb καθεξῆς which is unique to Luke-Acts in the NT and has provoked a great deal of controversy.[154] The best solution is to follow the author's own usage to

---

[147] Acts 9:29; 19:13. It is worth pointing out that in the LXX the negative shade is dominant, II Chron. 20:11; I Esd. 1:26; Esth. 9:25; II Macc. 7:19; 9:2; 10:15; III Macc. 6:24; 7:5; IV Macc. 1:5. It also appears in II Esd. 7:23 and II Macc. 2:29 (in the latter it applies to II Macc. by extension and is neutral).

[148] This is the majority view. Cf. Cadbury, *Beginnings*, 2:493-494; Brown, "The Prologues of Luke-Acts in their Relation to the Purpose of the Author," p. 2; Schneider, *Das Evangelium nach Lukas*, 1:38; Marshall, *The Gospel of Luke*, p. 41; Schürmann, *Das Lukasevangelium*, 1:7; Schweizer, *The Good News According to Luke*, p. 11.

[149] Cadbury, *Beginnings*, 2:505.

[150] Schürmann, *Das Lukasevangelium*, 1:12.

[151] *BAGD*, 61-62. The term is a hapax legomenon in the NT.

[152] *Rep.* 392D (see the discussion in chapter one); *Phdr.* 266E (a narrative in a speech).

[153] Diodoros 11.20.1; Dionysios of Halikarnassos 1.8.2; Josephos *BJ* 7.42, 274; *AJ* 1.67; 4.196; 11.68; 12.137; 20.157; *V* 336 (he also uses it in *AJ* 9.214; 12.136; 19.357); Lucian, *Hist. conscr.* 55. It is also used in II Macc. 2:32; 6:17.

[154] Lk. 8:1; Acts 3:24; 11:4; 18:23. Interpretations include the following. Successive or sequential without further specification: Cadbury, *Beginnings*, 2:505 and Schweizer, *The Good News According to Luke*, p. 12. Martin Volkel, "Exegetishce Erwagungen zum Verstandnis des Begriffs ΚΑΘΕΞΗΣ im Lukanischen Prolog," *NTS* 20 (1974): 289-299, argued that it meant to make the meaning of the events clear through *continua serie*. Franz Mussner, "Καθεξῆς im Lukasprolog," in *Jesus und Paulus: Festschrift für Werner Georg Kümmel zum 70. Geburtstag*, ed. E. Earle Ellis and Erich Graßer (Göttingen: Vandenhoeck & Ruprecht, 1975), pp. 253-255, built upon Volkel's research and tried to see a connection with "all" in v. 3. He suggested it meant "ohne Ausnahme, luckenlos." (In contrast to competing accounts which were circulating outside the bounds of orthodoxy.) Brown, "The Prologues

interpret it. The closest parallel to the use here is Acts 11:4, where Peter recounts the Cornelius episode to the Jerusalem church καθεξῆς, i.e., in sequence or order. In the prologue it would mean to write a narrative in good narrative order, i.e., sequentially.[155] The author thus considered his predecessors to have written narratives and proposes to write one himself.[156] They shared the common task of putting the apostolic tradition into narrative form.

There is, however, a further factor to consider. The very act of writing about the same material carries with it an implied criticism. What did the author find inadequate about his predecessors that caused him to pick up a reed? The basic difference between Luke-Acts and the known predecessors, Q and Mark, is the fullness of the material. The author appears to hint at this himself when stating his own procedure: ἔδοξε κἀμοὶ παρηκολουθηκότι ἄνωθεν πᾶσιν ἀκριβῶς. The participle παρακολουθέω has served as the occasion for an extended debate.[157] Patristic commentators understood this to refer to Luke's accompanying the apostles (understanding πᾶσιν to be a masculine).[158] Henry Cadbury likewise argued for this meaning in several articles he published on the Lukan preface.[159] This, however, stands against the earlier statement that distances the author from the eyewitnesses, i.e., the apostles. It also runs afoul of the modifying adverbs, ἄνωθεν and ἀκριβῶς, and the noun which serves as its object, πᾶσιν. Ἄνωθεν here is parallel to ἀπ' ἀρχῆς in

Luke-Acts in their Relation to the Purpose of the Author," p. 5, thinks it means "as follows." Others still prefer to see chronological or historical order: Marshall, *The Gospel of Luke*, p. 43 and Schürmann, *Das Lukasevangelium*, 1:12. Schneider, *Das Evangelium nach Lukas*, 1:39, thinks in terms of phases of salvation history. For further views and bibliography see the commentaries of Marshall and Fitzmyer.

[155] So also Dillon, "Previewing Luke's Project from His Prologue," pp. 219-223; Fitzmyer, *The Gospel According to Luke*, 1:298-299; and Tannehill, *The Literary Unity of Luke-Acts*, pp. 9-12.

[156] The only designation the author gives to his own work is the λόγος of Acts 1:1 which refers back to Luke. Cf. Philo, *Prob.* 1, Ὁ μὲν πρότερος λόγος . . . The word simply means "book" in these contexts.

[157] Other NT occurrences: [Mk. 16:17]; I Tim. 4:6; II Tim. 3:10. It is found twice in the LXX: II Macc. 8:11 (to fall upon); 9:27 (follow a policy [as I Tim. 4:6; II Tim. 3:10, follow a teaching]).

[158] E.g., Justin, *Dial.* 103; Tertullian, *Adv. Marc.* 4.2; Eusebios, *HE* 3.4.6.

[159] "The Knowledge Claimed in Luke's Preface," *The Expositor* 24 (1922): 401-422 and "'We' and 'I' in Luke-Acts," *NTS* 3 (1956-1957): 130-131. So also Jacques Dupont, *The Sources of the Acts*, trans. Kathleen Pond (New York: Herder and Herder, 1964), pp. 101-112. See below.

v. 2.[160] It must go back to the events in the gospel and probably to the infancy narrative. Ἀκριβῶς makes no sense whatsoever with "participate" or "accompany."[161] The πᾶσιν should be understood as neuter and refer back to the πραγμάτων of v. 1 instead of the αὐτόπται καὶ ὑπηρέται of v. 2, since there is nothing in the subsequent narrative which would support the latter.[162] What then does the participle mean? Fortunately we have a parallel text in Josephos' *Contra Apionem* which helps to elucidate the meaning here. Josephos argued that a historian had to know the facts ἀκριβῶς, ἢ παρηκολουθηκότα τοῖς γεγονόσιν ἢ παρὰ τῶν εἰδότων πυνθανόμενον.[163] The meaning here is "investigate" which makes the most sense in the Lukan preface as well.[164] This was a common *topos* among historians.[165] Our author's claim is that he investigated thoroughly, exhaustively, and accurately.

Ἐπιχειρέω, therefore, is used with a thin cutting edge. This really should not cause any surprise since criticizing predecessors was part of the stock and trade of Hellenistic historiography. It began with Hekataios of Miletos and continued throughout historiographical writings.[166] What is surprising here is how subdued the criticism is.

---

[160] So also Acts 26:4-5. Cadbury was forced to understand ἄνωθεν to mean "from a good while back." (*op cit.*, pp. 130-131 and "The Knowledge Claimed in Luke's Preface," p. 409). So also Dupont, *The Sources of Acts*, pp. 106-107. This is forced at best.

[161] The Fathers and Cadbury sensed this difficulty. For this reason Cadbury takes it with γράψαι. *Beginnings*, 2:504. This is again forced.

[162] Note also the statement in Acts 1:1: Τὸν μὲν πρῶτον λόγον ἐποιησάμην περὶ πάντων, ὦ Θεόφιλε, ὧν ἤρξατο ὁ Ἰησοῦς ποιεῖν τε καὶ διδάσκειν . . . The πᾶς here clearly refers to deeds (and teaching).

[163] *CA* 1.53. Cadbury, *Beginnings*, 2:502, incorrectly understood this to refer to Josephos' methodology in *BJ*. As we pointed out in the preceding chapter, παρηκολουθηκότα τοῖς γεγονόσιν refers to the *Antiquitates* and παρὰ τῶν εἰδότων πυνθανόμενον to *BJ*. This is clear from the following comments of Josephos where he claims that he has followed these two procedures in his own works: he translated the sacred writings and was himself a participant in the events of the war. (54-55). I do not see how "inquiring from those who know" can refer to *AJ* since it is clearly based on written records and not living witnesses. It therefore refers to *BJ* and "having investigated the things that have occurred" to *AJ*.

[164] So also *BAGD*, 619a. This is the traditional view.

[165] Historians frequently mentioned their investigations. E.g., Herodotos 1.1; Dionysios of Halikarnassos, *AR* 1.7.2-3; Lucian, *Hist. conscr.* 47; Cassius Dio 73.23.5.

[166] F 1. Cf. also Thukydides 1.21.1-2; Polybios 1.4.3-11 and book 12 which is largely a critique of Timaios of Tauromenium; Diodoros 1.3.1-4; Dionysios of Halikarnassos 1.6.1-3; 7.1; and 1.1.1, where he mentions that Anaximenes (380-320 B.C.E.) and Theopompos (fourth century B.C.E.) were both highly critical of others.

Perhaps his reticence should be understood within the context of Christianity where his sources had already achieved some standing.[167]

How should we account for this ambivalent stance which both identifies with and yet carries a subtle criticism? The best explanation is to remember Josephos' stance toward the LXX: he claims it as a precedent and yet criticizes its limitations as justification to write AJ[168]; so our author can claim Q and Mark as precedents and yet go on to write Luke-Acts.

The Traditio Apostolica. The basis for both the author's narrative and that of his predecessors is what παρέδοσαν ἡμῖν οἱ ἀπ' ἀρχῆς αὐτόπται καὶ ὑπηρέται γενόμενοι τοῦ λόγου (v. 2). Whether these are two groups or one—I prefer the latter—the emphasis on eyewitnesses should not be missed: they are guarantors of the tradition.[169]

The task our author has set before himself is to present Theophilos with an orderly narrative ἵνα ἐπιγνῷς περὶ ὧν κατηχήθης λόγων τὴν ἀσφάλειαν (Lk. 1:4). The stated purpose is to provide ἀσφάλεια of the λόγων. The λόγων here must echo the *traditio apostolica* of v. 2.[170] It is what the apostles have handed down about the "events fulfilled among us" that constitutes the substance of what the "many" have previously written and about which Theophilos has been instructed.[171] It is this tradition that he has accurately investigated from its very beginning and proposes to set forth for his reader. Through his investigation and orderly account he intends to

---

[167] Mark and Q must both have by this time since Matthew also uses them. On the reluctance to criticize see also Schürmann, *Das Lukasevangelium*, 1:7.

[168] AJ 1.10-13.

[169] Note also Diodoros 1.4.1, where personal presence is offered to buttress geographical knowledge; Josephos, *CA* 1.55; Lucian, *Hist. conscr.* 47 and also 29.

[170] Note the singular in v. 2, τοῦ λόγου, which is a *terminus technicus* for the word of God. I understand the plural of v. 4 to be various forms of instruction of this.

[171] Κατηχέω is a rare term prior to the NT. It does not appear in the LXX. It is only found 8t. in the NT, 4t. in Luke-Acts. The term can mean either "inform" as in Acts 21:21, 24, or "instruct" as in Acts 18:25. (In the other NT texts it means to instruct: Rom. 2:18 [Judaism]; I Cor. 14:19; Ga. 6:6 *bis* [Christian]) The interpretation one assigns to this term depends upon whether we conceive the audience to be Christians or non-Christians. Since I understand the audience to be Christians (see below), I prefer "instructed." So also Marshall, *The Gospel of Luke*, p. 43; Fitzmyer, *The Gospel According to Luke*, 1:301; Schürmann, *Das Lukasevangelium*, 1:15. *Contra* Cadbury, "The Purpose Expressed in Luke's Preface," *The Expositor* 21 (1921): 433-434 and *Beginnings*, 2:509.

provide certainty about the tradition.[172] The purpose is thus to define the tradition.[173]

Summary. The author saw the contents of his work as being the fulfillment of the OT. He was not the first to undertake the task of setting down a narrative about these events. His careful and thorough investigation, however, placed him in a position to offer a definitive account of these events.

Vv. 1-2	Vv. 3-4
Since many have undertaken	so I decided, after I had investigated everything carefully from the very beginning,
to present a narrative	to write to you, most excellent Theophilos,
concerning the events which have been fulfilled among us, just as those who were eye-witnesses	so that you could know the certainty
from the beginning and became ministers of the Word delivered to us,	of the matters about which you have received instruction.

Content

The author began with a preface designed to call attention to the literary intentions of the work. With these expectations we immediately encounter the most Semitic section of the work in an infancy narrative which parallels the births and early years of John and Jesus (1:5-2:52).[174] This is followed by a summary of John's

---

[172] Ἀσφάλεια occurs 3t. in the NT: Lk. 1:4; Acts 5:23; I Th. 5:3. It primarily denoted physical safety, but came to mean security, certainty, or reliability. The meaning here is well illustrated by the cognate ἀσφαλής in Acts 21:34; 22:30; 25:26, where the term denotes the reality of the matter (the term appears only 5t. in the NT) and ἀσφαλῶς in Acts 2:36 where the adverb means to know beyond question (the adverb appears elsewhere only in Mk. 14:44 and Acts 16:23 in the NT).

[173] The commitment to truth was a hallmark of historiography—at least formally. Cf. Diodoros Sikelos 1.2.7; Dionysios of Halikarnassos 1.1.2; Josephos, *BJ* 1.16 (and chapter five); Lucian, *Hist. conscr.* 40; Cassius Dio 1.2-3. The specific formulation in Luke 1:4 differs from that of any of these writers.

[174] I find the following parallels:

preaching and the preparation of Jesus for his ministry (3:1-4:13). Jesus' Galilean ministry (4:14-9:50) opens with a programmatic scene in which he is rejected by his own home town.[175] The ministry itself is primarily presented in a series of collections of controversy stories,[176] teaching material,[177] or miracles.[178] Unique to the third gospel is the extended journey of Jesus to Jerusalem (9:51-19:27). This is, however, not sustained as a journey[179] but allows for the inclusion of a great deal of teaching material which the evangelist again attempts to collect into meaningful units.[180] As in the gospel of Mark, Jesus' ministry in Jerusalem is presented in terms of conflict.[181] Luke has a distinctive passion narrative which, nevertheless, in the main follows the same line as the other evangelists (22:1-23:49). Like Matthew and John, he concludes with resurrection appearances (23:50-24:52).

Event	John	Jesus
Introduction of the parents	1:5-7	1:26-27
Announcement of the birth	1:8-23	1:28-38
Conception	1:23-25	2:6-7
Birth and naming of child	1:59-66	2:21
Response to the child's birth	1:67-79	2:22-38
Growth of the child	1:80	2:39-40, 52

[175] The author presents a rejection of Jesus at the beginning of every major section in the gospel: 4:14-9:50 (4:16-30, by the Nazarenes); 9:51-19:27 (9:51-56, by the Samaritans); 19:28-21:38 (19:39-40, by the Pharisees); and 22:1-23:49 (22:1-6, by Judas).

[176] Lk. 5:12-6:11 taken from Mk. 2:1-3:6.

[177] Lk. 6:20-49 (Q); 8:4-21 (4-15 = Mk. 4:1-20; 16-18 = Mk. 4:21-25; 19-21 = Mk. 3:31-35); 9:1-36 (1-9 = Mk. 6:6b-16; 10-17 = Mk. 6:30-44; 18-36 = Mk. 8:27-9:10 [Note the presence of the question in vv. 7-9, 18-22 and the answer in vv. 20, 35]).

[178] Lk. 8:22-56 = Mk. 4:35-5:43.

[179] 9:51-19:27 has precious little narrative. The author reminds us that Jesus is on his journey in 9:51-56, 57; 10:1, 38; 11:53; 13:22, 33; 17:11; 18:31, 35; 19:1 (11, 28). If it were not for these reminders the reader would easily forget that this is a journey.

[180] E.g., 10:25-42 (L; for 25-29 cf. Mark 12:28-34 [vs. 30-37 illustrate love of neighbor and vs. 38-42 love of God]); 11:1-13, prayer (1-4 = Mt. 6:9-13 [Q]; 5-8 = L; 9-13 = Mt. 7:7-11 [Q]); 11:37-54, woes against the Pharisees (37-41 = Mark 7:1-9; 42-52 = Mt. 23:25-26, 23, 6-7, 27-28, 4, 29-32, 34-36, 13 [Q]); 14:1-24, rules for dining (1-6 = L, 7-11 = L, 12-14 = L, 15-24 = Q [16-21 = Mt. 22:2-10]); 15:1-32, the love of God (1-3 = L, 4-7 = Mt. 18:12-14 [Q], 8-10 = L, 11-32 = L); 16:1-13, the dishonest steward (1-8a = L, 8b-9 = L, 10-12 = L, 13 = Mt. 6:24 [Q]). Manson, "The Life of Jesus," p. 395, called Lk. 15-19 "the Gospel of the Outcast." This reflects the overall concern reflected in 15:1-32; 18:1-8, 9-14; 19:1-10.

[181] 19:28-21:38 which in the main follows Mark 11:1-13:37.

Acts opens with a secondary preface (1:1-3) and recapitulation of the end of Luke (1:4-14). Within this opening section the author provides a programmatic statement indicating how the reader can expect the events to unfold: "you will be my witnesses in Jerusalem, in all Judea, in Samaria, and even to the ends of the earth" (1:8). That this indicates the plan of the work is supported by the way the narrative generally follows this scheme: Jerusalem (2:1-8:3), Judea and Samaria (8:4-12:25), and the ends of the earth (13:1-28:31). Before the narrative proper can commence the apostles must be joined by Matthias as Judas' replacement (1:15-26). With this completed, the church in Jerusalem is presented in five major narrative threads: 2:1-47, the beginning of the church; 3:1-4:35, the first instance of persecution[182]; 4:36-5:16, the first problem; 5:17-42, the second case of persecution; 6:1-8:3, the second problem and third occasion of persecution. Each of the first three lines of narrative culminates in a summary statement in which the church is cast in utopian terms.[183] The final instance of persecution involves the defense of Stephen (7:2-53) whose speech serves to provide a theological justification for the next major unit. The second section of Acts (8:4-12:25) contains five narrative threads all of which go back to the persecution which culminated in Stephen's martyrdom. Four of the five are designed to show how the church moved away from a strictly Jewish setting towards a universal stance.[184] The middle section is thus a hinge around which the early narratives of the Jerusalem church and the later Pauline mission turn. The third section of Acts presents the career of Paul both as a missionary (13:1-21:17) and as

---

[182] Note the similarity between chapters two and three-four:

Event	Two	Three-Four
Miracle	1-4	1-8
Reaction	5-13	9-10
Explanation	14-21	11-16
Sermon	22-36	17-26
Response	37-41	1-4
Summary	42-47	32-35

[183] 2:42-47; 4:32-35; 5:12-16.

[184] 8:5-40, the activities of Philip (conversion of the Samaritans and Ethiopian eunuch); 9:1-30, the conversion of Saul (this anticipates 13:1-28:31); 9:32-11:18, the activities of Peter culminating in the conversion of Cornelius; 11:19-30, the mission of the Hellenists; 12:1-23, the persecution of Herod. The last rounds out the material on the activities of Peter by contrasting the fate of Herod with the ineluctable spread of the word of God (12:24).

a prisoner (21:18-28:31). Paul's missionary work is narrated through a series of three major journeys around the Eastern half of the Mediterranean.[185] Between the first and second journeys the author placed the Jerusalem council to stress the unity of the church after the first mission and before the European mission (15:1-35). Following Paul's arrest in Jerusalem, the author records five trials.[186] At the conclusion of the fourth, Paul appealed to Caesar—the fifth is ostensibly to determine the exact charges. The appeal issues in a dramatic sea voyage (27:1-44) and Paul's arrival in Rome (28:1-16). The narrative comes to a conclusion on the note that Paul spent two years in his own dwelling κηρύσσων τὴν βασιλείαν τοῦ θεοῦ καὶ διδάσκων τὰ περὶ τοῦ κυρίου Ἰησοῦ Χριστοῦ μετὰ πάσης παρρησίας ἀκωλύτως.[187]

The contents of Luke-Acts are thus not about a single individual nor a collection of individuals, but about a movement. The gospel does not begin with Jesus, but with John. As the gospel ends, Jesus commissions the disciples leading us into Acts. The description of the early disciples focuses on Peter but never forgets the larger picture of the church in Judea and the Mediterranean seaboard. Even the hero of the second half of Acts can stand backstage when the occasion demands it (ch. 15). Luke-Acts tells the story of Christianity from its beginnings through its transformation from a Palestinian sect into an empire-wide movement some seventy years later. It is, therefore, not the story of Jesus nor of Paul. It is the story of Christianity, i.e., of a people. In this sense it is reminiscent of historical works which relate the story of a particular people.[188]

---

[185] 13:1-14:28; 15:36-18:22; 18:23-21:17.

[186] 22:1-21; 23:1-9; 24:1-23; 25:6-12; 26:1-32.

[187] 28:31. If Acts were a biography, it should include an account of Paul's death. It is interesting that the ending has always posed difficulties. The Pastoral Epistles fill in details of Paul's subsequent career in the Mediterranean. *I Clement* 5.7, claims Paul went to the West (i.e., Spain—Rom. 15:24, 28). This is repeated again by the *Actus Vercellenses* or *Acts of Peter* 1-3. The *Acta Pauli* has a different plot as it traces Paul's journey from Damascus to Rome for the second time. Modern scholarship is generally united in thinking that Paul died in Rome without being released, but just as divided as the ancients about the significance of the ending of Acts.

[188] Aune, *The New Testament in Its Literary Environment*, pp. 140-141, very correctly speaks of "the 'national consciousness' of Luke-Acts."

Form

Luke-Acts does not have a direct literary parallel.[189] In order to understand its form, then, we must ask first about influences on it and second, about specific literary forms within it.

1. *Literary Influences*

a. *Mark*.[190] The first model for our author was the gospel of Mark. The importance of Mark for our understanding of Luke-Acts should not be understated. Of the 661 verses which are part of the authentic text of Mark, c. 350 are reproduced in Luke including about 53% of the actual vocabulary.[191] The substance of Mark thus became a determinative source for the gospel.

Of even more importance for our question is the fact that the Markan framework became the basic structure of our gospel.[192] If our suggestion about composition is valid (i.e., Acts is modeled on Luke), then Mark also indirectly influenced the structure of Acts.

The author did not, however, take Mark—or Q or L—over wholesale.[193] Probably the most famous tradition about the gospel of Mark in antiquity is that of Papias who said: Μάρκος μὲν ἑρμηνευτὴς Πέτρου γενόμενος, ὅσα ἐμνημόνευσεν, ἀκριβῶς ἔγραψεν,

---

[189] So also Aune, *The New Testament in Its Literary Environment*, p. 78.

[190] I have not attempted to analyze the impact of Q on Luke-Acts since it is a Sayings Gospel rather than a Narrative Gospel.

[191] Streeter, *The Four Gospels*, pp. 159-160.

[192] There are, of course, well known exceptions: the greater omission of Mark 6:45-8:26 at Luke 9:17 and the lesser omission of Mark 9:41-10:12 at Luke 9:50. On the Markan material in Luke see Tim Schramm, *Der Markus-Stoff bei Lukas: Eine literarkritische und redaktionsgeschichtliche Untersuchung.* SNTSMS 14 (Cambridge: Cambridge University Press, 1971). I would attribute more of the alterations of Mark to the author than Schramm who distinguishes between Markan material and Markan material influenced by variants in the tradition.

[193] It is worth pointing out that the title which appears at Mark 1:1, Ἀρχὴ τοῦ εὐαγγελίου Ἰησοῦ Χριστοῦ [υἱοῦ θεοῦ], is avoided by our author. The exact force of this title is uncertain—does it go with 1:2-13 or with the entire book—and we have no way of knowing how the third evangelist understood it except to say that he avoided it. In fact, εὐαγγέλιον which is so important to Mark (1:1, 14, 15; 8:35; 10:29; 13:10; 14:9 [and 16:15]) does not appear in Luke and only twice in Acts (15:7; 20:24). The reverse is true if we examine the verb: it does not occur in Mark and is found 10t. in Luke and 15t. in Acts. The preface suggests that the author understood Mark to be a διήγησις rather than an εὐαγγέλιον. For the author of Luke-Acts the "good news" is not a document but something an individual does. *In nuce*, it is a verb not a noun.

οὐ μέντοι τάξει, τὰ ὑπὸ τοῦ κυρίου ἢ λεχθέντα ἢ πραχθέντα.[194] Our author apparently agreed with the assessment about order. On seven occasions he altered the order in an effort to provide a smoother or more credible narrative.[195] Just as Josephos united different strands of OT texts, so Luke shapes the Markan material into a flowing story—a procedure fully in keeping with Hellenistic historiography.[196]

The refinement of Mark does not stop at structure but extends to phraseology as well. Some of the most characteristic features of Markan expression are altered as they come into the third gospel.[197] The ubiquitous καί of Mark is frequently replaced with δέ or τε. The following chart will provide a rough idea of the different usage.[198]

Connective	Mark	Luke	Acts
καί	1083	1482	1127
δέ	158	543	559
τε	0	9	160

If we keep in mind the difference in length between the two gospels the variation becomes quite impressive. This is especially true when we remember how often καί introduces Markan verses. This pattern extends to the transformation of the paratactic structure of Mark to a more hypotactic structure in Luke through the use of either a genitive absolute or the substitution of a participle for a finite verb.[199] The third evangelist is also sensitive to vulgarisms—although he is

---

[194] Eusebios, HE 3.39.15. On this text see Kürzinger, Papias von Hierapolis und die Evangelien des Neuen Testaments, pp. 43-67, who understands Papias' assessment to be a rhetorical judgment of Mark's gospel.

[195] On the transpositions see Fitzmyer, The Gospel According to Luke, 1:71-72. I am generally indebted to his discussion on Markan composition in 1:63-106.

[196] According to Lucian a narrative should flow smoothly without gaps, Hist. conscr. 48, 55. Jacques Dupont, "La Question du Plan des Actes des Apôtres à la Lumière d'un Texte de Lucien de Samosate," NT 21 (1979): 220-231, has studied the structure of Acts in light of this principle.

[197] One of the most helpful studies along this line is still Cadbury, The Style and Literary Method of Luke, pp. 115-205.

[198] Unless otherwise indicated all word counts are my own and based on H. Bachmann and W.A. Slaby, eds., Computer Concordance to the Novum Testamentum Graece, 2nd ed. (Berlin/New York: Walter de Gruyter, 1985).

[199] Cf. Cadbury, The Style and Literary Method of Luke, pp. 133-136, for examples.

not completely consistent[200]—and Aramaic expressions.[201] Only
one of the 151 historical presents in Mark is preserved in Luke.[202]
Finally, we should point out that while Mark has only one optative
(11:14), it appears with some frequency in Luke-Acts.[203]

Mark thus served as a major source for Luke and provided the
basic structure of Luke and indirectly of Acts. At the same time, the
author transformed Mark in the same direction Josephos transformed the language of the LXX. The scope of Luke-Acts also goes
well beyond that of Mark. We need to account for the additional
material and for the inadequacy of Markan style for our author's
palate.

b. *LXX.* It is universally acknowledged that the author of Luke-
Acts knew the LXX.[204] In what ways did the LXX affect the formation of Luke-Acts?

The language of Luke-Acts at times betrays a heavy Semitic
tinge. A great number of theories have been invented to account for
this: Semitic sources, Hebraisms, and Aramaisms.[205] While there

---

[200] Note the replacement of κράβαττος in Mark 2:4 with κλινίδιον in Lk. 5:24.
Κράβαττος occurs in Mark 2:4, 9, 11, 12; 6:55. It does not appear in Luke, but
is found in Acts 5:15; 9:33.

[201] The third gospel removes Aramaic expressions through omission (ὡσαννά,
Mk. 11:9 and Lk. 19:38; αββα, Mk. 14:36 and Lk. 22:42; ῥαββί, Mk. 14:45 and
Lk. 22:47; γολγοθά, Mk. 15:22 and Lk. 23:33) or by offering a Greek substitute
(Καναναῖος, Mk. 3:18 and ζηλωτής, Lk. 6:15; ῥαββί, Mk. 9:5 and ἐπιστάτα, Lk.
9:33; ῥαββουνί, Mk. 10:51 and κύριε, Lk. 18:41; ὡσαννά, Mk. 11:10 and δόξα,
Lk. 19:38). Once again, the evangelist is not entirely consistent and has σίκερα
(1:15), πάσχα (2:41; 22:1 [Mk. 14:1], 7 [Mk. 14:12], 8, 11 [Mk. 14:14], 13 [Mk.
14:16], 15), ἀμήν (4:24; 12:37; 18:17, 29; 21:32; 23:43 vs. 13 times in Mark),
σατανᾶς (10:18; 11:18; 13:16; 22:3, 31 [Mk. 6t.]), Βεελζεβούλ (11:15, 18, 19),
γέεννα (12:5 [Mk. 3t.]), and μαμωνᾶ (16:9, 11, 13 ([L and Q]). The omisson of
Aramaic expressions was noted as early as Jerome, (*Ep.* 20.4.

[202] Mk. 5:35 = Lk. 8:49. Although it should be noted that Luke does use the
historical present: Luke, 10t.; Acts 13t. It is still with much less frequency.

[203] Of the 67 uses of the optative in the NT, 28 occur in Luke-Acts: 11 in Luke
(1:29, 38, 62; 3:15; 6:11; 8:9; 9:46; 15:26; 18:36; 20:16; 22:23) and 17 in Acts
(5:24; 8:20, 31; 10:17; 17:11, 18, 27 (*bis*); 20:16; 21:33; 24:19; 25:16 (*bis*), 20;
26:29; 27:12, 39. On the distribution in the NT see the convenient chart printed
in A.T. Robertson, *A Grammar of the Greek New Testament in the Light of Historical
Research*, 3rd ed. (Nashville: Broadman Press, 1934), p. 1408. James Hope Moulton thought that the use of the potential optative in Luke-Acts established "Luke
as the only *litterateur* among the authors of the New Testament" in Moulton,
Wilbert Francis Howard, and Nigel Turner, *A Grammar of New Testament Greek*, 4
vols. (Edinburgh: T. & T. Clark, 1906-1976), 2:7.

[204] The most important treatment of the LXX in Acts is that of William K.L.
Clarke, "The Use of the Septuagint in Acts," in *Beginnings*, 2:66-105.

[205] The most famous example is that of Charles Cuttler Torrey, *The Composition*

may be Jewish material beneath some of the Semitisms of Luke-Acts, most of them have parallels in the Septuagint and should be considered deliberate Septuagintalisms by the author.[206] I say deliberate because the jarring the reader experiences as she/he moves from the prologue to the infancy narrative can not be accidental.[207] The author can write in more than one literary style and appears to choose his style consciously.

Nearly every phrase in the opening pericope is an echo of an OT text. We begin with a transitional phrase in OT writing: ἐγένετο ἐν ταῖς ἡμέραις.[208] Once the temporal frame is in place, we are introduced to a priest whose wife shares the name of the first high priest's spouse.[209] The piety of both parents is stated in three phrases redolent of numerous OT texts: ἦσαν δὲ δίκαιοι ἀμφότεροι ἐναντίον τοῦ θεοῦ (Gen. 7:1; Jb. 32:2; 35:2), πορευόμενοι ἐν πάσαις ταῖς ἐντολαῖς (III Kgdms. 8:61; Ps. 118:1) καὶ δικαιώμασιν τοῦ κυρίου ἄμεμπτοι.[210] The pericope concludes by setting the stage for the narrative in terms that are distinctly reminiscent of Abraham and Sarah: καὶ οὐκ ἦν αὐτοῖς τέκνον, καθότι ἦν ἡ Ἐλισάβετ στεῖρα, καὶ ἀμφότεροι προβεβηκότες ἐν ταῖς ἡμέραις αὐτῶν ἦσαν.[211]

An interesting feature of the Septuagintal influence in Luke-Acts is that it principally occurs at the beginning of each book: in the infancy narrative of Luke (1:5-2:52) and the early chapters of Acts (esp. 1-12). In each instance the beginning of Jesus' ministry and the early years of the church are anchored in the language of the OT. It is not until we come to the second half of Acts that the style of the

---

and Date of Acts. HTS 1 (Cambridge: Harvard University Press, 1916), who argued that Acts 1-15 was translation Greek. He posited an Aramaic source which Luke translated.

[206] For recent treatments on the issue of Semitisms see Max Wilcox, The Semitisms of Acts (Oxford: The Clarendon Press, 1965); Nigel Turner, A Grammar of New Testament Greek, 4:45-63 and Fitzmyer, The Gospel According to Luke, 1:113-127. Fitzmyer lists undisputed Septuagintalisms on pp. 114-116.

[207] Lucian, Hist. conscr. 16, criticized a historian who began in Ionic in his preface and then shifted to the vernacular.

[208] E.g., Ex. 2:11; Judg. 15:1; Ruth 1:1 [A]; I Kgdms. 4:1; 13:22; 28:1.

[209] Ex. 6:23.

[210] The collocation of ἐντολή and δικαίωμα is common in the OT. E.g., Gen. 26:5; Ex. 15:26; Deut. 4:40; 6:1, 2; 7:11; 8:11; 10:13 et al.

[211] Gen. 18:11: Αβρααμ δὲ καὶ Σαρρα πρεσβύτεροι προβεβηκότες ἡμερῶν, ἐξέλιπεν δὲ Σαρρα γίνεσθαι τὰ γυναικεῖα. We should also remember that the first thing we learn about Sarah in the Genesis narrative is that she was barren (Gen. 11:30).

prologue begins to re-emerge.[212] The effect this has on the narrative is to match the march of the narrative from Jerusalem to Rome with a style that moves from heavily Septuagintal—the infancy narrative—through a more uniform style—the larger part of Luke-Acts—to a more Hellenized style in the final chapters of Acts. Interestingly, Lucian urged historians to make their language suitable to their subject.[213]

Granted that the author knew the LXX well enough to consciously imitate it, we would also expect it to have influenced the thought and form of his work. In particular, we would expect the narrative portion to have significance for him.[214] Of this material the story of Israel related in Genesis-IV Kingdoms promises to offer the most help in understanding Luke-Acts.[215] Modern scholarship recognizes two distinct historical works in this material: P = Genesis-Numbers and the Deuteronomistic history = Deuteronomy through II Kings.[216] We should not, however, assume that they were distinct for our author. While we recognize different agendas for each work, it is questionable whether our author would. It would therefore be a mistake to argue that Luke-Acts used the

---

[212] Note Acts 15:24-26; 17:22-31; 26:1-32; 27:1-44. A distinct exception to this is the sermon of Paul to the elders of Ephesus at Miletos, 20:18-35, where the influence of the Septuagint is again apparent.

[213] *Hist. conscr.*, 45.

[214] Clarke, "The Use of the Septuagint in Acts," pp. 69-77, compared the vocabulary of the LXX and Luke-Acts. He concluded that among the apocrypha, the author reflects the language of II and III Maccabees, Tobit, Judith, and possibly the Wisdom of Solomon. I have independently attempted to locate the Septuagintalisms frequently used in Luke-Acts within the LXX as a whole. Examining ἀποκριθείς . . . εἶπεν/λέγει, ἐνώπιον, καὶ ἰδού, κατὰ πρόσωπον + genitive, and πορευθείς + finite verb, I found that these expressions are most common in Genesis, Deuteronomy, Judges, Tobit, Daniel, and I Maccabees. A strong case can also be made for I-IV Kingdoms.

[215] I do not see any evidence to indicate that the Chronicler's history was significant for Luke-Acts.

[216] I am following the lead of Martin Noth which has been widely accepted. This is not, however, the only view. J. Wellhausen thought that JE extended to the end of Joshua. This was supplemented by the Dtr material gradually until it eventually reached II Kings. J. Van Seters has recently attempted to reverse this analysis by arguing that the Deuteronomistic work was the first history and that J and P followed as an extension of the Deuteronomistic work. R. Rendtorff proposed a Deuteronomistic school which was responsible for all of the material. The school shaped not only Genesis through Numbers, Deuteronomy, and Joshua-II Kings, but welded them all into a single unit. For an excellent summary with bibliography see Suzanne Boorer, "The Importance of a Diachronic Approach: The Case of Genesis-II Kings," *CBQ* 51 (1989): 195-208.

Deuteronomistic history as a model to the exclusion of P or vice versa. While it is impossible for us to remove ourselves from our way of thinking of the works, we should also keep in mind that it is a modern perspective.

P is a modern designation for the scribe(s) who finally assembled Genesis-Numbers probably c. 550 B.C.E. It thus spans the period from creation to the plains of Moab. The work is structured in two distinct forms. Genesis consists of the arrangement and composition of material under ten genealogical headings.[217]Exodus-Numbers are set up around twelve different stations: six from Egypt to Rephidim and six from Sinai to the plains of Moab.[218]On another level, the work has a biographical focus concentrating on Abraham, Jacob, Joseph, and Moses.[219]The promises made to Abraham and his descendants are the driving force of the narrative and are repeated throughout the work.[220]What becomes apparent is that God controls history to accomplish the divine will, i.e., the fulfillment of the promises. In Genesis the patriarchs are tested to see if they believe the promises; in Exodus the descendants of Abraham begin their trek toward the promised land from Egypt and become a nation at Sinai; in Leviticus the cultic procedures necessary for the covenant between the LORD and Israel are given; and in Numbers the people reach the edge of the promised land. The concern for order also extends to the periodization of history. There are three covenants in the text which differentiate four periods of time: Adam, Noah, Abraham, and Moses.[221]

The Deuteronomistic history embraces Deuteronomy through II Kings.[222]It thus covers the period from the plains of Moab to the

---

[217] Gen. 2:4a; 5:1; 6:9; 10:1; 11:10, 27; 25:12, 19; 36:1 and 9 (both refer to Esau); 37:2.

[218] My understanding of P here is largely built on the work of Frank Moore Cross, *Canaanite Myth and Hebrew Epic: Essays in the History of the Religion of Israel* (Cambridge: Harvard University Press, 1973), pp. 308-317.

[219] I understand Isaac to be more of a link between Abraham and Jacob than a principal character in his own right.

[220] The promise motif was originally a major theme of the Yahwist, the epic historian of Judah who is dated between 950-800 B.C.E. The promises are found in Gen. at 12:1-3 (a J text), 7; 13:15-17; 15:5, 7, 18-21; 17:2, 4, 5-8, 16; 18:18; 22:17-18; 26:4; 28:4, 13-14; 32:12; 48:21-22; 50:24; Ex. 2:24; 3:15-17; 6:3-8; 32:13; 33:1-3; Lev. 26:42; Num. 32:11.

[221] Gen. 9:8-17; 15:1-21; Ex. 19-24. On the theology of P see Walter Brueggemann and Hans Walter Wolff, *The Vitality of Old Testament Traditions*, 2nd ed. (Atlanta: John Knox Press, 1982), pp. 101-113.

[222] Martin Noth, *The Deuteronomistic History*, trans. by E.W. Nicholson.

release of Jehoiachin. As with the priestly work, this is not a fresh
composition, but represents a combination of earlier material and
composition: the editing of Deuteronomy-II Samuel and the composition of I and II Kings.[223]

The work is bound together by a common theological understanding of history: God blesses the righteous and punishes the
wicked.[224] This understanding of history is openly stated in two
major theological/historiographical statements: Judg. 2:6-3:6[225]; II
Kgs. 17:7-23. Although this is a different expression of historical understanding than that of P, it shares the same basic presupposition:
history is the record of how the will of God has been enforced among
humanity. The result of this view is that the Deuteronomist schema-
tizes his historical presentation—although not to the point of completely overriding the sources.[226] So we have cyclic history in
Judges (the people sin, are sold into slavery, repent, and God raises
a saviour ["judge"] who delivers them)[227] and formulaic summaries of the kings in I and II Kings which measures each ruler in
religious and cultic terms.[228] The same theological understanding

---

JSOTSup 15 (Sheffield: JSOT Press, 1981 [first German edition 1943]), first argued for the existence of a unified work. He pointed out that the work was framed
by speeches (Josh. 1:11-15; 23; I Sam. 12:1-25; I Kgs. 8:12-41) and argued that
the theme was irreversible doom which was addressed to the exiles (c. 550 B.C.E.)
in order to explain their plight. Subsequent research has accepted Noth's analysis
and attempted to refine it. One of the more important contributions is that of Cross,
Canaanite Myth and Hebrew Epic, pp. 274-289, who argued for two editions: the first
under the reign of Josiah (622-609 B.C.E.) and the second in the exile (561-520
B.C.E.). Three very important recent monographs are Mohse Weinfield, *Deuteronomy and the Deuteronomic School* (Oxford: The Clarendon Press, 1972); John Van
Seters, *In Search of History: Historiography in the Ancient World and the Origins of Biblical
History* (New Haven/London: Yale University Press, 1983) and Baruch Halpern,
The First Historians: The Hebrew Bible and History (San Francisco: Harper & Row,
1988).

[223] It appears that the scribe(s) furnished an introduction and conclusion to
Deuteronomy, revised Joshua, revised Judges and added an introduction,
minimally revised I and II Samuel, and composed I and II Kings. The key to the
work is the distinctive theology which unites this disparate material. (See below)

[224] E.g., Deut. 28; Josh. 1:12-18; Judg. 2:10-23; II Sam. 7:5-15; I Kgs. 15:3-4.

[225] This is one of the texts which Van Seters, *In Search of History*, pp. 342-343,
attributes to P since it presents the presence of the nations as a test for Israel rather
than a threat to the divine plan.

[226] See the excellent discussion of Halpern, *The First Historians*, pp. 219-228.

[227] Stated in Judg. 2:11-19: 11, 14, 18, 16.

[228] The introductory formula for introducing the kings of Israel is: date of accession which is synchronized with the date of the king of Judah; the name of the
capital (sometimes); the length of the king's reign; a condemnation of each king

of history is expressed in a number of speeches throughout the work: Joshua's farewell address,[229] Samuel's farewell speech,[230] and Solomon's prayer and speech at the dedication of the temple.[231]

John Van Seters has identified the following literary techniques which characterize the work[232]: parataxis (repetition of a formula or pattern as a connective within a *logos*,[233] speeches or editorial comments to state the theme of a unit or serve as a transitional device, the periodization of history,[234] the association of themes with principal figures (e.g., the temple of Solomon), a pointed interest in prophecy and its fulfillment,[235] and the use of analogies between the historical figures.[236] We should also add that as with P the presentation is biographically oriented.

How have these works influenced Luke-Acts?[237] First and fore-

---

(except Shallum); and the mentioning of the king's father (except for Zimri and Omri). For the kings of Judah it is: the date of accession synchronized with the king of Israel (obviously omitted after Israel's fall); the age at accession (except for Abijam and Asa); the length of reign; the name of the king's mother (except for Jehoram and Ahaz); and an appraisal of the king's reign. There is also a concluding formula: reference to source; statement of the king's death (and sometimes place of burial); and the name of the successor. There are two standard formulae for measuring a king. He either ויעש ... הרע בעיני יהוה (I Kgs. 11:6; 14:22; 15:26, 34; 16:19, 25, 30; 21:20, 25; 22:53; II Kgs. 3:2; 8:18, 27; 13:2, 11; 14:24; 15:9, 18, 24, 28; 17:2, 17; 21:2, 16, 20; 23:32, 37; 24:9, 19 [cf. also 21:15]) or ויעש הישר בעיני יהוה ... (I Kgs. 15:5, 11; 22:43; II Kgs. 12:3; 14:3; 15:3, 34; 18:3; 22:2 [cf. also I Kgs. 11:33, 38; 14:8] and II Kgs. 16:2 where it is used with a negative). The second formula is that "he walked" בדרכי (I Kgs. 11:33), בדרך אביו (I Kgs. 15:26; 22:43, 53 [cf. also II Kgs. 21:21]), בדרך ירבעם (I Kgs. 15:34; 16:2, 19, 26; 22:53), בדרך מלכי ישראל (II Kgs. 8:18; 16:3), בדרך בית אחאה (II Kgs. 8:27), בדרך יהוה (II Kgs. 21:22), or בדרך דוד (II Kgs. 22:2).

[229] Josh. 23:2-16.
[230] I Sam. 12:1-25.
[231] I Kgs. 8:12-61.
[232] *In Search of History*, p. 358. Cf. also his summary of the techniques in Kings on p. 321.
[233] One pattern Van Seters notes is the theme of the divine election and rejection of a king, e.g., Saul, Solomon, Jereboam (I Kgs. 14:7-16), and Baasha (I Kgs. 16:1-4). *Ibid.*, p. 312.
[234] *Ibid.*, p. 276, argues that the Deuteronomistic scheme divides Israel's history into three periods: the exodus and conquest, the age of judges, and the rise of the monarchy (based upon I Sam. 8:8; 10:18-19; 12:6ff.).
[235] E.g., I Kgs. 8:24; 22:38; II Kgs. 1:17; 7:17-20; 9:36-37; 15:12; 17:23. On a broader plane, the speech of Moses in Deut. 28 becomes a type of advance summary of what the history will unfold.
[236] E.g., the desert theophany and the dedication of the temple; Jereboam's centralization of apostasy vs. Josiah's reform. *Ibid.*, pp. 310 and 314, respectively.
[237] The most important essay along these lines is that of Daryl Schmidt, "The

most they have provided the author with his understanding of what history is. The common denominator between P and the Deuteronomistic history is their confessional stance towards the activity of God in human activities. We have already seen how the Deuteronomistic history served as a major factor in the work of Josephos who employed the Hellenistic concept of πρόνοια to describe God's control of human history. Luke-Acts follows this pattern although it uses different vocabulary and has a distinctive nuance. The key terms[238] in Luke-Acts are ἡ βουλὴ τοῦ θεοῦ,[239] δεῖ,[240] and the verbs denoting God's determinations of the course of history (ὁρίζω,[241] προορίζω,[242] and προοράω[243]). The author also demonstrates God's control over history by narrating key events as the actions of God. So Jesus pours out the Spirit in Acts 2, 8, and 10 to

---

Historiography of Acts: Deuteronomistic or Hellenistic?,'' pp. 417-427. The paper was designed as a prolegomenon.

[238] For treatments of the terms see Conzelmann, *The Theology of St. Luke*, pp. 151-154 and Fitzmyer, *The Gospel According to Luke*, 1:170-181.

[239] Βουλή is found 12t. in the NT, 9t. in Luke-Acts. It is used of God's will in Lk. 7:30; Acts 2:23, 4:28; 13:36; 20:27 (cf. also Acts 5:36-37). Other uses are in Lk. 23:51; Acts 27:12, 42, where it refers to human decisions. The will of God is found 23t. in the LXX: II Es. 10:3; Jud. 2:2, 4; 8:16; Ps. 32:11; 105:13; 106:11; Prov. 19:21; Wis. 6:4; 9:13, 17; Mic. 4:12; Isa. 4:2(?); 5:19; 14:26; 19:17; 25:1, 7; 46:10; 55:8; Jer. 27:45; 30:14; 39:19. A particularly important text is Isa. 46:10 which affirms that God's βουλή will be established. A related term is θέλημα which is found 62t. in the NT, but only once in Mk. (3:38). It is found seven times in Luke-Acts, four of which refer to the divine plan (Luke 22:42; Acts 13:22; 21:14; 22:14).

[240] Δεῖ occurs 101t. in the NT: 6t. in Mk., 8t. in Mt., and 40t. in Luke-Acts. It is undoubtedly of more significance to Luke-Acts than to Mark or Matthew. In Mark it refers to the passion (8:31), the fulfillment of Scripture (9:11), the course of events in the apocalyptic discourse (13:7, 10, 14), and an individual's lot (14:31). It is found 18t. in Luke and 22t. in Acts. It occurs 37t. in the LXX. There is no Hebrew equivalent for it there; it generally translates an infinitive construct with the preposition ל in a purpose clause. In apocalyptic texts it transforms a simple future reference (מה די להוא) into a necessity (ἃ δεῖ γενέσθαι), Dan. 2:28, 29, 45. The use in Luke-Acts, however, differs. It is not a compulsion through fate (μοῖρα) as in Greek thought nor an apocalyptic plan of history. While some texts reflect LXX influence, in others δεῖ is the divine necessity which propels historical events: Jesus' life and death (Luke 2:49; 4:43; 9:22; 13:33; 17:25; 22:37; 24:7, 26, 44; Acts 3:21), the course of Paul's life (Acts 19:21; 23:11; 27:24, 26).

[241] 8t. in the NT: 6t. in Luke-Acts. It denotes the preordained course of events in Lk. 22:22; Acts 2:23; 10:42; 17:31. (Other uses in Acts 11:29; 17:26) Other NT texts are Rm. 1:4; Heb. 4:7. It is found in the LXX 20t.

[242] 6t. in NT: only once in Luke-Acts, i.e., Acts 4:28. It is not in the LXX.

[243] 4t. in NT. Three of these are in Luke-Acts, but only one in the sense of God's plan (Acts 2:31). Cf. also Acts 2:25 (citing Ps. 15:8 [the only reference in the LXX]) and 21:29.

indicate the will of God.[244] The Spirit of God even controlled the movements of the missionaries.[245] History is thus under a divine constraint to move according to the βουλὴ τοῦ θεοῦ.[246]

What is striking about the formulation of this in Luke-Acts is that the divine will is essentially seen in the theme of fulfillment.[247] This is made clear by the connection of δεῖ and the fulfillment of Scripture.[248] Our author is recording the fulfillment of OT promises and prophecies in the life of Jesus and the early church.[249] That the life of Jesus and the church constitute the fulfillment of OT prophecy is a common Christian understanding of the OT.[250] What is unique to Luke-Acts is the writing of history from the perspective of the fulfillment of both the promises and prophecies.[251] The plan of God is in the OT in the form of promise. Luke-Acts represents an attempt to write out the record of its fulfillment.

Where did the author derive his concept? The distinctive Christian interpretation suggests that the primary impulse came from a

---

[244] The significance of these actions is brought out in Acts 10:47; 11:17; 15:8. The point is that no one can argue with God's actions. God has communicated the divine purpose by stepping onto the stage of human history directly.

[245] Acts 16:6-7.

[246] It is hard not to think of Polybios when we speak of history under divine will. There is now a Yale dissertation on this concept, John Squires, "The Plan of God in Luke-Acts," (Ph.D. dissertation, Yale University, 1988). I have not seen it.

[247] Two fundamental essays which helped to establish this are Paul Schubert, "The Structure and Significance of Luke 24," in *Neutestamentliche Studien für Rudolf Bultmann*, ed. W. Eltester (Berlin: Topelmann, 1957), pp. 165-186 and Nils A. Dahl, "The Story of Abraham in Luke-Acts," in *Studies in Luke-Acts*, pp. 139-158. Cf. also Franklin, *Christ the Lord*, pp. 119-124 and David L. Tiede, *Prophecy and History in Luke-Acts* (Philadelphia: Fortress Press, 1980), pp. 23-33; Schmidt, "The Historiography of Acts," pp. 420-421. Note the criticisms of Charles H. Talbert, "Promise and Fulfillment in Lucan Theology," in *Luke-Acts: New Perspectives from the Society of Biblical Literature Seminar*, pp. 91-103.

[248] Lk. 22:37; 24:7, 26, 44; Acts 1:16; 17:3.

[249] Luke alone among the evangelists stresses the fulfillment of the promises. The noun ἐπαγγελία occurs 52t. in the NT and only in Luke-Acts among the gospels where it appears 9t. References to the promises in the OT include Acts 7:17; 13:23, 32 (where its fulfillment is interpreted); 26:6. Cf. also Acts 3:25; 7:3. The verbal cognate, ἐπαγγελίζομαι, is used in Acts 7:5 of the promise made to Abraham. The verb occurs once in Mark 14:11, but in reference to the chief priests' promise to pay Judas for his act of betrayal.

[250] The covenanters at Qumran represent an antecedent movement with the same understanding. See especially 1QpHab.

[251] Matthew writes the life of Christ from this perspective, but I understand Matthew more in terms of biography than history.

Christian attempt to relate the life of Jesus and the church to the OT.
At the same time, there was an OT model for such a procedure in
Genesis-II Kings. The story of God's people was told in terms of
promise-fulfillment there. The author's intimate knowledge of the
LXX suggests that this formed a precedent for his own efforts. The
concept of history in Luke-Acts is thus indebted to the Israelite histories within the LXX both for its confessional understanding of history and its specific expression of the execution of God's will.[252]

The author did not, however, take over this concept without alter-
ing it significantly. What was the promise and what is its fulfillment?
P saw the fulfillment of the promises in terms of Israel and the Deuteronomistic history is the story of Israel and Judah alone. The story
of Luke-Acts, on the other hand, is the record of salvation for all of
the world.[253] In this sense it may be called salvation history.[254]
While the scheme of Luke-Acts is similar to P and the Deuteronomistic history, the actual presentation is distinctly Christian.

Did the general understanding of history extend to specific forms
or techniques? Taking up Van Seters' observations on the Deuteronomistic history, we find the following. Acts does use formulae
to mark transitions although not with the rigor of Kings.[255] Related
to this is his concept of analogy. Again there is absolutely no doubt

---

[252] So also Dahl, "The Story of Abraham in Luke-Acts," p. 152, who wisely
does not intend for this judgment to exclude all Hellenistic influence and Schmidt,
"The Historiography of Acts," pp. 417-423. Note the caution of Balch, "Acts as
Hellenistic Historiography," pp. 430-432.

[253] It is worth pointing out that Luke-Acts uses the group of salvation terms
more frequently than any other gospel. Σώζω occurs 107t. in the NT: Mk. 14t.,
Lk. 17t., Ac. 13t., Mt. 16t. Note especially Lk 19:10, where Jesus' mission is
presented in these terms. Σωτήρ appears 24t. in the NT. Luke is the only gospel
to use it: Lk 2t. and Ac. 2t. Σωτηρία is found 46t. in the NT: 4t. in Luke and 6t.
in Acts. It does not appear in the other gospels. Σωτήριον surfaces 4t. in the NT,
three of which are in Luke-Acts: Lk. 2:30; 3:6; Ac. 28:28. To point out the predilec-
tion for this terminology does not establish this as *the* major theological motif in
Luke-Acts; this is established by the narrative.

[254] I realize that this is a loaded term. The contemporary debate began with
Conzelmann, *The Theology of St. Luke*, who argued that Luke-Acts attempted to
come to grips with the delay of the parousia through the placement of the church
into the frame of *Heilsgeschichte*. This is virtually universally rejected today as the
major aim of Luke-Acts. Recent works which understand salvation to stand at the
center of Luke-Acts' presentation include Marshall, *Luke: Historian and Theologian*,
pp. 77-215 and O'Toole, *The Unity of Luke's Theology*.

[255] There are a series of summary statements which are not identical, but all
mark the progress of the church. Acts 6:7; 9:31; 12:24; 16:5; 19:20; 28:31.

that Luke-Acts uses patterns. The difficulty is that these were also very common in Greco-Roman literature, e.g., Vergil.[256]

Another possible point of contact is the speeches of the Deutero-nomistic history and those of Acts. Once again we meet with a phenomenon which occurs in different traditions.[257] In this case, I do not think that Luke-Acts exclusively used the speeches of the OT as a model. As we have seen, the speeches in the Deuteronomistic history are vehicles for the scribe to express his own theological in-terpretation of history; the speeches of Luke-Acts function in a much wider capacity and with much greater frequency. (See below) More apposite is the inclusion of prayers in Acts which remind the reader of the prayers incorporated in the OT narrative.[258]

Since the work of Conzelmann, students of Luke-Acts have noted a periodization of history.[259] Conzelmann thought in terms of three periods: Israel, Jesus, and the church. The trend in more recent research is to see two stages, promise and fulfillment, with a bifurca-tion of the latter into the period of Jesus and the church. Our analy-sis concurs with the more contemporary view.[260] I would like to suggest that the author of Luke-Acts worked his view out in literary terms.

The period of promise is the LXX; the period of fulfillment is

---

[256] Talbert, *Literary Patterns, Theological Themes and the Genre of Luke-Acts*, pp. 5-7.

[257] The strongest case can be made for the farewell discourses in Lk. 22:14-38 and Acts 20:18-35. These, however, occur in both Jewish and Greek traditions. Jewish: Gen. 47:29-49:33; Deut. 31:1-34:12; Josh. 23:1-24:29; I Sam. 12:1-25; I Kgs. 2:1-10; Tob. 14:3-11; I Macc. 2:49-70; Jvb. 21; Josephus *AJ* 4.309-326; 5.115-116; 7. 383-388; 12.279-284; T. 12 Patr.; T. Job; T. 3 Patr.; T. Mos.; T. Sol.; T. Adam. Greek: Plato, *Phaedo*; Plutarch, *Cato Minor* 66-70 and *Otho* 15-17; and Diogenes Laertios 10.16-22.

[258] Acts 1:24-25; 4:24-30. There are of course prayers in the gospel tradition, but they tend to be very brief with the exception of Jn. 17. I think it more likely that a prayer such as Acts 4:24-30 is incorporated on the basis of texts like I Kgs. 8:22-53. Both prayers interpret the course of events.

[259] *The Theology of St. Luke*, pp. 12-15, 149-151. The title in German is more descriptive of Conzelmann's views, *Die Mitte der Zeit*.

[260] Lk. 24:46-47 indicates that both Jesus and the church belong to the phase of fulfillment. Examples of a bipartite division are Eugene A. LaVerdiere and Wil-liam G. Thompson, "New Testament Communities in Transition: A Study of Matthew and Luke," *TS* 37 (1976):586-589, especially 587, and Richard, "Luke—Writer, Theologian, Historian," p. 5. Talbert, *Literary Patterns, Theological Themes and the Genre of Luke-Acts*, pp. 103-107, argues for four stages: the law and the prophets, Jesus, the apostolic age, and the post-apostolic age.

Luke-Acts subdivided into the age of Jesus (Luke) and the church (Acts). The key to the division of the last two is the coming of the Spirit.[261] After Jesus received the Spirit at his baptism, his first public act was his sermon in the synagogue at Nazareth. Here he reads "the Spirit of the Lord is upon me, because the Lord has anointed me to announce the good news to the poor . . ."[262] He then claims that this Scripture has been fulfilled in their presence. The programmatic nature of Lk. 4:16-30 and the claim mark this as not only the beginning of Jesus' ministry, but also of a new age. The same pattern is repeated in Acts 2 where the Spirit is poured out in fulfillment of prophecy.[263] The key to the prophecy as it is interpreted in Acts is that the coming of the Spirit signals the offer of salvation. Peter thus extends the offer in the name of the Messiah.[264] With this event the church is born. This analysis is confirmed by the author's references to the "beginning." The author uses the noun ἀρχή in a temporal sense on two occasions. In Luke 1:2, it refers to the period of the eyewitnesses, i.e., the time from the baptism of John.[265] The second instance is in Peter's report of the conversion of Cornelius: "the Holy Spirit fell on them just as it did on us ἐν ἀρχῇ."[266] There are thus two "beginnings." Did the author of Luke-Acts derive the concept of epochs of history and if so from what tradition? It is, of course, possible that it was his own creation, necessitated by the recognition that the life of Jesus was in the past. If we look for a precedent we are soon frustrated: the division of history into epochs is such a common pattern that it is impossible to pinpoint a single tradition.[267] It is, however, significant that it is present in a work which is known to be a major source for the author's thinking and writing.[268]

---

[261] So also Leonhard Goppelt, *Theology of the New Testament*, 2 vols. trans. by John Alsup (Grand Rapids: Wm. B. Eerdmans Publishing Co., 1981-1982), 2:278.

[262] Isa. 61:1.

[263] Acts 2:1-4, 17-21.

[264] Compare v. 21 and 37-41.

[265] Cf. Acts 1:22, where the participle is used to indicate the period of time one must have accompanied Jesus in order to be an eyewitness, ἀρξάμενος ἀπὸ τοῦ βαπτίσματος Ἰωάννου . . . Note also the statements in Luke 23:5 and especially Acts 10:37, where the verbal form is used and traces the beginning back to Galilee.

[266] Acts 11:15.

[267] The concept of ages in the world is widely attested. Hesiod, *Op.* 106-201, is of course the outstanding Greek example and Jewish apocalyptic the foremost Jewish representative. E.g., Dan. 2 and 7 with the four kingdoms.

[268] The fact that P divides ages by covenants and Luke-Acts by the coming of the Spirit argues against any wooden borrowing.

The same ambivalent view must be maintained about the writing of a narrative through a series of main characters. In the Greek world this is as old as Herodotos as we saw in chapter two. It is certainly present in P and the Deuteronomistic history, but this can not be pressed.

The LXX was thus of central importance for Luke-Acts. It provided the language for sections of the work, the concept of history which pervades it, and may have supplied some of the forms themselves.[269] More important than this is the realization that our author conceived of his work as the *continuation* of the LXX. His deliberate composition in Septuagintal Greek and the conviction that his story was the fulfillment of the promises of the OT imply that as a continuation, Luke-Acts represents *sacred narrative*.[270]

c. *The Hellenistic Jewish Historians.* As important as the LXX is, we have seen that it is inadequate to explain some of the techniques of Luke-Acts. More than that it can not account for the effort of Luke-Acts to place Christianity in a broader framework. There were, however, Jewish writers who had made this attempt for Judaism. Did they influence Luke-Acts? Since these historians retell the OT text, the two speeches in Acts which retell the OT provide a basis for our comparison. Of these two the speech of Stephen (Acts 7:2-50) comes closest to an actual rehearsal of the OT.

What is intriguing about the speech as a whole is that the selection of material corresponds to our fragments of the Hellenistic Jewish historian Artapanos. If we analyze the speech according to subject

[269] Other treatments of the debt of Luke-Acts to the LXX include Barrett, *Luke the Theologian in Recent Study*, pp. 15-19, who argues that the confession of faith in God's saving acts in Luke-Acts is due to the LXX; Marshall, *Luke: Historian and Theologian*, p. 56, the concept of a divine plan is due to the OT; Drury, *Tradition and Design in Luke's Gospel*, pp. 46-81, who contends that the historical works of the OT were Luke's models; and Schneider, *Die Apostelgeschichte*, 1:107, 124, who suggests that the linking of episodes in Acts imitates the historical works of the OT; Schmidt, "The Historiography of Acts," who compares the findings of Van Seters and Weinfield on the Deuteronomistic history and suggests that the techniques are the same; and David P. Moessner, *Lord of the Banquet: The Literary and Theological Significance of the Lukan Travel Narrative* (Minneapolis: Fortress Press, 1989).
[270] So also Gasque, "A Fruitful Field," pp. 120-121, who argues from the Semitic cast of the narrative and the central position of Jerusalem. Brown, "The Prologues of Luke-Acts in Their Relation to the Purpose of the Author," p. 4, suggests that the ἔδοξε κἀμοί of Lk 1:3 is echoed by Acts 15:28. Since the apostolic decree was the definitive document which established the relation between Gentile and Jewish Christians, Brown suggests that the ἔδοξε κἀμοί of Lk 1:3 implies "canonical intent." This places far too great an implication on a very slender basis.

matter we find the following: Abraham (vs. 2-8), Joseph (vs. 9-16), Moses (vs. 17-43), and the temple (vs. 44-50). It is striking that the three figures which the author emphasizes are the three of the fragments of Artapanos. Is this purely coincidental or are there other points of contact?

If we examine the occasions where the author departs from the biblical text (both MT and LXX) in the speech, we find two texts which share the same perspective as the Hellenistic Jewish historians. It is well known that the author has transferred the call of Abraham from Haran to Mesopotamia.[271] Why this telescoping of the biblical text? It would have suited the argument of Acts 7 to have the call in Haran just as well as in Mesopotamia: both were far removed from the promised land. It is worth remembering that Pseudo-Eupolemos also telescoped the biblical narrative.[272] Pseudo-Eupolemos pictures the astronomer Abraham responding to God's commands in Ur just as the author of Luke-Acts does.[273] The same type of general agreement occurs in the description of Moses. The early years of Israel's greatest hero are presented in the categories of Hellenistic biography: ἐγεννήθη . . . ἀνετράφη . . . ἐπαιδεύθη.[274] The final element in this trio is stated in v. 22: καὶ ἐπαιδεύθη Μωϋσῆς [ἐν] πάσῃ σοφίᾳ Αἰγυπτίων, ἦν δὲ δυνατὸς ἐν λόγοις καὶ ἔργοις αὐτοῦ. What is especially noteworthy about this comment is that it does not simply embellish the biblical text but contravenes it.[275] Encomiastic treatments of Moses are all pervasive in Judaism.[276] The question which we need to raise is which tradition accented Moses' *Egyptian* education? Our analysis of the

---

[271] Acts 7:2 places the call of Abraham in Mesopotamia which corresponds to Gen. 11:27-30 instead of in Haran where Abraham received the call according to Gen. 11:31-12:3.

[272] It would be possible to attribute this to Polyhistor's abbreviation; however, this would not simply be a reduction but an alteration. I prefer to attribute it to Pseudo-Eupolemos.

[273] F 1.3-4. Philo, *Abr.* 60-88, esp. 72, also places Abraham's call in Mesopotamia.

[274] Acts 7:20-22. Cf. Philo, *Mos.* 2.1: Ἡ μὲν προτέρα σύνταξίς ἐστι περὶ γενέσεως τῆς Μωυσέως καὶ τροφῆς, ἔτι δὲ παιδείας καὶ ἀρχῆς. The same pattern is present in *Flac.* 158 and Acts 22:3. For other references see W.C. Van Unnik, *Tarsus or Jerusalem: The City of Paul's Youth*, trans. George Ogg (London: The Epworth Press, 1962), pp. 18-27. Cf. also the form of the encomium prescribed by Anaximenes, *Rhetorica ad Alexandrum* 35.

[275] Ex. 4:10: כי כבד פה וכבד לשון אנכי and ἰσχνόφωνος καὶ βραδύγλωσσος ἐγώ εἰμι.

[276] Sirach 45:3, omits any reference to Moses' slowness of speech in praising him.

Hellenistic Jewish historians suggests that it was the apologetic tradition.[277] These references do not suggest that the author had a particular text before him, but that he was familiar with the treatments of the OT attested in the Hellenistic Jewish historians.

A more ambiguous possibility is the escape of Peter from Herod's prison. It is hard not to think of Artapanos' account of Moses' release: both accounts have the hero thrown into prison, mention the time as night, and have the doors open automatically.[278] The details, however, vary: both mention the guards but Acts offers no explanation for what they are doing as Peter makes good his escape while Artapanos explains that they are either asleep or dead and their weapons are shattered. Further, Acts adds a number of details not in Artapanos. The broad nature of the agreement and the frequency of this theme in ancient literature precludes any ascription of dependence. We should only note that Artapanos is one of many possible literary models.[279]

Our findings are too meager to argue that the author of Luke-Acts knew the Hellenistic historians directly. We can not therefore argue that they served as models for him. What the evidence does suggest is that the author's understanding of the OT was influenced by Hellenistic Judaism. The attempt to transform a biblical text into categories known to the Hellenistic world would not have been entirely new to him.[280]

d. *Josephos*. The case is more substantial when we examine the similarities between Luke-Acts and Josephos. The relationship between the two has been debated for well over a hundred years now. In the course of the argumentation every conceivable position has been held.[281] After examining the texts myself, I must conclude

[277] Artapanos F 3.3-4; Josephos *AJ* 2.236-237 (his education), 275-276 (difficulties in speech are converted into being a commoner, Ex. 4:10). Cf. also Philo, *Mos.* 1.20-24, where he masters both the learning of Egypt and Greece.

[278] Acts 12:3-19 and Artapanos F 3.23.

[279] Cf. also Euripides, *Bacch.* 447-448; Ovid, *Metam.* 3.699-700 and our discussion under Artapanos in chapter five.

[280] See the similar judgment of Plümacher in *RESup*, s.v. "Lukas als griechischer Historiker," 14:241.

[281] Some of the most significant treatments of the various positions are as follows. Luke-Acts was dependent upon Josephos: M. Krenkel, *Josephus und Lukas. Der schriftstellerische Einfluß des jüdischen Geschichtschreibers auf den christlichen nachgewiesen* (Leipzig: Haessel, 1894), the most extensive argument for this view (*non vidi*); *ERE*, s.v. "Josephus," by Niese, 7:577; and F. Crawford Burkitt, *The Gospel History and Its Transmission*, 3rd ed. (Edinburgh: T. & T. Clark, 1911), pp. 105-110, a sane statement of this view; Streeter, *The Four Gospels*, pp. 556-558, who suggested

with the majority of scholars that it is impossible to establish the dependence of Luke-Acts on the *Antiquitates*.[282] What is clear is that Luke-Acts and Josephos shared some common traditions about the recent history of Palestine. The stalemate along these lines has led some researchers to explore similarities between the two.[283] The

---

that Luke heard Josephos lecture in Rome and is dependent on his lectures not the written text of *AJ*. The relationship is insoluble: Cadbury, *Beginnings*, 2:355-358; F.J. Foakes-Jackson, *The Acts of the Apostles.* MNTC (London: Hodder and Stoughton, 1931), pp. xiii-xv. Luke-Acts did not use Josephos: the dominant position represented recently, for example, by Bruce, "The Acts of the Apostles," ANRW II 25.3:2590. Luke-Acts and Josephos are independent and depend on traditions which were common in the first century: Heinz Schreckenberg, "Flavius Josephus und die lukanischen Schriften," in *Wort in der Zeit: Neutestamentliche Studien* (*Festgabe für Karl Heinrich Rengstorf*), ed. by Wilfrid Haubeck and Michael Bachmann (Leiden: E.J. Brill, 1980), pp. 179-209, who provides a balanced summary of all of the textual evidence.

[282] The key texts are Acts 5:36 and *AJ* 20.97-98; Acts 12:19-23 and *AJ* 19.343-350; and Acts 21:38 and *BJ* 2.261-263. The first set represents the strongest possibility of dependence. In a speech attributed to Gamaliel, the author cites Theudas and Judas as examples of revolutionaries who had followings but came to grief. There are, however, major difficulties with the account as it stands: Gamaliel is ostensibly speaking c. 30 C.E., yet mentions Theudas who was not active until 44/45; he places Judas (6 C.E.) after Theudas; and implies that Judas and his followers quickly passed from the scene—an implication which runs contrary to the facts as we know them. Intriguingly, Josephos mentions them in the same order with the same basic story. There are, nonetheless, significant differences: Acts gives a number for Theudas' followers, Josephos does not; in the case of Judas, Josephos is dealing with his sons, Acts with Judas; and finally, Josephos omits recording Judas' fate which Acts narrates. The second set is a description of the death of Herod Agrippa I. Both accounts set the story in Caesarea, at the time of a feast, mention the garments of Herod, record his acclamation as god, attribute his death to this cause, and offer similar descriptions of his death. They differ in several significant features: Acts ascribes the response of the people to a speech of Agrippa, Josephos to his clothing; Acts has Herod smitten by an ἄγγελος κυρίου, Josephos maintains continuity with his earlier narrative by having an owl serve as a ἄγγελος of his death (see 18.195). Both of these variations could easily be transformations by the author of Acts. Acts does, however, also include a section on Blastos, the king's chamberlain which has no parallel in Josephos and can not be explained on the basis of Josephos' text. The last set of texts again have similarities and differences: both mention the Egyptian in connection with the desert—only Josephos has him lead the people from the desert to the mount of Olives. They differ in the number of followers: Acts 4000, Josephos 30,000. (Note: Could there be a confusion of Λ [30,000] and Δ [4,000]?) It used to be common to compare Lk. 3:1 with the references in Josephos to Lysanios (*AJ* 18.237; 19.275; 20.138; *BJ* 2.215, 247. Cf. also *AJ* 14.330-332; 15.92, 344; *BJ* 1.248, 398, 440). It has now been established through epigraphical evidence that there was a second Lysanios. See Schreckenberg, "Flavius Josephus und die lukanischen Schriften," pp. 188-189 and Fitzmyer, *The Gospel According to Luke*, 1:457-458.

[283] H.W. Montefiore, "Josephus and the New Testament," *NovT* 4 (1960): 139-160, 307-318, who compared the prodigies in *BJ* before the temple was destroyed with Christian traditions (his interpretations are more incredible than the

results so far have been negligible or too general to allow for any conclusion other than that our author and Josephos both utilized some of the same techniques and perspectives.[284] An area which has not received the attention it deserves is the common historiographical perspective between the two. The closest analogies with the prefaces of Luke and Acts are statements of Josephos. For the sake of convenience I have set them side by side. I have italicized the common vocabulary in the first text as a way of pointing out the close similarity. It should be noted that the first text from Josephos is not a preface, but an explanation of his historiographical procedures. It is also not from the *Antiquitates* but from *Contra Apionem* where Josephos makes explicit what he had argued for implicitly in the former.

Historiographic Concerns

CA 1.53	Lk. 1:1-4
Φαῦλοι δέ τινες ἄνθρωποι διαβάλλειν μου τὴν ἱστορίαν *ἐπικεχειρήκασιν* ὥσπερ ἐν σχολῇ μειρακίων γύμνασμα προκεῖσθαι νομίζοντες, κατηγορίας παραδόξου καὶ διαβολῆς, δέον ἐκεῖνο γιγνώσκειν, ὅτι δεῖ τὸν ἄλλοις *παράδοσιν πράξεων* ἀληθινῶν ὑπισχνούμενον	1 Ἐπειδήπερ πολλοὶ *ἐπεχείρησαν* ἀνατάξασθαι διήγησιν
	περὶ τῶν πεπληροφορημένων ἐν ἡμῖν *πραγμάτων*
(55πλείστων δ᾽ *αὐτόπτης γενόμενος*) αὐτὸν ἐπίστασθαι ταύτας πρότερον *ἀκριβῶς*,	2 καθὼς *παρέδοσαν* ἡμῖν οἱ ἀπ᾽ ἀρχῆς *αὐτόπται* καὶ ὑπηρέται *γενόμενοι* τοῦ λόγου
ἢ *παρηκολουθηκότα* τοῖς γεγονόσιν ἢ παρὰ τῶν εἰδότων πυνθανόμενον.	3 ἔδοξε κἀμοὶ *παρηκολουθηκότι* ἄνωθεν πᾶσιν *ἀκριβῶς* καθεξῆς σοι γράψαι . . .

prodigies in the text!); Benjamin J. Hubbard, "Luke, Josephus and Rome: A Comparative Approach to the Lukan *Sitz im Leben*," in *Society of Biblical Literature 1979 Seminar Papers*, edited by Paul Achtemeier (Missoula, Montana: Scholars Press, 1979), 1:59-68, who attempted to compare the similarities of Luke-Acts to *BJ* in terms of relationships to Rome (both positive) and Israel (both negative to one particular group); F. Gerald Downing, "Redaction Criticism: Josephus' *Antiquities* and the Synoptic Gospels (II)," *JSNT* 9 (1980): 29-48, Luke and Josephos share a common redactional method; idem, "Ethical Pagan Theism and the Speeches in Acts," *NTS* 27 (1981): 544-563, Dionysios (*AR* 6.6.1-9.5), Josephos (*AJ* 2.20-31), and Acts (13:16-47; 2; 3) all share a common pattern in speeches (1. God is powerful; 2. we must therefore be virtuous; 3. we will then enjoy the good life; 4. and escape punishment); idem, "Common Ground with Paganism in Luke and in Josephus," *NTS* 28 (1982): 546-559, both Luke-Acts and Josephos offer a humane theism as high-minded entertainment.
   [284] I have noted a couple of conceptual agreements: Acts 10:35; *CA* 2.210 and Acts 17:25; *AJ* 8.111 (a Stoic concept).

Secondary Prefaces

CA 1.1-2	Acts 1:1-3
Διὰ μὲν οὖν τοῦ προτέρου βιβλίου,	1 Τὸν μὲν πρῶτον λόγον ἐποιησάμην περὶ πάντων
τιμιώτατέ μοι Ἐπαφρόδιτε,	ὦ Θεόφιλε,
περί τε τῆς ἀρχαιότητος ἡμῶν ἐπέδειξα,	ὧν ἤρξατο ὁ Ἰησοῦς
τοῖς Φοινίκων καὶ Χαλδαίων καὶ Αἰγυπτίων	ποιεῖν τε καὶ διδάσκειν,
γράμμασι πιστωσάμενος τὴν ἀλήθειαν	2 ἄχρι ἧς ἡμέρας ἐντειλάμενος
καὶ πολλοὺς τῶν Ἑλλήνων συγγραφεῖς	τοῖς ἀποστόλοις διὰ πνεύματος ἁγίου
παρασχόμενος μάρτυρας,	οὓς ἐξελέξατο ἀνελήμφθη.
τήν τε ἀντίρρησιν ἐποιησάμην πρὸς Μανεθῶνα καὶ Χαιρήμονα καί τινας ἑτέρους.	
2 ἄρξομαι δὲ νῦν τοὺς ὑπολειπομένους	3 οἷς καὶ παρέστησεν ἑαυτὸν ζῶντα . .
τῶν γεγραφότων τι καθ᾽ ἡμῶν ἐλέγχειν.	

As we have seen, the presence of common vocabulary can not be used as a decisive proof. What we are looking for is whether or not the two shared the same historiographical orientation.[285] Josephos claims that there are two acceptable historiographical methods: careful investigation (*Antiquitates*) and eyewitness report (*Bellum Judaicum*). Luke combines the two by affirming that the tradition which he has carefully investigated rests upon eyewitness testimony. The secondary prefaces follow an identical pattern: reference to the first book, address to the patron, a summary of the first book, and an introduction to the second.

The historiographical agreements do not end here. Both authors attempted to tell the story of a given people through the rewriting of texts from within their group. Technically they differed in scope: Josephos retold the entire story; the author of Luke-Acts was a continuator. Yet in another way they agree: both tell the story of their people from the beginning point of their records. More importantly they both emphasize the antiquity of their movement: Josephos through a chronological reckoning and Luke-Acts by insisting that

---

[285] Plummer, *The Gospel According to S. Luke*, p. 5, dismissed this parallel. Van Unnik, "Remarks on the Purpose of Luke's Historical Writing," p. 12, has more correctly pointed out that while it would be foolish to posit dependence on the basis of these similarities, the more elaborate account of Josephos helps to elucidate the abbreviated comments in Luke.

Christianity was not new, but a continuation. Linked to their use and understanding of the LXX is their conviction that their narratives are sacred history. Josephos wrote as a priest/prophet and the author of Luke-Acts narrated the fulfillment of the OT text. The common presupposition is their shared emphasis on prophecy which is largely due to the fact that their concept of history was informed by the LXX, particularly the Deuteronomistic history. Intriguingly both Jewish and Christian author divide history into epochs on a literary basis. As we will see below, the texts of each functioned in a similar—but not identical way.

The author of Luke-Acts thus shared common historical[286] and historiographical traditions with Josephos. This does not mean that Luke-Acts is dependent upon Josephos,[287] but that they were cut out of the same bolt of cloth. The crucial issue now becomes whether Luke-Acts consciously hellenized Christian traditions as the Hellenistic Jewish historians and Josephos had hellenized Jewish material.

2. Hellenistic Forms and Elements

There are a number of forms and elements within Luke-Acts which are unambiguous indicators of the movement of Christian traditions into the larger Greco-Roman world.

The opening sentence of Luke is a clear declaration of the author's orientation. In contrast to Mark who begins *in medias res*, Matthew which offers a genealogy, and the rhythmic affirmation of the Logos in John, Luke starts with a literary preface. This *genus litterarium* is in clear accord with Hellenistic historiography which *required* a preface and well beyond the bounds of OT historiography which lacks any equivalent.[288] The narrative continues this process.[289] At

---

[286] It should also be noted that the reference to Saul's forty year reign in Acts 13:21 has no OT support. It is, however, attested in Josephos, *AJ* 6.378 (*contra* 10.143 where his reign is only twenty years).

[287] Or the much more improbable view that Josephos was dependent on Luke-Acts.

[288] Lucian, *Hist. conscr.* 23, 52.

[289] Danker, *Jesus and the New Age*, has collected a great deal of material demonstrating this. He calls the author a "cultural bridgebuilder," pp. 3-4. The bulk of Danker's presentation deals with the content rather than literary forms. See also the penetrating essay of Ronald F. Hock, "Lazarus and Micyllus: Greco-Roman Backgrounds to Luke 16:19-31," *JBL* 106 (1987):447-463, who interprets this parable in light of Lucian's *Gallus* and *Cataplus* and is able to elucidate the point

the conclusion of the infancy narrative, the most Semitic section of the whole work, the author presents Jesus as a child prodigy in much the same terms Josephos had presented himself. While in Luke the pericope serves a Christological purpose, it remains a form widely used in the Hellenistic world.[290]

A second example of this feature is the presence of four banquets which the author presents in terms reminiscent of symposia, Lk. 5:29-39; 7:36-50; 11:37-54; 14:1-24.[291] The essential features of a symposium are the *dramatis personae* (a host who is notable for wealth or wisdom, a chief guest who is particularly distinguished by wisdom, and other guests) and the structural arrangement (a "news item," *fait divers*, which serves as the beginning point of the discussion and the gradual introduction of the guests during the discourse).[292] These four units in Luke all share the same structure: setting at a banquet (5:29; 7:36; 11:37; 14:1), *fait divers* (5:29; 7:37-38; 11:38; 14:2-6), reaction (5:30; 7:39; 11:38; 14:2-6), Jesus' response (5:31-32; 7:40-48; 11:39-44; 14:7-14 [7-11, 12-14]), further question or statement (5:35; 7:49; 11:45; 14:15); and Jesus' response (5:34-39 [34-35, 36-39]; 7:50; 11:46-52; 14:16-24). What is noteworthy about this is that the common structure was made at the level of authorial redaction rather than in the tradition.[293] The

---

of the parable through these Cynic stories by demonstrating that within this context the rich are assumed to be hedonistic. The rich man is, therefore, not condemned simply because he is rich, but because he is evil.

[290] Lk. 2:41-52. Cf. Josephos, *V* 9 and n. 17 in chapter six. Rudolf Bultmann, *The History of the Synoptic Tradition*, trans. John Marsh, rev. ed. (New York: Harper & Row, 1976), pp. 300-301, has collected a wide range of parallels. Fitzmyer, *The Gospel According to Luke*, 1:437, has correctly pointed out the Christological function of the unit.

[291] The most important essays dealing with this are X. de Meeûs, "Composition de Luc., XIV et Genre Symposiaque," *ETL* 37 (1961): 847-870; J. Delobel, "L'onction par la pecheresse," *ETL* 42 (1966): 415-475; and E. Springs Steele, "Luke 11:37-54—A Modified Hellenistic Symposium?" *JBL* 103 (1984): 379-394.

[292] Steele, "Luke 11:37-54—A Modified Hellenistic Symposium?," pp. 380-381, has a convenient summary. He adds an explicit invitation to the chief guest under the heading of structure and arrives at this sequence: invitation, *fait divers*, discourse. For definitions see J. Martin, *RAC*, s.v. "Deipnonliteratur," 3:659 and Hans Gärtner, *KP*, s.v. "Symposium-Literatur," 5: 540. Symposia are attested for the following Greek authors: Plato, Xenophon, Speusippos, Aristotle, Aristoxenos, Epikuros, Syndeos, Persaios, Hieronymous of Rhodes, Menippos of Gadara, Prytanis, Didymos, Heraklides of Iarentum, Plutarch, Lucian, Athenaios, Methodios, and Julian.

[293] There are serious difficulties with locating the source for some of this material, e.g., how does Lk 7:36-50 relate to Mk. 14:3-9 (cf. also Mt. 26:6-13; Jn. 12:1-8)? Other evidence is fortunately not as complicated. 5:27-39 combines two Markan pericopae: vv. 27-32 = Mk. 2:13-17 and vv. 33-39 = Mk. 2:18-22. The

author thus demonstrates Jesus' wisdom in a banquet setting. Why? The parallels between the structure of a symposium and these banquets suggests that the author utilized a known Hellenistic form which the readers would find meaningful.[294]

When we come to Acts the evidence is even more obvious.[295] There are a number of citations or allusions to pagan literature within the work. Any student who has read the *Apology* of Plato can not fail to hear an echo in the apostles' retort to the Sanhedrin in Acts: πειθαρχεῖν δεῖ θεῷ μᾶλλον ἢ ἀνθρώποις.[296] The openness to Hellenistic literature becomes patent in Acts 17:28 when the author quotes from Aratos, *Phaenomena* 5. Other possible allusions include references to Thukydides[297] and Euripides[298] which, however, are more likely citations of Hellenistic proverbs. This openness sets Luke-Acts off from the other gospels and forces us to look for Hellenistic parallels in form as well.

---

combination enables the author to present a more substantial discourse after the meal. 11:37-38 betray clear signs of redaction (thus the setting and the *fait divers* are placed at the level of the author). It is also likely that 11:39-40 (Mt. 23:25-26), 42 (Mt. 23:23), 43 (Mt. 23:6), 44 (Mt. 23:27), 46 (Mt. 23:4), 47-48 (Mt. 23:29-32), 49-51 (Mt. 23:34-36), 52 (Mt. 23:13) are from Q. The banquet has become a means to give these sayings a setting. 14:1-24 is a clear composite of two L traditions (1-6 and 7-14) and a Q tradition (15-24 [Mt. 22:1-14, in an entirely different setting; *Gos. of Thom.* 64]). For details on the sources see Fitzmyer, *The Gospel According to Luke*, 1:587-588, 594-595; 1:684-686; 2:942-944, 1038-1052.

[294] It is important to note with Steele, "Luke 11:37-54—A Modified Hellenistic Symposium?," p. 390, that the author has modified the scheme by dropping the bipartite nature of Hellenistic symposia (meal followed by drinking with discourse) and diminishing the speeches of others to the vanishing point.

[295] The work of Pieter W. van der Horst, "Hellenistic Parallels to the Acts of the Apostles: 1:1-26," *ZNW* 74 (1983):17-26; "Hellenistic Parallels to the Acts of the Apostles (2.1-47)," *JSNT* 25 (1985): 49-60; and "Hellenistic Parallels to Acts (Chapters 3 and 4)," *JSNT* 35 (1989): 37-46, should be noted. He has been collecting Hellenistic parallels to words, phrases, and statements in Acts.

[296] Acts 5:29 (cf. also 4:19). Plato, *Ap.* 29D: πείσομαι δὲ μᾶλλον τῷ θεῷ ἢ ὑμῖν. The thought is common to Judaism as well. Cf. Dan. 3:16-18; II Macc. 7:2; Josephos, *AJ* 17.159. Foakes Jackson and Lake, *Beginnings*, 4:45, say that while the idea was common it was not commonplace. The issue of whether or not there is an allusion here depends upon whether there are other clear allusions in Acts to Hellenistic literature. Since there are, I am inclined to hear an echo here.

[297] Acts 20:35, the dominical logion is very similar to Thukydides 2.97.4. Note, however, that the specific formulation is reversed. Thukydides gives the opposite practice of the Persian custom: λαμβάνειν μᾶλλον ἢ διδόναι. This may well be a common Hellenistic proverb. So Haenchen, *The Acts of the Apostles*, pp. 594-595, n. 5. I Clem. 2.1 also (independently) cites this logion.

[298] Acts 26:14: σκληρόν σοι πρὸς κέντρα λακτίζειν is reminiscent of Euripides, *Bacc.* 794-795: θύοιμ' ἂν αὐτῷ μᾶλλον ἢ θυμούμενος/πρὸς κέντρα λακτίζοιμι θνητὸς ὢν θεῷ. The saying was, however, a common proverb. Cf. also Aeskylos, *PV* 323; *Ag.* 1624; Julian, *Or.* 8.246b.

The most obvious form is the presence of twenty-four speeches.[299] Speeches were a common trademark of Greek historiography.[300] Most of the speeches can be grouped into several discernible categories: missionary sermons to Jews,[301] sermons to pagans,[302] and defense speeches.[303] In one of his most important contributions to Acts, Martin Dibelius analyzed the speeches of Acts and concluded that with the noted exception of the missionary speeches they stood in the line of Greek historiography.[304] Dibelius argued that the speeches in chapters 10, 17, 20, and 22 all transcend the immediate narrative by illuminating the significance of the narrative for the reader.[305] He thought that the missionary sermons

---

[299] I have not counted minor one verse summaries of speeches here. The main speeches are those of Peter (1:16-22; 2:14-36, 38-39; 3:12-26; 4:8-12, 19-20; 5:29-32; 10:34-43; 11:4-17; 15:7-11), Paul (13:16-41; 14:14-17; 17:22-31; 20:18-35; 22:1-21; 24:10-21; 26:1-23, 25-27, 29; 27:21-26; 28:17-20 [cf. also 28:23, 25-28]), Stephen (7:2-50 [the longest in Acts]), James (15:13-21); non-Christians (5:35-39 [Gamaliel]; 19:25-27 [Demetrios]; 19:35-40 [Town clerk]; 24:2-8 [Tertullus]; 25:24-27 [Festus]). The speeches (and the letters [15:23-29; 23:26-30]) are of decisive significance in determining the historical nature of Acts for Berger, "Hellenistische Gattungen im Neuen Testament," pp. 1275-1277, especially 1276.

[300] The two most significant statements about speeches in antiquity are Thukydides 1.22.1 and Polybios 12:25a.5-25b.1. Cf. also Lucian, *Hist. conscr.* 58-59, who opens the door wide to rhetorical flourishes as long as the speaker and speech are suitable. Pervo's statement that the adaptation of speeches of one speaker to appropriate contexts is not in the realm of historiography but of romances is at direct odds with Lucian's comment. See *Profit with Delight*, p. 76.

[301] Acts 2:14-36, 38-39; 3:12-26; 4:8-12, 19-20; 5:29-32; 10:34-43; 13:16-41. These have been analyzed by Eduard Schweizer, "Concerning the Speeches in Acts," in *Studies in Luke-Acts*, pp. 208-211, 215-216, who locates the common elements within the speeches. Richard F. Zehnle, *Peter's Pentecost Discourse: Tradition and Lukan Reinterpretation in Peter's Speeches of Acts 2 and 3.* SBLMS 15 (Nashville/New York: Abingdon Press, 1971), has attempted to analyze the composition of Acts 2 and 3 and place them within the framework of Acts as a whole.

[302] Acts 14:14-17; 17:22-31. The bibliography for the latter is huge. For works through 1981 see Schneider, *Die Apostelgeschichte*, 2:227-229.

[303] Acts 22:1-21; 24:10-21; 26:1-23, 25-27, 29. According to Quintillian 3.9.1-5, there should be five components in a forensic speech: prooemium, narratio, probatio, refutatio, peroratio. Fred Veltman, "The Defense Speeches Of Paul in Acts: Gattungsforschung and its Limitations," (Th.D. dissertation, The Graduate Theological Union, 1975) and his "The Defense Speeches of Paul in Acts," in *Perspectives on Luke-Acts*, pp. 243-256, argues that none of the speeches in Acts fits this pattern precisely. Jerome Neyrey, "The Forensic Defense Speech in Acts 22-26: Form and Function," in *Luke-Acts: New Perspectives from the Society of Biblical Literature Seminar*, pp. 210-224, contends that the defense speeches of Paul can be classified as forensic speeches.

[304] "The Speeches in Acts and Ancient Historiography," in *Studies in the Acts of the Apostles*, pp. 138-185. Note, however, the qualifications Dibelius put on his conclusions on pp. 174-185, where he concludes that at heart Luke is a preacher.

[305] *Ibid.*, pp. 150-165.

reflected the preaching of the author's day and served as models of how it should be done. C.H. Dodd had earlier contended that the missionary speeches were based upon the original preaching pattern of the early church.[306] Ulrich Wilckens critiqued both by showing that just like the other speeches of Acts, the missionary sermons were the compositions of the author and were inseparable from the narrative.[307] Building on Wilckens, Eckhard Plümacher has attempted to show that the speeches are not about the author's present, but are designed to present past preaching in an effort to explain the growth of the church and therefore stand in the same historiographical tradition as those of Dionysios of Halikaranassos and Livy.[308] With this analysis, I agree: the missionary sermons are the dynamic which drives the growth of the early church. Further, as I indicated in the summary of the contents, Stephen's speech should be read as a theological defense for the narratives which follow. It is widely recognized that it answers the charges leveled against Stephen in a very indirect and circuitous way at best.[309] The number and suprahistorical significance of the speeches combined with the prologue point to a work written within the tradition of Hellenistic historiography.

This has been further buttressed by the work of Plümacher who has explained the deliberate imitation of the LXX in the missionary speeches.[310] Plümacher effectively argues that the literary movement which served as a basis for this imitation technique was Atticism.[311] The author combined this with an archaizing tendency in

---

[306] *The Apostolic Preaching and Its Developments* (New York: Harper, 1936).

[307] *Die Missionsreden der Apostelgeschichte: Form und traditionsgeschichtliche Untersuchungen*, 2nd ed. WMANT 5 (Neukirchen-Vluyn: Neukirchener Verlag des Erziehungsvereins GMBH, 1963), especially pp. 56-71.

[308] *Lukas als hellenistischer Schriftsteller: Studien zur Apostelgeschichte* (Göttingen: Vandenhoeck & Ruprecht, 1972), pp. 32-79, especially 32-38.

[309] The charges are in 6:13-14: he has spoken against the temple and the law. The two major themes of the speech are: the persistent resistance of the Jews to God's will (vv. 27-28, 35, 39-43, 51-53) and God's dealings with people outside the promised land (vv. 2, 30-34, 38, 44, 48-50). These themes are best understood with the narratives which follow: Jewish rejection leads to a wider mission; God has previously dealt with individuals outside the promised land and temple and will do so now.

[310] *Lukas als hellenistischer Schriftsteller*, pp. 38-50.

[311] *Ibid.*, pp. 51, 63. He cites Dionysios of Halikarnassos (pp. 52-56), Arrian, Appian, Cassius Dio, Philo (pp. 56-58), Chariton of Aphrodisias, Achilles Tatios (pp. 58-60), Josephos (p. 62), and several Latin authors (pp. 64-66) as examples of the same phenomenon. We ought to point out that Jewish authors also employed this technique. Among the finds at Qumran were five MSS of the Pentateuch and

an effort to provide the *Urzeit* with a patina of holiness.[312] In both instances he was following known Hellenistic techniques. The same phenomenon explains the dramatic nature of episodes which the author inserts into the narrative.[313] The use of known Hellenistic techniques was deliberate on the part of our author who realized that as Christianity moved out into the world, so would the form of its story.[314] The author was convinced of the historical significance of Christianity and wrote its story in that light.

Summary. Luke-Acts is thus a complex work which combines Christian, Jewish, and Hellenistic elements into a form of Hellenistic history. Is there any specific tradition which adequately accounts for the presence and interplay of these elements? I believe that there is: apologetic historiography. Narratives within this genre relate the story of a particular people by deliberately hellenizing their native traditions. This is precisely what Luke-Acts does. It now remains for us to consider whether Luke-Acts shares the same functions as apologetic historiography.

Function

The stated purpose of Luke-Acts was to provide Theophilos with certainty about the *traditio apostolica.* (Lk. 1:4) In order to understand the implications of this statement we first need to determine the audience.

Audience. The author addressed his work to κράτιστε Θεόφιλε.[315]

---

fragments of Job which used a paleo-Hebrew or "Samaritan" script, probably as a way of indicating the antiquity the scribes attributed to writings. See Frank Moore Cross, *The Ancient Library of Qumran and Modern Biblical Studies* (Garden City, New York: Doubleday & Company, Inc., 1958), pp. 33-34, 25-26 n. 46 and G.R. Driver, *The Judaean Scrolls: The Problem and a Solution* (New York: Schocken Books, 1965), pp. 413-414, 447-448.

[312] *Ibid.*, pp. 72-78. By archaizing he means the use of archaic christological titles etc.

[313] Plümacher contends that Acts has an episodic style in which the author argues through the presentation of vivid episodes, e.g., 25:13-26:32 (pp. 80-84), 18:12-17 (pp. 84-85), 10:1-11:18 (pp. 86-89), 22:17-21 (pp. 89-90), 8:26-40 (pp. 90-91), 14:8-18 (pp. 92-95), 16:16-40 (pp. 95-97), 17:16-33 (pp. 97-98), 19:23-40 (pp. 98-100). Cf. also the treatments on pp. 106-110. The episodes are insertions into the text which allow the author to press his theses in a vivid and impressive way. This not only makes the narrative dramatic, but allows the reader to have a sense of participation. Other Hellenistic examples of this technique are found in Livy, Kleitarchos, Duris, and Curtius Rufus (pp. 111-136).

[314] *Ibid.*, pp. 16, 16-25, 137-139.

[315] Lk. 1:3. The κράτιστε is dropped in Acts 1:1. I understand Theophilos to be a real person not a symbolic address to any "lover of God." We know nothing more

Interestingly, the only other occasions he uses the adjective κράτιστος are in addresses to Roman governors.[316] We, therefore, immediately want to ask whether Theophilos might be a Roman official. At first glance this appears plausible and would fall neatly into the pattern we have seen in Berossos, Manethon, and Josephos. It will not, however, stand up under scrutiny. It is very difficult to imagine Roman officials reading Luke-Acts to learn about Christianity. The author assumes that the readers can recognize the style of the LXX or there would not be any point in imitating it. He offers virtually no help for his readers. Allusions requiring a knowledge of the context of the OT are left unexplained.[317] There are no explanations given for customs such as we find, for example, in Dionysios' or Josephos' *Antiquitates*. The reader is simply expected to know them. There is not even any help given for key Christian theological terms. Not only this, but if the author intended for Roman officials to read it, he made a very poor statement of his case. Why did he allow statements like Lk. 1:32-33 to stand in his book? These factors exclude a pagan audience as the primary target.

These same arguments demonstrate that the primary audience must be Christians. Theophilos was probably a *patronus* for the author as Epaphroditos was for Josephos. The audience for which Luke-Acts was intended has traditionally been understood to be Gentile Christians.[318] There are a number of reasons for this.[319]

---

about him. The later tradition in Ps.-Clementine, *Recognitiones* 10.71, should be considered legendary.

[316] Acts 23:26; 24:3; 26:25.

[317] E.g., Lk. 4:25-27. How would a reader who is ignorant of the careers of Elijah and Elisha understand the significance of the comparison between Jesus and Israel's great prophets? The text demands a knowledge of the OT which is greater than what is immediately supplied.

[318] For a summary of recent views on the audience see Mary A. Moscato, "Current Theories Regarding the Audience of Luke-Acts," *Currents in Theology and Mission* 3 (1976): 355-361. In his recent survey of scholarship, Gasque has grouped the views as follows (all presuppose the readership is Christian): predominantly Gentile (traditional); Jewish (minority but growing); mixed (minority but growing). See "A Fruitful Field," pp. 119-120. LaVerdiere and Thompson, "New Testament Communities in Transition," p. 583, is a good representative of this view.

[319] Some of the reasons which have traditionally been adduced to establish a Gentile readership are faulty since they only demonstrate the Hellenistic nature of the audience, e.g., the Hellenistic nature of Luke-Acts as a work. If this same argument were applied to the writings of Philo, it would disqualify a Jewish readership for them. Hellenistic does not equal Gentile.

The general course of the narrative is to demonstrate the spread of the gospel to non-Jews.[320] This concern for a universal salvation is also evident in specific texts throughout the work.[321] Furthermore, in the gospel a number of Jewish concerns are omitted in the redaction of Mark.[322] To these should be added the argument of Jack T. Sanders that Luke-Acts pronounces a blanket condemnation of the Jews. If Sanders is correct, the audience was not Jewish.[323]

There are reasons, however, not to accept such a blanket assessment. We have already noted that the author has a keen interest in God-fearers and suggested that the author was either one himself or was Jewish. The question naturally arises: Was the envisioned audience composed of God-fearers who like the author had become Christians? Besides the particular interest the author displays in them, the presupposition that they knew their LXX thoroughly suggests—at least—that they have read and studied it for years. While it is possible that this familiarity was a result of their Christianity, it seems more likely that a good number of them had formerly been attached to synagogues.[324]

This leads us to ask if the audience could have consisted of Jewish Christians.[325] The work of Jacob Jervell, in particular, has raised

[320] We should not fail to remember that Acts ends on this note, 28:25-28.

[321] E.g., Lk. 2:32; the extension of the quotation from Isaiah 40:3-5 to include the phrase "all flesh will see the salvation of God" (Lk. 3:4-6; Mk. 1:3; Mt. 3:3); the tracing of the genealogy back to Adam instead of to Abraham as in the first gospel (Lk. 3:23-38; Mt. 1:2-17); 24:47; Acts 1:8; 9:15.

[322] E.g., Mk. 7:1-23 (part of the large omission of Mk. 6:45-8:26).

[323] *The Jews in Luke-Acts* (Philadelphia: Fortress Press, 1987) and his summary article, "The Jewish People in Luke-Acts," in *Luke-Acts and the Jewish People*, pp. 51-75.

[324] So also Schneider, *Die Apostelgeschichte*, 1:145-147, especially 146 and the important treatment by Philip Francis Esler, *Community and Gospel in Luke-Acts: The Social and Political Motivations of Lucan Theology.* SNTMS 57 (Cambridge: Cambridge University Press, 1987), pp. 30-45. Esler goes too far when he denies that there is a single example of a conversion of a Gentile who was formerly a worshipper of idols. Acts 14:20 and 17:34 imply the existence of such converts. Esler's suggestion that the converts of 17:34 (mentioned after the Areopagitica) are some of the God-fearers mentioned in association with the synagogue in 17:17 is *petitio principii*. See p. 41. Jacob Jervell, "The Church of Jews and Godfearers," in *Luke-Acts and the Jewish People*, pp. 11-20, also contends that there were no pagan converts and that the Gentiles of Acts are God-fearers.

[325] E.g., A.J. Mattill, "The Purpose of Acts: Schneckenburger Reconsidered," in *Apostolic History and the Gospel: Essays presented to F.F. Bruce*, ed. by W.Ward Gasque and Ralph Martin (Grand Rapids: Wm. B. Eerdmans Publishing Co., 1970), pp. 108-122, who thinks that it was written to defend Paul against charges leveled by Jews in Jerusalem and Rome.

this issue to the center of discussion.[326] Jervell argues that the church is not the "new Israel," but that the promises are fulfilled among Jewish Christians with whom the gospel found great success. These Jewish Christians in turn brought the gospel to Gentiles. To view Acts as a document of Gentile Christianity is "fatal to the understanding of the history of the early church."[327] Jervell is correct in pointing out the prevalence of Jewish elements in Acts.[328] The question is how do these concerns function. I am convinced that they serve to define Gentile Christianity vis-à-vis Israel rather than to make Israel the dominant audience.

Were there Jewish Christians in the audience or was it exclusively Gentile? There is a fairly consistent pattern in Acts with regard to the establishment of churches in the Pauline mission. Paul and his company regularly go to the synagogue and then turn to the Gentiles when the Jews reject the message.[329] Yet even after turning to the Gentiles in one locale, Paul continues to preach to the Jews as he moves to a new location. More importantly, after turning away from the synagogue in Corinth and Ephesus Paul continued to preach to Jews with some success.[330] If Acts reflects the churches of the author's day to any extent, then we may presume that there were some Jewish Christians in both the implied and real audience.[331]

We have seen then, that the audience was mixed. The composition of the audience was probably mainly God-fearers with Jews and

[326] *Luke and the People of God: A New Look at Luke-Acts* (Minneapolis, MN: Augsburg Publishing House, 1972) and *The Unknown Paul: Essays on Luke-Acts and Early Christian History* (Minneapolis, MN: Augsburg Publishing House, 1984), especially pp. 11-51. For some of the ensuing discussion see the collection of essays edited by Joseph B. Tyson, *Luke-Acts and the Jewish People.*
[327] *The Unknown Paul*, p. 40.
[328] Cf. also J.L. Houlden, "The Purpose of Luke," *JSNT* 21 (1984): 54-56, who collects the evidence for the positive aspects of Judaism in Luke-Acts.
[329] Acts 13:45-47; 18:4-7; 19:8-9; 28:25-28. On this pattern see the essay by Robert C. Tannehill, "Rejection by Jews and Turning to Gentiles: The Pattern of Paul's Mission in Acts," in *Luke-Acts and the Jewish People*, 83-101, who suggests that the tension between the promises made to Israel and fulfilled in Jesus with the rejection by the Jews is never resolved in Acts.
[330] Acts 18:8 (cf. 9-11 as well); 19:10 (although here they are residents of Asia generally, not Ephesus specifically).
[331] It is worth noting that the author frequently describes the composition of churches as mixed. Cf. Acts 13:43; 14:1; 17:4, 12; 18:4. All of these references describe the response to Paul's preaching in the synagogue. Cf. also 19:10. Moscato's theory that the Jewish Christians of the audience were "Nazoreans" is very speculative at best. Cf. "Current Theories Regarding the Audience of Luke-Acts," pp. 359-361.

LUKE-ACTS

Gentiles forming smaller groups. Were these readers in one locale[332] or was Luke-Acts addressed to a broader geographical constituency?[333] The issue of the relationship of Christianity to the empire addressed by Luke-Acts and the conception of the work as *sacred narrative* suggests to me that the implied audience was wider than a single community.

Function. How did Luke-Acts function among the mixed communities it addressed? The stated purpose was to define the *traditio apostolica*. The means by which this was accomplished was the writing of a historical narrative. Why a historical narrative rather than a circular epistle or theological treatise? At the end of the first century, the author of Luke-Acts recognized Christianity had emerged within the Roman empire as a distinct movement.[334] Years ago Rudolf Bultmann correctly saw the presentation of Christianity in Luke-Acts *"as an entity of world history."*[335] That it is an entity is clear from the fact that Christianity as a movement receives its own designations: it is called a αἵρεσις[336] and ἡ ὁδός.[337] Nor should it be overlooked that two of the three NT uses of Χριστιανοί occur in Acts.[338] The tie of this entity to world history is clear from the chronological synchronisms of the work.[339]

With this recognition also came the realization that Christianity

---

[332] So Esler, *Community and Gospel in Luke-Acts*, pp. 25-26, who bases his conclusions largely on Acts 20:18-35 where he thinks the author comes closest to addressing his contemporaries. He suggests Antioch-on-the-Orontes as the locale (p. 231 n. 36).

[333] So LaVerdiere and Thompson, "New Testament Communities in Transition," p. 585 and Robert Karris, "Missionary Communities: A New Paradigm for the Study of Luke-Acts," *CBQ* 41 (1979): 96-97, who thinks these are major missionary centers and their daughter communities.

[334] Cf. I Cor. 10:32 where Paul distinguishes among Jews, Greeks, and the church of God. The concept of Christianity as a third race would later develop from this.

[335] *Theology of the New Testament*, 2 vols. trans. by Kendrick Grobel (New York: Charles Scribner's Sons, 1951-1955), 2:116.

[336] Acts 24:5, 14; 28:22. In Acts 5:17; 15:5; 26:5, it is used of Jewish sects just as it is in Josephos.

[337] Acts 9:2; 19:9, 23; 22:4; 24:14, 22.

[338] Acts 11:26; 26:28. Cf. also I Pet. 4:16 where again the relationship between Christians and society is to the fore. The use of the term indicates an awareness of how the followers of Jesus were perceived by the outside world. It was coined by non-Christians to designate followers of Χριστός in much the same way as Ἡρωδιανοί in Mk. 3:6; 12:13; Mt. 22:16 or Καισαριανοί in Epiktetos 1.19.19. Cf. BAGD, 886.

[339] Lk. 2:1-2; 3:1-2; Acts 11:28.

had to be defined. I do not mean to imply that no one had previously offered a definition of Christianity. Paul offered his readers an understanding of Christianity even if he did not present it systematically. The same could be said for Mark, Matthew, and John. What is new about Luke-Acts is the perspective in which Christianity was both seen and defined. Luke-Acts argues *de rigueur* that Christianity has taken its rightful place *in history*. It must, therefore, be defined not only in relation to itself, but in relation to the larger world in which it exists. The difference between reading Mark and Luke-Acts is the difference between reading an account of a religious group from the perspective of the group as a self-contained unit and an account which presents the interaction of the group within society at large.[340] While not exclusive, one focus is inward, the other outward. For the sake of clarity I will analyze this self-definition from three perspectives moving from the inside to the outside in the pattern of concentric circles.

Christianity. It is a commonplace today to note the variety which characterized so much of first century Christianity. This has not always been the case! The fact that it was not is largely due to the image of the church presented in Luke-Acts: Christianity was a unified movement beginning with Jesus, extending through the twelve, and finally reaching Paul. This is perhaps the rationale for the literary parallelism between the gospel and Acts.[341] It also helps us to understand the Paul of Acts in contrast to the Paul of his letters: Paul had to be brought closer to the center.[342] The incongruity between

---

[340] This can be illustrated from my own religious tradition. In the nineteenth century Disciples of Christ, Christian Churches, and Churches of Christ all constitued one religious movement. By the beginning of the twentieth century a split had occurred. Historians writing from within the movement frequently boasted of the group's unity through the Civil War and attributed the split to purely theological differences. In recent years, however, a number of researchers have viewed the movement from the perspective of how it fit into the larger history of the United States. The result was the realization that the split occurred along the Mason-Dixon line. Theology suddenly had to accommodate the social forces of sectionalism. The seminal works were David Edwin Harrell, Jr., *A Social History of the Disciples of Christ*, vol. 1: *Quest for a Christian America* (Nashville: The Disciples of Christ Historical Society, 1966) and vol. 2: *Social Sources of Division in the Disciples of Christ 1865-1900* (Atlanta: Publishing Systems, Inc., 1973).

[341] So also Gasque, "A Fruitful Field," p. 123. Note also the more elaborate comments of Talbert, *Literary Patterns, Theological Themes and the Genre of Luke-Acts*, pp. 96-103.

[342] The old Tübingen view that Acts was a synthesis is not without any basis. I do not, however, accept the schema of a synthesis between Jewish and Gentile

the situation of the church as we know it to have been and the portrait in Luke-Acts is telling. The author has imposed unity on the
church. It is this unbroken chain which constitutes the *apostolica
traditiq.*

But why define the tradition? We should remember that much of
the ancient world saw truth in terms of unity; discordant voices were
of themselves proof of error.[343] It is possible that the author was
confronted by a threatening movement which he felt must be countered.[344] The major difficulty with this interpretation is that the evidence is too opaque for any specific identifications. It is better to allow the general nature of the work to stand as it is and understand
the record as a definition of Christianity in an age when competing
voices were frequent.[345]

We also need to consider the historical sense of the author. By the
early nineties, the first generation of Christians had passed from the
scene and the second generation was preparing to join them. This
meant that contact with the living voice was about to cease. In these
circumstances a third generation Christian—depending upon a second generation Christian, Luke the traveling companion of Paul—
set out to define what the apostolic tradition was. The emphasis on
the apostles' role as eye-witnesses and on the "we" served to offer
credibility for the tradition. Just as Josephos had offered Judaism a
new definition after the fall of Jerusalem, Luke-Acts offered Christians a definition of Christianity as the church moved into the post-
apostolic age.[346] For this definition the author looked to the past

---

Christianity worked out in the second century. For a summary of the Tübingen
school see Gasque, *A History of the Acts of the Apostles*, pp. 21-54.

[343] E.g., Josephos, *CA* 1.15-18, where he ridicules the Greeks for their lack of
unity and 37-38, where he claims accord for Jewish records. The Shepherd of Her-
mas, *Vis.* 3.5.1, looked back at the apostolic age as a pristine era in which unanimity prevailed. The concept that error arose after the apostles became a commonplace. E.g., *I Clem.* 1.2-2.8; Hegesippos in Eusebios, *HE* 3.32.7-8; 4.22.4.

[344] Charles H. Talbert, *Luke and the Gnostics: An Examination of the Lucan Purpose*
(Nashville: Abingdon, 1966), argued that Luke-Acts was a response to Gnosticism.
I do not think Luke-Acts is specific enough in its argumentation to support this.

[345] So also Fitzmyer, *The Gospel According to Luke*, 1:9.

[346] Philipp Vielhauer, "On the 'Paulinism' of Acts," p. 49 and Ernst
Käsemann, "Ministry and Community in the New Testament," in *Essays on New
Testament Themes*, trans. by W.J. Montague (Philadelphia: Fortress Press, 1982
[original date of essay 1949]), pp. 89-94 and "Ephesians and Acts," in *Studies in
Luke-Acts*, pp. 288-297, have called Luke-Acts a representative of early catholicism.
This, however, appears to go too far. I prefer the analysis of Schneider, *Die Apostel-
geschichte*, 1:147-154, who calls it "nachapostolisch." It represents a mid-point be-
tween Paul and Justin.

rather than an experience of the present. Identity as a Christian meant maintaining continuity with the tradition of the past, specifically the tradition of the apostles.

Israel. A historical viewpoint, however, meant that the author would have to account for some of the historical changes which had taken place since the inception of Christianity. The most significant of these was the emergence of Christianity as a historically distinct movement from Judaism. The author's concern for this issue is reflected in the recurring theme of Israel's rejection from the programmatic text of Lk 4:16-30 to the final declaration placed on the lips of Paul in Acts 28:25-28.[347] This would be a particularly acute problem if the author were himself a Jew.[348] The answer Luke-Acts offers is that Christianity is not a new movement, but the *continuation* of Israel. Jewish rejection of Jesus is not surprising since as Stephen told the Sanhedrin: "you always oppose the Holy Spirit; you are just like your fathers."[349]

Rome. The connection of Christianity to an ancient movement is also bound up with its relationship to Rome. Since this has important implications for our conclusions as a whole, we should recapitulate previous interpretations of the political perspective of Luke-Acts before offering our own.[350]

In the past it was fashionable to think of the audience of Luke-Acts as Roman and the work a direct apology. For some Luke-Acts was a defense of Paul at his trial.[351] This, however, necessitates the early date and led a large number of scholars to conclude that rather than a defense of Paul, Luke-Acts was a defense of Christianity, i.e., the *religio licita* theory.[352] The death knell to these views is the

[347] As I argued above under Audience, I do not see this rejection as being total.
[348] Paul struggles with this problem from this perspective in Rom. 9-11.
[349] Acts 7:51. A much more adequate treatment of this whole issue may be found in Esler, *Community and Gospel in Luke-Acts*, pp. 46-70.
[350] For critical summaries of views see Paul W. Walaskay, *"And so we came to Rome:" The Political Perspective of St. Luke.* SNTSMS 49 (Cambridge: Cambridge University Press, 1983), pp. 1-14 and Esler, *Community and Gospel in Luke-Acts*, pp. 205-214.
[351] George S. Duncan, *St. Paul's Ephesian Ministry: A Reconstruction (With Special Reference to the Ephesian Origin of the Imprisonment Epistles* (New York: Charles Scribner's Sons, 1930), pp. 96-100; Mattill, "The Purpose of Acts: Schneckenburger Reconsidered,"; and Munck, *The Acts of the Apostles*, pp. LV-LXI.
[352] This has enjoyed a very broad range of support in critical literature. Recent advocates include: Dibelius, *Studies in the Acts of the Apostles*, p. 149; Conzelmann, *The Theology of St. Luke*, pp. 138-144; Plümacher, *Lukas als hellenistischer Schriftsteller*,

audience: Luke-Acts is addressed to Christians not Romans.[353]

There is also some material in Luke-Acts which is indecorous to Christianity as politically innocent. This material led Paul W. Walaskay to reverse the traditional argument and suggest that instead of an *apologia pro ecclesia* addressed to Romans, Luke-Acts is an *apologia pro imperio* addressed to Christians.[354] The greatest difficulty with Walaskay's view is that it reverses the perspective of the text: the narrative presents trials of Jesus and Paul. Nor is Roman justice always portrayed in the best possible light. After all, Jesus did die on a Roman cross and Paul was held without cause.

A third alternative was proposed by Richard Cassidy who has argued that there was no political apology.[355] For Cassidy the political material is best explained by an "allegiance and witness theory." According to Cassidy the author wanted his audience to know that Jesus and earlier Christians had undergone trials and that while the outcome' was not always predictable, the stedfastness of their predecessors' witness was. He therefore presented them with what they needed in order to maintain their own witness.[356] Cassidy's work has the merit of explaining how this material related to Christians, but is faulty on two counts. It is difficult—impossible in my opinion—to sweep the universal verdict of innocent given at the trials under the rug. The corruption of Roman officials which Cassidy points out was commonplace. I do not find it to condemn Roman justice in Luke-Acts any more than I do in Cicero. Second, the thrust of Luke-Acts is to move Christianity out into the larger world. Cassidy's view would withdraw such an approach and keep the

---

p. 84; Hengel, *Acts and the History of Earliest Christianity*, p. 60; Fitzmyer, *The Gospel According to Luke*, 1:10 (subordinate purpose); Bruce, "The Acts of the Apostles: Historical Record or Theological Reconstruction," p. 2598. The term itself is Tertullian's and not a legal term in the Roman empire. See H.J. Cadbury, "Some Foibles of New Testament Scholarship," *JBR* 26 (1958): 215-216.

[353] C.K. Barrett, *Luke the Historian in Recent Study*, p. 63, has often been quoted in this connection: "No Roman official would ever have filtered out so much of what to him would be theological and ecclesiastical rubbish in order to reach so tiny a grain of relevant apology."

[354] "*And So We Came to Rome*", esp. pp. 64-67, for his conclusions.

[355] *Jesus, Politics, and Society: A Study of Luke's Gospel* (Maryknoll, New York: Orbis Books, 1978) and *Society and Politics in the Acts of the Apostles* (Maryknoll, New York: Orbis Books, 1988), esp. pp. 145-155. See also the important collection of essays he edited along with Philip J. Scharper, eds. *Political Issues in Luke-Acts* (Maryknoll, New York: Orbis Books, 1983).

[356] *Society and Politics in the Acts of the Apostles*, pp. 158-170.

perspective within Christianity itself. I can not accept this on literary grounds.

Philip Esler thought he solved the difficulties in the evidence by suggesting that there were Romans in either a military or administrative capacity in the audience who would be personally concerned about relating their faith to their allegiance to Rome.[357] The question here is whether such an elaborate motif in Luke-Acts was designed for a handful of individuals.

Before offering my own conclusions, we need to briefly review the major evidence for the apologetic dimension of the work. Both Henry Cadbury and Vernon Robbins have pointed out that the language of the prologue reappears in the second half of Acts in the trials of Paul. Each concluded that the prologue should be interpreted in light of these echoes: it provides "certainty" that the charges against Christians are groundless.[358] Horst R. Moehring argued that the placement of Jesus' birth at the time of the census was a political claim. Since the origins of the revolutionary movement were linked to the census,[359] the author demonstrated that the founder of Christianity had nothing to do with the seditionists.[360] A text which has been overlooked in the discussion is the genealogy of Lk. 3:23-38.[361] It is common to recognize a connection between the declaration of Jesus' Sonship at his baptism and the genealogy's

---

[357] *Community and Gospel in Luke-Acts*, p. 210. Esler critiques the *religio licita* school on pp. 211-214, where he points out that Christians did not practice all the regulations of Judaism and claims that to bring Christianity under the aegis of Judaism would impose the *fiscus Iudaicus* on Christians. The latter might have been true in Rome under Domitian, but as we have seen this was regarded as an aberration.

[358] Cadbury, *Beginnings*, 2:510; *idem*, "The Purpose Expressed in Luke's Preface," pp. 431-441; and Robbins, "Prefaces in Greco-Roman Biography and Luke-Acts," pp. 199-203.

[359] Acts 5:37.

[360] "The Census in Luke as an Apologetic Device," in *Studies in New Testament and Early Christian Literature: Essays in Honor of Allen P. Wikgren*, edited by David E. Aune. NovTSup 33 (Leiden: E.J. Brill, 1972), pp. 158-159. He has been followed by Gerd Luedemann, *Paul, Apostle to the Gentiles: Studies in Chronology*, trans. by F. Stanley Jones (Philadelphia: Fortress Press, 1984), pp. 18-19.

[361] There are well-known problems with the genealogy. For a summary of the material see Fitzmyer, *The Gospel According to Luke*, 1:488-505. See also Marshall Johnson, *The Purpose of the Biblical Genealogies: With Special Reference to the Setting of the Genealogies of Jesus*, 2nd ed. SNTSMS 8 (Cambridge: Cambridge University Press, 1988), pp. 229-252, who thinks that the genealogy helps to define the meaning of Sonship and connects Jesus to a prophetic lineage through David's son Nathan (vs. the royal line as in Matthew).

conclusion that Jesus is ultimately the Son of God (vv. 22, 38) or that
the genealogy provides a universal perspective (vs. the Matthean).
We need, however, to also ask if the genealogy makes a claim for antiquity. What strikes me about the genealogy is that just like Berossos, Manethon, Demetrios, and Josephos, it takes a tradition all the
way back to the beginning of time. If there were no ancestral theme
in Luke-Acts, this suggestion would not carry much weight.
However, the presence of the theme suggests that the rooting of the
founder in such a hoary past is no accident. The most important text
in the gospel is the trial scene of Jesus before Pilate. The distinctive
aspect of the Lukan account is the political concern which runs
throughout. Only the third gospel specifies the political charges
against Jesus.[362] Three times—the author counts them for us—
Pilate declares Jesus innocent.[363] Again, these declarations are
unique to the third gospel.[364] It is hard not to see some concern for
the political innocence of Jesus in such a presentation.[365]

The primary evidence in Acts is the presence of the numerous trials of Paul.[366] The charges filed against Paul throughout the narra-

---

[362] Luke 23:2. Note also vv. 5, 14. Mk 15:3 only says that the chief priest accused him of "many things." There is a political implication, however, as the question of Pilate in v. 2 makes clear. The charge in Jn. 18:30 is similarly vague. Only
Luke offers concrete political charges in this trial.

[363] Lk. 23:4, 14-15, 22. Note the declarations of the thief in vv. 40-41 and the
centurion in v. 47. Pilate's desire to release Jesus is again emphasized in Acts
3:13-14; 13:28.

[364] Lk. 23:4, 14-15 are unique to Luke among the synoptics. V. 22a = Mk.
15:14a; 22b is unique (it is the declaration of innocence); v. 23 = Mk. 15:14b. In
the third declaration our author has taken Mark's simple question (τί γὰρ ἐποίησεν
κακόν;), repeated it (v. 22a) and expanded it. The fourth gospel is much closer to
Luke here and has three declarations of innocence: Jn. 18:38; 19:4, 7. Note in particular Lk. 23:4b and Jn. 18:38c. Jn 19:1-15 does not have an equivalent in Lk. 23.

[365] Three important and different interpretations of the trial are Conzelmann,
The Theology of St. Luke, pp. 83-87, who accents the political implications; Cassidy,
Jesus, Politics and Society, pp. 68-71, 172-173 n. 40 and his "Luke's Audience, the
Chief Priests, and the Motive for Jesus' Death," in Political Issues in Luke-Acts, pp.
146-167, who contends that the trial narrative is designed to place the blame of Jesus' death on the chief priests and does not have a political motive (I do not see how
the guilt of the chief priests negates the political concerns especially since they surface throughout Luke-Acts); Daryl Schmidt, "Luke's 'Innocent' Jesus: A Scriptural Apologetic," in ibid., pp. 111-121, who contends that Jesus' innocence is bound
to his understanding that the Messiah must suffer according to prophecy, but does
not deny that a political theme may be present (p. 118).

[366] Acts 18:12-17, before Gallio; 22:1-21, before the people of Jerusalem;
23:1-9, before the Sanhedrin; 24:1-21, before Felix; 25:6-12, before Festus;
26:1-29, before Agrippa II.

tive vary from political[367] to religious[368] to a combination of the two.[369] As was true with Jesus, the political charges are always shown to be covers for religious differences. More importantly, the defense speeches of Paul make the issue the fulfillment of prophecy.[370] The defense is that Christianity is simply the extension of the Old Testament and therefore politically innocent.[371] Acts thus makes the same claim the apologists made: each stands within an ancient tradition. With this every Roman judge in Acts agrees![372] The repetition and uniformity of these verdicts of political innocence must be given their due.

We must now attempt to determine how an apologetic of Christians directed towards Christians makes sense. There are ten NT instances of ἀπολογέομαι: eight of which are in Luke-Acts.[373] In all eight of these cases the verb always denotes a defense before outsiders.[374] I would like to suggest that Luke-Acts served to help Christians understand their place in the Roman empire. The emergence of Christianity as a separate movement made it vulnerable to persecution. Under these circumstances the status of Christianity had to be addressed.[375] The claim that Christianity was a continuation of Judaism was a way of claiming the standing Judaism enjoyed. It is hard not to compare Josephos and Luke-Acts in this regard. Each pleads for respectability and uses precedents in the

---

[367] Acts 16:20-21; 17:6-7.

[368] Acts 21:28; 28:17.

[369] Acts 18:13 (where the charge is ostensibly against Roman "law" but is understood by Gallio correctly as Jewish "law"); Acts 24:5; 25:8.

[370] Acts 24:14-15; 26:6-8, 22-23; 28:20.

[371] The ancestral theme has long been recognized. E.g., Dibelius, *Studies in the Acts of the Apostles*, pp. 172, 174; Haenchen, *The Acts of the Apostles*, p. 102; Fitzmyer, *The Gospel According to Luke*, 1:10; Esler, *Community and Gospel in Luke-Acts*, pp. 214-218.

[372] Acts 18:14-15, Gallio; 23:29, Claudius Lysias the Roman chiliarch who witnessed the trials of Paul before the people of Jerusalem and the Sanhedrin; 25:18-19, 24-27, Festus; 26:31-32, Festus and Agrippa II. Cf. also 28:18.

[373] The other two are Rom. 2:15; II Cor. 12:19.

[374] Lk. 12:11; 21:12-14; Acts 19:33; 24:10; 25:8; 26:1, 2, 24. Note also the noun ἀπολογία in Acts 22:1, Paul before the Jerusalemites; 25:16, the right of a Roman citizen. The noun is found a total of 8t. in the NT.

[375] A definite date can not be given for this recognition. Tacitus, *Ann.* 15.44, implies that Christians were recognized as a distinct group in Rome as early as 64. Even if we grant this, it does not mean that provincial officials would have had any awareness of their distinctiveness. The very fact that Pliny wrote to Trajan in the second century indicates the difficulties facing local officials.

form of *acta* or trials to argue their case. There is, however, a difference: Josephos made his case *directly* to the Hellenistic world; Luke-
Acts makes its case *indirectly* by offering examples and precedents to
Christians so that they can make their own *apologia*.[376] It is here
that I part company with the *religio licita* school of thought.[377] Luke-
Acts is like the Hellenistic Jewish historians who addressed their
works to Jews in an effort to provide them with identity in the larger
world.

This leads us to another consideration as well. In a recent article,
Abraham Malherbe has suggested that we need to broaden the scope
of the apology by considering the social perception of Christians in
the Roman empire.[378] With this I agree and would only add that
the social and political concerns are inextricably bound together. It
is the social unacceptability of Christians that made them targets of
political pressures. *In nuce*, respectability and rights went hand in
hand as the *Antiquitates* demonstrates.

Summary. Luke-Acts defines Christianity both internally and ex-
ternally. The two are related by the recognition that Christianity is
a movement in history. It must understand both itself and the world
in which it exists. It was essential therefore to define Christianity in
terms of Rome (politically innocent), Judaism (a continuation), and
itself (*traditio apostolica*).[379]

SIGNIFICANCE

Did apologetic historiography play a decisive role in the writing of
Luke-Acts? I believe it did. The author shared the same outlook as
the writers of this genre: they belonged to subgroups within the
larger Greco-Roman world. It was this consciousness which led
them to write the story of their group (Content). Common to all of

---

[376] My conclusion is thus close to that of Cassidy, *Society and Politics in the Acts
of the Apostles*, pp. 158-170. The difference between our approaches is that I still see
a concrete apology in Luke-Acts which is designed to serve as a model.

[377] It was not essential for the author to remove all potentially embarrassing
material since non-Christians were not expected to read it.

[378] " 'Not in a Corner:' Early Christian Apologetic in Acts 26:26," *Second Century* 5 (1985-1986): 193-210.

[379] So also Aune, *The New Testament in Its Literary Environment*, pp. 136-138 and
Esler, *Community and Gospel in Luke-Acts*, pp. 16, 46, who uses the categories of Peter
L. Berger and L. Luckmann (*The Social Construction of Reality*) to argue that Luke-
Acts offers "legitimation" to its readers through the construction of a symbolic
universe.

the works is the emphasis on the antiquity of the group. The way the author made their case varied: it could be chronological as in Berossos, Manethon, Demetrios, Eupolemos, and Josephos; it could be through cultural claims as in the tradition before Josephos; or it could be by claiming continuity with a tradition recognized for its antiquity as in Luke-Acts. In any event, the claim is unmistakably present and betrays a defensive mentality in the historian who wants to gain respectability for his group.

The awareness of the group's place in the larger world led directly to the Hellenization of the group's traditions (Form). Again the specific ways that a historian chose to hellenize those traditions varied. In the case of Luke-Acts, as with Josephos, Hellenistic historiography provided the basic methodology. There is still a great deal of work to be done in this area. In particular I think II Maccabees might prove to be an important work to compare with Luke-Acts.[380]

The function of all the works in this tradition is to define the group: a function the prologue of Luke declares to be the purpose of Luke-Acts. Early in the tradition, native authors responded to the misrepresentations of their groups by Greek ethnographers. By the time of Luke-Acts this was no longer necessary: Greeks and Orientals had lived side by side for several centuries. The concern now was the social and political standing of the group within the empire.[381] This could be addressed either directly as with Berossos, Manethon, and Josephos or indirectly as with the Hellenistic Jewish historians and Luke-Acts. In both cases, however, the apology was present.

Our analysis has shown that Luke-Acts stands within the tradition of apologetic historiography. I would not go so far as to call it an *Antiquitates Christianae*. The author would have had to retell the OT from a Christian perspective to be considered a full equivalent of Josephos' *magnum opus*. It does, however, use the same conventions to relate the full story of a new group.

---

[380] Robert Doran has emphasized the apologetic element in II Macc. in *Temple Propaganda: The Purpose and Character of 2 Maccabees*. CBQMS 12 (Washington, DC: The Catholic Biblical Association of America, 1981). I would not place II Macc. in the category of apologetic historiography since its scope is too narrow, but do think it shares a number of historiographical concerns with Luke-Acts.

[381] I do not mean to imply that the authors of the Hellenistic world did not have political agendas: I have already argued they did. There is, however, a shift in the texts away from the cultural debate per se to a more overt political position.

Writing the Christian story in this genre had implications for the
understanding of Christianity which it presented. In the first place
it altered the definition itself. Luke-Acts was by no means the first
Christian document to employ Hellenistic forms: Paul's use of them
is too well known to require documentation. There is, however, a
gap between the orientation of the two. The clearest demonstration
of this is visible in the *Areopagitica* attributed to Paul in Acts
17:22-31. In a famous essay, Philipp Vielhauer pointed out how
Acts and Paul (Rom. 1:18-23) used Stoic natural theology for entirely different purposes: Paul used it to pronounce a sentence of condemnation on society; our author saw it as a forerunner for Christian faith.[382] Although the author can offer no *Kulturbringer*, he
clearly laid claim to Hellenistic culture as a prelude to Christianity
and in this regard anticipates the apologists of the second century.
The positive assessment of pagan culture and the willingness to define Christianity in relation to it demonstrates a movement away
from the *Mentalität* of a Palestinian sect to a group seeking social acceptance within the empire.

The willingness to identify *with* rather than to set oneself over
against (as in the Apocalypse) must have been somewhat revolutionary to the first readers. I do not mean the story-line of movement
from Jerusalem to Rome, but the intellectual undergirding of the
narrative. I think that our author was like Polybios who wrote his
history after he grasped the worldwide significance of Rome.[383]
The expansion of Christianity was a *fait accompli* by the end of the
first century. The intellectual undergirding of that expansion had
not yet, however, been grasped in historical terms. This is what our
author saw and why he wrote. It was an attempt to move Christianity into the larger world intellectually and socially as well as phys-
ically.

The author did not, however, send Christians into this world
without any parameters. He gave them a sense of identity through
the *traditio apostolica*. Paradoxically, this limited the perspective
through defining it in historical terms.[384] The structure this pro-

---

[382] "On the 'Paulinism' of Acts," pp. 34-37.
[383] 1.4.1-2.
[384] Cf. the observation of Hartog, *The Mirror of Herodotus*, pp. 288-289: "Writing amasses and preserves, and the ethnologist is the first or, on the contrary, the
last to witness a particular ceremony or to hear a certain song (for in this domain
you could well say that the first are also the last)."

vided did not, however, stifle the growth of the church but if anything helped it. The creative transformation of apologetic historiography laid the basis for subsequent Christian historiography.[385]

---

[385] Dibelius, *Studies in the Acts of the Apostles*, pp. 123-137, calls Luke the "first
Christian historian." Cf. also Aune, *The New Testament in Its Literary Environment*,
p. 139. Plümacher, *RESup*, s.v. "Lukas als griechischer Historiker," 14:263,
prefers to give the honor to Eusebios.

CONCLUSIONS

We now need to reassemble the evidence and show how the authors we have studied relate to the tradition as a whole. The antecedents of Greek historiography arose under the Persian empire when the birth of Ionian science and the heightened awareness of foreign peoples and lands stimulated by their incorporation into a common empire combined to foster the desire to describe the world and its inhabitants. The most significant early effort was that of Hekataios of Miletos who both corrected the map of Anaximander and wrote a commentary on it. His treatment of individual lands within this commentary, the *Periēgēsis Gēs*, became the basis for subsequent works on individual countries. These works form a distinct genre of prose writing and may be grouped together under the heading of ethnography. The fragments which remain suggest that each described a particular land and people (content) by presenting their land, history, wonders, and customs (form) in an effort to define who these people were for other Greeks (function).

The *heir extraordinaire* of Hekataios was Herodotos whose investigations into both ethnography and the conflict between the East and West have properly earned him the sobriquet *pater historiae*. Although ethnography continued to exist independently of "history," both genres were heavily influenced by Herodotos' *Histories*: histories would contain ethnographic sections and ethnographies would tend to become more historical.

The overthrow of the Persian empire at the hands of Macedon's military prodigy profoundly altered not only the political institutions of the eastern Mediterranean and Near East, but their cultural values as well. The fragmentation of Alexander's empire and the increasing importance of philosophy soon became evident in the literature of the period. Fittingly, it was another Hekataios (of Abdera) who laid the foundations for the transformation of ethnography. The court philospher of Ptolemy I wrote what in content appears to be another ethnographic treatment of Egypt, but what in form and more particularly in function veered markedly away. Instead of describing Egypt in a tone of wonder as Herodotos had done, Hekataios claimed that Egypt was the mother of all civilization— presenting her through the lens of philosophy in utopian terms.

Realizing the difference between his picture of the "gift of the Nile" and his ethnographic predecessors, he attacked the methodology of Herodotos by affirming that only native texts could serve to define a people. Egypt had not been properly understood: an ignorance Hekataios attempted to correct through a redefinition.

The competitive matrix of the Hellenistic world soon found expression in a similar way in the work of Megasthenes who like Hekataios presented his respective country, India, in a philosophically colored portrait. As a true Greek he claimed that Dionysos and Herakles established Indian culture in the remote past. Antiquity had thus become the battleground of cultural superiority.

The difference between ethnography proper and the works of Hekataios and Megasthenes is primarily one of perspective. Earlier ethnographers wrote to fellow Greeks within the context of the Greek world. Hekataios of Abdera and Megasthenes wrote as Greeks in adopted homelands. Each began the process of fusing their allegiances. They remained, however, outsiders to the country they celebrated.

The situation changed dramatically when a Babylonian priest named Berossos picked up a reed on behalf of his *patria*. The priest of Bel began his work in good ethnographic fashion with an autobiographical introduction and description of the land. At this point, however, his work begins to "translate" native Babylonian sources: *Enuma elish*, a flood account similar to the *Epic of Ziusudra*, and the Neo-Babylonian chronicles. The result was a brand new form of writing: apologetic historiography. The hybrid nature of his work must have seemed as strange to a Babylonian who chanced to read it as it did to the Greeks at the court of Antiochos I to whom he addressed it. The purpose of the work was to define the greatness of Babylon from a native perspective. So Berossos could claim that all of civilization had been revealed to the Babylonians long before other nations existed.

Berossos' contemporary, Manethon, soon wrote an Egyptian equivalent. The Egyptian priest, however, did not incorporate the normal forms of Greek ethnography, but depended solely upon his own sacred native sources. Like Berossos, Manethon traced the course of Egyptian civilization from before creation until a point close to his own time. His elaborate chronological reconstruction of Egypt's dynasties served notice of Egypt's great antiquity. Aware of the differences between his presentation and Greek ethnography, he harshly criticized Herodotos. The Greeks had not understood the Egyptians because they did not know the native sources.

The work of Berossos and Manethon established apologetic historiography as a distinct form of historical writing. In content it matched Greek ethnography: it told the story of a particular people. It is not by accident that their works have come down to us with Greek ethnographic titles. The shift from outsider to insider perspective, however, had an important consequence for the form. Instead of eyewitness reporting and investigation, the basis for the form of the new genre became the native records. This carried a built-in tension: How much emphasis would be given to the native tradition and how much to the Hellenistic form in which it was being clothed? Authors varied in their judgments. The function of the new genre was again similar to ethnography: it defined a people. The difference is that apologetic historiography is a reaction to Greek ethnography in its inception and to misconceptions in the larger world at a later date.

The most extensive tradition of apologetic historiography in antiquity belongs to the Jews. Toward the end of the third century B.C.E., Jewish and Samaritan authors began telling their story in Hellenistic categories. In contrast to Berossos and Manethon, these historians were more open to the acceptance of Hellenistic forms for their works—perhaps as a result of the continued advance of Hellenism. The authors experimented with specific forms: Demetrios with chronology, Artapanos with national legends, Pseudo-Eupolemos with Oriental and Greek myths, and Eupolemos with a more straightforward form of national historiography. What they shared in common was their effort to recast the biblical text in Hellenistic forms to the glory of the Jewish people. They also moved away from Berossos and Manethon by addressing their works—in part anyway—to their own people. They addressed both the issue of who the Jewish people were in the Hellenistic world and how they should relate to it. In true apologetic fashion they informed their readers that they were the founders or bringers of civilization.

Jewish tradition reached an apex in the *Antiquitates Judaicae* of Flavius Josephos. Like his predecessors, Josephos retold his people's story. In direct line with Berossos and Manethon he insisted upon the sacred texts as his sources. He differed with them by claiming the gift of prophecy and regarding his own work as a sacred text. Following the lead of the Hellenistic Jewish historians, Josephos recast the OT text in a Hellenized form. They served as precedents which helped to indicate the general direction (chronological emphasis, legends, and national historiography), but failed to provide an adequate model for the scope of his own undertaking. For this he turned to Dionysios of Halikarnassos who served him in much the same way that Eratosthenes served Demetrios. *AJ* offered a self-definition of Judaism just as the writings of the Hellenistic Jewish historians did, only Josephos reversed the emphasis in audience: he addressed it primarily to Greeks and secondarily to Jews. Unlike the indirect apology of the Hellenistic historians, the apologetic of *AJ* is direct. His message is that the antiquity and previous rights of the Jews ought to be respected in the Hellenistic world.

At the same time Josephos was writing his *Antiquitates*, a third generation Christian undertook the task of telling the story of Christians for the first time. Like Josephos, he hellenized his native sources by moving them into the realm of Hellenistic historiography. Unable to claim chronological age for his movement, he argued that it was a continuation of Israel of old: it is therefore not a new movement but an ancient one. He did this through arguing that Christianity was the fulfillment of the OT. As the narrative of fulfillment he regarded his work as sacred narrative. He thus provided Christians with a new self-definition which served to help them locate themselves both religiously and politically.

This analysis demonstrates the Janus-like nature of the tradition: it looks both to the outside world and to the group itself. Authors such as Berossos and Manethon concentrated on the audience of outsiders. Others, like the Hellenistic Jewish/Samaritan historians and the author of Luke-Acts, direct their attention to the group itself. Josephos explicitly addressed both although his focus on the former is clear. Regardless of the specific orientation, all of the works attend to the interplay between the group and the larger outside world.

It is intriguing that just as the Rabbis withdrew from the larger world, Hellenistic Jewish historiography came to an end. At the same time, just as Christianity established itself throughout the Roman world, Hellenistic Christian historiography began. The apex of Hellenistic Jewish historiography reached in the *Antiquitates Judaicae* of Josephos is complemented by Luke-Acts which not only marks the end of the same tradition, but serves as the beginning of another.

BIBLIOGRAPHY

Primary Sources

Aeschylus. *Aeschyli Septem Quae Supersunt Tragoedias.* Edited by Denys Page. OCT. Oxford: The Clarendon Press, 1972.

Aharoni, Yahanan. *Arad Inscriptions.* Translated by Judith Ben-Or. Jerusalem: The Israel Exploration Society, 1981.

Aland, Kurt; Black, Matthew; Martini, Carlo M.; Metzger, Bruce M.; and Wikgren, Allen, eds. *The Greek New Testament.* 3rd ed. Münster: United Bible Societies, 1975.

Aland, Kurt, ed. *Synopsis Quattuor Evangeliorum: Locis parallelis evangeliorum apocryphorum et patrum adhibites.* 11th ed. Stuttgart: Deutsche Bibelstiftung, 1976.

Aristotle. *The 'Art' of Rhetoric.* Edited and translated by John Henry Freese. LCL. Cambridge: Harvard University Press, 1926.

———. *Politics.* Edited and translated by H. Rackham. LCL. Cambridge: Harvard University Press, 1944.

Arrian. *Anabasis Alexandri et Indica.* 2 vols. Edited and translated with Appendices by P. A. Brunt. LCL. Cambridge: Harvard University Press, 1983.

Attridge, Harold W. and Oden, Robert A., Jr. *Philo of Byblos, The Phoenician History. Introduction, Critical Text, Translation, Notes.* CBQMS 9. Washington, DC: The Catholic Biblical Association of America, 1981.

Austin, M. M. *The Hellenistic World from Alexander to the Roman Conquest: A Selection of Ancient Sources in Translation.* Cambridge: Cambridge University Press, 1981.

Avigad, Nahman and Yadin, Yigael, eds. *A Genesis Apocryphon: A Scroll from the Wilderness of Judea.* Jerusalem: Magnes Press, 1956.

Bartlett, John R. *Jews in the Hellenistic World: Josephus, Aristeas, the Sibylline Oracles, Eupolemus.* Cambridge Commentaries on Writings of the Jewish and Christian World 200 BC to AD 200 1.1. Cambridge: Cambridge University Press, 1985.

Bowman, John. *Samaritan Documents Relating to their History, Religion and Life.* Pittsburgh Original Texts and Translation Series 2. Pittsburgh: The Pickwick Press, 1977.

Burstein, Stanley. *The 'Babyloniaca' of Berossus.* Malibu, CA: Undena Publications, 1978.

Charles, R. H. *The Apocrypha and Pseudepigrapha of the Old Testament in English.* 2 vols. Oxford: The Clarendon Press, 1913.

Charlesworth, James H., ed. *The Old Testament Pseudepigrapha.* 2 vols. Garden City, New York: Doubleday & Company, Inc., 1983-85.

Cicero. *The Works of Cicero.* 28 vols. Edited and translated by H. Caplan *et alii.* Cambridge: Harvard University Press, 1954.

Denis, Albert-Marie. *Fragmenta Pseudepigraphorum quae supersunt Graeca una cum historicorum et auctorum Judaeorum hellenistarum fragmentis.* (Published with M. Black, *Apocalypsis Henochi Graece*). PVTG 3. Leiden: E. J. Brill, 1970.

Dio Cassius. *Dio's Roman History.* 9 vols. Edited and translated by Earnest Cary. LCL. Cambridge: Harvard University Press, 1914-1927.

Diodorus Siculus. *Diodorus of Sicily.* 12 vols. Edited and translated by C. H. Oldfather, C. T. Sherman, C. Bradford Welles, R. M. Greer, and F. R. Walton.

LCL. Cambridge: Harvard University Press, 1933-1967.
Diogenes Laertius. *Lives of Eminent Philosophers*. 2 vols. Edited and translated by R. D. Hicks. LCL. Cambridge: Harvard University Press, 1925.
Dionysius of Halicarnassus. *The Roman Antiquities*. 7 vols. Edited and translated by Earnest Cary. LCL. Cambridge: Harvard University Press, 1937-1950.
——. *The Critical Essays*. 2 vols. Edited and translated by Stephen Usher. LCL. Cambridge: Harvard University Press, 1974-1985.
Donner, H., and Röllig, W. *Kanaanäische und aramäische Inschriften*. 4th ed. 3 vols. Wiesbaden: Otto Harrassowitz, 1962-1979.

Elliger, K.; Rudolph, W.; and Ruger, H.P. eds. *Biblia Hebraica Stuttgartensia*. Editio minor. Stuttgart: Deutsche Bibelgesellschaft, 1983.
Eusebius. *Ecclesiastical History*. 2 vols. Edited and translated by Kirsopp Lake and J. E. L. Outlton. LCL. Cambridge: Harvard University Press, 1926-1932.
Euripides. *Euripidis Fabulae*. 3 vols. Edited by Gilbert Murray. OCT. Oxford: The Clarendon Press, 1902-1913.

Fitzmyer, Joseph A. *The Genesis Apocryphon of Qumran Cave 1: A Commentary*. 2nd ed. Biblica et Orientalia 18A. Rome: Biblical Institute Press, 1971.

von Gall, August Freiherrn. *Der hebräische Pentateuch der Samaritaner*. Giessen: Alfred Topelmann, 1918.
Gaster, Moses. *The Asatir: The Samaritan Book of the "Secrets of Moses."* London: The Royal Asiatic Society, 1927.
Gifford, Edwin Hamilton, ed. and trans. *Eusebius: Preparation for the Gospel*. 2 vols. Oxford: The Clarendon Press, 1903; reprint ed., Grand Rapids: Baker Book House, 1981.

Hélidore. *Les Éthiopiques*. 3 vols. 2nd ed. Edited and translated by R. M. Rattenbury, T. W. Lumb, and J. Mailn. Paris: Société d'Édition 'Les Belles Lettres,' 1960.
Heliodrus. *An Ethiopian Romance*. Translated with an introduction by Moses Hadas. Ann Arbor: The University of Michigan Press, 1957.
Herodotus. *Herodoti Historiae*. 2 vols. 3rd ed. Edited by Carol Hude. OCT. Oxford: The Clarendon Press, 1927.
Hieronymus. *Liber de viris illustribus*. Edited by Ernest Cushing Richardson. TU 14.1. Leipzig: J. C. Hinrich, 1896.
Holladay, Carl R. *Fragments from Hellenistic Jewish Authors: Volume 1: Historians*. Texts and Translations Pseudepigrapha Series 20. Chico, California: Scholars Press, 1983.
Q. Horatius Flaccus. *Opera*. 2nd ed. Edited by Edward C. Wickham and H. W. Garrod. OCT. Oxford: The Clarendon Press, 1906.

Jacobson, Howard J. *The 'Exagoge' of Ezekiel*. Cambridge: Cambridge University Press, 1983.
Jacoby, Felix. *Die Fragmente der griechischen Historiker*. 3 vols. in 16 parts. Leiden: E. J. Brill, 1923-69.
James, M.R. *The Biblical Antiquities of Philo*. 2nd ed. with an introduction by Louis H. Feldman. The Library of Biblical Studies. New York: Ktav Publishing House, Inc., 1971.

Kirk, G. S.; Raven, J. E.; and Schofield, M. *The Presocratic Philosophers*. 2nd ed. Cambridge: Cambridge University Press, 1983.

Lake, Kirsopp, ed. *The Apostolic Fathers*. 2 vols. LCL. Cambridge: Harvard University Press, 1912-1913.

Lemaire, André. *Inscriptions hébraïques. Tome I: Les Ostraca: Introduction, Traduction, Commentaire*. Paris: Les Éditions du Cerf, 1977.

Lignée, H. "L'Apocryphe de la Genèse." In *Les Textes de Qumran*, 2: 205-242. Edited by J. Cargmignac, E. Cothenet, and H. Lignée. Paris: Letouzey et Ané, 1963.

Long, A. A., and Sedley, D. N. *The Hellenistic Philosophers*. 2 vols. Cambridge: Cambridge University Press, 1987ff.

Lucas, D. W., ed. *Aristotle: Poetics*. Oxford: The Clarendon Press, 1968.

Lucian. *The Works of Lucian*. Edited and translated by K. Kelburn. Vol. 6. LCL. Cambridge: Harvard University Press, 1959.

Meiggs, R. and Lewis, D., eds. *A Selection of Greek Historical Inscriptions*. Oxford: The Clarendon Press, 1969.

Mras, Karl, ed. *Die Praeparatio Evangelica*. GCS 43:1. Berlin: Akademie Verlag, 1954.

Nenci, Giuseppe. *Hecataei Milesii Fragmenta*. Florence, 1954.

Nestle, Eberhard; Nestle, Erwin; Aland Kurt; and Aland, Barbara, eds. *Novum Testamentum Graece*. 26th ed. Stuttgart: Deutsche Bibelstiftung, 1979.

Niese, Benedictus, ed. *Flavii Iosephi Opera*. 7 vols. Berlin: Weidmann, 1887-1889; reprint ed., 1955.

Pelletier, André. *Lettre d'Aristée à Philocrate*. SC 89. Paris: Les Éditions du Cerf, 1962.

Philo. *The Works of Philo*. 12 vols. Edited and translated by F. H. Colson, G. H. Whitaker, J. W. Earp, and Ralph Marcus. LCL. Cambridge: Harvard University Press, 1929-1962.

Philostratus. *The Life of Apollonius*. 2 vols. Edited and translated by F. C. Conybeare. LCL. Cambridge: Harvard University Press, 1912-1950.

Plato. *The Works of Plato*. 12 vols. Edited and translated by H. N. Fowler, W. R. M. Lamb, Paul Shorey, and R. G. Bury. LCL. Cambridge: Harvard University Press, 1914-1927.

Plutarch. *Lives*. 11 vols. Edited and translated by Bernadotte Perrin. LCL. Cambridge: Harvard University Press, 1914-1921.

Polybius. *The Histories*. 6 vols. Edited and translated by W. R. Paton. LCL. Cambridge: Harvard University Press, 1922-1927.

Pritchard, James B. *Ancient Near Eastern Texts (Relating to the Old Testament)*. 3rd ed. 2 vols. Princeton: Princeton University Press, 1969.

Pseudo-Callisthenes. *The Life of Alexander of Macedon*. Translated and edited by Elizabeth Hazelton Haight. New York: Longmans, Green and Co., 1955.

Pseudo-Callisthenes. *Der griechische Alexanderroman Rezension B*. Edited by Leif Bergson. Acta Universitatis Stockholmiensis 3. Stockholm/Göteborg/Uppsala: Almquist & Wiksell, 1965.

Pseudo-Philo. *Les Antiquités Bibliques*. 2 vols. Translated and edited by Daniel J. Harrington. SC 229-230. Paris: Éditions du Cerf, 1976.

Quintilian. *Institutio Oratoria*. 4 vols. Edited and translated by H. E. Butler. LCL. Cambridge: Harvard University Press, 1920-1922.

Rahlfs, Alfred, ed. *Septuaginta*. Editio Minor. Stuttgart: Deutsche Bibelgesellschaft, 1935.

Reardon, B.P., ed. *Collected Ancient Greek Novels.* Berkeley/Los Angeles/London: University of California Press, 1989.
Riessler, Paul. *Altjüdisches Schriftum ausserhalb der Bibel.* Augsburg: Benno Filfer, 1928.

Schmeling, Gareth L. *Chariton.* Twayne's World Author Series 295. New York: Twanye Publishers Inc., 1974.
Schwanbeck, E. A. *Megasthenis Indica.* Bonn, 1846.
Sperber, Alexander, ed. *The Bible in Aramaic.* 4 vols. Leiden: E. J. Brill, 1959-1973.
Stählin, Otto; Früchtel, Ludwig; Treu, Ursula, eds. *Clemens Alexandrinus.* Vols. 2-3. GCS. Berlin: Akademie Verlag, 1985, 1970.
Stearns, Wallace Nelson. *Fragments from Graeco-Jewish Writers.* Chicago: The University of Chicago Press, 1908.
Stephan von Byzanz. *Ethnika: Stephani Byzantii Ethnicorum quae supersunt ex Recensione Augusti Meinekii.* Berlin: G. Reimar, 1849; reprint ed., Graz, Austria: Akademische Druck-u. Verlagsanstalt, 1958.
Stern, Menahem. *Greek and Latin Authors on Jews and Judaism.* 3 vols. Jerusalem: The Israel Academy of Sciences and Humanities, 1974.
Suetonius. *Lives of the Caesars.* 2 vols. Edited and translated by J. C. Rolfe. LCL. Cambridge: Harvard University Press, 1912-1913 (Vol. 1 revised 1951).

Tacitus. *Cornelii Taciti Annalium.* Edited by C. D. Fisher. OCT. Oxford: The Clarendon Press, 1906.
Tcherikover, Victor A., ed. *Corpus Papyrorum Judaicarum.* 3 vols. Cambridge: Harvard University Press, 1957-1964.
Thackeray, H. St. J.; Marcus, Ralph; and Feldman H. *Josephus.* 10 vols. LCL. Cambridge: Harvard University Press, 1926-1965.
Thucydides. *Thucydidis Historiae.* 2 vols. Revised ed. Edited by Henry Stuart Jones and John Enoch Powell. OCT. Oxford: The Clarendon Press, 1942-1963.

VanderKam, James C. *The Book of Jubilees: A Critical Text.* 2 vols. CSCO 510-511. Louvain: E. Peeters, 1989.

Waddell, W. G., ed. *Manetho.* LCL. Cambridge: Harvard University Press, 1980.
Walter, Nikolaus. "Fragmente jüdisch-hellenistischer Exegeten: Aristobulus, Demetrios, Aristeas." In *Unterweisung in lehrhafter Form*, Bd. 31, Lfg. 2, pp. 257-296. JSHRZ, ed. W. G. Kümmel. Gütersloh: Gerd Mohn, 1975.
———. "Fragmente jüdisch-hellenistischer Historiker." In *Historische und legendarische Erzählungen*, Bd. 1, Lfg. 2. JSHRZ, ed. W. G. Kümmel. Gütersloh: Gerd Mohn, 1976.
Weber, Robert, ed. *Biblia Sacra.* 2nd ed. 2 vols. Stuttgart: Württembergische Bibelanstalt, 1975.
Whittaker, Molly. *Jews and Christians: Graeco-Roman Views.* Cambridge Commentaries on Writings of the Jewish and Christian World. Cambridge: Cambridge University Press, 1984.

Reference Works

Arndt, William F.; Gingrich, F. Wilbur; Danker, Frederick W. *A Greek-English Lexicon of the New Testament and Other Early Christian Literature.* 2nd ed. Chicago/London: The University of Chicago Press, 1979.

Bachmann, H. and Slaby, W. A. *Computer Concordance to the Novum Testamentum Graece.* 2nd ed. Berlin/New York: Walter de Gruyter, 1985.

Blass, F. and Debrunner, A. *A Greek Grammar of the New Testament and Other Early Christian Literature.* Translated and revised by Robert W. Funk. Chicago/London: The University of Chicago Press, 1961.

Brown, Colin. ed. *Dictionary of New Testament Theology.* 3 vols. Grand Rapids: Zondervan Publishing House, 1975-1978.

Brown, Francis; Driver, S. R.; Briggs, Charles A. *A Hebrew and English Lexicon of the Old Testament.* Oxford: The Clarendon Press, 1980.

Černý, J. *Coptic Etymological Dictionary.* Cambridge: Cambridge University Press, 1976.

Crum, W. E. *A Coptic Dictionary.* Oxford: The Clarendon Press, 1939.

Hatch, Edwin, and Redpath, Henry A. *A Concordance to the Septuagint.* 2 vols. Oxford: The Clarendon Press, 1897; reprint ed., Graz, Austria: Akademische Druck-u. Verlagsanstalt, 1975.

Kittel, Gerhard and Friederich, Gerhard, eds. *Theological Dictionary of the New Testament.* 10 vols. Translated by Geoffrey W. Bromiley. Grand Rapids: Wm. B. Eerdmans Publishing Co., 1964-1976.

Klausner, T., ed. *Reallexikon für Antike und Christentum.* Stuttgart: Hiersemann, 1950ff.

Liddell, Henry George; Scott, Robert; Jones, Henry Stuart; McKensie, Roderick. *A Greek-English Lexicon.* Rev. ed. Oxford: The Clarendon Press, 1968.

Lisowsky, Gerhard. *Konkordanz zum hebräischen Alten Testament.* 2nd ed. Stuttgart: Deutsche Bibelgesellschaft, 1981.

Morgenthaler, Robert. *Statistik des Neutestamentlichen Wortschatzes.* 3rd ed. Zürich: Gotthelf, 1982.

Moulton, James Hope; Howard, Wilbert Francis; and Turner, Nigel. *A Grammar of New Testament Greek.* 4 vols. Edinburgh: T. & T. Clark, 1906-1976.

Powell, J. Enoch. *A Lexicon to Herodotus.* 2nd ed. Hildesheim: Georg Olms Verlagsbuchhandlung, 1977.

Rengstorf, Karl Heinrich. *A Complete Concordance to Flavius Josephus.* 4 vols. with 2 Supplements. Leiden: E. J. Brill, 1973-1986.

Robertson, A. T. *A Grammar of the Greek New Testament in the Light of Historical Research.* 3rd ed. Nashville: Broadman Press, 1934.

Roth, Cecil, gen. ed. *Encyclopaedia Judaica.* 16 vols. Jerusalem: The Macmillan Company, 1971-1972.

Wissowa, G.; Kroll, W. *et alii* eds. *Paulys Real-Encyclopädie der classischen Altertumswissenschaft.* I 1-24; II 1-10; Suppl. 1-15. Stuttgart: Alfred Druckenmüller, 1893-1978.

Ziegler, K. and Sontheimer, W. *Der kleine Pauly, Lexikon der Antike.* 5 vols. Stuttgart: Alfred Druckenmüller, 1964-1975.

SECONDARY LITERATURE

Aharoni, Yohanan. "Hebrew Ostraca from Tel Arad." *IEJ* 16 (1966): 1-7.
——. "The Use of Hieratic Numerals in Hebrew Ostraca and the Shekel Weights." *BASOR* 184 (1966): 13-19.
——. "Arad: Its Inscriptions and Temple." *BA* 31 (1968): 2-32.
——. *The Archaeology of the Land of Israel: From the Prehistoric Beginnings to the End of the First Temple Period*. Translated by Anson F. Rainey. Philadelphia: The Westminster Press, 1978.
von Albrecht, Michael. "Dionyios von Halikarnassos," in *KP*, 3: 70-71.
Alexander, Loveday. "Luke's Preface in the Context of Greek Preface-Writing." *NovT* 28 (1986): 48-74.
Allan, J.; Haig, T. Wolseley; Dowell, H. H., *The Cambridge Shorter History of India*. Reprint ed., Delhi: S. Chand & Co., 1969.
Altshuler, David. "The Treatise ΠΕΡΙ ΕΘΩΝ ΚΑΙ ΑΙΤΙΩΝ 'On Customs and Causes' by Flavius Josephus." *JQR* 69 (1978): 226-232.
Amaru, Betsy Halpern. "Land Theology in Josephus' *Jewish Antiquities*." *JQR* 71 (1980): 201-229.
——. "Portraits of Biblical Women in Josephus' *Antiquities*." *JJS* 39 (1988): 143-170.
Anderson, Graham. *Ancient Fiction: The Novel in the Graeco-Roman World*. Totowa, New Jersey: Barnes & Noble Books, 1984.
Argyle, A. W. "The Greek of Luke and Acts." *NTS* 20 (1973-1974): 441-445.
Armayor, O. Kimball. "Herodotus' Influence on Manethon and the Implications for Egyptology." *The Classical Bulletin*. 61 (1985): 7-11.
Attridge, Harold. *The Interpretation of Biblical History in the "Antiquitates Judaicae" of Flavius Josephus*. HDR. Missoula, Montana: Scholars Press, 1976.
——. "Historiography." In *Jewish Writings of the Second Temple Period*, pp. 157-184. Edited by Michael E. Stone. CRINT. Philadelphia: Fortress Press, 1984.
——. "Josephus and His Works." In *Jewish Writings of the Second Temple Period*, pp. 185-232. Edited by Michael E. Stone. CRINT. Philadelphia: Fortress Press, 1984.
——. "Jewish Historiography." In *Early Judaism and Its Modern Interpreters*, pp. 311-343. Edited by Robert A. Kraft and George W. E. Nickelsburg. The Bible and Its Modern Interpreters. Atlanta: Scholars Press, 1986.
Aune, David E. "The Use of ΠΡΟΦΗΤΗΣ in Josephus." *JBL* 101 (1982): 419-421.
——. *The New Testament in Its Literary Environment*. Library of Early Christianity. Philadelphia: The Westminster Press, 1987.
Avigad, N. "A New Class of *Yehud* Stamps." *IEJ* 7 (1957): 146-153.

Badian, E. "Alexander the Great and the Unity of Mankind." *Historia 7* (1958): 425-444.
Bailey, James L. "Josephus' Portrayal of the Matriarchs." In *Josephus, Judaism, and Christianity*, pp. 154-179. Edited by Louis H. Feldman and Gohei Hata. Detroit: Wayne State University Press, 1987.
Baird, J. Arthur. "Genre Analysis as a Method of Historical Criticism." In *Society of Biblical Literature 1972 Proceedings*, 2: 385-411. Edited by Lane C. McGaughy. Missoula, Montana: Scholars Press, 1972.
Balch, David L. "Two Apologetic Encomia: Dionysius on Rome and Josephus on the Jews." *JSJ* 13 (1982): 102-122.
——. "Acts as Hellenistic Historiography." In *Society of Biblical Literature 1985 Seminar Papers*, pp. 429-432. Edited by Kent Harold Richards. Atlanta: Scholars Press, 1985.

Baldry, H. C. "The Idea of the Unity of Mankind." In *Grecs et Barbares*, pp. 167-204. Entretiens sur l'Antiquité Classique 7. Genève: Fondation Hardt, 1962.

Baldson, J. P. V. D. "Some Questions about Historical Writing in the Second Century B. C." *CQ* n.s. 3 (1953): 158-164.

Barber, Godfrey Louis. "Megasthenes," in *The Oxford Classical Dictionary*, 2nd ed.

Barish, David A. "The *Autobiography* of Josephus and the Hypothesis of a Second Edition of his *Antiquities*." *HTR* 71 (1978): 61-75.

Baron, Salo Wittmayer. *A Social and Religious History of the Jews*. Vol. 1: *The Beginning of the Christian Era*. 2nd ed. Philadelphia: The Jewish Publication Society of America, 1952.

Barr, David L. and Wentling, Judith L. "The Conventions of Classical Biography and the Genre of Luke-Acts: A Preliminary Study." In *Luke-Acts: New Perspectives from the Society of Biblical Literature Seminar*, pp. 63-88. Edited by Charles H. Talbert. New York: Crossroad, 1984.

Barrett, C. K. *Luke the Theologian in Recent Study*. London: Epworth Press, 1961.

Barth, Hannelore. "Zur Bewertung und Auswahl des Stoffes durch Herodot (Die Begriffe θῶμα, θωμάζω, θαμάσιος, and θωμαστός)". *Klio* 50 (1968): 93-110.

Basser, H. W. "Josephus as Exegete." *Journal of the American Oriental Society* 197 (1987): 21-30.

Beck, B. E. "The Common Authorship of Luke and Acts." *NTS* 23 (1976-1977): 346-352.

Belkin, Samuel. *The Alexandrian Halakah in the Apologetic Literature of the First Century C. E.* Philadelphia: The Jewish Publication Society, 1936.

Berger, Klaus. "Hellenistische Gattungen im Neuen Testament." In *Religion (Vorkonstantinisches Christentum: Leben und Umwelt Jesu; Neues Testament, Forts [Kanonische Schriften und Apokyphen])*, pp. 1031-1432. ANRW II 25.2 Berlin/New York: Walter der Gruyter, 1984.

——. *Formgeschichte des Neuen Testaments*. Heidelberg: Quelle & Meyer, 1984.

Bevan, Edwyn Robert. *The House of Seleucus*. 2 vols. London: Edward Arnold, 1902; reprint ed., New York: Barnes & Noble, Inc., 1966.

Bickerman, Elias J. "Origenes Gentium." *Classical Philology* 47 (1952): 65-81.

——. "The Jewish Historian Demetrios." In *Christianity, Judaism and Other Greco-Roman Cults: Studies for Morton Smith at Sixty*, pp. 72-84. Edited by Jacob Neusner. SJLA 12. Leiden: E. J. Brill, 1975.

——. *The Jews in the Greek Age*. Cambridge/London: Harvard University Press, 1988.

Bilde, Per. *Josefus som historieskriver*. Bibel og historie 1. København: G. E. C. Gad, 1983.

——. *Flavius Josephus between Jerusalem and Rome: His Life, his Works, and their Importance*. JSPSup 2. Sheffield: Sheffield Academic Press, 1988.

Blenkinsopp, Joseph. "Prophecy and Priesthood in Josephus." *JJS* 25 (1974): 239-262.

Bloch, Heinrich. *Die Quellen des Flavius Josephus*. Leipzig: B. G. Teubner, 1879; Reprint ed., Wiesbaden: Dr. Martin Sandig OHG., 1968.

Boedeker, Deborah, ed. "Herodotus and the Invention of History." *Arethusa* 20 (1987): 1-282.

Boer, Emilie. "Timaios," in *KP*, 5: 835-837.

Boorer, Suzanne. "The Importance of a Diachronic Approach: The Case of Genesis-Kings." *CBQ* 51 (1989): 195-208.

Bousset, Wilhelm and Gresmann, Hugo. *Die Religion des Judentums im späthellenistischen Zeitalter*. 4th ed. HNT 21. Tübingen: J. C. B. Mohr (Paul Siebeck), 1966.

Bovon, F. *Luc le théologien: Vingt-cinq ans de recherches (1950-1975)*. Le monde de la Bible. Neuchâtel/Paris: Delachaux et Niestlé, 1978.
——. *Luke the Theologian: Thirty-Three Years of Research (1950-1983)*. Translated by K. McKinney. Princeton Theological Monograph Series 12. Allison Park, PA: Pickwick Publications, 1987.
Brandon, S. G. F. "Josephus, Renegade or Patriot?" *History Today* 8 (1958): 830-836.
Braun, Martin. *Griechischer Roman und hellenistische Geschichtschreibung*. Frankfurter Studien zur Religion und Kultur der Antike. Frankfurt: Vittorio Klostermann, 1934.
——. *History and Romance in Graeco-Oriental Literature*. Oxford: Basil Blackwell, 1938.
——. "The Prophet Who Became a Historian." *The Listener* 56 (1956): 53, 56-57.
Breasted, James Henry. *A History of Egypt: From the Earliest Times to the Persian Conquest*. 2nd ed. New York: Charles Scribner's Sons, 1909.
Breebaart, A. B. "Weltgeschichte als Thema der antiken Geschichtsschreibung." *Acta Historiae Neerlandica* 1 (1966): 1-21.
Bright, John. *A History of Israel*. 3rd ed. Philadelphia: Westminster Press, 1981.
Brock, Sebastian. "Some Syriac Legends Concerning Moses." *JJS* 33 (1982): 237-255.
Brown, Schuyler. "The Prologues of Luke-Acts in Their Relation to the Purpose of the Author." In *Society of Biblical Literature 1975 Seminar Papers*, 2: 1-14. Edited by George MacRae. Missoula: Scholars Press, 1975; reprinted in *Perspectives on Luke-Acts*, pp. 99-111. Edited by Charles H. Talbert. Special Studies Series 5. Danville, VA: Association of Baptist Professors of Religion, 1978.
Brown, Truesdell Sparhawk. "The Reliability of Megasthenes." *American Journal of Philogy*. 76 (1955): 18-33.
——. *Timaeus of Tauromenium*. Berkeley: University of California Press, 1958.
——. "The Greek Sense of Time in History as Suggested by Their Accounts of Egypt." *Historia* 11 (1962): 257-270.
Brown, W. Edward. "Some Hellenistic Utopias." *The Classical Weekly* 48 (1955): 57-62.
Broyde, I. "Demetrius," in *The Jewish Encyclopedia*, 4: 512-513.
Bruce, Frederick Fyvie. "Josephus and Daniel." *Annual of the Swedish Theological Institute* 4 (1965): 148-162.
——. "The Acts of the Apostles: Historical Record or Theological Reconstruction?" In *Religion (Vorkonstantinisches Christentum: Leben und Umwelt Jesu; Neues Testament [Kanonische Schriften und Apokryphen], Forts.)*, pp. 2569-2603. ANRW II 25.3. Berlin/New York: Walter der Gruyter, 1985.
——. "Paul's Apologetic and the Purpose of Acts." *BJRL* 69 (1986-1987): 379-393.
Brueggemann, Walter and Woff, Hans Walter. *The Vitality of Old Testament Traditions*. 2nd ed. Atlanta: John Knox Press, 1982.
Buchner, Edmund. "Zwei Gutachten für die Behandlung der Barbaren durch Alexander den Grossen?" *Hermes* 82 (1954): 378-384.
Büchsel, Friedrich. "ἱστορέω," in *TDNT*, 3: 391-396.
Bultmann, Rudolf. "Evangelien," in *RGG*, 2: 418-422.
——. *Die Geschichte der synoptischen Tradition*. 9th ed. Göttingen: Vandenhoeck & Ruprecht, 1979.
——. *Theology of the New Testament*. 2 vols. Translated by Kendrick Grobel. New York: Charles Scribner's Sons, 1951-1955.
Burkitt, F. Crawford. *The Gospel History and Its Transmission*. 3rd ed. Edinburgh: T. & T. Clark, 1911.
Burton, Anne. *Diodorus Siculus: Book I, A Commentary*. Études Préliminaires aux

Religions Orientales dans l'Empire Romain 29. Leiden: E. J. Brill, 1972.
Bury, J. B. *The Ancient Greek Historians*. Reprint ed., New York: Dover Publications: 1958.
———. "Greek Literature from the Eighth Century to the Persian Wars." In *The Persian Empire and the West*, pp. 469-521. Edited by J. B. Bury, S. A. Cook, and F. E. Adcock. CAH 4. Cambridge: The University Press, 1969.

Cadbury, Henry J. *The Style and Literary Method of Luke*. HTS 6. Cambridge: Harvard University Press, 1920; reprint ed., New York: Kraus Reprint Co., 1969.
———. "The Purpose Expressed in Luke's Preface." *The Expositor* 21 (1921): 431-441.
———. "The Knowledge Claimed in Luke's Preface." *The Expositor* 24 (1922): 401-420.
———. "Lexical Notes on Luke-Acts: II. Recent Arguments for Medical Language." *JBL 45 (1926): 190-206.*
———. *The Making of Luke-Acts*. New York: Macmillan Co., 1927; reprint ed., London: SPCK, 1961.
———. "Lexical Notes in Luke-Acts: V. Luke and the Horse-Doctors." *JBL* 52 (1933): 55-65.
———. "'We' and 'I' Passages in Luke-Acts." *NTS* 3 (1956-1957): 128-132.
———. "Some Foibles of New Testament Scholarship." *JBR* 26 (1958): 213-216.
Cagnazzi, Silvana. "Tavola dei 28 Logoi di Erodoto." *Hermes* 103 (1975): 385-423.
Caizzi, Fernanda Decleva. "Pirroniani ed Accademici nel III Secolo A.C." In *Aspets de la Philosophie Hellénistique*, pp. 147-183. Entretiens sur l'Antiquité Classique 32. Genève: Vandoeuvres, 1986.
Callan, Terrance. "The Preface of Luke-Acts and Historiography." *NTS* 31 (1985): 576-581.
Case, Shirley Jackson. "Josephus' Anticipation of a Domitianic Persecution." *JBL* 44 (1925): 10-20.
Cassidy, Richard J. *Jesus, Politics, and Society: A Study of Luke's Gospel*. Maryknoll, New York: Orbis Books, 1978.
———. *Society and Politics in the Acts of the Apostles*. Maryknoll, New York: Orbis Books, 1988.
Cassidy, Richard J., and Scharper, Philip J., eds. *Political Issues in Luke-Acts*. Maryknoll, New York: Orbis, 1983.
Charlesworth, James H. "Jewish Astrology in the Talmud, Pseudepigrapha, the Dead Sea Scrolls, and Early Palestinian Synagogues." *HTR* 70 (1977): 183-200.
Charlesworth, M.P. "The Flavian Dynasty." In *The Imperial Peace A.D. 70-192*, pp. 1-45. Edited by S.A. Cook, F.E. Adcock, and M.P. Charlesworth. CAH 11. Cambridge: Cambridge University Press, 1969.
Cobet, J. *Herodots Exkurse und die Frage der Einheit seines Werkes*. Historia Einzelschriften 17. Wiesbaden: Steiner, 1971.
Cohen, Naomi G. "Josephus and Scripture: Is Josephus' Treatment of the Scriptural Narrative Similar Throughout the *Antiquities* I-XI?" *JQR* 54 (1963-64): 311-332.
Cohen, Shaye J. D. *Josephus in Galilee and Rome: His "Vita" and Development as a Historian*. Columbia Studies in the Classical Tradition 8. Leiden: E. J. Brill, 1979.
———. "Respect for Judaism by Gentiles According to Josephus." *HTR* 80 (1987): 409-430.
———. *From the Maccabees to the Mishnah*. Library of Early Christianity. Philadelphia: The Westminster Press, 1987.

Collingwood, R. G. *The Idea of History*. Oxford University Press, 1946.
Collins, Adela. *Crisis and Catharsis: The Power of the Apocalypse*. Philadelphia: The Westminster Press, 1984.
———, ed. *Early Christian Apocalypticism: Genre and Social Setting. Semeia* 36. Decatur, GA: Scholars Press, 1986.
Collins, John J., ed. *Apocalypse: The Morphology of a Genre. Semeia* 14. Missoula: Scholars Press, 1979.
———. *Between Athens and Jerusalem: Jewish Identity in the Hellenistic Diaspora*. New York: Crossroad, 1983.
———. *The Apocalyptic Imagination: An Introduction to the Jewish Matrix of Christianity*. New York: Crossroad, 1984.
Collins, John, and Poehlmann, Bill. "Artapanus." Unpublished paper from NT Seminar 201, Harvard University, 1970.
Collomp, Paul. "La Place de Josèphe dans la Technique de l' Historiographie Hellénistique." *Études historiques de la Faculue des Lettres de Strasbourg* 106: *Mélanges* 1945, 3, *Études Historiques* (Paris, 1947): 81-92.
Connor, W.R. "Historical writing in the fourth century B.C. and in the Hellenistic period." In *Greek Literature*, pp. 458-471. Edited by P.E. Easterling and B.M.W. Knox. The Cambridge History of Classical Literature. Cambridge: Cambridge University Press, 1985.
Conzelmann, Hans. *The Theology of St. Luke*. Translated by Geoffrey Buswell. New York: Harper and Row, 1960.
———. *Heiden-Juden-Christen: Auseinandersetzungen in der Literatur der hellenistisch-römischen Zeit*. BHT 62. Tübingen: J. C. B. Mohr, 1981.
Croce, Benedetto. *Aesthetic: As science of expression and general linguistic*. Rev. ed. Translated by Douglas Ainsile. Farrar, Strauss and Giroux, 1922.
Cross, Frank Moore, Jr. *The Ancient Library of Qumran and Modern Biblical Studies*. Garden City, New York: Doubleday & Company, Inc., 1958.
———. *Canaanite Myth and Hebrew Epic: Essays in the History of the Religion of Israel*. Cambridge: Harvard University Press, 1973.

Dahl, Nils A. "The Story of Abraham in Luke-Acts." In *Studies in Luke-Acts*, pp. 139-158. Edited by Leander E. Keck and J. Louis Martyn. Philadelphia: Fortress Press, 1980.
Dahlquist, Allan. *Megasthenes and Indian Religion: A Study in Motives and Types*. Stockholm: Almquist & Wisell, 1962.
Dalbert, Peter. *Die Theologie der hellenistisch-jüdischen Missions-Literatur unter Ausschluss von Philo und Josephus*. TF 4. Hamburg-Volksdorf: Herbert Reich, 1954.
Daniel, Jerry L. "Anti-Semitism in the Hellenistic-Roman Period." *JBL* 98 (1979): 45-65.
Danker, F. W. *Benefactor: Epigraphic Study of a Graeco-Roman and New Testament Semantic Field*. St. Louis, MO: Clayton, 1982.
Daube, David. "Typology in Josephus." *JJS* 31 (1980): 18-36.
Dawsey, J. "The Literary Unity of Luke-Acts: Questions of Style—A Task for Literary Critics." *NTS* 35 (1989): 48-66.
Delobel, J. "L'onction par la pecheresse." *ETL* 42 (1966): 415-475.
Denis, Albert-Marie. *Introduction aux Pseudépigraphes Grecs d'Ancien Testament*. SVTP 1. Leiden: E. J. Brill, 1970.
———. "L'Historien anonyme d'Eusèbe (Praep. Ev. 9, 17-8) et la Crise des Maccabées." *JSJ* 8 (1977): 42-49.
Derrett, J.D.M. "Megasthenes," in *KP*, 3: 1150-1154.
Dever, W. J. "Tel Malhata." *IEJ* 17 (1967): 272-273.
Dewald, Carolyn, and Marincola, John. "A Selective Introduction to Herodotean Studies." *Arethusa* 20 (1987): 9-40.

Diamond, Frances Henderson. "Hecataeus of 'Abdera: A New Historical Approach." Ph.D. dissertation, UCLA, 1974.

Dibelius, Martin. *Die Formgeschichte des Evangeliums.* 6th ed. Tübingen: J. C. B. Mohr, 1971.

———. "The Structure and Literary Character of the Gospels." *HTR* 20 (1927): 151-170.

———. *Studies in the Acts of the Apostles.* Edited by H. Greeven. Translated by Mary Ling. London: SCM, 1956.

Dihle, Albrecht. "Die Evangelien und die biographische Tradition der Antike." *ZTK* 80 (1983): 33-49.

———. "Zur hellenistichen Ethnographie." In *Grecs et Barbares,* pp. 205-239. Entretiens sur l'Antiquité Classique 7. Genève: Fondation Hardt, 1962.

Diller, Hans. "Die Hellenen-Barbaren-Antithese im Zeitalter der Perserkriege." In *Grecs et Barbares,* pp. 37-82. Entretiens sur l'Antiquité Classique 7. Genève: Fondation Hardt, 1962.

Dillon, Richard J. "Previewing Luke's Project from His Prologue (Luke 1:1-4)." *CBQ* 43 (1981): 205-227.

Dodd, C. H. *The Apostolic Preaching and Its Developments.* New York: Harper, 1936.

Donahue, John R. *"Are You the Christ?" The Trial Narrative in the Gospel of Mark.* SBLDS 10. Missoula, Montana: Society of Biblical Literature, 1973.

Doran, Robert. *Temple Propaganda: The Purpose and Character of 2 Maccabees.* CBQMS 12. Washington, DC: The Catholic Biblical Association of America, 1981.

———. "The Jewish Hellenistic Historians Before Josephus." In *Rise and Decline of the Roman World,* pp. 246-297. Edited by Wolfgang Haase. ANRW II 20.1 Berlin/New York: Walter de Gruyter, 1987.

Dormeyer, Detlev, and Frankemölle, Hubert. "Evangelium als literarische Gattung und als theologischer Begriff. Tendenzen und Aufgaben der Evangelienforschung im 20. Jahrhundert, mit einer Untersuchung des Markusevangeliums in seinem Verhältnis zur antiken Biographie." In *Religion (Vorkonstantinisches Christentum: Leben und Umwelt Jesu; Neues Testament [Kanonische Schriften und Apokryphen], Forts),* pp. 1543-1704. ANRW II 25.2. Berlin/New York: Walter de Gruyter, 1984.

Dornseiff, F. "Lukas der Schriftsteller: Mit einem Anhang: Josephus und Tacitus." *ZNW* 35 (1936): 129-155.

———. "Antikes zum Alten Testament." *ZAW* n.s. 15 (1938): 64-85.

Dörrie, Heinrich, and Dörries, Hermann. "Erotapokriseis," in *RAC,* 6: 342-370.

Doty, W. G. "The Concept of Genre in Literary Analysis." In *Society of Biblical Literature 1972 Proceedings,* pp. 413-448. Edited by L. C. McGaughy. Missoula: Society of Biblical Literature, 1972.

Downing, F. Gerald. "Redaction Criticism: Josephus' *Antiquities* and the Synoptic Gospels (II)." *JSNT* 9 (1980): 29-48.

———. "Ethical Pagan Theism and the Speeches in Acts." *NTS* 27 (1981): 544-563.

———. "Common Ground with Paganism in Luke and in Josephus." *NTS* 28 (1982): 546-559.

Drews, Robert. "Diodorus and His Sources." *American Journal of Philology* 83 (1962): 383-392.

———. "Ephorus and History Written κατὰ γένος." *American Journal of Philology* 84 (1963): 244-255.

———. *The Greek Accounts of Eastern History.* Washington: Center for Hellenic Studies, 1973.

———. "The Babylonian Chronicles and Berossus." *Iraq* 37 (1975): 39-55.

———. "Ephorus' κατὰ γένος History Revisited." *Hermes* 104 (1976): 497-498.

Driver, G.R. *The Judean Scrolls: The Problem and a Solution.* New York: Schocken Books, 1965.

Droge, Arthur J. "The Interpretation of the History of Culture in Hellenistic-Jewish Historiography." In *Society of Biblical Literature 1984 Seminar Papers*, pp. 135-159. Edited by Kent Richards. Chico, California: Scholars Press, 1984.
——. *Homer or Moses?: Early Christian Interpretations of the History of Culture*. HUT 26. Tübingen: J. C. B. Mohr (Paul Siebeck), 1989.
Drury, John. *Tradition and Design in Luke's Gospel: A Study in Early Christian Historiography*. London: Darton, Longman & Todd, 1976.
Dubrow, Heather. *Genre*. New York/London: Methuen, 1982.
Duncan, George S. *St. Paul's Ephesian Ministry: A Reconstruction With Special Reference to the Ephesian Origin of the Imprisonment Epistles*, New York: Charles Scribner's Sons, 1930.
Dupont, Jacques. *The Sources of the Acts*. Translated by Kathleen Pond. New York: Herder and Herder, 1964.
——. *Études sur les Actes des Apôtres*. Lectio Divina 45. Paris: Cerf, 1967.
——. "La Question du Plan des Actes des Apôtres à la Lumière d'un Texte de Lucien de Samosate." *NovT* 21 (1979): 220-231.

Earl, Donald. "Prologue-form in Ancient Historiography." In *Von den Anfängen Roms bis zum Ausgang der Republik*, pp. 842-856. ANRW I 1.2 Berlin/New York: Walter de Gruyter, 1972.
Eddy, Samuel K. *The King is Dead: Studies in Near Eastern Resistance to Hellenism 334-31 B. C.* Lincoln: University of Nebraska Press, 1961.
Ehrenberg, Victor, *Alexander and the Greeks*. Translated by Ruth Fraenkel von Velsen. Oxford: B. Blackwell, 1938.
Elliott, John H. *A Home for the Homeless: A Sociological Exegesis of I Peter*. Philadelphia: Fortress Press, 1981.
Ellis, E. Earle. *Eschatology in Luke*. Philadelphia: Fortress Press, 1972.
Esler, Philip Francis. *Community and Gospel in Luke-Acts: the Social and Political Motivations of Lucan Theology*. SNTSMS 57. Cambridge: Cambridge University Press, 1987.

Farmer, Wiliam Reuben. *Maccabees, Zealots, and Josephus: An Inquiry into Jewish Nationalism in the Greco-Roman Period*. New York: Columbia University Press, 1956.
——. *The Synoptic Problem: A Critical Analysis*. New York: The Macmillan Company, 1964.
Feldman, L. H. "Abraham the Greek Philosopher in Josephus." *TAPA* 99 (1968): 143-56.
——. "Hellenizations in Josephus' Portrayal of Man's Decline." In *Religions in Antiquity: Festschrift E. R. Goodenough*, pp. 333-53. Edited by J. Neusner. Studies in the History of Religions 14. Leiden: E. J. Brill, 1968.
——. "Hellenizations in Josephus' Version of Esther (Ant. Jud. 11.185-295)." *TAPA* 101 (1970): 143-70.
——. "Josephus as an Apologist to the Greco-Roman World: His Portrait of Solomon." In *Aspects of Religious Propaganda in Judaism and Early Christianity*, pp. 69-98. Edited by Elisabeth Schüssler Fiorenza. University of Notre Dame Center for the Study of Judaism and Christiantiy in Antiquity 2. Notre Dame: University of Notre Dame Press, 1976.
——. "Josephus' Portrait of Saul." *HUCA* 53 (1982): 45-99.
——. *Josephus and Modern Scholarship (1957-1980)*. Berlin/New York: Walter de Gruyter, 1984.
——. "Flavius Josephus Revisited: the Man, His Writings, and His Significance." In *Religion (Hellenistisches Judentums in römischer Zeit: Philon und*

Josephus), pp. 763-862. ANRW II 21.2 Berlin/New York: Walter de Gruyter, 1984.

——. "Josephus as a Biblical Interpreter: The *'Aqedah.*" *JQR* 75 (1985): 212-252.

——. "The Omnipresence of the God-Fearers." *BAR* 12 (1986): 58-63.

——. "Hellenizations in Josephus' *Jewish Antiquities*: The Portrait of Abraham." In *Josephus, Judaism and Christiantiy*, pp. 133-153. Edited by Louis H. Feldman and Gahei Hata. Detroit: Wayne State University Press, 1987.

——. "Josephus' Version of Samson." *JSJ* 19 (1988): 171-214.

——. "Prophets and Prophecy in Josephus." In *Society of Biblical Literature 1988 Seminar Papers*, pp. 424-441. Edited by David J. Lull. Atlanta: Scholars Press, 1988.

Feldman, Louis H. and Hata, Gahei, eds. *Josephus, Judaism, and Christianity*. Detroit: Wayne State University Press, 1987.

Finegan, Jack. "The Original Form of the Pauline Collection." *HTR* 49 (1956): 85-103.

Fischer, J. B. "The Name *Despotes* in Josephus." *JQR* 49 (1958): 132-138.

Fischer, Ulrich. *Eschatologie und Jenseitserwartung im hellenistischen Diasporajudentum* BZNW 44. Berlin/New York: Walter de Gruyter, 1978.

Fitzmyer, Joseph A. "The Priority of Mark and the 'Q' Source in Luke." In *Jesus and Man's Hope*, 1: 131-170. Perspective Books. Pittsburgh: Pittsburgh Theological Seminary, 1970; reprinted in *To Advance the Gospel: New Testament Studies*, pp. 3-40. New York: Crossroad, 1981.

——. *Luke the Theologian: Aspects of His Teaching*. New York/Mahweh: Paulist Press, 1989.

Flender, H. *Luke the Theologian of Redemptive History*. Translated by R. Fuller and I. Fuller. Philadelphia: Fortress Press, 1967.

Foakes Jackson, F. J. *Josephus and the Jews: The Religion and History of the Jews as Explained by Flavius Josephus*. 1930; reprint ed., Grand Rapids: Baker Book House, 1977.

Fornara, Charles W. *Herodotus: An Interpretative Essay*. Oxford: Clarendon Press, 1971.

——. *The Nature of History in Ancient Greece and Rome*. Berkeley/Los Angeles/London: University of California Press, 1983.

Fox, Robert Lane. *Alexander the Great*. London: Allen Lane, 1973.

Franklin, Eric. *Christ the Lord: A Study in the Purpose and Theology of Luke-Acts*. Philadelphia: Westminster Press, 1975.

Franxman, Thomas W. *Genesis and the Jewish Antiquities of Flavius Josephus*. Biblica et Orientalia 35. Rome: Biblical Institute Press, 1979.

Fraser, P. M. *Ptolemaic Alexandria*. 3 vols. Oxford: The Clarendon Press, 1972.

Freudenthal, J. *Alexander Polyhistor und die von ihm erhaltenen Reste jüdischer und samaritanischer Geschichtswerke*. Hellenistische Studien, Heft 1 & 2. Breslau: H. Skutsch, 1875.

Friedländer, M. "La Propagande Religieuse des Juifs Grecs avant l'ère Chrétienne," *REJ* 39 (1895): 161-181.

von Fritz, Kurt. "Herodotus and the Growth of Greek Historiography." *TAPA* 67 (1936): 315-340.

——. "Die Bedeutung des Aristoteles für die Geschichtsschreibung." In *Histoire et Historiens dans l'Antiquité*, pp. 83-145. Entretiens sur l'Antiquité Classique 4. Genève: Vandoeuvres, 1956.

——. *Die Griechische Geschichtsschreibung*. Bd. 1: *Von den Anfängen bis Thukydides*. Berlin: Walter de Gruyter & Co., 1967.

Frye, Northrop. *Anatomy of Criticism: Four Essays*. Princeton: Princeton University Press, 1957.

Gabba, Emilio. "True History and False History in Classical Antiquity." *JRS* 71 (1981): 50-62.
———. "Greek Knowledge of Jews up to Hecataeus of Abdera." *Protocol of the Colloquy of the Center for Hermeneutical Studies* 40. Responses by Erich S. Gruen, John W. Leopold, and Kenneth Sacks. Berkeley: The Center for Hermeneutical Studies, 1981.
Gager, John G. "Pseudo-Hecataeus Again." *ZNW* 60 (1969): 130-139.
———. *Moses in Greco-Roman Paganism.* SBLMS 16. Nashville/New York: Abingdon Press, 1972.
———. *The Origins of Anti-Semitism: Attitudes Toward Judaism in Pagan and Christian Antiquity.* New York/Oxford: Oxford University Press, 1983.
———. "Jews, Gentiles, and Synagogues in the Book of Acts." *HTR* 79 (1986): 91-99.
Gardiner, Sir Alan. *Egypt of the Pharaohs.* London/Oxford/New York: Oxford University Press, 1961.
Gärtner, Hans. "Symposium-Literatur," in *KP*, 5: 450-451.
———. "Synkellos," in *KP*, 5: 456.
Gasque, W. Ward. *A History of the Criticsm of the Acts of the Apostles.* Grand Rapids: Wm. B. Eerdmans Publishing Co., 1975.
———. "A Fruitful Field: Recent Study of the Acts of the Apostles." *Interpretation* 42 (1988): 117-131.
———. "Recent Commentaries on the Acts of the Apostles." *Themelios* 14 (1988): 21-23.
Gaster, Moses. *The Samaritans: Their History, Doctrines and Literature.* London: Oxford University Press, 1925.
Gauger, Jörg-Dieter. "Zitate in der jüdischen Apologetik und die Authentizität der Hekataios-Passagen bei Flavius Josephus und im Ps. Aristeas-Brief." *JSJ* 13 (1982): 6-46.
Gelzer, Heinrich. *Sextus Julius Africanus und die byzantinische Chronographie* 2 vols. Leipzig, 1898; reprint ed., New York: Burt Franklin, n.d.
Gentili, Bruno and Cerri, Giovanni. *History and Biography in Ancient Thought.* London Studies in Classical Philology 20. Amsterdam: J. C. Gieben, 1988.
Georgi, Dieter. *The Opponents of Paul in Second Corinthians.* Philadelphia: Fortress Press, 1986.
Gerhart, Mary. "Generic studies; Their Renewed Importance in Religious and Literary Interpretation." *JAAR* 45 (1977): 309-325.
———. "Generic Competence in Biblical Hermeneutics." *Semeia* 43 (1988): 29-44.
Giblet, J. "Eupolème et l' Historiographie du Judaïsme Hellénistique." ETL 39 (1963): 539-554.
Ginzburg, Louis. "Artapanus," in *The Jewish Encyclopedia*, 2: 145.
Gisinger, F. "Periplus," in *RE*, 19: 841-850.
Goldenberg, David. "Josephus Flavius or Joseph ben Mattithiah." *JQR* 70 (1979): 178-182.
Goldstein, Jonathan. *I Maccabees.* AB 41. Garden City, New York: Doubleday & Company, Inc., 1976.
———. *II Maccabees.* AB 41A. Garden City, New York: Doubleday & Company, Inc., 1983.
Gomme, A. W.; Andrewes A.; and Dover, K. J. *A Historical Commentary on Thucydides.* 5 vols. Oxford: The Clarendon Press, 1945-1981.
Goodenough, Erwin R. "The Political Philosophy of Hellenistic Kingship." *Yale Classical Studies* 1 (1929): 53-102.
Grant, Michael. *The Jews in the Roman World.* [n.pl.]: Dorset Press, 1984.
Gray, G. Buchanan. "The Foundation and Extension of the Persian Empire." In

The Persian Empire and the West, pp. 1-25. Edited by J. B. Bury, S. A. Cook, and F. E. Adcock. CAH 4. Cambridge: University Press, 1969.

Gruen, Erich S. *The Hellenistic World and the Coming of Rome.* 2 vols. Berkeley/Los Angeles/London: University of California Press, 1984.

Guelich, Robert. "The Gospel Genre." In *Das Evangelium und die Evangelien: Vorträge vom Tübinger Symposium 1982*, pp. 183-219. Edited by Peter Stuhlmacher. Tübingen: J. C. B. Mohr (Paul Siebeck), 1983.

Gundry, Robert H. "Recent Investigations into the Literary Genre 'Gospel.'" In *New Dimensions in New Testament Study*, pp. 97-114. Edited by Richard N. Longenecker and Merrill C. Tenney. Grand Rapids: Zondervan Publishing House, 1974.

———. *Matthew: A Commentary on His Literary and Theological Art.* Grand Rapids: Wm. B. Eerdmans Publishing Co., 1982.

Guthrie, W. K. C. *The Greeks and their Gods.* Boston: Beacon Press, 1950.

Gutschmid, A. *Kleine Schriften*, 5 vols., ed. by F. Rühl. Leipzig: B.G. Teubner, 1888-1894.

Güttgemanns, E. "In welchem Sinne ist Lukas 'Historiker'? Die Beziehungen von Luk 1, 1-4 und Papias zur antiken Rhetorik." *LingBib* 54 (1983): 9-26.

Hadas, Moses. *The Third and Fourth Book of Maccabees.* JAL. New York: Harper, 1953.

———. *Hellenistic Culture: Fusion and Diffusion.* New York/London: W. W. Norton & Co., 1959.

Hadas, Moses, and Smith, Morton. *Heroes and Gods: Spiritual Biographies in Antiquity.* Religious Perspectives 13. New York: Harper & Row, Publishers, 1965.

Haenchen, Ernst. "Das 'Wir' in der Apostelgeschichte und das Itinerar." *ZTK* 58 (1961): 329-366.

———. "The Book of Acts as Source Material for the History of Early Christiantiy." In *Studies in Luke-Acts*, pp. 258-278. Edited by Leander E. Keck and J. Louis Martyn. Reprint ed., Philadelphia: Fortress Press, 1980.

Hägg, Thomas. *The Novel in Antiquity.* Oxford: Basil Blackwell, 1983.

Hahn, Ferdinand. "Der gegenwärtige Stand der Erforschung der Apostelgeschichte: Kommentare und Aufsatzbände 1980-1985." *TRev* 82 (1986): 178-190.

Halpern, Baruch. *The First Historians: The Hebrew Bible and History.* San Francisco: Harper & Row, Publishers, 1988.

Hamilton, J. R. *Plutarch Alexander: A Commentary.* Oxford: The Clarendon Press, 1969.

———. *Alexander the Great.* London: Hutchinson University Library, 1973.

Harnack, Adolf. *Luke the Physician: The Author of the Third Gospel and the Acts of the Apostles.* Translated by J. R. Wilkinson. 2nd ed. Crown Theological Library. New York: G. P. Putnam's Sons, 1909.

Harrell, David Edwin, Jr. *A Social History of the Disciples of Christ.* Vol. 1: *Quest for a Christian America.* Nashville: The Disciples of Christ Historical Society, 1966.

———. *A Social History of the Disciples of Christ.* Vol. 2: *Social Sources of Division in the Disciples of Christ 1865-1900.* Atlanta: Publishing Systems, Inc., 1973.

Hartog, Francois. *The Mirror of Herodotus: The Representation of Other in the Writing of History.* Translated by Janet Lloyd. The New Historicism: Studies in Cultural Poetics 5. Berkeley/Los Angeles/London: University of California Press, 1988.

Hata, Gohei. "*The Jewish War* of Josephus: A Semantic and Historiographic Study." Ph.D. dissertaion, Dropsie University, 1975.

———. "Is the Greek Version of Josephus' *Jewish War* a Translation or a Rewriting of the First Version?" *JQR* 66 (1975-76): 89-108.

——. "The Story of Moses Interpreted within the Context of Anti-Semitism." In *Josephus, Judaism, and Christianity*, pp. 180-197. Edited by Louis H. Feldman and Gohei Hata. Detroit: Wayne State University Press, 1987.

Heidel, Alexander. *The Gilgamesh Epic and Old Testament Parallels*. 2nd ed. Chicago: University of Chicago Press, 1949.

——. *The Babylonian Genesis: The Story of the Creation*. 2nd ed. Chicago: The University of Chicago Press, 1951.

Heinemann, I. "Josephus' Method in the Presentation of Jewish Antiquities." *Zion* 5 (1939-1940): 180-203.

——. "Moses," in *RE*, 16: 359-375.

Helck, W. "Die Ägypter und die Fremden." *Saeculum* 15 (1964): 103-114.

——. "Manethon," in *KP*, 3: 952-953.

Hellholm, David. "The Problem of Apocalyptic Genre and the Apocalypse of John." In *Society of Biblical Literature 1982 Seminar Papers*, pp. 157-198. Edited by Ken Harold Richards. Chico, California: Scholars Press 1982; reprinted in *Early Christian Apocalypticism: Genre and Social Setting*, pp. 13-64. Semeia 36. Decatur, Georgia: Scholars Press, 1986.

Hemer, Colin J. "Luke the Historian." *BJRL* 60 (1977-1978): 28-51.

——: *The Book of Acts in the Setting of Hellenistic History*. Edited by Conrad H. Gempf. WUNT 49. Tübingen: J.C.B. Mohr (Paul Siebeck), 1989.

Hengel, Martin. "Anonymität, Pseudepigraphie und 'Literarische Fälschung' in der jüdisch-hellenistischen Literatur." In *Pseudepigrapha I: Pseudopythagorica-Lettres de Platon-Littérature pseudépigraphique juive*, pp. 229-329. Entretiens sur l'Antiquité Classique 18. Genève: Vandoeuvres, 1972.

——. *Judaism and Hellenism: Studies in their Encounter in Palestine during the Early Hellenistic Period*. 2 vols. Translated by John Bowden. Philadelphia: Fortress Press, 1974.

——. *Acts and the History of Earliest Christianity*. Translated by John Bowden. Philadelphia: Fortress Press, 1979.

——. *Jews, Greeks and Barbarians: Aspects of the Hellenization of Judaism in the pre-Christian Period*. Translated by John Bowden. Philadelphia: Fortress Press, 1980.

——. "Luke the Historian and the Geography of Palestine in the Acts of the Apostles." In *Between Jesus and Paul*, pp. 97-128. Translated by John Bowden. Philadelphia: Fortress Press, 1983.

Hernadi, Paul. *Beyond Genre: New Directions in Literary Classification*. Ithaca/London: Cornell University Press, 1972.

Heumann, C.A. "Dissertation de Theophilo, cui Lucas Historiam Sacram Inscripsit." *Bibliotheca Historico-Philogico-Theologica*, Classis 4 (1721): 483-505.

Hill, H. "Dionysius of Halicarnassus and the Origins of Rome." *JRS* 51 (1961): 88-93.

Hirsch, E. D., Jr. *Validity in Interpretation*. New Haven/London: Yale University Press, 1967.

Hobart, William Kirk. *The Medical Language of St. Luke: A Proof from Internal Evidence that 'the Gospel According to St. Luke' and 'the Acts of the Apostles' were Written by the Same Person, and that the Writer was a Medical Man*. Dublin University Press Series. Dublin: Hodges, Figgis, & Co., 1882.

Hock, Ronald F. "Lazarus and Micyllus: Greco-Roman Backgrounds to Luke 16: 19-31." *JBL* 106 (1987): 447-463.

Holladay, Carl R. *"Theios Aner" in Hellenistic-Judaism: A Critique of the Use of This Category in New Testament Christology*. SBLDS 40. Missoula, Montana: Scholars Press, 1977.

——. "Demetrius the Chronographer as Historian and Apologist." In *Christian*

Teaching: Studies in Honor of Lemoine G. Lewis, pp. 117-129. Abilene, Texas: Abilene Christian University, 1981.

Hölscher, Gustav. *Die Quellen des Josephus für die Zeit vom Exil bis zum jüdischen Kriege.* Leipzig, 1904. Summary in Heinz Schreckenberg, *Bibliographie zu Flavius Josephus.* ALGHJ 1. Leiden: E. J. Brill, 1968. Pp. 148-49.

———. "Josephus," in *RE*, 9: 1934-2000.

Holzberg, Niklas, *Der antike Roman: Eine Einführung.* München: Artemis, 1986.

Hornblower, Jane. *Hieronymus of Cardia.* Oxford Classical and Philosophical Monographs. Oxford: Oxford University Press, 1981.

Houlden, J. L. "The Purpose of Luke." *JSNT* 21 (1984): 53-65.

How, W. W. and Wells, J. *A Commentary on Herodotus.* 2 vols. Oxford: The Clarendon Press, 1928.

Hubbard, Benjamin J. "Luke, Josephus and Rome: A Comparative Approach to the Lukan *Sitz im Leben.*" In *Society of Biblical Literature 1979 Seminar Papers*, 1: 59-68. Edited by Paul Achtemeier. Missoula, Montana: Scholars Press, 1979.

Immerwahr, Henry R. *Form and Thought in Herodotus.* Philological Monographs 23. Cleveland: The American Philogocial Association, 1966.

Jacobsen, Thorkild. *The Sumerian King List.* The Oriental Institute of the University of Chicago Assyriological Studies 11. Chicago: University of Chicago Press, 1939.

Jacoby, Felix. "Über die Entwicklung der griechischen Historiographie. . ." *Klio* 9 (1909): 80-123.

———. "Eupolemos," in *RE*, 6: 1227-1229.

———. "Hekataios aus Abdera," in *RE*, 7: 2750-2769.

———. "Hekataios von Milet," in *RE*, 7: 2667-2750.

———. "Herodotos," in *RESup*, 2: 205-520.

———. "Hieronymous," in *RE*, 8: 1540-1560.

———. *Griechische Historiker.* Stuttgart: Alfred Druckenmüller, 1956.

Jaeger, Werner. *Diokles von Karystos: Die griechische Medizin und die Schule des Aristoteles.* Berlin: Walter de Gruyter & Co., 1938.

———. "Greeks and Jews: The First Greek Records of Jewish Religion and Civilization." *JR* 18 (1938): 127-143.

Jellicoe, S. *The Septuagint and Modern Study.* Oxford: Oxford University Press, 1968.

Jeremias, Joachim. *Jerusalem in the Time of Jesus: An Investigation into Economic and Social Conditions during the New Testament Period.* Translated by F. H. and C. H. Cave. Philadelphia: Fortress Press, 1969.

———. *Die Sprache des Lukasevangeliums: Redaktion und Tradition im Nicht-Markusstoff des dritten Evangeliums.* Kritisch-exegetischer Kommentar über das Neue Testament. Göttingen: Vandenhoeck & Ruprecht, 1980.

Jervell, Jacob. *A New Look at Luke-Acts. Luke and the People of God.* Minneapolis, MN: Augsburg, 1972.

———. *The Unknown Paul: Essays on Luke-Acts and Early Christian History.* Minneapolis, MN: Augsburg, 1984.

———. "The Church of Jews and Godfearers." In *Luke-Acts and the Jewish People*, pp. 11-20. Edited by Joseph B. Tyson. Minneapolis: Augsburg Publishing House, 1988.

Johnson, Marshall. *The Purpose of the Biblical Genealogies: With Special Reference to the Setting of the Genealogies of Jesus.* 2nd ed. SNTSMS 8. Cambridge: Cambridge University Press, 1988.

de Jonge, Marianus. "Josephus und die Zukunftserwartungen seines Volkes." In *Josephus-Studien: Untersuchungen zu Josephus, dem antiken Judentum und dem Neuen*

Testament, pp. 205-219. Edited by Otto Betz, Klaus Haacker, and Martin Hengel. Göttingen: Vandenhoeck & Ruprecht, 1974.

Karris, Robert. "Missionary Communities: A New Paradigm for the Study of Luke-Acts." *CBQ* 41 (1979): 80-07.

Käsemann, Ernst. "Ministry and Community in the New Testament." In *Essays on New Testament Themes*, pp. 63-94. Translated by W. J. Montague. Philadelphia: Fortress Press, 1982.

Kasher, Aryeh. *The Jews in Hellenistic and Roman Egypt: The Struggle for Equal Rights*. Tübingen: J. C. B. Mohr (Paul Siebeck), 1985.

Keck, Leander E., and Martyn, J. Louis, gen. eds. *Studies in Luke-Acts*. Philadelphia: Fortress Press, 1966.

Kee, Howard C. "Aretalogy and Gospel." *JBL* 92 (1973): 402-422.

———. *Community of the New Age: Studies in Mark's Gospel*. Philadelphia: The Westminster Press, 1977.

Kennedy, George A. *The Art of Persuasion in Greece*. Princeton: Princeton University Press, 1963.

———. *The Art of Rhetoric in the Roman World (300 B.C.-A.D. 300)*. Princeton: Princeton University Press, 1972.

Kingdon, H. Paul. "The Origins of the Zealots." *NTS* 19 (1972-73): 74-81.

Klotz, Alfred. "Zu den Quellen der Archaiologia des Dionysios von Halikarnassos." *Rheinisches Museum für Philologie* 87 (1938): 32-50.

Knox, John. "Acts and the Pauline Letter Corpus." In *Studies in Luke-Acts*, pp. 279-287. Edited by Leander E. Keck and J. Louis Martyn; reprint ed., Philadelphia: Fortress Press, 1966.

Koester, Helmut. "From the Kerygma-Gospel to Written Gospels." *NTS* 35 (1989): 361-381.

———. *Ancient Christian Gospels: Their History and Development*. London: SCM Press Ltd/Philadelphia: Trinity Press International, 1990.

Komorózy, G. "Berosos and the Mesopotamian Literature." *Acta Antiqua* 21 (1973): 125-152.

Körtner, Ulrich H.J. *Papias von Hierapolis: Ein Beitrag zur Geschichte des frühen Christentums*. FRLANT 133. Göttingen: Vandenhoeck & Ruprecht, 1983.

Kötting, B. "Euergetes," in *RAC*, 6: 848-860.

Kraabel, A. T. "The Disappearance of the 'God-Fearers.'" *Numen* 28 (1981): 113-126.

———. "Greeks, Jews, and Lutherans in the Middle Half of Acts." *HTR* 79 (1986): 147-157.

Krauss, S. "Eupolemus," in *The Jewish Encyclopedia*, 5: 269.

Kremer, J., ed. *Les Actes des Apôtres*. BETL XLVIII. Paris-Gemblous and Louvain: Duculot and Louvain University Press, 1979.

Krenkel, M. *Josephus und Lukas. Der schriftstellerische Einfluß des jüdischen Geschichtschreibers auf den christlichen nachgewiesen*. Leipzig: Haessel, 1894.

Kuhlmey, C. G. A. *Eupolemi Fragmenta prolegomenis et commentario instructa*. Berlin, 1840.

Kuhrt, Amélie. "Berossus' *Babyloniaka* and Seleucid Rule in Babylonia." In *Hellenism in the East: The interaction of Greek and non-Greek civilizations from Syria to Central Asia after Alexander*, pp. 32-56. Edited by Amélie Kuhrt and Susan Sherwin-White. Berkeley/Los Angeles: University of California Press, 1987.

Kümmel, Werner Georg. *Introduction to the New Testament*. Revised ed. Translated by Howard Clark Kee. Nashville: Abingdon Press, 1975.

Kurz, William S. "Luke 22: 14-38 and Greco-Roman and Biblical Farwell Addresses." *JBL* 104 (1985): 251-268.

Kürzinger, Josef. "Lk. 1, 3: . . . ἀκριβῶς καθεξῆς σοι γράψαι." *BZ* 18 (1974): 249-255.

———. *Papias von Hierapolis und die Evangelien des Neuen Testaments: Gesammelte Aufsatze, Neuausgabe und Übersetzung der Fragmente, Kommentierte Bibliographie*. Regensburg: Friedrich Pustet, 1983.

Ladenthin, Volker. "Betrachtungen zur antiken Geschichtsschreibung." *Geschichte in Wissenschaft* 36 (1985): 737-760.

Ladouceur, David Joseph. "Studies in the Language and Historiography of Flavius Josephus." Ph.D. dissertation, Brown University, 1976.

———. "The Language of Josephus." *JSJ* 14 (1983): 18-38.

Lambert, W. G. "Ancestors, Authors, and Canonicity." *Journal of Cuneiform Studies* 11 (1957): 1-14.

———. "Berossus and Babylonian Eschatology." *Iraq* 38 (1976): 171-173.

Lambert, W. G. and Millard, A. R. *Atra-Hasis: The Babylonian Story of the Flood*. Oxford: The Clarendon Press, 1969.

Laquer, Richard. *Der jüdische Historiker Flavius Josephus*. Giessen: Munchow, 1920; reprint ed., Darmstadt, 1970.

———. "Manethon," in *RE*, 14: 1060-1101.

———. "Synkellos," in *RE*, II 4: 1388-1410.

———. "Timaios," in *RE*, II 6: 1076-1203.

Lasserre, F. "Periplus," in *KP*, 4: 640-641.

LaVerdiere, Eugene A., and Thompson, Wilkim G. "New Testament Communities in Transition: A Study of Matthew and Luke." *TS* 37 (1976): 567-597.

Leon, Harry J. *The Jews of Ancient Rome*. Philadelphia: The Jewish Publication Society of America, 1960.

Lesky, Albin. *A History of Greek Literature*. Translated by James Willis and Cornelis de Heer. New York: Thomas Y. Crowell Co., 1966.

Levy, Isidore. "Moïse en Éthiope." *REJ* 53 (1907): 201-211.

———. *La Légende de Pythagore de Grèce en Palestin*. Paris: Bibliothèque de l'École des Hautes Études, 1972.

Lewy, Hans. "Hekataios von Abdera περὶ Ἰουδαίων." *ZNW* 31 (1932): 117-132.

Lieberman, Saul. *Hellenism in Jewish Palestine: Studies in the Literary Transmission, Beliefs and Manners of Palestine in the I Century B.C.E.-IV Century C.E.* Texts and Studies of the Jewish Theological Seminary of America 18. New York: The Jewish Theological Seminary of America, 1950.

Lindner, Helgo. *Die Geschichtsauffassung des Flavius Josephus im Bellum Judaicum: Gleichzeitig ein Beitrag zur Quellenfrage*. AGJU 12. Leiden: E. J. Brill, 1972.

Lloyd, Alan B. *Herodotus: Book II*. 3 vols. Leiden: E. J. Brill, 1975-1988.

Long, A. A. *Hellenistic Philosophy: Stoics, Epicureans, Sceptics*. New York: Charles Scribner's Sons, 1974.

Lowy, S. *The Principles of Samaritan Bible Exegesis*. SPB 28. Leiden: E. J. Brill, 1977.

Luce, T. J. "Ancient Views on the Causes of Bias in Historical Writing." *Classical Philology* 84 (1989): 16-31.

Luedemann, Gerd. *Paul, Apostle to the Gentiles: Studies in Chronology*. Translated by F. Stanley Jones. Philadelphia: Fortress Press, 1984.

———. *Das frühe Christentum nach den Traditionen der Apostelgeschichte: Ein Kommentar*. Göttingen: Vandenhoeck & Ruprecht, 1987.

Macan, R. W. "Herodotus and Thucydides." In *Athens*, pp. 398-419. Edited by J. B. Bury, S. A. Cook, and F. E. Adcock. CAH 5. Cambridge: University Press, 1969.

Macdonald, John. *The Theology of the Samaritans*. London: SCM Press Ltd., 1964.

MacLennan, Robert S. and Kraabel, A. Thomas. "The God-Fearers—A Literary and Theological Invention." *BAR* 12 (1986): 46-53, 64.

Maddox, Robert. *The Purpose of Luke-Acts.* Edited by John Riches. Edinburgh: T. & T. Clark, 1982.

Majumdar, R. C. *The Classical Accounts of India.* Calcutta: K. L. Mukhopadhyay, 1960.

Malherbe, Abraham. "'Not in a Corner:' Early Christian Apologetic in Acts 26:26." *Second Century* 5 (1985-1986): 193-210.

Malitz, Jurgen. *Die Historien des Poseidonios.* München: Beck, 1983.

Manson, T. W. "The Life of Jesus: A Survey of the Available Material. (3) The Work of St. Luke." *BJRL* 28 (1944): 382-403.

Marmorstein, A. "A Greek Lyric and a Hebrew Prophet." *JQR* 37 (1946-47): 169-173.

Marshall, I. Howard. *Luke: Historian and Theologian.* Grand Rapids: Zondervan Publishing House, 1970.

Martin, J. "Deipnon Literatur," in *RAC,* 3: 658-666.

Mason, Steve. *Flavius Josephus on the Pharisees: A Composition-Critical Study.* SPB 39. Leiden: E.J. Brill, 1991.

Matthews, Isaac George. "The Jewish Apologetic to the Grecian World in the Apocryphal and Pseudepigraphal Literature." Ph.D. dissertation, The University of Chicago, 1914.

Mattill, A. J., Jr. "The Purpose of Acts: Schneckenburger Reconsidered." In *Apostolic History and the Gospel: Essays presented to F. F. Bruce,* pp. 108-122. Edited by W. Ward Gasque and Ralph Martin. Grand Rapids: Eerdmans, 1970.

———. "The Good Samaritan and the Purpose of Luke-Acts: Halévy Reconsidered." *Encounter* 33 (1972): 359-376.

———. "Näherwartung, Fernerwartung, and the Purpose of Luke-Acts: Weymouth Reconsidered." *CBQ* 34 .(1972): 276-293.

———. "The Jesus-Paul Parallels and the Purpose of Luke-Acts: H. H. Evans Reconsidered." *NovT* 17 (1975): 15-46.

———. "The Value of Acts as a Source for the Study of Paul." In *Perspectives on Luke-Acts,* pp. 76-98. Edited by Charles H. Talbert. Special Studies Series 5. Danville, VA: Association of Baptist Professors of Religion, 1978.

Mattill, A. J. and Mattill, M. B. *A Classified Bibliography of Literature on the Acts of the Apostles.* NTTS 7. Leiden: E. J. Brill, 1966.

Mayer, Reinhold and Möller, Christa. "Josephus—Politiker und Prophet." In *Josephus-Studien: Untersuchungen zu Josephus, dem antiken Judentum und dem Neuen Testament,* pp. 271-284. Edited by Otto Betz, Klaus Haacker, and Martin Hengel. Göttingen: Vandenhoeck & Ruprecht, 1974.

Meeks, Wayne A. "Moses as God and King." In *Religions in Antiquity Festschrift E. R. Goodenough,* pp. 333-353. Edited by Jacob Neusner. Studies in the History of Religions 14. Leiden: E. J. Brill, 1968.

de Meeûs, X. "Composition de Luc., XIV et Genre Symposiaque." *ETL* 37 (1961): 847-870.

Meier, Christian. "Historical Answers to Historical Questions: The Origins of History in Ancient Greece." *Arethusa* 20 (1987): 41-57.

Mendels, Doron. "Hecataeus of Abdera and a Jewish 'Patrios Politeia' of the Persian Period (Diodorus Siculus XL, 3)." *ZAW* (1983): 96-110.

———. "'Creative History' in the Hellenistic Near East in the Third and Second Centuries BCE: The Jewish Case." *JSP* 2 (1988): 13-20.

———. "The Polemical Character of Manetho's Aegyptiaca." In *Purposes of History: Studies in Greek Historiography from the 4th to the 2nd Centuries B. C. (Proceedings of the International Colloquium Leuven, 24-26 May 1988),* pp. 91-110. Ed. H. Verdin, G. Schepens, E. de Keyser. Lovanii, 1990.

Merentites, K. I. 'Ο 'Ιουδαῖος Λόγιος 'Αρταπανὸς καὶ τὸ "Εργον Αὐτοῦ. Athens, 1961.

Meyer, Ben F. *Self-Definition in Early Christianity*. Protocol of the Colloquy of the Center for Hermeneutical Studies in Hellenistic and Modern Culture 37. Responses by Johyn T. Noonan, Mary Ann Donovan, and Ted Peters. Berkeley: The Center for Hermeneutical Studies in Hellenistic and Modern Culture, 1980.

Migliario, Elvira. "Per l'Interpretazione dell 'Autobiografia di Flavio Giuseppe." *Athenaeum* 59 (1981): 92-137.

Millar, Fergus. "The Background to the Maccabean Revolution: Reflections on Martin Hengel's 'Judaism and Hellenism.'" *JJS* 29 (1978): 1-21.

Mills, W.E. *A Bibliography of the Periodical Literature on the Acts of the Apostles 1962-1984*. NovTSup 58. Leiden: E.J. Brill, 1986.

Milns, R. D. *Alexander the Great*. London: Robert Hale, 1968.

Mitten, C. Leslie. *The Formation of the Pauline Corpus of Letters*. London: The Epworth Press, 1955.

Moehring, Horst R. "Novelistic Elements in the Writings of Jospehus." Ph.D. dissertation, University of Chicago, 1957.

———. "The Census in Luke as an Apologetic Device." In *Studies in New Testament and Early Christian Literature: Essays in Honor of Allen P. Wikgren*, pp. 144-160. Edited by David E. Aune. NovTSup 33. Leiden: E. J. Brill, 1972.

———. "The Acta Pro Judaeis in the Antiquities of Flavius Josephos." In *Christianity, Judaism and other Greco-Roman Cults: Studies for Morton Smith at Sixty*, pp. 124-158. Edited by Jacob Neusner. SJLA 12. Leiden: E. J. Brill, 1975.

———. "Joseph ben Matthia and Flavius Josephus: the Jewish Prophet and Roman Historian," in *Religion (Hellenistisches Judentums in römischer Zeit: Philon und Josephus)*, pp. 864-944. ANRW II 21.2 Berlin/New York: Walter de Gruyter, 1984.

Moessner, David P. "Luke 9: 1-50: Luke's Preview of the Journey of the Prophet Like Moses of Deuteronomy." *JBL* 102 (1983): 575-605.

———. "And Once Again, What Sort of 'Essence?:' A Response to Charles Talbert." *Semeia* 43 (1988): 75-84.

———. *Lord at the Banquet: The Literary and Theological Significance of the Lukan Travel Narrative*. Minneapolis: Fortress Press, 1989.

Momigliano, Arnaldo. "Intorno al *Contro Apione*." *Revista di Fillogia e di Istruzione Classica* n.s. 9 (1931): 483-503.

———. *Studies in Historiography*. London: Weidenfeld and Nicolson, 1966.

———. "The Place of Herodotus in the History of Historiography." *History* 43 (1958): 1-13; reprinted in Arnaldo Momigliano, *Studies in Historiography*, pp. 127-142. London: Weidenfeld and Nicolson, 1966.

———. *The Development of Greek Biography*. Cambridge: Harvard University Press, 1971.

———. *Alien Wisdom: The Limits of Hellenization*. Cambridge: Cambridge University Press, 1975.

———. "Time in Ancient Historiography." In *Essays in Ancient and Modern Historiography*, pp. 179-204. Middletown, Connecticut: Wesleyan University Press, 1977.

———. "Athens in the Third Century B.C. and the Discovery of Rome in the Histories of Timaeus of Taurominium." In *Essays in Ancient and Modern Historiography*, pp. 37-66. Middletown, Conneticut: Wesleyan University Press, 1977.

———. "Eastern Elements in Post-Exilic Jewish, and Greek, Historiography." In *Essays in Ancient and Modern Historiography*, pp. 25-35. Middletown, Connecticut: Wesleyan University Press, 1977.

———. "Greek Historiography." *History and Theory.* 17 (1978): 1-28.

Mommsen, I. "Cornelius Tacitus und Cluvius Rufus." *Hermes* 4 (1870): 295-325.

Montefiore, H. W. "Josephus and the New Testament." *NovT* 4 (1960): 139-160, 307-318.

Montgomery, James Alan. *The Samaritans: The Earliest Jewish Sect (Their History, Theology and Literature).* 1907; reprint ed. with an introduction by Abraham S. Halkin, New York: Ktav Publishing House, Inc., 1968.

Morgenthaler, R. *Die lukanische Geschichtsschreibung als Zeugnis: Gestalt und Gehalt der Kunst des Lukas.* ATANT 14/15. Zürich: Zwingli, 1949.

Moscato, Mary A. "Current Theories Regarding the Audience of Luke-Acts." *Currents in Theology and Mission* 3 (1976): 355-361.

Mosshammer, Alden A. *The "Chronicle" of Eusebius and Greek Chronographic Tradition.* Lewisburg: Bucknell University Press, 1979.

Müller, Klaus Erich. *Geschichte der antiken Ethnographie und ethnologischen Theoriebildung.* Vol I: *Von den Anfängen bis auf die byzantinischen Historiographen.* Studien zur Kulturkunde 29. Wiesbaden: Steiner, 1972.

Murray, Oswyn. "Hecataeus of Abdera and Pharaonic Kingship." *Journal of Egyptian Archaeology* 56 (1970): 141-171.

———. "Herodotus and Hellenistic Culture." *CQ* n.s. 22 (1972): 200-213.

Mussies, Gerard. "The Interpretatio Judaica of Thot-Hermes." In *Studies in Egyptian Religion: Dedicated to Professor Jan Zandee,* pp. 89-120. Edited by M. Heerma van Voss, D.J. Hoens, G. Mussies, D. van der Plas, and H. te Velde. Studies in the History of Religions 43. Leiden: E.J. Brill, 1982.

Mussner, F. "Καθεξῆς im Lukasprolog." In *Jesus und Paulus: Festschrift für W. G. Kümmel zum 70. Geburtstag,* pp. 253-255. Edited by E. Earle Ellis and Erich Graßer. Göttingen: Vandenhoeck & Ruprecht, 1975.

Myres, John L. *Herodotus: Father of History.* Oxford: Clarendon Press, 1953; reprint ed., Chicago: Henry Regnery Company, 1971.

Naveh, J. "The Excavations at Mesad Hashavyahu: Preliminary Report." *IEJ* 12 (1962): 89-99.

Navone, J. "Three Aspects of the Lucan Theology of History." *BTB* 3 (1973): 115-132.

Neusner, Jacob. *A Life of Yohanan Ben Zakkai.* 2nd ed. SPB 6. Leiden: E.J. Brill, 1970.

———. *From Politics to Piety: The Emergence of Pharisaic Judaism.* Englewood Cliffs, New Jersey: Prentice-Hall, Inc., 1973.

Neyrey, Jerome. "The Forensic Defense Speech and Paul's Trial Speeches in Acts 22-26: Form and Function." In *Luke-Acts: New Perspectives from the Society of Biblical Literature Seminar,* pp. 210-224. Edited by Charles H. Talbert. New York: Crossroad, 1984.

Nickelsburg, George W.E. *Jewish Literature Between the Bible and the Mishnah: A Historical and Literary Introduction.* Philadelphia: Fortress Press, 1981.

Nock, Arthur Darby. *Conversion: The Old and the New in Religion from Alexander the Great to Augustine of Hippo,* Oxford: The Clarendon Press, 1933.

———. "The Cult of Heroes." *HTR* 37 (1944): 141-174.

Noth, Martin. *The Deuteronomistic History.* Translated by E. W. Nicholson. JSOT-Sup 15. Sheffield: JSOT Press, 1981.

Oden, R. A. "Philo of Byblos and Hellenistic Historiogrpahy." *PEQ* 110 (1978): 115-26.

Olmstead, A. T. *History of the Persian Empire.* Chicago/London: The University of Chicago Press, 1948.

O'Meara, John J. "Indian Wisdom and Porphyry's Search for a Universal Way." In *Neoplatonism and Indian Thought*, pp. 5-25. Edited by R. Baine Harris. Studies in Neoplatonism: Ancient and Modern 2. Norfolk, Virginia: International Society for Neoplatonic Studies, 1982.

O'Neill, J. C. *The Theology of Acts in its Historical Setting*. 2nd ed. London: S.P.C.K., 1970.

Ormerod, H. A. and Cary, M. "Rome and the East," In *The Roman Republic 133-44 B.C.*, pp. 350-396. Edited by S. A. Cook, F. E. Adcock, and M. P. Charlesworth. CAH 9. Cambridge: Cambridge University Press, 1971.

O'Toole, Robert F. *The Unity of Luke's Theology: An Analysis of Luke-Acts*. Good News Studies 9. Wilmington, DE: Michael Glazier, 1984.

Otzen, Benedikt. "Noch Einmal das Wort *TRKB* auf einem Arad-Ostracon." *VT* 20 (1970): 239-242.

Overbeck, Franz. "Über die Anfänge der partristischen Literatur." *Historiche Zeitschrift* 48 (1882): 417-472; reprint ed., Darmstadt. Wissenschaftliche Buchgesellschaft, 1966.

Paul, André. "Flavius Josephus' 'Antiquities of the Jews:' An Anti-Christian Manifesto." *NTS* 31 (1985): 473-480.

Pearson, Lionel. "Herodotus on the Source of the Danube." *Classical Philology* 29 (1934): 328-37.

———. *The Early Ionian Historians*. Oxford: Clarendon Press, 1939.

———. Review of *Hecataei Milesii Fragmenta*, by G. Nenci. *Classical Review* n.s. 5 (1955): 263-265.

———. "Myth and *Archaeologia* in Italy and Sicily-Timaeus and his Predecessors." *Yale Classical Studies* 24 (1975): 171-195.

———. *The Greek Historians of the West: Timaeus and His Predecessors*. Philological Monographs of the American Philological Association 35. Atlanta: The American Philological Association, 1987.

Pédech, Paul. *La Méthode historique de Polybe*. Paris: Les Belles Lettres, 1964.

Pépin, Jean. "Le 'Challenge' Homère-Moise aux Premiers Siècles Chrétiens." *Revue des Sciences Religieuses*. 29 (1955): 105-122.

Perelman, Chaim. *The Realm of Rhetoric*. Translated by William Kluback. Notre Dame: University of Notre Dame Press, 1982.

Perry, Ben Edwin. *The Ancient Romances: A Literary-Historical Account of Their Origins*. Sather Classical Lectures 37. Berkeley and Los Angeles: University of California Press, 1967.

Pervo, Richard I. *Profit with Delight: The Literary Genre of the Acts of the Apostles*. Philadelphia: Fortress Press, 1987.

Petersen, Hans. "Real and Alleged Literary Projects of Josephus." *American Journal of Philology* 79 (1958): 259-274.

Pfeiffer, Robert H. "Hebrews and Greeks Before Alexander." *JBL* 56 (1937): 91-101.

Pilhofer, Peter. *Presbyteron Kreitton: Der Alterbeweis der jüdischen und christlichen Apologeten und seine Vorgeschichte*. WUNT II/39. Tübingen: J.C.B. Mohr (Paul Siebeck), 1990.

Plümacher, Eckhard. *Lukas als hellenistischer Schriftsteller: Studien zur Apostelgeschichte*. Göttingen: Vandenhoeck & Ruprecht, 1972.

———. "Lukas als griechischer Historiker," in *RESup*, 14: 235-264.

———. "Die Apostelgeschichte als historische Monographie." In *Les Actes des Apôtres: Tradition, rédaction, théologie*, pp. 457-466. Edited by Jacob Kremer. BETL 48. Leuven: University Press, 1977.

———. "Acta-Forschung 1974-1982." *TRu* 48 (1983): 1-56; 49 (1984): 105-169.

Plummer, Reinhard. *The Samaritans*. Iconography of Religions. Leiden: E. J. Brill, 1987.
Pohlenz, Max. *Herodot, der erste Geschichtschreiber des Abendlandes*. Neue Wege zur Antike 2 Series 7-8. Leipzig/Berlin: B. G. Teubner, 1937; reprint ed., Stuttgart: B. G. Teubner, 1961.
Porten, Bezalel. *Archives from Elephantine: The Life of an Ancient Jewish Military Colony*. Berkeley/Los Angeles: University of California Press, 1968.
Praeder, Susan Marie. "Luke-Acts and the Ancient Novel." In *Society of Biblical Literature 1981 Seminar Papers*, pp. 269-292. Edited by Kent Richards. Chico: Scholars Press, 1981.
Press, Gerald A. *The Development of the Idea of History in Antiquity*. McGill-Queen's Studies in the History of Ideas 2. Kingston/Montreal: McGill-Queen's University Press, 1982.
Pritchett, W. Kendrick. *Dionysius of Halicarnassus: ON THUCYDIDES*. Berkeley/Los Angeles: University of California Press, 1975.
Purvis, James D. *The Samaritan Pentateuch and the Origin of the Samaritan Sect*. HSM 2. Cambridge: Harvard University Press, 1968.

von Rad, Gerhard. *Genesis: A Commentary*. Revised ed. Translated by John H. Marks. OTL. Philadelphia: The Westminster Press, 1972.
Radermacher, Ludwig. "Dionysios von Halikarnassos," in *RE*, 5: 934-971.
Radin, Max. "The Pedigree of Josephus." *Classical Philology* 24 (1929): 192-196.
Rajak, Tessa. "Moses in Ethiopia: Legend and Literature." *JJS* 29 (1978): 111-122.
———. "Josephus and the 'Archaeology' of the Jews." *JJS* 33 (1982): 465-477.
———. *Josephus: The Historian and His Society*. Philadelphia: Fortress Press, 1983.
———. "Was There a Roman Charter for the Jews?" *JRS* 74 (1984): 107-123.
Ramsay, W. M. *St. Paul the Traveler and the Roman Citizen*. Reprint ed., Grand Rapids: Baker Book House, 1951.
Rappaport, S. *Agada und Exegese bei Flavius Josephus*. Wien, 1930.
Reardon, B. P. "The Greek Novel." *Phoenix* 23 (1969): 291-309.
Redford, Donald B. *History and Chronology of the Eighteenth Dynasty of Egypt: Seven Studies*. Near and Middle East Series 3. [N.pl.]: University of Toronto Press, 1967.
Reinhardt, Karl. "Hekataios von Abdera und Demokrit." *Hermes* 47 (1912): 492-513.
Rese, Martin. "Das Lukas-Evangelium. Ein Forschungbericht." In *Religion (Vorkonstantinisches Christentum: Leben und Umwelt Jesu; Neues Testament [Kanonische Schriften und Apokryphen]*, Forts), pp. 2258-2328. ANRW II 25.3 Berlin/New York: Walter de Gruyter, 1985.
Rhoads, David M. *Israel in Revolution: 6-74 C.E.: A Political History Based on the Writings of Josephus*. Philadelphia: Fortress Press, 1976.
Rhode, Erwin. *Der griechische Roman und seine Vorläufer*. 2nd ed. Leipzig; Breitkopf und Härtel, 1900; 4th ed., Hildesheim: Georg Olms, 1960.
Richard, Earl. "Luke-Writer, Theologian, Historian: Research and Orientation of the 1970's." *BTB* 13 (1983): 3-15.
Richards, G. C. "The Composition of Josephus' *Antiquities*." *CQ* 33 (1939): 36-40.
Rivkin, Ellis, *The Shaping of Jewish History: A Radical New Interpretation*. New York: Charles Scribner's Sons, 1971.
Robbins, Vernon K. "Prefaces in Greco-Roman Biography and Luke-Acts." In *Society of Biblical Literature 1978 Seminar Papers*, pp. 193-207. Edited by Paul Achtemeier. Missoula: Scholars Press, 1978.
———. "By Land and By Sea: The We-Passages and Ancient Sea Voyages." In *Per-*

spectives on Luke-Acts, pp. 215-242. Edited by Charles H. Talbert. Special Studies Series 5. Danville, VA: Association of Baptist Professors of Religion, 1978.

Rosmarin, Adena. *The Power of Genre*. Minneapolis: University of Minnesota Press, 1985.

Rostovtzeff, M. *The Social and Economic History of the Hellenistic World*. 3 vols. Oxford: The Clarendon Press, 1941.

———. "Ptolemaic Egypt." In *The Hellenistic Monarchies and the Rise of Rome*, pp. 109-154. Edited by S. A. Cook, F. E. Adcock, and M. P. Charlesworth. CAH 7. Cambridge: Cambridge University Press, 1954.

———. "*Syria and the East*." In *The Hellenistic Monarchies and the Rise of Rome*, pp. 155-196. Edited by S. A. Cook, F. E. Adcock, and M. P. Charlesworth. CAH 7. Cambridge: Cambridge University Press, 1954.

Roth-Gerson, Lea. "The Contribution of Josephus Flavius to the Study of the Jewish Diaspora in the Hellenistic-Roman Period." In *Josephus Flavius: Historian of Eretz-Israel in the Hellenistic-Roman Period*, pp. 185-201. Edited by Uriel Rappaport. Jerusalem: Yad Izhak Ben Zvi, 1982. (Hebrew with English summary)

Rowton, M. B. "Manetho's date for Ramesses II." *Journal of Egyptian Archaeology* 34 (1948): 57-74.

Runnals, Donna. "Moses' Ethiopian Campaign." *JSJ* 14 (1983): 135-156.

Russell, D. A. *Criticism in Antiquity*. Berkeley/Los Angeles: University of California Press, 1981.

Sacks, Kenneth S. *Polybius on the Writing of History*. University of California Publications in Classical Studies 24. Berkeley/Los Angeles: University of California Press, 1981.

———. "The Lesser Prooemia of Diodorus Siculus." *Hermes* 110 (1982): 434-443.

———. "Historiography in the Rhetorical Works of Dionysius of Halicarnassus." *Athenaeum* 61 (1983): 65-87.

Saldarini, Anthony J. "Johanan ben Zakkai's Escape from Jerusalem: Origin and Development of a Rabbinic Story." *JSJ* 6 (1975): 189-204.

Salmon, Marilyn. "Insider or Outsider? Luke's Relationship with Judaism." In *Luke-Acts and the Jewish People: Eight Critical Perspectives*, pp. 76-82. Edited by Joseph B. Tyson. Minneapolis: Augsburg Publishing House, 1988.

Sanders, E. P. *et alii*, eds. *Jewish and Christian Self-Definition*. 3 vols. Philadelphia: Fortress Press, 1980-1982.

Sanders, Jack T. *The Jews in Luke-Acts*. Philadelphia: Fortress Press, 1987.

———. "The Jewish People in Luke-Acts." In *Luke-Acts and the Jewish People: Eight Critical Perspectives*, pp. 51-75. Edited by Joseph B. Tyson. Minneapolis: Augsburg Publishing House, 1988.

Sartori, M. "Storia, utopia' e mito nei primi libri della Bibliotheca historica 'di Diodoro' Siculo." *Athenaeum* 62 (1984): 492-536.

Sauneron, Serge. "L'Avis des Egyptiens sur la cuisine Soudanaise." *Kush* 7 (1959): 63-70.

Schalit, Abraham. "Artapanus," in *EncJud*, 3: 645-646.

———. "Josephus Flavius," in *EncJud*, 10: 251-265.

———. gen. ed. *The World History of the Jewish People*. New Brunswick: Rutgers University Press, 1972. Vol. 6: *The Hellenistic Age: Political History of Jewish Palestine from 332 B.C.E. to 67 B.C.E.*, by Abraham Schalit.

———. "Die Erhebung Vespasians nach Flavius Josephus, Talmud und Midrasch. Zur Geschichte einer messianischen Prophetie." In *Politische Geschichte (Kaisergeschichte)*, pp. 208-327. Edited by Hildegard Temporini. ANRW 2.2 Berlin/New York: Walter de Gruyter, 1975.

Schaller, Berndt. "Hekataios von Abdera über die Juden. Zur Frage der Echtheit und der Datierung." *ZNW* 54 (1963): 15-31.
———. "Iosephos," in *KP*, 2: 1440-1444.
Schaublin, Christoph. "Josephus und die Griechen." *Hermes* 110 (1982): 316-341.
Schepens, G. "Lucas, hellenisme en christendom. Beschouwingen over 'De Handelingen der Apostelen.'" *Collationes* 30 (1984): 31-55.
Schierling, Stephen P. and Schierling, Marla J. "The Influence of the Ancient Romances on *Acts of the Apostles.*" *The Classical Bulletin* 54 (1978): 81-88.
Schiffman, Lawrence H. "The Conversion of the Royal House of Adiabene in Josephus and Rabbinic Sources." In *Josephus, Judaism, and Christiantiy*, pp. 293-312. Edited by Louis H. Feldman and Gohei Hata. Detroit: Wayne State University Press, 1987.
Schlatter, Adolf. "Eupolemus als Chronolog und seine Beziehungen zu Jospehus und Manetho." *TSK* 4 (1891): 633-703.
Schmidt, Daryl. "The Historiography of Acts: Deuteronomistic or Hellenistic?" In *Society of Biblical Literature 1985 Seminar Papers*, pp. 417-427. Edited by Ken Harold Richards. Atlanta: Scholars Press, 1985.
Schmidt, K. L. "Die Stellung der Evangelien in der allgemeinen Literaturgeschichte." In EYXAPIΣTHPION: *Festschrift H. Gunkel*, 2: 50-124. Edited by H. Schmidt. Göttingen: Vandenhoeck & Ruprecht, 1923.
Schnabel, Paul. *Berossos und die babylonisch-hellenistische Literatur*. Berlin: B. G. Teubner, 1923; reprint ed., Hildesheim: Georg Olms, 1968.
Schneckenburger, Matthias. *Über den Zweck der Apostelgeschichte*. Bern: Christian Fischer, 1841.
Schneider, Gerd. "Der Zweck des lukanischen Doppelwerks." *BZ* 21 (1977): 45-66.
———. "Zur Bedeutung von Καθεξῆς im lukanischen Doppelwerk." *ZNW* 68 (1977): 128-131.
———. *Lukas, Theologe der Heilsgeschichte*, Aufsätze zum lukanischen Doppelwerk. BBB 59. Königstein/Ts.-Bonn: Peter Hanstein, 1985.
Schramm, Tim. *Der Markus Stoff bei Lukas: Eine literarkritische und redaktionsgeschichtliche Untersuchung*. SNTSMS 14. Cambridge: Cambridge University Press, 1971.
Schreckenberg, Heinz. *Bibliographie zu Flavius Josephus*. ALGHJ 1. Leiden: E. J. Brill, 1968.
———. *Bibliographie zu Flavius Josephus: Supplementband mit Gesamtregister*. ALGHJ 14. Leiden: E. J. Brill, 1979.
———. "Flavius Josephus und die lukanischen Schriften." In *Wort in der Zeit: Neutestamentliche Studien* (*Festgabe für Karl Heinrich Rengstorf*), pp. 179-209. Edited by Wilfrid Haubeck and Michael Bachmann. Leiden: E. J. Brill, 1980.
Schubert, Paul. "The Structure and Significance of Luke 24." In *Neutestamentliche Studien für Rudolf Bultmann*, pp. 165-186. Edited by W. Eltester. Berlin: Topelmann, 1957.
Schuler, Philip L. *A Genre for the Gospels: The Biographical Character of Matthew*. Philadelphia: Fortress Press, 1982.
Schultze, Clemence. "Dionysius of Halicarnassus and his audience." In *Past Perspectives: Studies in Greek and Roman Historical Writing*, pp. 121-141. Edited by I.S. Moxon, J.D. Smart, and A.J. Woodman. Cambridge: Cambridge University Press, 1986.
Schunck, Klaus-Dietrich. *Die Quellen des I und II. Makkabäerbuches*. Diss. Greifswald. Halle (Saale): Niemeyer, 1954.
Schürer, Emil. *A History of the Jewish People in the time of Jesus Christ*. 3 vols. New York: Charles Scribner's Sons, 1885-1924.

——. *The Literature of the Jewish People in the Time of Jesus*. Edited with an Introduction by Nahum N. Glatzer. New York: Schocken Books, 1972.

——. *The History of the Jewish People in the Age of Jesus Christ*. 3 vols. Revised and edited by Geza Vermes, Fergus Millar, and Martin Goodman. Edinburgh: T. & T. Clark, 1973-1986.

Schwartz, Edward. "Hekataeos von Teos." *Rheinisches Museum für Philologie* 40 (1885): 223-262.

——. "Alexandros," in *RE*, 1: 1449-1452.

——. "Artapanos," in *RE*, 2: 1306.

——. "Berossos," in *RE*, 3: 309-316.

——. "Diodoros," in *RE*, 5: 663-704.

Schwartz, Seth. "The Composition and Publication of Josephus' *Bellum Judaicum* Book 7." *HTR* 79 (1986): 373-386.

Schweizer, Edward. "Concerning the Speeches in Acts." In *Studies in Luke-Acts*, pp. 208-216. Edited by Leander E. Keck and J. Louis Martyn. Reprint ed., Philadelphia: Fortress Press, 1966.

Sevenster, J. N. *Do You Know Greek? (How Much Greek could the first Jewish Christians have known?)*. NovTSup 19. Leiden: E. J. Brill, 1968.

——. *The Roots of Pagan Anti-Semitism in the Ancient World*. NovTSup 41. Leiden: E. J. Brill, 1975.

Shinan, A. "Moses and the Ethiopian Woman." *Scripta Hierosolymitana* 27 (1978): 66-78.

Shutt, R. J. H. *Studies in Josephus*. London: S.P.C.K., 1961.

Siegert, F. "Lukas—ein Historiker, d.h. ein Rhetor? Freundschaftliche Entgegnung auf Erhardt Güttgemanns." *LingBib* 55 (1984): 57-60.

Siker, Jeffrey. "Abraham in Graeco-Roman Paganism." *JSJ* 18 (1987): 188-208.

Silver, Daniel Jeremy. "Moses and the Hungry Birds." *JQR* 64 (1973-74): 123-153.

Smallwood, E. Mary. "Domitian's Attitude toward the Jews and Judaism." *Classical Philology* 51 (1956): 1-13.

——. *The Jews Under Roman Rule*. SJLA 20. Leiden: E. J. Brill, 1976.

Smith, Morton. "Palestinian Judaism in the First Century." In *Israel: Its Role in Civilization*, pp. 67-81. Edited by Moshe Davis. New York: Harper & Brothers, 1956.

——. "Prolegomena to a Discussion of Aretalogies, Divine Men, the Gospels and Jesus." *JBL* 90 (1971): 174-199.

——. *Palestinian Parties and Politics That Shaped the Old Testament*. New York/London: Columbia University Press, 1971.

Solberger, Edmond. "Graeco-Babyloniaca." *IRAQ* 24 (1962): 63-72.

Sontheimer, Walther. "Alexandros," in *KP*, 1: 252.

Speiser, E. A. *Genesis*. AB 1. Garden City, New York: Doubleday & Company, Inc., 1964.

Spoerri, Walter. *Späthellenistische Berichte über Welt, Kultur und Götter*. Schweizerische Beiträge zur Altertumswissenschaft 9. Basel: Friedrich Reinhardt, 1959.

——. "Beros(s)os," in *KP*, 1: 1548.

——. "Hekataios," in *KP*, 2: 976-980.

——. "Hekataios von Abdera," in *KP*, 2: 980-982.

——. "Hekataios von Abdera," in *RAC*, 14: 275-310.

Squires, John. "The Plan of God in Luke-Acts." Ph.D. dissertation, Yale University, 1988.

Stadter, Philip A. *Arrian of Nicomedia*. Chapel Hill: The University of North Carolina Press, 1980.

Starr, Raymond J. "The Circulation of Literary Texts in the Roman World." *CQ* 37 (1987): 213-223.

Steele, E. Springs. "Luke 11:37-54—A Modified Hellenistic Symposium?" *JBL* 103 (1984): 379-394.

Steichele, Hanneliese. *Vergleich der Apostelgeschichte mit der antiken Geschichtsschreibung: Eine Studie zur Erzählkunst in der Apostelgeschichte.* München: Hanneliese Steichele, 1971.

Stein, O. "Megasthenes," in *RE*, 15: 230-326.

Sterling, Gregory E. "Luke-Acts and Apologetic Historiography." In *Society of Biblical Literature 1989 Seminar Papers*, pp. 326-342. Edited by David J. Lull. Atlanta: Scholars Press, 1989.

Stern, Menahem. "Manetho," in *EncJud*, 11: 872-873.

Stern, M., and Murray, Oswyn. "Hecataeus of Abdera and Theophrastus on Jews and Egyptians." *Journal of Egyptian Archaeology* 59 (1973): 159-168.

Stoldt, Hans-Herbert. *History and Criticism of the Marcan Hypothesis.* Translated by Donald L. Niewyk with an introduction by William R. Farmer. Macon, Georgia: Mercer University Press, 1980.

Strange, John. "The Inheritance of Dan." *ST* 20 (1966): 120-139.

Streeter, Burnett Hillman. *The Four Gospels: A Study of Origins (Treating of the Manuscript Tradition Sources, Authorship, and Dates).* London: MacMillan & Co., Ltd, 1956.

Stuehrenberg, Paul F. "The Study of Acts before the Reformation: A Bibliographic Introduction." *NovT* 29 (1987): 100-136.

Sundberg, Albert C., Jr. "Canon Muratori: A Fourth Century List." *HTR* 66 (1973): 1-41.

Talbert, Charles H. *Luke and the Gnostics: An Examination of the Lucan Purpose.* Nashville: Abingdon, 1966.

———. *Literary Patterns, Theologiocal Themes and the Genre of Luke-Acts.* SBLMS 20. Missoula, MT: Scholars Press, 1974.

———. *What is a Gospel? The Genre of the Canonical Gospels.* Philadelphia: Fortress Press, 1977.

———. ed. *Perspectives on Luke-Acts.* Special Studies Series 5. Danville, VA: Association of Baptist Professors of Religion, 1978.

———. "Biographies of Philosophers and Rulers as Instruments of Religious Propaganda in Mediterranean Antiquity." In *Religion (Heidentum: Römische Religion, Allgemeines)*, pp. 1619-1651. Edited by Wolfgang Haase. ANRW II 16.2. Berlin/New York: Walter de Gruyter, 1978.

———, ed. *Luke-Acts: New Perspectives from the Society of Biblical Literature Seminar.* New York: Crossroad, 1984.

———. "Promise and Fulfillment in Lucan Theology." In *Luke-Acts: New Perspectives from the Society of Biblical Literature Seminar*, pp. 91-103. Edited by Charles H. Talbert. New York: Crossroad, 1984.

———. "Once Again: Gospel Genre." *Semeia* 43 (1988): 53-73.

Tannehill, Robert C. "Israel in Luke-Acts: A Tragic Story." *JBL* 104 (1985): 69-85.

———. *The Narrative Unity of Luke-Acts: A Literary Interpretation.* 2 vols. Foundations and Facets. Philadelphia: Fortress Press, 1986-1990.

Tannenbaum, Robert F. "Jews and God-Fearers in the Holy City of Aphrodite." *BAR* 12 (1986): 54-57.

Tarn, William Woodthrope. *Alexander the Great.* 2 vols. Cambridge: Cambridge University Press, 1948.

———. *Hellenistic Civilization* 3rd ed., Revised with G. T. Griffith. 1952; reprint ed., New York: Meridian, 1974.

Tcherikover, Victor. "Jewish Apologetic Literature Reconsidered." *Eos* 48 (1956): 169-193.

———. *Hellenistic Civilization and the Jews*. Translated by S. Applebaum. Jewish Publication Society of America, 1959; reprint ed., New York: Athenaeum, 1970.

Thackeray, H. St. John. *Josephus: The Man and the Historian*. New York, 1929; reprint ed., with an introduction by Samuel Sandmel, New York: Ktav Publishing House, Inc., 1967.

Thomas, D. Winton, ed. *Archaeology and Old Testament Study: Jubilee Volume of the Society for Old Testament Study 1917-1967*. Oxford: The Clarendon Press, 1967.

Thompson, R. Campbell. "The Influence of Babylonia." In *The Assyrian Empire*, pp. 226-250. Edited by J. B. Bury, S. A. Cook, and F. E. Adcock. CAH 3. Cambridge: Cambridge University Press, 1970.

Thraede, Klaus. "Das Lob des Erfinders: Bemerkungen zur Analyse der Heuremata-Kataloge." *Rheinisches Museum für Philologie* 105 (1962): 158-186.

———. "Erfinder II," in *RAC*, 5: 1191-1278.

———. "Euhemerismus," in *RAC*, 6: 877-890.

Tiede, David Lenz. *The Charismatic Figure as Miracle Worker*. SBLDS 1. Missoula, Montana: The Society of Biblical Literature, 1972.

———. *Prophecy & History in Luke-Acts*. Philadelphia: Fortress Press, 1980.

Tigsy, Jeffrey H. *The Evolution of the Gilgamesh Epic*. Philadelphia: University of Pennsylvania Press, 1982.

Timmer, B. C. J. "Megasthenes en de Indische Maatschappij." Disseration, Amsterdam, 1930.

Tinh, Tran tam. "Sarapis and Isis." In *Jewish and Christian Self-Definition*. Edited by Ben F. Meyer and E. P. Sanders. Vol. 3: *Self-Definition in the Greco-Roman World*, pp. 101-117. Philadelphia: Fortress Press, 1982.

Torrey, Charles Cutler. *The Composition and Date of Acts*. HTS 1. Cambridge: Harvard University Press, 1916.

Townsend, John T. "The Date of Luke-Acts." In *Luke-Acts: New Perspectives from the Society of Biblical Literature Seminar*, pp. 47-62. Edited by Charles H. Talbert. New York: Crossroad, 1984.

Tozzi, Periluigi. "Studi su Ecateo di Mileto: Ecateo ed Euripide." *Athenaeum* n.s. 41 (1963): 39-50.

———. "Studi su Ecateo di Mileto: Ecateo e la Cultura Ionica." *Athenaeum* n.s. 41 (1963): 318-326.

———. "Studi su Ecateo di Mileto: Lingua e Stile di Ecateo." *Athenaeum* n.s. 42 (1964): 101-117.

———. "Studi su Ecateo di Mileto: La ΙΣΤΟΡΙΗ di Ecateo." *Athenaeum* n.s. 43 (1965): 41-76.

———. "Studi su Ecateo di Mileto: La Fortuna." *Athenaeum* n.s. 45 (1967): 313-334.

Trigger, B. G.; Kemp, B. J.; O'Conner, D.; and Lloyd, A. B. *Ancient Egypt: A Social History*. Cambridge: Cambridge University Press, 1983.

Trocmé, Etienne. *Le 'Livre des Actes' et l'histoire*. Études d'Histoire et de Philosphie Religieuses. Paris: Presses Universitaires de France, 1957.

Troiani, Lucio. "Sui frammenti di Manetone nel primo libro del *Contra Apionem* di Flavio Giuseppe." *Studi Classici e Orientali* 24 (1975): 97-126.

Trüdinger, K. "Studien zur Geschichte der griechisch-römischen Ethnographie." Dissertation, Basel, 1918.

Turner, N. "The Quality of the Greek of Luke-Acts." In *Studies in New Testament Language and Text: Essays in Honour of George D. Kilpatrick on the Occasion of His Sixty-Fifth Birthday*, pp. 387-400. Edited by J. K. Elliott. NovTSup 44. Leiden: E. J. Brill, 1976.

———. "Eupolemus," in *IDB*, 2: 181.

Tyson, Joseph B. "The Jewish Public in Luke-Acts." *NTS* 30 (1984): 574-583.

———, ed. *Luke-Acts and the Jewish People: Eight Critical Perspectives*. Minneapolis: Augsburg Publishing House, 1988.

Ullman, B. L. "History and Tragedy." *TAPA* 73 (1942): 25-53.
Ulrich, Eugene Charles, Jr. *The Qumran Text of Samuel and Josephus.* HSM 19. Missoula, Montana: Scholars Press, 1978.
Unger, G. F. "Die Blüthzeit des Alexander Polyhistor." *Philologus* 47 (1888): 176-183.
van Unnik, Willem Cornelis. "De la regle Μήτε προσθεῖναι μήτε ἀφελεῖν dans l'histoire du canon." *VC* 3 (1949): 1-36.
——. *Tarsus or Jerusalem: The City of Paul's Youth.* Translated by George Ogg. London: The Epworth Press, 1962.
——. "Opmerkingen over het doel van Lucas' Geschiedwerk (Luc. i.4)" *Nederlands Theologisch Tijdschrift* 9, 6 (1955): 323-331; reprinted as "Remarks on the Purpose of Luke's Historical Writing (Luke I 1-4)," in *Sparsa Collecta: The Collected Essays of W. C. van Unnik*; 1: 6-15. Leiden: E. J. Brill, 1973.
——. *Flavius Josephus als historischer Schriftsteller.* Franz Delitzsch Vorlesungen, neue Folge. Heidelberg: Lambert Schneider, 1978.
——. "Luke's Second Book and the Rules of Hellenistic Historiography." In *Les Actes des Apôtres: Tradition, rédaction, théologie,* pp. 37-60. Edited by J. Kremer. BETL 48. Leuven: University Press, 1979.
van der Horst, P. W. "Hellenistic Parallels to the Acts of the Apostles: 1: 1-26." *ZNW* 74 (1983): 17-26.
——. "Hellenistic Parallels to the Acts of the Apostles (2.1-47)." *JSNT* 25 (1985): 49-60.
——. "Hellenistic Parrallels to Acts (Chapters 3 and 4)." *JSNT* 35 (1989): 37-46.
Van Seters, John. *The Hyksos.* New Haven/London: Yale University Press, 1966.
——. *In Search of History: Historiography in the Ancient World and the Origins of Biblical History.* New Haven/London: Yale University Press, 1983.
Varneda, Pere Villalba I. *The Historical Method of Flavius Josephus.* ALGHJ 19. Leiden: E. J. Brill, 1986.
Veltman, Frederick. "The Defense Speeches of Paul in Acts: Gattungsforschung and its Limitations." Th.D. disseration, The Graduate Theological Union, 1975.
——. "The Defense Speeches of Paul in Acts." In *Perspectives on Luke-Acts,* pp. 243-256. Edited by Charles H. Talbert. Special Studies Series 5, Danville, VA: Association of Baptist Professors of Religion, 1978.
Vermes, Geza. *Scripture and Tradition in Judaism: Haggadic Studies.* SPB 4. Leiden: E. J. Brill, 1961.
——. "A Summary of the Law by Flavius Josephus." *NovT* 24 (1982): 289-303.
Vielhauer, Paul. *Geschichte der ürchristlichen Literatur: Einleitung in das Neue Testament, die Apokryphen und die Apostolischen Väter.* Berlin/New York: Walter de Gruyter, 1975.
Vielhauer, Philipp. "On the 'Paulinism' of Acts." Translated by Wm. C. Robinson, Jr. and Victor P. Furnish. In *Studies in Luke-Acts,* pp. 33-50. Edited by Leander Keck and J. Louis Martyn. 1966; reprint ed., Philadelphia: Fortress Press, 1980.
Volkel, Martin. "Exegetische Erwägungen zum Verstandnis des Begriffs καθεξῆς im lukanischen Prolog." *NTS* 20 (1973-1974): 289-299.
Volkman, Hans. "Ptolemais I. Soter," in *RE*, 23: 1603-1645.
——. "Ptolemais II. Philadelphos," in *RE*, 23: 1645-1666.
Votaw, Clyde Weber. "The Gospels and Contemporary Biographies." *AJT* 19 (1915): 45-73; reprinted as *The Gospels and Contemporary Biographies in the Greco-Roman World.* Facet Books/Biblical Series 27. Philadelphia: Fortress Press, 1970.

Wacholder, Ben Zion. *Nicolaus of Damascus.* University of California Publications in History 75. Berkeley/Los Angeles: University of California Press, 1962.

——. "Pseudo-Eupolemus' Two Greek Fragments on the Life of Abraham." *HUCA* 34 (1963): 83-113.

——. "How Long Did Abram Stay in Egypt? (A Study in Hellenistic, Qumran, and Rabbinic Chronography)." *HUCA* 35 (1964): 43-56.

——. "Biblical Chronology in the Hellenistic World Chronicles." *HTR* 61 (1968): 451-481.

——. "Demetrius," in *EncJud*, 5: 1490-1491.

——. "Eupolemus," in *EncJud*, 6: 964-965.

——. "Hecataeus of Abdera," in *EncJud*, 8: 236-237.

——. *Eupolemus: A Study of Judaeo-Greek Literature.* Monographs of the Hebrew Union College 3. New York: Hebrew Union College-Jewish Institute of Religion, 1974.

Wagner, G., ed. *An Exegetical Bibliography of the New Testament. Volume 2: Luke and Acts.* Macon, GA: Mercer University Press, 1985.

Walaskay, Paul W. *"And so we came to Rome:" The Political Perspective of St. Luke.* SNTSMS 49. Cambridge: Cambridge University Press, 1983.

Walbank, F. W. *Polybius.* The Sather Classical Lectures. Berkeley/Los Angeles/London: The University of California Press, 1972.

Walsh, P. G. *Livy: His Historical Aims and Methods.* Cambridge: The University Press, 1961.

Walter, N. "Zu Pseudo-Eupolemus." *Klio* 43-45 (1965): 282-290.

——. "Zur Überlieferung einiger Reste früher jüdisch-hellenistischer Literatur bei Josephus, Clemens, und Eusebius." In *Studia Patristica* 7, pp. 314-321. TU 92. Berlin: Akademie Verlag, 1966.

——. "Jüdisch-hellenistische Literatur vor Philon von Alexandrien (unter Ausschluß der Historiker)." In *Religion (Hellenistisches Judentum in römischer Zeit, ausgenommen Philon und Josephus)*, pp. 67-120. ANRW II 20.1 Berlin/New York: Walter de Gruyter, 1987.

Walton, Francis R. "The Messenger of God in Hecataeus of Abdera." *HTR* 48 (1955): 255-257.

Warmington, Eric Herbert. "Periploi," in *The Oxford Classical Dictionary*, 2nd ed.

Waters, K. H. *Herodotus, the Historian: His Problems, Methods, and Originality.* Norman: University of Oklahoma Press, 1985.

Weinfield, Mohse, *Deuteronomy and the Deuteronomic School.* Oxford: The Clarendon Press, 1972.

Welles, C. Bradford. "The Discovery of Sarapis and the Foundation of Alexandria." *Historia* 11 (1962): 271-298.

Wenham, Gordon J. *Genesis 1-15.* Word Biblical Commentary 1. Waco, Texas: Word Books, 1987.

Westermann, Claus. *Genesis 1-11: A Commentary.* Translated by John J. Scullion. Minneapolis: Augsburg Publishing House, 1984.

von Wilamowitz-Moellendorff, Ulrich. *Greek Historical Writing and Apollo: Two Lectures Delivered Before the University of Oxford June 3 and 4, 1908.* Translated by Gilbert Murray. Oxford: The Clarendon Press, 1908.

Wilckens, Ulrich. *Die Missionsreden der Apostelgeschichte: Form und traditionsgeschichtliche Untersuchungen.* 2nd ed. WMANT 5. Neukirchen-Vlyn: Neukirchener Verlag des Erziehungsvereins GMBH, 1963.

Wilcox, Max. *The Semitisms of Acts.* Oxford: The Clarendon Press, 1965.

Wilken, Robert L. *The Christians as the Romans Saw Them.* New Haven/London: Yale University Press, 1984.

Wilson, Robert McL. "Jewish Literary Propaganda." In *Paganisme, Judaïsme,*

Christianisme: Influences et affrontements dans le monde antique (Mélanges offerts à Marcel Simon), pp. 61-71. Edited by André Benoit, Marc Philonenko, and Cyrille Vogel. Paris: E. de Boccard, 1978.

Winston, David. *The Wisdom of Solomon*. AB 43. Garden City, New York: Doubleday & Company, Inc., 1979.

———. *Logos and Mystical Theology in Philo of Alexandria*. Cincinnati: Hebrew Union College Press, 1985.

Wolfson, Harry Austryn, *Philo: Foundations of Religious Philosophy in Judaism, Christianity, and Islam*. 2 vols. Cambridge: Harvard University Press, 1947.

Woodman, A. J. *Rhetoric in Classical Historiography: Four Studies*. Portland, Oregon: Areopagitica Press, 1988.

Yavetz, Vi. "Reflections on Titus and Josephus." *GRBS* 16 (1975): 411-432.

Yoyotte, Jean. "L'Egypte ancienne et les origines de l' antijudaïsme." *Revue de l'Histoire des Religions* 163 (1963): 133-143.

Zehnle, Richard F. *Peter's Pentecost Discourse: Tradition and Lukan Reinterpretation in Peter's Speeches of Acts 2 and 3*. SBLMS 15. Nashville/New York: Abingdon Press, 1971.

Zeitlin, Solomon. "A Survey of Jewish Historiography: from the Biblical Books to the *Sefer Ha-kab-balah* with Special Emphasis on Josephus." *JQR* 59 (1968-1969): 171-214 and 60 (1969-1970): 37-68, 375-406.

Zimmerli, Walter. *Ezekiel*. 2 vols. Translated by Ronald E. Clements and James D. Martin. Hermeneia. Philadelphia: Fortress Press, 1979-1983.

COMMENTARIES ON LUKE-ACTS

Blaiklock, E. M. *The Acts of the Apostles*. Tyndale New Testament Commentaries. Grand Rapids: Wm. B. Eerdmans Publishing Co., 1959.

Bruce, F. F. *The Acts of the Apostles*. Grand Rapids: Wm. B. Eerdmans Publishing Co., 1951.

———. *Commentary on the Book of the Acts*. NICNT. Grand Rapids: Wm. B. Eerdmans Publishing Co., 1954.

Clark, Albert C. *The Acts of the Apostles: A Critical Edition with Introduction and Notes on Selected Passages*. Oxford: The Clarendon Press, 1933.

Conzelmann, Hans. *Die Apostelgeschichte*. HNT 7. Tübingen: Mohr, 1963.

——— *Acts of the Apostles*. Translated by James Limburg, A. Thomas Kraabel, and Donald H. Juel. Hermeneia. Philadelphia: Fortress Press, 1987.

Creed, John Martin. *The Gospel According to St. Luke*. London: Macmillan & Co. Ltd., 1930.

Danker, Frederick W. *Jesus and the New Age: A Commentary on St. Luke's Gospel*. Rev. ed. Philadelphia: Fortress Press, 1988.

Ellis, E. Earle. *The Gospel of Luke*. Rev. ed. NCB. London: Oliphants, 1974.

Ernst, Josef. *Das Evangelium nach Lukas*. RNT. Regensburg: Friedrich Pustel, 1977.

Fitzmyer, Joseph A. *The Gospel According to Luke*. AB 28 & 28A. Garden City, New York: Doubleday & Company, Inc. 1981-1985.

Foakes Jackson, F. J., and Lake, K., gen. eds. *The Beginnings of Christianity*. 5 vols. London: Macmillan, 1920-33; reprint ed., Grand Rapids: Baker Book House, 1979.

Foakes-Jackson, F. J. *The Acts of the Apostles*. MNTC. London: Hodder and Stoughton, 1931.
Geldenhuys, Norval. *Commentary on the Gospel of Luke*. NICNT. Grand Rapids: Wm. B. Eerdmans Publishing Co., 1951.
Godet, F. *A Commentary on the Gospel of St. Luke*. 2 vols. 5th ed. Translated by E. N. Shalders and M. D. Cusin. Reprint ed., Edinburgh: T. & T. Clark, 1976.

Haenchen, Ernst. *The Acts of the Apostles: A Commentary*. Revised translation by R. McL. Wilson. Philadelphia: The Westminster Press, 1971.
Harrison, Everett F. *Acts: The Expanding Church*. Chicago: Moody Press, 1975.

Knox, Wilfred L. *The Acts of the Apostles*. Cambridge: The University Press, 1948.

Manson, William. *The Gospel of Luke*. MNTC. New York/London: Harper and Brothers, 1930.
Marshall, I. Howard. *The Gospel of Luke: A Commentary on the Greek Text*. The New International Greek Testament Commentary. Grand Rapids: Wm. B. Eerdmans Publishing Co., 1978.
Marshall, I. Howard. *The Acts of the Apostles*. Tyndale New Testament Commentaries. Grand Rapids: Wm. B. Eerdmans Publishing Co., 1980.
Morris, Leon. *The Gospel According to St. Luke: An Introduction and Commentary*. Tyndale New Testament Commentaries. Grand Rapids: Wm. B. Eerdmans Publishing Co., 1974.
Munck, Johannes. *The Acts of the Apostles*. Revised by William F. Albright and C. S. Mann. AB 31. Garden City, New York: Doubleday & Company, Inc., 1967.

Neil, William. *The Acts of the Apostles*. NCB. London: Oliphants, 1973.

Pesch, Rudolf. *Die Apostelgeschichte*. 2 vols. EKKNT. Zürich/Einsiedeln/Köln: Benziger Verlag and Neukirchener Verlag, 1986.
Plummer, Alfred. *The Gospel According to S. Luke*. 5th ed. ICC. Edinburgh: T. & T. Clark, 1901.

Schneider, Gerhard. *Das Evangelium nach Lukas*. 2 vols. Ökumenischer Taschenbuch-Kommentar zum Neuen Testament 3.1-2. Würzburg: Gerd Mohn, 1977.
———. *Die Apostelgeschichte*. 2 vols. HTKNT. Freiburg/Basel/Wien: Herder, 1980-1982.
Schürmann, Heinz. *Das Lukasevangelium: Erster Teil*. HTKNT 3. Freiburg/Basel/Wien: Herder, 1984.
Schweizer, Eduard. *The Good News According to Luke*. Translated by David E. Green. Atlanta: John Knox Press, 1984.

Talbert, Charles H. *Reading Luke: A Literary and Theological Commentary on the Third Gospel*. New York: Crossroad, 1982.

INDICES

Page numbers connected by a dash indicate a reference on each page without implying continuous discussion. References to footnotes indicate either that the discussion took place in the note or would be difficult to locate quickly without the reference to the note. Where a reference is in both the text and a note on the same page, an asterisk (*) appears after the page number and before the footnote number.

INDEX OF ANCIENT AUTHORS AND TEXTS

Principles Governing the Index.
1. The following is a complete list of all texts cited up to the fifth century.
2. References to authors where no specific references to their texts were made are listed at the beginning of each entry under the name of either the author or the edition in order to enable the reader to trace the influence of a particular author. I have included all authors mentioned through the fifth century C. E.
3. For authors only extant in fragments:
   a. I have indicated the edition I have used. In the case of Hekataios of Miletos I have supplied the references to FGrH in parentheses beside the reference to Nenci. Where I have indicated the source of the fragment I have listed the fragment and the author of the fragment under his/her name but not the citation in that author's work.
   b. In the instances where I have used the major source in which the author is preserved, the references will appear under the extant source (e.g., most references to Hekataios of Abdera will be found under Diodoros Sikelos).

1. INDEX OF ANCIENT NEAR EASTERN TEXTS

The Dispute Between		5.1-44	111 n. 46
Cattle and Grain	111 n. 45		
		Epic of Ziusudra	112, 391
Enuma Elish	111-112, 391		
1.4	111 n. 46	*Gilgamesh Epic*	112, 116 n. 67
1.133-143	111 n. 46		
4.135-140	111 n. 46	*Journey of Wen-Amon*	
4.141-5.166	111 n. 46	*to Phoenicia*	71 n. 68

2. INDEX OF CLASSICAL TEXTS

Abydenos	106, 196, 260	*Prometheus Vinctus*	
		323	371 n. 298
FGrH 685		460	19 n. 390
F 1	108, 202 n. 305	904	243 n. 74
F 2	109		
F 2b	107 n. 26	Agatharchides	
F 3	109		
F 6	109	*FGrH* 86	61 n. 32, 63 n. 42, 70 n. 65, 89, 145, 249-250 n. 104
Achilles Tatios	373 n. 311		
Leukippe and Klitophon	185 n. 237	Agathemeros	21-22, 24-25
Aeschylos		Akousilaos	
Agamemnon		*FGrH* 2	246, 249 n. 104
1624	371 n. 298		

ALEXANDER POLYHISTOR	
FGrH 273	105 n. 15, 106-107, 116 n. 68, 141-142, 144-152, 156* n. 125, 159 n. 125, 168-169, 171 n. 186, 172, 184, 187, 191-193, 209-212, 220, 221 n. 405, 249 n. 104, 255-256, 263-264, 278, 280, 282-284, 302, 364 n. 272
T 1	144* nn. 41 & 42, 145 n. 46
T 2	144 n. 42
T 3	144* n. 43
T 7b	144 n. 43
F 70	148 n. 71
F 121	121 n. 72
ALKAIOS	139 n. 9
ANAXIMANDER	
FGrH 9	21-22* nn. 10 & 11, 24, 28, 390
ANAXIMENES OF LAMPSAKOS	
FGrH 72	314, 344 n. 166
Rhetorica ad Alexandrum	
35	364 n. 274
APION	
FGrH 616	
(*GLAJJ* LXIII)	164 n. 154
APPIAN	232 n. 31, 373 n. 311
Syriaca	
58	105 n. 10
APOLLONIOS MOLON	
GLAJJ XXIX	164-165
APULEIUS	
Metamorphoses (The Golden Ass)	185 n. 237
ARATOS	
Phaenomena	
5	371

ARISTOPHANES	
Acharnenses	
515-529	35
Ranae	
1032-1034	178 n.212
ARISTOTLE	7 n. 27, 55-56, 58-59 n. 15, 79 n. 101, 314
Ath. Pol.	
33.2	4 n. 10
De Generatione Animalium	
756b	50 n. 212
Metaphysica	
1.1-14-16 (981b)	71 n. 67
Poetica	
1.1	12
9.1-3	4
9.2	4 n. 10
17.5-8	337 n. 125
23.2-3	4 n. 10
Politica	
3.10	55
7.61	63 n. 42
Rhetorica	
1.3.1, 5	13-14 n. 69
1.4.13	4 n. 10
3.9.2	4 n. 10, 35 n. 138
Symposium	*370 n. 291*
ARISTOXENOS	370 n. 291
ARRIAN	373 n. 311
Anabasis	
5.6.2	92
5.65	36-37
7.6.1	57 n. 10
7.11.8-9	56 n. 6
7.12.2	57 n. 10
Indike	
1-17	94
2.1-3.8	94 n. 148
3.1	94 n. 148
3.6-7	95
3.6	94 n. 148 (3t.)
4.2-6	95
4.3-12	94 n. 148
5.1-6.3	94 n. 148
5.3	93
5.4-7	95
6.2-3	95
6.4-9	94 n. 148

434   INDEX OF ANCIENT AUTHORS AND TEXTS

3. INDEX OF OLD TESTAMENT TEXTS (MT AND LXX)

Introductory Note: References to both MT and LXX are only given where there is a discrepancy cited in the monograph. Specific use of either the MT or LXX is stated in the discussion. Books included in the LXX but not in MT are listed under the heading of the apocrypha.

5:24	215 n. 376	16:30	356-357 n. 228
5:25	215 n. 376	21:20	356-357 n. 228
5:26	215 n. 376	21:25	356-357 n. 228
5:27-32	215 n. 377	22:38	357 n. 235
5:32	215 n. 376	22:43	356-357 n. 228
6:2	217 n. 385		(*bis*)
6:15	214 n. 373 (*bis*),	22:51-II Kings	
	215 n. 377	17:28	248 n. 98
6:31	215 n. 377	22:53	356-357 n. 228
6:33-34	215 n. 377		(3t.)
7:13	215 n. 376		
7:14 (LXX 2)	215 n. 376	II Kings (IV Kingdoms)	
7:15 (LXX 3)	214 n. 373 (*bis*),	1:17	357 n. 235
	217 n. 385	3:2	356-357 n. 228
7:23-26	217 n. 385	7:17-20	357 n. 235
8:4	357 n. 235	8:18	356-357 n. 228
8:12-61	357		(*bis*)
8:12-41	355-356 n. 222	8:27	356-357 n. 228
8:22-53	361 n. 258		(*bis*)
8:22	215 n. 376 (*bis*)	9:36-37	357 n. 235
8:31	215 n. 376	12:3	356-357 n. 228
8:54	215 n. 376	13:2	356-357 n. 228
8:61	353	13:11	356-357 n. 228
8:63	217 n. 385	14:3	356-357 n. 228
8:64	215 n. 376	14:24	356-357 n. 228
9:11	215 n. 376	15:3	356-357 n. 228
9:12	215 n. 376	15:9	356-357 n. 228
9:14	215 n. 376	15:12	357 n. 235
9:15	215 n. 376	15:18	356-357 n. 228
9:27	215 n. 376	15:24	356-357 n. 228
10:11	215 n. 376	15:28	356-357 n. 228
10:12	215 n. 376	15:34	356-357 n. 228
10:16-17	217 n. 385	16:2	356-357 n. 228
11:6	356-357 n. 228	16:3	356-357 n. 228
11:15-17	217 n. 383	17:2	356-357 n. 228
11:33	356-357 n. 228	17:2	356-357 n. 228
	(*bis*)	17:7-23	356
11:38	356-357 n. 228	17:17	356-357 n. 228
14:7-16	357 n. 233	17:23	357 n. 235
14:8	356-357 n. 228	18:3	356-357 n. 228
14:22	356-357 n. 228	18:12-Dan 8	248 n. 98
15:3-4	356 n. 224	21:2	356-357 n. 228
15:5	356-357 n. 228		(*bis*)
15:11	356-357 n. 228	21:15	356-357 n. 228
15:26	356-357 n. 228	21:16	356-357 n. 228
	(*bis*)	21:20	356-357 n. 228
15:34	356-357 n. 228	21:21	356-357 n. 228
	(*bis*)	21:22	356-357 n. 228
16:1-4	357 n. 233	22:2	356-357 n. 228
16:2	356-357 n. 228	23:32	356-357 n. 228
16:19	356-357 n. 228	23:37	356-357 n. 228
	(*bis*)	24:9	356-357 n. 228
16:25	356-357 n. 228	24:19	356-357 n. 228
16:26	356-357 n. 228		

JUDITH
2:2
2:4
8:16
11:13

WISDOM OF
SOLOMON
6:4
7:1-2
9:13
9:17
10:20

SIRACH
Prologue
45:3

I ESDRAS

1:26
2:1-Esth 10:3

II ESDRAS
7:23
10:3

I MACCABEES

1:20-24
2:28
2:49-70
4:36-59
5:9-54
5:65
6:8-13
6:65-68
8
8:1-6
8:17

10:30
10:38
11:34

354 n. 214
358 n. 239
358 n. 239
358 n. 239
86 n. 118

354 n. 214
358 n. 239
151 n. 92
358 n. 239
358 n. 239
266

206 n. 323
252 n. 113
364 n. 276

250-251, 256
n. 134
342 n. 147
248 n. 98

342 n. 147
358 n. 239

213, 248
n. 97, 251,
318, 354 n. 214
220 n. 400
86 n. 120
361 n. 257
221 n. 402
220 n. 395
220 n. 395
304 n. 367
220 n. 395
210 n. 343
210 n. 343
207, 208
n. 337 (bis)
86 n. 120
86 n. 120
86 n. 120

12:16

14:22
14:24

II MACCABEES

1:10-2:18
1:18b-2:15
2:1-8
2:29
2:31
2:32
3-5
4:11

6:2

6:17
7:1-6
7:2
7:19
7:27
8:11
9:2
9:27
10:1-8
10:15
11:17
12:10-31

III MACCABEES

1:1-5
1:6-2:24
2:25-7:23
6:24
6:25
7:5

IV MACCABEES
1:5

208 n. 337
(3t.)
208 n. 337
208 n. 337

141 n. 19,
213, 318, 354
n. 214, 387
210 n. 343
210 n. 343
216 n. 381
342 n. 147
252 n. 113
342 n. 153
210 n. 343
208 nn. 334
& 335 & 337
188 n. 252,
205 n. 321
342 n. 153
216 n. 381
371 n. 296
342 n. 147
151 n. 92
343 n. 157
342 n. 147
343 n. 157
221 n. 402
342 n. 147
208
220 n. 395

90 n. 130,
318, 354
n. 214
154
154
154
342 n. 147
90 n. 131
342 n. 147

342 n. 147

6. INDEX OF PSEUDEPIGRAPHA

APOCALYPSE OF
ABRAHAM

II BARUCH

I ENOCH
7-8
8:3

307

307

195-201
179 n. 217
178 n. 210

65:14
72-82

75:3
81:5
82:1
83:1

198
178 n. 210,
198
178 n. 210
198
198
198

7. INDEX OF DEAD SEA SCROLLS

8. INDEX OF HELLENISTIC JEWISH LITERATURE IN GREEK

5.277	296 n. 318		244, 249-250
5.312	296 n. 318		n. 104
5.323	256 n. 133,	8.260-262	240 n. 68,
	298 n. 331		244, 249-250
5.336	256 n. 133,		n. 104
	298 n. 331	8.262	285 n. 244
6-11	290 n. 275	8.324	249-250
6-10	248		n. 104
6	248 n. 98,	8.379	304 n. 365
	250	9	248 n. 98
6.22	256 n. 133,	9.16	304 n. 365
	298 n. 331	9.87	304 n. 3
6.197	293 n. 302	9.208-214	250 n. 107
6.242-244	291 n. 291	9.208	253 n. 115
6.302	256 n. 133,	9.214	253 n. 115,
	298 n. 331		342 n. 153
6.307	296 n. 321	9.239-242	250 n. 107
6.371	293 n. 303	9.242	253 n. 117
6.378	369 n. 286	9.277-287	250
7	248 n. 98	9.282-287	249-250
7.10	298 n. 331		n. 104
7.31	291 n. 278	9.283	252 n. 113
7.36	291 n. 278	9.290	256 n. 133,
7.67	256 n. 133,		298 n. 331
	282 n. 232,	10	248* n. 98,
	298 n. 331		250
7.90-93	292 n. 296	10.7	304 n. 365
7.93	296 n. 321	10.18-20	249-250
7.95	296 n. 318		n. 104
7.101-103	249-250	10.20	260 n. 151,
	n. 104		261 n. 157
7.101-103	249-250	10.34b	249-250
	n. 104		n. 104, 260
7.284-285	291 n. 278		n. 151, 261
7.338	296 n. 318		n. 157
7.383-388	361 n. 257	10.35	250 n. 107
7.385	296 n. 318	10.78b-80	250 n. 108
8-10	250	10.88-95	250 n. 108
8	248 n. 98	10.102-107	250 n. 108
8.1	248 nn. 93 &	10.110-115	250 n. 108
	94	10.117-130	250 n. 108
8.11	367 n. 284	10.139	304 n. 366
8.50-56	220 n. 396	10.141	250 n. 108
8.55-56	220 n. 396	10.143	369 n. 286
8.63-98	250	10.156-180	250 n. 108
8.95	298 n. 331	10.185	267 n. 192
8.100	298 n. 332	10.210	292 n. 297
8.142	252 n. 113	10.214	296 nn. 317
8.144-147	249-250		& 318
	n. 104	10.218	252 n. 113
8.144	252 n. 113		(*bis*), 253
8.157	249-250		nn. 114 & 115,
	n. 104		255 n. 131,
8.253	240 n. 68,		260 n. 153

1.10	310 n. 401	4.219	309 n. 398
1.11	310 n. 401	4.366	309 n. 398
1.13-16	241	4.397	310 n. 401
1.15	241* n. 71	4.567	305 n. 373
1.16	241, 346	4.592-604	233 n. 33
	n. 173	4.616-621	233 n. 33
1.17-18	242 n. 73	4.622-629	233 n. 34
1.17	242, 252	4.622	309 n. 398
	n. 113, 264,	5.114	233 n. 35
	284 n. 240	5.151	252 n. 113
1.27	310 n. 401	5.224	281 n. 230
1.63	281	5.257	285 n. 244
1.248	366 n. 282	5.261	233 n. 35
1.398	366 n. 282	5.325-330	233 n. 35
1.440	366 n. 282	5.361	233 n. 35
2.137-138	230 n. 22	5.362-419	233 n. 35
2.215	366 n. 282	5.367	293 n. 299
2.247	366 n. 282	5.391-393	237 n. 56
2.261-263	366 n. 282	5.419	230 n. 20
2.316	231 n. 25	5.420	237 n. 57
2.320	231 n. 25	5.533	237 n. 57
2.345-404	231 n. 25	5.541-547	233 n. 35
2.388-389	310 n. 404	5.544	237 n. 57
2.411-429	231 n. 25	5.547	237 n. 57
2.430-432	231 n. 25	6.94	233 n. 35
2.433-448	231 n. 25	6.96-111	233 n. 35
2.457-465	231 n. 25	6.107	310
2.461-463	328 n. 90	6.112-114	237 n. 57
2.466-476	231 n. 25	6.118-120	233 n. 35
2.477-486	231 n. 25	6.124-129	233 n. 35
2.487-498	231 n. 25	6.312-313	237 n. 55,
2.499-555	231 n. 25		293 n. 299
2.562-571	232 n. 27 (*bis*)	6.356-357	305 n. 373
2.562	231 n. 25	6.365	233 n. 35
3.28	309 n. 398	7.42	342 n. 153
3.108	310 n. 404	7.45	328 n. 90
3.141-288	232 n. 28	7.46-62	299 n. 336
3.144	309 n. 398	7.82	309 n. 398
3.340-408	232 n. 31,	7.100-111	299 n. 336
	235 n. 49	7.158	234 n. 42
3.341	235 n. 49	7.218	299 n. 339
3.342	235-236 n. 49	7.274	342 n. 153
3.350-354	293 n. 299	7.318	309 n. 398
3.351	236	7.437-453	233 n. 39
3.352	229 n. 13	7.447-450	233 n. 39
3.354	226, 236	7.454-455	240 n. 68
3.391	236 n. 52	7.455	241-242
3.399-408	237 n. 55		
3.399-402	237 n. 55	*Contra Apionem*	11, 234-235,
3.400-402	293 n. 299		298, 304
3.408	233 n. 32		n. 370, 306
3.432-442	236 n. 53		n. 378, 309
4.11	252 n. 113	1.1-5	298 n. 329
4.147	305 n. 373	1.1-2	367-368

PHILO "THE ELDER" 146 n. 60, 264, 283

THEODOTOS 146 n. 60, 206 n. 326

9. INDEX OF RABBINIC TEXTS

MISHNAH
Aboth
2.8 — 230 n. 17

BABYLONIAN TALMUD
Megillah
9b — 225

Hagigah
9b — 230 n. 17

TARGUMIM
Targum Onqelos
Gen. 33:18 — 188-189 n. 255
Ex. 13:18 — 266 n. 180

MIDRASHIM
Genesis Rabbah
43 — 189 n. 256

Seder Olam Rabbah — 167

10. INDEX OF NEW TESTAMENT TEXTS

MATTHEW — 321-322, 330 n. 96, 335, 345 n. 167, 358 n. 240, 359 n. 251, 360 n. 253, 369, 379, 383 n. 361, 384
1:2-17 — 371 n. 321
3:3 — 376 n. 321
6:9-13 — 347 n. 180
6:24 — 347 n. 180
7:7-11 — 347 n. 180
18:12-14 — 347 n. 180
22:1-14 — 370-371 n. 293
22:2-10 — 347 n. 180
22:16 — 378 n. 338
23:4 — 347 n. 180, 370-371 n. 293
23:6-7 — 347 n. 180
23:6 — 370-371 n. 293
23:13 — 347 n. 180, 370-371 n. 293
23:23 — 347 n. 180, 370-371 n. 293
23:25-26 — 347 n. 180, 370-371 n. 293
23:27-28 — 347 n. 180
23:27 — 370-371 n. 293
23:29-32 — 347 n. 180,

23:34-36 — 370-371 n. 293, 347 n. 180, 370-371 n. 293
26:6-13 — 370 n. 293
26:61 — 335 n. 119
26:63 — 335 n. 119
28:18-20 — 333 n. 109
28:19-20 — 333-334 n. 110

MARK — 316 n. 29, 320-322, 330* n. 96, 338* n. 129, 341, 343, 345* n. 167, 350-352, 360 n. 253, 369, 379
1:1 — 350 n. 193 (*bis*)
1:2-13 — 350 n. 193
1:3 — 376 n. 321
1:14 — 350 n. 193
1:15 — 350 n. 193
2:1-3:6 — 347 n. 176
2:4 — 329 n. 92, 352 n. 200 (*bis*)
2:9 — 352 n. 200
2:11 — 352 n. 200
2:12 — 352 n. 200
2:13-17 — 370 n. 293
2:18-22 — 370 n. 293
3:6 — 378 n. 338

23	384 n. 364	ACTS	
23:2	384 n. 362	1-15	352-353
23:4	384 nn. 363		n. 205
	& 364 (*bis*)	1-12	353
23:5	362 n. 265,	1	332
	384 n. 362	1:1-13	323
23:14-15	384 nn. 363	1:1-3	323, 331,
	& 364		348, 367-368
23:14	384 n. 362	1:1	323, 331
23:22	384 nn. 363		n. 100, 343
	& 364 (3t.)		n. 156, 344
23:23	384 n. 364		n. 162, 374
23:33	352 n. 201		n. 315
23:34	336 n. 120	1:3	337 (*bis*)
23:40-41	384 n. 363	1:4-14	348
23:43	352 n. 201	1:4	335 n. 117
23:46	336 n. 120	1:5-12:25	323 n. 66
23:47	384 n. 363	1:8	335 n. 117
2350-24:52	347		(3t.), 348,
23:51	358 n. 239		376 n. 321
24	332, 337	1:15-26	348
24:7	358 n. 240,	1:16-22	372 n. 299
	359 n. 248	1:16	334 n. 115,
24:26	358 n. 240,		359 n. 248
	359 n. 248	1:19	328
24:36-53	322	1:22	335 n. 117,
24:44-49	333 n. 109,		362 n. 265
	334-335	1:24-25	361 n. 258
24:44	333, 334	2:1-8:3	348
	n. 115, 335	2:1-47	348, 358-359,
	n. 116, 358		362, 366-367
	n. 240, 359		n. 283, 372
	n. 248		n. 301
24:45	333 (*bis*)	2:1-4	332 n. 106,
24:46-47	333, 361		335 n. 117,
	n. 260		348 n. 182,
24:47	376 n. 321		362 n. 263
24:47-49	335* n. 118	2:5-13	348 n. 182
	(3t.)	2:14-36	372 nn. 299
			& 301
JOHN	347, 369, 379	2:14-21	348 n. 182
2:21	335-336	2:17-21	362 n. 263
	n. 119	2:21	362 n. 264
4:20-22	370 n. 293	2:22-36	348 n. 182
12:1-8	370 n. 293	2:23	358 nn. 239
17	361 n. 258		& 241
18:30	384 n. 362	2:25	358 n. 243
18:38	384 n. 364	2:31	358 n. 243
	(*bis*)	2:32	335 n. 117
19:1-15	384 n. 364	2:33	335 n. 117
19:4	384 n. 364	2:36	346 n. 172
19:7	384 n. 364	2:37-41	348 n. 182,
			362 n. 264

11. INDEX OF EARLY CHRISTIAN LITERATURE

INDEX OF ANCIENT PERSONS

Introduction: The following index contains the names of persons mentioned in the monograph who have a reasonable claim to historicity. I have omitted kings in king lists. For authors see the previous index.

INDEX OF MODERN AUTHORS